Mfundishi Jhutyms Ka

Spiritual Warriors Are Healers

Mfundishi Jhutyms Ka n Heru El-Salim

Cover, Logo design, and layout by Sn Khnum and Mfundishi Jhutyms Ka en Heru Hassan K. Salim. Inside Logo design, and layout by Dawit Lasanu and Mfundishi Jhutyms Ka n Heru El-Salim.

ISBN: 0-9747083-0-5

Published By: Kera Jhuty Heru Neb-Hu Publishing company.
P.O. Box 1396,Montclair, N.J. 07042.
Distributed By: Jhuty Heru Neb-Hu Publishing company.
P.O. Box 1396,Montclair, N.J. 07042.
First Printing 2003, Printed in the United States of America.
Second Printing 2009, Printed in the United States of America.

Nfr

PLEASE READ SLOWLY

You did not pick this book up by accident. If you live in the Western World, Europe, America, or under the rule of European Caucasian domination or live in a country that has been colonized by Europeans, then you are sick; maybe even insane and could be in critical condition. You may be involved in a suicide attempt, or responsible for the destruction of thousands of lives, and the unconscious destruction of nature. This book could possibly save your life. This particular volume was written primarily for Afrakans and any Melanin dominated People, but it could help anyone reconnect themselves to the human race. Find a comfortable chair, take a deep breath, but don't wait to exhale, just get busy!

Be On A Mission To Find :

Love * Truth * Happiness * Peace * Righteousness
Joy * Honesty * Spirituality * Innerstanding
** Justice * Your Goals * Your Dreams**
** Your Gifts * Afrakan-centeredness**
** Your Self * Your Soul-mate**
** The NTCHR In You**
The Creator
... then make it your Purpose to complete this mission.

Dedications

This book **Spiritual Warriors Are Healers,** is dedicated to the memory of all those giant Spiritual Warriors who are now ancestors, but who allowed me to stand on their shoulders while they were alive in their physical body-temples, like Dr. John Henrik Clarke, Omawale El Hajj Malik El Shabazz - Malcolm X, Dr. Cheikh Anta Diop, and Dr. Khalid Abdul Muhammad. May all their souls rest in peace, because their spirits are alive and well within me. I have been transformed and reborn because of their mighty spirits.

Dr. Clarke gave me the innerstanding of an Ourstorical Map. "History is a clock that people use to tell their political and cultural times of day. It is also a compass that people use to find themselves on the map of human geography. The role of history is to tell a people what they have been and where they have been, what they are and where they are. The most important role that history plays is that it has the function of telling a people where they still must go and what they still must be." Malcolm gave me the best example of Black manhood, and the innerstanding of Black Nationalism. Dr. Diop Kem-nected and connected me to ancient Kemet, as the foundation and source of our dynamic Deep Thought. Professor Cheikh Anta Diop said "Egyptian civilization is to African people what ancient Greek cilization is to European nations, that is, the historical source of their inspiration,..." And Khalid kept it real, as an Afrakan Warrior in its truest sense of the word, analyzing the true nature of the enemy, exposing the enemies, black and white, for the masses of Afrakan people, whom are too blind to see for themselves. These are living examples of Spiritual Warriors in my life-time; I shall continue the work of healing and liberating Afrakan people until my last human breath!

A special thank you goes out to all the leaders of Kemet Shrines and Ankh carriers that teach Ourstory, and Konsciously carry our collective ancestral memory! Duwa to the first known Kemet Shrine in New York by Heru Ankh Ra Semajh Se Ptah and Queen

Afua/Mut Nebt Het from the Smai Tawi Heal Thyself, Know Thyself Center. Duwa to Heru Ur and Nefer Nekhet and the New Kemet Society. Duwa to Heri Abu Khafra and the Shrine of the White and Gold Lotus. Duwa to Grand Master Kham and the Shrine of Kheper. Duwa to Priestess Akeru Aku Het Heru and the Temple of Mut em Uaa. Duwa to Priestess Kaitha and the Shrine of Het-Heru. Duwa to Abdel and Diane Salaam and sister Dela of the Forces of Nature and the Temple of the Living Book and the shrine of Bes. And a special Duwa to the Shrine of Jhuty Heru Neb-Hu: Snt Mut Seshatms Ma'atnefert (my right hand and hmt (wife)), Snt Sesheny Kheper, Sn Sheriff, Sn MBa-Heru, Snt Sia Seshat, Šnt Zuwena Iman, Sn Snjety, Sn Jhuty, Sn Bes, Snt Mut Khimarrah, Snt Ma'at Khepera, Sn Hassan Iman, Sn Khnum, and all of my initiates and extended family and friends.

A special thank you goes out to all the leaders of the Kupigana Ngumi and the Afrakan Martial Arts World. Duwa to the Shaha Mfundishi Maasi, Mganga Mfundishi Talo-Naa, Mfundishi Tayari Casel, Ahati Kilindi Iyi, Malenga Kenny Moody, Baba Ishangi, Mfundishi Vita, Mfundishi Khalid Maasi, Mwalimu Mwanzo and to all the Spiritual Warriors involved in the struggle for the liberation of Afrakan people.

Last but not least, Duwa to my family: my parents Bertha and William Hall and the Mokonde Nation in Tanzania, as well as the International Indigenous Society and Cherokee Nation from which our ancestral roots sprang. My brothers Robert, and Joe, my sister Sarah, my ancestral brother June, and spiritual brother Weusi Salim and their families. And a special Duwa to my children Zuwena and Hassan Iman Salim for choosing me as your father, I love you!

Mfundishi Jhutyms Ka en Heru's Journey Affirmation

"***SPIRIT*** of infinite miles, ***SPIRIT*** of infinite wisdom,
The Creator that allows space to be conceived,
Knowledge to be comprehended,
Allow me to sit at your feet ...
By myself, I am nonexistent,

Through you,
I am omnipowerful.
Through you,
Nothing can happen to me.
Through you,
My journey will be powerful.
Through you,
My innerstanding will be liberating.
Through you,
SPIRIT I am already there,
I am already enlightened.

Because of my Konsciousness and awareness of The Divine
NTCHR,
I am safe, and I will return safe.
Because I am the essence of the entire journey,
I have become through ***SPIRIT,*** the essence of a Spiritual
Warrior, Take hold of me, I invite you to become One with me.
Allow me to be One with you.
Now, I am ready to take my journey,
We are ready to take our journey through ***Spiritual Warriors Are Healers*** as One." ***AMEN-RA***

My journey, our journey is already successful before we started it, because I willed it to be so and now my ancestral spirit is all around me. I just gave them the highest praise, and what goes around, comes around...

Preface

I started my martial arts career in 1964 at the request of El Hajj Malik El Shabazz known as Malcolm X, under the organization of Afrikan American Unity, at that point Hassan Kamau Salim was born. Malcolm X stated three things were important: (1) Self-respect, (2) Self-determination and (3) Self-defense.

From 1965 to 1968, while attending J. P. Stevens High School, I was a county, district and regional champion in wrestling. My team was undefeated and was "State Champion" all three years. As a junior and senior, I was also "All County" and "All State Champion", in football and track. Team sports kept me in excellent condition for martial arts. From 1966 to 1971, I trained in Bondo under the great teacher, Mfundishi Maasi. In 1968, I received 36 scholarships as a "Scholar Athlete" from High School. I attended Norfolk State College, Norfolk, Virginia, where I received a Bachelors of Arts in History, specializing in Afrakan and Afrakan American History. I continued my martial arts training and simultaneously became a "Virginia State Wrestling Champion" for three consecutive years. I also studied Judo while attending Norfolk State. After graduating in 1971, I started training in Chinese Shaolin Kung Fu under Grand Master William Chung. I excelled to the level of Eighth Degree Black Belt (red sash), in the Chinese Shaolin Hung-Gar Kung Fu Federation.

In 1972, while attending Rutgers University, I pursued my Masters Degree in Philosophy of Education, specializing in Afrakan Studies. In that same year, I began teaching Kung Fu on the Livingston Campus of Rutgers University. In 1978, I founded Black Gold Afrakan Kultural Arts Center in New Brunswick, New Jersey, and started teaching Kupigana Ngumi (Afrakan Martial Arts) and Afrakan Philosophy. In 1985, I was promoted to Malenga (Physical and

Spiritual Leader) in Kupigana Ngumi, Afrakan Martial Arts.

Between 1971 and 1986, I traveled several times to the Afrakan continent with Dr. Ben Jochannan, visiting Kemet (Egypt), Sudan and Ethiopia. I have independently traveled extensively throughout East and West Afraka visiting Tanzania, Kenya, Congo (Zaire), Ghana, Nigeria, Togo, Benin, Ivory Coast, Senegal, Gambia and many others (a total of 25 countries to date). During my travels, I continued to study history, ourstory, religion, spirituality, philosophy and martial science. By 1986, while keeping abreast with martial arts, I attained over 150 trophies and became "Grand Champion" over 15 times in fighting, 5 times in weapons and 21 times in form or "Kata," in the Americas, Caribbean Islands and abroad. In 1987, I performed before the Royal Court in Ethiopia, as well as studied with a Coptic Priest and was awarded a special sword from the family of Haile Selassie as a "Warrior Priest". In 1989, I began teaching Kupigana Ngumi in New York City. On my 40th Earth day I became a Makonde Chief in Tanzania (my homeland) and also that same year a Nana Chief among the Ashante in Ghana. In 1993, the Kupigana Ngumi Pan Afrakan Federation promoted me to the rank of Mfundishi, Grand Master in the Afrakan Martial Arts, also in attendance was Baba Heru Semajh, Dr. Ben, Dr. Clark and the Key speaker was Dr. Leonard Jeffries. By 1996, I completed 3 Masters and a Ph'D

I shall continue to excel infinitely in the science of life. I shall teach those with the desire to learn, how to activate the Spiritual Warrior within for self-healing, community healing, Kultural healing and ultimately world healing, while I actively remain involved in my own personal healing and growth. As a Spiritual Warrior, I realize that I am still in the beginner's stages of impeccability. I train new Spiritual Warriors to say and internalize ... "Today is a good day to die! If you have nothing to die for, then you have nothing to live for. Fear prevents humans from living a full and satisfying mental, physical and spiritual life. Eliminate the fear from your life and nothing can stop you from living and fulfilling your visions, your purpose and the giving of your gifts." Join the Spiritual Warriors of Kemet, we are on a spiritual mission for Universal Wisdom, Power and Htp.

Shm e m Htp (I go in peace). Mfundishi Jhutyms Ka n Heru El-Salim

SPIRITUAL WARRIORS ARE HEALERS
By Mfundishi Jhutyms Ka-en-Heru Hassan K. Salim

KEMTENTS

Chapter ∩ l l (12) (continued)

Introduction

Mfundishi Jhutyms Ka en Heru Hassan Kamau Salim.

I am a Spiritual Warrior, all that I am is because of the Creator, and the Creator has blessed and manifested my spirit through Black Melanin Afrakan people. I chose to be reborn through my Afrakan parents in this time, at this age, because I am carrying some important pieces to the puzzle of Afrakan Unity, pieces that will aid in the healing of the Afrakan souls in America, Afraka and throughout the Diaspora.

I have been preparing for several lifetimes, in many forms on many dimensions, to give the gifts that The NTCHR has given me. Within the pages of this book is the beginning of my gift to you. We, Melaninated Afrakan people, have the power to heal ourselves. We have the power to liberate ourselves, and we have always had the power, because we are divine Ntchr-like spiritual beings. For those who are prepared to receive my blessings, may your eyes open, and may the Divine Spirit of the Moyo, and Sekhem or Heru Konsciousness fill your body-temple, guiding you towards Htp a state of Ma'at. With the Divine Spirit of Ma'at, you can heal yourself and help heal your families, you may even assist those who want to be healed, and then you must give your gifts to the world, expecting nothing in return. For my fellow Spiritual Warriors, who already have sight, who are illuminated by the light and who are already involved in the healing process, may we join hands in the healing of Afrakan people, our home-land Afraka, and the planet we now call Earth.

Open your mind and allow these words from ***Spiritual Warriors are Healers*** to have dialogue with your objective and subjective mind before you pass judgment on what I have to say or how I say it. Afrakans in the 21st century western time and 63rd century new Afrakan time are insane, collectively crazy, kulturally retarded and hooked on a deadly drug called European Caucasian domination or European centeredness (white supremacy), racism. And the first step towards healing Afrakan people is to confront our demons, our detrimental European behavior and thinking. We must re-Afrakanize, and re-Spiritualize the essence of our very being. Spiritual Warriors will have to "Deconstruct, Reconstruct, and Construct" a new Afrakan human from a new powerful Ma'atian centered Pan-Afrakan Worldview.

Afrakan people worldwide have to conquer our poor self-esteem and identity problem. Many Afrakans have forgotten who they are, some never knew, some are ashamed of what they have become and some are so pathologically and psychological damaged, they are just in denial or clueless. Regardless of the reasons, Afraka cannot heal itself and become strong with her children at home and the ones lost and scattered throughout the Diaspora in pain, diseased, drugged unconscious and disconnected from their parents. We must collectively come to the innerstanding that we are an Afrakan people, Ourstorically, and Kulturally. In addition, we must also innerstand that European Caucasian domination has created an illusion of an altered reality, but we are all an Afrakan people no matter where we are on the planet and no matter what language we speak. ***"We are Afrakans not because we were born in Afraka, but because Afraka was born in Us."*** Spiritual Warriors are teaching us that we must also innerstand that the Maangamizi disconnected us from our parents and from learning firsthand of the wisdom from our ancestors. This book, ***Spiritual Warriors Are Healers*** is a tool or instrument to be used for our re-Afrakanization and our development of a new powerful Ma'atian centered Pan-Afrakan Spiritual Worldview.

There are many people of Afrakan descent that are conscious and unconscious gate keepers of the Wazungu (the collective nature of aggression of European Caucasians) culture and western society, that are partners in the destruction of Afrakan Kulture and Afrakan people, mentally physically and spiritually. These gatekeepers are usually the most educated in our oppressors' culture, but mis-educated in Afrakan Kulture. They have obtained graduate degrees and other signs and symbols of western approval, and this is their badge of success, but they lack real knowledge of self or they dislike the Afrakan within themselves. They may even belong to a fraternal order or sorority, or even be masons, or Moors and they usually belong to a church or Masjid. They are placed in high positions for their loyalty and commitment to the oppressor's way of life and/or the American dream. The majority of these gatekeepers are unconscious collaborators of our common enemy. They hate that which is Afrakan in them, and love that which is Wazungu or none Afrakan in them, but they would never admit it openly, but watch their actions: the men usually have very short hair cuts so their natural tightly curled hair will never show or they have altered its natural kinky beauty. The male and female are also extremely proud of their straight Eurasian-like hair or features. The female Afrakan women gatekeepers usually straighten their hair in the same styles that Caucasian women wear or they weave it or wig it. Both will always wear European style clothes, even when it is not related to work. Culturally, they are as far removed from Afraka and the Afrakan Worldview as their Caucasian mentors. These gatekeepers are your educators (mis-educators), politicians, religious teachers and corporate professionals who aid our common oppressors in the enslavement of our minds, bodies and souls, and the truly sad part is that most of these western collaborators of Afrakan descent are unconscious that they are plugged into the matrix of European Caucasian domination, like the three C's, **C**larence Thomas, **C**ondoleezza Rice and **C**olin Powell or even Skippy Gates of Harvard. This book is for conscious and unconscious gatekeepers too.

It is extremely important for Afrakan people to utilize Afrakan terminologies and concepts in the rescue, restoration, reconstruction and reconnecting of our Afrakan Ancestral Memory. Theophile Obenga states, "*Language is the expression and the essence of Kulture, as well as, an internal paradigm that serves to gain insight and access to the spirit of civilization*". Most indigenous Afrakan languages have no letter "c" when expressed through European languages, and that sound is made with a European letter "k". Therefore, in the Afrakan language of Kiswahili, written in English, it would be written Afrika not Africa. The "k" in Afrika and in other English words that express Afrakan spirituality, are used throughout this book like ***Kultural*** **-** The Black Melanin Afrakan way of life that ***Kem-nects*** and connects us to a Pan-Afrakan Spiritual Worldview. ***Kemtrol*** - An Afrakan commitment of directing influence, from a Pan-Afrakan Spiritual and Kultural Worldview. ***Kemetik*** - The Black

Afrakan Deep Thought of spiritual expressions from ancient Kemet (Egypt). ***Kem-Unity*** - True community begins in the hearts of Afrakan people who have common ideas, love, respect and values, a place of being for spiritual and Kultural growth, development and protection. ***Afraka*** is an expression from ancient Kemet, and Kash, where deep spiritual thinking was at its very best. ***Afraka*** is the Mdw Ntchr (Medew Netcher - the classical written and spoken language system of ancient Kemet) expression of Afrika, another form of Kujichagulia, self-determination, naming ourselves and defining ourselves. ***"Afraka"*** is used throughout this book, ***Spiritual Warriors Are Healers;*** it is also used by many resurrected Kemetyu (Black melanimated people) of Kemet and traditional Afrakan Spiritual Systems, whom have seized Kemtrol and control of their minds, souls and destiny, by defining their own Worldview and spiritual reality. "Afraka," represents a line of demarcation between old ways and new ways of thinking for liberation, and empowerment. Afraka and Afrika both represent struggle and resistance against European Caucasian domination.

> **Af** - means the flesh, in relationship to the original Black Melanin human beings, molded from the Black Earth in relationship to this planet.
> ***Ra*** - means the light of the Ntchr of Creation or the light in all creation and in all things.
> ***Ka*** - means the living spirit in all human beings.
> ***Afraka*** - The land of the living Black flesh and spirit of the light, which gave birth, to Black humans in the physical form on Earth.
> ***Afrakan*** - Spiritual beings having a Black human experience, from Afraka. There is only one race, the human race. Black human beings were the first and original humans on Earth.

"Afraka," is also an "***Amharic***" word from ancient Kash, and modern Ethiopia meaning, "***Land of the sun.***" According to Dr. Yosef Ben-Jochannan, Afrika or Africa, it comes from a Greek word, and was not used as the name of the whole Black continent of Afraka, until 1675 B.C.E. or 5915 S.T., Sema Tawy - new Afrakan time, by

Europeans. As Spiritual Warriors, we must be masters of our own definitions and realities even while using our oppressor's language. There are also many Afrakan words from ancient Kemet, and many Kiswahili words used from East Afraka and a few other Afrakan languages used throughout this book, their definitions can be found in the glossary in the back of this book. The Afrakan languages in which our Afrakan ancestors spoke have been stolen from us, and we can retrieve them, our spiritual ancestors are waiting to teach us, because language is the best keeper and transmitter of Kulture. There are a few Afrakan words that are extremely difficult to translate into the Wazungu language, so they are left in their natural Afrakan form. This book, ***Spiritual Warriors Are Healers*** is to be used as a healing guide towards retrieving your lost or stolen Afrakan mind. Real healing cannot happen unless you retrieve your true mind. I know some of you will still resist, so I'm going to spell Africa like this because it's "good English". I say to you Htp (peace), but keep reading. We must seize the moment, re-educate ourselves, re-direct our focus towards Ma'at (truth, justice, righteousness and harmonious balance), re-capture our Afrakan identity through Kulture and language and rally around an Afrakan Spiritual Pan-Afrakan Worldview.

Afrakans in America are sick, out of their Afrakan minds, and desperately in need of a healing, because they are addicts of European Caucasian domination (racism), white supremacy. We are hooked on this deadly destructive drug that is destroying the whole human family and the Earth. This drug called European Caucasian domination is the European American Worldview, which perpetuates a Eurocentric political and economic system of aggression, exploitation and destruction (esfet). Like most destructive drugs, it controls our desires, our ambitions, and our minds, creating an illusionary self destructive reality that alters the way Afrakan Black humans would naturally function if they were in their right Afrakan mind!

Afrakan people not only need a healing, mentally, physically, and spiritually, but we need a new Worldview that has our own best interest at heart. Afrakans worldwide are insane, kulturally retarded, mis-educated, suffering from severe health problems, and mentally handicapped because our minds have been enslaved. The system of European Caucasian domination has mis-educated and spiritually abused Afrakans to the point that we hate ourselves, the images of our spiritual and Kultural deities, and what little we think we know of Ourstory and self-image. European Caucasian domination is in control of our desires. The desires of the western society is based on the psychological, physical, and spiritual desires of the European Caucasian man, Melanin deficient human kind. In addition, the Caucasian man is spiritually immature, with an unevolved soul. Caucasian women, because of thousands of years of mental physical and spiritual oppression by their Caucasian mates, are now acting and thinking like Caucasian men. Foreign men who are looking for success in America act like Caucasian men, and the so-called "most successful Afrakans" (economically), in this society, (male or female) are acting and thinking like Caucasian men. Plus, the Afrakan men that the dominant European Caucasian society keeps using as a good Afrakan example (like politicians, lawyers, businessmen, professors, and Christian religious leaders in general) all act like European Caucasian men or have Caucasian desires. Moreover, the desires of Caucasian men are anti-nature, anti-women, anti life-giving and anti life-sustaining values. The European Caucasian man's desires are destroying this planet, and it opposes Ma'at, the foundation of Black melanin Afrakan life and Spirituality.

The United States is the sole superpower in the world of the early 21st century western time. The U.S. stands first among industrialized countries in military technology, military exports, in Gross Domestic Products, health technology, and the number of millionaires and billionaires. This is the world of European Caucasian domination on one hand, but let us look at the other side of the same coin. The United States ranks twenty-first in eighth-grade math scores, twenty-fifth in education, and last in protecting our children against gun violence. White male supremacy says we need a strong military to protect us from our enemies outside our borders. Who is protecting American citizens inside the American borders from drugs, bullets, sickness, hunger, poverty, mis-education, homelessness and ignorance?

It seems like the United States investment priorities for a more secure America is morally bankrupt. Although the United Snakes is getting richer, Afrakans, other people of color and children are remaining poor. European Caucasian domination needs someone to exploit; this is the nature of capitalism and white male domination. Afrakans have been programmed for self-destruction. That is why we are eating ourselves sick first, before our early earthly death. The system of European Caucasian domination has a death wish for Afrakan people, and through years of negative programming, Afrakan desires are fulfilling this task by self-destructing. If you are of Afrakan decent and live in the United States or the western world, you are more likely to die sooner, and of a major disease, than members of any other ethnic group. By an alarming margin, Afrakans living in America lead in the mortality rate from the nation's biggest killers: heart disease, cancer, stroke, liver disease, infant mortality, accidental death, homicide, diabetes, and respiratory diseases. These health issues are largely because on a whole, Afrakans living in America have been programmed and conditioned or mis-educated for self-hate and for poor eating habits, which contribute to economic exploitation. The very foods that Afrakan people in America think they love, and that they consume the most of, are the worst foods for the human body, and specifically for Afrakan people. Soul food is an enslaved survival diet, not something we should be looking for in our diet of re-Afrakanization, and empowerment.

More than 30% of all the soft drinks (poisonous sugar water with no real nutritional value) consumed in the United States are consumed by Afrakans, a group who comprise about 12% of the entire population. The system of European Caucasian domination is in control of what we desire, what our aspirations are, and how we define success. It uses its school system of mis-education from pre-K to PhD level, plus the media of TV, radio, magazines, advertisements, newspapers, so that even what we think we want, we don't really want, we only desire them because the matrix say's it's desirable even though it is suicidal for us. We see the dominate European Caucasian society with these poisons and material things, so we think these things are good, but in reality they represent esfet (the destruction of harmony and life) for you and the planet. Afrakans in the highest economic positions, with the highest western degrees, are as sick as the poor, because they have both adopted insane, suicidal habits from the matrix of European Caucasian domination. Afrakans in America have a 70% higher rate of infant mortality. People of Afrakan decent are four times more likely to die of hypertension heart disease and four times more likely to die of chronic kidney diseases. Twice as many Afrakans suffer from cirrhosis of the liver, and Afrakans are five times more likely to die of tuberculosis. Afrakan women are five times more likely to die in childbirth. Obesity is one of the most serious health problems facing Afrakans in America next to ***Kultural Insanity***, especially for Afrakan women. Obesity is the second leading cause of preventable death in the United States, after smoking. Afrakans, through negative programming, consume on the average over 50 pounds of worthless sugar each year and it's rising. In addition, Afrakan children have become junk food junkies, which also lead to erotic and undesirable behavior. A powerful wholistic Afrakan-centered Pan-Afrakan Spiritual Worldview and Kultural programs must neutralize this negative programming from the system of European Caucasian domination.

The incidence of hypertension among Afrakans in America is higher than any other nation or ethnic group of people on Earth. Hypertension is the No. 1 cause of death among Afrakans in the United States, with a rate among Afrakan men of over 30 per 100,000 deaths annually. Moreover, 17% of all Afrakan men and 33% of women suffer from hypertension, while another 40% of men and 26% of women are estimated to have the disease without even being aware of it. The No. 1 cause of death for Afrakan men between the age of 15 - 35, is homicide, again we have internalized the hatred European Caucasian domination has for Afrakan men, and we destroy ourselves for them. The third leading cause of death among Afrakan males aged 15 - 24, in America is suicide and 70% of these suicides was with an illegal handgun, brought from the streets, while almost 50% of white male suicides were with legal shotguns they bought or their parents bought.

"How easy it is to defeat people who do not kindle fire for themselves." Afrakan proverb The system of European Caucasian domination has a death wish for Afrakan people, and our spiritual Black Afrakan Kulture and through hundreds of years of negative programming by the system of European Caucasian domination, perpetuated through the Maangamizi, Afrakan desires are fulfilling this task. Afrakans are self-destructing through self-hate, lack of self-respect, Kultural ignorance, spiritual insanity, political immaturity and a degenerative dietary code. What Afrakan people must realize is that only Afrakan people can change these conditions. Others can help through financial contributions, and re-educating their own communities and families. Afrakans must unite among themselves before uniting with others. However, all the citizens of America will have to work together from their own centers if America is to become a great nation for all of its citizens, not just the wealthy and the Caucasians and those who act like Caucasians.

The rise in Afrakan suicides has to do with wazungu terrorism, increased levels of Kultural insanity, along with the strain and stress on each generation of Afrakans to do better, achieve more success than their parents. The media has created the illusion of increased opportunities for Afrakan because of technology, but because racism is alive and well in Amerikkka, the reverse is happening. Moreover, because we never received therapy from the Maangamizi, and our children have never received proper therapy, as a result we have developed a collective craziness, the internalizing of Caucasian dreams, which is insanity for Afrakan people. None of these conditions will get better until Afrakans change their desires. Afrakan desires can only be changed through an Afrakan-centered Kultural and wholistic spiritual system, and a Pan-Afrakan political system that embraces all Afrakans regardless of Afrakan ethnical and geographical location. Afrakans in the 63rd century must go through a Whm Msu.

The Whm Msw (Weheme Mesu) means "repetition of the rebirth." An ancient Afrakan Kemetik spiritual practice of re-Afrakanization by going back to great Afrakan accomplishments in all fields of human survival, from Kulture, to governance and economic stability, and bring the best to the future. The Whm Msu is the Kultivation of Spirituality among Afrakan people by refocusing on our inner spirit. A primary goal of Afrakan centered spiritual leadership is to launch an Afrakan World Whm Msw designed to restore, resurrect or rebuild Ma'at within our Worldview and our everyday Kultural values, so that we not only end but destroy the Maangamizi.

Poverty is enslavement, and as long as Afrakan people are among the nations' poorest, sickest, most ignorant, and mis-educated, European Caucasian domination and racism will thrive. Afrakans have to make economic stability and Afrakan centered re-education their top priorities in the 21st century. Afrakans must manufacture all the clothes we wear, grow most of the food we eat, and write and produce most of the books and educational materials needed in our re-Afrakanization process. We have to support and develop our own healers. Afrakans in America have the economical means to liberate themselves and all the Afrakans in the Diaspora. Only when Afrakans in America wake up and seize the moment, by liberating ourselves will we be able to liberate Afrakans on our glorious continent Afraka, the richest land mass on the Earth.

Spiritual Warriors must stress, that we as new Afrakans have to be as meticulous about our diet, and the foods and drinks that we consume, as we are about the clothes we wear and the education we feed our minds and our children's minds. Some of our top scholars are intellectual giants, but are dietary degenerates. And these "dietary degenerates" are still drug addicts of ***European Caucasian*** domination. If our top scholars and intellectual giants are still drug addicts of European Caucasian domination, how can we unplug ourselves, and liberate ourselves?

The following are some of the major challenges facing Afrakan people in the 21st century western time and 63rd century new Afrakan time if we are serious about re-claiming our minds, our kulture, ourstory, our families and the continent of Afraka:

Challenges Facing Afrakans in 63rd Century

Kultural insanity, out of our Afrakan mind;

Poor self-esteem, we have been trained not to support things Afrakan - white ice is colder than Black ice;

Self- hate, our standard of beauty and importance is based on Europeans and the system of European Caucasian domination;

Colonization of the Afrakan Mind, and the Afrakan continent by European Caucasian domination, and Arabism under the disguise of Islam;

Wazungu enslavement of the Afrakan mind, spirit, and body. Seventy percent of the U.S.A. prison industrial complex systems are filled with Afrakans - 63rd century slavery, there are more Afrakan men in jail then in higher education, 21st century western slavery;

Economic instability, Afrakans are at the bottom of the economic ladder. Afrakans do not employ 2% of Afrakans in Amerikkka and the dollar stays in Afrakans hands about 10 minutes on the average;

Mis-education, a life-threatening training program for a job in the Euro-American, matrix system of white male domination;

Poor health, we are killing ourselves in the name of progress, on one hand and totally unprepared to address our health crises, like Aids and menticide on the other hand;

Spiritual Assassination, we have forsaken and we have been programmed to be ashamed of our own traditional Afrakan spiritual systems and religions, only to embrace the religions of our oppressors, which promises nothing but death to the Afrakan of the 63rd century;

The Afrakan has no national identity or collective Worldview as an Afrakan people that represents our security, health, education, political or economical future. We are not West Indian, Jamaican, Trinadians, African-Americans, We Are Afrakans!

Afrakans of the 63rd century cannot defend themselves against western world domination or Arab enslavement, theft and domination of Northern Afraka, and the saddest part of this dilemma, is that it is not on our agenda;

Suicidal music and an enslaving entertainment industry, that develops and supports music and movies that destroys the Afrakan community, self- esteem, and a positive spiritual life-style in Amerikkka or the world.

Destruction and dismantling of the Afrakan family, more then 70% of Afrakan families in the U.S. have no father in the home and children are raising children;

Poor visible Afrakan leadership, the leaders who have been chosen for Afrakan people are collaborators of the matrix, European Caucasian domination;

Afrakans have lost the ability to feed themselves, even with rich land in Afraka and in the Americas, because we are plugged into the matrix of European Caucasian domination, and it has a death wish for us.

Afrakans have not learned how to turn the billions of dollars that we generate in the U.S. gladiator-sports Industry into economic stability for the Afrakan Kemunity or communities, like Independent schools, homes or housing developments and Kultural Centers hear in America;

There are very few independent Afrakan schools, and the ones we do have are having financial difficulty and they are under siege and declining. Afrakans who have money and economic power are blind, dumb and ignorant of the real needs of their own people here or in our home-land Afraka.

We have inherited a collective crazy. The effects of the Maangamizi were so horrifying, so traumatic, that its horrific traumatization still affects the physiological and psychological soul of every Afrakan on the planet, because we are One people spiritually, even if we do not recognize our Oneness, it still exist. No Afrakan really wants to talk about our enslavement in any way shape or form by the savage and barbaric inhuman system set up by European Caucasians and Arabs between 700 C.E. and the 20th century western time. The pain is unexplainable deep with emotional side affects and scars that question the soul of your very being. The effects are a collective crazy, insane illusionary reality that masks the horrors of the real atrocities of the Maangamizi, and the shame of our surrender.

Afrakan people everywhere and anywhere in the Americas, the Caribbean, or Eurasia, we can feel the collective pain of our people, from the Maangamizi. When we look in each other's eyes, we know! When we see the rainbows of shades of Black melanin in the Diaspora, we remember the Middle Passage, The southern plantations and we can feel the pain from suffering of inhumane conditions. However, this pain and suffering are diminutive compared to the feverish emotions trapped in our collective minds, as millions of screaming women cry out from Wazungu rape. And part of every Black man dies because he cannot defend or save his wife, sister, mother, daughter, niece, aunt, friend, lover, or neighbor. This horrific traumatosis still affects the physiological and psychological soul of every melaninated Afrakan on the planet.

Many of the negative, suicidal habits and behaviors that have become reality for many Afrakans in the world today are the direct affects of the Maangamizi and this is the collective crazy I am talking about in this book. This collective crazy must be understood so it can be innerstood, corrected and healed. The re-Afrakanization process is not anti-white, it is pro-Black! The re-Afrakanization process for every Afrakan is part of the medicine received in therapy for the Maangamizi, which has not stopped. The Maangamizi is alive and well, and still destroying Afrakans, Melanin people, children and poor people worldwide.

NOTES OF A 63rd CENTURY AFRAKAN SPIRITUAL SCRIBE IN AMERICA

I speak only the truth before my sacred and great Spiritual Afrakan Ancestors.
The Afrakan suicide tendencies are so enormous, so addictive at this point in Ourstory,
That millions of Afrakans are already dead before they die.
Their madness caused by Kultural homicide, makes the killer disease Aids seem like an appetizer for genocide.
We have become the walking murdered, as we chain our babies to western ignorance as human sacrifices.
Afrakan youth disconnected and disjointed from the spirit of their Afrakan Divine ancestral roots.
Young boys bopping to the sounds of madness, with their pants hanging off.
Could be beautiful sisters disguising themselves in white dreams.
Black men roaming the streets in packs, jobless and unemployable, with the blues written on their faces.
Black women in training to be white men, imitating white women in training to be white men, and these white men are destroying all life as we know it, even the Earth.
Black executives sip champagne after a hard day's work of European-American prostitution.
Black Mayors and puppet, I meanpublic government officials guided and mentored by western pimps, inherit cesspools, and un-answered dreams.
Confused, Kulturally retarded parents lead their children off to slaughter houses in the name of education.
Black economics in America has evaporated along with white carnation milk and the destruction of Black Wall Street.
Poor children are dying or being killed before they know what life is or what it has to offer!
While their parents pray to white alien gods which are enemies of nature, women, Afrakan Kulture and spirituality.
As spiritual ignorance cherishes the progress of backwardness.
We are in the middle of a kultural-economical war with no offence.

Afrakans have been hypnotized and drugged white in deathly happiness and re-programed in Wazungu (white) desires.
Even Stevie Wonder can see where home is, but we can't recognize Afrika, or Kemet, or our kulture, languge, or our ancestral spirits dancing all around us...
We can't hear the sacred drums, because of cell phones and ipods, mass insanity...
Intuiton is confuesed with witchcraft or your daily horoscope.
Are you hot yet? Can you feel the urgency behind this poem?
Is it getting warm?
Are you mad? or at least smokin?
Because millions of us are already in the oven,
Being baked, well done, glowing in our Blackness,
With forks in our hands,
Smiling,
***With no idea,* We, Are Being Served ...**

Unless a new energy or Worldview is set in motion to offset the negative effects of European Caucasian domination on Afrakan people, these conditions illustrated above will continue to undermine and enslave the well being of Afrakan people, mentally, physically and spiritually. This new energy is a new Afrakan Kulture, which takes the best from the past and combines it with harmonious reasoning to lead us to a positive dynamic future. Pan-Afrakan Operational Unity will be one of the many vehicles or tools used to re-organize and re-energize Afrakan people to an Afrakan-centered Spiritual Worldview. Afrakan spirituality and Afrakan Kulture have within them the best medicine for Afrakan people to heal themselves, because no one else can or wants to liberate Afrakan people. The western or Eurasian cultures and political-economic systems are having too much fun exploiting us!

An Afrakan healing is what we need for the 63rd century new Afrakan time. Moreover, at the core of Afrakan Kulture through an Afrakan centered, wholistic dietary system, nature-centered spiritual system, lays the medicine that can heal and liberate Afrakan people.

No! Neither Christianity, Judaism, Islam, nor any of the other Asian spiritual systems will not, has not, cannot, save or liberate Afrakan people. All of these religions are good individually, up until a point, when it comes to Afrakan people. None of them can center Afrakan people, nor can they liberate us. They can help you if you are temporarily lost, insane, stressed and/or suicidal, and this destruction interferes with the western society. These systems were never designed to liberate Afrakan people. They all have foreign centers and cultures, plus these were the very same spiritual systems used by Europeans Caucasians and Arabs to enslave us and to destroy us as an Afrakan people and place us in the insane positions we now occupy in the world today, and they are all enemies of Afrakan Kulture, and Afrakan Spirituality. This means they are indirectly or directly enemies of Afrakan people. We must remember who our enemies are! Why do you think there are so many signs and posters in America saying," We will never forget September 11th 2001!".

My gift, "***Spiritual Warriors Are Healers***" starts with a Kemet Afrakan-centered innerstanding of the Creator and Creation, based upon the written records and ancestral memory left by our ancient Afrakan ancestors who lived in Afraka along the Hapy Valley. This First Chapter is called *The NTCHR*. What is important about this chapter is that we used indigenous Afrakan Kultures from the Rift Valley, and the indigenous Mdw Ntchr writings from ancient Kemet. The Kultural values, rituals, language and traditions traveled down the Hapy Valley from central and East Afraka, following Hapy, the great waterway we now call the Nile River.

Chapter Two is called *The Ntchru Of Ancient Kemet*, and the Ntchru are expressions of cosmic energies, with each Ntchr or Ntchrt representing a principle of nature in the harmonic unfolding of Creation. The Ntchru preside over all forms and functions, on several planes of reality, mental, physical and spiritual. The Ntchru reviewed in this book, ***"Spiritual Warriors Are Healers"*** are intended to be a guide for your own meditation or information and personal re-education towards higher Konsciousness.

Chapter Three is dedicated to the spirit of *Ma'at:* truth, justice, righteousness, harmonious balance and the law of reciprocity. Ma'at is at the center of Afrakan Spirituality, and Afrakan Kulture. European Caucaian domination has temporally separated us from our Kultural center in order to enslave our minds, bodies and control our desires. But the key to our survival is that we have never really been separated from our spiritual soul. The trauma of the drug European Caucasian domination has created an illusion of separateness, but the spirit that allowed us to survive the Maangamizi was our inner Afrakan Spirituality. This inner spirit changed the flavor of how we worshiped Christinanity or Islam. It has taken us this far, but in order to liberate ourselves and heal ourselves, and reclaim the best of our ancestral memory we will have to intertwine Afrakan Spirituality and Afrakan Kulture into one united philosophy, a new Pan-Afrakan Spiritual Worldview.

Chapters Four and Five journey into the spirit realms, *Spirits* and *Spirituality*. The land of infinite possibilities, the land where spirit, mind and matter meet. The Afrakan-centered perception of the universe is that everything is spiritual and part of The NTCHR. So through spirit we can communicate with anything and everything, because we are all interconnected. Innerstanding the spirits and living a life of spirituality are not the same. The Spiritual Warrior must have a degree of mastery of the innerstanding of the spirit realms while living a life of spirituality in the physical world. Harmonious balance is to have a degree of mastery in the mental, physical and spiritual worlds all at the same time.

Chapter Six explains who we are as Melanin dominated human beings. Afrakans are being manipulated and dominated by Melanin deficient human kind, because we don't know who we are, or who they are and why they are the way they are. Knowledge of the *Black Dot* may open up doors you will never be able to close again. It will become clear why Afrakans are the original scientists of the world and the authors of almost all known sciences until the eve of the modern era. We are truly the children of the sun, light beings having a human experience. We must learn to master our own energy of light, ***Be Enlightened.***

Chapter Seven addresses *Rituals* and how your Kulture reaffirms the necessary *Rituals* in your life, to keep you in tuned with the Creator, the spirits, and your day to day relationship with nature, community, family and self. *Rituals* can maintain Ma'at or they can be used for healing and for bringing Ma'at back into one's life. Spiritual Warriors teach that if you take good habits and repeat them for 42 straight days, you could correct bad habits and replace them with life-giving habits. These life-giving habits, now become part of your life style in the form of daily *Rituals*.

Chapter Eight is *Kulture and the re-Afrakanization* of Afrakan people worldwide. Kulture is the foundation that defines who you are as a living life-form. When another life-form superimposes their culture on you, than you literally die, or your dying is accelerated - a suicidal state of existence. A 12 point Afrakan Kultural re-Afrakanization program is introduced to reverse this death cycle Afrakan people are involved in, and temporarily trapped during the 63rd century new Afrakan time.

Chapter Nine looks at the Afrakan Holiday *Kwanzaa*, created in America as a healing ritual for Afrakan people. How can we recapture our Afrakan spirit and sense of family inside an insane crazy world of European Caucasian male domination.

Chapter Ten informs us and describes to us who are the *Spiritual Warriors*, why the real need for a *Spiritual Warrior*, and how to pursue this path if we want to be healers. *Spiritual Warriors* are human beings that are in constant pursuit of their own perfection and self-healing. We have the right to be right, to protect right, and the right to pursue righteousness.

Chapters Eleven and Twelve give us answers and maps to utilize, to help heal and liberate ourselves using very valuable tools from our Afrakan Kulture like Ma'at Akhw Ba Ankh, a spiritual meditative system of mastering your breath, your body-postures and

your focus for self empowerment. " ***To develop something of value or of beauty and not be able to defend it mentally, physically and spiritually is like not having it at all.*** " Ourstory rewards all research and it proves that the enemies of Ma'at are esfet in the form of European Caucasian domination and it will kill you, take what you have of value and claim it as its own. Also, look at the Americas, Afraka, Australia, Tasmania, New Zealand and the Caribbean Islands, only to name a few examples of what European Caucasian domination has done and continues to do to indigenous people. This mass destruction of human lives is not Mfundishi's imagination on a head trip, this is serious! ... it was them yesterday (indigenous people of melanin), and you, Afrakan people, tomorrow if you remain in your present state of insanity. Kupigana Ngumi, the Afrakan-centered Martial Science system, will help us use this information of self-empowerment and love to defend ourselves, family, Kem-Unity, communities and nation.

Chapter Thirteen captures the spirit of Heru, the Warrior energy through *The Asrian Drama.* Heru clearly defines, what we have to do today to be victorious against the forces of esfet, white male domination in the 63rd century new Afrakan time. Spiritual Warriors clearly define what a warriors is, and that our greatest battle will be within our own minds. We have to re-capture our own true Afrakan spirit, so that healing can take place in our own hearts. None of this can happen if we do not know who our enemies are and who are our allies, and most important, who we are!.

My final chapter, Fourteen, the beginning of my gift, is how to develop **Heart**, your ***Moyo***, your personal spiritual power so that you can liberate and heal yourself. Once you become Heru, the Spiritual Warrior, you can give your gifts to the world, and leave a legacy for our children and for all lost or uninspired souls to come. It is not so much what we say, but in the final moment, what we think is what we do!

Spiritual Warriors Are Healers is a tool or instrument for Afrakan liberation. In this book, I never refer to our collective experience as Afrakan people or our written or oral records of images issues and events of our glorious past, as *history*. Whenever we use the word *history*, we are automatically locked into a sexist, racist, backward none spiritual western concept of European Caucasian male domination, as well as an Asian Worldview. Spiritual Warriors innerstand that *history* and western civilization are synonymous and anti-Afrakan.

History celebrates the savagery and murder by European Caucasian domination through migratory Eurasian conquests of Afrakan people, Afraka and everyone that has been exposed to them over their last recorded four thousand years. We as Spiritual Warriors or Afrakan people must not be connected to the world in this type of insane, cancerous, murderous relationship with the planet and its inhabitants. It must be clear that the people we call the Wazungu, the Melanin deficient Caucasian humankind from the land we now call Europe and Asia, who migrated to North America, Australia, South America, New Zealand, Tasmania, South Afraka, and the Caribbean Islands are proud of their *history* of genocide, and barbaric destruction of land, resources, and people. Their present day museums are trophy cases of European Caucasian domination, white supremacy, displaying what they have stolen, plundered, or co-opted as their own in the name of western civilization. The real tragedy or madness here, is that the world has been tricked or hypnotized into accepting this insanity as normal and Okay. Eurasians have imposed this insane Worldview over all the world in the name of western civilization. We as new Afrakans must reject this concept of *history* in relationship to our human experience on this planet. Napolian Bonapart of France said,"History is the Lie agreed upon". Spiritual Warriors will tell Ourstory, good or bad, from a Ma'atian spiritual perspective or die in the attempt!

As a Spiritual Warrior, I want to make it crystal clear that even the most Afrakan-centered among us, at best are recovering addicts of European Caucasian domination, white supremacy.

If you have been indoctrinated into its religious institutions, worked in its capitalistic economic institutions, watch tell-a-lie-vision - TV regularly, or obsessed with western movies, then we are pluged into the Matrix of white male domination. We are also pluged in if we are dependent upon information only by western news, its newspapers and magazines, desire the American dream or are aroused by its standards of beauty and sexual perversion, than you are affected by this Wazungu cancerous virus, a drug more deadly than crack or cocaine combined. This drug has no friends, it destroys its own as it reaches inward and outward and it is on the verge of destroying the whole human family. This deadly drug is European Caucasian domination, Euro-centrism or white male supremacy. And like any recovering addict, you must remove yourself from the source of the problem, mentally, physically and spiritually. Next, the recovering addict must start a healing program that repairs what has been destroyed or taken away and rebuild a new person. This new person must be strongly rooted in Kultural values that are life-giving, life-sustaining and that is connected to their collective ancestral memory. They must also be spiritually centered in the love of life, and mentally focused on your gift of life. This new Black Afrakan must be initiated into this wholistic, spiritual Pan-Afrakan Worldview. Remember, just as every other addict the possibility of a relapse back into western insanity is not only great, but also guaranteed! Moreover, it does not matter how many books Molefe Asante has written, or how many Ph.D.'s Maulana Karenga has, or how many degrees Mfundishi has in Martial Arts, and it does not even matter how many public schools and streets we name after Dr. Martin Luther King Jr., and Malcolm X. It does not matter if you have read all the books on African History in your public library. If we, as Afrakan people, do not recognize our Divinity through Afrakan Kulture and Spirituality and develop a recovery program that re-Afrakanizes and re-connects the whole Afrakan family from an Afrakan-centered reality that is outside of the matrix of Caucasian domination, then we are doomed and powerless over this drug that is destroying the whole planet like a cancer. We can only defeat this addiction if we are in active wholistic, spiritual recovery.

Finally Spiritual Warriors and recovering addicts must be connected with like mind-sets that are wholistically involved in building institutions and families that will perpetuate this life-giving, life-sustaining, wholistic existence and Pan-Afrakan Spiritual Worldview in our homeland Afraka and throughout the Diaspora. Spiritual Warriors are ultimately preparing Afraka for its lost and stolen children, and we are preparing Afraka's children for a glorious homecoming, mentally, physically and spiritually.

This gift ***"Spiritual Warriors Are Healers"*** is our Afrakan ancestors' contribution to the liberation of our minds in the 63rd century, Sema Tawy, new Afrakan time. Mfundishi Jhutyms Ka en Heru Hassan Kamau Salim is only an instrument that the great and powerful ancestors used to express these thoughts. They do not belong to me, they just came through me to bring you wisdom where there is ignorance, clarity where there is confusion and hope where there is despair. I take responsibility for all mistakes because they are truly mine. Let us all grow in our innerstanding of the forces of nature, and the laws governing the cosmos, which is a small reflection of the All, The NTCHR. Internalize the knowledge of your wise fore-parents, for those who are skilled in the wisdom of your ancestors, surely will live forever. This is the essence of this gift. *Ee m htp me Ra jet* (I come in peace like Ra for eternity).

Kemet Chronology of Ancient Kemet

An Afrakan-centered Overview

In order to innerstand ancient Kemet, it is important to study the chronology of our ancient story. Kemet Ourstory was ancient and civilization in Afraka was in full bloom long before the so called 1st Dynasty. Afrakans along the Hapy (Nile River) had developed writing, mathematics, the 12 and 13 month Kalendar of 365 1/4 days, astronomy, masonry, a matriarchal political system based on native Black Afrakan Royalty, and a well defined spiritual system in place before 4240 B.C.E. The Heru m Akhety - Neb Hu was already over 5,000 years old, by the so called 1st Dynasty or the beginning of the First Golden Age of reunification, proving that a dynamic Afrakan civilization was living in the Hapy Valley while the rest of the known world was still sleep and barbaric.

4240 B.C.E. (Before Common Era) = 1 S.T. (Sma Tawi) or Prt Spdt hna Ra (the helical rising of Sirius together with the sun) = new Afrakan time.

(4240 B.C.E. to 2180 B.C.E.) from 1 S.T. to1160 S.T.
1st Golden Age, The Old Period: Kemet civilization fully established, writing, a kalendar, mathematics, astronomy, astrology, masonry, shipbuilding all in place by the so called 1st Dynasty. Mer Khutu (The Pyramids age) lasted for about 1,500 to 1,800 years. The 1st Golden Age ends around 2180 B.C.E. or 1160 S.T.

The Hapy Valley near Men-Nefer, showing the same type of architectural design of the great palace from Kash. This was also the design on the serek that denoted the Nswt RN (name).

The letter "b" in the figure above, shows the great palace with the Heru national symbol of rulership and leadership on top. Letter "c" is a front view of the great palace in ancient Kash or Ta Seti, the same logo was adopted by their ancestors and extended family in ancient Kemet. These images come from an incense burner from ancient Kash about 200 -300 years B.S.T. Before the reunification of Kemet by the Nswt Narmer.

A sitting statue of the Nswt Ntchr r Khet (Djoser or Zoser) of the 1st Golden Age, with traces of his beautiful dark brown hue, and right, Imhotep builder of the step Mr Khut for the Nswt Djoser. Imhotep was one of the first recorded multilevel Black geniuses of ancient Kemet and the World. He was an architect, scribe, doctor, priest, astronomer, counselor, and Vizier and Treasurer of the Nswt Ntchr r khet of ancient Kemet.

(2180 B.C.E. to 2040 B.C.E.) 2060 S.T. to 2200 S.T.

1st Period of Instability (internal disorder do to extrem draught): The first time large numbers of Asians invade Kemet, north east Afraka, but Kemet is still a Black Afrakan nation in the northern delta and almost all Black in the south, from Waset to Abu (Aswan).

(2665-1784 B.C.E.) 1575 S.T. to 2456 S.T.

2nd Golden Age (Literary Age): The so-called 11th Dynasty-founded by Mentchuhotep. Other dynamic leaders of this Middle Period were: MhatAmen SehotepibRa (Amenemhet 1) and SenUseret.

(1750 - 1552 B.C.E.) 2490 S.T. to 2688 S.T.

2nd Period of Instability: Foreign invasions by Hyksos and other Asian nomads in the Afrakan Kemet Delta. Also major invasions of North Afraka, southern Europe, Persia and India by the Indo-Europeans (Aryans).

(1552 - 1190 B.C.E.) 2688 S.T. to 3050 S.T.

3rd Golden Age (The New Period): Leadership from the south regains the glory and power back to Kemet. Several powerful Nswt and Hemut: HotepAmen Heqawaset (HotepAmen 111), Jhutyms, HatshepsutAmen, AkhenAten. The Hemut were HatshepsutAmen, Tiyi, Nefertsry and Nefertity. In the next ruling family was a powerful period of military leadership under the Sety and MessuRa Userma'atRa stp n Ra 11).

(1200 B.C.E.) 3040 S.T. Afrakans spreading spiritual knowledge and wisdom to the Olmecs in Central America.

** All the golden ages are led by native Black Afrakan royalty.*

(1000 B.C.E.) 3240 S.T.

3rd Period of Instability: Surrounded by foreign rule, but the masses of Kemetyu were still Black Afrakans.

(800 - 500 B.C.E.) 3440 to 3738 S.T. Afrakan influence on Krishna, India.

(760 B.C.E. or 3480 S.T.)

4th Golden Age (Last of the Golden Ages, also called the Late Period of ancient Kemet): The late period was a Revival Age. Strong leadership from Kash under the Nswt Kashta, Piankhy, Shabaka and Taharqa went back to the Old and Middle Period for Kultural models; the Shabaka Text was produced; the last period of political and Kultural rule of Kemet by native Afrakan royalty with an Afrakan Worldview.

(600 B.C.E.) 3640 S.T. Afrakan influence on Buddhism, India.

(550 B.C.E.) 3690 S.T. Afrakan influence on Confucianism, China.

(500 B.C.E.) 3738 S.T. Afrakan influence on Taoism - Lao Tzu, China.

Afrakan glory will retreat back into the interior of Afraka, constantly moving and evading European Caucasian and Asiatic invasions and influence. Powerful Afrakan leadership and glory will move back up south to Kash and westward towards western Afraka, and rule for another 1,000 years before Islam and European Caucasian domination chips away at Afrakan Kulture, spirituality and destroys or weakens an Afrakan Worldview.

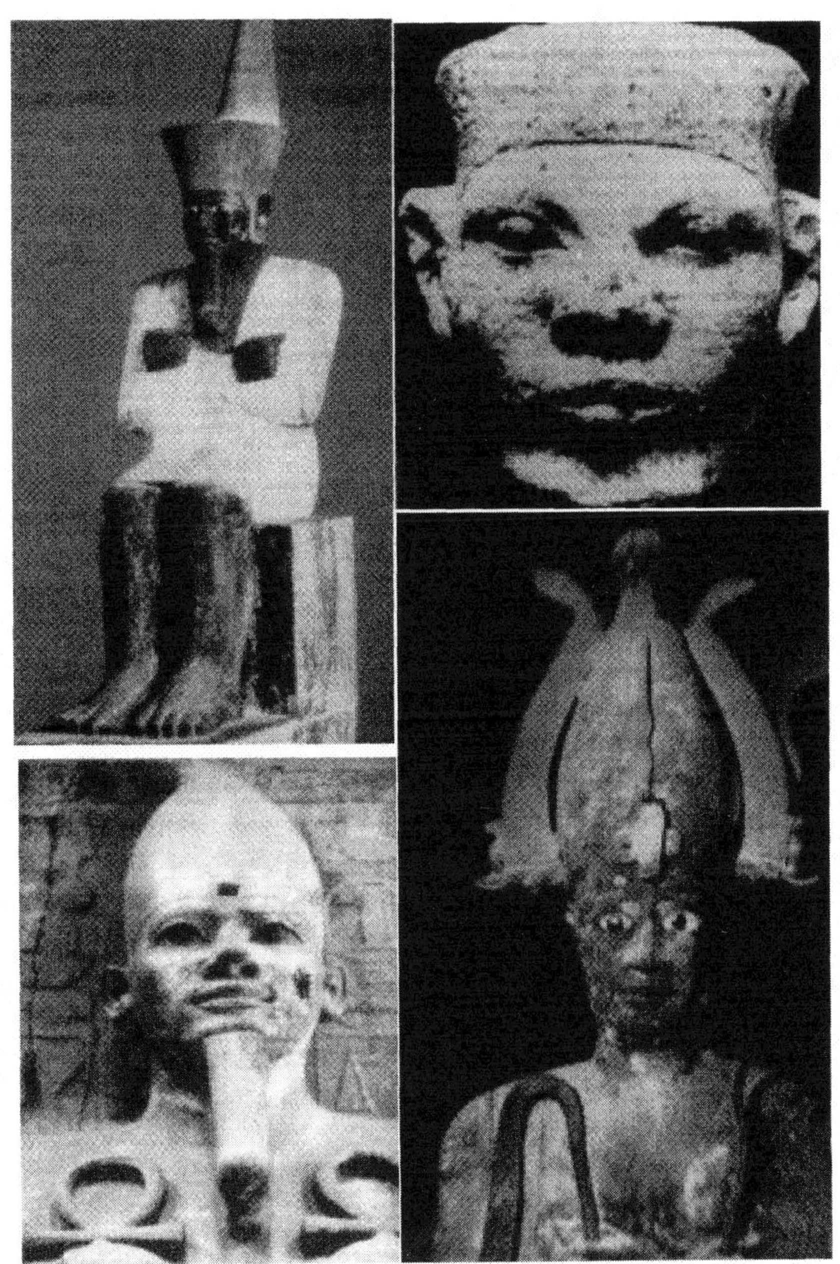

Bottom right is Asr, one of the oldest Ntchru of Ancient Kemet, and its first Nswt. Top right is Narmer, the first Nswt Of the re-unification of Ancient Kemet. Top left is Mentchuhotep one of the leaders and founders of the Middle Period. Bottom left is Senwosret KheperkaRa (Sebwosret 1) , also a leader of the Middle Period. All these leaders of ancient Kemet are Black Afrakans, like the majority of the Nswut and Hemut of ancient Kemet.

Top right is Heru em Akhety an Afrakan statue over 10,000 years old, showing the Afrakan genius in math, science, astronomy, astrology, architecture and masonry. Top left is Ast and Heru the great Black Mother and Son that the Hebrews and Christians will steal thousands of years after Kemet. Bottom left is Hemt Nswt Wrt Tiyi, ruler during three different Nswut of Ancient Kemet. Bottom right, Em-het-Amen (Amenemhet lll, a typical Black Afrakan Nswt of Ancient Kemet.

Mfundishi Jhutyms Ka-n-Heru El- Salim standing in front of a statue of Akh-en-Aten, a 3rd Golden Age Nswt (Ruler) of ancient Kemet, northeast Afraka, inside the Cairo Museum. Below, the symbol of Aten worshiped by Akh-en-Aten.

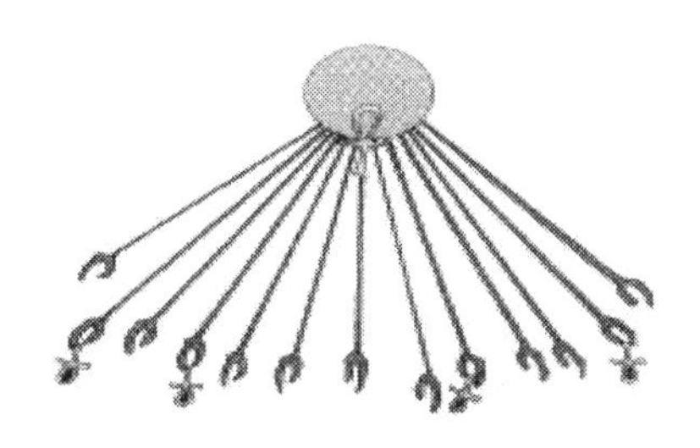

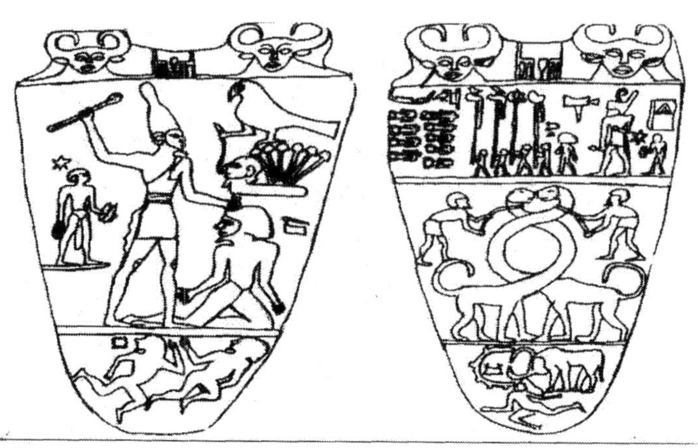

4240 B.C.E. or 1 S.T., -(Sema Tawy - unity of the two lands)= New Afrakan Time.

The Kemetik Priest Scientist believed that the new age of Taurus the bull and the new title of the Heru (ruler), The Bull, shown on the top of both sides of the palette came about around the same time. This Palette of Narmer shows the re-unification of Upper and Lower Kemet, and the Nswt Heru Narmer as a mighty bull defeating his enemies.

The Kemetik Kalendar

Month	Abed	Inundation	Coptic Name	Corresponding Gregorian Date
		First Season – Shemu		
	Meso-Ra	Birth of Ra	Mesore	August
	Jehewty	*Ntr* of Wisdom/Knowledge	Techit	September
	Menkhet	The Third Month	Paophi	October
	Het Heru	The House of Heru	Hathor	October – November
		Second Season – Peret		
		Growing		
	Ka-Her-Ka	The Ka Over the Ka	Khoiak	November – December
	Shefbedet	The Sixth Month	Tobi	December – January
	Rekh Wer	The Great Burning	Meshir	January – February
	Rekh Nedjes	The Small Burning	Phamenoth	February – March
		Third Season – Akhet		
		Harvest		
	Renutet	*Ntr* of the Harvest	Pharmouti	March – April
	Khonsu	Khonsu	Pachons	April – May
	Paini	The Festival of the Valley	Payni	May – June
	Ipet	The One of Ipet	Epipi	June – July

Major Foreign Invasions on Afraka

Hyksos - (1750 B.C.E. to 1552 B.C.E.) 2490 S.T. to 2688 S.T.

Persians - (525 - 405 B.C.E. and 343 -332 B.C.E.) 3915 - 3835 S.T.
and 3897 - 3908 S.T.

Greek and Macadamia Invasion - (332 - 30 B.C.E.) 3908 - 4210 S.T

Roman Invasion - (30 B.C.E. - 395 C.E.) (Common Era) 4210 S.T.- 4635 S.T.

Romans accept the Coptic Religon with Serapis and the destruction of Afrakan religious teachers. (315 C.E. or 4555 S.T.)

European and Asiatic Vandals (429 C.E.) 4669 S.T. (They came only to destroy and steal, Roman Empire overrun.)

Arab Invasion - (640 C.E.) 4880 S.T. They are still occupying our land as foreign conquerors. Arab civilization rises with the decline, or destruction of Afrakan civilization. Racism and genocide.

Moorish Conquest of their own people and southern Europe in the name of Islam and the invading Arabs, from (711 C.E. to 1492 C.E.) 4951 S.T. - 5732 S.T. and in northwest Afraka until the coming of the Europeans in the 15th century C.E..

(1000 -1500 C.E.) 5240 - 5740 S.T. Invasion of India by Muslims.

(1492 C.E.) 5732 S.T. - Europe was "land poor", "people poor", and "resource poor". Spanish inquisition and the ejection of the Moors by the Catholic Church.

(1496 C.E.) 5736 S.T. - European destruction of the native Americans, and their discovery of sugar cane, molasses and rum. Capitalism, racism and genocide.

(1510 C.E.) 5750 S.T. - Bartolome de las Casas - A Franciscan Bishop who initiated the Afrakan enslavement. Capitalism, racism and genocide.

(1516 C.E.) 5756 S.T. - The Asisento - Contracted to bring Afrakans to the Spanish new world. Capitalism, racism and genocide.

(1519 C.E.) 5759 S.T. - Cortez - Discovers the Aztecs in Mexico, for Europe and destroys their way of life. Capitalism, racism and genocide.

(1531 C.E.) 5771 S.T. - Pizarro - Conquest of the Inca civilization and the destruction of the people, and their culture, colonialism, capitalism, racism and genocide.

European slavery and enslavement of Afrakans - 1400's - 1900's C.E. colonialism, capitalism, racism and genocide.

Arab slavery, and enslavement of Afrakans - (640 C.E.) 4880 S.T. - present (Arabism under Islam) . Racism and genocide.

King James Version of the Old and New Testament. (1611 C.E.) A tool of European Caucasian male domination.

European Boers - (1652 C.E.) 5892 S.T. - present (white Caucaian male domination in south Afraka). colonialism, capitalism, racism and genocide.

European colonialism - White male domination of Australia & Tasmania - (1800's -C.E.)- 6040 S.T. - to the present. Over six million Blacks killed in 50 years by whites, they emptied the European prisons to destroy the indigenous Black people. - colonialism, capitalism, racism and genocide.

After this period, Europe was "land rich", "people rich" and "resource rich".

European colonialism -(1885 C.E.) - 6125 S.T. - present (Caucasian male domination of Afraka by Europeans, they partitioned Afraka up into pieces in a scramble for wealth for Europe - The Berlin Conference).

(2003 C.E.) - 6243 S.T. Afrakans and Afraka are still Politically, economically and spiritually colonized by Caucasian male domination and some of the very same boarders from 1885 C.E..

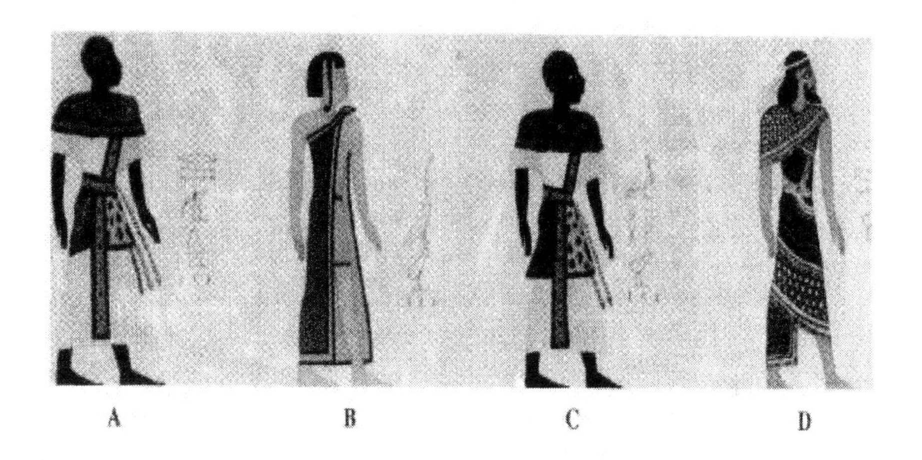

This painting from the tomb of Ramses 111 (1200 BC) shows that the Egyptians saw themselves as Blacks, and painted themselves as such without possible confusion with the Indo-Europeans [Caucasoids] or the Semites. It is a representation of the races in their most minute differences, which insures the accuracy of the colors. Throughout their entire history, the Egyptians never entertained the fantasy of portraying themselves by types B or D.

A) The Egyptian seen by himself, black type
B) The "Indo-European"
C) The other Blacks in Africa
D) The Semite

(From K.R. Lepsius: Denkmaler aus Aegypten und Aethiopien, Erganzungsband, plate 48)

Both of these illustrations, the bottom of the previous page and the top of this page clearly show how the Kemetyu or Remetchu, the indigenous people of Kemet and the Hapy Valley viewed themselves and their neighbors from Eurasia and the interior of Afraka during the Old, Middle and New Periods of ancient Kemet or the 1st, 2nd & 3rd Golden Ages of ancient Kemet.

How did the ancient Afrakans feel about the nature of the European Caucasians and Asiatics of their time. If we read their own words; we will not have to guess, because they will tell us and we all will know. ***From The Instruction Addressed To The Nswt MerikaRa***, the Second Golden Age, ancient Kemet the following words are used to describe the nature of the Wazungu of their time:

... Lo, the miserable Asiatic,
He is wretched because of the place he's in:
Short of water, bare of wood,
Its paths are many and painful because of mountains.
He does not dwell in one place,
Food propels his legs,
He fights since the time of Heru,...
He does not announce the day of combat,
Like a thief who darts about a group.

Translation by Miriam Lichtheim, Ancient Egyptian Literature, Vol l: Old and Middle Kingdom- pg 103 & 104.

Our Afrakan ancestors have given us all the healing images we need; we are just too blind to see them with our colonized eyes. Our ancestors have left us all the written documents we need, in stone, papyrus and wood, we are just too illiterate to innerstand the liberating messages with our colonized minds. Our ancestors have given us all the healing sciences and mathematical formulas we need to liberate ourselves in the architecture structures they left behind in ancient Kemet and Kash. We are so out of tune with nature we can no longer intuitively feel the healing sciences right in our faces or over our heads and even under our feet, because we are out of our Afrakan minds!

The Blue crown worn in ancient Kemet was the war crown, fashioned after and East Afrakan hair style of Afrakans that helped to liberate Kemet from the Hyksos in the so-called 17th Dynasty or New Peroid. This is the Third Golden Age in Kemet. It is time to go back to war, this time to liberate our minds!

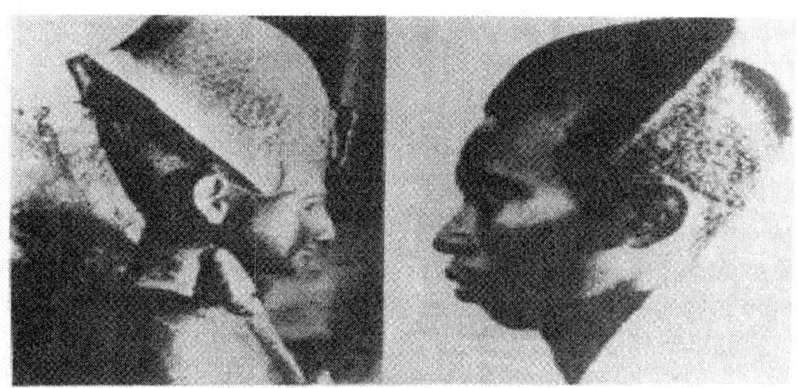

Plate 17. Ramses II, and a modern Batutsi.

As clear as Set stands before us, Ourstory, the Sankofa Spirit, is the foundation of our Worldview. Afrakans, we now know clearly, who the Europeans Caucasians are and who the Asiatics are. His-story and Our-story all equals the same story, Europeans and Asiatic collectively, are both the enemies of an Afrakan Worldview. They collectively are anti-Black Afrakans Kulture and Spirituality! As a Spiritual Warrior, this means the Wazungu- European Caucasians and Asiatics collectively are the enemies of Afrakan people.

Our real battle will be the ***re-Afrakanization*** of Afrakan people into an ***Afrakan Spiritual and Kultural Pan-Afrakan Worldview***. Once we see ourselves as ***Spiritual Beings*** having a human experience here on Earth, we will be able to Kultivate the mental, physical and spiritual aspects of our souls for liberation from the mental enslavement of Caucasian male domination and Arabism. We must see ourselves as the Ntchru, divine beings, spiritual expressions sent hear to maintain ***Ma'at***. This book, ***Spiritual Warriors Are Healers***, is part of my gift to you Afrakan people, from the ancestors who are operating through me. Take these words and digest them. Take these images and digest them. May each of us use only what we need, and together we will have the power and strength to ***liberate ourselves***, flourish and remain a ***sovereign people*** for ***eternity***.

Digest these images of yourself, so that you can be yourself. Nswut and Hemut aa of ancient Kemet: left top Kufu, Djedef-Ra, Pepi MeryRa (Pepi 1), Hatshepsut-Amen and bottom left; Tiyi, Sahu-Ra & Ankhenes.

CHAPTER I (1)

Somo la Kwanza

The NTCHR

The NTCHR is the "ALL." Everything that the human mind can conceive is part of the NTCHR. And everything that is incomprehensible, invisible, and even inconceivable is also part of The NTCHR. The NTCHR is the plants, the air, the mountains, the cosmos, the smallest microorganisms, the waters, the heartbeat, the thought, and even your dreams.

The NTCHR is all time and all space and the not yet existing time and space, this is also an aspect of the Divine Dichotomy. It is the infinite All or the infinite One. The NTCHR is nameless, hidden, formless, indefinableness, infinite Konsciousness, a self-existent, self-perpetuating force that created energy. It is intangible and yet it breathes its life in all of us. It is pure Konsciousness. It is intelligence underlying and supporting all matter and all existence. The NTCHR is the parents - Father and Mother of existence. The NTCHR is eternal, infinite and endures forever.

The NTCHR cannot be innerstood in it's totality for its very essence is unknowable to humans in this physical form. The NTCHR is everything and everything is part of the NTCHR.

The "Creation" of the Universe is mental, held in the mind of the "All", the greater intelligence, the NTCHR. The NTCHR is Spirit.

This Supreme Spirit, the infinite mind of The NTCHR, is the womb of the Universe. The Kemetyu (the black people of ancient Afraka) Spiritual Warrior Healer Scientists states that "Creation" has not been "Created." "Creation" is, in fact, mental manifestations, which are emanations of The NTCHR. These same ancient Kemetyu Priest Scientists tell us that we, our souls, are not only manifestations of The NTCHR, but that we are The NTCHR. As the Creator, The NTCHR alone exists. The NTCHR is the Creator and Creation.

It is The NTCHR, which causes time, space and the appearance of physical objects to exist. Physical science testifies that matter is no more than an illusion. Illusion is the only reality. The fact of the matter is that matter is not a fact. That which we call matter is merely energy, power, or force combined at various vibrational frequencies. The Spiritual Priest Scientists of the Kemet legacy say that what is perceived as energy and force is an outward manifestation, or projection, of the mind of The NTCHR. The NTCHR is absolute reality and is unfathomable. The absolute NTCHR is truly beyond the description of words or models. In order to truly innerstand and know the absolute, one must be "One" with the Absolute, a state of "Being", or "Becoming Heru", that can be accomplished by tapping into the infinite subjective mind. To recognize your Oneness with The NTCHR is a process, which involves removing the veil of ignorance and becoming a Spiritual Warrior. The closer Spiritual Warriors come to innerstanding themselves, the more enlighten they become and the greater their spiritual healing powers.

The Oneness of all things is Creation and all Creation is an aspect of the Absolute All, which is One, flowing in and out of all things. We humans are fascinated by the illusions of the many manifestations of the "One". We spend all of our time ignorant, unaware of its source, the "One," The NTCHR. Many spiritual thinkers believe that the entire Universe consists of duality like heaven and earth, good and evil, negative and positive, male and female, ying and yang, creator and created, etc. These dualities are contained within the much larger balanced whole - the infinite One, The NTCHR. However, the reality is that their are many realities

superimposed over and inside each other all at once and even this concept is only a very limited aspect of "The One," The NTCHR.

The Mission of the true Spiritual Warrior is to make yourself and your relationship to all other things the object of intense study. Only then will you find parallels with yourself and nature because you are nature and this is how one begins to comprehend and discover The NTCHR. As the west Afrakan Proverb states ***"Sometimes we cannot see the forest because of the trees."***

The Ntchr Ntchru

The Mdw Ntchr word Ntchr Ntchru is a way of trying to say the "ALL" or the Creation of the Supreme NTCHR. The Ntchr Ntchru cannot be designed into a diagram or model because of the limited innerstanding of the human mind and because we are trying to use words to describe and innerstand that which is incomprehensible in human form. Even to innerstand aspects of its essence, we would need to "BE" in order to "Know."

The Ntchr Ntchru is not only the act of "Creation" but sustains creation at every moment. Nothing exists without the will and the spirit of the Ntchr Ntchru. In the same manner as the sun supports life on Earth, the Ntchr Ntchru supports the sun and the Cosmic Universe and Innerverse.

The word God should not be used to describe The NTCHR or Ntchru because this is a very limited Western or Asiatic concept. There were no Gods and Goddesses in ancient Kemet, because the Kemetyu saw themselves as part of the infinite All. Moreover, the Kemet Ntchru, which are forces of energy, were aspects of themselves and nature. When we use the term "God" to describe these Ntchru, we superimpose Western and Asiatic thoughts, values and non-spiritual concepts on ancient Kemet, while undermining the original spiritual Kemet concepts. Actually ancient Kemet brought light to Western and Eastern Asia. God as described in the Holy Books of Judaism,

Christianity and Islam, was merely a portion of the innerstanding of the infinite All and should not be confused with The NTCHR. Never translate NTCHR or Ntchru as God! Or Gods! The Western world does not have a concept that is equivalent to NTCHR, so NTCHR should not be translated. Just like we do not translate the concept of Buddha into the English word as God, neither should we translate NTCHR or Ntchru into the word God or gods and goddess. Judaism and Christian and Islamic heirs proclaimed the original separation of humankind and nature. They claim a superiority of humankind over nature and all other life forms. And only humans are made in the image of God, and therefore he does not have to listen to the laws of nature and life. These religions: Judaism, Christianity and Islam are at war with nature, and the Earth. Not by Konscious words, but by their very actions that are anti-Ma'at. In Kemet, like most indigenous Afrakan spiritual systems, taught and still teach that all things are connected. The Earth is our father and mother. If we destroy and/or disrespect the Earth, we destroy and disrespect its children, which are all other life forms and their divine order. European Caucasian domination has a god complex, white men think they can control nature, and its life forms. European Caucasian domination wants to decide who lives and who dies, what creatures become extinct and which creatures they will save and allow to live. Caucasian men even think they are the chosen ones, and therefore they are above nature's life giving and life sustaining laws. According to the ancient Kemetyu, even Ra must follow the Divine Laws of NTCHR.

Ntchru

The Ntchru are created cosmic forces of The NTCHR and are simply the principles and laws by which the Universe and Innerverse operate. They, the Ntchru, are powerful manifestations or expressions of the Divine will of the " ALL" The NTCHR. The Ntchru cannot act independently of the will or order of The NTCHR because the Ntchru are only Spiritual expressions of that order. Today's modern Kemetyu Spiritual Warrior Priest Scientist, who possess ancient souls, are making it clear that the Ntchru, which are merely spiritual expressions of The NTCHR, are not Gods or Goddesses. White male domination has written and explained in every book on ancient Kemet (Egypt) that the Ntchru are gods and goddess, and this Caucasian-Eurocentric worldview is expressed in every museum and western library in the world. Who ever controls the situation defines the situation.

The Ntchru, which are cosmic forces or laws of the universe, are also present within us, and in all that is seen and unseen around us. We must innerstand that the same magnificent powers of the Ntchru, which we see in the cosmos, are also alive in each human being to a smaller degree. Therefore, as we learn about the cosmic universe, we are learning more about ourselves. This is why our Great Kemetyu Priest Scientists of yesteryear stated in stone "Know Thyself," for the gates of heaven are within each of us and the glory and the power of the Ntchru is ours. This is a lose translation behind some of the Kemet symbolism carved over doorways to sacred temples and tombs in ancient Kemet.

The higher your spiritual nature or your awareness of the Ntchr Ntchru the greater your Sekhem, or Ka (spiritual energy). This awareness allows you to tap into the collective Konsciousness of the universe, all of which lies within you. Your spirit directs your Konsciousness and is an aspect of the will of The NTCHR. The study of nature is the first thing on the ladder to greater innerstanding of self. The greater your Sekhem, the more profound your innerstanding of nature and the Ntchru. When humans tap into this infinite Oneness, we, like some of the Ntchru, can transcend normal physical laws of the Earth and experience limitless possibilities and enter into the realm of the supernatural or subjective world. When the Ntchr Jhuty, (articulate thought and speech) and the Ntchrt Ma'at, (harmonious balance), guide your soul, and the Ntchr Heru, (higher Konsciousness) guides your actions and your Konsciousness, you can be a great one here on Earth in your physical body as well as walk the path of a Spiritual Healer. As a Spiritual Healer your soul is open to recieve the many gifts of the infinite universe.

The Cosmic or Celestrial Ntchru: They are cosmic forces that aid in the maintenance and general operation of the Universe. These Ntchru are laws of Creation, and act as the managers of life. Some of the known names of the Cosmic Ntchru are: Amen, Ra, Ptah, Atum, Shu, Tefnut, Aten, Sekhmet, Seshat, Ma'at, Ma'at and Mwt-m-aa.

The Dwat Ntchru: They represent the Intermediate plane, such as Asr, Ast, Enpu, Nebt Het, Jhuty, Ma'at, Seshat, Heru and the Messu Heru. These Ntchru are realms of light that are responsible for transformation between the Spiritual World and Physical Material World. Some Ntchru exist on several levels or planes and dimensions.

The Natural or Terrestrial Ntchru : They represent nature and the natural functions of things on our Earthly plane, such as Hapy, the divine principle of the Nile; Apet, the divine principle of gestation; Bes, the divine principle of music, dance and protector of babies; Geb, the Earth and Nut, the Heavens or sky and livable atmosphere. Others are Set, Heru Ur, Ast, Asr, Nebt Het and also Heru and Enpu.

CREATOR AND CREATION

Creator (NTCHR)

Creation itself is Thought and it is sustained by Thought power which we call the mind or Konsciousness of The NTCHR. This NTCHR is formless. It is a Self-existent Energy, Force, intangible, beyond time and space, pure Konsciousness, Intelligence underlying and supporting self existence. Creation does not take place within time, rather, time is an effect of creation. The NTCHR Creator created itself before time was created, a state of pure Konsciousness from the Nwu or Nun (a state of nothingness) and it alone existed. The ancient Kemetyu knew we would need a reminder of our birth so they recorded it for us, the Book of Knowing the Creations of Ra. "I was alone", the Creator said. "I brought into my mouth my own name, and I, even I, came into being in the form of things which came into being, and I came in the form of the Creator." It is extremely clear: The NTCHR was alone, pure Konsciousness.

Supreme Spirit, the mind of the "ALL", The NTCHR, is the source of all creations and everything that comes forth from it. The Creator is The NTCHR. The NTCHR is the Center or Universal womb from which all things come from and must return. So that this can be innerstood from a human perspective, let's use the symbol of a black dot to represent The NTCHR, the Creator. ⊙ The NTCHR is the origin of all souls and spirits. The NTCHR is non-dual, there are no pairs of opposites or genders. NTCHR = CREATOR. Ntchr Ntchru = the CREATION. The Universe is a creation of The NTCHR.

Creation

From the Book of Knowing the Creations of Ra, we can see that the second stage of Creation was Divine Law. "***Not found I a place I could stand wherein. I enlightened with Divine Wisdom with my Will. I laid a foundation in Divine Law or Order (Ma'at) and I made every attribute. I was alone, not had I emitted Shu, not had I emitted Tefnut, not existed another who worked with me.***"

Afrakan cosmogony shows that before things can be made, a foundation based on Ma'at (Order) must be put into place. And this is why Ma'at does not really matter in modern science. Look at their Big Bang theory - where is the order, or divine law? The fact is that Ma'at does not exist in any other creation story - not from Asia or Europe, only Afraka, and therefore Ma'at must precede every thing we do as an Afrakan people, family, community and nation.

The NTCHR, the Creator projects from the center outward into itself. At the time of Creation, the Cosmos is created, after Divine Law. Time and space come into being, and is still becoming. This Cosmic Universe is like the Aura of The NTCHR. When creation is created from the "One," an apparent division occurs, which is only an extension of itself. Now there exists the illusion of two principles, which is really one. These encompass the notion of duality: male and female, up and down, in and out, positive and negative, giver and receiver, all together in the one Konsciousness called the "ALL", the Ntchr Ntchru, which is The NTCHR.

Creation is the Ntchr Ntchru, one part, The NTCHR "GIVES" the life force and then the Ntchru "RETURNS" it back to the source in a perpetual cycle. Nothing is ever gained or lost. Like the sound of the heart the in and out is all part of the one beat. No one can create, only The NTCHR Creates. All we can do is reorganize and transform that which is already in existence. The cosmos and everything in it, including all living beings on all planets and planes of existence, are in reality one Supreme Energy, The NTCHR viewed as separate entities by our limited and conditioned minds. The unity of this whole is represented as the symbols of the Ntchr Ntchru as depicted in the various Afrakan cosmogonies. They are called: **Jhuty, Ma'at, Ra, Amen, Atum, Ptah and the Psedjwt Ntchru** for simplicity and human comprehension, but in its essence, the "ALL" is unknowable in our physical bodies or objective mind set.

The "ALL" Creates in its Konsciousness, countless Universes, which exist for eternity, but to The NTCHR this is as simple as the twinkling of an eye. The NTCHR is the All and the All must be All that really is. There can be nothing existing out side of the All, else the All would not be the All. The NTCHR, which is the All, is infinite in space, limitless. The NTCHR is infinite in time, eternal. The NTCHR can never "not be", and it can not be destroyed, because all that there is, is The NTCHR.

Who are the Ntchru of Creation?

The Ntchru are created expressions of order created by The NTCHR, the Creator, and these cosmic forces aid in the operation of the Universes, known and unknown. The Ntchru follow the design of NTCHR and do not act independently of Divine Will or Divine Order.

During the time period before the Great Nswt (rulers of ancient Kemet) Aha and Narmer, the Ntchru were called Realms of Light. The two major Ntchru were Heru, who was Higher Konsciousness and power through unlimited will, in which all the Nswt identified, (Shemsu Heru - followers of Heru) and Het-Heru, the Great Mother, powerful female energy, in which all the Hemut identified, (the Great Mothers of the Throne of Kemet). The re-uniters of Upper and Lower Kmet into One United Land, also called Tawy, the United Two Lands or Ta Merry - The Beloved Land. The most common term the people of northeast Afraka used to identify

themselves and their land was Kemet and the Kemetyu. This term as the late great Professor Diop clearly states, is really a collective meaning: the Black people. Thus, the Black people of the United Two Lands commonly referred to their country as the Black Community or the City of Blacks. It is in ancient Kemet that we first receive the Divine Creation story, written on papyrus and etched in stone long before most western and eastern Asians had even emerged from a state of savagery and barbarism to developed a civilization.

The Ntchru of Creation had different names at different time periods in Kemet and at different regions of the country. Some of the earliest Cosmogonies of Ntchru were at Annu in the so-called Old Period, the Cosmogony of Khemmenu in the so-called Middle Period, the Cosmogony of Waset in the so-called New Period, and the Cosmogony of Men Nefer in the so-called late Period. The Ntchru were: Amen (unseen, hidden, ever present, formless, unlimited, and imperceptible aspect of The NTCHR beyond duality and description) and Heru (Great Sun and Sky Ntchr) which also represented the male energy. Other male energies were: Ra, Ptah, Set, Asr, Geb, Shu, Khnum, Jhuty and Khepera. Het Heru (the Great Mother) represented the female energy. Other female energies were: Apt, Amenit, Wajet, Mut, Sekhmet, Ast, Nebt Het, Tefnut, Nut, Seshat and Ma'at.

The Afrakan Cosmogonies were developed from the various Afrakan educational and Spiritual centers, and their main purpose was to prove the concept - As above (Pet = heaven) , so below (Ta = earth) NTCHR Creates the world. In innerstanding the Ntchru, we could innerstand ourselves as a microcosm of the universe macrocosm. The Cosmogonies represented a blue print for living, and that life was based on Divine Law, not emotions, likes or dislikes.

The Cosmogony from Annu

According to the Pyramid Texts, or Mer Khut Texts, book (1248) Atum came into being, in Annu, as one who comes extended. He put his penis in his hand, that he might achieve orgasm with it. The two twins were born - that is, Shu and Tefnut. But, the Mer Khut

Texts, book (1652 - 53a, 1655) states that:

Atum Kheper Ra! You have come up, as the Hill; you have arisen, as the benben, in the House of the Heron, in Annu. You have sneezed, as Shu; you have spat forth, as Tefnut. You have put your arms around them, as the arms of (a) Ka so that your Ka might be in them. Oh, great *ennead* that is in Annu! *Atum, Shu, Tefnut, Geb, Nut, Asr, Ast, Setsh, Nebt - Het*! Children of Atum! Extend his heart to his child, in your identity of Nine Bows.

In a third version from Annu, Mer Khut Texts, (1655), It states :

Atum creates himself by the projection of his own heart, and brings forth eight elementary principles which, together with himself, make up the nine which is, The Great Ennead of Annu: Shu and Tefnut, then Geb, the Earth and Nut, the Sky, and finally Asr and Ast, Setsh and Nebt Het, entities of cyclic life and renewal, of death and rebirth. It is written that none of these entities is separate from him, Atum.

Atum is formless Konsciousness and will, and is the chief representative of NTCHR as taught from Annu.

The Company of Ntchru of Annu.

The Cosmogony of Khemmenu

In the Cosmogony of Ntchru from Khemmenu, the primordial eight, are called the Ogdoad, which line in four couples:

Nwu (primeval waters, unformed matter)	**Nwunet** (heaven - creation, formed matter)
Huh (boundlessness)	**Huhet** (bound)
Kuk (darkness)	**Kuket** (light)
Amen (hidden)	**Amenet** (manifest)

Khemmenu is the city of the Ntchr Jhuty, Neb (master) of writing, numbers, measurements, time and articulate speech, articulate thought, wisdom, and articulate action. Jhuty states that the Nuw (Nun) is an indefinable substance, the eternal and infinite source of the Universe, for deep thinkers. But on a earthly plane, Jhuty also states that the lotus is a symbol of the five elements of creation. Its roots are in the *Earth*, its stem is in *Water,* its leaves and flowers opening out into the *Air,* receiving the rays of Ra, the *Fire,* and it emits its flowery-scent to the *Ether* which could be used by the common people of Kemet so that they could innerstand their national symbol.

Ra the principle of light comes forth from the primordial Lotus. The Eight Ntchru of Khemmenu are called the Fathers and Mothers of Ra. A common misconception is that Ra is the sun, but in reality Ra is the energy that allows light to come from the sun. (For many texts affirm that Ra penetrates the Solar globe and causes it to shine, so that he renders it luminous by his passage.) Thus Ra is not light but that which provokes the phenomenon of light and life. As stated from Khemmenu:

I am he who made sky and earth, formed the mountains and created what is above.

I am he who made the waters and created the celestial waves...

I am he who made the bull for the cow...

I am he who made the sky and the mysteries of the two horizons, I placed there the souls of the Ntchru.

I am he who opens his eyes, thus the light comes forth.

I am he who closes his eyes, thus comes forth obscurity.

On the order of whom Hapy's flood flows ..., whose name is not known by the Ntchru

I am he who made the hours, thus the days were born.

I am he who opened the New Year's Festival, who created the river.

I am he who made the Living Fire (Sekhem).

I am KheperRa in the morning, Ra at noon, Atum in the evening.

This Cosmogony of Khemmenu during the 2nd Golden Age, so-called Middle Period, focused on sound or the word as the prime mover or creative energy of NTCHR. Thus Ra is All. He is called Atum Ra at Annu, Ra Heru Akhty at Men-Nefer, and Amen Ra at Waset.

From left to right: Kheper: the morning Sun, Ra: the noon Sun, and Atum: the Sunset

Kheper - e Kheper Kheperu Kheper - kuy - m- Kheperu
I became, the becoming became. I have become in becoming.
N Kheper Kheper - m - sep Tepy
Of becoming, who came into being in the first time.

The Cosmogony of Waset

The Cosmogony of Ntchru from Waset was headed by Amen or Amen-Ra. (Amen the hidden, undefined, unlimited, hence imperceptible aspect of NTCHR, whose sacred animal is the Ram.) Ra manifested the life-force operating through the Sun. Ipet - Astu is the name of the group of Temples in Waset. Ipet Astu meant "the most select of places" or "the Holiest of places" . It should be innerstood that they were universities that taught Spirituality not religion, they also taught governance, and the sciences of the universe for in Ancient Kemet the spiritual, mental and physical disciplines were inseparable. The Great Triad at Waset was Amen - the Nswt and father , Mwt the Great Mother and the Wife of the Nswt

and Khonsu , the son. Khonsu is the energy of the moon and protectorate by way of mastering the emotions, through the breath or meditation. The Waset Priest Scientist wrote that Amen had three forms:

1. The Serpent, Kam-at-f, or (Kematef) "the one who has made his time" was equal to Amen-Ra.
2. The serpent, Ir-ta, or (Irta) "who makes the Earth" was equal to Min-Amen.
3. The Eight Primordials, one of whom is Amen, who thus regenerates himself, and the Solar Child who comes forth from the lotus at Khemmenu as Ra, is also Amen.

Amen represents the vital breath which lives in all things (Shu and Tefnut). The power Triad was Amen, Ra, and Ptah - they have no equal. He whose name is hidden is Amen, whose countenance is Ra and whose body is Ptah. But the Kemetyu innerstood that Amen, Ra, and Ptah are aspects of the One and the same entity NTCHR.

The Great Trinity: Amen, Ra, and Ptah or sometimes called the Power Trinity.

The Nswt giving an offering to the Triad at Waset Amen, Mut and Khensu

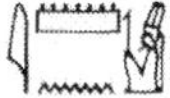

The Cosmogony of Het Ka Ptah

The Cosmogony of Ntchru from Het Ka Ptah (Men-Nefer) was Ptah the creative qualities, the blacksmith, together with his mate, Sekhmet (the powerful) symbolized as a lioness, and NeferAtum (the accomplishment of Atum), the son.

The metaphysical concepts of the Cosmogony of Ntchru from Het Ka Ptah, also Men Nefer of ancient Kemet have been recorded for Ourstory by the Great Kashite Nswt Shabaka, who was also the Nswt Heru Shabaka, who ruled Kemet in the 8th Century B.C.E. He was committed to preserving an ancient teaching of "the great ancestors". This venerable Black Afrakan leader preserved for the world the earliest known philosophical, theological, and cosmological principles of Ma'at from Het Ka Ptah in written form, now kept in the British Museum.

According to the teachings of the Shabaka Stone, the spiritual teachings were as follows: In the beginning only NTCHR existed and nothing else. Then, through its own Konsciousness The NTCHR became three, Amen - Ra - Ptah.

Ptah conceived in his heart all that would exist and at his utterance, created Nuw (Nun), the primeval waters (unformed matter).

Then, Ptah causes Nuw (Nun) to emerge from the primeval waters as the Primeval Hill, which is called Atum.

Ptah manifested himself as heart, he who manifested himself as tongue, in the likeness of Atum, is Ptah, the very ancient, who gave life to all the Ntchru. The heart and the tongue have power over all the other members, since the tongue describes what the heart conceives. Thus, Ptah re-creates the Great Ennead, and gives rise to all the qualities of things, through the desire of his heart and the word of his tongue. The four pairs of Ntchru are also called the Ogdoad:

Nuw, Nun (primeval waters, unformed matter) and Nuwnet (atmosphere, matter).
Huh (boundlessness) and Huhet (that which has boundaries).
Kuk (darkness) and Kuket (light).
Amen (the hidden) and Amenet (that which is manifested).

The Ntchru (Nuw, Nuwnet, Huh, Huhet, Amen, Amenet) are the lips and teeth of the mouth of The NTCHR which speaks the names of all things which come into existence...

...The NTCHR is found as the heart within all bodies, and in the mouth of each Ntchru and all humans as the tongue (will), of all things...

...That which the nose breathes, the eyes see, the ears hear: all of these (senses) are communicated to the heart. It is the heart (mind) which makes all knowledge and awareness manifest. The tongue is what repeats what the heart has thought...

...All divine utterances manifested themselves through the thoughts of the heart and the commandments of the tongue... "

The Nswt Kneeling before Ptah and Sekhmet

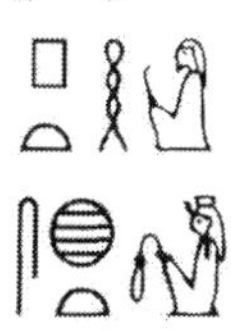

Ptah is also the embodiment of artistic creativity in Heaven and Earth. ***"All the divine decrees came into being in the thinking of the mind and the commanding of the tongue."*** This creation is made by Ptah in the form of Atum, the source of all that is created.

Thus, the Het Ka Ptah Cosmology formed the basis for many of the religious teachers of the world and we can see that it was postulated many centuries later in other parts of Afraka and in Asia in a variety of Kultures.

The Kemetyu forces of nature, the Ntchru can be followed to Nigeria where they become the Orishas of the Yoruba. Nigeria's Yoruba Kulture gave birth to Voodoo in Haiti, Shango in Trinidad, Candomble in Brazil via the European and Arab enslavement of Afrakans and trade from the 1500's to the eve of the 20th century.

The ancient Chinese Taoist philosophy of ying and yang mirror the much older Kemet philosophy of the Principles of complementary Forces as the basis of universal harmony and control. In the first Dynasty of Ancient China, Black men from East Afraka were involved in it's creation, The Shang. (See Dr. Ivan Van Sertima, African Influence In Early Asia).

Many elements of Judaism, Christianity and Islam have their roots in ancient Kemet, but these are not Kemetyu systems. Great nations like Sumer, Babylon, Assyria, India, Greece, Rome, etc., as well as the philosophers and theologians of the western world have very little to say about the Subjective essential state of the Creator. (Most at best, if anything is mentioned,) is that only chaos existed before the Creator or Creation. The Kemet Deep Thinkers explain the concept of the One, NTCHR and the state before Creation began, the Nuw or Nun, the Triple Blackness.

Ancient Kemet also gave the concepts of triads or holy trinities to the world. The most famous triad was Asr , Ast , and the son Heru . Judaism, Christianity and even Buddhism will all borrow sacred spiritual concepts from this famous triad from ancient Kemet. Asr is the ruler of eternity, Neb of everlastingness, Neb of nature, leader in front of the mighty bull of the Ament (west). Asr was also the sun after its disappearance in the west, but rising again the next morning. Asr means "Place of The Eye." Ast the Ntchr of mothership and maternal devotion; the divine mother, the great Black woman, mother of Heru, dutiful wife of Asr, who assists in his resurrection. Ast has often been equated with the Virgin Mary, in ancient Kemet she was also called Mery the beloved one. She is the Black Madonna holding the Christ, the anointed one known as Heru, later Jesus.

Asr  ***, Ast , and the son Heru***

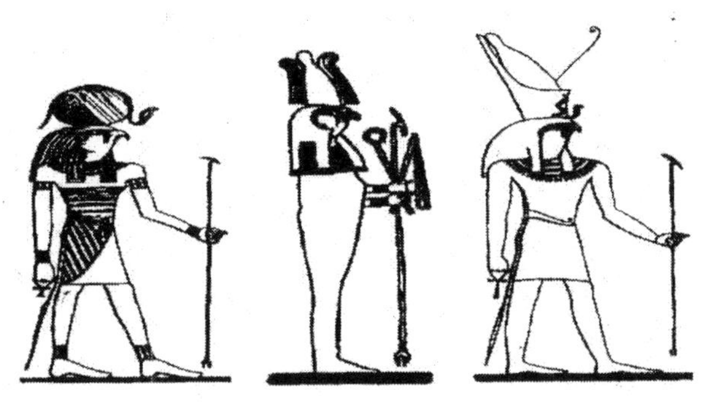

The Hawk Trinity: Ra, Seker, and Heru

Other triads were Khnum, the molder, who created man and woman from the Black Earth on his potters wheel. Khnum's mate is Anuket and their son Satet, from the city of Abu and Esna.

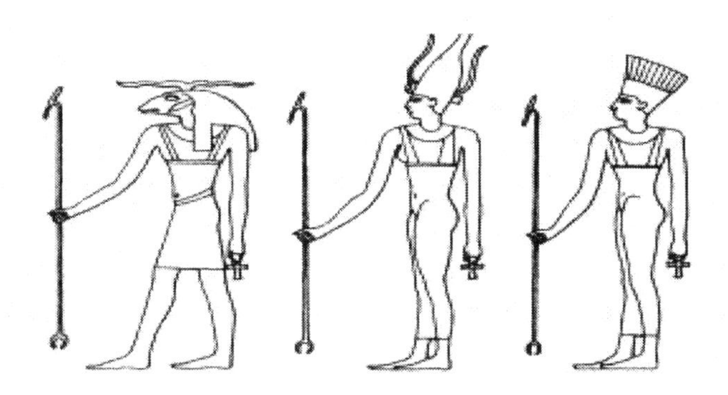

Khnum , Anuket, , Satet This triad was worshiped in the 6th cataract region, Khnum was also believed to have connections with inundation. Khnum is also another version of Ptah the Divine architect of the universe and patron to all crafts.

Set also heads up a triad from the delta with Nebt-Het his wife and their son Enpu the embalmer, or Tepy ju-f The one who is on top of his mountain. Set was basically the manifestation of blind force. The Ntchr of esfet, darkness, the opposite of his brother Asr. He ruled by might and force. Set was the sky by night, the downward motion of the sun. He was the third son of Geb and Nut, along with Asr, Heru Ur, Ast, and Nebt Het. Set was born on the third day of the Holy five days above the year at the wrong time and wrong place, by forcing his way through a wound which he made in his mother's side. Set's complement was Nebt Het, the mother of Enpu . In the Old Period he was the national Ntchr of the Delta, and during the Hyksos invasion, the King Apepa, made Set the greatest of all the Ntchru during his dominance. Set was the archetype of the Cain and Abel story, from Judaism and Christianity.

To the Remtch or Kemetyu of ancient Kemet and to modern Spiritual Warriors it is clear that the Ntchru Atum, Amen, Ra, Ptah, Asr, Ast, Shu, Tefnut, Geb, Nut, Jhuty, Heru, etc., are not gods, but attributes of the One, NTCHR. It is also very clear that the modern European and Asiatic Egyptologists, whose writings are the main source of popular understanding of the Kemet spiritual and religious system were lacking in the appropriate skills to explain Afrakan Spirituality and Deep Thought from ancient Kemet. They, modern Egyptologists did not know, and still do not innerstand Afrakan philosophy, theology, Afrakan Conceptual Deep Thinking, Hapy valley linguistics from an Afrakan Kultural Worldview that is needed to innerstand ancient Kemet and the concept of Ntchru, Ntchr Ntchru or NTCHR.

Ancient Kemet was the mouth piece of the Afrakan continent, all that we saw in ancient Kemet was Afrakan from the Black people through to their Afrakan Kulture, Afrakan Spiritual values and even all its spiritual and religious paraphernalia, originated in the interior of Afraka. The following is a list of common traits that further depicted the influence and similarities of ancient Kemet with the rest of Black Afraka, or the inside of the continent of Afraka.

1. The divine status of the mental, physical and spiritual leader, and his title the Nswt "The ruler from the South where the Swt plant grows." (Kash, Punt, Ta Khuy, Ta Ntchr, all from the interior of Afraka).

2. Royal bird symbol: Heru, Ṅekebet, Mut, Jhuty, Ra, etc...

3. The cult of the royal ancestors, lineage and blood line coming from up south from inner Afraka, the interior of the Kemetyu continent.

4. The preservation of the transformation of the Nswt bodies and High Priest. Sahu (mummifcation).

5. Common feasts and festivals, based on astrology, astronmy and nature.

6. The belief in the spirit world like a Guardian Spirit or Ancestor Spirits and the Great Creator Spirit.

7. Common root words, very scholarly expressed by Professor Cheikh Anta Diop in the following books" The Afrikan Origins of Ancient Egypt", " Cultural Unity of Black Afrika" and Dr. Theophile Obenga's books, "The Genetic Linguistic Relationships Between Egyptian, Modern Negro-African Languages", and "Ancient Egypt And Black Africa".

8. All the symbols in their language, the Mdw Ntchr, are Afrakan in origins. (Kash, Meroe and South of Kemet)

9. A Supreme NTCHR, the source of all life and all creation, the sum total of all existence, seen and unseen, perceivable and unperceivable, with many manifestations and shades of the One Konsciousness.

10. Ma'at, Divine Law is the foundation of all things in the universe, and came before Creation, so even the Ntchru must follow Divine Law.

11. Nuw, undifferentiated, unformed, undefined existence. It is inert, it is infinite, and it is enveloped by total darkness (double and triple Blackness). This is the state from which NTCHR Created itself through Konsciousness, therefore all things come from Blackness.

It is very important for all serious students of philosophy, religion, sciences, meditation, yoga, and martial science to innerstand the key role in which Afraka, ancient Kemet and ancient Kash played in the development of the body, mind, and spiritual disciplines of today.

Kemklusion

The NTCHR is, therefore, absolute, nameless, hidden, formless, Self-existent Energy, Force, intangible, beyond time and space, pure Konsciousness, intelligence underlying and supporting all existence, perceivable and incomprehensible. Thus, the mind of The NTCHR is the source of all Creations, and everything that springs forth from it. Ptah Heru is one of the names of this Konsciousness. Under the direction of Ptah Heru, Atum creates all things, meaning other Ntchru, as directed by Ptah Heru. The Ntchru are qualities of matter or enegies. Atum is the will-power to create, which is both male and female inside Ptah Heru: the mind.

The Ntchr Ntchru is creation. And this creation itself is thought and is sustained by the thought of the Supreme NTCHR. These Ntchru which are qualities of matter can be explained as dynamic principles of creation, Air - Fire - Earth - Water, and the basic mechanism by which they interact, Hot - Dry - Wet - Cold. Thus, the physical and astral universe is made of matter in various degrees of vibrational existence from gross (solid-lower frequency) to subtle (waves-higher frequency), thereby establishing the Principle of Complementary Forces as the basis of universal harmony and control. The universe is in a sense the total collection of all that is, which is NTCHR.

Below: The Kemet " Four Qualities and the Four Elements" also known as The Eight Point Pole Star.

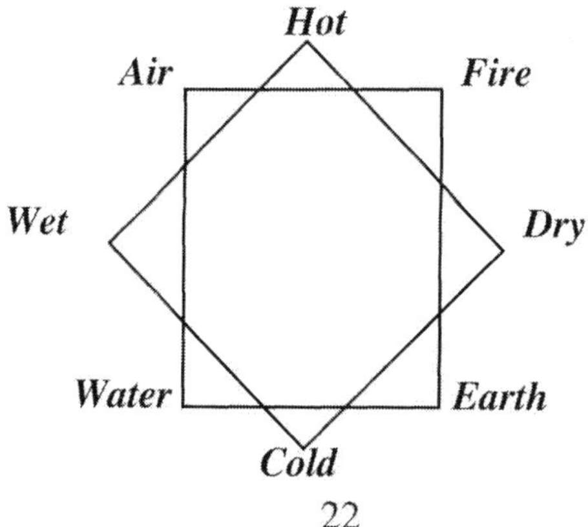

The Spiritual Warrior can find enlightenment by focusing in on the cosmic mind thereby creating a union between the two, which is really only One Konscious Mind. Since the universe is created by the mind of The NTCHR, it follows that all things, even our own mental ideas as well as what is called physical reality, are emanations from the cosmic mind of NTCHR. Yes, we are innately divine Ntchru. We too can reorganize matter with our minds. Not only ideas, but new physical realities as well, through the practice and exercise of our heart, which is your mind; and tongue, which is your will, the Moyo or Sekhem your Spiritual Power. It is only because we have been thoroughly convinced by the ignorance of the western world that we lack the power and the glory to do for ourselves, or to resurrect ourselves. Instead, we have been conditioned that we need assistance from outside of ourselves, and that we exist in a degraded, unevolved, depressed state, born in sin instead of divine.

The NTCHR is the underlying reality, the state of Heru Konsciousness, behind all events of the world. The NTCHR is that which is perceived and also the perceiver. Therefore, only The NTCHR exists. Nature does not exist as a separate entity from The NTCHR; The NTCHR is nature. The soul of all things, including man, is not separate from NTCHR, we are NTCHR. We are Spiritual beings having a human experience; this is the spirit of the Spiritual Warrior. This is the mystery of mysteries that must be known, not only "intellectually", but also "spiritually". All philosophical, religious, and scientific ideas originate from this source. Spiritual Warriors can only be healers when they have adopted the doctrine of Ma'at, which is Divine Order in their life, mental, physical, and spiritual harmony. This alignment allows you to see yourself as NTCHR. In addition, when the Spiritual Warrior sees itself as NTCHR their is no fear! Where there is no fear of death, life, and living becomes Divine!

The Ntchru are to be seen as particular emanations of The NTCHR or given qualities of the universal process. The statues of the Ntchru Heru or Jhuty are not worshipped and the image of Heru or Jhuty is not worshipped. The statues are just three - dimensional symbols that reflect the concepts and spiritual power of the dawning of universal wisdom in the heart of the beholder. By utilizing these sacred symbols of nature, we are petitioning their force, not from the statues of Heru and Jhuty, but from the depths of our immortal divine souls.

The various creation perspectives from the many different Afrakan centers are not competing doctrines but parts of a whole. Jacob Carruthers explains it beautifully in his book "Essays in Ancient Egyptian Studies". He states that these perspectives represent various points on the circle of perceptions as the creation, which is the focal point, is brought into view. This same phenomenon occurs when anything is viewed from several angles. Each point reveals a configuration somewhat different from, but not incompatible with all other viewpoints. All the Ntchru: Amen, Kheper, Ra, Ptah and Atum are manifestations of the One transcendental principle, sometimes viewed from different angles, different locations and various levels of Konsciousness. Amen is the omnipotent, forever present unseen spiritual essence of the universe. Kheper is the creative act of coming into being. Ra is omnipotent creative will. Ptah is the spark of life or creative architect of the universe. Atum is the creation. In Chapter Two, the list continues, however, all of these Ntchru are aspects of The NTCHR that exists simultaneously.

The Kemet teachings and Spiritual way of life was taught by Afrakan Priest Scientists throughout Afraka and to foreigners who came to Kemet to learn "The Way." This is the foundation of most of the world's great religious teachings and spiritual philosophies. Afraka is the foundation of Eastern deep thinking from Asia to the Native Americans. Afraka is also the foundation of all the Masonic secret societies and occult secret orders of Eurasia and much later Europe and finally the founding Masonic mason fathers of America all owe a depth to Afraka and Black Afrakan Deep Thought.

However, for the Afrakans unlike the foreigners, Ma'at was at the center of their hearts, so upon entering the doorway of Heru Konsciousness, the Afrakan Spiritual Warriors entered the inner Konscious mind of the collective ancestors which links them to the infinite past, present, and future. When Spiritual Warriors enter the state of Heru Konsciousness and experience the light, The NTCHR, they possess the Ancient Healing Wisdom. They were and are still called Sa Sat en Ra -"Sons and Daughters of Light." The ability to develop and maintain unity with the light, while you are in your mental and physical body is the ultimate healing power for human beings.

We, the Spiritual Warriors of the Afrakan Kemet Spiritual System, believe that the Afrakan Spiritual Initiation and/or the training of Priestship in the "Deep Thought System" of ancient Kemet is the path towards the Truth - (Ma'at), and like the words of Molefi Kente Asante in his book " Afrocentricity" - " the Truth travels through the air faster than any space vehicle. Truth is indivisible everywhere." We the modern Spiritual Warriors of the Afrakan Kemet Spiritual Order must return Ma'at back into ***The Great Wisdom Teachings of Ancient Kemet and Afrakans everywhere.*** This is the mission of the Spiritual Warriors of today, to re-capture our Afrakan minds, Heru Konsciousness and bring about a ***Healing, for Afrakans, Afraka and the world.***

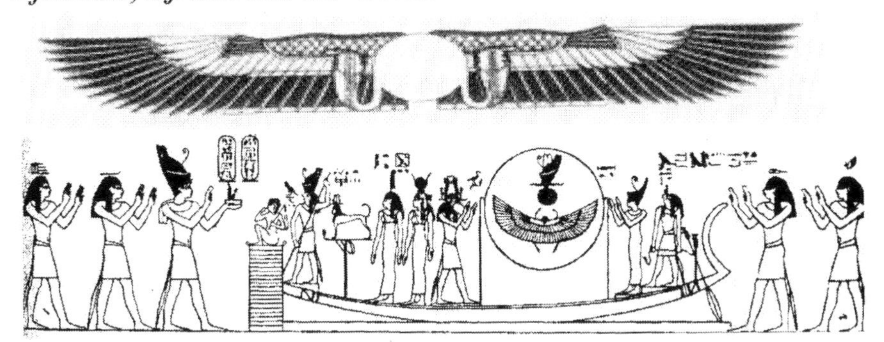

The above relief showing the Ntchru of the senses and their relationship to the Spirit (from the Temple of Heru at Edfu).

Afrakan Deep Thought was the foundation for eastern and western philosophy, and their spiritual systems.

The following is a list of educational centers around the world where the Kemet Spiritual ideas were taught:

The Great Temple in Waset, Kemet at Iput Isut Subordinate Lodges:

1. Kash (Ta-Sety)
2. Het Ka Ptah (Memphis), Kemet
3. Mali (Dogon)
4. Zimbabwe
5. Monomotapa (Southern Afraka)
6. Ghana (Akan)
7. Nigeria (Yoruba)
8. Kilwa (Eastern Afraka)
9. Media (near the Red Sea)
10. Palestine (at Mt. Carmel)
11. Assyria (at Mt. Herman in Lebanon)
12. India (at the banks of the Ganges River)
13. Babylon
14. Burma
15. Athens
16. Rome (at Elea Coton)
17. Rhodes
18. Delphi (temple at Orphic with the schools of Plato & Aristotle)
19. Miletus
20. Cyprus
21. Corinth
22. Ionian (temple at Didyma)
23. Crete
24. Megara (temple of Euclid)
25. Crotona (school of Pythagras)
26. Aztec (Mexico)
27. Olmec (Mexico)
28. Maya (Central America)
29. Inca (Peru, South America)
30. Shang (China)
31. Funan (Kambuja)
32. Kampa (southeast Asia)
33. Canaan (Phoenicia)

Afrakan Deep Thought was the foundation for world philosophy, religion and their spiritual systems.

North East Afraka	**Western Afraka**
Kemet	**Seven Afrakan Powers**
Jhuty	*Obatala*
Sobek	*Eloggua*
Heru	*Shango*
Heru-Ur	*Oggun*
Asr (wsr)	*Orunla*
Ast	*Yemaya*
Het-Heru	*Oshun*

The Kemet Ntchru of ancient Kemet and Kash gave birth to many civilizations and spiritual systems around the world with its innerstanding of The NTCHR as the Creator and Ma'at as Divine order. The southern and eastern Asians were awaken first, after they thawed-out from the last ice age, than followed by the Greeks who are the first Europeans to become civilized. The Romans come much later, but still earlier than most of the Europeans of western Asia.

Kemet -Kash	**Greek - Roman**
Afrakan (Kemetyu)	**European (wazungu)**
Heru	*Apollo*
Set	*Typhon*
Ast	*Demeter - Ceres*
Neith	*Athane - Minerva*
Min	*Pan - Faumus*
Amen	*Zeus - Jupiter*
Bast	*Artemis - Diana*
Jhuty	*Hermes , Thoth - Mercury*

The Afrakans are the first to perform circumcision for cleanliness and rights of passage, much later taught to the Hebrews, and the Black Hebrews passed this knowledge on to their Eurasian disciples. These Afrakans of the Hapy Valley set the first known eating codes, like no pig, scavenger fish, and the cow, which was later taught to India, through the spiritual system of Het Heru the Great Mother.

The NTCHR Is Love

The NTCHR is All
All is The NTCHR

The love of NTCHR is the love of life
Because The NTCHR is ALL life.

The Kemet Spiritual Legacy teaches that Ma'at is harmonious life
Only with the power of Ma'at can one love.

Love of self is a prerequisite of the knowledge of eternal life.
Knowledge of self creates the power to listen.

Listening creates the power to communicate.
Communication creates the power to innerstand.

Innerstanding creates the power to be in love
Loving The NTCHR is the key to all love and harmonious life...

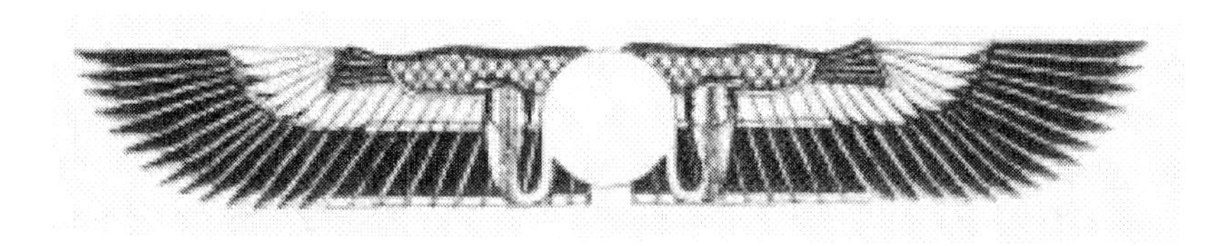

CHAPTER II (2)
Somo la Pili

THE Ntchru OF KEMET

The Ntchru are expressions of cosmic energy, with each Ntchr or Ntchrt representing a principle of nature in the harmonic unfolding of Creation. The Ntchru preside over all forms and functions, on several planes of reality, the celestial realm - energies and laws beyond our physical world here on Earth, that which is in Heaven; the terrestrial realm - energies on this earthly plane; and the under world, or Duat, the world of transformation.

Many of the Ntchru were merged with others during different time periods and changing political, spiritual and religious climates during ancient Kemet's Ourstory. Some of the Ntchru were raised to great heights in the worship of the Kemetyu, and then became almost forgotten. Other Ntchru are not well known even though the origins of some Ntchru extend beyond even Sema Tawy around 4240 B.C.E. or 1 S.T. (Sema Tawy).

Because of the mysterious, essentially "unknowable" nature of the Ntchru and the multiple layers of meaning attached to each Ntchru according to the philosophy of the Kemetik Spiritual System, it is to be innerstood that these humble definitions do not represent a "total" view of the Ntchru they describe. The Ntchru reviewed in Spiritual Warriors *are Healers*, are intended to be a guide or a springboard for your own meditation and personal Re-education towards Heru Konsciousness and your innerstanding of ancient Kemet. Use this guide to begin your journey toward inner knowledge of the Ntchru in your own life so that you can heal yourself.

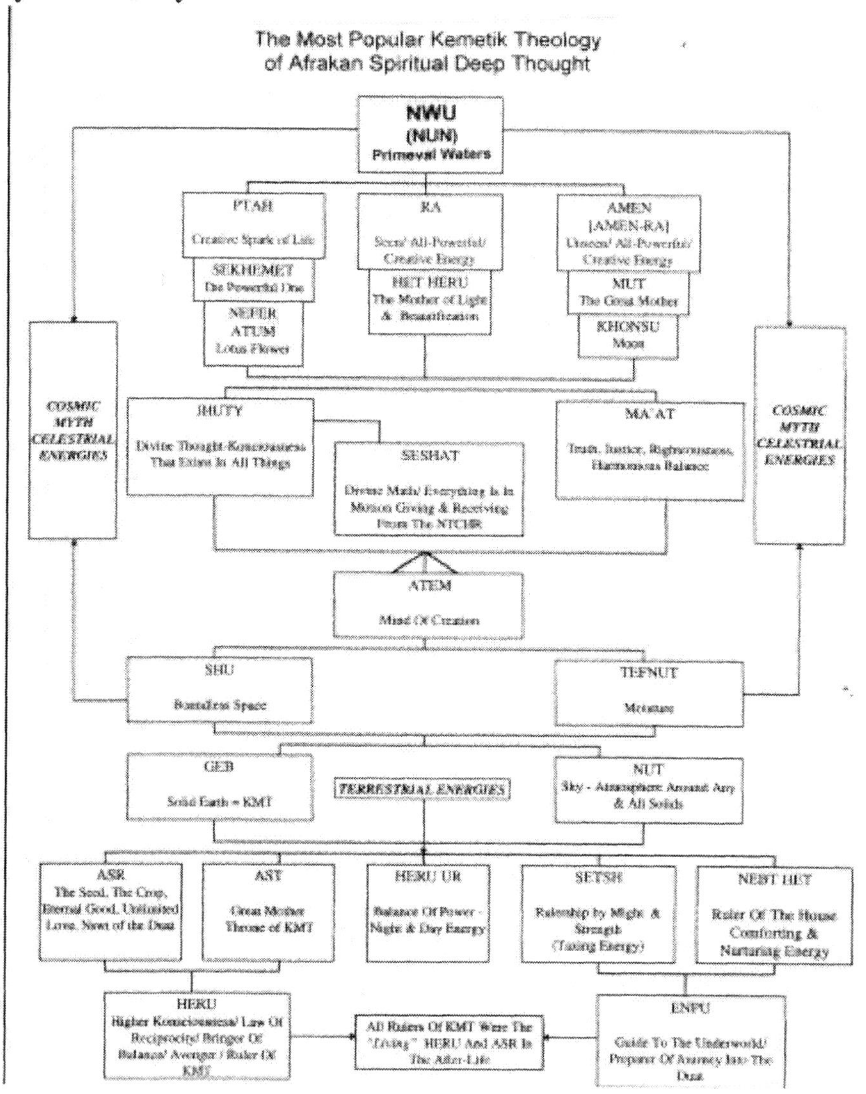

Workshops and Charts available on "The Most Popular Kemet Theology"
http://www.BlackGoldSacredLiving.com

"Ntchrw Astrological Chart" © 2008 developed by Black Gold Sacred Living Per Ankh (House of Life)

Ntchrw	Zodiac/ Element	Image	Color(s) / Planetary Aspect	Crystal(s)/ Stone(s)	Oil(s)/ Incense(s)/ Scent(s)	Herbs	Anatomy	Other Ntchrw
Amun, Amun-Ra	Aries/Fire	Ram (Goat)	Red/ Mars	Quartz Crystal *Ra: Bloodstone *Mars: Agate, Jasper *Color: Red Coral Aventurine, Fluorite, Malachite, (Diamond)	Cinnamon, Frankincense, Myrrh	Herb Flowers: Hibiscus Flowers, Mullein, Red Clover, Red Raspberry	Head Area	Asar
Haap	Taurus/Earth	Bull	*Ra: Green or Bluish-Green/ Venus	Quartz Crystal *Ra: Turquoise *Venus: Aventurine, Emerald *Color: Amazonite, Jade, Malachite. Carnelian, Rose Quartz, (Emerald)	Myrrh, Lotus, Rose	Herb Roots: Burdock Root, Dandelion Root, Dong Quai Root, Echinacea, Mullein, Nettle Root	Throat Area	Het Heru
***Shu/Tefnut**	Gemini/Air	Male/Female	Yellowish Orange/ Mercury	Quartz Crystal *Ra: Agate, Citrine *Mercury: Tiger's Eye *Color: Amber, Citrine Aquamarine, Rutilized Quart, Smoky Quartz, (Pearl)	Eucalyptus, Jasmine, Lemongrass, Lavender, Peppermint, Sage	Herb Fruit: Apricot, Bilberry, Blackberry, Blueberry, Cherry, Cranberry, Mullein, Pineapple, Saw Palmetto Berries	Shoulder/ Arms Area	Jhuty/Seshat
***Kheper**	Cancer/Water	Scarab	Blue, Silver or Grey/ Moon	Quartz Crystal *Ra: Moonstone	Lotus, Sweetgrass	Herb Leaves: Barley Greens, Dandelion Leaf,	Chest/ Breast Area	Nebt Het

*http://www.BlackGoldSacredLiving.com * Info@BlackGoldSacredLiving.com *1-866-227-3170 or 1-866-239-5313

				*Moon: Moonstone *Color: Blue-Laced Agate, Kyanite (Ruby)		Gotu Kola, Mullein Leaf		
Sekhmet	Leo/Fire	Lion (Lioness)	Orange or Gold/ Sun	Quartz Crystal *Ra: Carnelian, Golden Topaz, Onyx, Black Tourmaline *Color: Citrine Obsidian, (Peridot, Jade)	Frankincense, Musk, Patchouli, Sandalwood	Herb Flowers: Hibiscus Flowers, Mullein, Red Clover, Red Raspberry	Heart Area	Heru or Heru m Akhety
Ast	Virgo/Earth	Woman holding symbol of constellation of Virgo	Navy Blue, Grey/ Mercury	Quartz Crystal *Ra: Soldalite *Mercury: Citrine *Color: Lapis Lazuli Amber, Tiger's Eye (Sapphire)	Patchouli	Herb Roots: Burdock Root, Dandelion Root, Dong Quai Root, Echinacea, Mullein, Nettle Root	Stomach Area	Geb
***Ma'at**	Libra/Air	Scales	Blue, Lavender/ Venus	Quartz Crystal *Ra: Lapis Lazuli *Venus: Sapphire *Color: Amethyst, Soldalite Black Tourmaline, Lepodolite, (Opal)	Lavender, Rose, Sandalwood	Herb Fruits: Apricot, Bilberry, Blackberry, Blueberry, Cherry, Cranberry, Mullein, Pineapple, Saw Palmetto Berries	Kidneys	Ast
***Serkhet**	Scorpio/Water	Scorpion	Deep Red (Burgundy, Maroon)	Quartz Crystal *Ra: Coral *Pluto: Garnet	Pine	Herb Leaves: Barley Greens,	Reproduc-tive & Urinary	Anpu

"Ntchrw Astrological Chart" © 2008 developed by Black Gold Sacred Living Per Ankh (House of Life)

			Pluto	*Color: Ruby Boji Stone, Black Hematite, Black Tourmaline (Topaz)		Dandelion Leaf, Gotu Kola, Mullein Leaf	Organs Area	
*Khonsu	Sagittarius/Fire	Man & Horse with Bow & Arrow	Purple/ Jupiter	Quartz Crystal *Ra: Amethyst *Jupiter: Topaz *Color: Fluorite Carnelian, Lapis Lazuli, Obsidian, Soldalite (Turquoise)	Cinnamon, Lemon, Lotus, Patchouli, Peppermint, Rose, Sandalwood	Herb Flowers: Hibiscus Flowers, Mullein, Red Clover, Red Raspberry	Thighs & Hip Area	Khnum (Ram or Lion Head with Ram Horns)
Herishef	Capricorn/Earth	Goat & Fish (Sea Goat)	Dark Green, Brown/ Saturn	Quartz Crystal *Ra: Agate, Garnet, Black Onyx *Saturn: Lapis Lazuli *Color: Bloodstone, Tiger's Eye Black Hematite, Red Jasper, (Garnet)	Musk, Patchouli, Pine	Herb Roots: Burdock Root, Dandelion Root, Dong Quai Root, Echinacea, Mullein, Nettle Root	Knee Area	Khnum, Set
*Hapy	Aquarius/Air	Man Pouring Water onto a Fish, a Libation	Electric Blue, Indigo/ Uranus	Quartz Crystal *Ra: Amethyst, Garnet, Moss Agate, Opal *Uranus: Turquoise	Eucalyptus, Frankincense, Lavender, Patchouli, Sage	Herb Fruits: Apricot, Bilberry, Blackberry, Blueberry, Cherry,	Ankle Area	Ma'at

				*Color: Kyanite, Lapis Lazuli Jet, Onyx (Amethyst)		Cranberry, Mullein, Pineapple, Saw Palmetto Berries		
Hat-Mehyt	Pisces/Water	2 Fish	Pale Green, Turquoise/ Neptune	Quartz Crystal *Ra: Amethyst, Aquamarine, Bloodstone, Jade, Sapphire *Neptune: Aquamarine *Color: Aquamarine Coral, Lapis Lazuli, Soldalite (Aquamarine)	Frankincense, Jasmine, Lavender, Lotus, Sandalwood	Herb Leaves: Barley Greens, Dandelion Leaf, Gotu Kola, Mullein Leaf	Feet Area	Nut, Nanuet

***NOTES*:**

In 1912, the Jewelers of America organized an official list connecting each month with a specific stone. They added or changed the list according to what was most commercially viable, and not necessarily what was traditionally deemed the proper birthstone for that particular month. This list is still used today to identify particular stones. As a result, some stones are assigned gemstones according to an astrological sign and a month. For this reason, some older birthstone lists vary from today 's modern birthstones. ***In the chart above, the stones in parenthesis are mostly based on this 1912 list or one of the common birthstone lists used today. The other stones and colors in the chart are based on the planetary influence, characteristic/energy of the Ntchrw or the characteristics of the astrological personality.***

Precious Stones used in Ancient Kemet: Agate, Amethyst, Beryl (Emerald), Carnelian, Chalcedony (Quartz, i.e. Agate, Moss Agate, Carnelian), Coral, Granite, Hematite, Jade, Jasper, Lapis Lazuli, Malachite, Olivine, Onyx, Pearl, Peridot, Sard, Sardonyx, and Turquoise, Amber (a resin).

"Ntchrw Astrological Chart" © 2008 developed by Black Gold Sacred Living Per Ankh (House of Life)

The Kemetyu are considered to be the first to have used medical astrology that represent the "Astrological (Zodiac) Anatomy", illustrating the correspondence of body parts and systems for each Astrological (Zodiac) sign.

Astrology is a language of interconnectedness that demonstrates in a profound way the link between everything like, colors, crystals, health, people, signs, planets, herbs, etc. It establishes these connections through a very logical analysis of correspondences and polarities/ dualities in all things that are the mathematical principles used by our ancient ancestors, the Kemetyu.

The human body, crystals, planets, astrological (zodiac) signs and herbs contain elements found in nature. The body contains all of the five elements found in nature, Spirit/Ether, Air, Fire, Water and Earth that give it certain energetic qualities. (See the diagram of the Eight Polar Qualities). The human organism is an exact miniature duplicate of the solar system with the outer framework of the body corresponding to the signs of the Zodiac and the internal organs and body systems corresponding to the planets. Harmonious health (Seneb Ma'at) is represented by all five elements being in harmony (ma'at). The herbs and food we eat, our lifestyle and level of consciousness, the planetary cycles, which manifest in our mind and body: All will have an effect upon this balance. The Kemetyu saw astrology as a "black print" for how these energetic planetary patterns may influence one's health and wellness.

"Ntchrw Astrological Chart and Information" Contributed & Written by Spiritual Scientist, Abut Mwt Seshatms Ma'atnefert El-Salim

References:

- Abut Seshatms Ma'atnefert El-Salim and Mfundishi Jhutyms Ka n Heru El-Salim, Booklets on *"Guide to Crystals", © 2008, "Colorology 101" © 2008, Pamphlet on Self healing with Energy of Color & Crystals" ©, Workshop DVD-"Self Healing with the Energy of Colors & Crystals", ©2008.*
- Anatoly T. Fomenko, Tatiana N. Fomenko, Wieslaw Z. Krawcewicz, Gleb V. Nosovskii, *"Mysteries of Egyptian Zodiacs and Other Riddles of Ancient History. A Guide to Dating Ancient Astronomical Data." © 2001.*
- Bernardine Fine Art Jewelry, Cincinnati, Ohio.
- Dr. Llaila O. Afrika, N.D., *"Manual for Advance Naturopathic" Training © 2008* and African Holistic Health: A&B Publisher's Group, Brooklyn, NY, 2004, Accredited by the International Board or African Thinkers, Traditional Priests/Priestesses, Healers, and Religion Association.
- Lucus, A. and Harris, J. R. *Ancient Egyptian Materials and Industry, Precious and Semi-Precious Stones*: Edward Arnold, London, 1926.
- Rosemary Clark, *The Sacred Tradition in Ancient Egypt*: Llewellyn Publications, St. Paul, Minnesota, 2000.

The Ntchru of Ancient Kemet

The Ntchru Heru and Set, who live inside all humans representing the struggle between the Higher and Lower self.

Ammt

The devourer of the unjust, the eater of the souls of those who's hearts proved heavier than Ma'at. Amamt can only harm those who were unrighteous in their earthly lives, the wrongdoers, the followers of esfet. Amamt was a terrifying prospect for the ancient Kemetyu, because it meant that your soul could never meet Asr and live forever in the Fields of Peace with the sacred ancestors, who were true of voice. She was a combination of a crocodile, lioness and hippopotamus. Other names: Amam, Am-mit.

Amen

The hidden one, the almighty force, the Ntchr of air and wind. Perhaps originally a Ntchr of the breath of life. Amen was self produced at the beginning of time, self existent, almighty and eternal force, who created all the Ntchru and gave form to all things. Amen is the unknowable unconditional self. Amen is the unseen and "unseenable" creative force that is spirit, and all thoughts. From the Middle Period on he was believed to be the father of all the Nswt of ancient Kemet.

In the Old Period Amen was a local Ntchr of Waset. But when Mentuhotep and the powerful Middle Period Nswt ruled Kemet and Waset became the new capital of Kemet, Amen became the Nswt of the Ntchru. Later in the new period Amen was coupled with the Ntchr Ra, forming the composite Ntchr Amen-Ra, the source of all life in heaven (Pt), earth (Ta), and the underworld (Duat). Eventually the priests of Amen claimed that there was no other Ntchr like Amen, who was the "one one" and had "no second." Later the Hebrews, will borrow this concept, who said, "Yahweh our God is one Lord" (Deuteronomy 6:4).

In the Kemetyu art, Amen is usually portrayed as a black man with a beard, with a headdress of doubled plumes. In his right hand is the ankh, symbol of life, and in his left sometimes the scepter. The tail of a lion or bull hangs from his tunic. Sometimes Amen-Ra is given a hawk's head surmounted by the solar disk encircled by a serpent. or A ram, or ram headed man. Amen's sacred animals were the ram and the goose. Amen was self created at the beginning of time. The mate of Amen was Mwt and their son Khonsu formed the Triad of Waset. Variant spellings are Aman, Amon, Amun, Amun-Ra, and Emn or Imn.

"I give him praises to the height of heaven,
And over the breath of the earth,
I tell his might to traverse north and south; ...
You are Amen, the Neb of the silent,
Praise giving to Amen
I make for him adorations to his name.
Who comes at the voice of the poor;
When I call to you in my distress,
You come to rescue me,
To give breath to him who is wretched,
To rescue from bondage.
You are Amen-Ra, Neb of Wast,
Who rescues him who is in the Duat;
For you are he who is merciful,
When one appeals to you,
You are he who comes from afar."

Votive stela of Nebre with hymn to Amen-Ra, from Deir el-Medina.

Hymn to Amen-Ra

"Amen-Ra who first was Nswt, the Ntchr of earliest time,
The vizier of the poor.
He does not take bribes from the guilty, he does not speak to the witness, he does not look at him who promises, Amen judges the land with his fingers.
He judges the guilty, he assigns him to the East, the righteous to the West."

Apep

The Ntchr of evil and darkness. Each night Apep did battle with Ra, whose spells and flames destroyed him. This nightly combat took place just before Ra's ascension from the Duat, the underworld.

In the <u>Book of the Overthrowing of Apep</u>, a ritual is prescribed that was recited daily in the temple of Ra, and the power behind this ritual destroys Apep, as well as all his other spirits, shadows, and offspring of the night. Apep is depicted as a snake or serpent. The Greeks call Apep, Apophis. A variation of the name is Aaapef.

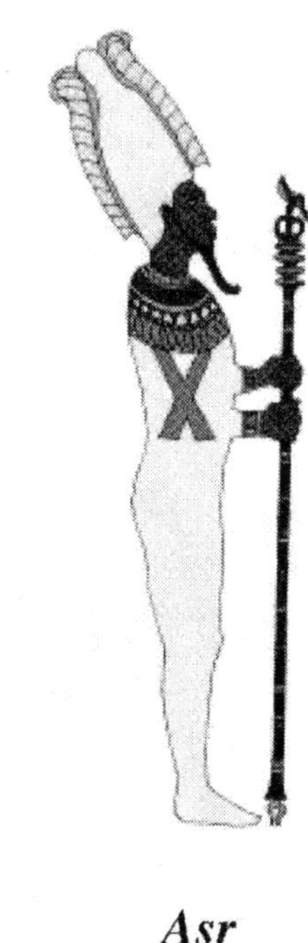

Asr

Asr is the ruler of eternity, Neb of everlastingness, Neb of nature, leader in front of the mighty bull of the Ament (west). Asr was also the sun after its disappearance in the west, but rising again the next morning. Asr is a very ancient Ntchr, as old as the discovery of agrikulture on the Afrakan continent, more than one hundred thousand years old. Asr was manifested as a water Ntchr in the very Old Period. Asr means "Place of The Eye."

Every ruling Nswt of ancient Kemet embodied the spirit of Asr and was buried in the Asrian position with his arms folded in front of the chest. Today people in the Masonic orders, many of the secret societies, some Muslims, the U. S. Military officers, all bury their dead in the Asrian position. This tradition was developed in the Hapy valley and has been in existence for more than 6,000 years.

According to the ancient Kemetik Afrakan Spiritual System, Asr came to earth in human form to teach man "The Way", The Truth; he is the bringer of civilization to Kemet. Asr is the principle of perpetual renewal of our earthly lives. He was called the great Black, even though sometimes he is depicted green in the underworld of the Duat. Remember black and green are the colors of the essence of life in the mineral, plant and animal systems of life on earth. The worship of Asr as an Afrakan deity is one of the earliest in the Hapy Valley. Asr maintained the position as judge in the Duat, Neb of justice, judge of new life, the son of the Ntchru Geb and Nut, the brother of the Ntchru Ast, Setsh, Nebt Het, and Heru Ur from the Old Period before 4240 B.C.E. to 30 B.C.E. when the Romans conquered Kemet.

One of Asr's manifestations was as a corn deity which was connected to Hapy and inundation, he was a symbol of new life, regeneration, fertility, and vegetation. Asr was sometimes called "the Crop" or "the Harvest" a personification of the seed or corn, which annually died and came to life again. The planting of the seeds were symbolic of being buried, resting in the darkness also symbolic of the Duat, and when the new seed germinated, this was symbolic of the resurrection. Asr was also known as "Un-Nefer" or Wen-n-Nefer "The Eternally Good Being," the Perfect One, after his resurrection.

The story of Asr is in chapter 13, called the Asrian Drama. In the Asrian Drama, Asr's life, death, and resurrection explains how the drama was studied in ancient Kemet. There are several sacred cities dedicated to the worship of Asr based upon the legend of the Asrian drama in ancient Kemet like Abju, where Asr's head was symbolically buried, making it a holy city. Pilgrimages were made once a year to visit the Neb of Abju. At Ta Rst (Dendera) there are scenes of transformation and resurrection on the walls of one of the great temples. There is no death in the Kemetik Spiritual System, only transformation, change, and periodic renewal. The ancient Spiritual Warriors and today's modern Spiritual Warriors are still teaching the same basic philosophy: No person escapes transformation (death), and every living soul is destined to resurrection.

From the Old Period, or the time of the Pyramid Texts, to the Roman Period, the Asrian myth was an example of how human beings could be resurrected and live forever. The Kemetyu believed that if you lived a life based on Ma'at like Asr, you would also be victorious in death and be resurrected by Asr. In every funeral inscription the deceased was identified with Asr during the funeral ritual. In Kemetik art Asr is usually portrayed as a mummy, wearing a beard and with the white crown upon his head and the Menat, an amulet associated with virility and fecundity, hanging from his neck. He sometimes appears as the Djed pillar, symbol of strength and stability in life and renewed power after death. Variant spellings are Wsr, Asar, Ausar, or the Greek form of Osiris, Osirus.

Asr is the elder of the Ancient Ones
Who establishes Ma'at on the two banks of the river
The son who is placed upon the seat
Who his father Geb praises
And who his mother Nut loves.

Ancient Kemet, Old Period.

Nebt-Het and Ast praying before the alter of life and stability.

Ast

The Ntchr of mothership and maternal devotion; the divine mother, the great Black woman, mother of Heru, dutiful wife of Asr, who assists in his resurrection. She is one of the four "Protector" Nchrtu, guarding coffins and Messu Heru jars; sister of Nebt Het, Setsh, Heru Ur and Asr. Ast is also the daughter of Geb and Nut. She gives birth to the ruling line of power that comes forth from her son Heru the power of truth and balance on Earth. Ast is associated with the art of healing and medicine. She is the great wife who loves her subjects and cares for the weak and helpless. Her spiritual Konsciousness is entirely selfless. She is the Divine Mother to whom we can turn to in times of grief and she offers warm and ready sympathy for our tears. Her name means " throne", sometimes worn on her head. She is The Great Hmt.

Ast has often been equated with the Virgin Mary. She is the Black Madonna holding the Christ, the anointed one known as Heru (later Jesus). Even the European city Paris in France, came from the worship of Ast at the Per Ast or House of Ast. Ast was also called Mery, the beloved one. She taught the art of growing corn, making cloth and designing garments. She also instituted and instructed her people in the art of healing diseases. Ast learns her magical powers from Jhuty. In ancient Kemet, Ast was the manifestation of the ideal wife, mother and loving companion and was worshipped and honored. The Greeks called her Isis: in Yoruba, she is Yemaya. The throne of Ast is a symbol of rulership of the emotions. Ast was represented by a woman with a vulture headdress or with a throne (seat of power and chair of royalty) on her head. Her temple is located near Aswan at the Island of Philae, near the sixth cataract. Later she was worshiped through out the entire Roman Empire

"Golden-tongued Ntchrt,
Whose voice shall not fail,
Skilled to command
Beneficent Aset,
Who rescued Her
brother."

-Stele of Amenmose, New Period

" I invoke you, Great Ast,
Ruling in perfect Blackness,
Mistress of the Ntchru of Heaven from birth."

-Michigan Papyrus 136 Coptic Period

Ast in the zoomorphic form of a cow, pouring libation for the soul of the Initiate, the beloved one.

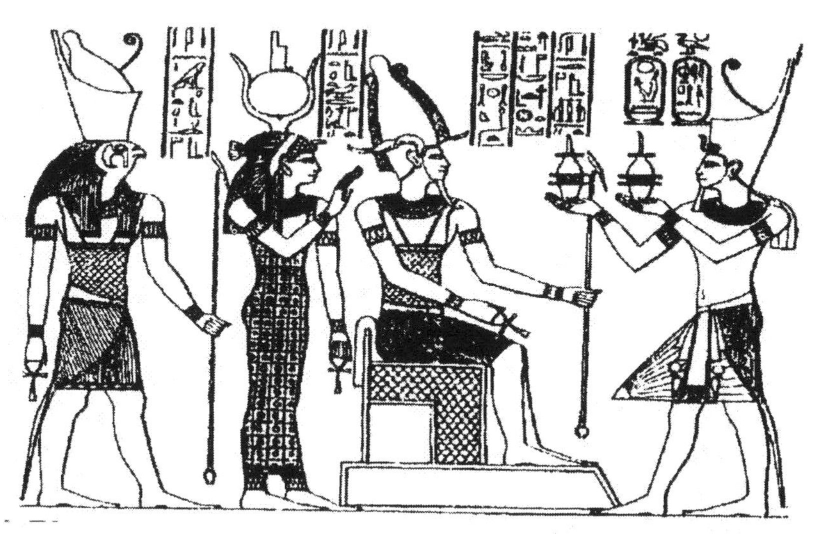

The most popular triad in ancient Kemet was of Asr, Ast, & Heru, being praised by the Nswt Ma'at- men- Ra.

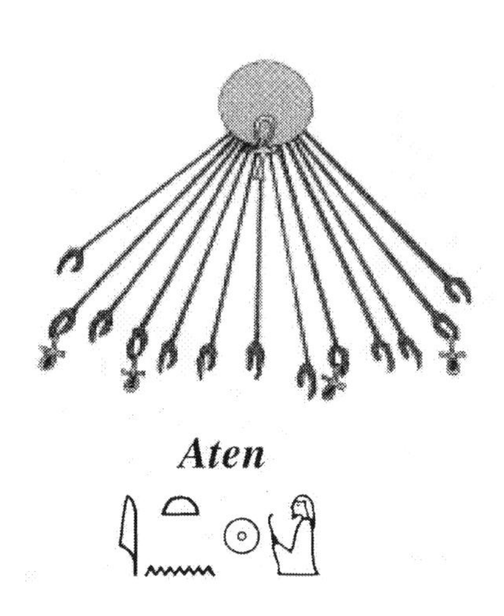

Aten

The Aten was the Ntchr of the sun, the solar disk of the sun, maker of the Ntchru, the creator of men, and self created. The Aten is an old Ntchr that was worshiped in the city Annu and later became popular in the New Period under the rulership of the Nswt Hotep Amen NeferkheperruRa (1372 - 1355 B.C.E.), who changed his name to Akhenaten, which may mean "glory of Aten." The great Nswt of upper and lower Kemet, Hotep Amen lll and Hemt Aa, Tiy, the parents of Hotep Amen llll, named their boat after this Ntchr. It was called "Aten-Neferu" (Beauties of Aten the giver of life).

Akhenaten's reign was dedicated to the worshiped of the Aten, which lasted for a little more than fifteen years. Amen-Ra was the main Ntchru worshiped in the capital city of Waset, so Akhenaten had to build a new city and capital, he called it Akhet Aten, the horizon of the Aten, now the spot where the city was is called Tell el-Amarna. His great wife was Nefertity, "the beautiful one has come," and she had six daughters with Akhen Aten. Nefertity was not of the royal blood. How she died or what happen to her during the last years of her husband's reign is unknown. Her daughters are married to several different Nswtu: SmenkhKaRa, married MerytAten, TutankhAmen, married AnkhesenpaAten and Ay, married TutankhAmen's widow, AnkhesenAmen and probably against her wishes since she was actually marrying her grandfather. Variant spellings are Aton, Atn, and Eton.

Hail to you, O living Aten!
Dawning in heaven he floods the hearts
Every land is in feast at his rising;
Their hearts rejoice in acclamations,
When their Neb, their maker, shines upon them.
Your son offers Ma'at to your face,
You delight in seeing him who came from you;
The son of eternity who came from Aten,
Who benefits his benefactor, pleases the heart of Aten

Hymn to the Aten and the Nswt. East Wall, columns 6 -10
A prayer in the tomb of Ay

AkhenAten and Neferiti below the Aten.

Bast

She is depicted as a cat Ntchrt, and often portrayed as a woman with the head of a Black cat. She sometimes carries a sistrum for music or is depicted as a complete cat. Bast is a lover of music, dance, and pleasure. Bast is a protector of pregnant women. She also protects you from diseases and evil spirits. She was commonly considered the personification of the beneficial, fertilizing power of the sun. Sekhmet is her counterpart. She the daughter and wife of Ra, mother of Khensu and Maahes. Her spiritual center is in the northern Delta at the city of (Per-Bast).

Bast is one of the oldest Ntchru on record. Her color is green and her stone is malachite. She is associated with fertility, warfare and the protection of the Nswt (divine rulers). Her temple was visited before battles. Bast is known as the Lady of Pleasure and Sexuality. She is sometimes called the "soul of Ạst" and associated with the sun and the moon. She is able to work and play in balance. A variant spelling of Bast is Bastet.

"... ***Bastet, Who protects the Two Lands.***"

"Hail to Thee ... Eye of Ra, Mistress of the Ntchru,
Plume wearer...
Sole one superior to Her father,
To whom no Ntchru can become superior,
Great of magic in the Bark of Millions of Years,
Sacred one dawning in the seat of silence...
Strife and peace are in Thy grasp ... Praise to Thee,
Who art stronger than the Ntchru; joy to Thee.''"

-Book of Coming Forth By Day, Utterance 164

Bes

Originally a lion Ntchr of protection, Bes is the Ntchr of art, music, dance, ceremonies and celebrations. The origin of Bes is in the region of Kilimanjaro at the beginning of Hapy, the equatorial region of Kemet. He represents joy and pleasure and is the protector of children, youth, and helper of women in childbirth. He is depicted as a bearded dwarf Ntchr, with bowed legs, a tail, and often playing a musical instrument. He is a domestic Ntchr, protector against snakes and various terrors. At the temple of the Nswt Hatshepsut Amen at Der al Behari, Bes is shown aiding in the birth of the great servant Hatshepsut Amen. His female counterpart is Beset.

Enpu

Enpu is the Jackal headed mortuary Ntchr of mummification and embalming. He embalmed the body of Asr, and swathed Asr's body in linen woven by Ast and Nebt Het. It resisted the influences of time and decay. He guards the doorway to the Hall of Judgement and the underworld or the Duat for the deceased, holding the title "opener of the way." Wp Wawt. He is the son of Set and Nebt Het, but from another point of view he was the son of Asr, and adopted by Ast,.and in another from, the son of Ra. He is the guard and protector of the balance of judgement that presides over the weighing of the soul (heart) before the soul is allowed to pass to the next world. In the text of Unas (line 70) he is associated with the Eye of Heru, and his duty as the guide of the dead in the Underworld on their way to Asr was well defined.Other titles of Enpu are: Tp-ju-f, "On top of his mountain" and Nb ta Jsr, Master of the Holy land. Some of the locations in which Enpu was especially worshipped are Abt, the Papyrus Swamps, Sep, Re-au, Heruti, Ta-hetchet, Saint, Sekhem, etc. Other name variation are Anpu, Inpu. and Anubis.

> ***"Hail Anpu, come to me.***
> ***The High and Mighty, Chief over the Mysteries***
> ***of those in the Underworld;***
> ***the Nswt of those in Amenti;***
> ***The Chief Physician;***
> ***the fair son of Asr,***
> ***He whose face is strong among the Ntchru,***
> ***You manifest Yourself in the Underworld***
> ***before the hand of Asr."***
>
> -Leyden Papyrus

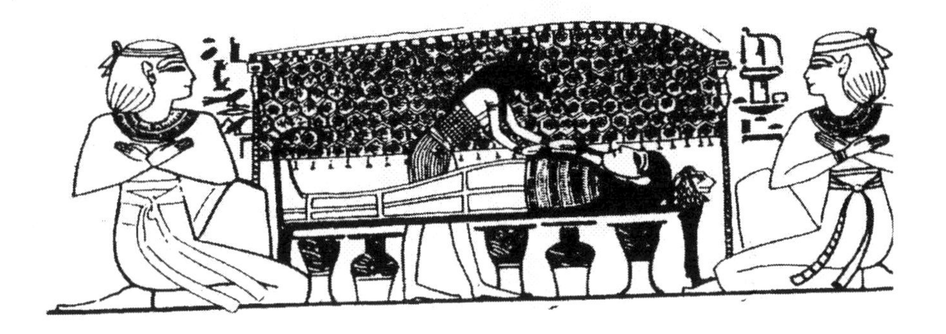

In the center is Enpu the Divine Embalmer, to the right is Nebt-Het, and to the left is Ast his Divine helpers.

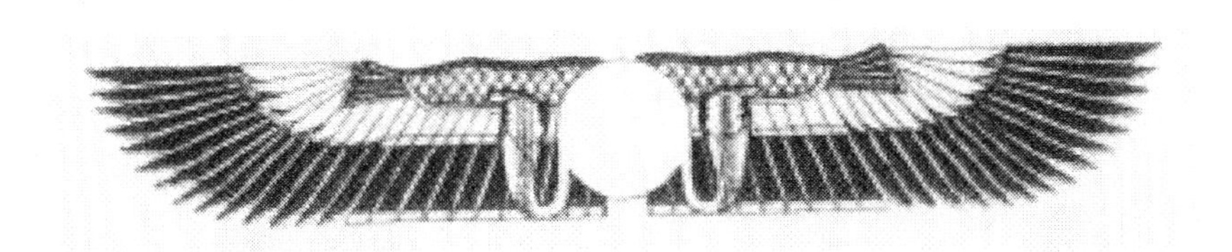

Geb

The Earth Ntchr or the Neb of Earth, is the source of terrestrial authority. Geb is a member of the Ennead of Annu. Shu and Tefnut are his parents, his mate and sister energy is Nut. Geb and Nut gave birth to five children, who represent the five days above the year: Asr, Setsh, Heru Ur, Ast and Nebt Het. He is also known as the father of the great Asrian Family. One legend in ancient Kemet says he is the great Cackler -The man with the golden egg from which the world sprang. He is symbolized by a bearded man with a goose upon his head; sometimes he is wearing the Atef crown. Geb can also be symbolized as a goose, the bird sacred to him. Other variants of his name are Kenken, Keb, Qeb, and Seb.

Geb is often depicted lying on his side under Nut, the Sky Mother, raised on one arm with one knee bent. Shu, his father, is shown standing in front of Geb with his arms stretched upward supporting Nut. Shu represents the atmosphere separating heaven (Nut) and earth (Geb).

Legend has it that Geb was separated from Nut by Shu at the request of Ra, who was jealous by the close relationship between Geb and Nut. Ra then declared Nut barren. So great and fierce was Geb's crying that he could be heard day and night and his tears filled the oceans and seas. Jhuty pitied Nut and was able to reconstruct five new days that did not fall under the jurisdiction of Ra. Hence, legend says that Geb and Nut gave birth to the great Asrian family.

Geb's color is green, which represents the fertility of the earth. Sometimes Geb is shown with an erect phallus perpetually seeking his lover Nut, also symbolic of the earth's power of procreation.

The Nswt receives his power of rulership from Geb, transmitted through Asr and then Heru. Heru therefore, is seen as a renewed form of Geb, and Geb's throne was given to Heru for his victory over Setsh.

"[Geb, Neb (lord) of the Ntchru, commanded]
That the Nine Ntchru gather to him.
He judged between Heru and Seth;
He ended their quarrel.
He made Seth Nswt of Upper Kemet
In the land of Upper Kemet,
Up to the place in which he was born, which is Su.
Up to the place in which his father was drowned
Which is "Division-of-the-Two-Lands."
Thus Heru stood over one region,
And Seth stood over one region.
They made Hotep over the Two Lands at Ayan.
That was the division of the Two Lands.

-Shabaka Stone, Columns 7-9

Hapy

The Ntchr of the Nile in inundation and the divine name for the Nile River was Hapy. The symbol of Hapy was a androgynous man with a beard, breasts of a woman, and pregnant to show the fertility of Hapy, from which all animal and plant life came. There were two forms of Hapy: Hap-Rst - Hapy of the south wore the cluster of lotus plants on his head. Hap-Meht - Hapy of the north wore the cluster of papyrus on his head. Hapy was also called the river of the south, because Hapy flows down north from the southern highlands of central Afraka. Hapy is over 4,160 miles or more than 6,825 kilometers long. It is the longest river in the world and supplies Kemet with 98% of its water.

Hapy was the artery of life and the blood for the entire Kemet civilization. Hapy and its magical waters was held to be as powerful as Ra. Although the sun transmitted light and heat, there would be no life without the vital waters of the Hapy River. Hapy is a very old Ntchru and it was also worshiped in Ta-Sty. Sometimes Hapy is colored blue to symbolize the water.

Hapy has three main sources: a) The White Nile, from Uganda, b) The Blue Nile, from the Ethiopian Lake Tena and c) the Atbara River also from Ethiopia, ancient Kash. Kemet was literally reborn annually as black silt from the waters from inner Black Afraka was added layer by layer to the soil. The Kemetik year was made up of three months of inundation and nine months of dry season; the nine months coincided with the human period of gestation. Other possibe names: Hapi.

"Adoration of Hapy
Hail to you, Hapy,
Sprung from earth,
Come to nourish Kemet!
Of secret ways,
To whom his followers sing!
Who floods the fields that Re has made,
To nourish all who thirst;
Let's drink the waterless desert,
His dew descending from the sky.

Food provider, bounty maker,
Who creates all that is good!
Lord of awe, sweetly fragrant,
Gracious when he comes.
Who makes herbage for the herds,
Gives sacrifice for every Ntchru.
Dwelling in the Netherworld,
He controls both sky and earth.
Conqueror of the Two Lands,
He fills the stores,
Makes bulge the barns,
Gives bounty to the poor."

-The Hymn to Hapy
Mer Khut (Pyramid) Text

Heru

The Ntchr Heru appears as a falcon, or a falcon headed man or a sun disk with falcon wings. Heru means that which is up, one who is up or "He who is above," or "that which is above," Up is symbolic of heaven, that which is righteous. Heru is the embodiment of what we call "Royalty" or divine rulership in Kemet. Heru was also the foundation of Ma'at in ancient Kemet. Each Nswt of ancient Kemet was the embodiment of Heru during their rule. Heru is the ultimate triumph, the ultimate transformation in human form.

There is an ancient prediction that Heru will one day return to recapture the kingdom of his father, when the golden age will be restored and the lion will unite with the lamb. Heru is believed to have a resurrection during the Aquarian Age. He is the prince of peace, bringer of order, redeemer of truth for humanity, resurrection and the life. He is able to right the wrongs of the past, free the oppressed, and restore Ma'at.

Heru is the life advocate, the warrior that fought falsehood. In the Asarian Drama in Chapter 13, Heru avenges his father's death by battling and defeating his uncle, Set. Set, Asr's brother was jealous of his brother's reign in Kemet and him.

The eye of Heru is the "all" seeing eye commonly known as the third eye. It is the eye of inner konsciousness which is actually our "first" eye. The left eye of Heru is the lunar (moon) eye. Since Heru means that which is above, he is associated with the heavens and the sun and moon are his eyes. The mastery of Heru is to return to the source or to be in a state of BEING. **Bhdt (Behdet)** - Winged Solar Disk - This is a form that the Ntchr Heru of Edfu takes in his battle with Setsh. The Ntchr Jehuty used his will to turn Heru into a sun-disk with splendid out stretched wings.The Greek terminology for Heru is Horus. Other names of Heru are : Hor , which translates as "face".

Heru had four (4) sons, Mesu Heru: Emst, Hapy, Duamutef, and Gebsenuf. They guarded the affairs of Asr, and are the four heavenly spirits of the four Ntchru of the cardinal points of the zodiac.

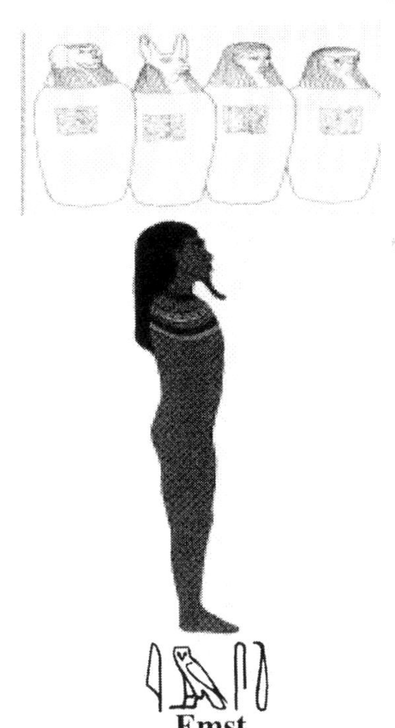

Emst

The Ntcher Emset had the head of a Man and represented the direction of the west. He protected and guarded the body organ of the liver. Emst's color is green, and his female guardian is Ast. The element for Emset is the earth which represents passive or receptive emotions.

Hapy

The Ntcher Hapy or Hapi had the head of a Baboon and represented the direction of the east. He protected and guarded the body organs of the lungs and heart. Hapy's color is blue, and his female guardian is Nebt Het. The element for Hapy is the air which represents characteristics of the intellect, activism, and being outgoing.

Duamutef

The Ntcher Duamutef had the head of a Jackal and represented the direction of the north. He protected and guarded the body organs of the stomach and large intestines. Duamutef's color is red, and his female guardian is Neith. The element for Duamutef is the fire which represents energy and creativity.

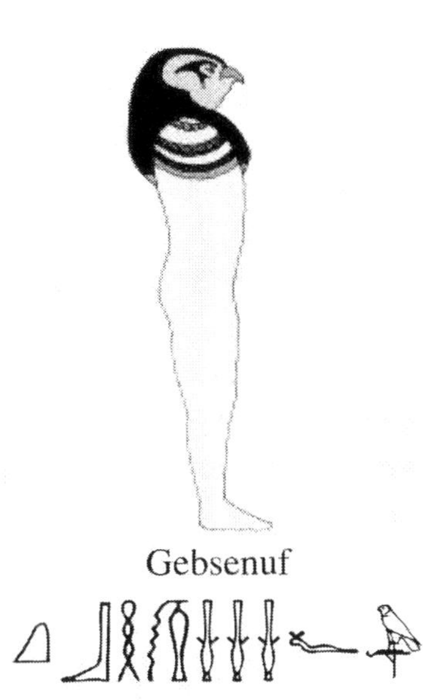

Gebsenuf

The Ntcher Gebsenuf had the head of a Falcon and represented the direction of the south. He protected and guarded the body organ of the small intestines. Gebsenuf's color is white and his female guardian is Serqet. The element for Gebsenuf is the water which represents purity. A variant spelling is Qebsenuf.

...Geb gave his heritage to Heru
Who was the son of his son...
Heru stood atop of the land
He united this land
Heru appeared as Nswt-Bity
Uniter of the Two Lands.
In fact, when Heru appears
Splendor is established under his laws
The road on which one passes is open
The two shores are made constant
Misconduct goes away
Wrong is departed
The land is in peace under its Neb
He gives disorder his back.

-DeBuck,

Readingbook

"Who is He?
He to Whom was assigned over the Ntchru
Is Heru the son of Ast,
Who was caused to rule in place of His father Asr."

-Coming Forth By Light
Utterance 17b

"The fire-child with glittering rays,
Dispelling darkness and gloom.
Child increasing in stature and sweet form,
Resting within His Eye."

New Period, Ancient Kemet

Heru is spiritual protection, life, stability and power.

Heru m Akhety

One of the oldest monuments in ancient Kemet; it has the body of a lion and the head of a Black man, a high priest. It is a symbol of human beings mastering their lower animal nature and rising to their highest spiritual potential in their physical body-temple. Neb Hu, master of your own senses. Today it is in Giza, Egypt standing over 60 ft. high and 240 ft. long carved out of solid rock. Heru is a symbol of higher Konsciousness as well as the sun giving energy and life, like the rising and setting sun of the two horizons. Kemet Priest scientist believe, this statue was originally a lion created 12,000 years ago during the age of Leo at the end of the last ice age.

"Hail to you, Heru Akhuty-Khepera, Who created Himself.
How beautiful is Your arising in horizon,
Illuminating the Two Lands with Your rays.
All Netcheru are in exultation when They see
The Nswt of Heaven, the Neb,
With the Uatchet abiding on His forehead.
Its place is made as Your symbol of power,
And the crowns of Upper and Lower Kemet
Are on Your brow."

-Stele for Tjeker-Jhuty, Late Period

Heru-Ur

The Ntchr Heru-Ur represents the perfection of Ra in Creation. Heru-Ur means "Heru the Elder", "Heru The Great" and also "Heru of the Future." In the Asarian Drama, Heru-Ur represents Heru after he had defeated Set and reestablished order and harmony in Kemet.

In the story of the Ennead, Heru-Ur is one of the Ntchru arising from Ra-Atem: Shu, Tefnut, Geb, Nut, Asr, Ast, Set, Nebt-Het, and Heru-Ur. Heru Ur is also the Uncle of Heru the son of Ast and Asr. In most Afrakan societies, the uncle is responsible for his nephew's development.

Het Heru (Het-Hert)

She is the golden one, or the golden Calf. She has many functions and attributes. She is a benevolent solar Ntchrt, with maternal and fertile aspects, who was also connected with rebirth. Het-Heru, the Ntchrt, mother of light, music, dance, happiness and womanship. She is often represented as a cow-headed woman, as a woman with cow ears and\or with a horned headdress or sometimes as a cow.

In Kemetik art she was often depicted as a woman wearing on her head a pair of horns within which rested the solar disk. The solar disk and horn headdress eventually was also attributed to the Ntchru Ast, with whom Het-Heru has much in common. In her hostile aspect she was Sekhmet. She is also known as Het Hert, Hathor by the Greeks. Het Heru literally means the "House of Heru" or "Mansion of Heru".

Het Heru is the "Cosmic Womb" from which Heru is born, the one who will retun to the source. Variant spellings of her name are Het Hert, Athyr, Athor, Hathor.

She signifies the spiritual strength to be gained by making contact with the Ntchrt force within us. Het-Heru was also called the *Lady of the Sycamore* and presided over all aspects of feminine principles and woman's beauty, such as makeup, perfume, adornment, clothing, jewelry, etc. The sistrum (ritual rattle) is associated with her and were held only by priestesses. Her image adorned the handles of sacred sistra and mirrors.

Het Heru was one of the oldest known Ntchrt of ancient Kemet, symbolizing the great mother or cosmic Ntchrt who conceived, brought forth, and maintained all life. Predynastic Kemetyu people saw in the cow a perfect symbol of motherhood, a gentle, patient provider of sustenance, like milk for her children.

She not only nourished the living with her milk, but she even supplied celestial food for the dead in the Duat, the underworld. She was the Mistress of the Western Desert. Her compliment was Heru, their son Ihi and their sacred city of Iwent (Dendera). They were also worshiped at Edfu. Interesting to note, her son, Ihi was portrayed as an infant playing the sistrum (a rattle-like musical instrument, whose sound was said to drive away evil spirits).

"I praise the Golden Ntchrt,
I exalt Her Majesty,
I raise high the Lady of Heaven,
I make praise for Het Heru,
And chants for My Mistress."

"Songs of Extreme Happiness"
Old Period, Ancient Kemet

"Het Heru, Lady of the West, Thou of the starboard side,
Lady of the Sacred Land, Eye of Ra in His forehead,
Beautiful of face in the Bark of Millions of Years,
Seat of rest for the doer of righteousness,

Ferryboat of the favored ones,
Whose place it is to provide the great Neshmet boat
To take the righteous across."

-Coming Forth By Day
Utterance 186

Imhotep

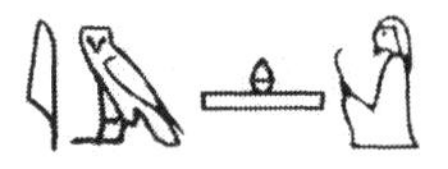

Imhotep was a great architect, vizier, physican, poet, mathematician and astronomer who lived during the so called 3rd Dynasty in ancient Kemet 5,000 years ago. He was the designer of the Step Pyramid for the Nswt Ntchr r Khet (Djoser), and he was the Nswt's personal physican. Imhotep became so famous that after his death, he was deified as the Ntchr of medicine, and the archtype of a Great Man. Even the early Greeks worshiped him as Aesculapius. As a deity he was considered the "son of Ptah" in Kemet.

Jhuty

The Ntchr of Good Speech, Intelligence and Wisdom, the Scribe of the Ntchru, the universal mind and balance. He is the Neb of divine words, time, universal balance and the judge of Heru and Setsh. Jhuty is self produced, the heart of Ra and the tongue of Ptah. It was Jhuty who spoke the sacred words which gave Ptah the energy necessary to affect the Creation of the universe. He is the Ntchr of arts and science, the Ntchr of law, both in heaven and upon Earth. Jhuty is the Neb of Mdw Ntchr, the great magician, the divine manifestation of writing and articulate speech, the recordner of time, teacher of the mysteries in Amenta. Jhuty means "the measurer." Jhuty is the Ntchr that taught medicine to the healers. He is the personification of learning, books, and libraries. In the Mer Khut Sabyat (Merkhut Text), it is stated that Jhuty is the oldest son of Ra. His sacred city is Khemennu, in middle Kemet, the city of eight with the secret four pair: night, obscurity, secret, and eternity. Since the Old Period, his consort or complements are in ancient times Seshat and Ma'at.

Jhuty is sometimes represented as a Baboon, Ibis crane bird or with a man's body and Ibis bird head wearing the crescent moon and disc on his head. The Greeks also called Jhuty, Thoth and Hermes. The word, thought and the process of correct and rationale thinking comes from the Greek word Thoth. (Jhuty is the divine recorder of yesterday, today and tomorrow or whatever is, was, and will be, has already been written by Jhuty.) In essence, he was the author of all life sciences, mentally, physically, and spiritually. His day is Heru Sesu (the sixth day of the week), he is associated with the moon (as the measurer of time), and his color is amethyst. ***Jhuty's wisdom's is that knowledge will be your strength, faith your sword, and silence your impenetrable armor.***

Jhuty presides over all forms of communication as the Divine Scribe. He is credited with the creation of written language: Mdw Ntchr, the "words of Ntchr." He is Neb of wisdom, "The Great Ntchr, Neb of Pt (Heaven)", the Divine Judge, He stands next to the scales upon which one's heart is weighed after death, prepared with his reed pen and papyrus scroll to record the results for eternity. Along with his other consort, Seshat, Ntchrt of records and Libraries, Jhuty records the names and deeds of all beings on the leaves of a sacred sycamore tree, the tree of life. Jhuty is "The Maker of Eternity and creator of Everlastingness." Other spellings of his name are Jhuty, I

Jhuty

Jhuty the prime minister and Chief Justice
Jhuty the messenger of Ra...
Jhuty the powerful of Tawy
Jhuty who puts all thing in their place.

An Ancient Kemetik Book of Heru, p. 34

"Give praise to Jhuty;
Make rejoicing to Him every day.
He Who gives breath to the weary-hearted one
And vindicates you against your enemies."

Coming Forth By Light
Utterance 18

"The vizier Who settles cases,
Who changes turmoil to hotep;
The scribe of Ma'at Who keeps the book,
Who punishes crime,
Who accepts the submissive,
Who is sound of arm,
Wise among the Ennead;
Who relates what was forgotten."

-From a Statue of Nswt Horemheb
New Period

Jhuty is further praised in a New Period text:

"Come to me Jhuty O letter writer of the Ntchru
Make me skillful in your calling
Your calling is better than all callings
It makes men great
He who masters it is found fit to hold office
I have seen many whom you have helped:
They are among the Thirty (the National Council)."

"Prayer to Jhuty" Ancient Egyptian Literature, vol. 2, p. 113.

Kheper-Ra

The Ntchr who represented the rising or morning sun and was closely associated with the scarab, the sacred beetle of ancient Kemet. Khepera was a symbol of resurrection and fertility. Khepera was among the original creation Ntchru and like the rising sun with which he is identified, he was said to be self-created, born of his own substance. According to one myth he copulated with his own shadow and from his semen came Shu, the air, and Tefnut, moisture; and from the union of Shu and Tefnut came Geb, the earth, and Nut, the sky. They in turn bore the great Ntchru Asr, Ast, Set, Heru Ur and Nebt Het. These nine deities formed a group worshiped in a cosmological system known as the Ennead or Company of Ntchru.

Since beetles were believed to be the incarnation of Khepera, beetle amulets were worn to attract the power of the Ntchr and secure its protection. In Kemetik funerary practice beetles or beetle amulets, often inscribed with a text from the Book of Coming Fourth by Light, were buried with the mummies to help insure their resurrection. Khepera was portrayed in Kemetik art as a beetle-headed man or sometimes simply as a beetle.

The Book of knowing the forms of Ra and of felling Aapep; words spoken by the Neb of the universe, which he said after he took form:

> *"I it is who took form (Kheper) as Khepri.*
> *I took form; (other) forms took form.*
> *All forms took form after I took form.*
> *Forms multiplied in emerging from my mouth,*
> *Before earth existed, before sky existed,*
> *Before snakes and worms were created in that place...*
> *I made all shapes alone, before I sneezed out Shu, before I spat out Tefnut, before any other took form and had acted with me."*

...Khepera, the scarab was worn by the living as protective amulets, and as symbols of triumphant acquittal in the Judgement Hall of Asr, and as emblems of the resurrection which was to be effected by the power of the Netcheru Khepera whom they represented, and the words of power of Chapter 30 in the book, Coming Forth By Light.

...The ancient Kemetyu believed that if scarabs were placed under the coffin no fiend or esfet could harm it, and their presence in a tomb gave to it the protection of the "father of the Netcheru."

The Wab Priest who performed the opening the mouth ceremony had to be ceremonial, clean and pure,

> ***"Who hath not eaten the flesh of animals or fish,***
> ***And who hath not had intercourse with women.***
> ***And behold, thou shalt make a scarab of green stone,***
> ***With a rim of gold,***
> ***And this shall be placed in the heart of a man (person),***
> ***And it shall perform for him the Opening of the Mouth.***
> ***And thou shalt annoit with anti unguent (sacred oil),***
> ***And thou shalt recite the words of power."***

-Chapter 30, Book of Coming Forth By Light

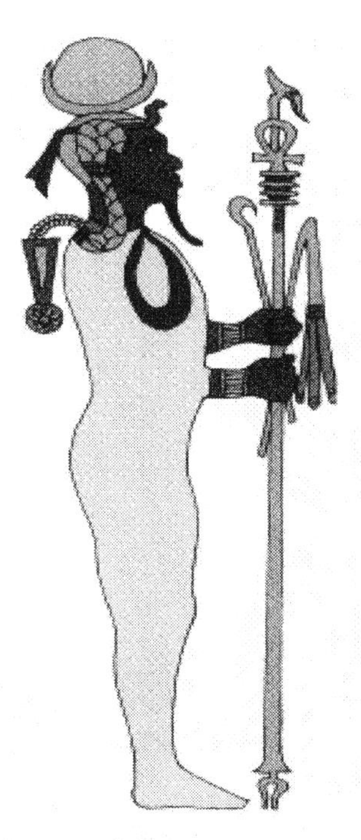

Khensu

Khensu was a moon Ntchr and the son of Amen-Ra and Mwt. His name derives from the root, "Khens" which means to travel, to move about to run. He was usually portrayed as a man with the head of a hawk and wearing the lunar disk.

Khensu was a very old Ntchr of ancient times. Khensu was associated with the moon and was considered a form of Jehuty by the Kemetyu of Wast, and it was in Wast that MessuRa Mery Amun (Ramesses 111) built the "House of Khensu in Wast, Nefer-hetep."

It was said that when Khensu caused the crescent moon to shine, women conceived, cattle became fertile, and all nostrils and every throat were filled with fresh air. In the Middle Period (12th Dynasty) in a papyrus on the dispute between a man and his Ba, states:

...May Jhuty judge me, he who appeases the Ntchru!
May Khensu defend me, he who writes truly!
May Ra hear my speech, he who calms the sun-bark!

Variations are Khonsu, and Khons.

Khnum

Khnum is the Ram headed divinity. Khnum's name literally means "molder." He is the divine potter who fashioned the world, the molder who created man from the black clay of the earth on his potter's wheel. He is the builder of man, the maker of things,the creator of water and life. He is the father of fathers. The four heads of Khnum symbolized the life and souls of Ra, Shu, Geb, and Asr, which also represented the four elements, fire, air, earth, and water.

Khnum was of "Ta Nahesy" (ancient Kash) origin, and was believed to be an aspect of Ptah that was given a local name. He is associated with the cities Abu and Esna. Khnum was usually represented as a ram-headed man, with long wavy horns adorned with plumes, a disk and a cobra. A variantion in the spellings of his name is Khenumu.

...The king is sustenance, his mouth is plenty,
He who will be is his creation.
He is the Khnum of everybody,
Begetter who makes mankind.

from the Deputy Chief Seal-bearer, Sehetep-eb-Ra. For the Nswt M-het-Amen NubmaatRa (Amenemhet lll).

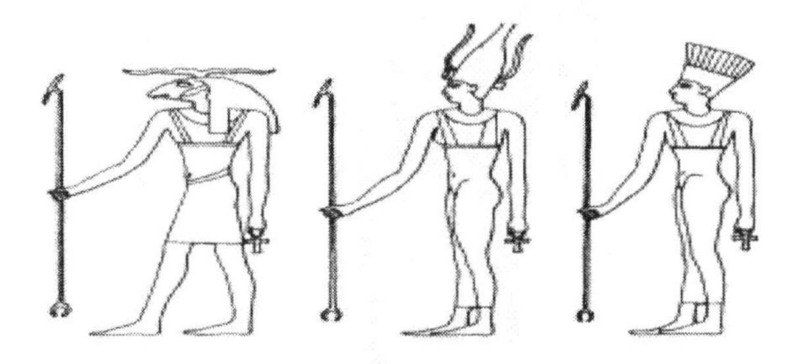

Khnum, Anuket, Satet.

This triad was worshiped in the 6th cataract region, Khnum was also believed to have connections with inundation.

Ma'at

Ma'at was the personification of the physical and moral law of the universe, such as the 42 Oracles of Ma'at. Both Ma'at and her complement Jhuty, took part in the creation of the world. Ma'at was called "daughter of Ra" or "eye of Ra." She was also called "Lady of Heaven," "Mistress of the Underworld." Variant spellings of her name are Maa, Maet, Maht, and Maat.

The principle of balance in life and in nature is called Ma'at. Ma'at was the foundation of Kemet and was thought of as right, true, truth, real, genuine, righteous, steadfast, and unalterable; there is no single word in English that embraces all the meanings of Ma'at. Like the Tao (Way) of ancient Chinese, Ma'at is the energy which holds creation together. Without Ma'at, esfet reigns unchecked. It is important for a person's heart to be as light as a feather and not weighed down with guilt.

In Kemetik art, Ma'at is portrayed in human form wearing a headdress with an ostrich feather attached to it. The ostrich feather - the symbol of herself is pure, colorless, light and billowing. However, in some depictions she holds the feather in her hand. Sometimes she has falcon wings. She is Cosmic order.

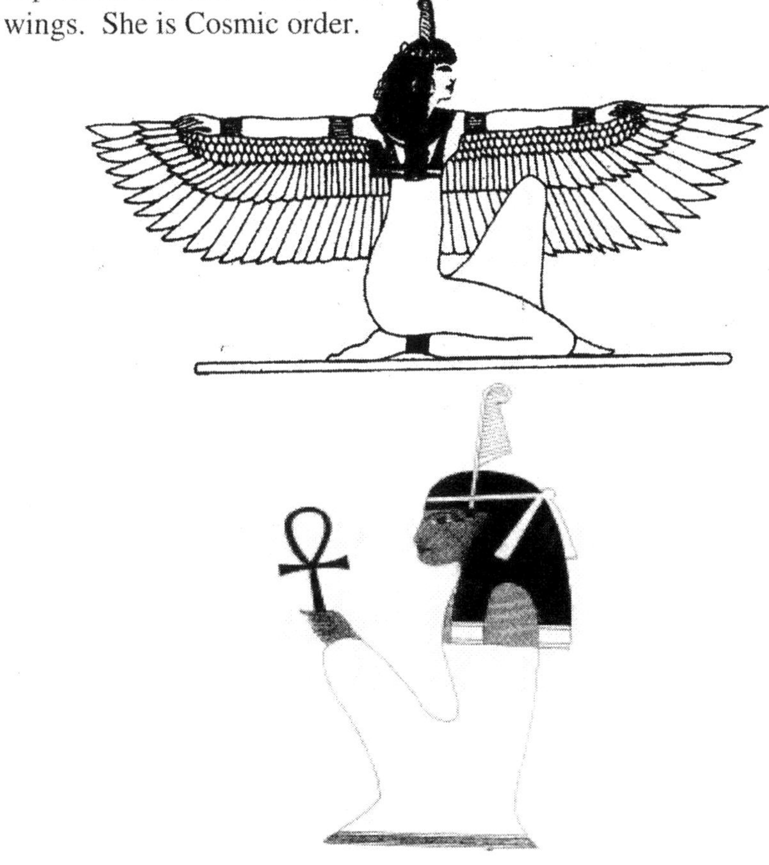

Ma'at

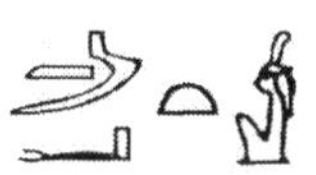

"Your right eye is Ma'at,
Your left eye is Ma'at,
Your flesh, your members are Ma'at...
Your food is Ma'at, your drink is Ma'at,
The breaths of your nose are Ma'at...
You exist because Ma'at exists
And Ma'at exist because you exist."

-Berlin Papyrus

"Ma'at is in every place that is yours...
You rise with Ma'at,
You live with Ma'at,
You join your limbs to Ma'at,
You make Ma'at rest on your head,
In order that She may take Her seat on your forehead.
You become young again in the sight of your daughter Ma'at
You live from the perfume of Her dew.
Ma'at is worn like an amulet at your throat;
She rests on your chest,
The Divine Entities reward you with Ma'at,
For they know Her wisdom...

-Berlin Papyrus

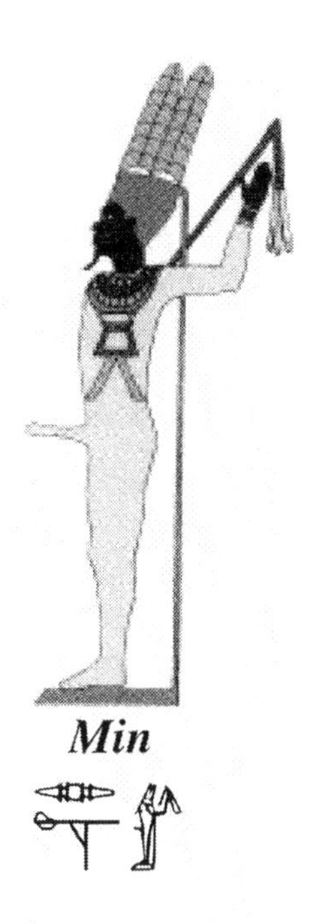

Min

Min was the Ntchr of fertility *par excellence.* One of the largest celebrations in ancient Kemet was the "Festival of the Coming Forth of Min." Min was one of the most ancient Kemetik Ntchru, a deity of fertility whose origins are lost in the mist of time.

The worship of Min was universal throughout Kemet; but two cities were particularly associated with him: Gebtu and Khen-Min. Gebtu lies on the east bank of Hapy some 40 km north of Wast, the capital of the 5th stp. Khent-Min (which means "The Shrine of Min") lies on the east bank of Hapy some 80 Km south of Assiut, capital of the 9th stp.

Min was usually depicted as a man standing upright wearing on his head a cap surmounted by two tall plumes. One arm, bent at the elbow, is raised and outstretched, its hand open; above it floats a flail. The other arm is tucked under his robe, from which projects his penis, huge and erect. And his skin is always painted Black.

Mentchu

Mentchu is a falcon-headed Ntchr of war and his main center was from Wast. At Ipet Astu (Karnak), Mentchu is Neb of Wast and his main temple lies north, the great temple of Amen. The Middle Period had a number of rulers who displayed the name of the Ntchr Mentchu like: Mentuhotep ("Mentchu is content"). Mentchu became the embodiment of the conquering vitality of the Kemetik rulers against esfet. Mentu's consorts are the Wast Ntchru Tjenenyet and the solar Ntchrt Raettawy.

Other centers where Mentchu was worshiped were ancient Medu, north-east of Wast- where a sanctuary founded by Senwosret KakhauRa (Senwosret 111 was expanded during the New Period and also in the Late Period. Another version of the Ntchr of wars name was Montu.

Mwt (Mut)

Mwt is the great mother; she is considered to be the great maternal power who conceived and gave birth to everything. Mwt is the compliment of Amen in the triad at Wast. She is the mother of Khensu the moon child.

In Kemetik art she is depicted as a woman who wears a vulture headdress and she holds the ankh and papyrus scepter called the uadj, symbolic of growth and expansion. Sometimes she is represented as a vulture. The vulture was regarded as sacred throughout Kemet and symbolizes the twofold nature of Mut. She was the great mother on one side and the devourer of the dead so that new seeds could come forth.

Mwt became identified with every Ntchrt that expressed the maternal principle, including Nut, Ast, Het-Hert, Apet, Sekhmet and Bast. She even became the "Eye of Ra" as the triad in Wast became stronger.

Nebertcher

Neb-er-tcher is the All-encompassing Ntchr, the great Kemetik Trinity of Amen-Ra-Ptah. Neb-er-tcher was also called Netcher Netcheru, the Trinity describes one Divinity or Ntchr which expresses three aspects of Oneness. "Everything is Amen-Ra-Ptah, three in one." Amit-Rai-Sekmet are complements, representing their dynamic power of manifestation.

"He whose name is hidden is Amen.
Ra belongeth to him as His face,
And the body is Ptah.
There cities are established on earth forever, Waset, Annu, Het-Ka-Ptah.

Neb-er-tcher Speaks:

I was alone, for the Ntchru were not yet born, and I had emmitted from myself neither Shu nor Tefnut. I brought into my own mouth, Hekau (the divine words of power), and I forthwith came into being under the form of things which were created under the form of Khepera."

Pert em Heru.

Nebt Het

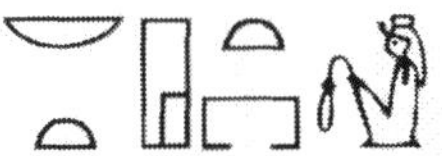

Nebt-Het, the "Ruler of the House". She is the great helper, the sociable part of harmony, peace and love. She is the daughter of the Ntchru Geb, and Nut, the wife of Set, sister of Asr, Ast and Heru Ur. Her color is green and the lotus flowers are her sacred symbols. She is the guardian, along with Hapy, of the lungs (air element) for the Mesu Heru jars. Nephthys is the Greek name for Nebt Het.

"Nebt Het, Divine Sister, the Eye of Ra,
Lady of the Beautiful House.
May She grant that my soul walks
Amongst those who are in Hotep."

-Papyrus of Ta-Shed-Khonsu

"I have encircled My brother Asr;
I have come that I may be thy magical protection.
My protection is around thee, forever;
Thy call has been answered by Ra."

Coming Forth By Light
Utterance 151c

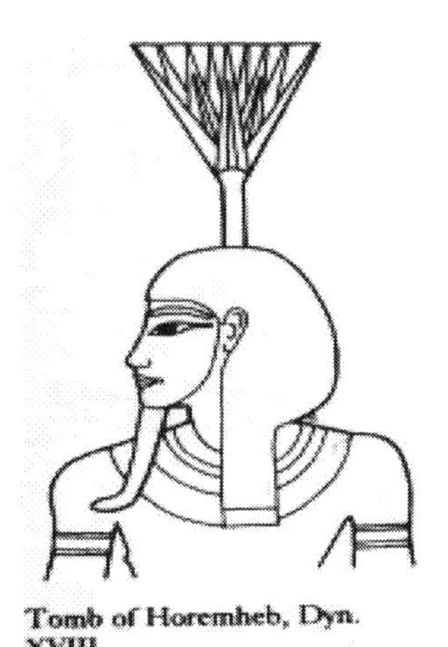

Tomb of Horemheb, Dyn. XVIII

Nefertem

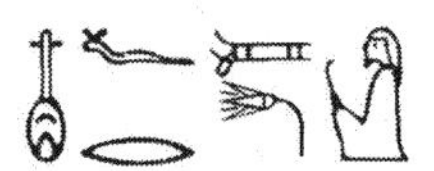

Nefertem the Ntchr of the primeval lotus blossom. The name Nerfertem has the notion of "perfection". Nefertem is the son of the lioness Ntchrt Sekhmet and Ptah. Similarly the feline Ntchrt Bastet also states, she is the mother of Nefertem. He is the blue lotus out of which, according to one myth, the sun rises. In a description in the Mer-Khut Texts (Pyramid) Nefertem is the lotus blossom in front of the nose of Ra.

In art form he is usally represented by an Afrakan man with a beard, wearing a head-dress in the shape of the lotus plant. As a child, he can be depicted seated on a lotus blossom. Variation of his name is Nefertum.

Neith (Net)

Net is the Ntchrt of spiritual protection for all aspirants of "The Way". She uses a bow and arrow to shoot down the enemies of righteousness (anger, hatred, greed, jealousy, envy, lust, and esfet). Her name Net means that which is real, true, and abiding. Neith was originally worshiped as an ancient war Ntchrt, who led the charge in battle. Her symbols, two crossed arrows and a shield, reflected her martial nature. She was the Ntchrt of the city of Sais. Like a great many Kemetik deities Net had a dual nature. She could be both fierce and gentle. She was a mother Ntchrt, a nourisher and sustainer of life and a protector of the dead, as well as a deity of war.

In the Mer Khut Saybyet (Pyramid Text) line 620-627, it is explained that the initiate is Sebek, the Ntchr who is the son of Net, and that the initiate rises like the son of Net. In the city of Net, Sobek is recognized as a form of Heru.

The Ntchrt Net gave birth to the Ntchru and to human beings, but she herself was not given birth, she brought herself into existence and gave birth without being impregnated. She was the primeval waters and she emerged as herself out of herself and all has come forth through and from her. She is self-existent, and her nature is secret, a mystery to all.

In Kemetik art, Net was usually portrayed as a woman wearing the crown of the North on her head and holding a scepter in one hand and the ankh emblem of life, in the other. Sometimes she is shown grasping a bow and two arrows. Variant spelling of her name are Neith, and Nit.

The following was inscribed on the wall of her temple:

" I am all that has been, that is, and that will be."

***"...Neith, Mother of mothers, Lady of Abu, the great lady,
Lady of the south, the great cow who gave birth to the sun,
Who made the germ of Ntchru and men, the mother of Ra,
Who raised up Tem in primeval time,
Who existed when nothing else had being, And who created
That which exists after she had come into being.
...with her mate, Khnemu."***

-From a Temple at Seni (Esneh)
Old Period

The following was inscribed from Mer Khut text line 606:

***"Net, together with Aset, Nebethet and Serqet, watched over the funerary bed of Asr.
The bandages and shrouds used for the sahu(mummy) of the deceased was given by the Ntchrt Net and through these she imparts her protection as well as her blessings in the form of spiritual power."***

NTCHR

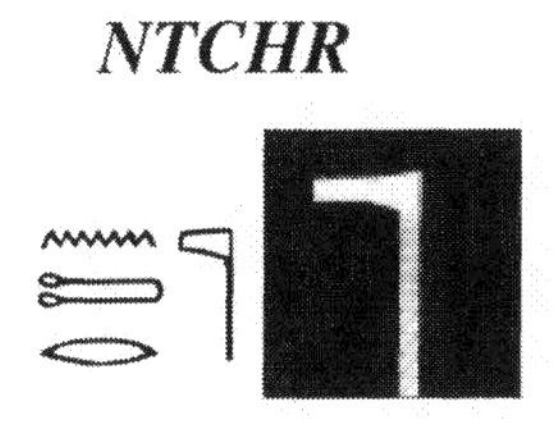

NTCHR, the universal force. The Spirit and soul of all creation. The NTCHR is the manifestation of spirit, the Creator, Divine nature, and the All. The NTCHR is represented by a white flag, a symbol of nature or the existence of the All, the totality of all life and all existence.

Ntchru

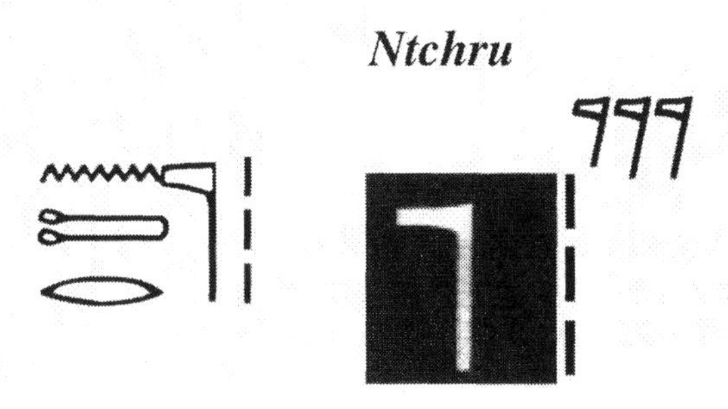

The Ntchru is the manifestations of the One spirit, aspects of divine nature, the laws by which the Creator governs the All. The Ntchru are the many forms of the One universal energy which is the All.

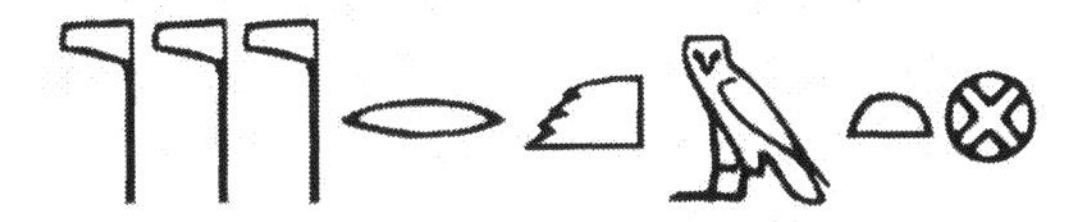

Nut

The Ntchrt who personified the sky or livable atmosphere. She was usually depicted as a woman bearing on her head a vase of water, with the medu Ntchr phonetic value of Nut. She sometimes wears a headdress of horns and the disk of the Ntchrt Het Heru, and holds a papyrus scepter in one hand and the ankh, emblem of life in the other. Sometimes she is shown as a woman spangled with stars, arched over the body of her husband Geb, or sometimes supported by her father Shu. The sun was thought to have been swallowed by Nut, passing Nut was

also regarded as friend and protector of the dead. She is frequently referred to as mother Nut, and is supposed to spread herself out over the dead in her name of "Governor of the Sky".

She was expected to supply the dead with food and drink, but because she was also their protector, is often portrayed on the inner side of coffin lids, where she could closely supervise what was happening to the dead person in the afterlife. The sycamore tree was sacred to her. One ancient Kemetik text reads:

"Hail, thou sycamore of the Ntchrt Nut! Grant thou to me of the water and of air which dwell in thee."

The branches of the sycamore tree became a place of refuge from the fiery heat of the summer sun. Weary travelers refreshed themselves in the tree's shade and ate of the tree's abundant fruit, on which the Ntchrt Nut herself subsisted. In one Kemetik myth, Ra passed between the Ntchrt Nut's two turquoise-colored sycamores at Annu when he began his journey across the sky each morning.through her body to be reborn every day.

O Asr Pepy, Nut, your mother, spreads herself above you,
She conceals you from all evil,
Nut protects you from all evil,
You, the greatest of her children!

-Sarcophagus Chamber, West Wall. Utterance 446

Nuw (Nun)

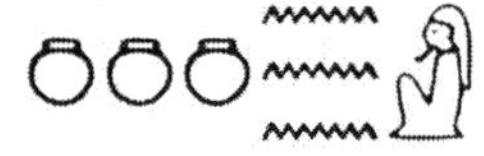

Nuw Ntchr personifying the primeval waters out of which emerged the Creator- NTCHR. Nuw is double Blackness, that which allowed the NTCHR to come into being before creation and Ma'at.

Nuw is an important spiritual Afrakan Deep Thought concept, but it has no religious rituals, no temples or priestship. Other variations of Nuw are Nun the consort of Nunet, as creator divinities in the Ogdoad.

Ptah-Nun, the father who made Atum.
Ptah-Naunet, the mother who bore Atum.
Ptah-the Great is heart and tongue of the Nine Ntcheru...
Old period, Heru and Ptah are One. From Het-Ka-Ptah

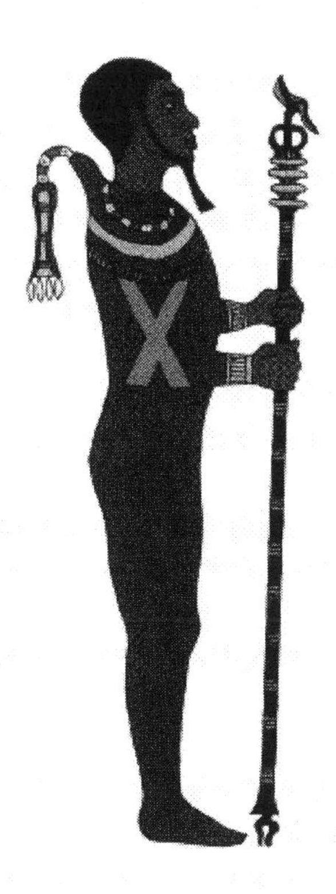

Ptah

It is written by Jhuty that Ptah created everything and brought all the Ntchru into being. Thus, he is indeed Ta-tenen (the Earth Ntchr form of Ptah). Ptah is the Ntchr who is the great architect of the universe, father of beginnings, grandfather of the Ntchru. Ptah is the spark of life in all existence, the Neb of life. The Greeks call him Hephaestos.

Ptah is the Neb of all artisans and all forms of construction. The patron of craftsmen and those who create such as sculptors, artisans, engravers, and painters . He is the chief worker in metals, thus the greatest smelter, caster and sculptor. As the master craftsman, he fashioned the Ntchru and made the cities.

He is the Ntchr of the Het-Ka-Ptah (Memphis). Ptah's complement and mate is Sekhmet and their son is Nefertum. Ptah is also the father of Tem or Atum. The heart of Ptah appeared in the form of Jhuty. He is the symbol of new inventions, skills and crafts. Ptah is pictured Black or brown in color and he is always represented as a man wearing a skull cap and a false beard signifying divinity and holding a scepter.

"His beauty is in every body.
Ptah has done this with His own hands, to rejoice His heart.
The pools are freshly filled with water,
The Earth brims over with love for Him."

-from a song inscribed in the tomb of Neb-Amen, Waset
New Period

"Homage to Thee, Ptah-Tenen, Thou Great Netcher
Whose form is hidden!
Thou openest Thy soul and Thou wakest in hotep,
O' Fathers of the Fathers of all the Netcheru,
Thou Disk of Heaven!
Thou illuminates it with Thy two eyes,
And Thou lightest up the earth
With Thy brilliant rays in hotep."

-Hymn to Ptah-Tenen, New Period

The Nswt kneeling before the Ntchru Ptah and Sekmet

Ra

Ra is a Ntchr of light and victory, of protection and of immeasurable power. He is the seen force of the universe, manifested by the sun and the symbol of the sun is used to describe energy. Ra is he energy that allows light to shine. As Khepera he is Creator, who came forth from himself: a light in the darkness, rolling life like a scarab rolls balls of dung into the light, from which its children spring as if by magic. Variants of his name are Re and Phra.

As Tem or Atum, he is the Creative Essence, the power of life and time which carries forth desire into reality. As Amen-Ra, the Hidden Neb, he is both the bright and blazing light of truth and the whispering wind of power. As Heru Khuti, he soars through the sky as a falcon,

seeing all, protecting the birds in his nest. The Great Ntchr Ra, father of the Ntchru and men, is one of the central Ntchru of ancient Kemet. Ra's power is infinite. Ra is in the fire of sunshine, the cries of falcons, the willful, determined work of Kheper, the scarab. Like the sun, he keeps us warm, offers life, marks the cycle of day and night, months and years, centuries and millennia.

All the Nswtu of Kemet in the Old Period believed themselves to be the sons of Ra. In ancient Kemet, the Kemetyu saw the themselves as the children of the sun. In Kemetik art, Ra is usually portrayed as a hawk - headed man or sometimes in the form of a hawk. He wears the disk of the sun encircled by a serpent on his head. When he appears in human form, he holds the ankh, emblem of life, in his right hand and a scepter, emblem of power, in his left.

The origin of the world itself seems to have been not so much an act of creation in the manner of the Judaeo-Christian concept where a god creates the world in a specific period of time; rather the creator and his creation emerged spontaneously out of the void before time and before matter. One text, among the most widely copied on coffins and funerary papyri, describes the Creator at the dawn of existence. Shorn of the extensive commentary interspersed through the text even in the earliest version, it provides the following opening verse:

...The word took form, all was mine, when I existed alone;
I am Ra in his first appearances,
When he shines forth from the horizon;
I am the great Ntchr who took form of himself,
Who created his name,
Neb of Enneads, who has no opponent among the Ntchru;
Yesterday is mine, and I know tomorrow.

- Coffin Text

"Arise, Ra. Arise Thou in Thy shrine,
So that Thou mayest engulf the winds,
Inhale the north wind,
Swallow the spine,
Spit out the day,
Kiss the truth." *-The Book of the Two Ways*
Coffin Texts 10029

Ra in his boat, sails over the body of Nut while Shu holds her body up and separates her from her complement Geb.

Ra traveing through the Duat within the body of Nut. From right to left: Nut holds Ra in an embrace and consumes him in the evening. Then Ra is renewed by three Ntchru, the first Ntchr is "Living years," then "Living eternity," then "Forever," then the Ntchrt Ma'at, and the Ntchr Hekau assist Ra in his rebirth as he creates a new day.

Seker (Sokar)

A Ntchr associated with Asr, but Seker came to represent absolute death when Asr triumphed over all Ntchru of death in Kemet. In Kemet art, Seker is portrayed as a hawk headed man in the mummified form. In the Old Period, Seker amalgamates with Ptah: Ptah-Seker. As such, Seker takes Sekhmet as his consort. His funerary aspect is important where he is known as Seker of 'Rosetau' or 'mouth of the passages' (into the Underworld). The festival of Sekar was as popular as the New Year festival of Opet. He is conveyed in an elaborate henu (boat) with Asr and Ptah.

In the Book of Coming Forth By Light, Seker is described as,

> ***"The great Ntchr who carrieth away the soul,***
> ***Who eateth hearts, and who feedeth upon offal,***
> ***The guardian of the darkness,***
> ***The Ntchr who is in the Seker boat. ..."***

-Book of Coming Forth By Light
Chapter 17, Line 11

The vulture, Nekhbet, holding the Sed festival symbol endows him...

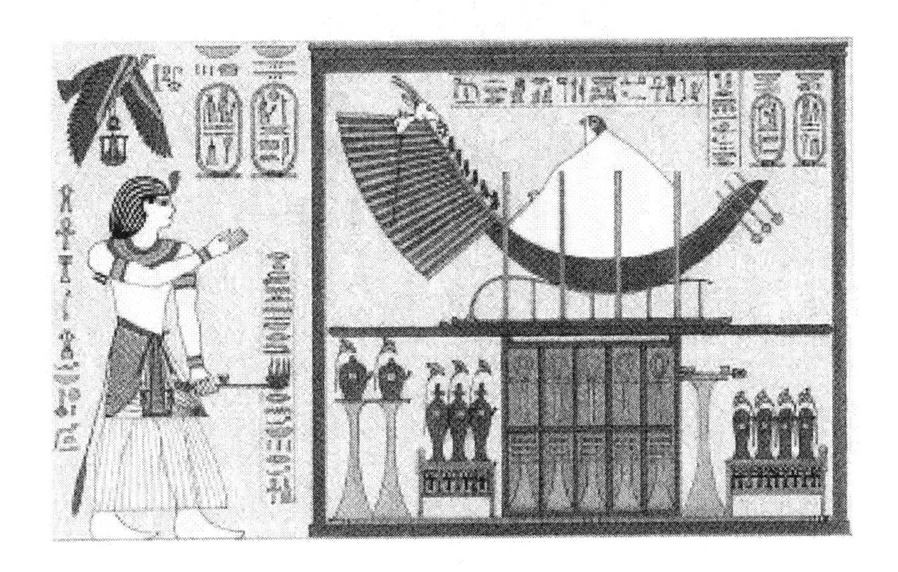

Censing the Hena Boat of Seker. "Protection, life, stability, all around him, like Ra, for eternity." (Within the shrine) "Words spoken by Seker Asr, the great Ntchr, Neb of heaven, who gives life, stability and power to the good Ntchr who makes monuments for his father Seker. Neb of the two lands, User-Ma'at-Ra, Beloved of Amen, Neb of Rising, Messu-Ra (Ramesses), Ruler of Iwnw."

Sekhmet

Sekhmet was a lioness Ntchrt that personified the fierce, destructive heat of the sun. Her name literally means "the powerful one." She was also the Ntchrt of war and battle, who could be both punitive and death dealing. Sekhmet is the daughter of Ra, consort of Ptah and mother of Nefertum. Sekhmet, Ptah and Nefertum was the divine triad at Men-nefer.

In the Kemet art , Sekhmet was portrayed as a women with the head of a lioness which wore a solar disk and uraeus on her head. She was also associated with the Eye of Ra, the Leopard Ntchrt Mefdet, Bast and Het-Heru. Her strength was legendary and she was invoked in all things involving healing and to turn back plagues and infections. As the daughter of Ra, she is his protector and avenger, who goes out into the world to ward off Ra's enemies. She is the Lady in Red, a powerful female whose vengeance is terrible and swift, a great mother who shields her children from all adversity with the fierce love of a lioness.

> ***"How strong She is! Without contender,***
> ***She honors Her name as Hmt of the Cities.***
> ***Sharp-sighted, keen as Ntchr's protector, Right Eye of Ra,***
> ***Disciple facing Her great Neb, bright with the Glory of Ntchr, Wise upon Her high throne,***
> ***She is Most Holy of Places,***
> ***A mecca the world cannot parallel."***
>
> -Leyden Hymn 10

Sekhmet in her feline aspect of her nature is a cat, and cats have a inimical relationship with serpents. In the ancient Kemetik mythology, the *Serpent of Darkness* is seen as the embodiment of ignorance and esfet, which threatens the nightly movements of Ra in his Night Boat, and the *Serpent of Darkness* threatens all spiritual aspirants from attaining enlightenment. Sekhmet is the one who paves the way for Ra and all spiritual aspirants by destroying the evil of ignorance and esfet in the Konsciousness of the human heart. She is seen as the warrior and champion of the Ntchru and all spiritual aspirants. ***Below is the Ntchrt Sekhmet as Mafdet the leopard.***

Selket (Serket)

She is the Kemet scorpion Ntchrt. She is the mistress and guardian of life, she is equated with Neith, and Ast. In the belief in the hereafter she plays a vital role as a protectress of the dead. Her full name is Serket hetyt meaning - she who causes the throat to breathe. The earliest reference to her as a Kemet Ntchrt occurs in the Old Period on the stela of Merika from Saqqara.

During the great Mèr Khut Age she has a protective role around the throne of the Nswt. During the Middle and New Period she was one of the guardians of Messu Heru (Sons of Heru). Her responsibility is to protect Qebehsenuef, Ntchr guarding the intestines. Also in a Middle Period karst composition known as the Book of the Two Ways, she watches over dangerous twists in the pathway in the under world. She is also credited with binding the hostile snake Apophis or Apep, who is an enemy of Ra.

Serket is usually represented as a lady whose head is surmounted by a scorpion with its tail raised ready to sting. She is a healer that deals with poisonous bites.

Seshat

Seshat says that everything is ordained by numbers. Creation begins when numbers begin, when it is possible to give something a name and an origin. She is the female Ntchrt of numbers, measurements, mathematics, letters, literature and mate of Jhuty. She is often shown as a woman wearing a seven rayed star on her head, carrying a reed pen and palette recording some deed for eternity and wearing a leopard skin dress. Sometimes she wears a seven rayed star on her head surmounted by two inverted horns. She is closely connected with the number seven, sefekh. She represent the seven colors in light, and the seven musical tones. She is the "Lady of the House of Books" and "Lady of Letters", the Ntchr of architecture, building and construction. In the Duat, she records the names of the deceased on her register, these are the names Jhuty will declare before Asr.

Seshat: Lady of the House of Books
"Words spoken by the great Seshat, Lady or Mistress of the House of Books.
Nekhbet and Edjo of Depyt have reared my Neb embracing his beauties, The Nswt of Upper and Lower Kemet, Men-Maem-Ra. Behold, it is command to record his Divine rulership, my hand writing his great lifetime according to what comes forth from the mouth of Ra, My reed pen forever, and paint for eternity, and the bowl of water for millions of great many Jubilee festivals For the Nswt of Upper and Lower Kemet, Men-Ma'at - Ra.

Sem Priest and Sem Priestess making an offering.

All Sem Priest and Priestess were closely associated with the Ntchrt Seshat the record keeper, the great mathematician, the keeper of books in the sacred library, the keeper of time, astrology and astronomy. They wear the leopard skin, as a symbol of the power to dispel ignorance, and esfet, and all forms of death, mentally, physically, and spiritually, by opening the mouth (mind) of the initiate.

Set (Setsh)

Set was basically the manifestation of blind force. The Ntchr of esfet, darkness, the opposite of his brother Asr. He ruled by might and force. Set was the sky by night, the downward motion of the sun. He was the third son of Geb and Nut, along with Asr, Heru Ur, Ast, and Nebt Het. Set was born on the third day of the Holy five days above the year at the wrong time and wrong place, by forcing his way through a wound which he made in his mother's side. Set's complement was Nebt Het, the mother of Enpu. In the Old Period he was the national Ntchr of the delta, and during the Hyksos invasion, the King Apepa, made Set the greatest of all the Ntchru during his dominance. Set was the archetype of the Cain and Abel story.

The Greeks called him Typhoon. Set's worship was one of the oldest in Kemet. The pig was associated with Set, but most often an unidentified animal. Other animals associated with Set were the crocodile, hippopotamus, black boar, and the ass.

Set, the Ntchr of strength stood at the brow of Ra's Boat, where he fends off the serpent of esfet from the Neb of limitless light.

Some texts describe Set as having red hair incidentally, some people with red complexions or red hair were often treated with great disdain in Kemet. Variants of Set's name are, Seth, Sethi, Sit, Sut, Setesh.

"Who is He.
He is Set.
He is the Great Wild Bull,
He is the soul of Geb."

-The Book of Coming Forth By Light

"I am Set, greatest in virility among the Ennead,
For I slay the opponent of Ra daily while I am
At the prow of the Bark of the Millions,
Whereas not any other Netcher is able to do it."

-The Contendings of Heru and Set

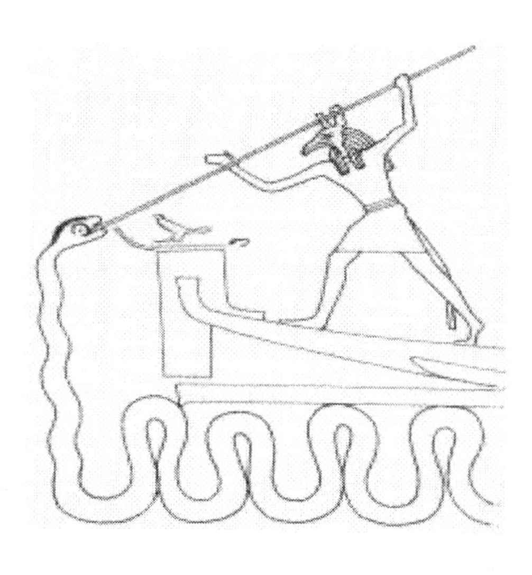

Shu

The Ntchr of dry air. He is boundless space, the breath of the Ntchru. Shu is a very old Ntchr along with his twin sister Tefnut. They were the first couple of the Ennead, a group of Ntchru worshipped at Annu.
Shu means "he who holds up".

It was Shu who separated the sky (Nut) from the earth (Geb) at Ra's request so that light and space were created as well as heaven above and earth below. Shu maintained the division with his upraised arms at the four pillars of life. Shu, along with his complement Tefnut, are also the parents of Geb and Nut. Many thousands of years later in the ancient Greek mythology, Atlas supported the heavens with his head and hands.

Shu is almost always portrayed in bearded male human form, wearing a great ostrich feather, or feathers, upon his heads. If he is not standing holding up Nut he has a scepter in one hand and an ankh in the other. Shu is the bringer of the eyes of Ra, daylight or sunlight. He represents the male element and the principle of dryness. The great temple at Philae is dedicated to Shu. The origin of Shu and his twin Tefnut is in southern Sudan, ancient Kash.

Hail, O waters brought by Shu,
which the twin springs raised,
In which Geb has bathed his limbs,
So that hearts lost fear, hearts lost dread.
Pepi was born in Nun before there was sky, before there was earth,
Before tere was mountatins, ...strife...fear...

Old Period, so-called 5th Dynasty

Sia

The Ntchr of the sense of touch, or feeling, and of knowledge and innerstanding. Sia appears in the Book of the Coming forth by Light as one of the Ntchru who watches the heart of the deceased being weighed during the great judgment scene. He is portrayed as a man with a fringed headband. Sia is the personifcation of innerstanding. A variant spelling is Saa.

Sobek

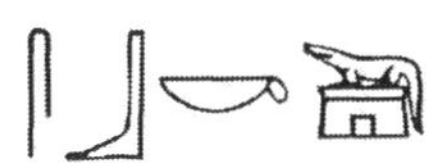

The crocodile Ntchr, representing the personification of power, esfet and death. In the city of Shedet the crocodile was sacred at Sobek's sanctuary. In the very early period of ancient Kemet, when the canals connected to Hapy dried up, the crocodile was able to wander about the fields at will, to kill and eat whatever came into its path. The Kemetyu came to regard this animal as a personification of the powers of esfet, and they associated it with the Ntchr Setsh.

The destructive power of Sobek was seen to be a necessary element in the process of transformation. The destructive powers that Sobek embodied were only destructive to those who became the tools of esfet and were caught in the matrix of the material trappings of the external world.

In Kemet art, Sobek is portrayed as a crocodile headed man wearing either a solar disk or ram horns. Sobek is sometimes depicted simply as a crocodile. Variants of the name are Sebek, Suchos.

"Unas has come today from the overflowing flood,
Unas is Sobk, green-plumed, wakeful, alert,
The fierce who came forth from shank
And tail of the Great Radiant one,
Unas has come to his streams
In the land of the great flowing flood,
To the seat of contentment
Which lies, green-pastured, in lightland,
Unas arises as Sobk, son of Neith;
Unas eats with his mouth,
Unas spends water, spends seed with his phallus;
Unas is Neb (lord) of seed who takes wives from their husbands
Whenever Unas wishes, as his heart urges.

-Utterance 317 Merkhut (Pyramid) Text

Asr the symbolic first Nswt stands on Ma'at the foundation of ancient Kemet, before his son Heru who stands victorious over Set, with his four sons the guardian Ntchru of Ma'at behind him.

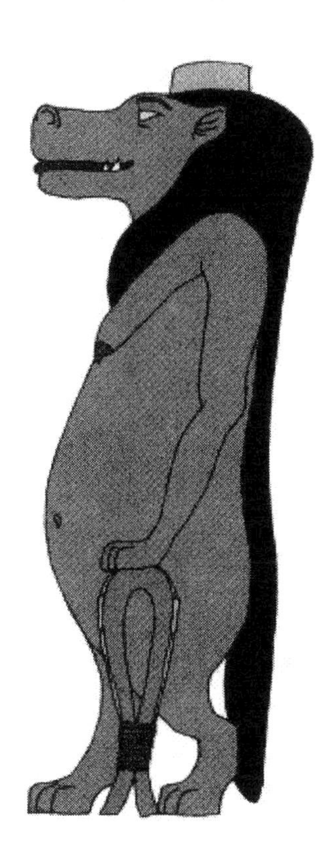

Taurt

A hippopotamus Ntchrt, a patron of childbirth and maternity, who was often identified with the Great Mother Het Heru. The literal translation of her name is "the great fat one." In Greek mythology, she is called Thoueris. Another spelling of her name is Taueret.

In Kemet art, she is depicted as a large female hippopotamus with who is standing upright on her legs. Sometimes in her paw rests the Sa, a symbol of protection represented by the stylized life preserver, made of papyrus, worn by river travelers.

Tefnut

The twin sister and complement of Shu, her father the Ntchr Ra-Atum, She is the Ntchr of water or moisture in the form of dew and rain. She is the intense humidity and heat of a Kemet summer. Tefnut is the fluid from which all life comes. She is the mother of Geb and Nut.

Shu and Tefnut complement each other and cannot exist separately. Theirs is the first union of opposites or complements in order to create the other Ntchru. They reflect the twin nature of the Spdt star system where one brilliant giant star and one highly potent dwarf star are caught in an eternal dance around each other.

As an "Eye of Ra" she appears lioness-headed. Shu can also take leonine form and the couple were worshipped as a pair of lions in the Delta.

Tem, Atum

The Ntchr Tem or Atum was the only Ntchr in ancient Kemet worshipped as the living Neb, Ankhu, the ever living one, the eternal Ntchr. The Tem was man perfected, the son of Ptah, Creator of eternity, enlightener of the double earth, the Kemet holy spirit, giver of breath, the divine law-giver, the original Adam before the Hebrew "borrowed" version. The Mdu Ntchr is symbolic of the sledge sign. He is represented as a man wearing the double crown of Kemet, holding the Was scepter. Atum is a director of motion, the Ntchr of Celestrial time. Tem's center was the city of Annu.

O Unas, you are not departed dead,
You have departed alive to be seated on the throne of Asr,
with your scepter in your hand, you issue commands to the living,
See, your staff has been installed in your hand.
Issue commands to the most secret of places!
Your upper arm is that of Atum, your forearms are those of Atum,
your belly is that of Atum, your back is that of Atum,
your rear is that of Atum, your legs are those of Atum,
your face is that of Atum, ...

The text for healing the living. Old Preoid

Ancient Kemet developed a dynamic and ingenious innerstanding of the cosmos. The NTCHR was the Creator and the Ntchru are manifestations of this Oneness. The laws or divine energies that maintained harmonious order were called Ntchr and Ntchrt in Kemet, but some of these same deities in central and western Afraka were called Orishas. The most popular were called the Seven Afrakan Powers. These 7 Powers were: Obatala, Eloggua, Shango, Oggun, Orunla, Yemaya and Oshun.

As the Afrakans were dispersed throughout the northern and southern hemisphere so was their spiritual knowledge and wisdom. The Seven Afrakan Powers can also be found in Brazil, Columbia, Cuba, Trinidad, Puerto Rico, Haiti, and most of the Caribbean Islands along with Afrakans in America, especially the southern states.

There are three levels of spiritual innerstanding of the One: Supreme NTCHR the All or Olorun by the Yoruba, Ntchru and Orishas, and the closes level of spiritual forces to man are the spirits of deceased relatives who are collectively known as the Ancestors.

Kemet	*7 Afrakan Powers*	*Greek*	*Roman*
Amen	....	Zeus	Jupiter
Ra	....	Helios	
Ptah	....	Hephastos	
Nut	....	Rhea	
Geb	....	Kronos	Saturn
Net	....	Athena	Minerva
Khensu	....	Heracles	Hercules
Set	....	Typhon	
Bast	....	Artemis	Diana
Bes	....	Dionysus	
Uadjit	....	Leto	
Asr	***Orunla***	Osiris Hades	Pluto
Ast	***Yemaya***	Isis Demeter	Ceres
Nebt-Het	....	Nepththys	Aphrodite
Enpu	....	Anubis	
HetHeru	***Oshun***	Hathor Aphrodite	
Heru	***Shango***	Horus Apollo	Horae
Jehuty	***Obatala***	Thoth Hermes	Mercury
Ma'at	....	Astraea or Themis	Faunus
Min	....		Pan
Imhotep	....		Asclepius
Sobek	***Eloggua***		
Heru Ur	***Oggun***		

In ancient Kemet and throughout much of Black Afraka birth or re-birth was defined as the beginning of physical life, and death is the end of it. But the essential energy of existence, your spirit-soul continues beyond physical life. Both life and death simply exist and are two sides of the coin of existence.

The ancient Kemetyu with their innerstanding of the Ntchru help to civilize the modern world. The Greeks are the first Wazungu to become civilized, as they sat at the feet of great Afrakan Kemet wisdom teachers of Deep Thought. But all of Eurasia owe a great deal to Kemet and the Spiritual Afrakan societies for bringing humanity and Ma'at into the innerstanding of the world.

CHAPTER III (3)

Somo la Tatu

MA'AT

"Ma'at is the Principle of Balance in the universe whether that balance refers to weights and measurements in the market, law in the courts, judgment of the heart of the dead or universal cosmological patterns," ... Jacob H. Carruthers, Essay in Ancient Studies.

The woman is great among women, yet she serves the children.
The hunter is great among hunters, yet he serves the village.
The soldier is great among soldiers, yet he serves his Chief.
The Ruler is great among Rulers, yet he serves his people.
(Wolof proverb - Western Afraka)

Ma'at is the principle of Universal Harmony and Balance as innerstood by the Kemetyu, ancient Black people of the Hapy Valley. Ma'at may also be defined as truth, justice, and righteousness. To the ancient Kemetyu, Ma'at represented a commitment to social order, based upon personal morality and compassion. It was said that the person of Ma'at was just, upright, and steadfast. Virtues are sometimes missing in today's mainstream Kemetyu (Afrakan) population with regard to the manner in which we treat each other and ourselves. The Black men and women of today should love, praise and honor each other. We should be our own best friends, and you should always avoid violence with your friends and family, both physical and psychological. The Afrakans of today have been taught to prey upon each other with vengeance as though attempting to put the finishing touches upon a job initiated centuries ago by our enemies called the Maangamizi. Caucasian Europeans and Asiatics who sought to exploit the Afrakan continent, its people and its natural resources. Our ancient Afrakan ancestors, who laid the foundation for science, art, spiritual practices, and social order, believed that a person operating upon a negative wavelength was infused with esfet (aggressiveness, selfishness, dishonesty, etc.) and had lost "The Way". On the other hand, there were the Priest Scientists in ancient Kemet and today Spiritual Warriors. They were self-mastered, calm, modest, wise and socially active. They are in tune with nature and the spirit world, they represented the embodiment of Ma'at also known as "The Way".

Ma'at, therefore, represents the posture of universal harmony. For example, the position of bearing of the body: state or condition at a given time in relation to other persons or things should all be in accordance with this universal harmony. Ma'at became the measuring stick by which all things were judged traditionally in the ancient Kemetyu society.

> ***"Indeed, national life was so integrated with the earth, moon, stars, and the wind that man's Ka (vital force) was viewed as coming from the heavens and returning to be mingled with the eternal stars..." Jacob H. Carruthers, Essays in Ancient Egyptian Studies.***

Ma'at represented, to the Kemetyu, the principle of cosmic order as well as eternal renewal. Ma'at is right order in nature and society as established by the act of Creation and hence means, according to the Kemet text, that which is right, correct, law, order, justice and truth. The Spiritual Warrior must stand on Ma'at. The Ancient Priest Scientists believed that the Ma'at state of righteousness must be preserved and established in great matters as well as small. "As Above, So Below," even the very foundation of Kemet was based on this Ma'atian Law of correspondence or Universal Truth. The nation was divided into two parts, Upper and Lower Kemet, with 42 Sput (Districts or Providences), which also corresponded with the 42 Laws of Ma'at. A Spt which was the geographical term that divided boundaries (districts), literally meant to make like the heavens. Many of the Mru (Pyramids), if not all were aligned with stars in the Kemet heavenly map called a zodiac today. "As ***Above, So Below."***

Ma'at was absolute truth, or Ma'at is absolute! According to the ancient teachings of our Black-human Afrakan ancestors of the Hapy Valley, the **TRUTH IS ABSOLUTE!** And each Spiritual Warrior must also know this to be true in their hearts. This Truth is Ma'at, which was the foundation of the entire Hapy Valley Civilization, northeast Afraka.

This Ma'atian Law of correspondence states that principles operating on one level operates on all levels. They knew that the human body was a microcosm of the earth - macrocosm. And by using the law of correspondence, they knew that the earth was a microcosm of the sun-macrocosm and so on. Through the innerstanding of the human body-temple and soul they could innerstand the very patterns of creation, along with the entire workings of the universe could be grasped. Correspondence is not analytical comparison. It is an innerstanding of nature on its most basic level. Viewing the world through this Ma'atian Law allows you to see the interconnectiveness of all things mental, physical, and spiritual.

In ancient Kemet, every aspect of the society was based on this Ma'atian law, from the workings of our innerstanding of creation, to the architecture, to spiritual worship were all in sacred harmony and proportion with the universe. The mathematical concept of Pi = 3.14 and the royal cubic = 1.61 or sometimes called the Golden Mean, was common knowledge in Ancient Kemet 6,000 years ago. All measurements in Ancient Kemet were based on the Golden Mean 1.61, from the building of the Mru, Ipet Astu at Waset and all their temples, monuments, art, language, star maps, kalendar making, even the measuring of farm land. Later the Greeks, who sat at the feet of Kemet Afrakan masters learned about this science and called it Phi, which equals 1.61. The Free Masons, all the Masonic orders use these measurements based on the royal cubic of Ancient Kemet. Much of Washington D.C.and its monuments, was laid out and designed on these same Afrakan principles, also the United Nation Building, the post cards at the U .S. Postal service and the list goes on.

Spiritual Warriors of the Kemet legacy teach that if you innerstand this Ma'atian law of correspondence, than you will have a greater innerstanding of yourself in relationship to the universe. Lets look at the golden mean, or royal cubic, the distance between your finger tips and your hand in proportion to your hand and elbow, this distance is consistent all over your body-temple. The ratio will be the same between all the joints on your body-temple like each finger, the ratio between the joints is the same ratio on your hand and elbow, between your forehead and chin, between your chest and waist, between your thigh to knee and knee to foot, between the joints on your toes and your ring size and foot size, glove size and head size will also be in the same ratio proportion of 1.61. This Kemet law of correspondence is Ma'at. And when any of these proportion are out of balance your challenges are greater to maintain harmony.

The classic Kemet grid upon which all reliefs, temples and human figures are laid out are in harmony with the Ma'atian law of correspondence. The Kemetyu drew objects from different aspects and the square grid was used to preserve proportions during construction from the plans. Common use of the Kemet grid of squares led to the concept of coordinates.

Even your spirit is in harmony with the spirit of the universe. If you breath correctly, as taught in Ma'at Akhu Ba Ankh or Kupigana Ngumi, your breath will be in rhythm with the heavens. On the average, it takes four seconds to complete a breath cycle. There are 86,400 seconds in one day. Therefore, you average 21,600 breaths in one day, this is equal to the ratio of 1.61. This is a perfect example of the law of correspondence. The sun travels at 21,600 miles per hour. The earth and the moon are 216,000 miles apart. The sun is 400 times further away (86,400,000 miles away) and 400 times larger than the moon. The moon's radius is 2,160 miles. One month in the grand year of the procession of the equinox is 2,160 earth years. And 12 of which make the grand year of 25,920 which is equal to the earth's circumference of 25,920 miles. Now you innerstand why the Mru , the largest man made structures were almost perfect, and why all the monuments and statues no matter how large seem to be always in perfect human proportions. ***"As Above, So Below."***

To the Spiritual Warrior, it is crystal clear that there is no task, no mission that is more important than the innerstanding of Ma'at. Even the very concept of Afrakan Deep Thought has to be based on Ma'at or there will be no dynamic action, just thought or philosophy, flowery words without action, void of soul and spirit or human progress. Ma'at is, therefore, not only right order, but also the object of human activity.

Ma'at is both the task which humans set for themselves and also, the state of awareness called Heru Konsciousness, the promise and reward which awaits them upon fulfilling Ma'at. The innerstanding of the conceptualization of Ma'at was an essential key in the articulation of the ancient Afrakan Worldview as expressed in Kemet and we must once again return to this foundation as an Afrakan people.

Ma'at originated with the Creation. The Great Nswtu of ancient Kemet, who considered themselves the" Sons of Ra", and "Followers of Heru," were also "Great Servants" of the Ntchrt Ma'at. As the Servants of Ma'at, they felt it necessary to constantly restore

Ma'at wherever it was needed. Today, we as Spiritual Warriors must look at ourselves also as servants of Ma'at with the Spirit of Heru. If we are to do any healing, we will have to do battle with esfet constantly so that we may restore Ma'at where it is needed. Healing is, in fact, a state of returning a condition of esfet back to Ma'at. This is done by creating harmonious wholistic conditions wherever Afrakan people are, a state of bringing balance back to a condition where it does not exist, mentally physically or spiritually.

"Ma'at is great, and its effectiveness lasting, it has not been disturbed since the time of Asr... " (From The Husia by Maulana Karenga) Ma'at out lasts human life, but human beings, however, are judged by Ma'at, and whoever is in accord with it is granted longevity, spiritual harmony and Htp. Thus, the Kemet Spiritual Warrior Priest Scientists believed that Ma'at was the spiritual and cosmic order, and the rightful order which the Nswt and Hem Sem-Tepy and every member of the society had to maintain as well as the just reward promised to those who kept it faithfully. Ma'at was, in fact, the heart of Kemetyu ethics, and we must return to those ethics of Ma'at if we, as Spiritual Warriors, are to truly empower ourselves to do the healing that is necessary among Afrakan people worldwide.

Ma'at was the basis of the Kemet legal system. The Vizier , who was responsible for the administration of justice, appointed by the Nswt, was from the Fifth Dynasty onward called "The Priest of Ma'at," or "the Neb of Ma'at." In later times, judges wore an image of Ma'at on a chain about their necks or on their clothing. Today's Kemetyu Priests, Priestess and Spiritual Warriors wear or carry an Ankh because the key of life must be based on Ma'at - truth, justice, righteousness, and harmonious balance. Other Kemet symbols are also worn called Sa, for spiritual protection.

In the _Pert-em-Heru_ *or The Book of Coming Forth by Light*, it clearly shows us that when each person's physical life is over, one enters the Double Halls of Ma'at in the underworld of the Duat (A spiritual realm of transformation). The deceased must then pass the confessions to Ma'at. These confessions should correspond to an ideal way of life which all should aspire. The *42 Laws of Ma'at* constituted a moral code which prevailed in ancient Kemet throughout much of its recorded Ourstory and history. Therefore, it stands to reason that one had to conform to Ma'at in both one's speech and in one's actions.

The deceased would have writings on their tombs describing acts of Ma'at to show their righteousness, such as:

> ***"I have given bread to the hungry man, clothes to the naked man ..."***
> ***"I carried over him that had no boat ..."***
> ***"I saved the weak from him who was stronger than he."***

Next to these are general confessions such as:

> ***"I have not inflicted pain".***
> ***"I have not made any man weep".***

These statements show clearly that the ancient Kemetyu believed in Ma'at and the harmonious order of the universe.

A person's heart is symbolic of the seat of intellect and will, as well as the life giving center of the physical body. This symbolic heart was weighed against a symbol of Ma'at (usually depicted as a feather), which served as an ethical standard. Enpu, the Neb of the West, was Master of Balance and Transformation. Enpu led the deceased to the way of the scales; Jhuty, the Master Scribe of the Ntchru, weighed the heart against the feather. He then recorded and announced the verdict, with the help of Seshat, the female Ntchrt scribe of mathematical order and harmonious rhythm. If the verdict should be unfavorable and Ma'at has not been upheld, the victim meets

Amamet, "the Devourer of the souls of the unjust." If the verdict should be favorable, the deceased becomes "the vindicated one" - True of voice, and is brought before Asr by Heru, the son of Asr and the Great Avenger of injustice and a Spiritual Warrior for Ma'at.

This judgement scene represented three levels of Ma'at. This scene clearly showed us that Ma'at stood for man's relationship with man on an earthly level, when the heart of the deceased, symbolically their actions was weighed against the feather of Ma'at. Man's relationship with the second level of life or the spirit world of the Duat also comes through in the judgement scene when Jhuty and Heru finalize the transformation to the spirit world. Finally, this scene stands for man's relationship with The NTCHR, and the Ntchr Ntchru, when the deceased is actually judged and declared "the vindicated one".

Ma'at is also truth, justice and harmonious balance for all that The NTCHR has created. So when someone defies the Laws of Ma'at, they also defy an established order of the universe. This act of disorder is called esfet (wrong doings, falsehood, evil, that which destroys balance). Esfet is the major reason for disease, the lack of harmony in the body-temple. The Spiritual Warrior must be like Heru, he who fights injustice for eternity. According to Spiritual Warriors, this act of returning esfet back to balance is healing, Htp.

The Spiritual Warrior must always maintain Ma'at on a wholistic level, which is peace, justice and righteousness both in our personal or individual lives as well as our universal one. We must strive for truth and justice in our hearts, the family, the village - community, or

nation, and we must maintain harmony in nature, and in our personal environment. The Spiritual Warriors of the so-called 18th Dynasty, New Period, left their legacy etched in stone. This is merely one of many examples of their infinite wisdom:

> ***"Tut-Ankh-Amen drove out disorder from the Two Lands and Ma'at is firmly established in its place; he made lying an abomination and the land is as it was at the first time."***

Ma'at, as defined by modern Spiritual Warriors has at least thirteen cardinal principles. They are truth, justice, balance, harmony, reciprocity, order, propriety, righteousness, straightness, uprightness, natural law, harmonious rule, and integrity. Spiritual Warriors who are healers must be a living testimony to these principles of Ma'at, which are essential ingredients to impeccability, giving your gifts, following your mission and fully living our daily lives in Htp.

Ma'at is the key to inner light, enlightenment and spirituality. The Kemetyu have always placed Ma'at first in the founding and maintenance of our societies when we were in control of our own lives mentally, physically and spiritually. Therefore, Ma'at becomes essential for Afrakans to wholistically incorporate Ma'at back into our lives while we are living here in Amenta, the land founded on esfet. As the Kemetyu or descendants of Afrakans, we must never forget how we got to North America, the Caribbean, and South America. We did not come here on the Mayflower or on a cruise ship. We were brought here by a people who were practicing esfet as a world order in the new names of capitalism, colonialism and racism. Kemetyu were stolen, abducted, hijacked, tricked and forcefully removed from Afraka and enslaved. This Black Holocaust was called the Maangamizi. It must be clear, thieves, bandits, pirates and inhuman barbaric savages with the help of backward greedy Afrakans and Arab opportunist and collaborators who assisted in our enslavement for Europeans, Arabs and European Caucasian colonist brought Kemetyu here illegally. Europeans Caucasians Christian, and Arabs who claimed to be civilized Muslims treated Afrakans inhuman like a horse or a cow or a chicken. Spiritual Warriors of Afrakan descent you are in America, but you must never surrender your souls to esfet, never be about the business of what America stands for or European Caucasians, Ma'at must always be at our center..

IN AMERICA, NOT OF AMERICA

Peaceful creatures and puppets have no future in America
That's why there are no more buffalos
Red men are on reservations
And our presence here is out of an economic act of exploitation
Our Blackness is a constant reminder of white racism
As we dangle from strings made in Japan like puppets, that were broken like limbs from Afrakan trees with European Caucasian images carved upon our Ebony masks
We are in America
But not of America!

As Kemetyu who are Spiritual Warriors, we must prepare ourselves to defend Ma'at wholistically, which is the first step in mental defense. You and your family must be able to defend yourself mentally by re-learning our true legacy in Kemet, and in the Diaspora. Knowledge is the key to power, like ignorance is the key to perpetual enslavement, which means we must learn the skills necessary to liberate ourselves and to control our lives on every level. We must also be able to defend ourselves and our families physically. We must always be healthy and in excellent physical condition. We should learn some basic forms of martial arts and/or weaponry. Kupigana Ngumi is a Kemetyu based martial arts with a Ma'atian spiritual system for the development of the New Afrakan of the 21st century. It is the type of martial arts that allows the involvement of the entire family. Kupigana Ngumi physical training includes: hand to hand combat, grappling, anti-grappling, weaponry, dance, meditation and survival training in nature. The last step is spiritual defense. You must prepare yourself and your family on how to defend Ma'at spiritually. If you are of Afrakan decent, a Afrakan Religion or Spiritual system like Kemet, Akan, Yoruba, Voodoo, Candomble, Shango, etc. should be part of your spiritual existence, but it must be rooted in Ma'at and reflect your Kulture. I also recommend some form of meditation. People of Afrakan decent should probably practice a form of meditation that is centered in their Kulture, like Ma'at Akhw Ba Ankh, Egyptian yoga or Ari Ankh Ka because this will help you center yourself with the NTCHR. There is, of course, much to learn from other spiritual and meditative systems of other cultures, but your own Kulture always has the medicine you need, so a strong Afrakan Kultural and spiritual system is medicine for Afrakan people. Other cultural systems can help you if you are lost and have no program as an individual, maybe even supplement missing survival skills, but they cannot center Afrakan people as a whole and they can not liberate us.

Ma'at is "The Way" for The Spiritual Warrior. Ma'at is perfect health and is the state where healing can take place. It causes everything to heal and it maintains order and harmonious balance. Ma'at Konsciousness is one of the quests for Spiritual Healers. You must use the scales of Ma'at to judge everything you do mentally, physically, and spiritually. (Moderation and equanimity in all events and situations are the deeper implications of the scales of Ma'at in your life-style.)

Below are the "Double Scales" of Ma'at.

Ma'at Konsciousness of The Spiritual Warrior

1. Right Thinking: Thought based on Ma'at. Thought has infinite power; focus your thoughts on harmonious goals and objectives to reach the goals with a wholistic plan based on Ma'at. Focus your thoughts on listening to The NTCHR, and the wisdom of Ma'at will enter your life daily.

2. Right Innerstanding : See the world as The NTCHR and maintain Ma'at in everything you do. Use Ma'at in your relationships with people, things and nature; always bring harmony and balance to your innerstanding.

3. Right Speech: Allow the Ntchr Jhuty, which is Higher Spiritual Konsciousness, to guide your words through reason and knowing based on Ma'at. It is also knowing what to say, how to say it, when to say it, and when to remain silent.

4. Right Action: Movement guided by Higher Konsciousness. Action is the instrument of thought. Kemetyu liberation must be guided by Right Action and Right Thought from a Kemetyu centered reality.

a) Never take any life without a just cause, based upon Ma'at.
b) Never take anything which is not freely given.
c) Never abuse your Ntchru given powers, mentally, physically or spiritually.
d) Never speak without Ma'at in your heart.
e) Never abuse your mental, physical, or spiritual body by consuming life threatening foods or substances like drugs.

5. Right Livelihood: Make a living in such a way as to benefit oneself, the family and all others based on the laws of Ma'at. Do work that is in keeping with your Ntchru gifts, goals, mission and aspirations.

6. Right Meditation: High Konsciousness that teaches you to transcend esfet and live by Ma'at, through the innerstanding of Oneness with The Ntchr Ntchru. Right Meditation is also a period of silence that allows your

physical body-temple to tune in and align itself with the mind and spirit. Right Meditation is also objective and subjective, non-judgmental reflection.

7. <u>Right Breathing</u>: Innerstand that Shu is the breath of The NTCHR, and through the correct use of Shu in our physical body, High Konsciousness can be obtained. This leads to liberation, mentally, physically, and spiritually. Only through Right Breathing can Moyo (your internal unlimited vital force) be developed and utilized to send forth unrestricted energy to all points of the body temple.

8. <u>Right Mindfulness</u>: Have an awareness of everything that one does at all times. Act with Konsciousness, or simply tune in to the Oneness of the Spirit. Right Mindfulness is the awareness that Right Thinking must supersede all Right Action.

9. <u>Right Spirituality</u>: Innerstand that your spirit is undying, unconquerable and one with the NTCHR. You can then use "The Spirit" to guide your life mentally and physically as a Spiritual Warrior.

10. <u>Right Rest</u>: Sleep is a state where your Konscious mind be comes one with your unkonscious mind, or your subjective mind becomes one with your objective mind, a form of recharging your energy, which should happen at least 5 to 9 hours every 24 hours.

11. <u>Right diet</u>: The consumption of life giving foods as fuel and not life threatening substances that some humans eat and call food. Fuel for human beings that have the greatest efficiency and nutrition are: fruits, vegetables, grains, legumes, nuts and clean water. Right diet also means not over consuming even of the right foods. Everything must be in moderation, this is Ma'at. Never consume more than two large meals in one day, and make sure more than 50% is raw organic foods, which readily allows the body to utilize and transform the fuel into usable energy. Try to consume at least 32 oz. of clean water every 24 hours. Try to avoid eating and drinking together, as the water washes away the digestive juices needed in digestion.

12. Right Exercise: The body is a Holy Temple created by The NTCHR to house the spirit, which directs the mind, which directs the body. Keep the body temple healthy, strong and supple through moderate exercise in all areas of the body-temple with a consistent routine. Right Exercise can be one or a combination of the following exercises: Ma'at Akhw Ba Ankh, Ari Ankh Ka, meditation, yoga, Kupigana Ngumi, Martial Arts, aerobics, running, walking, bicycling, weights, and the various sport games.

13. Right cleanliness: Keep the Holy Body Temple clean. Wash the body several times daily. Always wash before eating, praying, entering your personal space from the outer world activities and before and after any sexual acts. Make these acts a ritual.

14. Right Reciprocity: Perform selfless service at least once every day. Expect no reward in return, but with the innerstanding that what goes around, comes around. A Spiritual Warrior must always give more than they expect to receive. This is also the ultimate act of healing and bringing Ma'at back into our lives, even to those who are among the walking murdered. The walking murdered are the unkonscious suicidal addicts of western capitalism and European culture superimposed over their unkonscious Afrakaness.

So for the Spiritual Warrior, one must do Ma'at, by speaking truth, doing justice, and living by "The Way" every day through eternity. This harmony creates a sense of Konscious unity between self and the cosmos or NTCHR. The Spiritual Warrior sees no split between the material and spiritual aspects of knowing the world. The Spiritual Warrior internalizes each human lesson with spirit, transforming thoughts and actions into perfection, this impeccability is innerstanding the divine within. This is "The Way" to the Spiritual Warrior, thus the process of growth and development are the true meanings of joy in ones life.

The Articulate Farmer

During the long reign of the Nswt Pepy, Kemet began to decline. Many reasons have been suggested for the fall of the Old Period. The climate seems to have continued to get drier and years of low Hapy led to famines and weakened the peoples' faith in their Nswt. Unwisely, the Old Period rulers gave away many of the royal lands to reward their officials and even allowed them to pass on their jobs to their sons. This made the civil service less efficient and more independent and was particularly dangerous in the case of the officials who governed the Sptu (districts). These governors grew rich and powerful and began to rule their Sptu like petty kings. Wars broke out between them and for the century known as the First Intermediate Period (c2134-2020 B.C.) Kemet was divided and weak. The story of the Articulate Farmer is set in this period when Kemet was full of corrupt officials but the old ideal of impartial justice - Ma'at was still remembered in the minds and hearts of the masses of Afrakan people.

In the reign of the Nswt Nub-Kau-Ra, a farmer call Khunanup lived with his family by an oasis in the Western Desert. He worked hard all year round to gather food to trade with in Kemet but he was still a poor man. One day Khunanup said to his wife, "I'm going down to Kemet to barter for food for our children. Measure out what's left of our grain."

When she brought the grain from their storeroom, Khunanup divided it into two uneven parts. "Keep these twenty measures to feed you and the children while I'm away but take these six measures and make them into bread and beer for my journey."

The farmer loaded his two donkeys with bundles of rushes, sacks of salt and natron, jackal hides and ostrich feathers. When the bread and beer were ready he said good-bye to his wife and children and led the donkeys south towards the city of Nekhen. Some days later, as he was traveling through the district of Perfefi, Khunanup's donkeys were noticed by an official called Nemtynakht. This official was a greedy and ruthless man and when he saw the laden donkeys he decided to take them from the farmer. The house of Nemtynakht stood close to a narrow path which had a corn field on one side and the Hapy River on the other.

The official sent one of his servants to fetch him a sheet and he spread it across the path with its fringe in the corn and its hem hanging over the river.

As Khunanup came along the path Nemtynakht called out, "Be careful, farmer don't let your filthy donkeys tread on the sheet I'm drying!" "Whatever you say," answered the farmer cheerfully, and he urged his donkeys up into the field to avoid the sheet. "You wretched farmer! " shouted Nemtynakht. "Now you're trampling my corn!" "can't help trampling the corn if your sheet is blocking the path," said Khunanup reasonably but at that moment one of his donkeys seized and ate a wisp of corn. "Thieving beast! I shall take this donkey," announced the official, "as payment for my stolen corn." "My donkey is worth far more than one wisp of corn!" protested Khunanup. "I know that this estate belongs to the High Steward Rensi. He is an enemy to every thief and he won't let me be robbed on his own land!"

Nemtynakht was furious with the farmer for arguing. "It is me you have to deal with, not the High Steward!" He beat Khunanup with his staff and seized both the donkeys. The poor farmer sat down on the path and wept. "Stop wailing, "snapped Nemtynakht, "or I'll send you to the Neb of silence!" "First you rob me, then you beat me and now you forbid me to complain; but you can't stop me from asking the Ntchru for Justice (Ma'at)!"

For ten days Khunanup hung around the house of Nemtynakht, hoping to persuade him to give back the donkeys and their loads. When he saw that it was no use, the farmer walked to the city Nni-nsw to look for the High Steward Rensi. He found Rensi standing on the river bank with a group of judges, waiting for a barge to take them to the courthouse.

The high steward never refused a plea for Ma'at and he ordered one of his scribes to stay behind and write down the details of the farmer's complaint. As they boarded the barge the other judges said to Rensi, "Surely there is no need to punish an official for a few skins or a trifle of salt. The farmer probably belongs to him and has been caught trying to sell his master's goods."

Rensi said nothing, but he was very angry with the judges because he knew that Nemtynakht was dishonest. It also saddened him to think how hard it was for a commoner to get a fair hearing.

The very next day the high steward read the details of Khunanup's case and summoned him before the court. Confident that Rensi was a just man, the farmer knelt down and began to speak; "O High Steward, greatest of the great, when you go down to the Sea of Ma'at, you shall have fair winds. No storm will strip away your sails and your mast will never snap. Truth will bring you safely to harbor for you are a father to the orphan, a husband to the widow, a brother to the helpless. You are free of greed, an enemy of lies and a friend of truth. You are a Neb of Ma'at who hears the voice of the oppressed. Hear my plea, heal my grief, do me justice!"

Rensi, who was used to coaxing a few words out of silent or stammering commoners, was astonished to hear such an articulate speech. He promised Khunanup that he would hear the case in full the next day and hurried to the palace. Rensi bowed before the Nswt Nub-Kau-Ra and said in great excitement, Nswt Bety, Neb of the beloved land, my Neb, I have discovered a farmer who cannot read or write but who speaks with wonderful eloquence! He is a poor man and one of my officials has robbed him of his donkeys and trade goods so he has come to me asking justice."

The Nswt was intrigued, "As you value my happiness, Rensi, detain this farmer for a while. Be silent when he pleads and have someone write down everything he says. Make sure that he has enough to live on and that his wife and family are provided for. These farmers only come to Kemet to trade when their storerooms are nearly empty. Help them, but in secret!"

Everything was done as the Nswt commanded. Rensi saw that the towns people offered food to Khunanup and messages were sent to the oasis with orders that the farmer's wife and family were to be cared for. The next time Khunanup came into court, Rensi frowned and spoke coldly to him, but the farmer was not daunted. "Great Neb of Ma'at, justice is the rudder of heaven; you are the rudder of Kemet, the equal of Jhuty who keeps the Balance and is the most impartial of judges. If you support the thief, who is there left to punish crime? The desperate can steal without reproach, but you are great and rich and powerful. Neb of Ma'-at , be generous, be just!"

Rensi listened with secret pleasure to the farmer's speech and a scribe hidden behind a curtain wrote it all down. When it was over the high steward rose left the court without a word and Khunanup went away dejected.

The next morning the farmer came back to the court and made a fierce speech attacking judges who were greedy or corrupt. Rensi said nothing but the courthouse guards gave Khunanup a thrashing for his insolence and Nemtynakht looked on and laughed.

For five more days the farmer came to court and pleaded his case but the High Steward would not answer him. By the ninth day Khunanup was desperate. He knew that the rations he had left for his family would be used up by now and without him they might starve. The farmer went into the court knowing that if he could not get justice that day he would have to go home.

For the last time, Khunanup knelt before the High Steward. "Great one, do justice for the sake of the Neb of Ma'at and shun esfet. When the just man dies his name is not forgotten on Earth and his spirit is blessed in the Realm of the Dead; this is the law of the Ntchru. Speak justice, do justice, for it is mighty and endures for ever!"

The farmer looked up at the high steward but Rensi was silent and gave him no sign. "A man who once saw has now become blind," said Khunanup sadly. "A man who once heard has now become deaf. For nine days I have pleaded in vain, now I shall complain of you to the Ntchru!" He stood up and strode out of the court but Rensi ordered two guards to bring him back. Khunanup was sure that he was going to be punished for his bold words. "When death comes, " he said steadily, "it is like a cup of water to a thirsty man".

For the first time the High tewards smiled at him. "Good farmer, do not be afraid. Stand there and listen to your pleas for justice." Khunanup was astounded when a scribe came forward and read out the nine speeches from a papyrus scroll. "Come with me now to the palace,".

said Rensi and the farmer soon found himself kissing the ground before the throne of the Nswt Nub-Kau-Ra. The Nswt read the speeches and was delighted that a commoner should speak so well and so bravely. He smiled on Khunanup and ordered the high steward to judge his case.

A terrified Nemtynakht was dragged into the throne room and beaten until he confessed his crimes. Then Rensi ordered that all the official's land and goods be given to Khunanup. So the articulate farmer returned to his oasis a rich man and justice ruled in Kemet.

These are the lessons we must teach our children, dynamic lessons from Ourstory, and our Kulture. Lessons that talk about honor and trust between spouse, and family responsibility, patience, living with no fear, and living by Ma'at by any means necessary. Khunanup was a Spiritual Warrior even though he had never been officially trained by the Priest. He was a warrior because he innerstood the principles of "Being." He had embodied the spirit of Jhuty into his very soul and just like Jhuty was a lover of the NTCHR which is Ma'at, this was the spirit of Khunanup **and it must be the spirit of the Spiritual Warrior Today!**

Kemklusion

Ma'at was created by The NTCHR at Creation. Ma'at is the Ntchrt of Balance in the Universe and Innerverse on all levels, mentally, physically and spiritually. Ma'at is the center principle that is the mate or complement of Jhuty, the Ntchr of articulate thought, speech, writing and dynamic action. Ma'at is that quality that keeps a person or the Ntchru in line with harmonious balance among the universal cosmological patterns.

Ma'at is the scales of justice in the underworld or spiritual world of the Duat, called the Double Halls of Ma'at. Even in the Duat, Ma'at was the code by which the heart of the deceased, symbolic of intellect and earthly will, must be measured against. Ma'at is an ideal way of life to which all should aspire, in order to become "the vindicated one" and return to The NTCHR, along with the Sacred Ancestors (also called Pt (Heaven) to the Kemetyu of ancient Kemet).

On a human level, Ma'at exists in our lives through the 13 cardinal principles of the Spiritual Warrior. These are truth, justice, balance, harmony, reciprocity, order, propriety, righteousness, straitness, uprightness, natural law, harmonious rule and integrity. As a value system, we can use the *42 Laws of Ma'at* to guide our daily lives using tradition and reason so that it is updated to innerstand the times of today.

Declaration of Innocence to Ma'at
(Commonly known as the 42 Laws of Ma'at)

(1) Say, whose long of stride, who comes forth from the city of Enu, I have not done wrong doings.

(2) Say, who embraces fire, who comes forth from the city of battle - Khraha, I have not robbed with violence.

(3) Say, one who is of the divine nose, who comes forth from the city of Khemennu (Hermopolis), I have not been rapacious (evil minded).

(4) Say, eater of shades, who comes forth from the temple of Qrnt (Elephantine), I have not killed people. (twice)

(5) Say, decayer of bodies, who comes forth from heaven, I have not acted deceitfully.

(6) Say, the Ntchru in the form of two lions who comes forth from heaven, I have not acted deceitfully.

(7) Say, whose eyes are fire, who comes from Saut, I have not stolen or seized the property of the Ntchru.

(8) Say, flames who come forth from and go back, I have not spoken falsehood.

(9) Say, breaker of bones, who come forth from the city of the Nswt Henen (young ruler), I have not carried away the bread offering.

(10) Say, commander of flames, who comes forth from the city of the house of the soul of the Creator - Het Ka Ptah (House of Ptah, located in Men-Nefer, Kemet (Egypt), I have not sullen (cause pain through harsh words).

(11) Say, Qrrty, who comes forth from the West, I have not committed sodomy, nor have I committed fornication to myself.

(12) Say, his face is behind him, who comes forth from his caravan, I have not made anyone to cry.

(13) Say, Bsty, who comes forth from the secret place, I have not swallowed my heart.

(14) Say, who has legs of fire, who comes forth from the darkness, I have not gone astray.

(15) Say, eater of squirting blood, who comes forth from the offering block, I have not acted deceitfully.

(16) Say, eater of entrails (inwards parts), who comes forth from Mabetu, I have not robbed conveyed land.

(17) Say, Neb of truth and righteousness, who comes forth from the city of double truths, I have not listened to the discussion of others.

(18) Say, who goes astray or backwards, who comes forth from the city of Bast (Bubatis), I have not departed.

(19) Say, Srdyu (divine gleaming one), who comes forth from the city of Enu, I have not disputed about anything.

(20) Say, he who is doublely wicked, who comes forth from the city of Aty, I have not defiled the wife of a man.

(21) Say, double serpent, who comes forth from the temple of executions, I have not defiled the wife of a man.

(22) Say, who looks at what is brought to him, who comes forth from the temple of Amsu, I have not copulated excessively.

(23) Say, who is the highest of the great ones, who comes forth from Amemt (a wooden tree), I have not made terror.

(24) Say, Khyu (destroyer), who comes from Gyu, I have not gone astray.

(25) Say, disposer of speech, who comes forth from the city of Wryt (Unes), I have not been hot tempered.

(26) Say, child, who comes forth from the city of Uab, I have not been deaf on myself concerning the words of truth and righteousness.

(27) Say, Knnemety who dwells in darkness, who comes forth from the city of Knnemet (darkness), I have no secrets.

(28) Say, bringer of his offering of peace, who comes forth from the city of Sau (Sais), I have not gone forth by arm force.

(29) Say, Sre Khru (one who's voice foretells), who comes forth from the city of Wnest, I have not stirred up strife.

(30) Say Neb of faces, who comes forth from the city of Njft, I am not hasty of heart.

(31) Say, Sekhryu (one who governs), who comes forth from Uten, I have not listened to the discussion of others.

(32) Say, Neb of two horns, who comes forth from the city of Sauty (Sais), I have not multiplied my words (talked too much).

(33) Say, beautiful Tm, who comes forth from the city of the house of the soul of the Creator, Het Ka Ptah, I have not done wrong doings nor have I done evil.

(34) Say, Tm one who is of all seasons, who comes forth from the city of Djedu, I have not made hostility or sedition against the Nswt (Ruler), or great ancestors.

(35) Say, who works in his heart, who comes forth from the city of Tebu, I have not fouled or polluted upon the water.

(36) Say, sistrum player, who comes forth from the primordial waters Nun, I have not haughty my voice (loud voice).

(37) Say, provider of humans, who comes forth from the city of Sau, I have not questioned the all existing force of the universe (Ntchr).

(38) Say, Nehhb Ka (uniter of attributes), who comes forth from his hiding, I have not exalted the son of wrong doings.

(39) Say, beautiful Nehb Nfrwt, who comes forth from his caravan, I have not defrauded the offerings of the Ntchru (the all existing forces of the universe).

(40) Say, controlled head, who comes forth from the secret shrine, I have not taken away the offerings from the beneficent ones (Spirits of Light).

(41) Say, bringer of his arms, who comes forth from the double city of truth and righteousness - Ma'at, I have not taken away the food of the infants. I have not scorned the Ntchr of my city.

(42) Say, who has white teeth, who comes forth from the land of the lake - Ta she, I have not slaughtered the sacred cow.

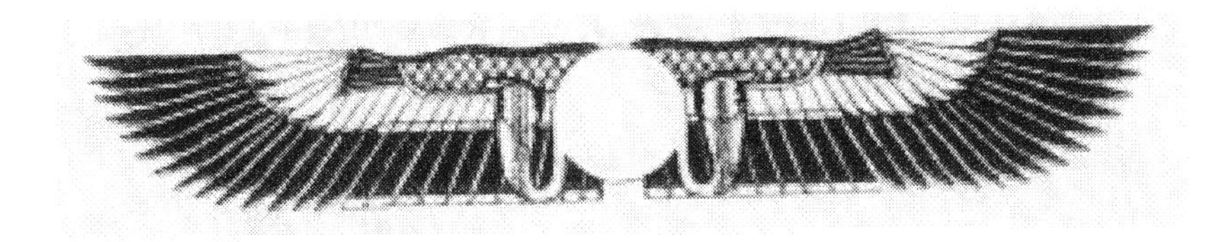

Oracles of Ma'at

This is the most popular translation by Europeans and Euro-American Egyptologist.

(1) I WILL DO NO WRONG.
(2) I WILL NOT STEAL.
(3) I WILL NOT ACT WITH VIOLENCE.
(4) I WILL NOT KILL.
(5) I WILL NOT BE UNJUST.
(6) I WILL NOT CAUSE PAIN.
(7) I WILL NOT DESECRATE HOLY PLACES.
(8) I WILL NOT LIE.
(9) I WILL NOT WASTE FOOD.
(10) I WILL NOT SPEAK EVIL.
(11) I WILL NOT COMMIT SODOMY.
(12) I WILL NOT CAUSE THE SHEDDING OF TEARS.
(13) I WILL NOT SOW SEEDS OF REGRET.
(14) I WILL NOT BE AN AGGRESSOR.
(15) I WILL NOT ACT GUILEFULLY.
(16) I WILL NOT LAY WASTE THE PLOWED LAND.
(17) I WILL NOT ENTER INTO CONSPIRACY.
(18) I WILL NOT BEAR FALSE WITNESS.
(19) I WILL NOT BE WRATHFUL AND ANGRY EXCEPT FOR A JUST CAUSE.
(20) I WILL NOT COMMIT ADULTERY.
(21) I WILL NOT COMMIT ADULTERY.*
(22) I WILL NOT POLLUTE MYSELF.
(23) I WILL NOT CAUSE TERROR.
(24) I WILL NOT POLLUTE THE EARTH.
(25) I WILL NOT SPEAK IN HOT ANGER.
(26) I WILL NOT TURN FROM WORDS OF RIGHT AND TRUTH.

(27) I WILL NOT UTTER CURSES EXCEPT AGAINST EVIL.
(28) I WILL NOT INITIATE A QUARREL.
(29) I WILL NOT BE EXCITABLE OR CONTENTIOUS.
(30) I WILL NOT PREJUDICE.
(31) I WILL NOT BE AN EAVESDROPPER.
(32) I WILL NOT SPEAK OVERMUCH.
(33) I WILL NOT COMMIT TREASON AGAINST MY ANCESTORS.
(34) I WILL NOT WASTE WATER.
(35) I WILL NOT DO EVIL.
(36) I WILL NOT BE ARROGANT.
(37) I WILL NOT BLASPHEME NTCHR.
(38) I WILL NOT COMMIT FRAUD.
(39) I WILL NOT DEFRAUD TEMPLE OFFERINGS.
(40) I WILL NOT PLUNDER THE DEAD.
(41) I WILL NOT MISTREAT CHILDREN.
(42) I WILL NOT MISTREAT ANIMALS.

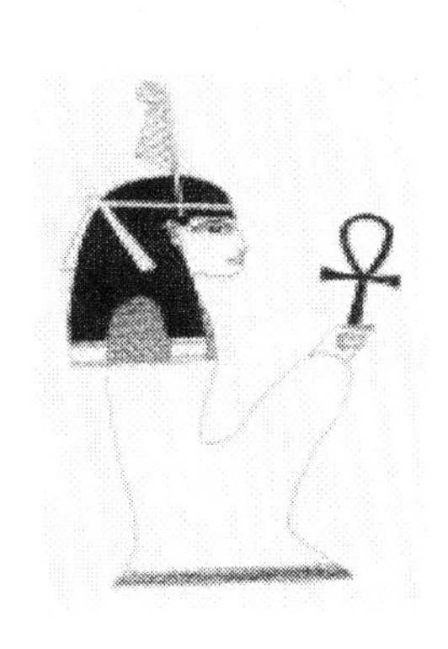

Ma'at

Declaration of Innocence to Ma'at written in Mdw Ntchr on the following pages
(Commonly known as the 42 Laws of Ma'at)

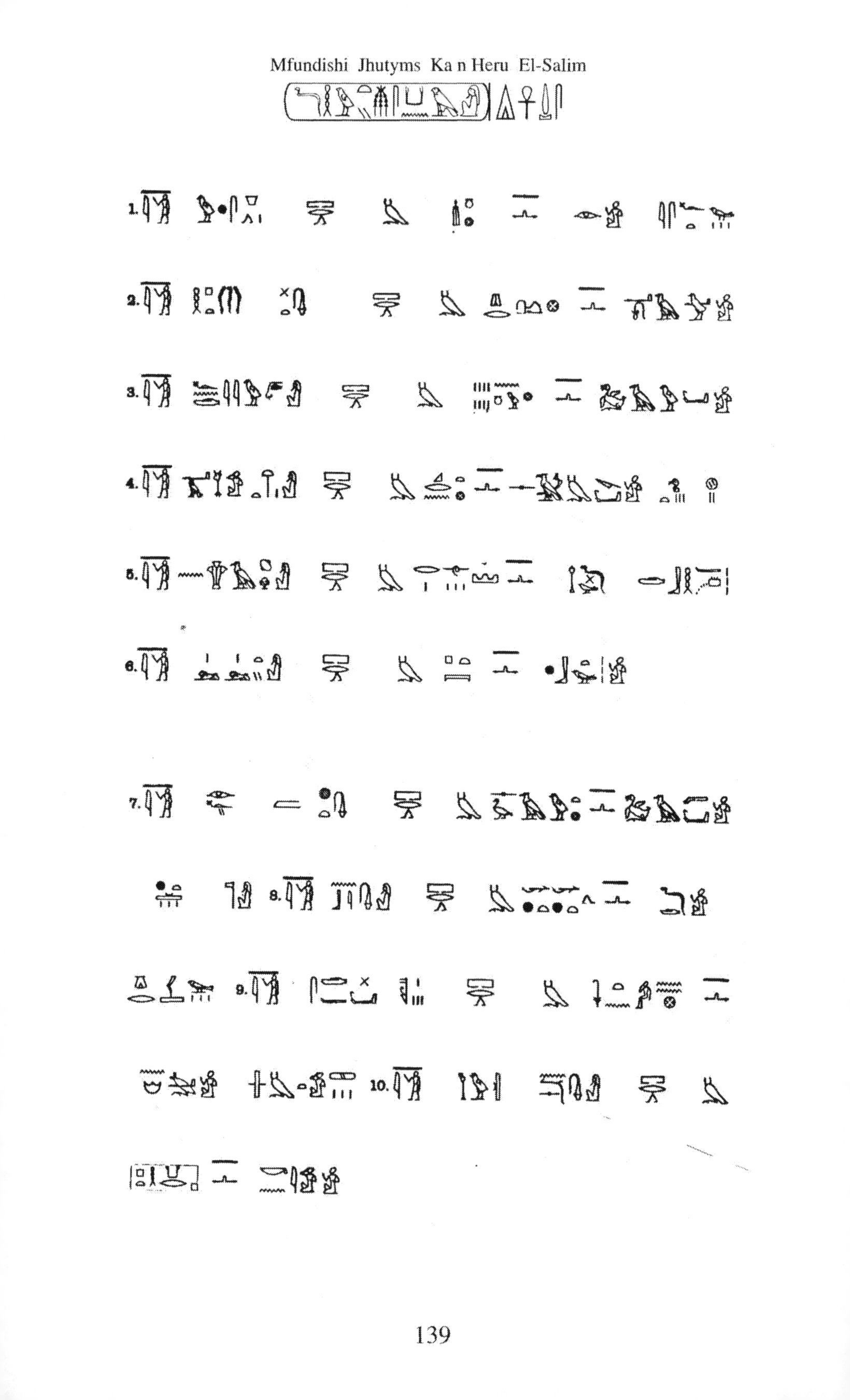

1.

2.

3.

4.

5.

6.

7.

8.

9.

10.

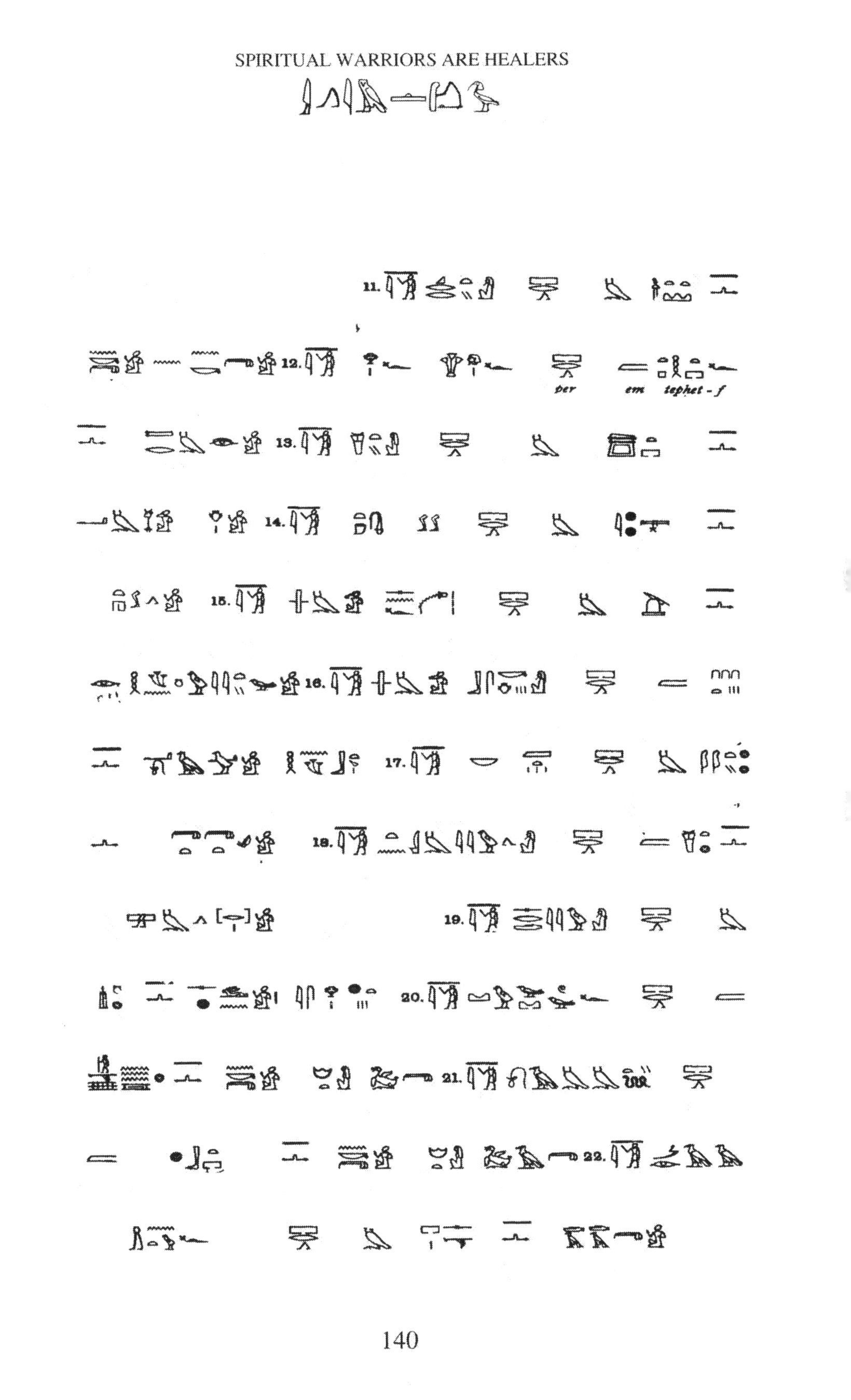

11.

12.

per em tephet-f

13.

14.

15.

16.

17.

18.

19.

20.

21.

22.

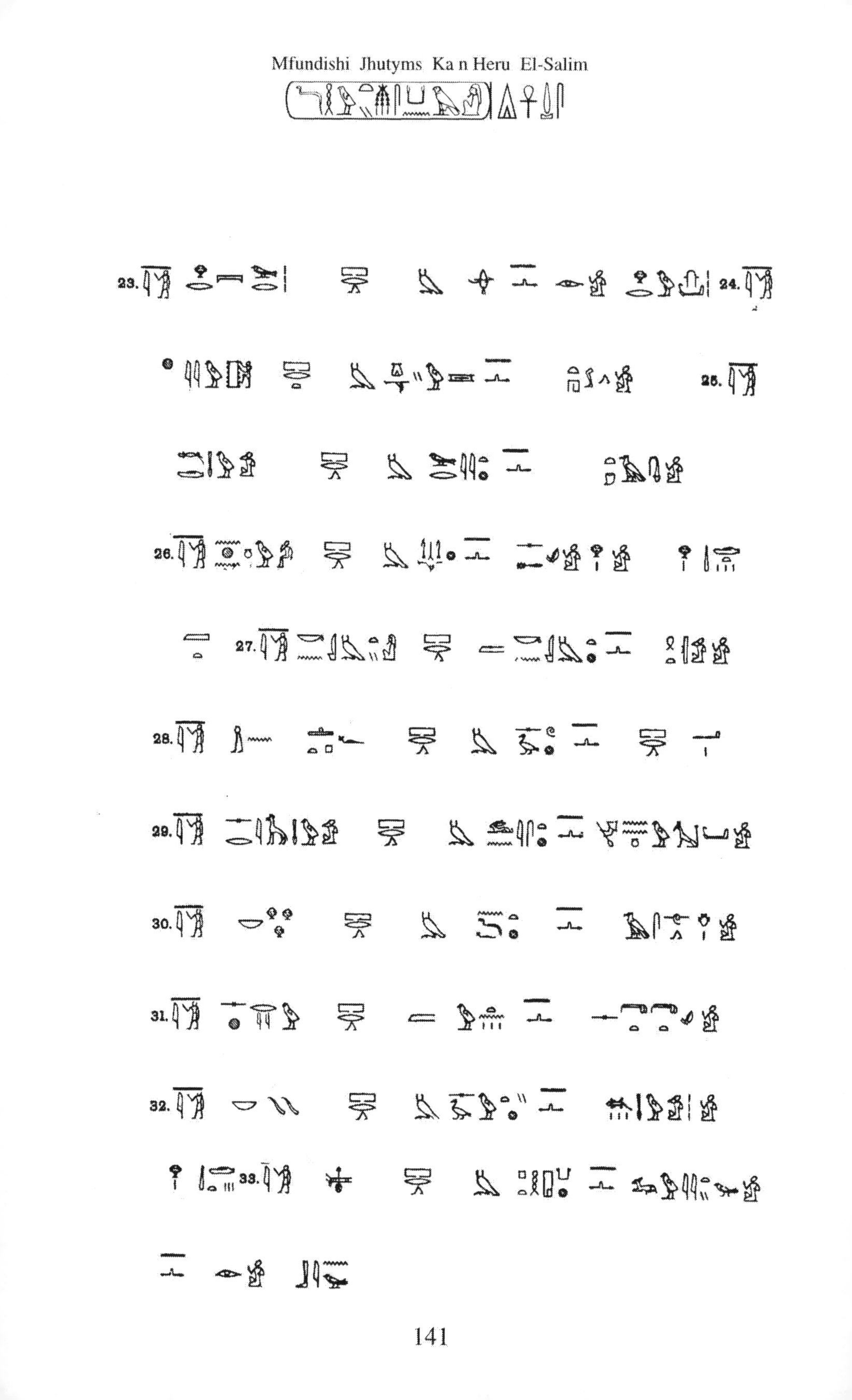

23. 24.

25.

26.

27.

28.

29.

30.

31.

32.

33.

34.

35.

36.

37.

38.

39.

40.

per

41.

42.

Many Spiritual Warriors of today also use the *7 principles of Kwanzaa, see Chapter 9* for more details on Kwanzaa and the Nguzo Saba.

NGUZO SABA

(The Seven Principles)

1. UMOJA (Unity): To strive for and maintain unity in the family, community, nation and race.

2. KUJICHAGULIA (Self - determination): To define ourselves, name ourselves, create for ourselves, and speak for ourselves instead of being defined, named, created and spoken for by others.

3. UJIMA (Collective work and responsibility): To build and maintain our community together and make our sisters' and brothers' problems our problems and to solve them together.

4. UJAMAA (Cooperative Economics): To build and maintain our own stores, shops and other businesses and to profit from them together.

5. NIA (Purpose): To make as our collective vocation, the building and developing our community in order to restore our people to their traditional greatness.

6. KUUMBA (Creativity) To do as much as we can, in the ways we can, in order to leave our community more beautiful and beneficial than we inherited it.

7. IMANI (Faith): To believe in all our hearts in Afrakan people, our parents, our Afrakan centered teachers, our Afrakan centered leaders, and the righteousness and victory of our struggle.

Ma'at is a healing force in our lives mentally, physically and spiritually. The Kemetyu must love each other with the same intensity that we love The NTCHR. Spiritual Warriors once again must become followers of Heru. We must battle injustice and esfet at every level, whenever and wherever we confront it.

"Those who live today will die tomorrow, those who live tomorrow will be born again; Those who live Ma'at will live eternal."

***AFRAKAN* VALUES**	***vs***	***EURASIAN VALUES***
(Kemetyu-centered)		***(Wazungu-centered)***

SPIRITUALITY / RELIGION

Afrakan Values	Eurasian Values
1) Our life love is the worship of nature (NTCHR) or the Creator for self-perfection.	**1) They use religion to control material wealth, land, and the minds of people.**
2) We enjoy thinking about the meaning of life.	**2) They delight in defining the meaning of life.**
3) We believe in law of reciprocity.	**3) They believe in everyone for themselves.**
4) We enjoy giving.	**4) They believe in taking, instead of giving.**
5) We believe in the ancestors and the spirit world as a part of the whole.	**5) They believe this is it, heaven and hell is on earth, so get it all now.**
6) In the sunset years of life, we renounce the world and prepare for the hereafter.	**6) They retire to enjoy the fruits of their labor on earth.**
7) We have an optimistic view of existence.	**7) They have a pessimistic view of existence.**
8) Communalism is a special virtue.	**8) Individualism is a supreme virtue.**
9) Monotheism - the principle of the oneness of the hidden, absolute, formless Creator.	**9) Polytheism, mythology, and personification of divinity (ancestral worship).**
10) No guilt of our existence and no original sin.	**10) Original sin with the woman at fault and at the bottom.**

NATURE

Afrakan Values	Eurasian Values
1) We are by nature passive (ma'at morality).	**1) They are aggressive. (esfet mentality)**
2) We accept nature (NTCHR) as it is.	**2) They aim to change nature according to their blueprint.**
3) We seek to live in peace with nature.	**3) They aim to impose their will on nature.**
4) We believe that nature is science and we learn through self inner-standing.	**4) They believe that science is on the outside and must be dissected to understand.**
5) We move, dance, and think in rhythm with nature and it is natural.	**5) Their movements, dance, and thinking is out of tune with nature and is anti-natural.**

LOVE

1) Our love is silent.	1) Their love is vocal.
2) Our love is personal, private, only a family affair.	2) They delight in showing their love to others.

RELATIONSHIPS

1) Our axiology is the highest value which lies in the interpersonal relationships between people.	1) Their axiology is the highest value which lies in the object or in the acquisition of the object.
2) Personal relationships are the most important thing.	2) Obtaining the object is the most important thing (woman - wealth).

MARRIAGE

1) We marry first, then we love.	1) They love first, then they marry.
2) Marriage is the beginning of a life long love affair, with your partner (Kemantik).	2) Their marriage is the end of romance and the beginning of ownership.
3) Marriage can only be dissolved by families, not individuals.	3) Marriage is a contract of individuals.
4) We have can have more than one mate. (extended family / sharing)	4) They can only have one mate. (individual possession / no sharing)

FAMILY

1) We have matrilineal families.	1) They have patrilineal families.
2) Wife keeps family name.	2) Wife loses family name.
3) Wife can divorce because it is a family affair.	3) Wife cannot divorce because she is property.
4) All children raised within the village.	4) Excess babies killed.

CHILDREN

1) We were born divine.	1) They were born in sin.

EDUCATION

1) Our Priest Scientists and scholars wrote right to left predominantly, but they also wrote left to right for balance and symmetry. They also wrote from top to bottom.	1) Their priests learned writing from Afrakans then later changed their writing from left to right only.
2) The Afrakan-centric genius descends from the absolute information.	2) The Euroasian genius descends from man to God.

3) Our method of processing information is called Ntuology - all sets are interrelated through human and spiritual networks.	**3) They process information through technology - all sets repeatable and reproducible.**
4) Our epistemology is affective. One knows through symbolic imagery and rhythm.	**4) Their epistemology is cognitive. One knows through counting and measuring.**
5) Our logic is Diunital - union of complements.	**5) Their logic is Dichotomous - either or.**

ECONOMICS

1) We are taught from birth to want less and conserve more.	**1) They are urged everyday to want and want and consume more.**
2) We are taught simplicity in living and, only use what one needs is a part of spiritual elevation.	**2) To them simplicity and not having a lot is degradation and poverty.**
3) Land is collective property and belongs to everyone.	**3) Land is private property and belongs to whoever can take it or buy it.**
4) We have an attraction to things foreign (worldly out-look)	**4) They have fear of things foreign, so they only deal with themselves.**
5) Agrikultural and hunting is subsistence.	**5) Pastoral and hunting is subsistence.**
6) We live for the moment, but we prepare for the after-life and not retirement.	**6) They retire to enjoy the fruits of their labor on earth.**

DEATH

1) We have burial / funeral rites.	**1) They have cremation funeral rites.**
2) We believe life and death are part of one existence.	**2) They believe that death is the end.**

TIME

1) We live in the infinite now, yesterday, today, and tomorrow are all in one. Afrakan people exist in time, but are not bound by time.	**1) They live by time - it is important to control man's actions so they are imprisoned by the exactness of time.**
2) We have 12 months to get things done.(hot climate), so we take our time	**2) They have only three (3) to four (4) months to get things done (for growing of food, etc.) (cold climate). They must do it right away (fast).**

DEFENSE / SECURITY

1) We like to contemplate before action.	**1) They just like to act (right or wrong).**

POLITICAL OUTLOOK

1) We believe in freedom of silence while your deeds speak for you.	**1) They believe in freedom of speech and not your deeds.**
2) We enjoy being at rest (sedentary).	**2) They are always on the move (nomadic).**
3) Matrilineal succession of power.	**3) Patrilineal succession of power.**

Below is the characteristics of Cheikh Anta Diop's Two Cradle Theory, which reinforces Mfundishi's concepts that we as Afrakan people must take almost the opposite mission in life as the Wazungu, and even if we both want a similar goal, our approach towards achieving it must be different, but based on our Kultural and Spiritual Worldview.

Southern Cradle	Northern Cradle
1. Abundance of vital resources	1. Bareness of resources
2. Sedentary agricultural economy	2. Nomadic - hunting economy (piracy)
3. Gentle idealistic peaceful nature endowed with a spirit of justice	3. Ferocious warlike nature with spirit survival
4. Matriarchal family	4. Patriarchal family
5. Emancipation of women in domestic life	5. Debasement/enslavement of women
6. Territorial state	6. City, state
7. Xenophilia	7. Xenophobia
8. Cosmopolitanism	8. Parochialism
9. Social collectivism	9. Individualism
10. Material solidarity of right for each individual which makes moral or material misery unknown	10. Moral solitude
11. Ideal of peace, justice, goodness and optimism	11. Disgust for existence, pessimism
12. Literature emphasis novel, tales, fables and comedy	12. Literature favors tragedy and horror

Kemklusion

Ma'at was the foundation of the Afrakan value system that gave the world one of its greatest Spiritual civilizations. Spiritual Warriors have recaptured the warrior spirit of our ancient ancestors and with this spirit, we can rise again up the pyramid of life and become the creators we were suppose to be. Ma'at keeps life in harmony and in perfect balance. We must rescue, learn and protect Ourstory, our languages, our value system, our families and our Afrakan Kulture. The center of the Afrakan world must be Afrakan-centered Konsciousness. An Afrakan-centered world-view must be the way of life for Afrakan people every where, and we must reject white male domination and all value systems that seek to make Afrakans foreigners to their own Kultural world. Because this Euro-centric value system is turning the world upside down, brother against brother, sister against sister, and sister against brother and the society against nature. This system of white male domination destroys life and creates disharmony. Only when human beings adopt the value system and culture of foreigners does it reduce their dignity. Afrakans at home and in the Diaspora, we must abandon white male domination and their Euro-centric value system and that includes their religions, standards of beauty and their economic and political Worldview or we will all perish, or forever remain enslaved.

European Caucasian ice is not colder than Afrakan ice. The western world is sick and morally and spiritually retarded, they the wazungu and the Asiatics have killed more people in the name of religion than any other cause of death! Yet, this same killer with their European, Asiatic religions and worldview want you and me to believe that these same religions have the answers to the sickness and backwardness of the world. This is not good common sense. We, Afrakans are the parents of Spirituality. Afrakans are the inventors of religious theology from which everyone has borrowed or stolen. To believe in a Supreme Being, a Divine Force or Creator is thoroughly Afrakan. So why are Afrakans looking outside Afraka for Spiritual guidance and religion. Afrakan Kulture will lead you to Spirituality; this path will lead you to the Creator "NTCHR". This innerstanding of the Divine Creator is the foundation of Ma'at, truth, justice, righteousness and harmony.

We must return to Ma'at, the foundation of Afrakan values, Spirituality, and our Afrakan Spiritual Worldview, which will lead us to Heru Konsciousness, and liberation, but not just for Afrakan people, but for the planet Earth.

Sifa Kwa Ma'at

Sifa yote kwa Ma'at
Sifa yote kwa wetu Muumba - NTCHR
Sifa yote kwa maisha ya Afraka
Sifa yote kwa Babu wetu wa Afraka
Sifa yote kwa watu wa Afraka
Sifa yote kwa asili kwaida ya Afraka
Sifa yote kwa Mama na Baba wa Afraka
Sifa yote kwa Watoto wa Afraka
Sifa yote kwa Taifa wetu wa Afraka
Sifa yote kwa wetu Muumba - NTCHR
Sifa yote kwa Ma'at
All Praises to truth, justice and righteousness
All Praises to our Afrakan Creator
All Praises to Afrakan life
All Praises to our Afrakan ancestors
All Praises to Afrakan people
All Praises to Afrakan Traditions and kustoms
All Praises to Afrakan Mothers and Fathers
All Praises to Afrakan Children
All Praises to our Afrakan Nation
All Praises to our Afrakan Creator
All Praises to truth, justice and righteousness

Ma'at is Love

Love is an expression of Ma'at
The spiritual harmony between two forces that become one
Follow your spirit to harmony
By listening to your eternal soul
The soul loves because it needs to be loved
Let your love bind your soul and spirit together as one
Your love of life as well as, the love of your life
As for the love of your life, let there be space in your togetherness
Even two great oaks trees with roots as strong and as long as
Ourstory itself, cannot grow in each others shadow
Let your love be like a never ending tide pulsating along the shore
of your eternal soul
Love gives nothing but itself
Love takes nothing but itself
The harmony of love does not possess and it will not be possess
For love is sufficient unto love
Love is Ma'at - truth, justice, righteousness, reciprocity and
harmonious balance
When two forces learn to grow together into one harmonious path
You learn that you cannot direct love
Love, if it finds you worthy, will direct your course
Love has no other desire but to fulfill itself
Give each other your love, but not all your thoughts
Because all your thoughts are not expressions of love
Give through innerstanding, unasked, but willingly
When two forces have found this harmony
You will hear the sounds of eternal silence
This is the silence of all ages, chanting simple truths that govern
the cosmic universe
Ma'at is love...

CHAPTER IIII (4)

Somo la Nne

The Spirit

Spirit is the living mind. The NTCHR, which is All, is mind. And the whole cosmic universe is mental, a Divine Creation of The NTCHR. The word spirit means "real essence" or the living mind. Spirit is the energy of The NTCHR directed by thoughts or Konsciousness, and only the NTCHR can direct the spirits of the Divine Creation, manifesting itself in many forms. Spirit is the essence of all things, and because spirit is the living link to the NTCHR, all things are spirit, alive and connected by Divine Spirit through the Ntchr Ntchru. Creation is and continues to be an act of Divine Will, which is the Konsciousness of NTCHR expressing itself outward and inward within itself.

Spirit lives on many levels. There are spirits we can see and there are those we cannot see. There are spirits we can feel and comprehend, as well as spirits we cannot feel and cannot comprehend. There are Ancestor Spirits, Nature Spirits, Animal Spirits, Guardian Spirits, and Clan Spirits these and others, all exist through the Ntchr Ntchru, because only the NTCHR exist.

All humans are Spiritual beings regardless of race or color. There is nothing that exists hat does not have spirit. All humans have the same access to The NTCHR, although all may not have the same Konsciousness or innerstanding of the Ntchr-Ntchru. Some humans became less Konscious of the spirit world and "The Way", as they lost their Melanin life-force in the extreme weather conditions of the last ice age. As humans traveled northward into the colder zones they mixed with humankind a Melanin deficient life-force, whose nature, consciousness and perception of the world contrasted greatly from the original human beings from Afraka. The original Melanin dominated human beings, however, have evolved on this planet for millions of years in a warm tropical climate, and have a special, more sensitive or mature innerstanding and connection to nature and the cosmos. Our original Afrakan ancestors learned to survive through a Spiritual union with a host of Nature Spirits. And because they were One with these spirits, they were guided by a life-giving and life-sustaining force that today Spiritual Warriors simply call "The Way". Today we call this kind of Spiritual guidance instincts. All creatures on the planet seem to innerstand "The Way," a life giving and life sustaining philosophy, except the western and northern Asiatics, whom we call Europeans or Wazungu, and some northern Asiatic tribes. Their way is in direct conflict with "The Way". If their nature is to kill, destroy and take, like the nature of the tiger of Asia verses the nature of the lion, who only kills when necessary, and never for a sport. We as Afrakan people the Kemetyu, Melanin dominated humans need to innerstand this so we can deal with them, the Wazungu, Melanin deficient humankind intelligently, without losing *our way, which is synonymous with "The Way" and Ma'at.*

The Melanin energy which is the core of the animal family and key to bringing harmony to our souls, carries the keys to innerstanding and connecting us with all that exists in the animal family, plant family and mineral family. The Melanin dominated human beings, therefore, have a special relationship and bond with nature. Our Melanin acts as keys that are locked in our DNA codes that can unlock the secrets of the universe. This information can be spiritually downloaded into our ancestral memory, it paints a clearer picture of our unique mission and our responsibility to the planet and all that exists on it. On the other side, we have Melanin deficient humankind who came from a cold climate. It seems by nature, that they are at war with the forces of nature on this planet, and with the spiritual powers of harmony. Ma'at is an irrelevant concept to the Wazungu and most Asiatics. They have developed a very aggressive nature and seem to have very different feelings about nature. Feelings we call human and humane are alien to them. The Wazungu (Melanin deficient humankind from Eurasia) their understanding of nature was great for survival, but devastating in terms of a harmonious existence with any other life-force. They felt the need to control, hoard and dominate instead of sharing and living in harmony with your environment. The Kemetyu believed in Ma'at, a live and let live sharing relationship with nature and our environment. The Wazungu believed in esfet, kill or be killed relationship, therefore everything and everybody is the enemy, nothing personal just survival.

Who are you? What are you? Where are you from? Based upon the previous questions, can you plot where you are going? Remember, the body-temple only exists as an extension or container for the soul, which is an aspect of the spirit. We are the sum total of divine Melanin energy recorded through our ancestral memory and manifested through time and space, which has absorbed all earthly and cosmic spiritual energies since creation. This Ntchr Ntchru Konsciousness is also known as Heru Konsciousness. Melaninated human beings, the Kemetyu, in their right Afrakan spiritual mind set, can reflect visions of the very act of Creation within the very spirit of our souls using our minds. Spirit creates our reality from inside to the outside. Anything you can feel or see in your inner subjective mind, where Heru Konsciousness exist, can be transferred to your outer objective mind, which is largely shaped by your personal experiences. If there exists some kind of harmonious balance, between your soul, Konsciousness and the Divine Spirit - inner subjective mind and your outer objective mind, you can achieve anything, there are no limits on your possibilities.

Spiritual knowledge is "knowing" Divine Order, which is Ma'at. Spiritual acts deliver Divine Will through presenting your message or gifts to life thereby fulfilling your unique purpose in life as designed by The NTCHR. The Divine Spirit, through many spiritual energies, helps us in this learning process. Ancient Afrakan beliefs says that returning souls are coming to complete a mission. Our spiritual cosmology speaks of each person's incarnation objectives and purpose. We are not just here on earth to live lascivious, pleasurable, materialistic, Wazungu consuming, meaningless lives, we have all returned with goals to be accomplished and we are also equipped with gifts and talents called tools to aid us on this mission.

The higher your spiritual Konsciousness, the greater your energies. If your concentration is great through your innerstanding of the Divine Spirit, then your Sekhem or Moyo, your personal spiritual power will expand, this energy will also be great, along with the innerstanding of the Divine Order in your life. Now all those tools or gifts and talents allow you to become master of yourself, fully expressing your unique gifts, fulfilling your divine purpose.

The Spiritual Warrior must innerstand that one of our primary missions in life should be to manifest our purpose by keeping our spirit in alignment with The NTCHR. When we are in alignment with the Ntchr Ntchru or nature, we can recognize our purpose in life and this allows us to accept the lessons the various spirits are trying to teach us.

The most basic Divine Law of the Afrakan Spirit World is simply " To Be" and To Be was to follow "The Way" which is Ma'at. A "Spiritual Warrior " is the human embodiment of Ma'at when they are fulfilling their purpose. This is a state when one recognizes their own divinity and connection with nature and the universe. When the Spiritual Warrior unites with their greater spiritual self, esfet is transformed into Ma'at, this transformation is called healing and this is the state of " **Being**".

Spiritual Warriors of ancient Kemet and Kash, the most powerful Warriors in the world, mentally, physically and spiritually. These Afrakans were the prototype of the" Priest Warrior " of ancient Asia.

SPIRITS

Spiritual energies in general do not interfere or ask to come forward into your world. They will always wait to be invited into your Konscious reality, whether that reality is a deeper innerstanding of the universe or a shallow understanding. Sometimes unconsciously, or through ignorance you venture into their world, the spirit world unprepared and therefore not in a position to innerstand your new reality. It is possible that you could perish (transform from one state of energy to another). You may even be trapped in a dual reality unable to deal with either, (classified as crazy, or unstable) you may have a revolutionary experience that could change your life one way or the other, or you could possibly be so far out of touch with yourself that you are oblivious to the whole experience.

The assistance of the spiritual energies may come in many forms: as dreams, as inspirations, or as opportunities. The great Kemetyu Ancestors teach us through folklore that there is no such thing as luck or coincidence. What we perceive as good luck or bad luck is our ability to take advantage of certain opportunities that come our way, based upon alertness or our ability to listen to our ancestors. For example, say two brothers are walking to work. One brother steps on a $100 dollar bill unconsciously because he is caught up in the rituals and chaos of the world. The second brother who is open to and in tune with the Ntchru, feels the money first, then quickly focuses on it with his eyes, and picks up the $100 dollar bill. The first brother who stepped all over it says, "Man! You sure are lucky."

Reality is only what you perceive it to be, or not to be, based upon your understanding or your innerstanding. Spiritual Warriors who are aligned with the spirit will always be in pursuit of their purpose through their mission. The spirits will always be with them, along with the power and the glory of the NTCHR.

There are many spiritual levels and spirits on the planet we call Earth. All physical life forms that we collectively perceive as reality belong to either the mineral, plant, or Animal Spirit world. Afrakan

Kulture also teaches us that the elements are also very powerful spirits: fire, water, earth, and air, plus their qualifiers like hot, cold, wet and dry. We can align ourselves to any and all of these spirits, because they all belong to and are part of The NTCHR, which also means all of these energies are connected to all of us.

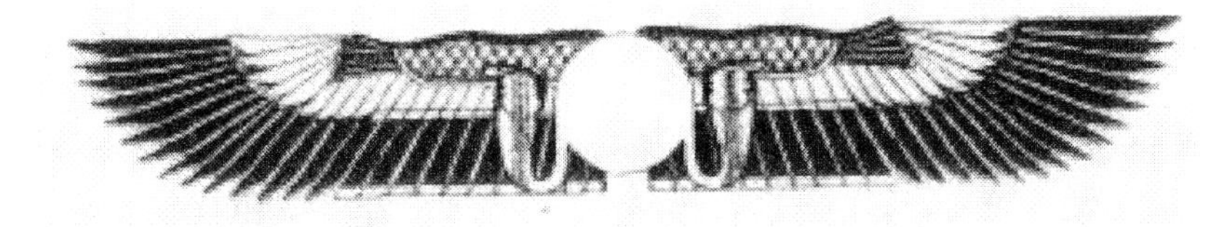

Soul Spirits

Within each human being, spirit is the divine essence or energy that is immortal. It cannot die or be destroyed. This divine essence can only be innerstood through Konsciousness. In the ancient Kemetik legacy, this Higher Konsciousness was Heru Konsciousness or using the eye of the Ntchr Ra. This Higher Konsciousness linked you to all information through the power of the One Divine NTCHR.

Heru Konsciousness was the quest of all the Nswtu of ancient Kemet, thus they called themselves the Followers of Heru (Shemsu Heru). The Nswtu were the great leaders of ancient Kemet. The western definitions of King and Pharaoh do not apply to the Nswtu, for they were the mental, spiritual and physical leaders of the people who were the upholders of Ma'at. They were also the highest of the High Priest. Heru was the power behind each ancient Nswtu. Ma'at was their guide and Jhuty their voice. From the so called Fifth Dynasty on, all of the ancient Kemetik Nswtu also called themselves Sons of Ra, and their priests were called divine servants.

The Nswtu and their Priests and Priestesses were the Spiritual Warriors and healers of ancient Kemet. Their lives were dedicated to the maintenance and development of Ma'at. These Spiritual Warrior Priest Scientists developed a system for innerstanding and developing this Divine Spirit in humans also called the soul. They divided the spirit of the soul into nine parts: Ka, Ba, Khat, Ab, Khaba, Akhu, Sahu, Sekhem and Ren.

I. Ka:

"Whatever is, in the first place, is spirit." (Jedi Shemsu Jehewty) The Divine Spirit endows all things, and survives past the physical life of the individual. The human aspect of this Divine Spirit is also called the abstract personality or ego. This ego is your subkonscious desires and it develops the concept of self. Ka is also called the energy body or the double. It is the Ka that reincarnates, by seeking another physical vehicle in order to continue the work of self perfection. The Ka is portrayed as a pair of arms outstretched towards heaven.

II. Ba:

Ba is "The Soul" which dwells in the Ka with the power of metamorphosis. The soul is your "Higher Self" and it is an invisible source of energy, like electricity behind all visible functions. The soul, which is an aspect of the self, can be dialogued with and can be a spiritual guide to the Spiritual Warrior.

The Ba or soul through Konsciousness projects and maintains the union of the physical body. When the soul has no more use for the physical body, it discards it and returns to the Divine Ka or Universal Spirit. The

Divine Spirit will redirect its energy based upon its state of enlightenment or balance with Ma'at. If the soul is enlightened, it may join all enlightened souls in Pt (heaven). If the soul is not enlightened, it will return to the elements and reincarnate into another life form.

The Ba is immortal. The soul is also the transformation of the breath of life. Through this breath, the spirit of the ancient ancestors can be transmitted to its descendants. The soul can never be destroyed, only transformed, it will always exists, for energy cannot be destroyed. The Ba is represented as a human headed bird, usually a falcon.

The Ba of a human is immortal.

Immortality to the Kemetyu was achieved when a person innerstood their divine mission and purpose, had developed their special gifts and shares them unconditionally with those who are prepared to receive their blessings. At this point, a person becomes a Spiritual Warrior and is able to unite the Ka and Ba in alignment with Heru Konsciousness. This formula is connected to the ultimate goal of all Spiritual Warriors and Spiritual Healers.

III. Khat:

The Khat is the physical body of the human being, and the concrete personality. This body is not immortal, it is a temporary container for your spiritual energy. When a human recognizes their divinity, the body is sometimes called 'the Body - Temple'.

IIII. Ab:

Ab represents the heart. It is the symbol of the mind, representing Konscious and unconscious feelings, intent and desires of the body. Spiritual Warriors must strive to purify their Ab. Each of us who are striving to become One with the NTCHR must learn to listen to our hearts through the voice of the inner soul. Only then can the essence of universal peace be innerstood. In the Kemetyu *Book of Coming Forth by Light*, Anui version, we see the Ab undergoes examination by Jhuty, the scribe of wisdom and innerstanding. One's own heart will fashion one's own fate according to one's will and desires, which is based on one's innerstanding about one's true self. ***"The Konscience (Ab) of a person is their own Ntchr"***

The Spiritual Warriors must first innerstand that the entire Universe and Innerverse are only mental manifestation of The NTCHR. The greater your level of Konsciousness the more evolved your innerstanding of your spirit. The greater your level of wisdom, the more expansive your innerstanding of reality. One's level of Konsciousness can be raised by a Konscious effort to grow in wisdom through the practice of Ma'at Akhw Ba Ankh and Kupigana Ngumi. This will help align your virtues, self discipline and the study of nature through your Kultural and Spiritual Center.

> ***"Strive to see with the inner eye, the heart. It sees the reality not subject to emotional or personal error; it sees the essence. Intuition then is the most important quality to develop."***
>
> **Ancient Kemetyu proverb**

It is one's own heart which will fashion one's own fate (coming into being) according one's will and desires, which are based on one's innerstanding (wisdom) about one's true Self.

IIIII. Khaba or Khabait :

Khaba is also called the shadow and it produces emotion and motion. The Khaba represents sensory perception and the phenomena of color, total harmony and the circulation of blood. It also receives nourishment from the Ba.

IIIIII. Akhu:

Akhu is the spiritual soul, the seat of intelligence and mental perception. The Akhu is characterized by attributes like judgement, analysis, and mental reflection, all of which can be trained and disciplined to be dedicated to serve higher expressions of being. It is an Ethereal Force and is immortal.

IIIIIII. Sahu:

Sahu is the spiritual body that houses the Ba and the Akhu. The Sahu is the goal of all aspirations. It is the reason for human existence to become NTCHR-like while you are still in your human body-temple.

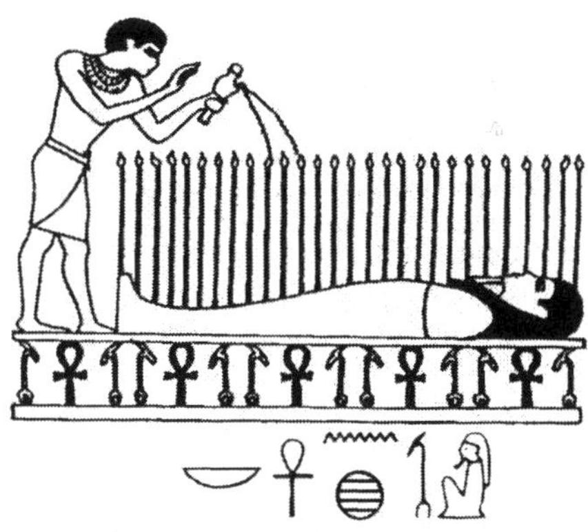

Light rays, in the form of beams tipped by tiny flames, emitted from the body-temple of Asr, the Neb Ankh.

When the Spiritual Warrior reaches enlightenment, the spiritual and mental body become one, expanding and evolving your realities, and your perception on nature and the cosmos.

IIIIIIII. Sekhem:

Sekhem is the spiritual power that is the personification of the Ntchr Ntchru that exists in every life force in which we as human

beings are connected. This power is not usually manifested until a being reaches puberty or adolescence and becomes the true Sekhem at maturity. This is based upon their spiritual level of Heru Konsciousness. This spiritual process is also called the development of the Moyo.

IIIIIIIII. Ren:

Ren is the name, or the essential attribute to the personification of a being. It is a power that can feed itself, and it can generate its own kind. The Ren can also bring about the union of the brain and the mind, so that the will and intent become one. This conducts the mental maturity of the individual. The symbol of the water recalls the image of energy, and the symbol of the mouth represents utterance, thus Ren relates to Konsciousness manifesting through names, words and sound transforming energy.

The Soul can align itself with the Divine Spirit, becoming One. This is part of our sacred purpose in our life experiences. This sacred task can be accomplished through the study of Kupigana Ngumi - Afrakan martial arts, and or Ma'at Akhw Ba Ankh - Afrakan spiritual meditation, as a way of developing and practicing spiritual virtues and Kemtrol and control of the mind. As expressed before, these systems are Kulturally rooted and in tune with Ma'at. Most human beings only have a general understanding of the Khaba and the Ren, and mainly just deal with the ego personality, leaving them very incomplete. We must learn how to join with our higher self and this can only happen when you have an innerstanding of all nine aspects of the Soul.

" Follow your heart throughout your life. Do more than is required of you. Spend no more time on daily cares than required by your household, when wealth ultimately arrives, then too follow your heart for wealth does no good if you are downhearted." **Kemetyu Proverb**

Through innerstanding the nine levels of the Spirit we can tune into the ultimate truth, which goes far beyond our mind, senses and body. Alignment with the Divine Spirit will allow you to listen to your soul and heart, which is listening to intuition. The NTCHR is the source of your intuition. Only through following your intuition can you find your purpose and your life mission in this physical life form.

Heru Konsciousness is knowing yourself through Divine Spirit. Each Spiritual Warrior wants to develop their Heru Konsciousness so that they can overcome worldly desires and destructive ignorance. The Spiritual Warrior must master their spiritual self and their physical self. Spiritual Warriors who are healers have a high level of mastery of self. To knowthyself is to know the Ntchru, which is to know the universe. True healing can only happen when the action is in alignment with Ma'at.

The Ancestor Spirits

Ancestor Spirits may be those persons in the family, community, race or nation who have since passed on and their physical bodies have transformed into another state of energy. This represents a spirit we can no longer see in our regular Konscious lives. These Ancestor Spirits are energies that can be communicated with and can guide us to the truth by showing us Ma'at in its truest form.

Worship of the sacred Kemetyu Ancestors and Ancestor Spirits are an integral part of traditional Kemetyu Spiritual Kulture. It represents Ma'at by living the law of reciprocity, by paying respect to those energies who were responsible for greatness, both theirs and ours. It is also a method of honoring and giving praise to the great ones who have laid the foundation of life in which we follow. Some of the ways to honor the sacred ancestors are by calling their names, praying for or to them (mentally or out loud) at a shrine or sacred location. When you give them energy they become more aligned with The NTCHR and in return they help you in your alignment with the Spirit. We also pay homage and respect to our Ancestor Spirits through the maintenance and continuation of their work, ideas, land, and institutions. This is one of the highest forms of honor and worship.

According to ancient Afrakan Spiritual philosophy, it is spirit helping spirit that fulfills the work of The NTCHR. As humans of Kemetyu descendents, we should recognize our Ancestral Spirits as vital parts of our spiritual growth and evolution as a people. As Spiritual Warriors, it becomes vital that we keep that high spiritual energy alive through

recognition, honor and veneration. Kemetyu tradition also states that we start all our functions, small or large, by giving praise and honor not only to the NTCHR, but also to our Sacred Ancestors, by simply thanking them for protection, innerstanding and spiritual guidance.

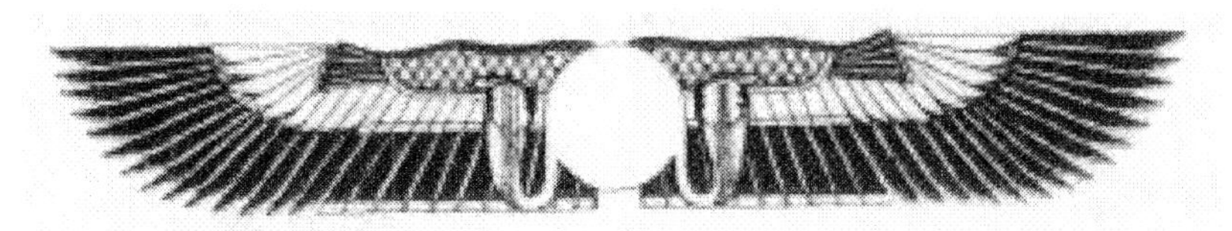

Nature Spirits

Traditional Afrakan Kulture teaches that we must recognize spirit on all levels. Spirits of air, water, fire and earth are called Nature Spirits. Nature Spirits are also all the energies in the mineral and plant families. They provide us with essential elements that support our physical life.

In the Kemetyu Spiritual Kultural system of the Hapy Valley, Nature Spirits were called Ntchru. The Ntchr Shu represented air or boundless space, the breath of The NTCHR. The Ntchrt Tefnut, represented moisture, fluidity, and is the complement of Shu. Other Ntchru of nature were: Geb, which represented mass or the earth and its complement, Nut, which represented the atmosphere or the visible sky. At a higher level, Nut represented the force field of energy which emanates from every mass, like the human aura that surrounds each human being.

These Ntchru are natural laws of Creation. The NTCHR directs these laws so that they may maintain Ma'at in the universe. These Nature Spirits or Ntchru provide guidance so that we can align ourselves with spirit. Through their continuous examples and natural laws it provides us with opportunities to bring ourselves into alignment with Ma'at. When we are in alignment with the Divine Spirits, we can recognize and accept the lessons in life which will lead us to a fuller, richer, and more wholistic existence by fulfilling our divine purpose.

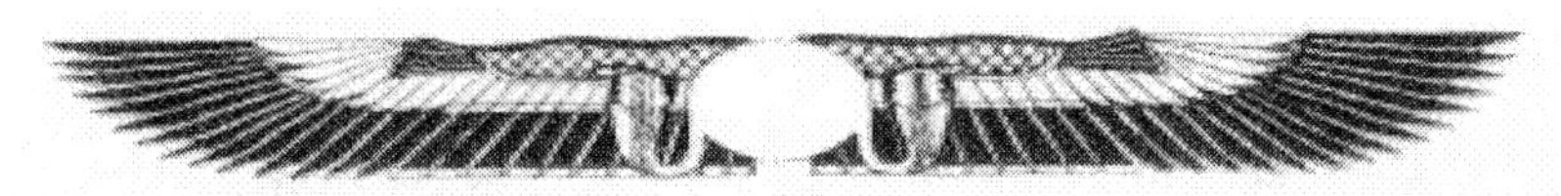

Animal Spirits

Animal Spirits represent the basic instincts of all living, moving, crawling, walking, swimming, and flying creatures surviving and thriving on the Earth's provisions. The natural impulse or innate propensity that incites all members of the animal domain to actions which are essential to their existence, preservation, and development are called instincts. These natural instincts are direct messages from The NTCHR. They are simple or sometimes very complex, unlearned, adaptive responses to some situations or experiences for life and harmony.

Melaninated human beings in their right Afrakan mind, with Heru Konsciousness, and the correct Kultural center, have instincts that maintain Ma'at with nature and the cosmos. The Spiritual Warrior's greatest attribute is his or her ability to follow their spiritual guides, which are called instincts or intuition.

Animal Spirits in many Kultures may be revered as the protectors of humanity in general. Many of the animals chosen seem not to allow any distractions to stop them from accomplishing their goals. They all seem to be extremely focused, confident and efficient. Many of these characteristics humans lack, especially in a very undisciplined society like America or the Western world. In many Afrakan myths, like in ancient Kemet, figures such as Simba the Lion and Heru the Falcon use their ferocity and unparalleled strength to overcome their enemies. In some Native American myths, figures such as the Raven and Coyote use cleverness rather than ferocity to protect humans from their enemies.

Animals are frequently seen as sacred guardians of humans, especially in Shamanistic and Kemet Kultures. Shaman Priests, like Kemet Priest Scientists, often draw healing and visionary powers from an Animal Spirit who acts as his or her personal protector and guide in the spirit world.......

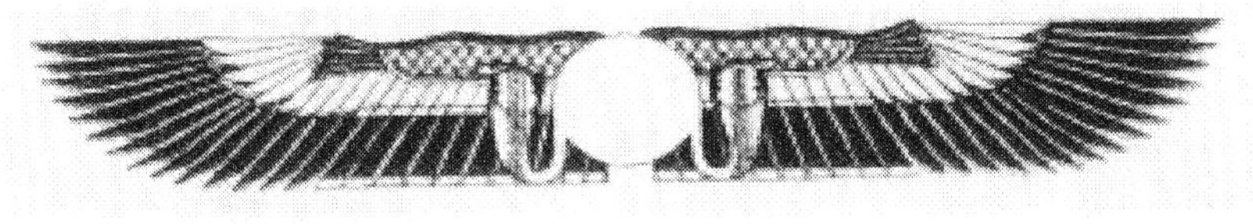

Guardian Spirits:

Guardian Spirits are specific energies that walk through life with you. They can be seen as a protective spirit that assist you on your life journey, and we all have at least one. We may not be Konscious of its presence because we are not in tune with ourselves. The Guardian Spirit can take the form of any spirit; Ancestral Spirit, Animal Spirit, Nature Spirit, or it can be some other benevolent force whose spiritual evolution is dedicated to assisting living beings on Earth.

Most Guardian Spirits are Ancestral Spirits because they have a vested interest in the survival of their descendants. They do not have to be members of the immediate family but usually are members of the same ethnic group, because the perpetuation of the Kulture is equally important. The Guardian Spirits, like the other spirits we have mentioned exist outside of your physical body. At the same time they are connected to you like your aura or personal force field. All living things have a protective force connected to it, and everything is part of the One, The NTCHR. The Guardian Spirit, however, is within your spiritual reach at all times. It will not interfere with the choices or decisions of your Konscious or unconscious mind. In times of need or danger, this spirit will give guidance and insight in the form of thought or Dynamic Action.

How do we communicate with our Guardian Spirits in our everyday lives? The best and most effective ways are through prayer and meditation. We must simply be open and willing to let the Guardian Spirits in, so that we can meditate on the Oneness of The NTCHR and the mission of our existence. The Guardian Spirits can provide Divine Power to our life and a sense of universal intelligence that cannot be learned in books, or found in any university.

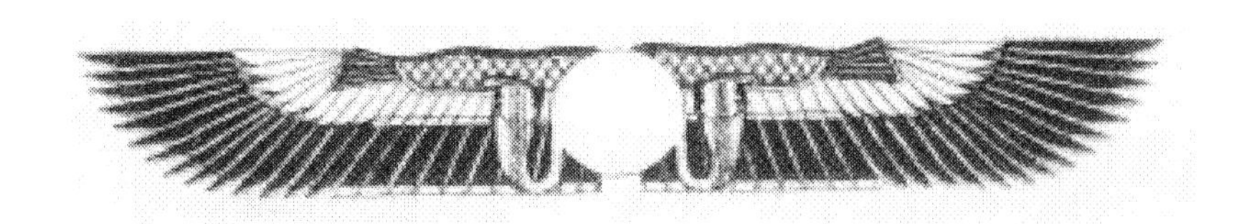

Clan Guardians

Afrakans, Asians and Native Americans have many anthropomorphic animal figures, revered as Clan founders, helpers and spirit guardians. These figures, which include; falcons, cranes, eagles, lions, panthers, snakes, crocodiles, baboons, etc. are depicted on totem poles, walls of sacred temples, artifacts and heraldic clan emblems. These Spirit Guardians watch over the person, the Village or a particular place over which the carved figure of the Clan Ancestor stands guard. An encounter with the ancestor is central to many rituals in traditional Afraka.

Afrakan Spiritual Healers and Shaman Priests sometimes use animal energies to protect or help heal human energies. Sometimes they transform themselves into various special animals to travel to the spirit realm or world in order to recover the lost or kidnapped soul of a sick person. Sometimes the symbols of birds may also represent the flight of the human soul between the world of the living and the spirit world or the world of transformation.

Initiation into the Kemetyu Society means that the initiate would have to innerstand these animal energies. If they were being initiated into the Kemetyu healing science as a priest or priestess the initiate enters a trance, during which the animal ancestor appears and gives guidance and clarity to the mission, so that the various animal energies could be accessed for healing. Animal energies are depicked within the Ntchru that are symbolic of the spirits in the inner and outer world "So is above, so is below"..

The sacred triad at Wast: Asr, Ast & Heru. Even here animal symbolism is every where. They are powerful and inspiring symbols to the initiate and just art to the uninformed.

Kemklusion

The Spirit is the light, the energy emanating from The NTCHR through the Ntchru. Thus, there is nothing that is without spirit. A Guardian Spirit, who assists us on our life path so we can fulfill our purpose by delivering our gifts to the world, favors us as human beings. In the Afrakan Kemet Spiritual System, the Ntchr Jhuty and his spiritual mates Ma'at and Seshat are your Spiritual Guides that allow you to discover the keys to the Ntchr Ntchru inside yourself. The Afrakan Spiritual System teaches us that we have Ntchru existence, instinct, and self-reflective Konsciousness. This complex universal knowledge is Divine Spiritual energy on all levels and with it comes great responsibilities. This dynamic energy can be extracted from a rock (like a crystal) used to heal or to feel by seeing. This Divine Spiritual energy can be extracted from a plant or an animal as medicine or fuel for energy to aid in healing or the visualization process in special rituals. The greater the innerstanding of ones spiritual connection the greater the universal human innerstanding of nature. The more you know about nature, the more you will know about yourself. The more one is in tune with self, the easier it is to be receptive to the spiritual energy emanating from the rock, the plant, and the animal or some other benevolent spiritual force sent here to guide you.

Afrakan Spirituality is the one missing tool and healing medicine in our formula for Afrakan liberation. It is the correct Spiritual path and Kultural path for Afrakan people. An Afrakan destiny without Afrakan Spirituality will lead you to a confused worldview, which will lead you to insanity and back to slavery. Slavery is when you are under the physical, mental and spiritual influence of other people. Afrakans today worldwide are under the spiritual influence of other people through their religions, which are anti-Afrakan Kulture and anti-Afrakan Spirituality, and we are hypnotized into thinking we are free. This of course is insane and retarded thinking and behavior, and it will not get you a nation but it will surely put you back on the plantation. If Afrakans are to be liberated, whole, healed and have sovereignty, we must honor the Creator, our Afrakan Ancestors, our Kulture and our Afrakan Spirit through Afrakan Spirituality.

All Afrakan languages have a word for the Creator, spirit and spirits, but none have a word for religion. This is because Spirituality was central to Afrakan kulture and an Afrakan worldview. Below are two other systems from West Afraka That are very simular to the Kemet Spiritual System:

Yoruba Spiritual System

1. *Olorum - Creator.*
2. *Orisha - Spirits.*
3. *Ori - Head, destiny, or personal Orisha.*
4. *Ori inu - Inner Self.*
5. *Oriki - One's praise name.*
6. *Ori alasinwaye eda - Destiny or the meaning of life.*
7. *Okan - Seat of soul or the heart.*
8. *Orun - Ancestral world.*
9. *Emi - Mind soul that animates the Ara.*
10. *Ire - Good fortune or goodness.*
11. *Ara - Physical body.*
12. *Ato - Long life in good health.*

Akan Spiritual System

1. *Onyankopon or Nyame - Creator.*
2. *Obosom - Spirits.*
3. *Okra - Soul or life force in people given from Nyame.*
4. *Mogya - Blood from mother or one's ancestral power.*
5. *Dzen - One's name.*
6. *Nkrabea - Destiny or the meaning of life.*
7. *Sunsum - Spirit personality from the father.*
8. *Samanadze - Ancestral world.*
9. *Osanam - Spirit personality after death.*
10. *Krado - Shoulders or seat of the soul.*
11. *Honam / ho - Physical body.*
12. *Obra bo - Truth and Ethical Living.*

The Dogon Nation of Mali, West Afraka, who traces their place of origin to the Hapy Valley, Ancient Kemet, has a spiritual term called, the Nommo - The power of the Word. The Dogon Spiritual Priest Scientists say that the Nommo is a Spiritual life force, a unit of spiritual and physical fluidity. The Nommo also is giving life to everything, penetrating everything, and causing everything to "Be."

The Nommo awakens all "sleeping" forces and strengthens weak ones according to the will of the Divine speaker. If the human spirit is in alignment with The NTCHR, words uttered in a particular rhythm and tone can bring a rock to "ACTION," cause rain to fall, or heal a sick person many miles away. Many Afrakan Kultures also believe that when properly played, the drums create sound or energy that manifests a similar energy or a spiritual form of the Nommo. The drum can send messages to the Universal Intelligence and receive answers. All things in the universe have a constant effect on each other, inter-connectedness with all of creation. As Spiritual Warriors, we believe everything can be interpreted as having spiritual significance and essence and we are assistant directors in maintaining its harmony through Ma'at.

We are an Afrakan people, and at the center of our world, there must be Afrakan Spirituality. This Afrakan Spirituality connects us to The Creator, our ancestors, our Kulture, our relationship to nature and all other life forms; it is our lifeline to immortality and excellence. If we are to liberate ourselves, heal ourselves, and become whole again it will be because of our innerstanding of spirit, and our use of Afrakan Spirituality in the building and maintaining of our souls, families, businesses, institutions, communities, towns and nation.

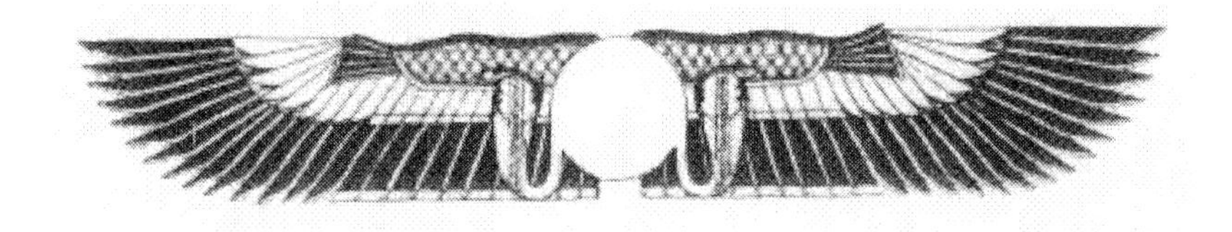

The Nature Of Self

The nature of self is to innerstand the nature of the Ntchru
The eye with which we see the Ntchru
Is the same eye with which the Ntchru sees us
We must learn to see with our hearts
For it is only with the heart that one can see righteously
What is essential is invisible to the eye
Seeing is feeling with the spirit
And when one feels with one's heart
It will show you that the nature of The NTCHR is a circle of which the center is everywhere and the circumference is a reflection of the center.
The self says, I am
The heart says, we are
The Spirit says, we are ONE, which is everything...

I Am Eternal Spirit

I have always existed
I am spirit
Heru Konsciousness
I am you
And we have the power
We have always had the power
We are NTCHR
And The NTCHR is all
We were born to be reborn
Our rebirth is an unending act
Life is eternal and an interwoven continuous miracle
On a journey towards the light
Which is the Spirit
Heru Konsciousness
The power that brings Ma'at
Our purpose is to bring forth healing, balance, truth, justice, righteousness and eternal harmony.
I have always existed
I am you, Afrakan
The sum total of everything that has ever happened
I am everything that has been and the potential to Be
Your Heru Konsciousness
I am eternal spirit...

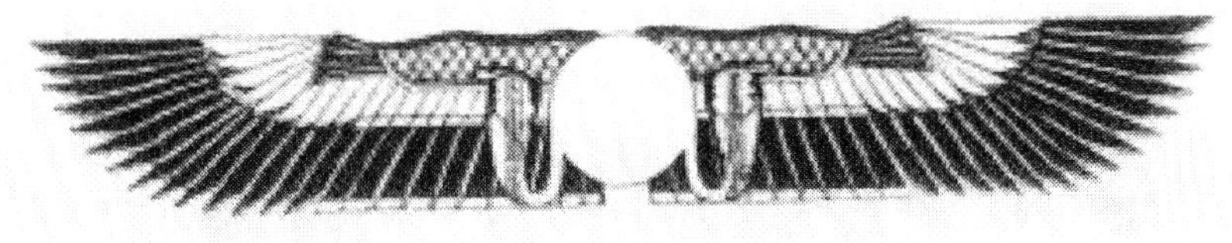

CHAPTER IIIII (5)
Somo la Tano

SPIRITUALITY

If the Divine Spirit directs the Ntchr Ntchru, then to live a life by spirit is to live a life of Spirituality. If we are spirit, and the spirit is the living Konsciousness of the human mind, which directs the body - temple, then Spirituality requires a harmonious alignment between spirit, body and mind. This Spirituality is a Oneness within and without, making you aware of the wholeness of life, connecting you to every living force in nature and the universe. The greater your level of innerstanding of your Spirituality the greater your level of peace, harmony and a sense of becoming complete.

The journey of Spirituality is the daily path of growing, learning, and expanding your Konsciousness. It is using the Divine Spirit to bring clarity to your innerstanding of The NTCHR, which is the source of your power and all power. There is nothing mystical about Spirituality as most people think. In fact, it is the simplest and least complicated approach to life's happiness, joy, and fulfillment.

Many Spiritual Warriors are not connected to a Church, Mosque, Synagogue or Temple. Spirituality to them is not a religion nor does it take the place of religion. Spirituality is your personal connection with the Creator, and the Ntchr Ntchru (nature and the forces of nature). That Spiritual connection is your guiding force of

Warriorship. The greatest and highest levels of Afrakan Spirituality and Warriorship brings you peace, harmony, and Ma'at. The fulfillment of your mission through living your divine purpose in life is happiness and joy through the giving of your gifts to your people and the universe.

In order to live a life of Spirituality, one must develop and use your First Eye, the "Ujah," the eye of The NTCHR. When using the eye of The NTCHR, your perception is expanded beyond your personal experience. Your Konsciousness has no limits, not even earthly limits, because you can see the truth and beauty in all life forces. Spirituality is a never-ending journey inward and outward connecting you to the pulse of the universe as it is expressed through your being. Remember we are Spiritual beings having a human experience.

One of the greatest battles of the Spiritual Warrior is to conquer his or her own personal fears, which feeds esfet (hate, anger, loneliness, wrong doings and imbalance). When these things are taken out of your life the void is filled with the Konscious Spirit of the Ntchr Ntchru, which is the essence of love, innerstanding and purpose. Therefore, Spirituality is a method of growing and learning by using the power of the Divine Spirit, the Ntchr Ntchru, to innerstand your Oneness and your purpose in life as designed by The NTCHR.

A life of Spirituality teaches us that there are no limits in life. You can accomplish your dreams, visions, and goals through love, innerstanding, gratitude, and being One with the Divine Spirit, and all of its various aspects and Spiritual manifestations that exist on various levels. A few of these levels are Ancestral Spirits, Nature Spirits, Animal Spirits and Guardian Spirits. They are all here to help you become better teachers and students at the same time. Spirituality is a life expression that is lived through following your ancestors Kulture and your divine mission to reach your purpose. ***"We are either learning a lesson, teaching the lesson or the object by which the lesson will be taught."***

Each Spiritual Warrior must learn to love unconditionally and trust intuitively by using forgiveness, honesty and patience. These

Spiritual tools will help you learn from every experience in life. As a Spiritual Warrior your greatest tools will be knowledge of self, your people, and your enenmy along with prayer, meditation, and breathing the spiritual life force of Shu through Geb and Nut. Ma'at Akhw Ba Ankh can give you an excellent foundation in innerstanding the breath, and utilizing it to expand your Sekhem or Moyo, our Spiritual life force. The Moyo is also the internal vital life energy at the heart of Heru Konsciousness. These spiritual tools are perfect ways of keeping your Konsciousness focused. This focus will bring clarity and only with clarity, power and **Divine Will**, can you develop and perfect your gifts and give it to the world with grace, so that your purpose can be fulfilled.

As Afrakan people liberate themselves from the deadly drug of white male domination, Spirituality and Afrakan-centeredness will have to be the foundation and food from which we are to draw our strength. The Spiritually of the Eurocentric soul is trapped in an infant stage of moral stagnation. They are spiritually unevolved like children with scientific technical knowledge with the ability to destroy the planet or its life giving, life sustaining, ecosystem. The Europeans or Wazungu have grasped the mystery of the atom, but they are clueless in innerstanding the essence of the human being, the spirit or our soul and the dynamics of our connection and innerstanding of nature. Western humankind under the system of white male domination is stumbling blindly through spiritual darkness while toying with the pre-carious secrets of life and death like a two year old. The western world has achieved "deathly" brilliance without spiritual wisdom, and power without the innerstanding of peace or universal Konsciousness. The world in the 63rd century S.T., new Afrakan time, is a world of nuclear giants and ethical infants. Western man knows more about killing than they know about living. As Afrakans and descendents of the Kemetyu of Kemet, we must reject all aspects of Eurocentrism and white male domination. We cannot and will not cure ourselves of this deadly drug by having more of it: better plantation jobs, more European degrees, more money, bigger house, newer cars, longer vacations, and just one more charge card! In the final analysis, Afrakan Spirituality must be used as a tool to heal the Afrakan individual, family, community, and our Afrakan Nations.

In one of my favorite Afrakan folktales, called "*The Frog and the Scorpion,"* the main lesson taught, is that we must innerstand our nature and the nature of our friends and enemies or we are destined for self-destruction. Like the scorpion, the Wazungu has not changed his nature since we discovered them in the caves of western Asia. Their clothes have changed, but their diminutive use of spirit, and their destructive nature has not. The main difference between us then and us, the Kemetyu now, is that we have lost " The Way". We have lost our personal power or surrendered our personal and collective will to our oppressors, white male domination. Afrakan people in Afraka and throughout the Diaspora in the 63rd century S.T., have lost the power to control the will of our Spirit - Heka. We no longer utilize the power of the Divine Spirit to protect our families, our people or our nations, so we have failed to hold esfet in check, because we have lost "The Way" as a people. The Ntchr Heru gives us magnificent examples of what we are to do. Our Afrakan ancestors etched out our blueprints for liberation on the walls of Kemet, and the Wazungu through esfet have spread them all over the world, but we are still blind. We can't even see that the mighty Warriors from Kemet were and are **US**. Now we all are floundering in the wake of a self-destructive technology which, instead of honoring nature or NTCHR and evolving in harmony with the Spiritual principles that formed us, seems intent only on destruction. Human beings everywhere are desperately searching for some deeper meaning to life in the spiritual vacuum that white male domination has created wherever they control or have major influences.

Afrakans everywhere have been tricked out of our Spirituality. Today Afrakans are very religious, but Spiritualy very sick. However, the spiritually retarded, immature European Caucasians have replaced our Afrakan Spirituality with their desires. And as long as we are enslaved, and trapped in their Worldview, holding on to their desires and values we can never get free. Freedom from oppression is not a place you escape to... Freedom is a state of Konsciousness you first create in your mind, then with the right tools, plan and Spiritual support, you can manifest it into a physical reality. Afrakan Spirituality connected to a Pan-Afrakan, Afrakan-centered Worldview is the medicine we need as Afrakan people to get off the deadly drug of white male domination and truly become free to **"Be"**. **We have the right to be right. We must become Heru, fighting esfet for eternity, so that Ma'at may return into our Konsciousness. Only as Heru can we find our divine purpose, by fulfilling our mission of living a life of Spirituality and to give your gifts to all of humanity, the planet and the cosmos.**

Kemklusion

Today, one of our greatest challenges is to recreate a Spiritual Afrakan Worldview that is aligned with our ancestral lineage of Afrakan Spirituality. Once again, knowledge of self and your-story is a prerequisite. The greater your Heru Konsciousness, a Konsciousness that is rooted in Ma'at manifested in your kulture and guided by The NTCHR, the greater your Spiritual energy. This Spiritual energy is also known to many Kemetyu as the Sekhem or Moyo. The greater your Sekhem or Moyo, the deeper and clearer your innerstanding of self and the universal Ntchru, which are various spirits that are reflections of The NTCHR that exist inside **YOU**. We are all living with the power of our Ancestral Spirits; all of the spirits are alive in us.

When you operate your life with Spiritual awareness, you are aligned with The NTCHR. This alignment allows you to know your divine purpose. Your purpose propels your mission, your direction in everything you do, as you are giving your gifts to the world. Our great and sacred Afrakan ancestors from Kemet taught us that the fundamental purpose of Afrakan Spirituality is to give. "de ankh" this is Spiritual living or Spirituality. Afrakan Spirituality is a celebration of life and Kulture. To know that the Ntchru exist is not enough. Knowledge without wisdom and action is irrelevant. We must act on what we know with Ma'at guiding our hearts. The Ntchr Jhuty inspires your unlimited Konsciousness, and the Ntchr Heru protects all that you have developed and inspired. When one is living a Spiritual life, it is also the most direct and simplest form of living. ***Htp***.

FOLLOW YOUR SPIRIT TO FREEDOM

All souls are not to be trusted
It is only the Divine Spirit that can guide us to the truth
Uncolored, unevolved, untrustworthy European and Asiatics
Came to the shores of our most ancient land Afraka
with bad intensions, they did not come to share...
We welcomed them, fed them, helped them survive...
Our reward for our kindness was war, and human betrayal,
as they stole and enslaved our children, families, land and
most precious, our dreams
Despite efforts to shackle the souls and spirits of Afrakan
people
The human spirit would not be contained
We refused limitations and replaced them with Black genius
Treasures that knew no bounds
These treasures are to touch every walk of life in America
Through simple acts of spiritual courage
Our spiritual genius, like our great Afrakan ancestors of
yesteryears
Still develop as we prepare to balance the wrongs and
injustices done to our people, our land Afraka and the
souls and dreams of righteousness
The Maangamizi has titled the scales of righteousness
For only Ma'at can bring back harmony and truth
Let reparations fill the halls of reciprocity
We will follow the Divine Spirit to freedom...
And we will not rest until freedom, Blackness, beauty and
harmony become the Konscious Spirit of Afrakan people
everywhere.
Amen.

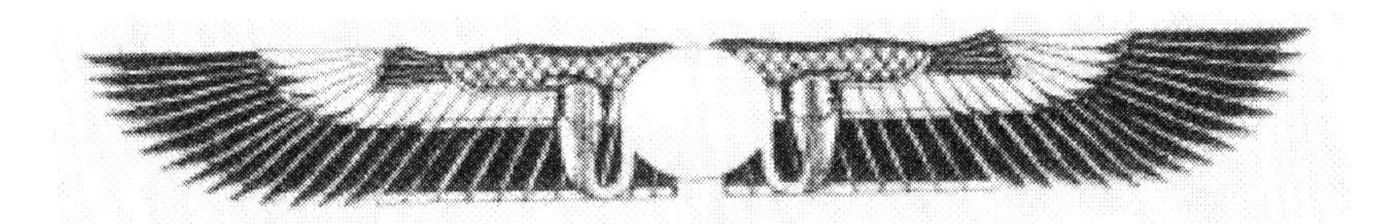

WE ARE DIVINE SPIRIT

We are Divine Spirit
Healers, bringers of light
Look inside yourself, the answers are waiting, glowing...
Feel this Divine Essence
For those among us who are asleep
Rise from your ignorance
You are not just your mind
You are not just your body
You are the Spirit
Yes, you were born of the elements
But we must realize that our home is far beyond this Earth
You are a manifestation of the Light
Light Beings, Aluminous Spirits
The Spirit of the Divine NTCHR is within you
Konsciously join your spirit, become One with your inner self
Prepare your soul for enlightenment
The Konscious blending with the Eternal Light
The Divine NTCHR

All great human beings have seen the Light, and followed the Light to righteousness
Do not seek to follow in the footsteps of great leaders, teachers, sages, healers...
For their prints will not liberate you
Seek what they sought
The Light, The Divine Spirit, Ma'at, enlightenment
Their greatness may have opened doors
Maybe even your eyes
But you must enter Heaven alone
Creating your own footprints...
As you follow the Divine Light
Amen.

SPIRITUALITY IS WAITING

The NTCHR is the totality of all spirits
Therefore, through the Ntchru we can make a spiritual connection
Harmonious order... Infinite peace... Spiritual Oneness...
This divine greatness exist within us and all around us
However, most of us miss it! Not even close!
Because we are too involved in the wrappings of the rituals
of abstract life
Change is not possible because it's not on our daily agenda
The alignment of spirit, mind and body has to be a priority
We have to seek spiritual guidance daily
Spirituality is not an accident, or coincidence
We live with our ancestral spirits, they are alive in us
However, we must look inside ourselves
The morning light is soft...
A light breeze rustling through trees
The rhythmical pulse of the universe
Like a dance, can't you feel it...?
Please don't miss this groove...
Can't you see it...? Close your eyes and look with your mind
There is only One Master Drummer in the universe
And everything is moving to The Creators beat...
Echoing magical heart melodies of life
We, Afrakans are the baddest drummers on earth, because we
were the first, the original Melaninated Earth Spirits,
obedient children and dynamic students of nature
Afrakan drum beats imitating heartbeats
As we echo the sounds of life, the sounds of spirits
We are part of all that there is...
Each moment is new, yet ancient and wonderful
There is nothing outside the Spirit
There is only the infinite now, harmonious order...
Spiritual Oneness... Infinite peace...
If you are a Konscious part of it, smile back at the ancestors
The evening sunset is soft in its nakedness
I celebrate the anniversary of each new breath...
As the NTCHR fills me with Divine Spirit.
Amen

CHAPTER IIIII (6)
Somo la Sita

Black Dot

Definition: Blackness, as symbolized by the Black Dot, is the seed of humanity - the archetype of humanity, the Black hidden doorway to the collective inner-Konscious, the mind's timeless memory banks of Ourstorical knowledge of one's ancestors. Thus, the Black Dot is the hidden doorway that leads one to Heru Konsciousness, the hidden doorway through which unkonscious ideas pass as they become inner-Konscious. It is that which connects us to infinite time and knowledge.

The profound symbol, Black Dot ☉ is an ancient Kemetyu symbol for Blackness, as found in the Kemet Mdu Ntchr. This symbol often characterizes the Ntchr Ra . It also means energy of the sun, or energy of light, that allows the sun to exist or illuminate and give life. Heru is another symbol of the energy of the sun or that which gives light. Heru represents the synthesis of the male principles (logical, left brain) and female (emotional, right brain). By tapping into your Heru Konsciousness you're aligning yourself with the same energy of the Black Dot.

Collective Inner Konscious: The collective is part of the human mind which contains the mental records of one's ancestors. The libraries of our mind are infinite, endless, containing the wisdom of all man's ancestors, the past, present, and even the future. This collective Konsciousness, when innerstood, brings into being a sense of unity, universal knowledge, universal life, harmony and peace. Daily trials then become trivial when innerstood against the back drop of infinite time.

Melanin acts as a super highway that allows the inner Konscious thought from the Black dot to flow to your Konscious mind. There is only one race of humanity on this planet Earth, the Black Melanin dominated race, with many shades of Black. Black is the essence of all humanity and this humanity ranges from Black Black to white Black. White Black is the absence of hue or melanin in major parts of the body but mainly in the skin, eyes, hair, inner Konsciousness of the pineal gland and ancestral memory. We are all part or indirectly connected to Black Afrakans. Human beings and humankind are expressing different styles of Konsciousness, different pathways shaped by different geological environments. But, we all have to pass through the same Black doorway to our Black Dot - higher selves in the same spiritual energy of The NTCHR in order to awaken our Heru Konsciousness.

Hu = God in Sanskrit, Man = Mind, so we are God minded beings. Human = Hu-man. Hu(e) = color, man = being (homo sapien) in Latin. Therefore, 'human' means God minded beings with color. The original form of human is the Black human. Everyone else is a copy of or comes from the original Black human and the xerox copy many times removed is a White - Black human or a yellow - Black human. The Wazungu or melanin deficient being from western Asia and Asia are humankind, or kind of like the original Black human or kind of melaninated or melaninated to a small degree. The Black human Konsciousness has no limits, in a enlighten state, not even earthly limits, We are spiritual beings having an earthly physical experience.

Melanin was found in high concentrations in the skin of almost all the sahu (mummies) from Kemet and Kash. The sahu (mummies) that were melanin deficient, belonged to foreigners, invaders and a few from mixed marriages to royal families in ancient Kemet.

Melanin is the organizing molecule present in the human body. Melanin seems centrally involved in control of all physiological and psychological activity.

The Black Dot

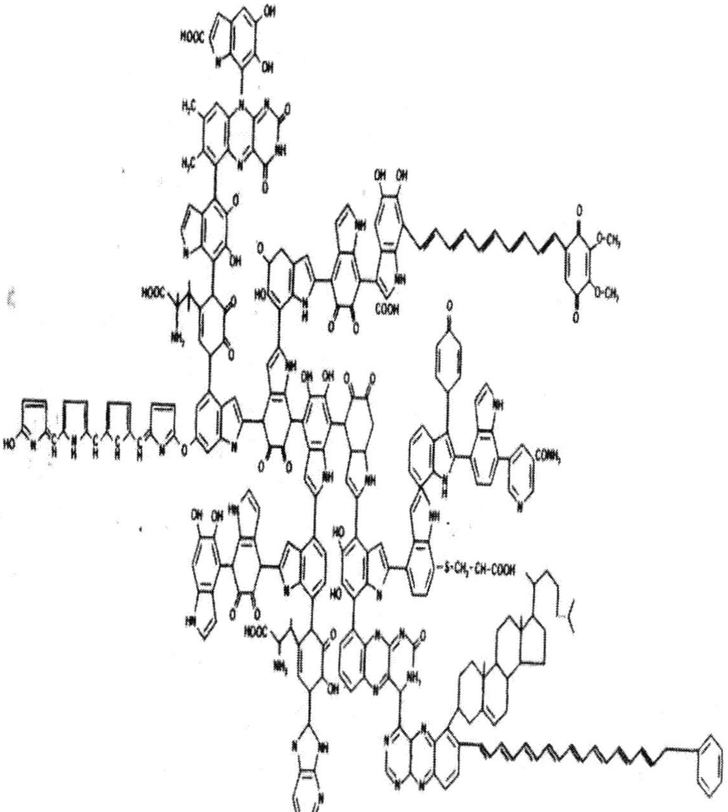

The Melanin Molecule

Listed below are just a few beneficial properties of Melanin:

- It is the main primitive and universal pigment in living organisms, present at the inception of life and directs development.

- Neuromelanin increases with higher forms of life, reaching a peak in human beings (12 centers)

- Melanin has semi- conductive properties with physiological response to stimulation by light, sound, and electricity.

- Melanin is synthesized in most cells that are intimately involved in the Immune System for delivery throughout the body to areas of need, especially injury sites.

- Melanin acts as a semi- conductor, regulating igniting of nerve cells.

- Melanin is extremely stable, highly resistant to experimental analysis.

Melanin is one of the most unique and strategically important biochemicals (biopolymer) found in the BLACK HUMAN. The term "MELANIN" is used to represent the biological substance that ranges in color from golden - brown to black and is manufactured in the body from small chemical units such as the following:

- Phenylalanine
- Tyrosine
- Dopamine
- Norepinephrine (Noradrenaline)
- Epinephrine (Adrenaline)
- Serotonin
- Melatonin

Melanin is a polycyclic polymer of high molecular weight and may contain in its structure various combinations of the chemical units cited above. Once formed, Melanin is insoluble in most solvents and is extremely difficult to dissolve in strong acids and bases.

Melanin is concentrated in the nervous system, skin, eyes, ears, facial structures, endocrine gland, heart, liver, arteries, muscles,

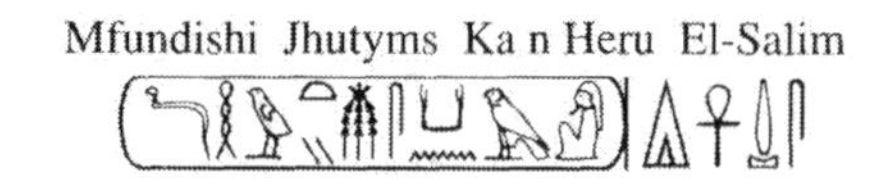

digestive tract, and several organs. Brain melanin is concentrated in a region that functions as a gateway for all the sensory, motor, emotional and motivational input and output, as well as a region that mediates Konscious awareness in general.

Because of melanin's complex reorganization of other molecules via its two - way capacity to convert energy, the melanin model potentially offers a powerful scientific rationale for therapies that rely on biofeedback, light, color, sound, acupressure, acupuncture, altered states, and self-regulations rather than drugs and surgery.

1. Because of melanin's ability to aid in tissue repair and re-generation, the best asset for self - healing would be a subtle ability to shift the Konsciousness to effect the direct current. For this reason, Kemet priest spent long periods of time meditating in order to control the Konsciousness and direct the Sekhem as the ultimate healing force. The force of Sekhem in the Mdw Ntchr, this is the energy from The NTCHR, the vital force of the universe within each human-being.

2. Melanin organizes "free radicals," the unpaired electrons blamed in the aging process. According to one current theory, aging may result from exhaustion of the melanin system. To protect the melanin, one must live wholistically and eat foods that preserve and perpetuate melanin. Kupigana Ngumi, Ma'at Akhw Ba Ankh and Ari Ankh Ka training is one of the best potent melanin exercises available, giving you physical and spiritual stability and the ability to protect whatever you develop. It provides breathing and meditative postures which empowers one with a high level of concentration and focus which strengthens one's spirituality. Kupigana Ngumi and Ma'at Akhw Ba Ankh also teaches you Your Story and Kulture which will help to develop your strong life-giving mentality.

The BLACK HUMAN is known to have high levels of MELANIN in external organs as the skin, eyes, and hair. What is not known to the average lay person is that the BLACK HUMAN also has high levels of MELANIN in major functional regions of the body. These include the following areas:

- Central/Peripheral nervous system - the brain has 12 black MELANIN sites

- Diffuse neuroendocrine system-pineal / pituitary gland, thyroid, thymus, adrenal, etc.

- Inner ear or auditory nerve

- Visceral areas - heart, sexual organs, muscles, arteries, liver, gastrointestinal tract

The pineal gland, which was named by ancient Kemet Priest Scientists - "The Eye of Heru", is the eye of inner vision. The ancient Kemtyu also called it "The Eye of Ra" or our "First Eye". This form of vision or Konsciousness which was the very goal of the entire educational process of the ancient Kemetyu of Ta- Mrry, Kemet, Ta Nhsy, Kash, Punt, and Ta Khuy (These were names of ancient countries in Afraka along the Hapy valley). True education for the Human helps to bring out of one's Black inner mind, that which is already in you, which is connected to the Divine Creator, The NTCHR.

Pineal Gland- The pineal gland releases two hormones into the body:

1. Serotonin is released into the bloodstream during sunlight hours by the pineal gland. Serotonin is somewhat of a memory storage hormone. It increases the flow of memories from the cortex into the blood stream. (Black Afrakans are heavy melanin dominated people, therefore, the sun instantly gives the Kemetyu greater capacity of memory - that is why they say Afrakans are the children of the sun. Melanin transforms sunlight into energy.)

2. Melatonin is released into the bloodstream during darkness by the pineal gland. Melatonin is a memory read out hormone that increases the flow of memories into the cortex. More importantly, melatonin initiates dreams or R.E.M. sleep by activating the locus coeruleus, the Black Dot, the 12th and uppermost in a chain of 12 deeply pigmented nuclei found in the brain stream of all humans. Dreams have long been considered by many to be a royal road to the inner Konsciousness, making visible the soul, spirit, body and mind of various realms of Konsciousness. In the inner Konscious mind, through the hidden door of Heru all things are possible. Within Heru Konsciousness there is only the infinite now, which means yesterday, today and tomorrow are all one and can be expressed at any moment.

The pineal gland is found in the exact mid-line of the brain between the masculine left cortical hemisphere and the feminine right cortical hemisphere.

Why is the chemical - melanin - important to the Kemetyu? Melanin has many functions in the human body and is indeed the most important molecule and chemical of the Kemetyu (Black human). Melanin that is functioning healthy and wholistically is the key to the Kemetyu functioning on a high mental, physical, and spiritual level. If the above is true, then one can conclude that if your melanin is not properly functioning on a high level, the Kemetyu mental, physical, and spiritual levels will be retarded. Below are some critical conditions controlled by melanin.

- Memory
- Motivation
- Mental maturation
- Mental organization
- Integration of sensation
- Consuming environmental energy
- Dreaming
- Emotion
- Motor output
- Anti - immune system
- Anti -aging

The conditions we have just reviewed, have the potential to be greatly amplified or de-amplified in the Kemetyu depending on the "energy state" in which melanin exists. These energy states, if they are healthy and high, are helpful to the Kemetyu. But if their energy states are low and unhealthy, They become toxic to the Kemetyu in the conditions described above especially after puberty and adult maturaity.

The Spiritual Warrior Priest Scientists of Kupigana Ngumi and the Kemetik legacy believe that the best way to protect melanin, the Black Dot, is to eat, think, work, create, protect, and sleep Black, from a Kemetik or Afrakan-centered perspective. If the center of our world is Eurasian or "Western" and you, by nature, are a Afrakan BLACK HUMAN, then your melanin function will be retarded and severely suppressed and altered due to abnormal social, Kultural, and technological contact with the opposing world view of western society or white male domination.

European Caucasian domination and the Western world, through the facade of Euro-centricity, has caused an acute case of psychological and mental degradation to the Kemetyu (Black human). This degradation is indiscriminate, and it affects the rich and the poor, the young and the old, this is the root or foundation to our collective crazy.

If one can analyze the true Ourstory of civilization among the humans on this planet, one would conclude that life of the first humans began in Afraka and the first civilized human was an Afrakan BLACK HUMAN. For tens of thousands of years, the Afrakan BLACK HUMAN developed all branches of the known sciences of today, from math to astronomy to astrology, writing to poetry and prose, government to religion and philosophy, masonry to pyramid building, agrikulture and the development of cities. How then can White Supremacy exist? (The teaching that says that human kind is the creator of all of the above). Euro-centricity not only teaches that they, (Human kind) white BLACK HUMANS, the Wazungu started civilization, but that all this greatness came about since the Greeks. Some white Black Western Asiatics even teach that the Kemetyu were white BLACK HUMANS in ancient Kemet and we learned civilization from them. Logically, this does not make sense to even

those who propose this? In order for BLACK HUMANS to believe these lies, the white human kind had to distort the BLACK HUMAN'S whole world view and his own.

The "negative" feelings and opinions that BLACK HUMANS express about melanin and their Blackness are a direct psychological problem or disease that has infected most of the Kemetyu or Afrakan BLACK HUMANS in America and the Diaspora. Extreme examples of these "negative" psychological behavior patterns are:

(a) The BLACK HUMAN feels that their large features, thick lips, wide nose, large buttocks, big feet, long arms, big hands, are unattractive and prefer the smaller features associated with the human kind. Some BLACK HUMANS "internalize" these feelings and are psychologically affected all of their lives. BLACK HUMANS who have become severely psychologically deranged may have cosmetic surgery to remove thick lips, wide noses, dark skin, etc.

(b) Black humans suffer with a "complex" about their "Black" skin complexion. Black - BLACK HUMANS tend to choose other BLACK HUMANS that are light skinned so they will not reproduce themselves (self- hate). An extreme case is where a BLACK HUMAN chooses a humankind (European) for their mate.

(c) BLACK HUMANS, ashamed of their tightly curled beautiful hair, sometimes called "nappy" (and not in an affectionate way), straighten it to look like human kind (white blacks, Western Asiatics called Europeans), brown Blacks and other Asians like those who are yellow Black. These BLACK HUMANS want to look like anybody else but themselves. They are totally ignorant of the power in their own naturally tightly curled hair, which is the most versatile hair on the planet!

(d) BLACK HUMANS think that the eye coloring of human kind looks better, sexier, and thus superior. So they change their eye coloring with contact lenses, not innerstanding that dark or heavy melaninated eyes have superior vision in speed, depth and field.

(e) Abnormal behavior patterns : thinking and acting like human kind, adapting human kind speech patterns, hobbies, diets and culture.

(f) BLACK HUMANS standards of beauty are anti-Black, the closer BLACK HUMANS are to human kind standards of beauty, the prettier the BLACK HUMAN feels. The world is being conditioned by "White magic" (TV, movies, magazines, newspapers, advertising, bill boards, public schools, colleges, universities and corporate America). These are instruments of white male domination used to distort reality and create an illusion that will become the new reality of insanity. BLACK HUMANS who are mentally insane feel that human kind Wazungu, white features are attractive and human characteristics, especially the BLACK HUMAN, is unattractive.

(g) Lost and stolen Ourstory: BLACK HUMANS have little or no knowledge of their true story. Humankind have stolen BLACK HUMAN's story and distorted it and rearranged everyone's story from a perspective of white male domination from a Euro-centric point of view.

(h) The results are, human kind are proud of history (his - story), BLACK HUMANS are ashamed of Ourstory from his-perspective.

The BLACK HUMAN must innerstand that living a "lifetime" with the above depressing thoughts, changes ones body chemistry. If the Kemetyu, the BLACK HUMANS, do not innerstand their Kulture which is based on their genetic make up and story, they are destined for self destruction. Spiritual Warriors, and Kemet Priest Scientists believe that the reasons for the destruction to Afrakan Kulture from Kemetyu (Black human) is because of ignorance, not knowing the

greatness of who they were, and as a result, BLACK HUMANS become ashamed of the Greatest Kulture the world has ever seen, known, or created. If you follow someone else's culture that is opposite to yours, it will cause extreme stress, depression, anxiety, diseases, and early earthly death. If melanin is in a retarded state, it can be extremely dangerous and toxic. Melanin has high binding capabilities for the following drugs:

- Cocaine	- Caffeine
- Marijuana	- Nicotine
- Codeine	- Agent Orange
- Morphine	- Amphetamine

which means that these drugs are much more dangerous and more addictive to the melanin of the BLACK HUMAN than anyone else in the society.

Afrakan Spiritual Warrior Priest Scientists believe that the chemical melanin is an excellent molecule to support the Kemetyu mentally, physically, and spiritually in all activities. Melanin is the key to virtually all life's functions. So, Afrakancentricity is a must for the Kemetyu, the Black human in this world, if we are to develop and maintain healthy minds, bodies, and souls. Knowing and loving thyself is the key to our using the Black Dot, the door of Heru Konsciousness to recapture our traditional greatness. Only with healthy functioning melanin can we rebuild, re-create, the genius that is inside the Afrakan mind that conceptualized the pyramids (Mer Khut) and re-plot the correct course for the humans to follow towards their highest self.

If we, the Kemetyu are out of our right minds, which is our Afrakan mind as a whole, is it not amazing that we are still the most dynamic athletes, entertainers, dancers, singers, scientists of today? Can you imagine us in our right minds? As a people we would surpass our great ancestry because hidden in our inner Konscious minds exist everything we knew. So Afrakan BLACK HUMANS, let's embrace our own Afrakan Kemet Deep thinking and Afrakan-centered Worldview. Remember that healthy melanin in the pineal gland has the greatest potential. That is why the Black human is responsible for the creation of the majority of all known sciences of today, including chemistry, mathematics, medicine, engineering, law, philosophy, astronomy and agrikulture, even the science of Ma'at was first conceptualized in a BLACK HUMAN'S mind.

The superior, physical abilities (motor output) of the BLACK HUMAN have been alluded to in "Western society" in connection with athletics, dancing, and other forms of entertainment. It is also accepted that BLACKS do not show signs of aging as dramatically as members of the white Black human kind family and that the BLACK HUMAN has a low incidence of skin cancer. This low incidence of skin cancer is due to the free radical scavenging or neutralizing properties of MELANIN. This property keeps all organs in the body (external and internal) from aging rapidly; thus keeping the BLACK HUMAN appearance, as well as mental and physical performance youthful. These observations merely scratch the surface of the importance of MELANIN in determining the quality of life for the BLACK HUMAN.

Melanin is to BLACK HUMAN as chlorophyll is to plants, and as carbon is to the mineral world. We as Afrakans must learn to Kultivate our melanin, so that it can operate at maximum efficiency. Europeans or the Wazungu have melanin in their outer skin, but to a lesser degree than the BLACK HUMAN or brown humans, but they need it. Sometimes they are even obsessed with it. Melanin deficent human kind crave melanin psychologically, as well as physically. That's why they lie out in the hot sun like someone with no sense, they are trying to get some more sense from melanin by any means necessary. **Spiritual Warriors can never be anti- white... We are pro-Black, pro-life.** Kupigana Ngumi, and Ma'at Akhw Ba Ankh are physical and spiritual systems or programs that embrace Afrakan Kulture and the Kemet legacy and they are all ways to innerstand our Blackness. This Blackness that links us to the Black Dot is also that which gives us our spirituality and our innerstanding of NTCHR.

The Kemet philosophy of religion was really spirituality, a total way of life. To worship "the life force" that binds all existence, was a 24 hour tribute, everyday of the Kemetyu's life. The Kemet Priest Scientists put a special interest into seven major functions of the Kemetyu and they called them the seven Kemet powers:

1. Remembrance of the Ancestors
2. Celebration of new birth and naming ceramonies
3. Fertility rites
4. Prayer to the unborn
5. Rites of passage
6. Purification rites
7. Prayer and special rituals to praise the Ntchru- the eternal and all existing forces which are also reflections of the internal and external lifeforce within each of us.

Religion varied among Afrakan nations, depending on geographic location and environmental conditions. Nearly all Kemetyu on the continent believed in a single Higher Divine Force, from which all things came. Much has been written about the many spirits, methods of worship, etc. It must be innerstood that these practices are a product of centuries, millenniums, may be even hundreds of thousands of years and cannot be counted in a few minutes or days. For more information contact the spiritual leaders or Priest Scientists of the Kemet Spiritual Systems or other Afrakan Spiritual Systems; Akan, Yoruba, Voodam, Ma'at Akhw Ba Ankh teachers. Or contact indigenous Kemetyu Priests still in the heartland Afraka, like the Bambara, Dogon or the Twa Priests of the Khalahari. When one is seeking the knowledge of the Light of Blackness, don't look aimlessly for the master, just prepare yourself. Spend all your time developing the self and mastering life and "The Spirit of Perfect Blackness" will find you!

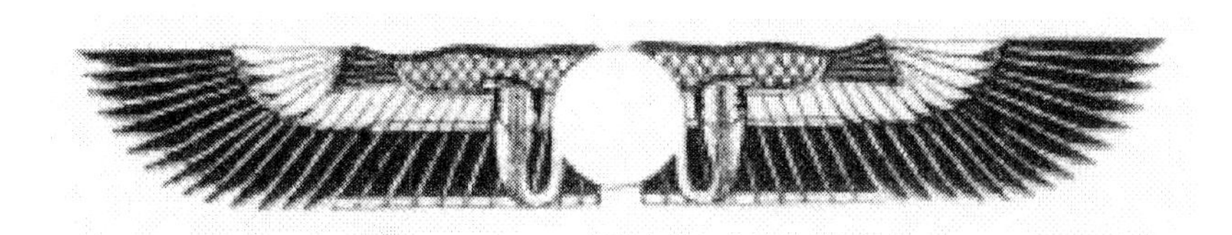

Kemklusion

In kemklusion, MELANIN chemistry must be carefully controlled for optimum mental, physical, and spiritual performance. Most of these conditions are suppressed or altered due to social, cultural, and technological contact with "western society," white male domination.

MELANIN is a significant component in all bodily functions. Studies must be conducted that center around MELANIN in the BLACK HUMAN. Such research would eliminate many of the social and kultural problems, as well as many diseases associated with BLACKS.

MELANIN is refined, complex, and a highly functional molecule. The impact of this chemical on living organisms is phenomenal. Some of the fascinating qualities of MELANIN are outlined in these concluding statements:

MELANIN can convert light energy to sound energy (music) and back again to light energy!

MELANIN can convert light energy to heat and electrical energy!

MELANIN is self-organizing (auto-polymerizing) and may reproduce itself!

MELANIN is extremely stable and resist analysis!

MELANIN is centrally involved in controlling all physiological and psychological activities!

MELANIN is an ancient chemical that was present at the inception of life and has existed for millions of years!

MELANIN is found in high concentrations in the skin of mummies from Ancient Kemet and the Hpy Valley!

MELANIN can bind and release all elements known on Earth!

MELANIN can cause altered states of Konscious - ness as the "shouting", and "speaking in tongues" experienced in BLACK religious ceremonies, the creation of jazz music, and even "spiking the football in the end zone!"

MELANIN is present at the site of tissue repair, regeneration (cuts, wounds), and infectious diseases!

MELANIN is centrally involved in keeping the human body Konscious!

MELANIN granules are mini - computers and may analyze and initiate responses and reactions without reporting to the brain!

MELANIN has the ability to absorb light, sound, and magnetism and this in turn allows the BLACK HUMAN to demonstrate physical, chemical, and mental abilities that are closely related to the properties of light, sound, and magnetism!

MELANIN encourages the creation of BLACK Kultural traits that are similar to its chemical properties. For example the "Blues Brothers" look (dark glasses and dark suits) and black- on black designs in clothing and decor!

MELANIN is capable of undergoing many chemical reactions at once (oxidation- reduction; processing many data points) and thus gives the BLACK HUMAN smooth movements and rhythm. MELANIN eliminates robotic movement (due to the processing of few data points) and is responsible for the multi-rhythmic music and dance associated with BLACKS!

MELANIN is located in melanin centers within the brain and are responsible for coordinating and controlling body movement as well as controlling brain power (thinking abilities, smartness). The white race has fewer MELANIN centers in the brain and throughout the body and therefore lacks coordination, body control (this is seen and demonstrated perfectly when one observes their dancing, robotic movement and athletic performances-awkwardness) and brain power when compared to the BLACK HUMAN. Since MELANIN controls both mental and physical activities, one can conclude that the white race brain power is equal to their abilities to dance and perform athletic activities which has been demonstrated to be poor. This could be why they fear, and destroy first.

MELANIN is present in the early stages of development and plays a vital role in the formation of the fetus of the BLACK HUMAN!

MELANIN can become toxic to the BLACK HUMAN because of its superior binding properties. MELANIN becomes harmful when it combines with drugs such as: cocaine, amphetamines, psychedelic hallucinogens, neuroleptics (tranquilizers),

marijuana, agent orange (dioxin), parquets, and tetracyclines. To prevent death and the retarding of our melanin, these drugs must be removed from the environment of BLACKS!

MELANIN behaves as a sedative or harmonizing agent and has a calming, relaxing effect on the body which promotes a caring, civilized society!

MELANIN holds the key to solving a wide variety of physical problems including: mental instability (manic depression and schizophrenia), cardiovascular disorder, immunological disorders (allergies and infections), aging; and cancer!

MELANIN pigmentation in the eye is directly related to reaction time or quickness of movement!

MELANIN can conduct electricity without offering any resistance to the flow of electrons or electricity. This is called super- conduction!

MELANIN is responsible for the existence of civilization, spirituality, religion, philosophy, truth, and justice!

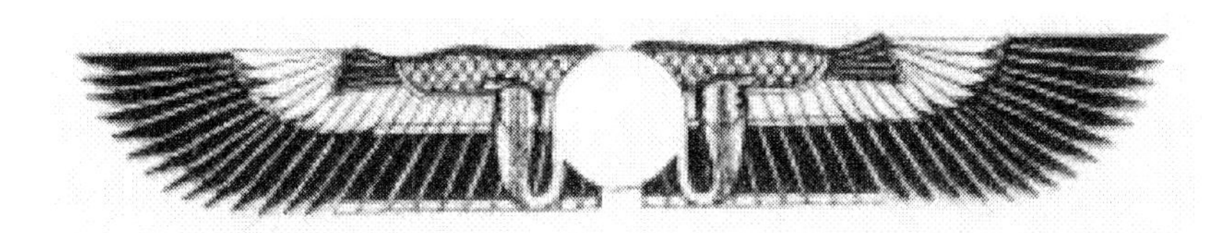

BLACK SILENCE

Can you feel the silence of the Black night
Wisdom waiting for the meditative mind
Ancestral knowledge bathing in an internal sea of Melanin
Black Silence can be educating
Black Silence can be empowering
A source of infinite inspiration and strength
Oneness with the Creator

Can you hear the silence of the Black night
Sound muffled by the heaviness of darkness
Invisible shadows motionless
A kool dark breeze unheard and unseen
Sending unknown messages
As infinite as time itself

Can you see the silence of the Black night
Darkness waiting to be recognized
By black eyes
That peer the unseen
Knowing the unknowable
Conceiving the unthinkable
This blackness is beauty that is undefinable
Immeasurable
Strong, mysterious but silent
Black Silence
Infinite hues of Black faces
Waiting in the silence of the Black night
Waiting for us to recognize how powerful and
How Beautiful We Really Are!

CHAPTER IIIIIII (7)
Somo la Saba

Ritual

Ritual and Afrakan Spirituality

With knowledge of our environment and a harmonious relationship with nature came our first rituals. Early humans found that through certain repetitive behavior they could gain spiritual insight, enlightenment, and guidance. These spiritual rituals empowered them, allowing them to be Konscious of their union with NTCHR. These first Black human beings, the parents of all humankind, developed rituals that engaged their environment in a life-giving, life-sustaining way. Thus, the spiritual essence of life became the yardstick by which all things were measured in the Afrakan Worldview. Afrakan-centered rituals combine real everyday life with artistic expression. Ritual is the ultimate philosophical expression of the Afrakan Worldview. It is the uniting of matter and spirit in divine alignment, where a higher spiritual being, The NTCHR that dwells within every human being, is achieved. It is through ritual that the unexplainable is innerstood, through which seeming chaos is put into cohesive order within the logic of tradition.

Life for the Black human became a spiritual experience, where each member of the clan or society gave their divine gift, filling in the puzzle pieces of their divine existence. These particular daily rituals forged Afraka's first Kulture. Kulture became a collection of repetitive rituals acted out daily in a ritual drama. This ritual drama used music, and dance, to express Afrakan spirituality, Ourstory, governance, and ideology, essentially their Afrakan Worldview.

Rhythm, dance and song are quintessential aspects of the Cosmic Afrakan universe.

Each clan assigned certain individuals who possessed certain spiritual powers with the awesome responsibility of memorizing these rituals until they became woven into the heart and soul of the person. Later societies called these powerful people, Spiritual Healers, Priests and Priestesses, Wisdom keepers, Sages, Shamans and Prophets.

Black Afrakans in East Afraka along the Hapy Eteru (the Nile), developed a Spiritual System later called the Mysteries by the Wazungu (European and Asiatic invaders). The purpose of the Kemet Spiritual System was to provide spiritual rituals that developed the whole human being, the whole family, and the whole society through the spiritual power of the Sekhem. Ritual is to celebrate the affirmation of a sense of community, a feeling of togetherness, because all who have gathered and participated in the ritual become one.

***"Its better to have an Afrakan heart without words, than Afrakan words without a heart."*"** **Afrakan proverb.**

Following is a list of a few Afrakan centered attributes that ritual confirms.

1. The souls of all human beings are of One Divine Essence.

2. The soul of no human being is ever separated from its divine source, The NTCHR.

3. Not all human beings are equally Konscious of their divine nature, their soul. This then, accounts for the varied spiritual enlightenment and moral behavior of human beings and human kind.

4. Every human can seek divine aid for personal regeneration and immortality within NTCHR. This spiritual Konsciousness is the Sekhem, or your own spiritual essence or soul, which is part of the Divine reality.

5. No human is deprived of the right of communication to the ultimate source, The NTCHR. The poor and the rich have the same source. The Priestship is no more divinely qualified for this union of humanity with The NTCHR, than the most humble station in life.

6. When one is seeking a Konscious union with The NTCHR, you experience an exalted state of Konsciousness, a sensation of liberation of body and mind from the microcosm. This is Oneness with the Divine Source, the ultimate force, The NTCHR. This state of absorption with the wholeness of The Divine NTCHR is called, and was termed by Kemet Priest Scientists of the ancient Kemet Spiritual School, as a mystical experience.

7. This mystical experience can be achieved in many different ways, on many planes, and can take on many manifestations as it provides a regeneration of the self. This force that regenerates the self is called Moyo by Kupigana Ngumi, and Sekhem by Ma'at Akhw Ba Ankh Priest Scientists and Afrakan Spiritual Warriors.

"It is a meticulous being like the tortoise who can see another tortoise in the bush." (An alert person is aware of the trickery of others). Yoruba proverb.

Kemet was a very spiritual and religious society. Ritual and praise to the Ntchru was common practice in the every day life of the Kemetyu. Only through initiation could certain Kemetyu become Priestesses, Priests and leaders in the Kemet society. After the initiate had passed their basic Afrakan Spirituality initiation test, it could take them up to 42 years or even a lifetime to become one of the sun's of light or son and daughter of the sun. The sun's of light had to master the sacred books of Jhuty. There were 42 books of Jhuty and these books were divided into 6 classes:

1) 1- 10 Books - Ma'at, Sacred laws of The NTCHR and the general wholistic education of the Priestess/Priest.

2) 11-20 Books - Service of The NTCHR - sacrifices, offerings, and forms of Kemet worship and rituals.

3) 21-30 Books - Ourstory of the world, geography and the Mdu Ntchr.

4) 31-34 Books - Astronomy and astrology.

5) 35-36 Books - Spiritual and Religious compositions and ritual.

6) 37-42 Books - Medicine, herbology and natures cures.

"Be not arrogant because of your knowledge. Take up counsel with the ignorant as well as with the wise, for the limits of knowledge in any field have never been set and no one has ever reached them. Wisdom is rarer than emeralds and yet is found among the women who gather at the grindstones." **The Book of Ptah-Hotep**

Kemet Priests taught that life was immortal and that it does not begin or end here on Earth. But there is an immortality of the spirit and physical life on Earth is only a stage in the totality of the infinite life of the Ntchru.

In Kemet, there were three realms: Heaven, Earth and the Duat. The Ntchru were the casual powers - primary causes and secondary causes of everything that manifests itself in the universe. They are the principles, agents, and functions of these manifestations. The worlds or "states" of the universe are aspects of The NTCHR that have been given different names by the Kemet Priest Scientists. They have summed them up in one formula "That which is in heaven, on Earth, and the Duat."

A. <u>That which is in "heaven" or the celestial world</u>: The world of Ba, the universal Divine Soul, source of all Ba's. The world of the principles, and the creator powers. The abstract, impersonal, impressive world, which contains within itself all possibilities.

Mwt em Uaa - The great mother, Mother of the Ntchru, the mate of Amen, the Ntchrt that brings forth all life.

Amun - Amen- the never born unseen force of The NTCHR. The Creator of the Ntchru.

Ra - The universal light that contains the Atum. The seen force of the Ntchru, who was self created.

Ptah - The world of Ptah, the innate fire of terrestrial matter, who created it, the very spark of life.

Aten - The self created Ntchr, which brought all life into existence and sustains all life.

Atum - Creator of Shu, Tefnut, Geb, and Nut the Ntchru of fundamental functions. Atum also created the four (4) elementary constituents of matter fire, air, water, and earth, with, Dry, Wet, Warm, and Cold to their most complex combinations: stars, all minerals, and other life forms.

B. "That which is in the Duat" or the intermediate world: This is the world of Asr (Wsr), overseer and master of the transformations in the Duat. The Duat is the world of transition between the abstract world of the casual powers and the concrete world of phenomena or world of nature. The state of in between" Becoming" or towards a "Return." Two levels of Duat:

1. Moves towards the terrestrial genesis.

2. Emerges from terrestrial existence and now in a state of waiting to return once more to Earth or to ascend, through the necessary transformation, towards its spiritual home. It is the world of Kau. Ntchru -

(Five divisions of Solar Ntchru - Asr, Ast, Setsh, Neb Het, and Heru). As in Heaven and Earth, the sun shines eternally.

Jhuty - The scribe of the Ntchru, and the keeper of records.
Enpu - The opener of the way, the roads of eternity.
Amamet - Devourer of the unjust souls in the Duat.
Ma'at - The truth, the feather which represent the way, the standard by which life was measured and balanced.

C. "That which is on Earth, " or the concrete and terrestrial world. This is the world of bodies (Khat). The world of Asr Un - Nefer, the master and regenerator of vegetative life. Asr who is master over all cycles of renewal in nature. Asr is also the state of perfect Black. A few of the other Ntchru are:

Het- Heru - The house where the great Falcon lives or a state of Higher Konsciousness. The house of higher Konsciousness.
Heru - The protector of positive energy, the creator of balance through struggle. The son of Asr and Ast.
Shu - The Boundless space and the father of Nut and Geb.
Nut - The sky, the physical atmosphere where human beings dwell. Nut is also the cosmic virgin of whom it is said: "I am that which is, that which will be, that which has been."
Jhuty - The Messenger of Ra, tongue of Ptah and heart of Amun. The scribe of the Ntchru, the creator of knowledge wisdom, speech and writing.
Enpu - The embalmer and opener of the way, the roads of eternity. Enpu is an energy like Heru and Asr that exists in the Duat as well as in the terrestrial realm.
Sokar - The Fire energy Ntchru.
Serket - The breathing in, the Scorpion Ntchr-)
Sekhmet - The Cleansing energy, the fire eyes of Ra. The mate of Ptah.
Net Ntchr - The breathing out.
Wadjit - The Vegetative life.

A Spiritual Warrior innerstands that as attractive as the modern European Caucasian world appears with its material abundance, it is repulsive with its spiritual and emotional poverty. Wherever there is European Caucasian domination and western technology, there is a general degeneration of the spiritual realm. The European-American corporate world along with Christianity are technological machines that ravaged and continues to ravage the indigenous world and Afraka; as well as Afrakans everywhere who embrace European Caucasian domination or who live under their systems.

Western machine technology, or rather western use of machine technology is a spirit of death made to look like life. The world of takers makes life seem easier, comfortable, cozy, but the price one has to pay includes the dehumanization and degeneration of the self. Caucasian domination has made the natural way of living look primitive, famine-ridden, diseased, ignorant and impoverished. This is so that we would appreciate our enslavement to the machine and enjoy being dope addicts of European Caucasian domination.

The Western World, the world of white European-American male domination is the enemy of Afrakan people and it can never serve us, because it can't serve. It needs servants. It is the culture of the takers. It is like having an enormous white elephant in your home as a pet or guest. First it will destroy your home, crush your Kultural values, and endanger the lives of your family, not to mention the energy spent to find 200 pounds of food every day, and 50 gallons of water a day. How can this compensate for what you would get out of this relationship? Any Afrakan whose genius is wrapped up in this madness must devote their whole life to it and be disconnected from Afraka, Afrakan people, your sacred ancestors and even the Ntchru.

Spiritual Warriors are in America but not of America, we are recovering addicts of white male domination. We have heard our souls screaming and we have learned to heal the suffering of the soul through Kultural and Spiritual Konsciousness. Afrakan Kultural rituals are the medicine we need in order to recover our Black Afrakan minds, and heal the suffering of the soul and to make peace with displaced, disjointed, lost, and stolen Afrakan ancestors. Only the spirit of the wise and sacred ancestors through ritual can deliver us and bring glory and harmony back into our lives. This harmony is "The Way" or Ma'at. We must first recognize the need for healing, the need for wholeness, the need to be one Konsciously with The NTCHR. Second, we must slow down and listen to ourselves, breathing the breath of The NTCHR with Konsciousness, allowing the spirit to teach you and guide us to wellness and wholeness in our human form. This can be done anywhere since The NTCHR is everywhere, but each human should have their own personal sacred spaces to do life-giving rituals.

Spiritual Warriors are rare in this mechanical machine, enslaved society. Most Afrakans live separated from their Afrakan Kulture and their spiritual souls in this European Caucasian centered culture. There are many cases of unconscious Afrakans actually ending their physical lives. Afrakan suicide and homicide is the highest in America. Most of these Afrakans never knew who they were or innerstood the dynamics of their Afrakan self. They die unconscious as they surrendered their souls to the enemy. Afrakans in America are insane. They still do not innerstand that Afraka is our home and we can go home any time we want. Afrakans are still destroying themselves because they have no Konscious sacred Afrakan home to go to, and lack the knowledge of any kind of spiritual ritual to receive and heal their souls.

When Spiritual Warriors wear ceremonial garments in public or Afrakan clothes in European and American settings it is not a random act. This is a ritual statement. The Afrakan Kultural clothes are a display of Afrakan Kulture with the intention of showing pride, dignity, the beauty and continuation of our way of life, even in the madness of confusion. In some cases the wearing of ceremonial Afrakan garments act as a healing medicine, and hope to unkonscious Afrakans who are addicts of white male domination. Spiritual Warriors intend to continue to weave and embroider Afrakan life in the intricate way that has been passed to them from their ancestors. Our Afrakan ancestors are angry and the Earth is angry with Afrakan people, the original people of this planet, because we have lost our way with the light of spirit all around. We have become takers instead of leavers and givers of life. Some of us have thrown away our Kulture for another and many of us remain ignorant of Ourstory and Kultural greatness. In either case, rather we plead ignorance or stupidity, the ancestors are insulted and angry. Our dead cannot find peace, and as a result, we are paying for this with ills, disease and a poisoned planet. Our future, if we continue on this course of action is a nightmare about to explode into non-existence. On the Afrakan continent many Afrakans are worshiping western machines and culture, which have replaced The NTCHR, the Ntchru and the worship of our ancestors. In the western world, Afrakans are imitating this termite like destructive frenzy of European Caucasin life, characterized by a work-obsessed culture, which is symptomatic of an illness that is equivalent to a drug addict unable to help itself, because it has been blinded by the drugs of European Caucasian domination.

Spiritual Warriors innerstand that rituals are called for because our soul communicates things to us that the body translates as need, or want, or absence. So we enter into ritual in order to respond to the call of the soul. Purpose is the driving force that contributes to the effectiveness of ritual. All Spiritual Warriors use ritual as a prerequisite to earthly events, to assist the spirit and to act as a form of communication with the Spirit, in regards to the elements, the principles, the deified ancestors and the Creator, The NTCHR. This is the spirit that should precede human involvement with the world and with each other.

The NTCHR is the All, everything that can be perceived and all that is outside of our comprehension is NTCHR. The spirit is the essence of The NTCHR, its Konsciousness, Therefore the spirit and the ritual is the act that connects us to our spirit, nature, the cosmos, the ancestral realm and the Ntchru inside and out of our Konsciousness. The Afrakans or Kemetyu of ancient Kemet thought that it was innately inscribed within the Kemetyu to do rituals. Rituals exists in every aspect of their lives as expressed through their Kulture, so ritual draws from the area of human existence where the spirit plays a life-giving role. The force field or Sekhem we create within a ritual is something coming from the spirit, not something coming from us. Spiritual Warriors are only instruments or healing tools in this kind of interaction between dimensions, between realms of unlimited energy.

There is ritual each time a spirit is called to intervene in human affairs. Ceremony is what we call the structure or foundation of the ritual. In each ritual, we have participants, the Spiritual Warrior who acts on behalf of the community, family or individual that are asking or presenting a request to the spirits to intervene in their affairs. The presence of the spirits, their coming, turns our ceremony into a ritual. Spiritual Warriors teach that spirit is our channel through which every challenge in life can be met. They also teach that the spirit realm will not take care of their challenges without our Konscious participation. The ritual itself acts as the blueprint for spirit to follow.

Libations are to give praise and thanks to the sacred Afrakan ancestors. It is a way of remembering those on whose shoulders we stand. We are calling on The Supreme Spirit, our ancestors for guidance, support and strength. This ritual puts us back in connection with "The Way." It guides us with a direct line to the sacred aspects of existence, we begin to feel expanded and liberated, this ritual opens us to our creativity and our infinite capacity for inventing solutions to our daily challenges. In our ancient Afrakan tradition of communalism, we as Spiritual Afrakan Warriors should and must start all rituals with libations.

Libations is usually led by an Afrakan Priest, elder or some knowledgeable person whose life is in concert with Ma'at. They usually ask everyone to stand and honor the wise and sacred ancestors. Water, the substance of life, is poured into a plant or on to the ground, and everyone participates by responding in an Afrakan tongue to reclaim and reconstruct our Afrakan centeredness and our humanity. Here are a few Afrakan languages that are commonly used by Afrakans in America.

Mdu Ntchr- "Amen", "Hotep", or "Duwa". Yoruba- "Ashe", Akan- "Ya ol", Zulu- "Yebo". In essence we are saying, "Praises, so be it, it is done". This is an example of a complete call and response to libation:

The Call: *In the name of the great Afrakans who began the march of humanity and civilization, in the womb of Mother Afraka's Great Lake Region, East Afraka, we ask these Afrakans to be with us to strengthen us and give us vision for a great Afrakan future.*

Response: *Duwa!*

The Call: *In the name of the Great Afrakans who began the march of civilization along the Hapy Valley establishing their High Kulture, building their temples, great monuments, pyramids and tombs to The Ntchr and Ntchru, we ask these great Afrakans to be with us and give us vision for a great Afrakan future.*

Response: *Duwa!*

Call: *In the name of the great Afrakan Ancestor Spirits who began civilization and opened it up to Afrakans on our glorious continent like: Kemet, Kash, Nubia, Zimbabwe, Kilwar, Mali, Ghana, Yoruba, Ibo, Ba Congos, the Dogon, the Ashante, and the Zulu. We give praise to the Afrakans who strengthened neighboring lands like: the Greeks, The Arabs, the Indus Kush Valley, India and Sumaria. We ask these Afrakans to be with us, to strengthen us, and to give us vision for a great Afrakan future.*

Response: *Duwa!*

Call: *In the name of the great Afrakans who were stolen out of Afraka during the Maangamizi, but who kept the spirit of greatness in their hearts, and the love of The NTCHR in their being, who fought for liberty, and justice as they were put into the ships of enslavement, as they were brought across the Atlantic Ocean in the horrible Middle Passage, to the shores of South America, North America and the Caribbean. We need strength from the spirit of these Afrakans who left a legacy of struggle and freedom that cannot be matched. To resist enslavement, they went into the highlands of Brazil at Palmares and created the first Free Republic in the Americas by non-indigenous people. To resist enslavement, they went into the mountains of Jamaica and other Caribbean islands and created the Maroon communities. To resist bondage and enslavement, they escaped to the mountains of Hispanola and through the Afrakan Spirit of Voodun and its mighty priests like Boukman and Deasalines and brave generals like Toussant L. O'verture defeated the French becoming the first Afrakan liberated nation in the Western Hemisphere, where slavery was abolished forever. We ask these Afrakans to be with us, to strengthen us, and to give us vision for a great Afrakan future.*

Response: *Duwa!*

Call: *In the name of the great Afrakans who were enslaved here in North America and who fought injustice and inhumanity by resisting bondage and enslavement, who went into the swamps of the backwoods of Florida and Georgia and linked up with the Seminoles who were also fighting for their lives against white male domination and genocide. These great Afrakans, we ask their spirits to be with us, in the tradition of Nat Turner, Denmark Vesey, Gabriel Prosser, David Walker, Henry Highland Garnet, Harriet Tubman, Sojourner Truth, Benjamin Banneker, and Frederick Douglas. We ask these Afrakans to be with us, strengthen us and give us vision for a great Afrakan future.*

Response: *Duwa!*

Call: *In the name of the great Afrakans here in the 20th Century whose spirits we have seen or have been touched by and whose shoulders we are still standing like W.E.B. DuBois, Marcus Mosiah Garvey, Carter G. Woodson, El Hajj Malik el Shabazz, Dr. John Henrik Clarke, and countless unnamed, forgotten Afrakans who renewed our contributions to science, who helped developed the light bulb and telephone, electricity, agrikultural and science. We ask these great Afrakans to be with us and to give us vision for a great Afrakan future.*

Response: *Duwa!*

Call: *And last but not least, to the great Afrakans who are here physically, who are still involved in the fight for freedom, justice, equality, and the liberation of the mind. And to the unborn who are with us and give us strength as we continue our quest to retain our greatness and to rebuild a new Afrakan nation, so that we can reclaim the land of our great ancestors. All those Afrakan spirits involved in this mission, we ask that you give us strength and vision for a great Afrakan future.*

Response: *Duwa!*

So it has been said, so let it be done! Duwa (everyone may be seated).

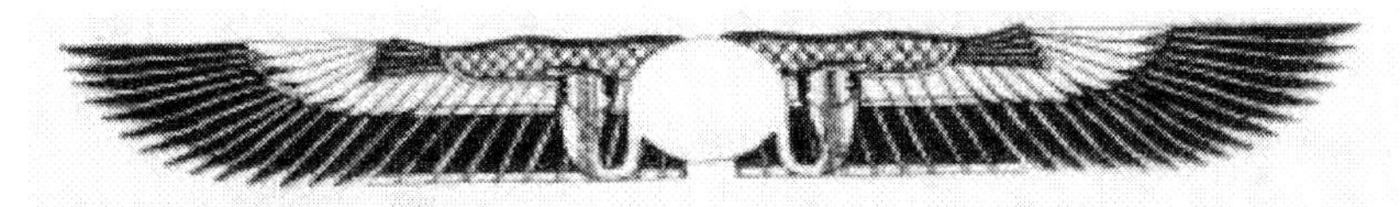

INVOCATION:

Invocation is to invoke the spirit by calling upon the invisible. It is an important part of the ritual ceremonial structure. *Invocation is a call placed by a person to a spirit.* The callers language must be a humble request to the spirit. Humility is the key in expressing yourself, so that the spirit may allow the Moyo to travel from The NTCHR to you. Malidoma Some, a Dagara spiritual Warrior from Burkina Faso, gives a typical invocation prior to a journey: **"I greet you spirits of my ancestors; I greet you spirit guides, friends of the invisible. You that see without looking, you that know without learning, I come to tell you I am about to go on a journey. How can a blind man travel? My feet can't hold me, my eyes can't show me the way, my wit can't guide me through traps. So I come to give myself away to you, that you may be my feet, my eyes and my wit; that I may see through you, that I may walk with you, that I may feel you. For it is with you that this journey can happen as a journey. May it be safe."**

All powerful Rituals have structure. The ritual space is opened whenever the sacred spirits are invoked. Many times this structure is opened with libation if it is an Afrakan ritual.

1) Libation is to give praise and thanks for our existence and for bringing us to this point. We honor you, for the entire universe dwells within your spirit. Water is poured and the spirits are welcomed.

2) Invocation. Humans call on the spirit for a specific purpose.

3) Dialogue. We enter into a conversation with spirit and with ourselves.

4) The Message. Actions or ceremonial structure in the rituals are the same each time. The dance, songs, Hekau and the type of enlightenment may vary. The experience will be different each time, but the structure will be the same.

5) Thanking. All of the spirits must be properly thanked and given respect on behalf of the spiritual presenters.

6) Closing. The spirit is sent away symbolically, not dismissed. The ritual space is closed when the spirit is thanked and sent away.

The spirit structure is what is basic to indigenous Afrakan Ritual. This is the message Spiritual Warriors are trying to bring to Afrakans in the diaspora. We must recapture our spirituality, and begin to perfect our gifts so that we can give them back to the world, so that we can heal ourselves, our people and the planet.

Spirituality is the Oneness within and without making you aware of the wholeness of life, connecting you to every living force in nature and the cosmos. The essence of this spirituality is expressed through rituals.

Spiritual Warriors innerstand that they are spirit and that spirit is in everything and everywhere at the same time. So from the Afrakan Worldview all rituals are spiritual. All Afrakan rituals belong to one of the five major types. They are; 1 - communal rituals, 2 - clan, ancestral or family rituals, 3 - Individual rituals, 4 - organizational or religious rituals, 5 - Nature or Ntchru rituals. Some of these rituals overlap, having more than one function.

Communal Rituals

1) The communal Rituals are designed to bond the larger community together as a single unit in harmony with each other. All the adult members of the community are obliged to attend. These gatherings mend the people together and reaffirm its unity under one spirit, one purpose and one aim. Communal rituals are also Kultural rituals that reaffirm who you are in relationship to The NTCHR and your relationship with your people or clan.

Without a community you cannot be yourself. The community is where we draw the strength needed to effect changes inside of us. Community is formed each time more than one person, or family meet for a purpose. Developing a community depends on what the people involved consent. An Afrakan community is a place of self definition. Any group of people meeting and living together with the intention of connecting to the power within is a community. Most Afrakans living in America do not live in communities. Instead we live in neighborhoods, where we are disconnected from each other and there is no communal bond.

True community begins in the hearts of people who have common ideas, love, respect and values, a place of being. Malidoma in his book "Ritual", states that **"the elder cannot be an elder if there is no community to make him an elder. The young boy cannot feel secure if there is no elder whose silent presence gives him hope in life. The adult cannot be who he is unless there is a strong sense of presence of the other people around. This interdependency is what I call supportive presence."**

Spiritual Warriors innerstand that we have to rebuild our neighborhoods into powerful communities that will function as home away from home or a place where healing can take place, because the spirit is watching over us. There are certain things we must have, the following are some important ***characteristics of real community***:

1. **Unity of Spirit.** The group has to want to be together as a community. The community feels an indivisible sense of unity. Each member is like a cell in the human body. The group needs the individual, and the individual needs the group.

2. **Trust.** Everyone is moved to trust everyone else by principles and having a common value system. If everyone is connected to The NTCHR the same way with the same Kultural values, then trust becomes natural to Ma'at and the well being of the community.

3. **Openness**. People are open to each other unreservedly. This means that individual problems quickly become community problems and they are solved together. There is strength in unity, trust and openness.

4. **Love and Caring**. A fair distribution of wealth. Your good or bad fortune is shared with the community.

5. **Respect for the Elders.** The Elders are the pillars and the collective memory of the community. They hold the wisdom that keeps the community together. They initiate the young ones, prescribe the rituals for various occasions and monitor the dynamics of the community.

6. **Respect for Nature.** Nature is the principal book out of which all wisdom is learned. It is the place where initiation happens. It is the place where your food and medicine comes. And nature is where you live. Life in harmony with Ma'at must be the yardstick by which you measure your existence and respect to and for nature. Have communty clean up once a month. Develop a community garden and have community block parties. Develop a community study group, create an atmosphere of growth and love.

7. **Ancestor reverence.** The ancestors are not dead. They live in the spirits in our community. We name streets after them, buildings, parks, rivers and even our children. We build monuments in there honor to guide and inspire the community.

We need ritual to confirm our community because it is an expression of the fact that we recognize the difficulty of creating a different and special kind of community. A community that doesn't have common rituals cannot exist in unity. This is why Black people, Afrakans in America can be divided and conquered and kept in a state of confusion and crisis, because there is no strong Afrakan community with experienced elders to constantly fight for your best interest. Ritual must be constantly invoked as an opportunity for the weak and ignorant to become strong and knowledgeable of themselves, their Kulture and the ways of the enemy. Ritual also allows the strong to get even stronger.

A corporate neighborhood, or your integrated American neighborhood, or slums full of people who have no place else to go, are not communities. They are conglomerations of individuals in service of an insatiable soulless entity that acts as your pimp or pusher for the life threatening drug, capitalism and white male domination.

Clan, Ancestral or Family Rituals

2) Family rituals are performed under the guidance of the family head and in the presence of every responsible family member. Any initiated person is considered responsible and must attend family rituals.

There are family rituals, which can be a subcommunity honoring of certain spirits in the name of family unity. Afrakans in the West are just beginning to retrieve family rituals from the pits of our ancestral Konsciousness. Family reunions are becoming more common today in America. Naming rituals are powerful family rituals that bind the family closely together.

Funerals have always been a powerful family ritual. It is a ritual that involves everyone, both the living and the ancestors. The family is in charge of the ritual, but the community, as well as individuals outside the immediate family and community, can participate and grieve on behalf of the deceased. Everyone has an invitation to unleash grief. If grief is allowed to be a cleansing force, it acts as a healing tool to all those who knew the deceased. After the family and friends have cleansed their soul through grief they want to celebrate because they have paid their dues to the dead and the ancestors. The other side of real grief is real joy.

Malidoma also states in his book on Ritual that " **When there is an opportunity for humans to mourn their losses, the horizon for rites that heal will be pure and bright, and healing will come pouring into the souls in a great moment of reunion."**

Spiritual Warriors also innerstand that there are family rituals that include the extended family or your ethnic group or clan only. Sometimes we call spirits into a circle of family, the Afrakan family, in order to help achieve goals that cannot be achieved in any other way. This calling needs to remain in safe containment, the way a baby remains hidden in the sacred womb prior to being reborn into the physical world. Safe containment means keeping the space away from any impurities, any unwanted intrusions or from human kind who do not share your Kulture or spiritual purpose.

Individual Rituals

3) First we must respect the rights of the individual, because individual rituals are just as important as family rituals and community rituals. Rights of passage rituals are probably the most famous of the individual rituals and they may happen in a person's life many times, from birth to childhood, to adolescence, to manship, to womenship, to leadership to eldership, and finally to ancestrialship. These Rights of passage rituals are the processes of developing the necessary tools and knowledge that will allow a human being to navigate into maturity, so that one can travel through their missions as captain of their own human and spiritual vessel or

life-force, enabling them to give their gifts to the world as they complete their life's purpose.

Spiritual Warriors are powerful humans because of their constituency with their individual rituals everyday, which allows the Moyo to manifest through them, this is spiritual power. The Sekhem is invisible, yet its presence can be felt in terms of gentleness, love, sharing and compassion, and yet pure power and strength in time of conflict or war. Spiritual Warriors who live in constant touch with the invisible realm of incomparable power are always in a good temperament and very innerstanding of other human situation and challenges. There is discipline and strength that allows the tranquility of peace to be or to come into being. Therefore, as a Spiritual Warrior the individual rituals will assist in preparing you to do battle in order to be who you need to be, not only for yourself, but for your people.

Spiritual Warriors innerstand the more ritualized their personal space, the more spiritual their lives. A sacred life is a ritualized life, that is one that draws constantly from the realm of the spiritual to handle even the smallest situation or challenge on all realms of existence.

The Spiritual Warriors must use their Moyo or Sekhem to help create and develop communities that meet the intrinsic need of the Afrakans inside it. With this type of strong Afrakan community the Afrakan individual can finally discover within the community something to relate, something to be apart of, something to protect with their lives if necessary. When this type of community exist it can truly honor the individual human, or Spiritual Warrior. Through the Spiritual Warrior, healing works both ways, the individual heals the community and the community can then help heal the individual.

Organizational or Religious Rituals

4) Religious ceremonies are rituals that connect you with the divine. The intimacy with the divine is the spirit which flows through you as a result of the ritual. So the Religious Ritual is not just an elegant

procession of music and dance, that lifts the soul, but it is an intimate experience with spirit through words, song, Kulture or just divine feelings that connects or creates awareness between your Konsciousness to NTCHR. Belonging to an organization is how we are connected to the societies we reside. If you are Afrakan you should belong to some type of organization that is working towards the upliftment, and /or development of your people, mentally, physically or spiritually. What goes around comes around. If you do nothing to develop your people, your people will not develop, and any people who are not developing are dying. Many Afrakans in the world are embracing Western white European culture hoping to rescue themselves from the entrapment of white male domination. Only to become sicker, and insane just like a drug addict who thinks more drugs or different drugs will solve their problem. The illness of white male domination cannot be healed with pills or drugs or alcohol, or shopping at the mall, or being tranced out of your Afrakan mind in front of the TV screen, or surprisingly by making more money. For Afrakans without real Afrakan Rituals based upon Afrakan Kulture, there is only illness and more illusions waiting for you.

Spiritual Warriors are healers because they are living, walking examples of the best of their Kulture. They are spiritual beings directed by spirit. Their souls are at peace and they are giving their gifts and living by divine order which is Ma'at. Where there is no divine rituals, the soul runs out of its real nourishment, and then all kinds of social, emotional, economic, physiological and political problems ensue. As Spiritual Warriors, our only recommendation would be to embrace your own spiritual and physical Kulture. Only Kultural rituals can put Afrakans back in touch with their real soul. By bringing the spirit into our lives, we bring the Creator, NTCHR. Through NTCHR all things are possible, especially divine peace and happiness, Htp.

The road towards wellness is a road that leads to wholeness and both roads lead towards a spiritual ritualized life. This means first slowing down and learning how to breath so you can invoke the spirits or things spiritual into your life. This means embracing wholistic health and excellent physical conditioning of the sacred body-temple. This also means being able to pray out loud, and alone, being true to oneself. There are Spiritual Warriors that can help you on this journey, but at some point it will be just you and the Divine Creator. You will have to surrender to your higher self, and to your ancestral spirits, remember you are your ancestors, you are your people. So it becomes extremely important that your religion holds your Kulture in divine reverence. Because if your holy land is not in Afraka and you are Afrakan, you probably have the wrong religion. If your holy people, wisemen, and great sages, prophets, spiritual mentors, ancestors don't look like you, than you are in the wrong Kulture and the wrong religion. And on top of all that you are unconsciously insane, and disconnected from your people, ancestors and you're Kulturally, and spiritually dead. Ourstory rewards all research and it clearly shows that Islam, Judaism, Hinduism and Christianity are enemies to Afrakan people, Afrakan Kulture, and the spiritual reverence to Afrakan ancestors and their indigenous spiritual way of life. These religions are psychologically oppressive, anti-Black, anti-Afrakan Kulture, and anti the Afrakan Worldview. The healing that can liberate and empower you must feed your soul through spiritual rituals. Your spirituality or religion should be in alignment with your Kulture, which helps build positive self esteem. When there is alignment between your spirituality and Kulture, then your actions will be an example for your children and to our Afrakan spiritual and Kultural way of life. Your Kulture should inspire and empower tomorrows Afrakan children for eternity, Amen.

Nature or Ntchru Rituals

5) The study of astronomy and astrology are the study of the sciences that deal with the location, sizes, motions, and the celestial bodies influence on human affairs or rituals that occur repetitively. In ancient Kemet the flooding of the Hapy Eteru (Nile river) was a natural ritual that happened every year and the Kemetyu (the Black people) would have special ritual celebrations to align themselves with these spiritual and physical forces of nature. Humans have developed rituals around nature and the Ntchru for millenniums and it shows our spiritual connection with nature and our life giving environment. In many cases, our survival

depended on our keen observation of nature. Nature rituals sometimes dealt with food and medicine: the gathering, preserving or usage of foods and herbs. Some Nature rituals were developed around the change in seasons or the change in temperatures that may determine survival in certain areas during certain times of the year.

Spiritual Warriors must allow Nature rituals to direct your life towards your NTCHR given gift. Learn to start and end every day with prayer and praises to The NTCHR. All things of value are accomplished through the blessings of NTCHR. Every morning say a word or two, a small prayer to the ancestors, those that are here and those in our homeland Afraka. It is private and effective, for now those spirits will watch over you.

Some rituals of nature revolved around animals, others vegetation and some on the emotional pull of certain celestial energies like the sun, moon and various planets on the human body, and environment.

Nature and Ntchru rituals are the essence of spiritual worship among Afrakan people. The general philosophy expressed by Spiritual Warriors is that ritual should precede human involvement with the world and with each other. So planting begins with offering a sample of that which is going to be planted. In a way, the planting already happens at a divine level before happening physically. Afrakan rituals show the divine connection between the mental, physical and spiritual energies call the Ntchru.

Afrakan Spiritual Warriors teach that visible wrongs on the physical level have their roots in the spirit. To deal only with their visibility is like trimming the leaves of a weed when you mean to uproot it. Ritual is the mechanism that uproots these dysfunctions. It offers a realm in which the unseen part of nature or the dysfunction is worked on in ways that affect the seen.

The only place where abundance is warranted is in nature. Humans who wastes are people who insult nature, Ntchru and The NTCHR. In the Afrakan world view, the land belongs to everyone and could not be owned or hoarded for selfish personal use. If nature was good to you this season you shared with those less fortunate, this is the Afrakan law of reciprocity. There cannot be a giver who does not receive. There cannot be a receiver who does not give.

Kemklusion

Ritual is the prerequisite to all things, mentally, physically, and spiritually. The European Caucasian and the Arabs, as conquerors, have deprived Afrakans of the right to call on their Creator in a language of their own Kultural creation and in an image of their own Kultural Afrakan self. Spiritual Warriors must lead in our Re-Afrakanization by example. The more ritualized our space the more ritualized our lives. The more ritualized our lives the closer you are to innerstanding your life's purpose. As a Spiritual Warrior, I am suggesting that our homes reflect our Afrakan Kulture if you are of Afrakan descent. And that every home must have a sacred ritual space with a shrine dedicated to the family and great Afrakan ancestors, the elements of nature, and your sacred spiritual principles like the sun, moon and various planets that effect the human body, and environment. Each Afrakan home should also have a sacred Afrakan Drum. The Afrakan drum connects us to the rhythm of the universe, which is in rhythm with The NTCHR. Every community that has a large Afrakan population should have a Kultural space for community rituals. If a Kultural space does not exist as a Spiritual Warrior, your job is to create one. All those who are in the act of becoming Spiritual Warriors, must discipline your lives first and lead by example. Afrakanize your personal name, and your family name. Afrakanize yourself by becoming as natural and as Afrakan-centered as possible, from a natural hair style to the clothes you wear, to the Afrakan artwork in your home, to the books you buy and read. Only through the spirit of the heart can we manifest the Moyo. And the Moyo will be the spiritual power that will help us return Afrakan people to their traditional greatness and will save this planet. Rituals are our servants and not our masters. We must use them to serve the needs of humanity and not be enslaved by them.

Spiritual Warriors must use the power of discipline to Kemtrol and control the breath, your focus, and your posture. With this kind of discipline the Spiritual Warrior can devote time, energy, money or personal resources to attain the gifts and knowledge needed to complete your purpose. Kultural rituals are your riches resource for life-giving information. Afrakan Numerology is an example of some of the Kultural rituals that can be incorporated into our lives:

Dagara Cosmology

The Dagara people of West Afraka have devised a system for recalling your life's purpose based upon connecting the elements with the last number of your birth year (Example, born in 1970 would make you an earth person).

Earth (Last number of the birth year is 0 or 5) - The earth person loves the world and earth. Earth people are nurturers who want everyone to feel fed, content, respected, and loved. Earth people can't stand the sight of scarcity; they would give away everything they have before giving anything to themselves. Making others feel good, makes them feel good. The earth person takes care of other people spiritually, materially, and emotionally. They can empower others. They feel responsible for our groundedness, our sense of identity and our ability to nurture and support one another. Earth deals with comfort.

Mineral (Last number of the birth year is 4 or 9) - Mineral people are storytellers, fascinated with myth, tradition, and rituals, versed in dealing with metaphors and symbols. They constantly remind us in stories, proverbs, songs, and poems the deep healing person's love for argument, for different ways of saying the same thing, and for the eloquent ways of saying nothing can baffle the non-mineral person. A mineral person is extroverted, and they almost always have a point. The gift they present to society is an ability to help us to remember our origins and purpose, give us the means to communicate and make sense out of what others are saying. They remind people of things they forget. Mineral people are socially easy to connect with.

Water (Last number of the birth year is 1 or 6) - The water person is slow, shows great innerstanding, and is eager to make things work for the greatest good. He or she perceives the world in terms of possibilities. The water person thinks of the community relationship, love and harmony. Peace, focus, wisdom and reconciliation are the characteristics of water. Water people are peace makers.

Nature (Last number in the birth year is 3 or 8) The nature person is a person with great power to adjust, to change shape and shift. They are witches, magicians

and tricksters. Nature challenge people to be real. A nature person is like a child who loves to play and sees life as a challenging play. Nature people also help us to go through major changes and life threatening situations. Nature brings change, magic and laughter into our lives.

Fire (last number in the birth year is 2 or 7) The fire person is someone who does not fit well within their Kulture. This person is viewed as eccentric. Fire people have a strong connection to ancestors and spirit, and are a gateway between this world and the spirit world. Shamans fit into this category. A fire person has powerful dreams, innerstands dream imagery and can translate and interpret dream images to people. Fire people also live in the future, and therefore find the average person too slow. A fire person cannot stay idle. The fire person exhibits a great deal of emotions. His or her fire can be translated into a warm, gentle flame that keeps a whole community aware of its vital relationship to other worlds. Fire people keep our connection to the self, the ancestors and keep our visions alive. Fire is our ability to act, emote and intuit.

All Afrakan healers and Spiritual Warriors, who remember our powerful Afrakan ancestral rituals from the Dagara, Dogon, Akan, Yoruba, Masi, Makonde, Zulu, ancient Chaldean and ancient Kemet, and the list could go on, because the content of Afraka is rich in spiritual Kultural expressions and these rich Kultural expression that are manifestations of Ma'at must be used in our lives and we must celebrate our life in it's highest mental, physical and spiritual form. Only this state of impeccability should be the yardstick by which our lives and their relationships should be measured, in a life-giving and life-sustaining way. DUWA!

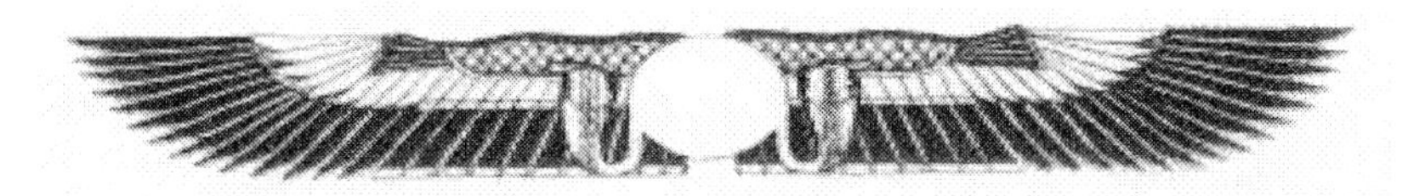

KEMET

Kemet was the great country of the Blacks
Standing in front of Heru em Ackhet (the great Sphinx)
Looking south
In the direction from whence my ancient ancestors came
Somewhat mesmerized from the awesome power of Hapy
Reflections from timeless tombs and temples
Completely blanketed by blackness
That twinkle star light messages not yet decoded by modern man
I smile to myself
Thinking how glorious are the wonders of the world

Only a people from the sun
Enriched and inspired by the sun
Could have created the temples of the sun
Reflecting truth, wisdom, knowledge and innerstanding
Through the esoteric symbols of nature
So precisely, yet so simple
That they reveal the forces that aid in the control of the Universe.

For the forces that govern the heavens outside the temples
Also govern the heavens within the temples of humans
Blackness and Melanin are synonymous
Afrakan and Blackness are synonymous
Afraka was the birthplace of Melanin and Humanity
Afraka was the seeds and the fruits of High Kulture in the world
So it was in the beginning
Now we shall return
Black and Beautiful
Amen Ra

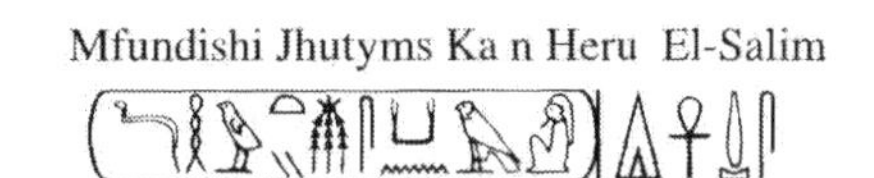

Chapter IIIIIIII (8)
Somo la Nane

Kulture and Re-Afrakanization

From Culture to Kulture

Culture as defined by European Caucasians and European Americans Caucasians, is the whole behavior and technology of the dominate people that is passed on from generation to generation; the acquired ability of a people to recognize and appreciate generally accepted esthetic and intellectual excellence for control and power. The dominate European Caucasian society expects all other ethnic groups, from all other countries to conform to their standard of "beauty", "excellence", and "control". Culture to European Caucasians is something that they feel they must ***give*** to the world, and not something that the rest of the world already has, and this is also how you control the world.

European Caucasian culture is to maintain European Caucasian nationalism, and European Caucasian nationalism means cultural imperialism and the destruction of all other cultures. The nature of European Caucasian culture is inherently expansionism in the form of imperial and colonial domination. European Caucasian-centered is not only different from Afrakan-centeredness, but it is the very opposite. We believe in Ma'at, and the harmonious order of the universe. The Afrakan-centered Worldview is predicated on Ma'at and a harmonious interrelationship with nature. The Afrakan Worldview encomposses the ancestors, the living and the not yet born, all living in harmony within the infinte now. They, the Wazungu, say they want peace also, but peace to them is rational order void of feelings, spirit, and intuition. Wazungu order means European Caucasian control, which also means it opposes harmonious organic order and must replace it with a rationale, technical and mechanical order, that they, the collective European Caucasians or Wazungu must control. Therefore, in order for white supremacy to exist, it must systematically destroy positive self-images of Afrakans and any other culture other than European culture, the foundation of European Caucasian domination.

The European Caucasian culture in the United States was set up to develop the Wazungu self-image (the collective Caucasian ethnic groups of Europe or western Asia, Australia, and Caucasian South Africans etc.). Moreover, this self-image is based on the white male personality. Let us take a closer look at the Caucasian male, these are the traits their culture wants to produce: aggressive, assertive, competitive, dominate, independent, ambitious, forceful, non-spiritual, but self-reliant. All their leaders, C.E.O's and breadwinners must follow this path. The female personality was supposed to be warm, sensitive, loyal, affectionate, gentle, understanding, compassionate, and loving towards children. They did not even want their women to be spiritual; remember the European Caucasain "Witch hunts" in the colonies and the millions of women murdered and destroyed in Europe by the Christian Church.

The European Caucasian culture distrusts any form of spiritualism and humanism in the Afrakan Kulture because they cannot control it, or define it. Afrakan rituals scare them and make them feel inadequate and incomplete. Therefore, they have given us their fears, and we now fear our own personal power and spiritual essence. The western world is based on psychological individualism and cosmic disorder. Moreover, they take pride in them-selves for the despiritualiztion of the western world, and all the countries they politically control. European Caucasain power is based on the ability to manipulate and control (colonization). Since all spirituality conflicts with Wazungu concepts of power, the possibility of spirit threatens its achievement; European Caucasians' success depends on the destruction of all other spiritual Kultures especially Afrakan, the very foundation of all spiritual Kultural centers around the world.

Capitalism is the economical system that supports their culture, and capitalism is exploitative in principle. It must forever seek new markets to control, and new resources to exploit. It can never be a system at rest or at peace. Now, it becomes clear why Rome was always at war or the sun never set on the British Empire, and you can see why the western world like, Germany, Russia, America must be in a war or conflict to feed this capitalistic monster.

European Caucasian culture can never be self reliant, it must control or exploit someone else for its wealth or life-force, like cancer, it needs a host... Without "others", there is no possibility of Caucasian European power. Europe itself is barren, depending on the natural resources, creative talent, and spiritual wealth of others for its existence. Europe, America or any of the other predominately Caucasian male dominated countries would destroy each other if there were no Afrakans and other unorganized cultures to exploit or prey on, this is their nature, study their history in Europe.

Think about this European American Caucasian culture, if you go to school in America you will be programmed from a Caucasian male European American middle class, Judaic, Christian, value system and cultural perspective. All of our public education through primary, secondary and "higher" education is predicated on European Caucasian standards. Even your intelligence is evaluated according to a European American Caucasian I.Q. Test, which is a European American Caucasian culture test. In America, the majority people of the world are told they are minorities, like Chinese 26%, Indian 20% and Afrakans 15%. When in reality all these people have greater populations than all the white people on the planet 8%. All of these people are taught or trained to operate from a European American Caucasian male Worldview, if they want to be successful working in the western world. While working for a capitalist U.S. American Institute, everyone would be automatically expected to wear European suits and ties, European dresses or slacks. The culture of European Caucasians automatically harnesses and suppresses other cultures. Caucasian European culture fears and destroys before it tries to understand other Kultures. White male domination feels it must control the situation. The cultures of the Chinese, Indian and Afrakan are much more complex and refined at their best, than the American Caucasian and older than the foundation of European Caucasian culture, like the Greeks, Romans and Brits of antiquity, which is the foundation of European Caucasian civilization. Afrakan Kulture was ancient, in harmony with nature and science before western European Caucasian culture was born. They really fear and hate Black Afrakan Kulture, which they associate with spiritual power, a power that they can neither possess, create, nor control. Therefore, the Wazungu created racism. Prejudice and racism is normal business in Amerikkka, nothing personal. This is an example of culture in America. Now, I think you innerstand why we as Afrakans must move from culture to Kulture. We are in America, but we do not have to accept the mentality of the American Caucasian culture in order to be successful. European Jews and Indians from India have proven that you can have a different culture and different values and still be successful in America. They have become a nation within a nation within the matrix of European Caucasian domination.

Afrakans who live in the modern world should know who the Europeans are culturally, and we should innerstand their history, so that we can innerstand the nature of their value system and their collective world-view. Ourstory rewards all research, and it clearly shows that the Afrakans, Melanin dominated human beings and Caucasian Europeans, Melaninated deficient humankind life-forms are, by nature, different. Our values and Worldview are not only different, but also diabolically opposed. Afrakans see and feel everything from the spirit first. The Afrakan Worldview is spiritual and they believe spirit is in all things and all things are inter-connected and part of the One. Through humanity an expression of Ma'at, we have the potential to ultimately live in harmony within the cosmos. The Caucasian European world is anti-spirit, and emotionally impoverished, void of humanity. The European Worldview is "Them" versus "All Others". Therefore, to Caucasian Europeans everyone else is the enemy and therefore threatening. They have spread their culture through Caucasian male domination, racism and genocide, and because we were ignorant of their culture and nature they have been successful in destroying Afrakans and other melaninated people in Afraka, the Americas, the Caribbean Islands, Australia, Tasmania, New Zealand, and every place they have conquered. The Arabs have employed the same philosophy of Afrakan genocide in North Afraka, hiding behind the banner of Islam, but it is Kultural genocide, and the theft of Afrakan land. The lessons that must be mastered here, are whenever you surrender your

Kulture, and spiritual ancestral connection you are destroying the very roots of your people. And a people without strong roots will destroy themselves, even when the enemy is not physically present, because you become the enemy when you embrace the enemy's culture.

Spiritual Warriors must re-stress the importance of Kulture to Afrakan people. It is the first medicine we should take when under attack by any foreign entity. The best of our Afrakan ancestral spirits are waiting within the rituals of traditional Afrakan Kulture to help us. Within the ancestral memory lies unlimited, preserved treasures of the knowledge and wisdom of your own ancestral story and Kultural traditions. Afrakan-centered elders are our Kultural custodians whom guide, build, and maintain families, communities, and the Kultural institutions that direct the desires, aspirations, education, foods, clothes, knowledge and life-style of a people. Without esteem Afrakan-centered elders, Afrakan people are doomed.

After knowledge of self, we innerstand that we are an Afrakan people, and then you learn the culture and history of your enemies, so that you can be clear about their nature and possibilities. As Kemetyu, Melaninated human beings, whose ancestors come from Afraka, we must be clear on who our enemies are and who our friends are. Our new Afrakan-centered Kulture teaches us that the Caucasian Europeans under the banner of Christianity and White male domination, and the Arabs, under the banner of Islam and all people who embrace capitalism, like the Japanese are all our enemies. Our first friends must be ourselves, the complete Pan-Afrakan world; we cannot look at ourselves as individual Afrakans. Afrakan Kultural heritage is one of the strongest links Afrakans have between the ancestors and the living generations of Afrakans today in Afraka and throughout the Diaspora.

Afrakans in America are operating from a clueless information bank when it comes to our own Afrakan Kultural Ourstorical Ancestral Memory. Part of the problem is that many Afrakans are still traumatized from the many horrific atrocities and cruelties from the Maangamizi. The Maangamizi is the deliberate destruction and enslavement of Afrakans by Caucasian Europeans and Arabs. This destruction was like several atomic bombs ripping Afraka apart, thus the destruction of the basic family unit, destroying our Afrakan Kultural and our Ourstorical ancestral memory. We are one of the few ethnic groups that send our children to our oppressors or enemy for education, without Kultural institutions in place to supplement what they will not learn in the public mis-educational school system. We have surrendered ourselves and our children's minds to the wolves. It is like sheep sending their calves off to wolf school, and then wondering why the wolves are getting fat, and your community is getting poorer and poorer. When the children of the oppressed have as their greatest aspirations, to be like the oppressor, we know that these children have received the wrong type of education, and we can begin to innerstand why some of our children are destroying themselves and each other. They have received the wolf education, only they are the sheep. The tragedy here is that these sheep will lead their fellow sheep and love ones to the slaughterhouse in the name of progress, better education, patriotism and the American way.

"A child does not give birth to itself" Afrakan proverb.

Families teach a people who they are, not only by their Kultural custodians, but also by everyday actions and activity in their human experience within that society. Children (Watoto) learn by watching our actions or lack of action, more than by listening to what we say, so the redevelopment of strong Afrakan families are the foundation of the watoto and wanafunzi long before they enter an Afrakan-centered school.

Spiritual Warriors must take total control of the education of our Afrakan children, mentally, physically and spiritually. We must develop Afrakan-centered educational boot camps to re-Afrakanize Afrakan children who are lost beyond the Afrakan-centered educational school system. Today, urban Afrakan children are being destroyed by a criminal, mis-educational system, which teaches about the negativity of Afrakans in the European American society, by the mass media, like TV, movies, magazines, billboards, newspapers, and other advertisements. Actions have always been more powerful than words. New Afrakans will have to master the control of their own images and actions by controlling our own media, and the very communities that we live in if we are to re-Afrakanize ourselves, our families and our children, to create a positive Afrakan future.

Spiritual Warriors will also have to de-program the general Afrakan population in Amerikkka, so they will be Konscious of subliminal racists advertisement, anti-health advertisement, anti-Ma'at advertisement and pro-capitalist advertisement.

Afrakan-centered education, developed, financed, defended and spiritually operated by Spiritual Warriors is a critical key to Afrakan peoples salvation, sovereignty and Nationship. We need to develop all male and all female re-Afrakanization centers. These re-Afrakanization centers must be in a rural, country setting, so that we can get reconnected with nature again. We, as Afrakan people have lost our way. And the first step towards finding your way is to admit that we are lost. Our glorious and dynamic legacy of who we were, will help us innerstand who we are. Once we have a human map, which is a positive Afrakan-centered curriculum, with excellent teachers, and committed families, we can find our way back to a positive reality for Afrakan people. Men will have to learn from other Spiritual Warriors who are men, and women will have to learn from other Spiritual Warriors who are women, on how to innerstand Ourstory. And together, how to innerstand our relationship with Spirituality, our relationship with nature, our relationships with ourselves and our own sexuality, and our responsibility to Afrakan families, the community and the Afrakan nation. We have the expertise, the problem is their are no operational agendas in place on a large scale. The International Afrakan-centered planning board of CIBI, Council of Independent Black Institutions, is a living example of what needs to happen throughout the Pan-Afrakan-centered world.

All classes are centered around the develoment of self, in relastionship to Afraka. We must make our parents and families great again.

How We Define Afrikan-Centered Education:
A Position Statement

CIBI defines Afrikan-centered education as the means by which Afrikan Kulture - including the knowledge, attitudes, values and skills needed to maintain and perpetuate it throughout the nationbuilding process - is developed and advanced through practice. Its aim, therefore, is to build commitment and competency within present and future generations to support the struggle for liberation and nationhood. We define nationbuilding as the conscious and focused application of our people's collective resources, energies, and knowledge to the task of liberating and developing the psychic and physical space that we identify as ours. Nationbuilding encompasses both the reconstruction of Afrikan Kulture and the development of a progressive and sovereign state structure consistent with that Kulture.

We, in CIBI, further believe, that in practice, Afrikan-centered education:

1. **acknowledges Afrikan spirituality as an essential aspect of our uniqueness as a people and makes it an instrument of our liberation;**

2. **facilitates participation in the affairs of nations and defining (or redefining) reality on our own terms, in our own time and in our own interests;**

3. **prepares Afrikans "for self-reliance, nation maintenance, and nation management in every regard";**

4. **emphasizes the fundamental relationship between the strength of our families and the strength of our nation;**

5. **ensures that the historic role and function of the customs, traditions, rituals and ceremonies - that have protected and preserved our Kulture; facilitated our spiritual expression; ensured harmony in our social relations; prepared our people to meet their responsibilities as adult members of our Kulture; and sustained the continuity of Afrikan life over successive generations - are understood and made relevant to the challenges that confront us in our time;**

6. **emphasizes that Afrikan identity is embedded in the continuity of Afrikan Kulture history and that Afrikan Kultural history represents a distinct reality continually evolving from the experiences of all**

Afrikan people wherever they are and have been on the planet across time and generations;

7. **focuses on the "knowledge and discovery of historical truths; through comparison; hypothesizing and testing through debate, trial, and application; through analysis and synthesis; through creative and critical thinking; through problem resolution processes; and through final evaluation and decision making";**

8. **can only be systematically facilitated by people who themselves are consciously engaged in the process of Afrikan-centered personal transformation;**

9. **is a process dependent upon human perception and interpretation. Thus, it follows that a curriculum can not be Afrikan-centered independent of our capacity to perceive and interpret it in an Afrikan-centered manner;**

10. **embraces the traditional wisdom that "children are the reward of life" and it is, therefore, an expression of our unconditional love for them. In order to best serve Afrikan children our methods must reflect the best understandings that we have of how they develop and learn biologically, spiritually and Kulturally.**

(adopted 11 November 1994)

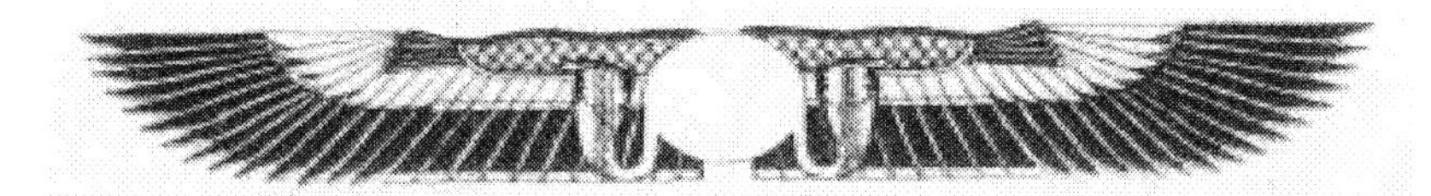

The future of the Afrakan world; re-Afrakanization and Nationbuilding is in the hands of Spiritual Warriors. These Afrakan Spiritual Warriors must reproduce themselves while giving their gifts to the Afrakan community, nation and the world. The Afrakan-centered Pan-Afrakan Worldview expressed through Ma'at is the spiritual center that is expressed in every aspect of our lives in relation to Nationbuilding.

The Spiritual Warrior innerstands that the family in all instances will be the central and most important factor in developing and maintaining Nationship. For this reason the family's involvement in Kupigana Ngumi for mental, physical and spiritual defense; Afrakan-centered re-education, Kultural re-Afrakanization and Afrakan-centered spirituality are critical.

Afrakan families must give birth to a new awareness and commitment to the goals of the Afrakan-centered Pan-Afrakan Worldview. Spiritual Warriors innerstand that the spirit is comprehensive and thorough, but it takes Kulturally committed, impeccable, competent, and confident Spiritual Warriors, who are uncompromising to lead Afrakan people to a spiritual and Kultural re-Afrakanization and Nationbuilding.

One of the many problems facing Afrakan people in the 21st century western time is that we are upset, mad, angry, insane, embarrassed and totally confused about where we are and who we are. The Spiritual Warrior teachings of the Kemet shrine of Jhuty Heru Neb-Hu, teaches us, ***do not look where you fell, but where you slipped*** if you are to correct a bad situation. We know that your Kulture is your life-line. Once you are cut off from your life-line, you are already doomed, destined for destruction and failure unless you can retrieve your life-line. When the sun is behind you, it caste a shadow in front of you. If we embrace the light of our past, the Ra of our glorious Kulture, it will take us far into the present. Just like the greatness of Afrakan Kulture in ancient Kemet was responsible for the flowering of Afrakan civilization. We, the Afrakans who have fallen, must re-Afrakanize ourselves through a new, yet ancient Afrakan Kulture based upon tradition and reason with the spirit of Ma'at.

Left: Hemet Ntchrt Seshatms Ma'atnefert El-Salim, center, Queen Afua / Mut Nebt-Het, and Mfundishi Jhutyms Ka n Heru El-Salim, Spiritual Warriors of the Kemet Legacy, and Healing Arts.

When a thorn gets into your toe, and European Caucasian domination is surely a thorn in the Afrakan toe, the whole body bends to get it out! The whole Pan-Afrakan community will have to bend together and remove Caucasian male domination, racism and capitalism from the Afrakan toe. **This process is Pan-Afrakan operational unity now or perish!** Spiritual Warriors must prepare Afrakan people to be reborn. The Birthing process itself is not beautiful, in fact, it is messy, but the outcome is magnificent and beautiful. Birth is a painful process but there is no progress without struggle. However, be aware of the progress trap. Caucasian male domination tells us we need more of what they have, European-American validation (European Caucasian culture), in order to make progress. Moreover, what they have (European Caucasian culture), is not just our problem, but also its the world's problem. Spiritual Konsciousness dispels the need for more European-American validation. Pan-Afrakanism must also be based on Spiritual Konsciousness, not imitating the Wazungu in Blackface.

Ancient Afrakan Spiritual Warriors viewed themselves as a divine part of the universe, and the universe is only a small part of The NTCHR, which expands far beyond our comprehension. In addition, all this is spiritual and divine. Therefore, Afrakans, Black humans, the original Melaninated humans were part of that divinity, and we are the parents of all other humans on earth. The Kemetyu (Black humans) saw themselves as eternal like the universe, and spiritual like the Ntchru. This was the foundation of the ancient Kemet Worldview and thought pattern that was basic to almost all indigenous Afrakan Kultures on the continent of Afraka, from Kemet in North Afraka, to the Zulus in South Afraka, we are divine!

A powerful Afrakan Kulture was the core of real identity and Nationship in antiquity and it must be at the core of our recovery now as we, the Pan-Afrakan community, the modern Kemetyu embark on the 21st century western time. We cannot survive as a whole people, if we continue to allow Europeans, or Caucasian European Americans, Melanin deficient humankind, especially our former enslavers and colonial oppressors to mis-educate, employ, feed, house, and care for our total well being, mentally, physically and spiritually. Ourstory and history clearly shows that they, the European Caucasians and Caucasian Americans collectively, have never helped Afrakans collectively. The testimony of history is that European Caucasians brought the worst that civilization could offer to Afraka and to Afrakans. The European and American Worldview and value system has meant and continues to mean death, enslavement, and Kultural destruction to Afrakan people. The European Caucasian and the European colonist called Americans and their system of capitalism is anti-spiritual, abstract, cold, materialistic, and promotes an individualistic value system that cannot liberate Afrakan people. If we are to heal as Afrakan people, we have to innerstand what is good for us and what is bad for us. It is unquestionable that the Indo-European culture and value system equal genocide for Afrakans, and all melaninted people.

War is one of the primary contributions of the Indo- European to contemporary world culture and civilization. It is the nature of the European Caucasian to take and destroy. Ourstory and collective ancestral memory will show that they fought, not only to defeat and subjugate their enemies, but also to terrorize their victims into devout obedience, or just total annihilation. In the Afrakan Worldview, you have to do something to us or threaten our existence to be our enemy. In the European Caucasian Worldview, anybody not European Caucasian is their enemy. Also, any culture that has something of value, that the Caucasian man can use, like rich land, natural resources, gold or other mineral wealth, puts it in jeopardy of becoming the Caucasian Europeans enemy. Look at Australia, Tasmania, the Caribbean Islands, South America, North America, and Afraka. None of these people considered themselves the enemy of European Caucasians, none of them attacked European Caucasians or Europe, none of them threatened European security, but they were all destroyed, or enslaved by European Caucasians.

It is ironic that Afrakans and Indians, with their great ancient Kultures, and with their great contribution to civilization, science, art, and human spirituality, now sit at the feet of Caucasian European cultures, begging for western validation or stamp of approval. Western culture, which is historically reckless and morally undisciplined, is posing as the cultural model for the world. Now, Caucasian males are teaching *us, the original humans,* lessons on life, success, family, nature, happiness and responsibility.

A Spiritual Warrior's inventory of the major contributions of the Wazungu, the collective European Caucasians to world culture are as follows: 1) Warfare and extreme and aberrant aggression, to take just because you can, and because you desire the possessions of others; 2) Racism and segregation based on color, with white on top and black on the bottom; 3) The subjugation, disdain, inferiority, and impurity of women; 4) The absence of respect and innerstanding of the planet Earth and its ecosystem; 5) The use of religion to subjugate, and enslave the body, souls and minds of people; 6) The distortion of his-story and the devaluation of everyone else's story, undermining their cultures. To the European Caucasian, history is the lie agreed upon by the ruling power; Ma'at to the Wazungu and Asiatics is an irrelevant concept; and 7) The creation of money so that they can dictate and control the wealth of the world. The irony here is that the Caucasian European and European American colonist are proud of these accomplishments, and are prepared to defend what they have stolen, or destroyed in the name of white male domination. 64.6% of the American gross national product goes into wars and the manufacturing of weapons. And in Caucasian countries like Australia and Israel, it's over 70%, only to name a few, because this is the norm among Caucasian European countries of the western world.

One of the best ways to heal and liberate Afrakan people is with a new Afrakan Kulture based upon the best of Afrakan tradition, and a Pan-Afrakan Spiritual Worldview. Afrakan tradition has to be combined with reason so that we have the correct direction on the map of humanity, and this new map of humanity will lead us towards and down the path to healing and recovery so that we can redevelop our Afrakan spirituality and become human, and humane as we become harmonious with the life-giving and life-sustaining force of the planet Earth.

Afrakan Kulture is the totality of values, beliefs, behavioral patterns, symbols, institutions, languages, Ourstory and actions that characterize Afrakan people, echoing from our ancestral collective memory and that defines Afrakan people. Everything that Afrakan peoples do is related to their Kulture, or lack of innerstanding of their Kulture. Afrakan Kulture must be utilized as an instrument of liberation for Afrakan people in the 63rd century, new Afrakan time, as we re-Afrakanize ourselves, by redefining ourselves. The new Afrakan Worldview that will liberate us has its foundation in Afrakan Kulture, which would also include a Pan-Afrakan standard of beauty, Afrakan truth based upon Ma'at and traditions and rituals that define the Afrakan reality. Afrakan Kulture is a composite of socially and Ourstorically determined behaviors handed down by way of our collective ancestral memory that will nourish Afrakan people and thereby define their unlimited intellectual and spiritual capacity to innerstand everything in the cosmos as The NTCHR.

Afrakan Beauty

Beauty has form, feeling and Kultural significance
Like Afraka
Black, strong, magical, and infinitely wise
Real beauty can never be denied
Like nappy hair
Always trying to return to its original form
Natural and uncontrollably divine
All the way to the mind
There lies the real beauty, in the mind
Which is transmitted by the soul
The beauty of the soul is manifested through self
The beauty of the self is manifested through knowledge
The beauty of knowledge is manifested through wisdom
The beauty of all wisdom is divine positive action
Positive action is the key to innerstanding
And only through the innerstanding of Ourstory and Kulture
Can you see yourself, your real self
The source of all personal beauty
You Black, gorgeous, dynamic melaninted creatures you!

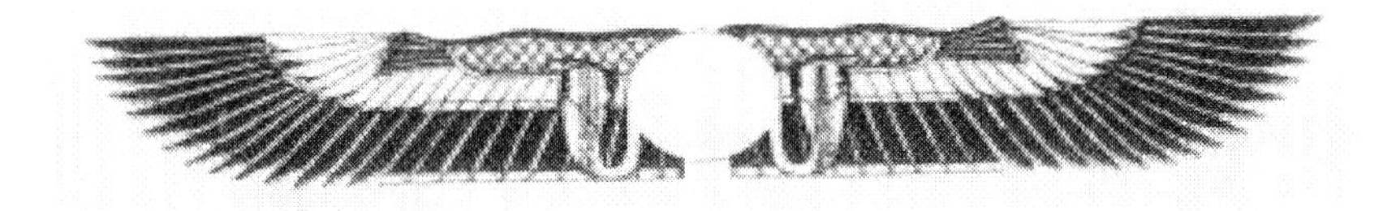

Sankofa and Afrakan Kulture

Sankofa plays a very important part in Afrakan Kulture for new Afrakans of the 63 rd century new Afrakan time. The knowledge from our Ourstorical past and collective ancestral memory banks will provide the binding information that keeps us Kulturally informed and prepared for the future. Our Afrakan Kulture will show us how the modalities such as languages, rituals, art, icons and symbols serve to facilitate the group to Afrakan Konsciousness, and a new and powerful social order. Ourstory rewards all research, and if we analyze Ourstory and learn of our great civilizations, and the spirituality that gave Afrakans their spiritual center, we will clearly see that this was the foundation for world civilization.

Sankofa allows us to retrieve this greatness, the best of our spirits, and bring them to the future. We must rescue, re-cover, re-construct, re-establish, and re-connect ourselves to the spirit of the best Afrakan Ancestors and the gifts they gave to the world. We must use this spirit to give birth to the new Pan-Afrakan Worldview and new Afrakan Kulture that will lead us out of the chaos of Caucasian male European domination. Without a Pan-Afrakan Worldview, Afrakan history and social science is almost irrelevant. Our Pan-Afrakan Worldview must embrace an Afrakan-centered Kulture and values, based on the best of Afrakan heritage, our classical language, the Mdw Ntchr and our cosmological and spiritual systems as taught by our Afrakan Deep Thinkers, Sages, and Spiritual Warriors from Kemet, Kash, and the best of our great Afrakan educational centers throughout the Diaspora. The more spiritual we become, the more we innerstand and practice our Afrakan Kulture. The more economically, psychologically, socially and politically distanced we become from the culture and center of European American civilization, ***the greater and more productive we will become, as Pan-Afrakan people world-wide.***

Spiritual Warriors must be at the foundation and in a leadership role as custodians of the new Afrakan peoples' Kulture. The Spiritual Warrior must bring enthusiasm, conviction, and ideological clarity, moral integrity and courage, as well as spiritual insight and knowledge, to the liberation struggle in the re-Afrakanization of our minds and souls. Spiritual Warriors are the keepers of rituals that maintain the Kulture and that connect us Konsciously to spirit. Spiritual Warriors are entrusted with the task of inculcating the essential values of Afrakan Kulture, and thereby guaranteeing its continuation. Sankofa will be one of the tools of liberation for all Afrakan Spiritual Warriors of the 63rd century new Afrakan time. Sankofa will help Afrakans innerstand the farther back we look, the further forward we as Afrakan people will be able to see. Sankofa will help Afrakans innerstand and appreciate the power of spirit. Spirit is the foundation of everything. Spirit is the path to NTCHR, and all relationships are related to NTCHR, especially among Afrakans in the Pan-Afrakan Black Kultural world.

Mfundishi at Black Gold in New Jersey. Afrakan Spiritual Warriors must be Kultural custodians for Afrakan people.

Mfundishi Jhutyms Ka - en - Heru returning to the source of our greatness, and recharging his crystal wand at the Step Mer-Khut of Heru Netcherekhet .
SANKOFA
Go back and retrieve your valuables, so you can go forward into the future.
Below
UserMa'atRa MeryAmen holding a power staff and UserMa'atRa Setep en Ra wearing his War Crown with the Heqa - Rulership staff.

BLACK GOLD
KERA JHUTY HERU NEB HU
KULTURAL ETHNIC GROUPINGS

Worldview	Afrakan	Asian	European
	(Entire Afrakan Continent and Indigenous peoples of color: Native Americans, aborigines of the South Pacific Islands) Black and brown people of Afraka.	(Central & Eastern Asian). The yellow and brown people of Asia.	(Western-Asian/ Euro-American). The white people of Eurasia and their descendants.
Axiology (The study of values, symbols, rhythms)	Higher value lies in the interpersonal relationship between people and NTCHR and Ntchru.	The highest value lies in the cohesiveness of the group.	The highest value lies in the object or in the acquisition of the object.
Epistemology (The study of how you know knowledge)	Affective Spirituality One knows through symbolic imagery and rhythm by being in a state of Being connected to the NTCHR.	Conative One knows through striving towards the transcendence.	Cognitive One knows through counting and measuring.
Logic (Reasoning)	Diunital The union of complements. Reasoning is based upon its nature.	Nyaya The objective world is conceived independent of thought and mind.	Dichotomous Either / or If one has the power to do it, the end justifies the means.
Process (How you use your knowledge)	Ntuology All sets are interrelated through human and spiritual networks.	Cosmology All sets are independently interrlated in the harmony of the universe.	Technology All sets are repeatable and reproducible.
Male-Female Relationships	Woman-man relationship to total environment.	Woman-man relationship to group.	Woman-man relationship to object of possession.
Ruler	The ruler is governed by Ma'at and the Keeper of harmony.	The ruler acts on behalf of the Divine Power - Ma'at not the most valuable law. But the end result justifies all actions and the right to control.	The ruler uses destruction and force to rule. Thier military is used to take other's land, natural resources and anything they desire. And the same militaryis used to protect what they have taken. Ma'at is an irrelevant concept.
Creator (How you define your knowledge source of the Creator)	NTCHR (The All) Creator The Self-Created Konscious mind that is the All, the Spirit of the Universe. Ma'at is the foundation of all things and all things are governed by Ma'at, and Creation is still coming into being.	Budda/ Allah/ Brahma/ Krishna/ Creator The Creator is worshiped as an entity beyond and outside the self.	God Judaism/ Christainity God is a jealous and vengeful god. End result justifies the means. He created the universe in six days, and then rested. Ma'at is an irrelevant concept.

Workshops available on "Kultural Ethnic Groupings"
Website: http://www.BlackGoldSacredLiving.com

SANKOFA!

I Afrakan, the original Melaninated human
Parents of civilization
Guardians of the truth
Sacred messengers of the Creator
Inventor of divine math
We are the ones who brought science into innerstanding so that we could comprehend ourselves in relationship to nature
SANKOFA! SANKOOOFAAA!

We, who plotted the stars before human-kind learned to speak
We, designed the Blackness in-between star lights, the essence by which light can be comprehended
So is above, so is below
Only positive action, through Ma'at is the way to go
The Universe and the Innerverse are reflections of the same verse, which exist within the Afrakan verse simultaneously as we converse
Konscious and unconscious Afrakans everywhere, wake up! And seize the moment!
Clear your head of this western nightmare
Pan-Afrakanism or none-existence!
Our ancient Afrakan ancestors created rituals that demand that we give, what we hope to receive.
Deliver your gift, live your mission, be true to your purpose
SANKOFA!

It is not a taboo, or the wrong thing to do
When you go back, to retrieve what you have forgotten
When the sun is behind you, it caste a shadow in front of you
If we embrace our glorious Afrakan past, it will take us far into the present.

The greatest of the ancient Afrakan ancestors are waiting to assist you with your great gifts, and to give you your Kultural tools and your Universal memory.
BUT, YOU MUST TAKE IT!
SANKOFA! SANKOOOFAAA!

Spiritual Warriors must teach us to go beyond the pain, the anger, the self pity, the embarrassment, the denial and deal with the problem directly.
Become Heru, your own hero or shero.
Intelligent, direct positive Action through unity is the only proper solution.
When a thorn gets into your toe, the hole body bends to get it out! Get the western world out of your hair, house, bed, off your back and out of your mind!
Let's move now Brothers-Sisters before we loose the whole foot.
Do not look where you fell, but where you slipped.
You are not the problem, its what you have become.
Your problem is what you have embraced - Wazungu culture
So you have become your enemy.
Before you were your enemy you were Afrakans, Black.
Before you were unconscious, you were Konscious. Creators.
Before you were at war with nature, you were in harmony with nature. Followers of "The Way".
Before you were anti-spiritual, you were spiritual.
Before you were African-americans, you were Afrakan.
Go back and fitch your mind, your soul, your ancient spirit. your collective ancestral memory.
SANKOFA!

Because, Afrakans everywhere, we are at war
For the liberation of our minds, Our families, Ourstory,
Our dreams, Our Blackness, Our Continent.
Our existence as Afrakans and life as we know it, on this planet
SANKOFA! Sankoofa!! Sankooofaaaaaaaaaaaaaaaa...

Pan-Afrakanism and Re-Afrakanization

Pan-Afrakanism, as expressed through the new Afrakan Kulture by Spiritual Warriors of the 63rd century means to facilitate and bring about a healing through Afrakan unity of Afrakan people throughout the world. Pan-Afrakanism can also restore what European and Arab enslavement, colonialism and religious conquest like Judaism, Christianity and Islam took away from an Afrakan spiritual people. All of the above are oppressors of Afrakan people. The first thing they all did was destroy traditional Afrakan Kulture. So it is clear we must restore a stronger and even more powerful new Afrakan Kulture in its place.

Pan-Afrakanism is an expression of re-Afrakanization by modern new Afrakan Spiritual Warriors. This re-Afrakanization is any effort on the part of Afrakan people to reclaim any portion of Afraka that has been taken away, mutilated, misunderstood, or misinterpreted by a non-Afrakan to the detriment of Afraka and Afrakan people everywhere.

The late Dr. John Henrik Clarke taught us that we have no friends in the modern world. Every ethnic group that could, has used our kindness and humanness as a weakness, and has exploited us; the Europeans Caucasians, the European Jews, the Arabs, the Indians, the Koreans, the Chinese and the Japanese. They all have come into our communities and opened up businesses and given nothing back in return. They can do this because we, Afrakan people are having an identity crisis. We don't know who we are, or don't like what we have become, so we want to be like anybody, except Afrakans. And because we are not united Afrakans these other united cultural groups can exploit us economically because we are divided and weak. Dr. Clarke said we owe them nothing but a whipping, because we Afrakans are all their parents and we are being disrespected, but don't get mad, get organized!

Pan-Afrakanism is the uniting of the Afrakan world in unity worldwide, including the continent of Afraka and throughout the Diaspora. It is part of the solution to our problem as Afrakan people. Afrakans are not just uniting against European Caucasian domination, but we, as Afrakan people are uniting for ourselves, as part of our healing. Our own love turned inwards to ourselves and towards Afrakan people is our medicine.

There are a billion Afrakan people on this planet. We only need ourselves to liberate ourselves. All we have to do is become our own best friend. Re-Afrakanization of our minds with a new Afrakan Worldview and Afrakan Kulture at the roots is a prerequisite for total Pan-Afrakan liberation and Nationship. Afrakan Kulture is the key and doorway to the foundation of Pan-Afrakan Nationbuilding. Malcolm X, El Hajj Malik El Shabazz, taught us you cannot hate the roots of a tree and not hate the tree itself. Well, Afrakan people cannot hate the roots of their naturally kinky hair, thick lips, wide nose, and dark melaninted skin without hating Afraka and Afrakans; it is a package deal. The new trend in Afraka is the straightening of the hair and bleaching of their skin by Afrakan women. Many of these Afrakan women on the continent still wear their traditional clothes and speak their own language, but they have adopted someone else's standard of beauty. Our sisters should recall the Afrakan proverb: ***Knowing nothing is bad, but to learn nothing is worse***. We are volunteering to throw away, or surrender, our dynamic Afrakan beauty and Kulture for European Caucasian acceptance and spiritual destruction. This is the promise that European Caucasian culture has for us, mental, physical, and spiritual collective death...

The concept of beauty is a fundamental element of a people's Worldview based upon their Kulture, and European Caucasian and Asiatics consciously undermined that concept as Afrakan civilization was destroyed. The perfection that was Blackness was distorted, rearranged, and replaced with evil, lies, and imperfection. This act of Afrakan people recreating the images of their conquerors, European Caucasians and Arab Muslims as their own is fundamentally an act of submission and insanity, and Kultural suicide. Moreover, we are still surrendering our souls to the enemy instead of fighting. Afros, dashikis, and the demand for Afrikan Studies in the sixties were a revolutionary act of war and rebellion against European Caucasian oppressors and our former enslavers from a Kultural perspective. Today, Konscious Afrakans are wearing locks, short natural hairstyles, Kente and Mud Cloth as a Kultural statement, because we are pro-Afrakan. We are at war for our minds, our souls, our Kultural integrity and the true natural spiritual beauty that has been hiding inside us, waiting to come forth like the mighty rays of the sun after a storm.

Dr. John Henrik Clarke also stated that Afrakan people have been rehearsing for over a hundred years for a show called "Liberation" and we are afraid to put it on. We have the right costumes, the right setting, the right conditions, we know our lines, and we have the right theme music and songs, but no show! You are still in a state of enslavement as long as you are dependent on other people *solely* for your jobs, your shelter, your transportation, your food, the cleaning of your neighborhoods, the education of your children, the images of yourselves on television and the movies, your image of beauty and the images of the Creator that are in your Churches, Mosque, or Temples. Under these conditions, you are still enslaved and destined for self-destruction, before you even know what your purpose in life is.

The very root of Afrakan Kulture, as expressed through Pan-Afrakanism and re-Afrakanization, is the liberation of our minds, mentally, physically, and spiritually. Living under these two principles, we can be free from dependency of other people's images of beauty, education, food, clothing, transportation, even houses. Most of all, we can be free from dependency on other people's interpretation of the Creator.

Kulture is responsible for one's relationship to Nation-building and developing a national Konsciousness, a Worldview. This national Konsciousness facilitates the development of a United States of Afraka or a Pan-Afrakan National Country that is not a puppet of the western world. Once there is a national Konsciousness, we can develop a nation within a Nation anywhere in the Diaspora, because it is linked to a nation not just a continent. Afrakan Kulture must develop and define our behaviors as a Pan-Afrakan people in relationship to ourselves, our families, values, Ourstory, language, institutions, and images of beauty. Spiritual Warriors must also develop a Pan-Afrakan defense system to protect what we develop worldwide, especially the precious minds of our watoto (children).

"Honor a child, or children and they will honor you." Afrakan Proverb.

Our children will not be able to honor us if we do not honor ourselves, by our integrity and our actions. We must reconstitute and revitalize our national Kultural identity. We must reestablish the Afrakan-centered perspective, the Konsciousness that defines us and links us with our great Afrakan ancestors. This linkage is our Kultural human map that our children can read and follow back to their right Afrakan minds. Minds that are in tune with The NTCHR. Only with our new Afrakan Kultural identity can we build the institutions necessary to lead us into immortality.

Spiritual Warriors must develop a new reality for Afrakan people. That new reality for Afrakan people must have at its foundation a Pan-Afrakan Worldview that embraces Afrakan Kulture, and not European-American Caucasian culture in black face. We must stop imitating and following the European American Caucasian reality, which is only an illusion and is not the correct reality or road map for Afrakans and their descendents.

Caucasian European American culture, in black face, will not get Afrakans a nation, nor will it get us any respect as a people. It will only put Afrakans back on the plantation. If we look at the European-centered Worldview of white-nationalism or Caucasian male domination who divided Afraka up in the 19th century western time, they are more united today in the 21st century or 63rd century new Afrakan time. If we could not stop the exploitation and oppression of Spain, France, Portugal, Belgium, England, etc. as individual vultures, then what chance have we got, divided and dis-organized against the Wazungu united? European Caucasians are looking at their position not just for today or tomorrow, but also for generations to come. The emergence of this new Pan-Afrakan-centered Konsciousness marks the rebirth of the new Afrakan personality and the re-Afrakanization of Afrakan people worldwide. With a new, but ancient re-vitalized Afrakan Kulture we will have the revitalization of Afrakan Nationality and by using our Afrakan Kultural 12 point system, Nation building can become a reality, not just a show that never happened. Afrakans, Pan-Afrakanism or perish - the Maangamizi continues until non-existence or two thousand more years of enslavement; the choice is ours.

Illusion

America's power is an illusion
Just like Afrakans' powerlessness in America is an illusion
Only we are living through a continuous nightmare
Which we think we have no control over
I think
We are afraid to face what we are
And we are petrified to think of what we have become
So we pretend
Spending more money on entertainment
Or entertaining spending more money
Than any other ethnic group in the world
Watch more TV.
Take in more movies
Somebody other than Afrakans, needs to tell us
More is not necessarily better
As we get lost in someone else's illusion.

Multi-dimensional Imhotep Spiritual Warriors who embraces the art of Warriorship, Education, Drama, Poetry, Dance, Drumming, Art, Fashions and Deep Thinking; Mama Makini Niliwambini and Mfundishi Jhutyms Ka n Heru El-Salim.

The 12 Point New Afrakan Spiritual Warriors Re-Afrakanization Kultural System

It does not take a mathematical genius or Imhotep to figure out that if your enemy is working 24/7, 365 days of the year to oppress you, and you, the oppressed, are only working part-time, mainly on weekends and during the summer, and you are working for the same enemy your trying to destroy, this is insane. With this formula, you will never liberate yourself from under the yoke of oppression; this equation equals more oppression, annihilation and eventually extinction, not liberation. Moreover, this formula of enslavement is what Afrakan people in America are operating under, which means the Maangamizi is still alive and well at the beginning of the 63 rd. century, new Afrakan time.

Afrakan Spiritual Warriors must prepare ourselves to work for ourselves, build liberating institutions, and to do battle 24/7, 365 days every year to liberate ourselves. Our ancient Afrakan ancestors in the Hapy Valley, northeast Afraka knew that we would need a formula for freedom and resurrection, so they etched on the walls of the sacred temples, time capsules also called tombs and giant monuments words of power and illustrations for liberation. They showed Afrakans, Black melanin men and women, the Kemetyu doing battle with all the races of the world and in victorious form. Nevertheless, we were mainly fighting the forces of esfet (evil, disharmony). In the ancient Kemetyu book called the ***Pert em Heru,*** there were 12 energies, Ntchru that sat on the council of judgment in the Double Halls of Ma'at in the Duat. Their responsibilities were to make sure only the righteous, and the truthful entered the gates of ***Heaven*** pt, so that the Afrakan way of life would be ritualized and immortalized for eternity. Afrakan Spiritual Warriors of today have redeveloped an Afrakan Worldview that will resurrect our Kulture. These Spiritual Warriors will reclaim our Afrakan Ourstory, an Ourstory of Afrakan civilization that was already old when Europe was born. We have developed 12 energies as in the ***Pert em*** ***eru, that*** will assist in the resurrection, reconstruction, and rebuilding of our Afrakan minds, mentally physically and spiritually. This 12-point system is as follows:

1) Intuitively knowning The NTCHR, as The All, The Supreme Spirit in all things. 2) Embracing Afrakan-centeredness and a Pan-Afrakan Worldview. 3) Maintaining an Internal and External Security and Defense System. 4) Utilizing a ritualized Spiritual System that reinforces Afrakancentricity and Spirituality. 5) Kultivating Afrakan-centered Educational Systems that supports a positive Pan-Afrakan Worldview. 6) Establishing Pan-Afrakan Political governance. 7) Believing in and supporting the Ujamaa Economy. 8) Utilizing an Afrakan Mental, Physical and Spiritual Healing and Health Development System. 9) Continuing the best of our ancient's ways by enforcing The Halls of Ma'at. 10) Developing and Kultivating an Afrakan-centered Science, Technology and Language System. 11) Embracing The Kuumba System of Art and Inner-attainment, and 12) The Maangamizi Never Again Memorial System.

These 12 points are the Soul Force, but not the only forces behind the development of a new Afrakan Nation, a new Pan-Afrakan Worldview and an all new Afrakan Spiritual Warriorship. The soul signifies the emotional fire of the spirit force or power that captures the pain and joy, the sorrow and the glory of the Afrakan experience, ancient and present in one collective expression. Soul is our Afrakan rhythm and music, our love and our pain. Soul is our connection to immortality, and it is our Afrakan survival and the essence of our Worldview. Soul moves Afrakan people towards liberation. The Soul Force shapes and defines the Black Human Being into a unifying Kultural structure for command of Black expression. The Soul Force is the key to the Spiritual Warriors healing powers because like Afrakan music, it unifies our individual and collective experience and affirms our Oneness with The NTCHR.

The new Afrakan Spiritual Warriors must ultimately expand on what the previous generations have left. Afrakans in America have developed a powerful pool of Afrakan-centered scholars in almost every field of scholarship. We have an elaborate list of Afrakan organizations that have some degree of Afrakan Konsciousness. We have developed several local and national newspapers and magazines that center on Afrakans in America and in the Diaspora. We have a growing list of Black millionaires by way of sports and the entertainment fields. The list of Afrakan doctors, lawyers, engineers, scientists and politicians have expanded extensively over the past 20 years. However, we, as Afrakans in America and in the Diaspora, are still enslaved by Caucasian European male domination. With all these Black Afrakan successes, why are Afrakans still suffering from Afrakan unemployment, which is as high as it was in 1963 when Afrakans marched on Washington D.C. or exploded in the Afrakan uprising in Watts, California? The Urban cities have more drugs in the Afrakan community than ever before and Black on Black and white on Black crime is up. The number one cause of death for an Afrakan man in America is homicide with a gun, by another Afrakan man. Afrakans with a college degree still make less than the average Caucsian male who only went to high school. There are more Afrakan men in prison, than in higher educational training. Yes, things are bad and as a Spiritual Warrior, I'd say it's worst than bad.

Illusions of What We Think We Know

Yes things are worse than bad
I see hidden souls screaming to be recognized
Pyramid builders, in unemployment lines
Now unconscious European Matrix slaves
Many unconscious of their former greatness
Lost to poetry from the ages
Totally unaware of the magnitude of their real existence
Walking contradiction
Blind to their own beauty
Invisible
Konsciously and unconsciously hating themselves
A total delusion
And this is BAD!
But what is worse than bad
Is that we believe this ugly illusion
As we imitate our oppressors, we confirm their desires
AND TOMORROW REFLECTS THE SORROWS OF MORE MADNESS...

For the first time since the physical enslavement of Afrakans in America, the Afrakan child knows less than their parents do. This is truly a sad note in Ourstory. As an Afrakan scribe and Spiritual Warrior, the facts already stated are just a few of my many observed tragic notes on the Afrakan in the 63rd century new Afrakan time. So surely, our proposed 12-point System, which is not new, is long over due. I think its time to put on one of the greatest shows of the 63rd century, LIBERATION! Liberation of our minds, souls and spirits from the illusions of white male domination as we return to **Ma'at**.

The point I am making here is that we need not debate on; rather we need a plan of action for Afrakan people. At this point in Ourstory the question is, "Are we ready to take on the challenge of our lives?" Afrakans in America are addicts of Caucasian European domination and we need a revolution to liberate our minds. Marcus Garvey told us in 1917 that, **"not until the Black man strikes out independently to do for himself and proves his nettle in nation building, commerce, industry, politics and war, will he be rated as one of the forces of the world."** This 12-point New Afrakan Kultural System is a means to our solution. This 12-point outline guide for New Afrakan Spiritual Warriors is a work in progress. Afrakans must relearn how to become fluent with life and nature. In this anti-nature society of Caucasian European domination, simplicity is one of the most difficult things to master because we have lost our way, "The Way". This book, ***Spiritual Warriors Are Healers***, is a simple guide back to "The Way". It defines an operational blue print of Pan-Afrakanism and Afrakan unity. Our New Afrakan Kulture tells us, we are AFRAKAN. We are Afrakan people wherever we are on the planet earth. Moreover, we are Afrakan no matter what language we speak or what colony or country we are from, or if your melanin is light Black-to-Black Black, tight curly hair, to lose curls, or even straight hair - be natural. These superficial abstract things do not define you. Western man has gotten you so caught up in self-importance that we cannot smell the poison in the air, taste the poison in the water and in the food, or see the monster that the European Caucasian domination has created out of the Maangamizi. If Afrakans are to save themselves, we need to know who we are now, where we have been, and where we are going, one step at a time as we move from addicts to recovering addicts in control of our destiny. "Today, liberation of our minds and bodies... Tomorrow liberation for Afrakan families and communities everywhere... Next the reunification and uniting of an Afrakan Nation, United States of Afraka." Ultimately as Spiritual Warriors, we must learn to "BE". Being has not been given its due. Only by Being, can you come into balance or into unity with ourselves and all other beings, which are only reflections of The One, NTCHR.

Two teachers and High Priests of the Kemet Spiritual System for over 25 years; Left, Baba Heru Ankh Ra Semahj Se Ptah, one of the earliest pioneers of the Kemet Legacy, and the founder and keeper of the oldest known Kemet Shrine in North America. Right, Mfundishi Jhutyms Ka n Heru El-Salim of Kera Jhuty Heru Neb-Hu, one of New Jersey's earliest Kemet pioneers. Right Photo, author of several books on Afrakan Kulture and politics. This Spiritual Warrior was a Pan-Afrakanist, Black Nationalist leader of the Mau Mau freedom fighters and he was the first Prime Minister of Kenya, Mzee Jomo Kenyatta.

12 Point Re-Afrakanization System

1. *The NTCHR and the Ntchru*

The NTCHR is nameless, hidden, formless, indefinable, infinite Konsciousness, a self-existent, self-perpetuating force. It is intangible and yet it breathes its life in all of us. It is pure Konsciousness. It is intelligence underlying and supporting all matter and all existence. Our ancient Kemetyu ancestors of the Hapy Valley call the essence of this self-perpetuating force Spirit or Ka, and its many powerful manifestations are called the Ntchru.

Everything, everywhere, all the time is endowed by this Essence, this Ka or Spirit. Moreover, the first Ntchr Created after Divine Konsciousness was Jhuty and Ma'at, Divine Konsciousness and Divine Order and harmony. To Afrakan people, the cosmos, as well as the world is a spiritual entity in divine order. Therefore, everything Afrakan people do is related to The Spirit and Ma'at. For Afrakan Spiritual Warriors, the greatest state of Konsciousness is to have Heru Konsciousness, which is to be Konscious of your divinity and your Oneness with The NTCHR, which brings Ma'at into your heart. This Heru Konsciousness is a state of "Being". Once Afrakan Spiritual Warriors become in tune with themselves, which is to know nature and their people, it becomes part of their sacred mission to lead by example. Afrakan people must abandon all foreign spiritual religious systems and embrace the Spirit of Afrakan Spirituality and Kulture, if we are to heal. We should be treating nature and all Afrakan people, especially Afrakan women, with dignity and respect as though each and every one is divine. We must re-establish our sacredness our connection to Ma'at between nature and the Afrakan Family and institutionalize this divinity.

POINT 1; GOAL: To develop and maintain Heru Konsciousness among the masses of Afrakan people, with an innerstanding that we as Afrakan people as well as nature are divine and One with The NTCHR. Black life is sacred, and the Black family is the center nucleus of this sacredness. It is the smallest unit of Nationship. So our 12 point System is designed to reclaim our sacred connection to NTCHR, while we are building and defending ourselves as an Afrakan people and a united Pan-Afrakan nation wherever we are.

2. Embracing Afrakan-centeredness

Second only to the concept of The NTCHR and Ntchru and its life-giving Spirit, is the central concept of Afrakan-centeredness, providing the love we must maintain to sustain the Afrakan family. Living an Afrakan-centered life will allow you to see the world through the all-seeing eyes of Heru Konsciousness, your First Eye, misunderstood as the third eye. As a result, you will see your own true Kulture and your true human story. The knowledge you will gain regarding the uniqueness of the Afrakan Kultural experience on earth, manifested through our dynamic Kulture, will serve to increase your vitality in the Afrakan movement. Ourstory, our mental, physical and spiritual collective responses and interactions with our environment for millenniums helped define Afrakan-centeredness. To deny the Kultural, spiritual, psychological and physiological consequence of our unique experience is insane. To Konsciously affirm this dynamic Afrakan Kulture in thought and behavior, through family and then to institutionalize that dynamic Afrakan experience is Afrakancentricity or Afrakan-centeredness.

Spiritual Warriors clearly innerstand that just like the all-existing power of The NTCHR is not a debatable topic to a Spiritual people, neither is Afrakancentricity to a liberated Afrakan. Afrakan-centeredness is sanity for Afrakan people. It is the new Afrakan method of survival with dignity. Afrakancentricity becomes the Soul-Force and meaning to a lasting development of re-Afrakanization for the Kemetyu of the new Pan-Afrakan World Order.

All Afrakan Spiritual Warriors and Afrakan Konscious families of the New Pan-Afrakan Worldview should surrender western enslaved names that were given to their Afrakan forefathers. This includes English, Spanish, French, Portuguese, Dutch, and all other European and Christian, Jewish, or Arabic foreign names. We must re-Afrakanize ourselves and our families with names that express our Afrakan Kulture and Afrakan Ancestry. Names should reflect your spirit and your commitment to humanity and nature, as well as your people.

Each citizen who receives a new name must also travel through a rites of passage program so that they are empowered by the re-Afrakanization process. We must sever the ties and cut the umbilical cord of slavery, enslavement and the Caucasian European domination and dependency that has held Afrakan people in psychological bondage.

As an Afrakan Spiritual Warrior who is a recovering addict of white male domination, I know what is going through your head: "I'm not changing my name, even if it is the oppressor's property; I would be disrespecting my family," or several other excuses. All this means is that you are still not ready to cut the umbilical cord of slavery and European domination. The prescription for Afrakan liberation prescribed by Afrakan Spiritual Healers is to engage in daily struggle against those activities and bonds which have Ourstorically weakened Afrakans, such as disunity and disorganized actions against Caucasian European domination. We are afraid to destroy our oppressor, because we have become so much like our oppressor we are afraid to destroy ourselves.

It is absolutely essential that Afrakans destroy these barriers and bonds that sabotage our liberation. Afrakan people must resolve, through strict will power and tenacity, to engage in daily struggle against our own weaknesses and to struggle against Caucasian European domination, even if this puts us outside of our current comfort zone. Knowing full well that this so-called comfort is a constricted version of the total greatness of ourselves, and is merely a token of the oppressor's cultural system. Embracing Afrakan Kulture is a prerequisite for our families and our collective liberation. All people of Afrakan descent must have knowledge of our Afrakan past from an Afrakan-centered perspective. This will aid us in kulturally defining ourselves, believing in ourselves and using Afrakan-centeredness as a tool for liberation.

Hippocrates, who the European Caucasians say is the "father of their medicine," was a student of the students of the great Afrakan Healer and medicine man Imhotep, who preceded him by over a thousand years.

Imhotep, a Black Afrakan from Kemet, in the Hapy Valley, northeast Afraka was a prototype of human scholarship and human science. He laid the foundation for not only medicine, but also Pyramid building, military strategy, philosophy, and poetry. So from an Afrakan-centered view, not only is it a lie, that Hippocrates is the father of medicine, but unethical; he did not even give credit to his teachers, who were giants compared to him.

We must now take a closer look at how we view the world we live on. Afraka is the birthplace of humanity and of the most ancient well-known civilizations, such as Kemet, Kash, and Punt, just to name a few. All these early great civilizations equated South with up and North with down. This also meant that Europe (western Asia) as well as central and eastern Asia are all below Afraka. From the Afrakan Worldview, the Sun (Ra) rises in the East, which is synonymous with left and Ra sets in the West, which is synonymous with right. Even today, if you look at a western map, people in Egypt refer to Southern Egypt as Upper Egypt and Northern Egypt as Lower Egypt.

Afrakancentricity says we must construct our own maps with the correct directions. We, as Afrakan people are having difficulty finding "The Way" because we are standing on our heads in order to view things from the Eurocentric perspective. Spiritual Warriors must teach us to stand firmly on our feet as Afrakans, and view the world from Ma'at.

After we have found our correct special perspective, it is equally as important that we correct our perception of time. Ourstorigraphical context of how we begin our dating system must be selected from an important ancient Afrakan event. Moreover, this event should not be based on conquest and destruction like the Eurocentric Caucasian male system, as well as the Asian systems, are based upon. As Spiritual Warriors we are suggesting the date 4,240 B.C.E. as the year "1" S.T., because it's a date that our astronomical Kalendar of 365 days came into being, or was widely accepted by the genius of Afrakan scientist in the Hapy Valley civilizations of Kemet and Kash.

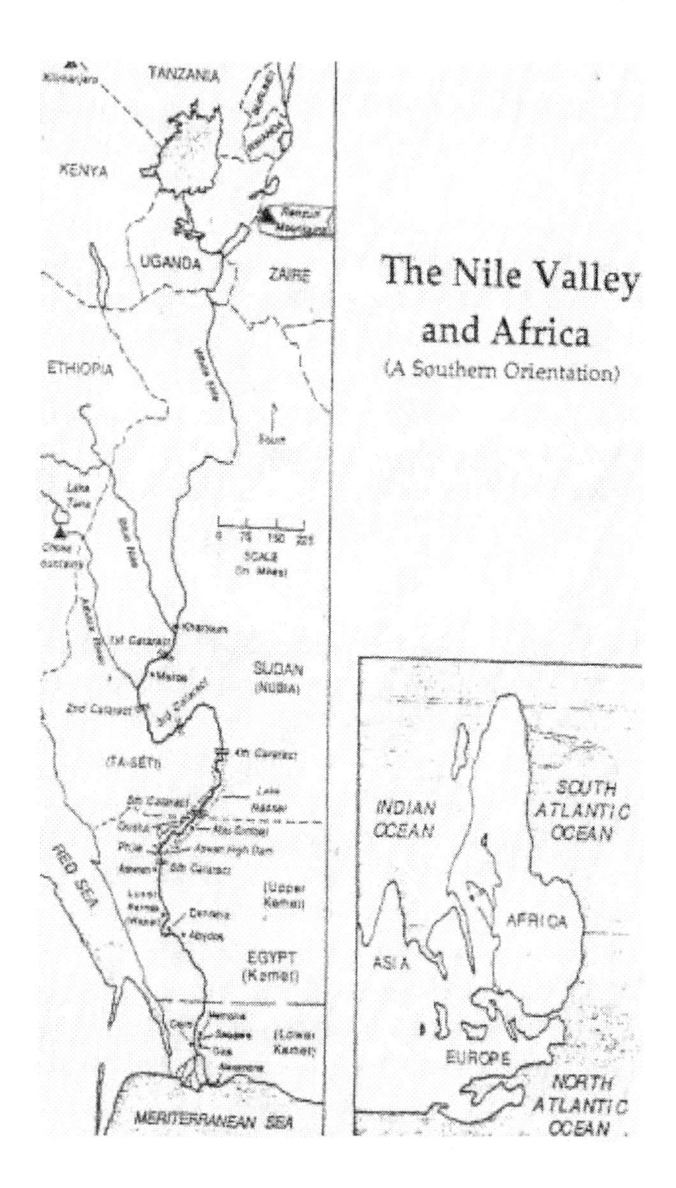

Kemet map of the Hapy Valley, northeast Afraka, with a southern spacial perspective.

The Afrakan Worldview must clearly use a kalendar based upon the greatness of our heritage to define our concept of time. Moreover, Ourstory must be delivered or told from that Afrakan-centered perspective. In the struggle to reclaim our Kulture, our families and the control of our minds, it is extremely important that Afrakan Spiritual Warriors recapture our right minds and place it in the right time spacial perspective. Time is a very subjective concept, and is determined according to your relationship with the Ntchru or nature. We are presently following a system of recording time (the Gregorian calendar) that, although has its origins in Afraka, the Hapy Valley, has been altered to suit the thought process and needs of Caucasian Europeans. Afrakans have been accurately recording time for at least 52,000 years, two sun years, by Spiritual Priests in the Hapy Valley East Afraka. Our Black melaninated Afrakan ancestors from the Hapy Valley created the first and most accurate kalendar that ever existed. They created kalendars based upon the movement of the pole stars, the moon, the sun and finally - around 4240 B.C.E., or the year i1 S.T. new Afrakan timeî- they created a kalendar based upon the heliacal rising of the star Spdt (Sirius A). This kalendar is mathematically more precise than the Gregorian calendar used today by most of the western world.

The Kemet Kalendar has 13 months. 12 months have exactly 30 days. The month is divided into three 10 day weeks. Each day has 24 hours. This adds up to 360 days. The kalendar has 5 intercalary days above the year to celebrate the birth of the first five earth born Ntchru (divine principles that control our relationship with nature, that exist inside each human being). This brings the total to 365 days, and the 13th month. The Kemetyu also innerstood and developed the leap year that came every 4 years. This brings the total to 365.25 days for a year. This kalendar is divided into three seasons of four months each: the inundation season (Shemu), the planting season (Prt) and the harvest season (Akhet

). Year, renpt -

Kemet Kalendars can be purchased by contacting Black Gold; Jhuty Heru Neb-Hu Publishing Company at www. blackgoldsacredliving.com or P.O. Box 1396 Montclair, N.J.07042

Spiritual Warriors innerstand that to be truly Afrakan-centered we must build all our institutions from a perspective that supports Afrakan-centeredness from all fronts. As Afrakan Warriors, we do not look for jobs or employment from our oppressors. We create our own employment opportunities through the spirit of giving our gifts to our people and the world. Sankofa, Spiritual Warriors - it is time for us to build institutions for our children and our families, like our ancient Afrakan ancestors of the Hapy Valley. Institutions that will stand for decades, centuries, millenniums, like the Mer Khut en Khufu (the great Pyramid of Khufu), or the Heru em Akhet, Neb-Hu (the so-called great Sphinx also in Egypt).

If the family is to be the major entity for socialization in the New Afrakan-centered Worldview, then children must cease being accidents and once again become priorities. Only properly functioning Afrakan families will produce healthy children, healthy relationships, and the proper environment for Afrakan-centeredness. The philosophy of Ma'at, reciprocity, spirituality, manners, the concepts of love, war, sharing, and caring are family-centered human values. Kulture is practiced at home first. The family becomes your first teacher and families that share similar Kultures make up communities.

Spiritual Warriors innerstand that not every house is a home. Houses and apartments have to be made into homes with love, planning, Kultivation and a lot of innerstanding. A Spiritual Warrior's home is a reflection of the world he or she wants to live in. Afrakan Spiritual Warriors must create Melanin enriched rejuvenating mini-learning environments. Haki Madhubuti, a Spiritual Warrior from Chicago expresses the idea that serious study should be like eating. Everyone should have at least one good healthy well-rounded meal each day and every Spiritual Warrior should read and or study two to three hours every day. Because knowledge is food for your mind and spirit. The watoto (children) learn by what they see us do, not by what we say do. If the watoto see writing, reading and us studying, they will want to do it too. Encourage study-time every day in your home, your mini-learning center, and everyone from grandparents through the entire extended family is studying, reading or discussing events that affect **Afrakan** people and the world. Turn the television off and buy a TV guide so that your family can watch life-giving, intelligent and responsible educational and Kulturally enriched programs. The average Afrakan teenager in America by the time they are 17, will have spent 17,000 hours watching TV, and only 11,000 hours in a school classroom.

One of the reasons that Afrakan people cannot remove the shackles of slavery, and enslavement from our minds is because our analysis of our enslavement position is faulty. The educational institutions, TV, newspapers, news stations and Eurocentric and Afro-American magazines contribute to the faulty information about the nature and cause of our enslavement. Until Afrakan people re-claim our families, turn our houses and apartments into homes that are clean, peaceful, warm, secure, rejuvenating with food for the mind and body which reflect the Worldview we want to live in, then we will continue to be exploited. If the families' nucleus is weak with faulty information, the watoto will remain lost and enslaved. Spiritual Warriors must teach and institutionalize the development of strong Afrakan families. Families must eat together in their homes, talk about each other's lives, and the world as it relates to Afrakan people. One of the keys to Afrakan peoples' liberation and Afrakan-centeredness is in its very definition itself. As long as Afrakan people accepts the conqueror's definitions of manship (manhood), womanship (womanhood), freedom, education, politics, business, trade, religion and even the very name that you are identified by, it will be difficult to imagine another Worldview, especially one Afrakan people control, with the Afrakan concept of Ma'at at the center.

Remember, the best teachers are good examples. At some point, our so-called great Afrakan scholars and business minds will have to stop working for the enemy, and work and teach out of institutions we as Afrakan people create from the genius of our own collective experience and Worldview. We have tried other people's formula in parts of Afraka for more than 2,000 years, in West Afraka for more than 1,000 years, in the Americas for more than 400 years and nowhere has it worked and it never will work. We, Afrakans are spiritual beings having a Black human experience and we must align ourselves with Ma'atian spiritual systems and an Afrakan-centered, new Afrakan Kultural Worldview in order to flourish.

POINT 2; GOAL: All Institutions, as well as its people, are operating from an Afrakan-centered System on all 12 points. The struggle for Afrakan-centeredness becomes each Spiritual Warrior's life, and the life of New Afrakans, also the developing of correct maps, kalendars and chronological perspectives. For Afrakan people to become reconnected and grounded to the very best of Afrakan Kulture and traditions of the past, we must embrace family, Afrakan-centeredness and our own Worldview.

This is the Ancient Kemet Zodiac that our Afrakan ancestors of the Hapy valley developed. Today's zodaic's system is based on this ancient Afrakan zodiac which was found in Dendera with a few minor changes, like Kheper, the Scarab, has been changed to Cancer, the Crab. And also, the Kemet Kalendar is based on this concept of the twelve houses.

3. ***Internal and External Security and Defense System***

Nationship is the only means by which modern civilization can completely protect itself. We must nationalize our Afrakan continent into one powerful Nation or a few Unified large Nations that make up a United Afrakan Order. Moreover, we, as Afrakan people in the Diaspora, must become a unified nation connected to that one Nation or Unified Order on the continent of Afraka. We must build and maintain a secure institutional infrastructure of an independent nationality, and project a Konscious commitment to advance the Afrakan Nation and families towards independence and freedom, and the human race towards greater humanity.

Afrakancentricity states that to develop a nation and not be able to protect it is like not having it at all. Afrakan Spiritual Warriors must mobilize our efforts into a true Pan-Afrakan security effort, linking the sons and daughters of Afrakans throughout the world.

It will take highly trained Spiritual Warriors on a level the world has not yet seen, to develop a clear innerstanding of the Ourstorical impediments and drawbacks that have plagued Afrakan liberation and development in the past. These Spiritual Warriors will then lead the way to correction and victory. They will develop institutions for defense that can analyze our impediments and provide a clear criteria for adjustments with solutions for identifying and handling those less obvious impediments to the advancement and safety of the race and the Afrakan Nation.

Kupigana Ngumi and Ma'at Akhw Ba Ankh will be part of the daily lives of the New Afrakan-centered nation. The objective is to impart self discipline and correct focus to masses of Afrakan people at such a high level, that discipline and focus become as normal as talking and eating, essentially becoming second nature. Spiritual Warriors will plant the foundation of correct breathing, correct posture and correct mental focus, along with innerstanding the value and proper use of silence. This will be the order of the new day for the New Afrakan Worldview.

As Spiritual Warriors, we must wage total war on the minds of Afrakan people. We must explain the Maangamizi in such a way that the intentions of Caucasian America against Afrakan people becomes totally and unquestionably clear. Afrakan people and other melanin people must be educated to the role America's allies play in oppressing Afrakans, as well as its treatment of nature itself. Caucasian male domination in all of its various forms, culturally or politically and militarily, are clearly the enemies of Afrakan people and Afrakan-centeredness as well as Pan-Afrakanism.

Afrakans lost power and control over their internal affairs and their ability to defend themselves when they surrendered to Caucasian male domination and this system of colonialism. Caucasian European male domination and its colonial system liquidated pre-existing states in Afraka and destroyed the moral foundations of great long standing Afrakan societies. Let us be clear, Caucasian male domination destroyed the right and ability of Afrakans to chart their own development and remain the authors of their own destiny. If Afrakans are to defend themselves they must destroy all traces of colonial rule in Afraka, the Caribbean, and any place Afrakans want to control their own destiny. We must become a nation within a nation with the ability to defend ourselves no matter where we are.

Afrakan militaries must stop imitating their colonial masters, and no longer accept military training and inferior, outdated military supplies and equipment. Afrakans have failed to develop indigenous defense industries. We must, at once, use the available technology to develop our own weaponry so we will no longer remain technological hostages of external Caucasian European male domination. Also, all Afrakans must develop a defense system that is Pan-Afrakan in nature, closely connected with Kupigana Ngumi, so that we can defend all Afrakan life anywhere and everywhere simultaneously.

Afrakan Spiritual Warriors must innerstand that our first battle is with our selves and Afrakan people. After we win the minds of Afrakan people back from the Caucasian European domination drug then we can begin to talk about Nation-building. Once we have redirected the spiritual energies of our people, victory will prevail like a mighty storm.

POINT 3; GOAL: Afrakan people must be able to protect Afrakan peoples' best interests, politically, economically, spiritually, and physically in all 12 areas of the 12-point Afrakan Kultural System for New Afrakans. We are the only people who can make universal promises to The NTCHR and keep them, because we have no designs on the lands or natural resources of other people. Part of the Afrakan Spiritual Warriors' mission is to deliver Afraka to Afrakans, in the spirit of Marcus Garvey. Kupigana Ngumi or an Afrakan Kulturally based martial arts system must be a part of each Afrakan family, as the first line of defense. Our second line of defense must be our communities and institutions wherever they are. Another part of our mission is to leave a new legacy of greatness that equals the building of the Pyramids for our Afrakan children. With this new Afrakan legacy we can give the whole human race a new definition of freedom and responsibility. This will be done by teaching the laws of living in concert with the Ntchru for The NTCHR.

Right, Our father of the back to Afraka movement, Marcus M. Garvey.

Spiritual Warriors of the Afrakan Martial Arts: Dr. Ndugu Khan, Bro. Nigel Ninns, author of Nuba Wrestling, and Mfundishi Jhutyms Ka en Heru.

4. Ritualized Spiritual Systems

Ritual is, in a sense, the ultimate philosophical expression of the Afrakan Worldview, for it is the modality through which the unity of the human and the divine are expressed. It is through ritual that the unity of spirit and matter is perceived. Moreover, it is through ritual that eternal moments are achieved. The New Afrakan Worldview must be centered in this unity as the Kultural leaders maintain the Spiritual focus of Nation-building, every moment and on every level.

Afrakan humans are divine, and we must treat each other as if we know that we are divine. Afrakans must develop a Konscious alignment between the spirit, soul, mind and body-temple, and this alignment and harmony must be at the height of our spiritual and or religious experience. This is true not only for Spiritual Warriors, but for each divine Afrakan citizen as the Moyo or Sekhem within us, and the power of the Ntchru manifest themselves in us as spiritual possessions or trance. As the result of this alignment, we are given divine guidance from the Ntchru that marks a clear direction of our glorious Afrakan-centered Worldview.

Our rituals must reinforce our spiritual system, and our traditional Afrakan morals. We must give praise to the elderly, and the ancestors, because they watch over Afrakan people and they make sure we are following the best of our traditional greatness.

Our spirituality must also be centered within the very essence of our Afrakan-centered Kultural foundation. We must embrace Afrakancentricity which will make sure that our mental, physical and spiritual realities are self-reflective and in harmony with our existence with nature. Afrakan people should follow a system that holds their sacred images as Ntchr-like and divine. Our spiritual system or religion must embrace Afrakan Kulture as redefined by our new Afrakan reality. Therefore, Afrakan people are divine. This does not mean that non-Afrakan people are not divine; we are just proclaiming our divinity as Afrakans. Our spiritual system must also embrace Afraka as our Holy Land, not Asia or Europe, or someplace that Europeans and Arabs created called the Middle East. Where is the middle west, and middle north and middle south and to what is it the middle of?

The Spiritual Warriors who are the vanguard of the New Afrakan-centered Worldview must live by the example of the spiritual laws of Ma'at (truth, justice, propriety, harmony, balance, reciprocity, and correct order), which is "The Way".

- *I am because we are, and because we are, I am.* *Afrakan proverb.*

We must practice spiritual rituals that foster the innerstanding of Ma'at in our daily lives. In order for Afrakans to restore Ma'at, back into our daily lives we have to be kem-mitted (totally committed from an Afrakan-centered perspective) to Afrakan-centered struggle. It is clear that if we want to restore the ecological balance we must restore the spiritual balance back into our Afrakan lives so that we can prevent the best of our ancient values from being eroded any further.

Afrakan people must be re-Afrakanizied through rituals that clearly affirm that family is the basic spiritual and moral unit. The family is the primary social, judicial, economic, political and spiritual unit in the society. Spiritual Warriors must help develop and maintain family rituals that maintain daily contact with the ancestors and us. Spiritual Warriors suggest that we make sure we have family meals as often as possible, at least one meal daily, and if this is not possible, then on the weekends. This simple ritual keeps us together in prayer and innerstanding of what is happening in our daily lives. At least once a month invite extended family members over or visit them, eat together, share your lives with each other. We Are Family have to be more than just a slogan. Yearly or every two-year total extended family gatherings called family reunions must be kept alive with a section for rites of ancestral veneration, which are methods of communion and communication. These rituals allow our ancestors to become immortal. As longs as we remember them, they continue to be part of the Afrakan family, community and nation.

POINT 4; GOAL: To transmit the knowledge of Afrakan spiritual tradition, and develop an appreciation for Afrakan tradition and the wisdom of our ancestors through rituals. These rituals will establish the Afrakan-centeredness in our Kulture as the major principles to self, family, community and the Afrakan Nation. To develop an Afrakan National Spiritual System that is based on Afrakan tradition and modern reasoning, that has the best interest of Afrakan people and Afraka at the center of its physical terrestrial philosophy. This Afrakan Spiritual Institution must have a innerstanding of Afrakan values and skills of leadership that are essential to liberation and redevelopment of Afrakan people and an Afrakan Worldview.

Queen Afua, a master of the healing rituals with her book, Sacred Women, and Zuwena Kheper Salim from the Shrine of Jhuty Heru Neb Hu.

5. *Afrakan-Centered Educational System*

Education is an essential key in the re-Afrakanization of our minds. Afrakan-centered education becomes the perpetual will or soul of Afrakan people's ability to recover, recreate and perpetuate our Kultural Heritage. As a dynamic enterprise, it enriches Afrakan Kulture, as it acts to illuminate it, simultaneously attempting to re-Afrakanize the people who are collective and Ourstorical experiences shape and is shaped by that Kulture. Afrakan-centered education is as important to the National Kulture as childbearing is to the human species. Afrakan-centered education assures the continuation and permanence of the Afrakan Worldview and Afrakan people or acts as a tool in the development of knowledge, attitudes, values and skills needed to maintain and perpetuate the nationbuilding process. Afrakan-centered education represents an attempt by Afrakans in America to reconnect themselves to an Afrakan past from which they had been violently disassociated.

Civilization is an Afrakan invention, and any analysis from the primacy of classical Afraka must include the ancient Hapy Valley. Having a strong vision and identity with our Afrakan past is the only sound basis for reconstructing an independent Afrakan future. Our education must also firmly anchor the Afrakan liberation movement in the fundamentals of Afrakan spirituality. All people of Afrakan descent must embrace this fundamental philosophy of Afrakan Oneness, regardless of the hue of our melanin, sex, accent, or where we are on the planet. We must be prepared, and not fall prey to the old divide and conquer method that Caucasian Europeans have historically used to keep us fragmented and easily controlled. "Afraka for Afrakans home and in the Diaspora." Whether we are speaking of Afrakans in America, Afrakans in Haiti, Jamaica, South America, India, or Australia, we are all one people, fighting for national and Kultural liberation. We must maintain clarity in thought, as we re-educate ourselves. Spiritual Warriors cannot over-emphasize the necessity to re-educate Afrakans towards a new Afrakan survival. We must learn that we are all divine, and the grade of our hair will not make us less, or more divine. The darkness of the hue of our skin will not determine the level of our divinity either. Our divinity isbased in our Konsciousness. Our Afrakan-centered Konsciousness recognizes that The NTCHR is Divine and that we are the original humans, directly connected to the divine. However, **we** must make that spiritual connection. We, as new Afrakans must, within our divinity, preserve, worship and protect ourselves and nature.

Our Afrakan-centered education must teach us who our friends are and who our enemies are, based upon clear analytical Ourstorical and historical research. Spiritual Warriors, without apologizing or allowing their egos to collapse in the presence of our enemy, clearly state that we must learn that the Caucasian man, Europeans, European-Americans, the Wazungu collectively, are our enemies. Also anyone or group who thinks as they do collectively, or who embraces their ideology and their individualist capitalistic system, **are our enemies!**

Afrakan-centered education is the Konscious statement, and record of Afrakans in the process of Afrakanizing our own images, and interests. Afrakan-centered education is a solution towards developing and maintaining a positive Afrakan identity, positive self-esteem and making sure the images of your story and origins of your achievements are immortalized. This clear picture allows a people to see where they have been, how they got to where they are, as well as where they are going, and where they must go, according to their own make up and internal directional human map.

The foundation of Afrakan-centered education must also be rooted in Ma'at. Afraka is the cradle of humanity and the birthplace of civilization. Black humans created the first civilizations in the world, pre-dating other humans by millenniums. Fossil evidence, molecular biology, logic, reasoning and human Ourstory proves conclusively that the earliest and most modern humans were Afrakans; that all other so-called races of the human family are recent and that they are our distant children. All DNA codes link humanity to the original Black, melanin dominated Afrakan Family.

Spiritual warriors clearly agree on the following principles:

1. Afraka is the cradle of early humans, of all six early hominid.
2. Afraka is the cradle of modern humans, homo sapiens.
3. Afraka is the cradle of civilization.
4. Afraka once held a position as world teacher, including the teachers of the western and eastern worlds.
5. Their existed a unified Kultural unity of the Afrakan content.
6. Afrakan migration populated the world over thousands of years.
7. Afraka has been under siege for more than 2,500 years and only recently from European enslavement and colonization, Asiatics, Greeks, Romans, and Asiatics under Islam and lastly Europeans have taken turns invading and sometimes colonizing the Afrakan continent. This siege and destruction of Afraka and Afrakan people is called the maangamizi.
8. Afrakans are all over the world today, the third largest ethnic group of the human family.
9. Afrakan people have resisted domination stubbornly on the continent and in the Diaspora for more than 2,500 years.
10. Even under the Maangamizi of Caucasian European enslavement, colonization, segregation, apartheid, and extreme racism under Caucasian male domination, Afrakan people have made monumental Kultural contributions in the arts, sciences, humanities, politics, music, sports and in every facet of the human experience.

All records show that these early Black Afrakan civilizations started in eastern-central Afraka, and migrated in all directions, west, south and to northeast Afraka, following great waterways like lake Nwanza, the Congo River, the Niger River, and the Hapy River Valley (the Nile). Kemet became the center voice of this body of ancient Afrakan wisdom and knowledge, spirituality, philosophy, and science, as it spread to other lands through, trade, travel, students and Initiates. The indigenous people of ancient Kemet were Black Afrakans of the same type as their tropical western, central, eastern and southern Black Afrakan brothers and sisters.

Other early Afrakan civilizations of west, central and southern Afraka, including Ghana, Nork-Ife, Zimbabwe empires date back before 2,000 B.C.E. or 2,240 S.T. new Afrakan time, and were trading partners with ancient Kemet. Afrakans of the Ancient Zhing empire smelted iron, used the red, black and green flag to represent their nation, which was located in Central-east Afraka predate Kemet by thousands of years. Civilization started in the interior of Afraka and traveled down north into the Hapy Valley. Afrakans of Ancient Kemet, Kash, Punt, and other great Afrakan Civilizations established and maintained trade and relationships between Asian civilizations and indigenous Americans B.C.E. Several of their civilizations were profoundly influenced by Afrakan contact.

Afrakan-centered education in American communities for Afrakans must and should operate on the same principles and the same goals as Afrakans in Tanzania, Ghana, Ethiopia, and South Afraka. The essential goals are genuinely self-sufficiency, self-determination, and Nationship and Pan-Afrakan unity.

The Kultural ideological spacial perception of the educational system must be clear to every member of the Afrakan community. Afrakans of the 63rd century must innerstand that our membership requires an active role in helping to develop and maintain our educational system through work, and active intellectual and Kultural growth. Education must reflect the totality of the Afrakan-centered Kultural expression. These expressions include philosophy or Afrakan Deep Thought, morality, spirituality, ethics, politics, ideology, aesthetics, science, law, defense, security and relationships. Each expression of the Afrakan Kulture must factor in the economic processes of sustaining the educational Institutions. In return, the Educational Institutions will serve to perpetuate the entire Afrakan Kultural reality, through an Afrakan Worldview in relationship to Afrakan Nationship.

Wherever Caucastian male domination exists, Afrakan youth experience a racial and Kultural identity crisis, which leads them to display racially dysfunctional behaviors. If one looks even closer, one will find that they come from families that lack Afrakan Kultural centeredness. This backward phenomena is by design, and occurs whenever you are not in control of your own educational system. Information on their Kulture and Afrakan-centered Ourstory concerning our common oppression, and the need for collective Afrakan commitment to ensure our liberation is not transmitted to Afrakan youth during their early critical developmental years at home or in their schooling. This is why Afrakan-centered educational Institutions are necessary for Afrakan people. If there is no Afrakan-centered school available, at least create an after school Kultural program or weekend Kultural educational supplementary program that will teach what you know the public schools will not.

The Council of Independent Black Institutions (CIBI) is laying down some beautiful groundwork for future Independent Afrakan-centered schools to follow. Recently, there have been a growing number of Afrakan so-called independent schools who have changed their status to chartered schools to receive government funding. It is this author's view that chartered schools cannot be, and are not, independent of the very hands that are responsible for their problems. I do not support these schools; they are also part of our problem, for creating a diversion and an illusion of Afrakan-centeredness, when they are part of the system of white male domination in Blackface. We must sponsor and finance our own liberation and we should not be going backwards, but forever forward. At the same time, I innerstand that an Afrakan-centered chartered school is better than having our children's minds completely controlled by this European American mis-educational system, (if this is only a step towards total control.) However, we must be clear that an Afrakan-centered chartered school is an oxymoron.

Let us be extremely clear as Afrakan people, our public schools are operating in a mis-educational oppressive system that supports Caucasian male domination, we are teaching our Afrakan children to have a death wish by teaching them European culture from a Eurocentric worldview, which is controlling their desires. Desire takes over your wishes, dreams, wants, behaviors, and perceptions, so it is not an accident that the urban school districts are the worst in the nation. It is not an accident that the urban youth have developed a sub-culture based on the worst European values, and criminal behavior, with unlimited funds to perpetuate the negative Rap artist and culture. It must be clear that negative Rap and Hip Hop music was created, and funded by the desires of Caucasian male domination. This negative music perpetuates European Caucasian male domination. The system of European Caucasian male domination could not last without the constant perpetuation of insane desires. The European Caucasian American educational system is the carrier of this deadly disease, along with capitalism and its supporting political system.

Spiritual Warriors must make it clear to the Afrakan population how important Kulture is to your educational system. It is your educational system along with your family values, that controls your desires, and your desires control your aspirations or lack of positive realistic goals. The more Afrakans in political office in America, the more Afrakans in jail, because we carry out the same insane desires as white male domination in Blackface, and that is what they represent. Black men are 7 times more likely to be arrested than white men are, and 23 times more likely to be jailed than white men are. Unemployment for Black men between the age of 18 and 29 is over 50%. One of four Black men in the urban cities between the ages of 18 to 29 is in jail or on the probation system. Homicide is the number one reason for death among Black men in America between the ages 18 to 35. We are being programmed for death in the American mis-educational system. America is a criminal country and it is set up like the Mafia. America has more people in prison than all the rest of the nations of the world combined. Prisons are the new plantations and enslaved prisoners are the new slaves of the 21st century, western time or 63rd century new Afrakan time. Caucasian men are the overseers or police and they are not arresting Caucasian men at the same rate they are arresting the rest of the population. What the American mis-educational system is not telling us is that Caucasian men are the master criminals, killers, thieves, psychopaths, and serial killers. We must remember, that is how Afrakans got to Americas and the rest of the Diaspora in the first place.

In the urban school setting, 20% of Afrakan male students are receiving the grade C or better and 80% are failing. 50% of all suspensions in the New York and New Jersey schools are Afrakan males. We are carrying out the wishes of white male domination through black-on-black crime, poor health and poor health habits, which increases high blood pressure, causes heart disease, etc. Caucasian produced desires are designed to destroy your health, mind and spirit. Moreover, Afrakan educators and politicians are perpetuating Caucasian male domination through their ignorance of their own Afrakan Kulture. Moreover, the few positive Afrakan thinking Afrakans in the public schools, are looked on as the bad people, and at best are band-aids, when major surgery is needed.

Afrakan Spiritual Warriors must be in control of our Afrakan-centered educational system. Afrakan Kulture must be at the center of all Afrakan peoples' education. This is the only way to control the desires of Afrakan people. How we relate to other people and to ourselves will depend on our desires. Our educational institutions must teach us to manufacture our own desires, while at the same time removing the desires for white male domination. These are also the steps towards creating new Afrakans and a nation within a nation.

There must be at least three levels to Afrakan-centered education: (1) Independent Afrakan-centered schools as defined in the CIBI charter; (2) Afrakan-centered institutions in a rural setting on a campus with dormitories that simulates a nation within a nation. Afrakans in the urban cities must develop schools in liberated zones outside the urban jungles. These Afrakan-centered schools must also have campuses with dormitories to house these youth, so that we can Kemtrol and control, not only their education, but also their desires, through the mass media an a powerful loving Afrakan-centered family life; and (3) Afrakan-centered boot camps to house and re-Afrakanize Afrakan wanafunzi (students) who are damaged beyond the reach of normal Afrakan-centered institutions. They will have no TV, no movies, no radio, no signs of Caucasian European domination spacial perspective, but a strong Afrakan-centered military discipline program to undo the damage of Caucasian European domination, while rebuilding useful citizens and warriors for our new Pan-Afrakan communities and Nationship. In addition, all three levels must have highly trained teachers and administrators who are Spiritual Warriors or who were at least trained by CIBI for an Afrakan centered Worldview.

No one said this struggle for our minds and the minds of our children was going to be easy. We must activate powerful Sankofa Spirits along with equally powerful Spiritual rituals to resurrect the essence of our soul. Only Afrakan Spiritual Warriors, as teachers and jegnoch, and Father/ Mother nature, along with the Ntchru can nurture Afrakan people back to their right Afrakan minds and Heru Konsciousness.

As Spiritual Afrakan Warriors, we must create an **Afrakan** Critical Think Tank, or a council of Afrakan-centered respected Elders, nationally and by regions. Once it is operational, 24/7, 365 days of a year from an Afrakan-centered perspective, we will have a core group whose purpose is to identify and implement strategies that will eliminate the causes of our Afrakan downfall, and Maangamizi. Then and only than will we be in a position to reclaim our worldwide freedom. The Afrakan-centered educational Institutions will be at the center of this new liberation and Nationship for Afrakan people, worldwide.

Spiritual Warriors must create the environment that puts us into a position where we are controlling our own environment and perpetuating a powerful independent positive future. Only by developing our own independent schools, not chartered, not Afro centric public schools, can this happen. This does not mean that Afrakans do not have the right to go to "the public" institutions, or any school that we choose. We as Afrakan people just need our own Afrakan institutions that define our own reality and that is engaged in the dialogue of human progress from an Afrakan-centered perspective. The following are examples of the Konsciousness and leadership we must take as Afrakan Warriors in our independent schools, with positive Afrakan centered Black Afrakan teachers.

The CIBI pledge is done by the whole shule (school) every morning in all the CIBI schools. In addition, each shule has their own Afrikan Pledges, songs and positive affirmations. At Afrakan People's Action School (APAS), these healing rituals are done the first thing in the morning and just before going home in the late afternoon. Songs like <u>Red, Black and Green, Nkosi Sikelel' Afrika, and Lift Every Voice and Sing.</u>, And Msamafo! (Ancestors). We, as Afrakan people must teach, train and program our watoto to love each other and to have our own best interest at the center of our development, mentally physically and spiritually.

The CIBI PLEDGE

We are Afrikan people struggling for national liberation,

We are preparing leaders and workers to bring about a positive change for our people,

We stress the development of our bodies, minds, souls and Konsciousness,

Our commitment is to self-determination, self-defense and self-respect for our race.

The APAS PLEDGE

We struggle today for a Black tomorrow
Pamoja tutashinda
Together we build a nation strong
Pamoja tutashinda
We remember and study our Afrikan roots
Pamoja tutashinda
Afrikan people with Afrikan minds, all members of one family
It's nation time! It's nation time!
Time for Afrikan Kazi

(Pamoja tutashinda means "together we will win,"
Kazi means "work".)

We are a strong Afrikan people
Ready to work
Ready to learn
Ready to re-build our new world

LEADERSHIP PLEDGE

I am the Spirit of Afrakan People,
I am a representative of Ma'at

I will lead not follow,
I will create not destroy, I will love not hate,
I am a force like Heru, ready to fight the enemies of our people and the enemies of "The Way".
I am an Afrakan leader,
I will defy the odds and I will succeed!

Pledge on Black Manship and Afrakan-centeredness

I am the Black Man, an Afrakan
Some knew me as Aha Heru, Imhotep, Mentuhotep, Hannabal, Sundiata Keita, Shaka Zulu ,from ancient Afraka or Hale Salaie, Kwame Nkruma, Julius Nyerere, Steven Biko and Patrice Lumba of modern Afraka.
Others in America knew me as Nat Turner, Denmark Vasey, Gabrel Processor, Martin Delany, David Walker, and Frederik Douglass yesterday or as Marcus Garvey, W. E. B. DuBois, Elija Mohammad, Osajifu El Hajji Malik El Shabas today.
I am all of them.
From this day forward I pledge my life to the liberation of Afrakan people at home - Afraka and throughout the Diaspora.
I will put the Creator first in my life,
with Ma'at as my guide.
Afrakan women will feel safe and secure when they see me.
I will be a supportive, responsible, protective, and loving mate.
I am the original Black human.
The most powerful yet gentle Warrior on the planet.
The one that other men are afraid of.
Because they know whenever I've been given the opportunity
Isucceed!!!

The Afrakan Konsciousness pledge is done in my 7th and 8th grade classes at Afrakan Peoples Action Shule (APAS) every Friday as part of our re-Afrakanization Program along with the Nguzo Saba, Kiswahili, Mdw Ntchr, Afrakan-Kemet studies and Pan-Afrakan current events.

"Afrakan Konsciousness"

1. Love for The NTCHR is first, for The NTCHR is love, and it is you and you are the world, and the world is NTCHR.

2. Develop knowledge of your Afrakan heritage. Embrace the spirit of Sankoka, go back and fetch what is yours and bring it to the future. Embrace Mdw Ntchr, our classical language and other Afrakan languages like Kiswahili, Wolof, Ashante Twe, Yuroba, for language is the key to innerstanding Kulture.

3. Develop respect for yourself, your family, your elders, your brothers and sisters, which is the core to the Afrakan Nation and our Afrakan Worldview.

4. Develop a clear and open line of communication between parents, children, the extended family, elders, educators and the institutions of the Pan-Afrakan community.

5. Develop institutions in the Afrakan community that equitably provide and distribute, for all its members, goods and services which include food, clothing, housing, transportation, education, recreation, health care, energy, sanitation and protection.

6. Develop immediate, middle, and long range goals and firm objectives for yourself, and your family in relationship to your people and nation.

7. Develop and maintain strong rights of passage programs for the development of dynamic men and women.

institutions. They will have no TV, no movies, no radio, no signs of white male domination spacial perspective, but a strong Afrakan-centered military discipline program to undo the damage of white-male domination.

8. Develop your knowledge of the world through Ourstory, and develop and maintain educational institutions to teach them from an Afrakan-centered Worldview, because education is a key link to economic and spiritual strength.

9. Develop a clear innerstanding of Ma'at, so that ideologies and philosophies can be based on truth, justice and righteousness and harmonious balance (Ma'at).

10. Develop a spiritual belief system based on the Kemetik spiritual science with an Afrakan Kultural foundation. Afrakan spirituality is an essential aspect of Afrakan people and we must use it as an instrument of our liberation.

11. Develop discipline, control, and focus so that you can guard against lust, desire, greed, fear and sheer materialism.

12. Develop and maintain an Afrakan-centered Worldview with a positive life-giving Afrakan Kulture at your center.

13. Develop our Homeland Afraka, our place of origin and to develop it to our fullest potential because to develop something of value or something of beauty and not be able to defend it is like not having it all.

Only your own powerful Afrakan institutions that stand behind your people rooted in a Spiritual Pan-Afrakan Worldview in economic development, social development, Kultural development, intellectual development, scientific development, and defense development can legitimize who you are in an insane, totally crazy world controlled by Caucasian European male domination.

Afrakan-centered educators: Dr. Asa Hilliard the first Vice President of ASCAC, Professor, psychologist, Ourstorian and author of SBA; The Reawakening of the Afrikan Mind, with Mfundishi Jhutymes Ka en Heru at an ASCAC conference.

Afrakan-centered educators; Dr. Theophile Obenga, a giant in the field of Afrakan Studies and a master teacher, lecturer, and author, teaching a Mdw Netcher workshop at an ASCAC conference.

Afrakan-centered educators: Left, Dr. Leonard Jeffries second Vice President of ASCAC & Dr. Jacob Caruthers, The First Presidents of ASCAC, The Association for the Study of Classical Afrikan Civilization. Right, Sis. Rhkety Amen in the center, after lecturing on Mdw Ntchr and Afrakan Spirituality, with community educators Mfundishi Salim and Bro. Kames Haki.

Afrakan-centered educators: Bottom left, Mr. & Mrs. Dr.Wade Nobles. Right, Bro. Ashra Kwesi & Dr. Barashango.

Mfundishi with 9 year old CIBI Imhotep science award winner Khalif from Minneapolis, Minasota with his mother and teacher at the Imhotep Science Academy,2oo3.Below CIBI Ndundun members Mfundishi Salim and the CIBI Science Expo Coodinatior Karume Jumal from Omowale Ujamaa Shule, Pasadena, Calafornia.

POINT 5; GOALS: Afrakan Spiritual Warriors must be able to develop Afrakan-centered educational institutions that are soulfully committed to the reconstruction of Afrakan Kulture for Afrakan Sovereignty and Nationship. Through the reclamation of Afrakan Ourstory, history and critical and creative analysis of all knowledge and experiences from an Afrakan-centered perspective. The goal is to develop and institutionalize a complete and more comprehensive Ourstorical Konsciousness, from antiquity to the contemporary, that will be the basis of Pan-Afrakan unity worldwide. This Konsciousness must be a part of our school system from Nursery school through the University level education. These Afrakan-centered educational Institutions must be completely financially independent of any government funding, unless it is in the form of grants and reparations, for whoever controls the institution financially eventually directs the course of the institution. Teach real education that inspires Afrakan people to live by the natural laws of the Earth. The teachers in our Afrakan-centered institutions can only be systematically facilitated by people who themselves are Konsciously engaged in the process of Afrakan-centered personal transformation. Afrakans must learn to innerstand life as we find it, and learn the skills necessary to make it better. Spiritual Warriors must transmit this Afrakan-centered information from one generation to the next. This knowledge and wisdom has been accumulated from the best of our society and must be disseminated to our young people to prepare them for the future membership of our new Afrakan community. The youth must be trained so that they can actively participate in the continued maintenance of this new Pan-Afrakan Worldview. Every child can learn if motivated. We believe that approaching education from an Afrakan Kultural context and Worldview is an important means of providing educational motivation for Afrakan children and adults. Education should challenge Afrakan students to apply the skills they acquire in the service of their community and its needs. We as Spiritual Warriors embrace the traditional Afrakan wisdom that "children are the reward of life" and it is, therefore, an expression of our unconditional love for them, that we build, maintain, protect and financially support Afrakan-centered institutions.

6. *Pan-Afrakan Political Governance and Collective Ethos*

Effective Pan-Afrakan political governance and leadership requires an Afrakan-centered vision in administrative skills, with the ability to motivate and inspire Afrakan people. When the Afrakan leaders are Afrakan-centered, there is a greater clarity in ideological and moral consistency. In order to develop and maintain an ideology of Afrakan unity and liberation, there must be dedicated groups of Afrakan-centered scholars, researchers, and activists who are committed to extracting from Ourstory, from our contemporary experience the principles that guide Afrakans to liberation, independence and self-determination towards an Afrakan Worldview and Afrakan Nationship.

Pan-Afrakan political leaders must embrace Afrakan Kulture, and the development of a United States of Afraka, utilizing the concept of a nation within a nation wherever we are. Afrakan political leaders must be committed to protecting Black life, mentally, physically and spiritually, even with their last breath. The laws governing the society must protect Afrakans, and those Afrakans living in that society must feel a sense of Nationship. Feeling like one nation is the highest ideal of all people in a nation.

Afrakan Spiritual Warriors must embrace the political leadership of the Afrakan community so that an appreciation of the need to foster an Afrakan-centered Kulture and political unity among all Afrakan people everywhere can become a reality. Part of this Afrakan political commitment is to an Afrakan Kultural unity. Afrakan Kulture, from a political perspective, requires that Afrakans throughout the Diaspora and the continent of Afraka support a United States of Afraka. In America, this means that we support a nation within a nation and the political leaders must represent a national council of elders who have only Afrakan people's best interest at heart and mind. Black collective leadership is a primary requirement for the 63rd century. Black elected government officials are suppose to represent all the people, and they are the protectors of white male domination in black-face, so they can't by the nature of the beast represent, protect and defend Afrakan people and our communities, but we must learn how to make them at least double agents.

Because of the Caucasian tyranny against Afrakan people world-wide, it is mandatory that all Afrakan people and people of Afrakan descent work together towards the creation of a new Afrakan world order. Therefore, Afrakans must develop Afrakan-centered Information and Strategy Centers that are completely owned, funded and run by Afrakan-centered Spiritual Warriors if we are to become liberated and stay liberated. Afrikan American elected officials of the Matrix cannot, and will not, save us.

This network of highly trained Spiritual Warriors must provide Pan-Afrakan leaders with relevant information, intelligence, strategies and tactics to use for liberating Afrakan people from their various oppressors.

Afrakan people are not enslaved mentally, physically and spiritually because they are not intelligent or powerful warriors. Afrakans are oppressed worldwide because we lack the intelligent information outlining the who, what, why, and causes of our oppression. Therefore, we do not have effective plans that will, from an Afrakan-centered perspective, correct this oppression, bringing balance into being. Because we lack this special intelligent information, it becomes increasingly difficult to develop dynamic, necessary blue prints to set in place a strategy for becoming strong and independent.

Spiritual Warriors of the 63rd century will have to develop the network of intelligence that can answer the questions of how do we as Afrakans, gain power over our destiny, mentally, physically and spiritually. How do we fund this Afrakan-centered intelligence agency? Spiritual Warriors clearly innerstand that this agency must be totally funded by the Afrakan and Pan-Afrakan community. Afrakans in the United States have the money; we earn over $500,000,000.00 annually. It is just not a priority in our backward, western programmed, enslaved drugged out thinking process. However, this would change with our new Afrakan Kultural re-Afrakanization process. Spiritual Warriors will have to staff it with expert blue print technicians and intelligent operators who can scope out Afrakan problems, detect the presence of barriers, find ways of entering closed places, set agendas, plan political strategies, and act upon agreed-on Afrakan-centered objectives.

The strategic purpose of the Afrakan-centered intelligence agency is to define what Afrakan people, organizations and nations should and can do in order to succeed in the 63rd century. Spiritual Warriors have to become first class spies in order to get some of the information we need to end Afrakan oppression. However, like any other nation, Afrakans will be no stronger than our information and intelligence. Spiritual Warriors will have to be impeccable Warriors in order to keep the world of esfet in control, within its own borders.

There is some basic information this Afrakan-centered intelligence agency must research, analyze and publish or make known to the Afrakan-centered leadership of Esteemed Elders. Answers are needed to some basic questions:

* What are the most critical obstacles standing in the way of developing Afrakan-centered, Afrakan owned schools in America, Afraka and the Diaspora?

* What are the underlying principles causes for Afrakan insanity, the love of white death?

* What states, cities and congressional districts offer the best opportunities for building Afrakan political strength in America?

* What, in order of importance, are the current forces that pose the greatest obstacles to the progress of Afrakans locally, nationally and worldwide?

* What are the major steps in developing a United States of Afraka on the Afrakan continent, and making the O.A.U. Real?

* How can Afrakans stop corruption in government on the Afrakan continent and disband all European Caucasian concepts of government?

* What are the principal steps in securing the raw materials that Afraka already has, so that it can develop its own mass transportation network, from plane, train, ship and car manufacturing?

* What are the obstacles, in order of priority that Afrakans must address to rebuild the infrastructure of all Afrakan cities on the continent, so that they are in order with Ma'at and in harmony with the new Pan-Afrakan Kulture and Worldview ?

* Do Afrakans need to relocate to specific areas in America for greater control of our destiny and for greater safety based on the innerstanding of the nature of Caucasian male domination?

* How does Afraka go about reclaiming her natural resources, like the gold in South Afraka and the diamond mines stolen by Europeans, who still control them even though the country has disbanded the legal racist system of apartheid, without causing a world war or race war?

* What are the very best steps towards re-claiming and re-building the Afrakan family in America and in the Carib-bean?

* How do we re-organize the Afrakan entertainment and music Industry so that they are reflective of a Pan-Afrakan Worldview?

* What are the major steps in controlling our sports and athletic teams and athletes so that the Afrakan Community will benefit from the billions of dollars that are generated yearly from these gladiator sports.

In order to conquer and rule Afrakans, Europeans used the old divide and conquer methodology. To accomplish these divisions and foster conflicts among Afrakans, the Europeans deliberately divided Kultural groups inside new colonial boundaries and combined different, unrelated ethnic groups to effectively pit Blacks against each other. This formula was used repeatedly throughout Afraka, the Caribbean, South America and here in the United States. Consequently, as Marcia Sutherland states in her book Black Authenticity, "Afrakans have surrendered to tribalism." Even without Europeans present, Afrakans on the continent will be engaged in; tribal wars and border conflict for the next hundred years, unless we begin to take Pan-Afrakanism seriously. Spiritual Warriors can clearly see that because we, as Afrakan people failed to form alliances with each other when we first encountered the white man and the invading Arab Muslims, our common enemy, they were able to destroy our way of life through divide and conquer, and we lost our independence. As *Afrakan people in the 63rd century, we will have to form alliances with each other.* It is the only road back to independence, self-reliance and self-respect. This alliance today is called Pan-Afrakanism. The importance of Afrakan people forming alliances around Afrakan Kulture and the development of a United States of Afraka is as essential as air itself for the survival of Afrakan people. We must always consider the political implications of what we say, what we do and what we write. Afrakans must face the undeniable fact that we all have a common enemy, white male domination, and as long as we stay divided we will continue to be oppressed by white male domination. Therefore, we have a common struggle, and a common goal. Afrakan people must unite under a national Konsciousness, rooted and growing from our new Afrakan Kultural identity. This cannot be over-emphasized, **we must unite Yesterday!**

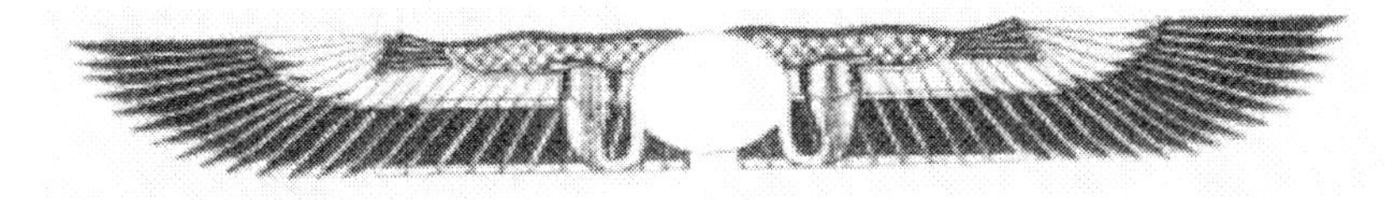

Afrakan nations and Afrakan people are being used as pawns in a world power game that we have not learned how to play. We know the nature of the Caucasian Europeans, the Wazungu and the nature of Arabs, but we are not listening to what the records are showing us. re-read ***Things Fall Apart***, and ***Two Thousand Seasons***. Neither the European nor the Arabs came to Afraka to share power with Afrakan people; one look at history and Ourstory, will confirm this fact. They both came to Afraka as uninvited quest and stayed as conquerors. Our Pan-Afrakan political governance teaches Afrakan people that Caucasian Europeans and Arabs, and their way of life, is anti-Afrakan. Therefore, they are our enemies.

Dr. Asa Hilliard in the beginning of his book ***SBA: The Reawakening of The African Mind***, states, "Our first mistake was that we thought of freedom as a place, rather than as a continuation of a struggle. Tyranny never sleeps. Our second mistake was that we thought of freedom as a goal, rather than as a launching pad from which to reach our goals. Without purposes, freedom hardly matters. Our third mistake was we thought that freedom made us free. That, however, is license - not freedom at all. Freedom is being shackled to identity, purpose and direction, and being in constant pursuit."

Spiritual Warriors of political Konsciousness: The late Dr. Kwame Nkruma the first President of Ghana and a giant spirit of Black Nationalism. left, and Professor James Small right, Professor, lecturer, community and political activist, President of the Organization of Afrakan American Unity with Mfundishi El-Salim at the funeral of another great Spiritual Warrior Dr. Khalid Muhammad.

POINT 6; GOALS: Afrakan political leaders must develop and maintain an ideological clarity and spiritual love for Afrakan people. We must be committed to organizing and unifying a productive and dynamic Afrakan nationality for Afrakans in America a nationality that will be connected to Afrakans worldwide and ultimately in the United States of Afraka. To develop Pan-Afrakan political leaders who are part of the Afrakan community and who are committed to developing, building and maintaining Afrakan Institutions that will train children to be leaders like the best of our ancient Afrakan ancestors. To develop an infrastructure that will be able to spot and train leaders early and begin to instill in them an undying love for Afraka and Afrakan people. Pan-Afrakanism is the only ideology for the construction of a united and prosperous Afrakan Worldview. To develop an Afrakan-centered intelligence agency and strategy center that will answer the needed questions dealing with Afrakan liberation and total Pan-Afrakan independence. Our lives will become powerful and respected only when Pan-Afrakanism Is enshrined in our daily attitudes and practices. Only then, will we as Afrakans become liberated and stay liberated, while recovering our land, our human integrity, our Kulture and our traditional greatness and prosperity.

Left, Dr. Yosef ben-Jochannan The father of modern Kemetology & Dr. Molefi Asante, the father of the political concept of Afrikancentricity.

7. The Ujamaa Economic System

We as Afrakan people and Afrakan Spiritual Warriors must embrace an Afrakan-centered economic system if we are to survive in the 63rd. century. We certainly agree that Afrakan people must demonstrate greater self-reliance and self-determination in improving the economic conditions of Afraka and Afrakan people worldwide. We are proposing the Ujamaa Economic system of "do for self," along with Network Marketing. An Afrakan-centered economic system must have Pan-Afrakanism at the heart. A Pan-Afrakan economic system reflects Afrakan values and Kulture, which are fundamental and indispensable to the development and upward mobility of a United States of Afraka or any Afrakan nation or community. The Ujamaa Economic System embraces a unified Afrakan Continent concept in its planning. As Afrakan Spiritual Warriors, we are committed to the philosophy that Afrakan people must work towards this goal of economic sovereignty.

Afraka is the richest continent in natural resources in the world. These resources include valuable minerals and energy exports like gold, diamonds, uranium, oil, and the raw materials needed for modern technology. Afraka is the last geographic mineral reservoir in the world. However, the Caucasian western world receives about 85% of Afraka's natural useable resources. The majority of the world's gold and diamonds come from Afraka. Nevertheless, Black Afrakans receive very little of this enormous wealth. There is uranium in Ethiopia, Cameroon, Nigeria, and the Sahara, along with the Republic of the Congo, Ghana, Zambia, Mozambique, Uganda and South Afraka. There are oil deposits in Gabon, Nigeria, Senegal, Angola, and the Congo. And these are only a few of the great energy sources within Black Afraka which, in themselves, could make the United States of Afraka one of the most highly industrialized countries in the world.

Afraka is the home of the longest river in the world and many other great waterways and lakes. Black Afraka leads the world in hydraulic energy with its reserves of thousands of billions of kilowatt-hours representing about half the total world resources. A few of these great river sources are the Nile, the Niger, the Zaire River, and the Sanaga River. The hydroelectric power of the Zaire Basin alone (Inga and Kisangani dams) could supply all of the United States of Afraka or the Afrakan continent with electricity.

Another energy source that exists in Afraka is wind energy. Properly utilized trade winds along the west coast of Afraka could supply Afraka with an enormous amount of energy. Afraka is also rich in thermal energy. All of East Afraka (Ethiopia, Kenya, Uganda, Tanzania and the entire Rift Valley region) would be eminently suited for the installation of plants powered by geothermal energy. It is also important to note that hydraulic energy, solar energy, wind energy, thermonuclear energy, volcanic and geothermal energy, all of these Afrakan energies, are non-polluting to the environment unlike the oil, coal, nuclear and atomic energies primarily used in the west.

Afraka also has rich fertile land conducive to agrikulture. However, Afraka, once an agrarian giant, the land where agrikulture started, has lost the ability to feed itself. Of the continents in the world, Afraka is the only one in which, if present trends continue, the majority of her people will be living in poverty and will remain in increasing poverty, while the rest of the world is on course to eliminating poverty. Afraka and Afrakans worldwide have become mass consumers. Afraka plays no significant role as producer of manufactured goods, contributing an estimated 0.5 % to the world production (Kodjo, 1987).

The Ujamaa Economy stresses and supports a United States of Afraka. It also stresses the elimination of colonialism, Caucasian male domination, its western imposed borders and the disengagement of the western economic system, along with its European political systems. Afraka and Afrakans worldwide, must support and practice Pan-Afrakanism, an interracial Afrakan controlled economic structure that benefits Afraka and Afrakans throughout the Diaspora. Afrakans are the third largest ethnic group in the world. All we need to do is support ourselves and become our own best friends. New Afrakans will have to create our own Afrakan economic financial system, based upon the wealth of Afraka and Afrakan people. Moreover, as Spiritual Warriors, we must be able to defend our institutions with our very lives. We already know the nature of the Wazungu and Asiatics; we must now revolutionize our economic security forces, as well as our national security against esfet.

Afraka must first invest in rural agrikultural development to meet its domestic needs. The only way to do this is to eliminate Caucasian European male domination from all of its institutions and the minds of Afrakans everywhere. For the Spiritual Warrior it is clear that education also works hand in hand with your economic system. All attention now must be turned within the mental, spiritual, and physical boarders of Afraka and Afrakans. Once Afraka attains a level of productivity to generate a surplus of food, then those funds should be directed toward research, training, health-care, education, and technology for Pan-Afrakan progress and development.

We, as Afrakan people, must support other Afrakans to the extent that we become a nation within a nation wherever we are. Ujamaa Economics means that we buy Black, and build with Afrakan builders and designers who are Afrakan-centered. We must invest Black, sell Black, and circulate the Black dollar several times before it leaves Afrakan communities. We must be as prosperous as Black Wall Street was in Tulsa Oklahoma in 1920, which circulated the dollar 36 to 100 times, sometimes taking a year for currency to leave their community "Little Afrika". Today in the 21st. century, western time, a dollar leaves the Black community in 10 minutes. Spiritual Warriors clearly innerstand that Afrakan economic success depends on us spending our money with Afrakan people first. There are over a billion Afrakan people, and more than two billion Black people in this world. All we have to do is to learn how to support ourselves, defend ourselves and love ourselves. Then we can solve all of our economic and political problems.

Afrakan Kulture must direct and generate the foundation and conditions that controls the mode of Afrakan production. This is the only way that Afrakans worldwide can build, expand and perpetuate an Afrakan- centered future. Afrakans who embrace the Ujamaa Economy must build all their institutions using the Moyo, or the Afrakan Soul force. By using the new Afrakan Kultural guide, Afrakans are guaranteeing their soul expression be expressed in the economy, schools, universities, community centers, housing developments, Afrakan trade, cottage industry, technology, scientific research, Afrakan corporate Institutions, parks, farms, music, literary productions, communication and distribution.

The Ujamaa Economy is also part of the re-Afrakanization process for Afrakan people, if we are to become a nation within a nation or have sovereignty. As long as Afrakans in America spend huge amounts of money and consume indiscriminately from non-Afrakan businesses and service establishments, who contribute little or nothing to our economic growth and stability, Afrikan communities will remain poor. As long as we do not circulate our dollars in our own business and service establishments, we will remain enslaved to a process that is destroying our community's ability to do for itself. We will always be at the bottom of the world economic ladder if we do not embrace the Pan-Afrakan Ujamaa Economy. We can use our own power of economic strength with Network Marketing of Businesses, Investments, as well as human and natural Afrakan resources to solve all of our own problems in America, in the Diaspora, and Afraka itself. Remember Afrakans in America spend more money than the gross national product of Canada, more than $500,000,000. Afrakans in America having the potential to be the ninth wealthiest Nation in the world, if we operated from a national Pan-Afrakan Konsciousness System. However, the reality is that we do not operate or spend our money as a united, Konscious Afrakan family. According to the U.S. Census Department and the Economic Census Report for 1997, businesses owned by Afrakans in America accounted for only one third of one percent of all businesses in the U S. This means that for every $100 spent with businesses in America, Afrakan businesses earned $.35 cents. This is economic slavery in the 21st. century western time. Caucasian male domination has painted the picture that Afrakans in America are doing fine, but the reality again is that we have been Had! Bamboozled, we have been economically enslaved in this country since 1619. That is why we were kidnapped, stolen, rapped, robed and brought here to America, and those blacks who were here, their land stolen, and very little has changed. During the savage period of the Maangamizi when Afrakans were treated as chattel slavery, we had to be close to 1/3 of one percent of the economy. In 400 years, America has only changed the name of the game, but the reality is still economic enslavement, racism and Kultural exploitation with white on top and black on the bottom. Why can't we as Afrakan people see that a snake is a snake, is a snake! The Wazungu or the Caucasian European economic system has not changed; his nature has not changed at all.

Afrakans in America, Afrakans on the continent and Afrakans throughout the Diaspora must not think as a minority, but as a majority, and as a Pan-Afrakan international family. With this new wholistic, spiritual Afrakan Worldview, Afrakan people can begin to produce every single item essential to our survival from the things we wear, the food we eat, to the cars we drive. The Ujamaa Economy also involves training our Afrakan children to follow our positive Pan-Afrakan footsteps, to complete the mission. We can employ ourselves by producing for ourselves, and then purchasing products and services from each other. The mission will be self-sustaining, self-reliance, self-employment, and self-defense all of this is sovereignty. This is also Network Marketing of Business and Institutions.

Before we knew Europeans and Asians existed, we fed ourselves, clothed ourselves, housed ourselves, traded among ourselves and created the world's most dynamic civilizations. We need to regain our confidence in ourselves, so that we can do for ourselves again. If we truly analyze our true story, we will see that we have always been a rich people. Afrakans are rich in Kulture, rich in ideas and rich in imagination. Only through a Pan-Afrakan economic system, based on our new Afrakan Kulture and Worldview, can we re-empower Afrakan people economically.

Solar energy is the energy of the future since it will exist as long as there is a sun or we can receive its light. Afraka is the home of unlimited solar energy as it houses the largest desert in the world. The Sahara is almost the size of the entire United States, and Afraka is the hottest continent in the world, with a land mass of almost 13 million square miles.

The entire Afrakan continent lies in the tropical or subtropical zone, and is the home of an abundance of natural reusable nontoxic energy sources. We must use our greatest resources, our Afrakan minds, our own Afrakan genius to empower us economically.

POINT 7; GOALS: For Afrakan people to embrace the Ujamaa Economy, an Afrakan-centered, and Pan-Afrakan economic base system of survival. This Afrakan-centered economy strengthens the community because it allows the community to become a nation within a nation, by reshaping its spending, consumption and investment patterns and organizing its Konsciousness in ways which best serve the Afrakan community and Afraka. When you have a nation within a nation, all non-Afrakan Institutions and companies must contribute to the Afrakan community and support that community if they want the business of Afrakan people and to remain in that community. The process of accomplishing these Afrakan-centered economic goals will radically and positively transform the Afrakan-centered and Pan-Afrakan socioeconomic community to a state of self-sufficiency. Afrakan governments must embrace a Pan-Afrakan Worldview and create the environment for Afrakans in the Diaspora to respond with Ma'at. Only after we as Afrakan people re-create a new powerful spiritual Afrakan world order will Afrakan people invest their faith, confidence and economic power in Afraka. Hence, the Kultural Konsciousness is essential in order to release our creativity and positive Heru energy in order to build a better world For Afrakans and all of humanity. When Afrakan people reclaim their right Afrakan mind and our own Pan-Afrakan Spiritual Worldview, which will nurture and perpetuate a strong mental, physical and spiritual control over our lives, then the planet will be able to heal itself, because we are the soul of the planet!

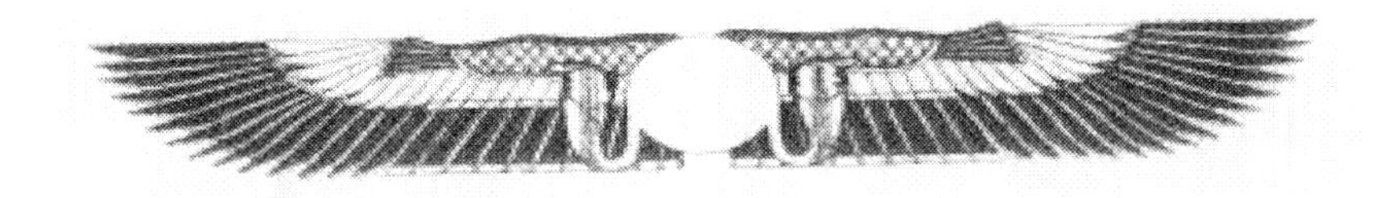

Left, Haki Madhubuti is a leader in Pan-Afrakanism and self-determination. He is a Spiriual Warrior who believes in taking control of the institutions that control your children and therefore your future. Bro. Haki Madhubuti is a poet, essayist, author, community activist, educator and publisher of Third World Press. Right, Bro. Anthony Browder with his daughter Atlantis. Tony Browder is an author, publisher, cultural historian, artist, and educational consultant, but most of all, he is a Spiritual Warrior of Self-Determination. Bottom left, Dr. Barbara Ann Teer founder of the National Black Theatre and right, Susan Taylor of "Essence Magazine" with Designer Natchura Hapi of Chicago.

8. *Psychological, Spiritual and Physical Health and Healing Systems.*

Afrakan Kulture must dictate the spiritual, psychological and physical nature of how healing takes place, so that the Kulture can be the healing tool that it is. All aesthetics and concepts of beauty find their source in spiritual, emotional, and intellectual reflections of your own Kultural essence. Afrakan healing and beauty are reflections of our own ideal versions of ourselves, of our Black Afrakan Kulture.

How Afrakan people view and internalize beauty has a lot to do with our mental, physical and psychological health. If Afrakan people spend most of their lives in pursuit of what is unnatural for them, and therefore, dangerous and unhealthy, the physical body will be weakened and placed in a state that will allow disease to enter the body-temple. Afrakan Kulture must promote the development of a sense of beauty and righteousness that is Afrakan-centered. That which is good or Ma'at from an Afrakan-center is beautiful. The standard of beauty within a race is determined by that which is outstanding, typical within but unique to that race. Afrakan people must celebrate that which is Black, melanin, and typical of Afraka and Afrakan people.

An Afrakan-centered psychological and spiritual outlook on the world is concerned with the acquisition of self-determination, self-respect, self-esteem, self-sufficiency, as well as, self-defense, for Afrakan people. Spirituality, the ultimate truth for Afrakan-centered Spiritual Warriors, is to humanize ourselves in concert with the Earth; this humanization of our spirit promotes optimum health.

The poor state of health, mentally, physically and spiritually, in the Afrakan community in America, in the Diaspora and on the Afrakan continent itself, has to do with the defeat of Afraka and Afrakan people by foreign cultural systems like Arabs under Islam and Caucasian male domination under Christianity. Afrakans have surrendered their continent, along with Afrakan Kulture. This was a result of the physical and psychological destruction of Afrakan civilization by the European, Asian and Arab invaders, conquerors and enslavers of Afrakan people. This initial destruction was then followed by the Maangamizi and compounded with Caucasian European male domination. This genocidal destruction was equivalent to ten atomic bombs on the Afrakan continent, and Afrakan people are still suffering from its devastating traumatic effects today.

Afrakan people's mental and physical health is directly related to our psychological state of being. Therefore, re-Afrakanization into a new Afrakan-centeredness is not an option or luxury; it is mandatory for our health and our survival as Afrakan people. The list of European or Wazungu - white people's attacks on Black people and Afrakans is long and dreary. It is this list, under Caucasian male domination that continues white on Black violence, which is chiefly responsible for the psychological backwardness and poor health of Afrakan people in America. It is the European Caucasians psychological system of white male domination that has been internalized by Afrakan people, that molds our suicidal attitudes and behaviors of self-destruction. The culture of Caucasian male domination is insane for Afrakan people. It is insane for Afrakan people to eat and prepare our foods like the Wazungu, have the same kind of relationships with nature and ourselves as Caucasian Europeans, and worship the same European religions as whites. In addition, it is this insanity that leads to Black on Black violence in its many various forms. Historical and contemporary forms of white on Black racism and violence, projected through their system of Caucasian male domination, induce and maintain in varying degrees, the backward, self-dependent, economically weak, suicidal nature, and poor health of Afrakans in the world today.

Afrakans worldwide are in a health crisis, and we will remain in a serious health crisis until we reclaim our minds through a revised new Afrakan Kulture. Afrakan healing will only take place when the re-Afrakanization of Afraka and Afrakans, through a new Afrakan Kulture linked to Pan-Afrakanism takes place. Our Afrakan Kulture must re-Afrakanize and re-organizes the Afrakan family, because we are in a state of war. Remember the family is the smallest unit of a community, state or nation. Non-functioning families will produce non-functioning people and a non-functional community is destined for self-destruction. Afrakan people must be re-connected to themselves through their Kulture. Afrakan spirituality re-connects us to the Earth by way of Ma'at, which is life-giving and life-sustaining. Only through a positive Pan-Afrakan re-Afrakanization program can Spiritual Warriors re-connect our families, re-connect us to nature and our relationship with The NTCHR. This re-connection to Afrakan Spirituality and Kulture will be synonymous with healing mentally, physically and spiritually for Afrakan people.

Only Afrakan Spiritual Warriors are equipped to deal with the colossal, retarded, backward, insane state that we as Afrakan people are in today. This book, Spiritual Warriors Are Healers, is part of the medicine that Afrakan people will have to take, if we are to meet the challenge of wholeness, liberation and self-determination. Afrakan people have to move beyond the state of knowing what to do; we have to ***do* it!** Action speaks louder than all words. Spiritual Warriors, we must rise to the occasion and heal our people before we self-destruct. The damage that has been done to Afrakan families via the Maangamizi is catastrophic.

Moreover, just like our families and health is in a state of crisis, so is the Afrakan leadership worldwide. There are large numbers of Afrakan leaders who are very insane and unkonscious of whom and what they are. They are ignorant to what they have become, and openly express their love for their former slave colonial oppressors. Marcia Sutherland in Black Authenticity lists several of these Afrakan societies where self-hatred is perpetuated: Bermuda, the Cayman Islands, the islands of the Netherlands Antilles, Martinique, Guadeloupe, French Guiana, the British Virgin Islands, and Anguilla. These societies steadfastly refuse to become fully independent of their former European colonial powers. In fact, the only remaining pressure for independence comes from the Europeans themselves, who no longer profit from their oppression economically. This is an example of how psychologically and kulturally retarded we have become. Therefore, you can innerstand why we cannot even deal with principal health issues like AIDS, infant mortality, suicide, inadequate water supplies, poor sanitation,

Poverty, tribal war, or the large numbers of refugees in Afraka, whose health issues go far beyond the bounds of this report.

Afraka's health crisis is directly related to her National Kulture Crisis, and International Spiritual Crisis. And because there is a National Kulture and Spiritual Crisis, Afrakans are unwilling to come together as a Pan-Afrakan family, with One aim, One goal, One destiny to solve its worldwide health problems. Afrakans are afraid to eradicate all the old European imposed borders that cut through ethnic groups and in many cases make no sense. Why do independent Afrakans continue to keep these insane borders that support and help to enslave them economically, psychologically, and most of all spiritually, is beyond any logical reasoning.

Afraka and Afrakans cannot be helped by the IMF (the World Bank), America, Europe or foreign aid from the United Nations. None of these powerful energies can free the minds of Afrakan people. Many Afrakans have entrapped their minds in chains of inferiority, "defeatist" thinking and European and Arab culture, as a result of trusting the above European and Arab families, culture, and spiritual systems. Afrakan Spiritual Warriors must be armed with a new, powerful national Afrakan Kulture, and Spiritual system, with a national platform and common Pan-Afrakan goals. With a cooperative struggle, we can heal the minds and promote psychological, spiritual and physical healing for Afrakan people.

POINT 8; GOALS: To innerstand that psychological, spiritual and physical healing for Afrakan people must come from our Afrakan-centered Kulture, which has its own healing system that is spiritual and harmonious with nature. Traditional Afrakan healing systems were spiritual, herbal and wholistically in tune with nature and Ma'at. Modern Spiritual Warriors must learn how to use tradition and reason, so that we can utilize the very best from both traditional and modern worlds, but from an Afrakan-centered perspective. Healing Afrakan people will only happen when Afrakan people take the healing of their families and their destiny into their own hands, worldwide. Only then can we unify our land from a Pan-Afrakanist political perspective. Once we unify our Kulture, based on the best

of our ancestral traditions, along with modern reasoning, then we can develop an Afrakan Worldview that will guide Afrakan healing. We have to feel good about ourselves, as a people, with positive Afrakan self-esteem, mentally, physically, and spiritually in order to heal ourselves on a national scale.

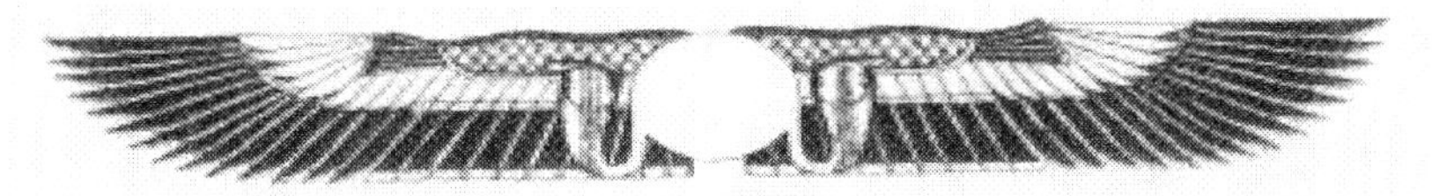

Left, is Spiritual Warrior Imhotep Laila O. Afrika, Holistic Healer, Lecturer, Historian and Author of Afrikan Holistic Health, Nutricide and The Gullah.

Right, Dr. Sebi, Herbologist and founder of the world renowned Usha Research Institute, Honduras, Central America.

The USHA Research Institute has successfully treated thousands of people in the United States and around the world for pathologies such as AIDS, cancer, diabetes, leukemia, sickle cell anemia and many other types of illnesses like female and male dysfunctions, etc.

9. The Halls of Ma'at

Afrakan people, lead by Afrakan Spiritual Warriors, must be able to protect and defend Afrakan people and Afraka. All the members of the Afrakan-centered society, which creates the nation, or the nation within a nation, must feel safe and protected from esfet and white male domination. Ma'at must take-on and represent a powerful meaning in the Afrakan-centered community, where a firm Afrakan-centered identity and Konsciousness, guided by a deep and abiding sense of spirit, Ourstory and Afrakan Kulture, protect women, children and Afrakan youth.

The Double Halls of Ma'at in ancient Kemet gave direction, as well as examples, on how to maintain Ma'at and to overcome esfet. Afrakan Spiritual Warriors of today, 63 rd. century new Afrakan time will have to recreate new and wholistic laws and rules for an Afrakan and humanitarian responsible Worldview. Afrakan-centered Kulture is the key. We must take control and ownership of the media (print, advertisement, news and self-images), educational institutes, economic institutions, and the Kultural arts associated with the Afrakan community or nation. Afrakans must not ask permission to set up our own defense force and legal council of esteem elders to carry out the function of developing and maintaining Ma'at in our families and communities where ever we are. When someone tries to destroy an Afrakan relationship the Afrakan legal system, The Pan-Afrakan Defense force and esteem elders steps in and re-establish Ma'at within the relationships that had become broken or strained and that objective is best achieved by the reconciling parties through the legal council of Ma'at. One of the primary tasks of the new council of esteem elders, The Double Halls of Ma'at will be to smooth out personal difficulties as well as to settle legal issues. The Ḥalls of Ma'at will have a separate judicial system for settling legal matters. This legal system must be Afrakan-centered, as well as rooted in Ma'at. When the Afrakan community feels safe, and protected, the law of reciprocity will yield unlimited support. What goes around comes around, an Afrakan concept of Ma'at.

Afrakan Spiritual values and morals will govern the behavior of the new Afrakan. Spiritual laws with Kultural responsibility will revitalize the need for re-Afrakanization. So Afrakan collaborators, uncle-tomism, community sell-outs, traders, drug dealers, drug users, hustlers and prostitution - mentally, physically and spiritually will have to find a new home outside the Afrakan community. The first Afrakan spiritual law is the law of reciprocity, which means a system of retribution. This law stands ready as the standard Afrakans will use as we deal with any entity that violates Afrakan life, Kulture, spirituality or the Afrakan nation itself.

Afrakan Spiritual Warriors are persons of Kulture, who are Afrakan-centered, spiritually authentic, and have a undying love for Afrakan people. At this level of Konsciousness, Spiritual Warriors are healers; and as healers, they are functioning on the premise that our powerful new Afrakan Kulture will create the realities of unity, reciprocity, harmony with nature and respect for the sacredness of Afrakan life along with the Afrakan Kulture and the spiritual guidance of Ma'at. These are essential tools for a National Council of Spiritual Warriors to lead the masses of Afrakan people to Afrakan liberation.

POINT 9; GOALS: To develop and maintain an Afrakan Nation that is in existence to maintain Ma'at, for all its citizens, and the laws of which reflect that harmonious balance. But it must also have sharp knives or a capable defense system ready for unrighteous intruders. To develop Afrakan citizens who have a strong and just social and moral code with high self-esteem and a high self-regard for fairness, decency and the laws of Ma'at. To develop and practice Ma'at in the courts or legal Afrakan judicial system by the principle of leveling compensation. Whereever imbalance exists, compensation is granted until there is balance. To eliminate all existing European or colonial judicial systems that govern Afrakan people under Afrakan control. To have a National governing council of Spiritual Warriors lead the Nation, and the spokes persons are only the voices of the National council. If our enemy kills the spokes person, a new Spiritual Warrior takes his place. Cut off the head, and the body grows a new one. There is only one national party based on Pan-Afrakanism and Afrakan spirituality, all in harmony with Ma'at.

10. Science, Technology and Language Systems

New Afrakans must provide a common Afrakan language that houses our Kulture and our unique way of communicating with the world. We embrace Kiswahili as our common everyday language and Mdw Ntchr as our Classical Afrakan language, but we encourage the learning of any of the relevant ingenious Afrakan languages on the Afrakan continent. Mdw Ntchr is the oldest language in the world, having a vast and varied literature. Every Afrakan Kulture evolves its unique language. This unique language embraces its own social patterns and symbols. Language is one of the best ways to express a Kulture. Language is the voice of your Kulture. This is why it is important for Afrakan people in the Diaspora to know at least one Afrakan Language. We must learn operational unity, to move as a collective group with a common agenda. When we are operating as one people, we will be scientifically and technologically unlimited.

Being in control of defining where we are now, and in the future as Afrakan people, has to come from our new Pan-Afrakan Kultural focused center. This Kultural focused center will direct our technological and scientific research depending on how efficiently we make the transformations we need as a people towards controlling our own destiny. We cannot control our own destiny until we develop the United States of Afraka or a Pan-Afrakan Nation that has all Afrakan peoples interest at heart first. Moreover, this can only happen if we become unified under a common Afrakan Kulture. Pan-Afrakan operational unity will allow us to be a nation within a nation wherever we are in the world. Expressing and defining our destiny through an Afrakan language is the best way to express our soul force and Afrakan-centered Kulture. The newly formed United States of Afraka will embrace a trade language like Kiswahili for the Nation. All the indigenous Afrakan languages will still remain intact, in their various villages, but the Pan-Afrakan language, the new Afrakan Kultural language would be Kiswahili. Kiswahili will and can link all Afrakan people together, around the world if we will it. If a small non-resourceful country like Portugal can dictate its language to a large country like Brazil with the correct spirit we can control an Afrakan language. Tanzania in East Afraka would be a living working example of unifying people around a language.

Left, Dr. Charles S. Finch, historian, lecturer, medical research scientist and author of The African Background to Medical Science, and Echoes of the Old Dark Land: Theme From the African Eden. Right, Dr. Ivan Van Sertima, professor of Afrikan-American Studies, lecturer, Linguist, author, They Came Before Columbus, and Editor; "The Journal of Afrikan Civilization," The Afrikan Presence in Early Europe/ Egypt Revisited/ Nile Valley Civilization/ Black Women In Antiquity/ Great Black Leaders: Ancient & Modern, and The Moors. Bottom, Mfundishi Salim inside the Mer Khut of Khufu (the Great Pyramid) explaining the science of the Mer Khut to his Children, Zuwena and Hassan I. Salim.

Spiritual Warriors cannot build a Re-Afrakanization movement today or tomorrow if we are not healing and teaching the watoto (children).

Kiswahili

Kiswahili is an East Afrakan language. It is spoken over a broader geographical area and in more countries than any other traditional Afrakan language, allowing it to become an excellent trade and communication language. It is the national language of Tanzania. It is spoken widely in Kenya and Uganda, and is used in parts of the Republic of the Congo, also in the Congo and Mozambique. Because of the international character of the language, many independent Afrakan-centered schools have chosen Kiswahili as a principal Afrakan language in their school curricula. These schools recognize the primary role language plays in Kultural transmission and provide Kiswahili as a means of strengthening the students' personal identification with values and things Afrakan. In addition, the Pan-Afrakan Kultural community from the early sixties adopted Kiswahili as the Afrakan language of choice. All the Afrakan words in the Afrakan-American celebration of Kwanzaa are in Kiswahili. In addition, many of these Afrakan Kultural Pan-Afrakanist were the founders of many of the CIBI schools, Afrakan Study programs and concepts like Afrakancentricity.

Originally, Kiswahili was written in an indigenous Afrakan script, like the Mdw Ntchr, but foreign conquest destroyed the original written script. Afrakan scholars and Linguist like the late Dr. Cheikh Anta Diop has traced a large percentage of Kiswahili words back to the Mdw Ntchr. During the East Afrakan colonial period, Kiswahili was written in Arabic characters. When the British became the new exploiters, Christian missionaries introduced the English alphabet. Although Kiswahili is a relatively easy language to pronounce, it will take perfect practice and consistency, that will lead to perfection and greater innerstanding of yourself and the language Kiswahili. One of the best guides is listening to native speakers in their day-to-day conversation.

Some frequently used Kiswahili terms and phrases are provided here as general introduction to the language. If you cannot attend a Kiswahili class, try to join a Kiswahili study group at your closes Afrakan-centered school, also, audio tapes and books are available.

Pronunciation of Vowels

a pronounced as 'a" in father
e pronounced as "a" in day
I pronounced as "e" in Egypt
o pronounced as "o" in go
u pronounced as "oo" in moon

Year- Mwaka
Next year - Mwaka ujao
Last year - Mwaka uliopita
Month- Mwezi
Days- Siku
Day before yesterday- Juzi
Day after tomorrow- Kesho kutwa
Last month- Mwezi uliopita
Next month- Mwezi ujao
Today- Leo
Allday - Kutwa
Tomorrow- Kesho
Date- Tarehe
Yesterday- Jana
Week- Wiki

January - Mewezi wa mosi (kwanza)
February- Mwezi wa pili
March- Mwezi wa tatu
April- Mwezi wa nne
May- Mwezi wa tano
June- Mwezi wa sita
July- Mewezi wa saba
August- Mewezi wa nane
September- Mewezi wa tisa
October- Mewezi wa kumi
November- Mewezi wa kumi na moja
December- Mewezi wa kumi na mbili

Jumamosi- Saturday
Jumapili- Sunday
Jumatatu-Monday
Jumanne-Tuesday
Jumatano- Wednesday
Jumasita- Thursday (Alhamisi)
Jumasaba- Friday (Ijumaa)

Moyo	- heart
Hapana	- no
Ndiyo	- yes
Kuangalia	- pay attention
Anamu	- ready
Kuanza	- begin
Sasa	- now
Nisemehe	- excuse me
Asante	- thank you
Asante sana	- thank you very much
Kwaheri	- goodbye
Ngapi?	- how much?
Vangapi?	- how many?
Sifahama	- I don't understand
Pole Pole	- slowly, quietly
Unafahama?	- do you understand?
Hapa	- here
Upesi	- quickly
Pia	- also
Tu	- only, quite
Usiku	- night
Usiku kucha	- all night
Alfajiri	- before dawn
Asubuhi	- morning
Alfajiri	- before daybreak
Mchana	- Noon, daytime
Halafu	- Later
Mapema	- Early
Saa nyingi	- Late

Alasiri	- Afternoon
Jioni	-evening
Karibu	- near
Pamoja	- together
Sikukuu	- Holiday

KISWAHILI PHRASES:

Ninataka kukwenda choo tafadhali?	- May I go to the bathroom please?
Tafadhali?	- please?
Tafadhali sema tema	- please repeat
Simameni kisaskari	- stand like soldiers
kazi yake nzuri sana	- his/her work is very good
Je chakula tayari?	- is the food ready?
Vitabu kumi na vitano	- fifteen books
Watu kumi na wawili	- twelve people
Chakula chema	- food for good health
Kupigana Ngumi	- method of fighting with fist
Siku ya Kuzaliwa	- Birthday
Siku tatu ziliziopita	- three days ago
Mwanzo wa juma	- Beginning of the week
Kesho kutwa	- the day after tomorrow
Kivazi	- uniform
Amkia	- greeting
Kituo	- stop
Kwenda mbio	- run
Kukaa	- sit down
kulala	- lie down
Kusimama	- stand up
Piga Ngumi	- punch
Piga Teke	- kick
Fagia	- to sweep
Kulinda	- block
Nyatia	- stalking
Kwa Heri	- goodbye

Asante	- thank you
Si Kitu	- you are welcome
Tafadhali	- please
Hujambo	- how are you
Sijambo	- I am well
Kupigana	- method of combat
Ngumi	- fist
Mpigana	- one who practices Kupigana Ngumi
Shule	- school
Shikamoo	- to bow (greeting); respectful greeting to kneel at someone's feet
Anamo	- prepare to stand, be ready
Angalia	- attention
Anza	- begin
Maliza	- stop
Basi	- dismissed
Punazika	- to relax
Kaa	- to sit down, stay
Moyo	- spiritual heart energy (soul force)
Kongowea	- salutation to Kupigana Ngumi Trinity
Mambo Ya Peponi	- spiritual world
Mtaktifu (Amun)	- holy spirit
Ulimwengo	- natural laws (mannifestation of the holy spirit)- the universe
Ulimwengo mfano	- a form of standing meditation (symbolic of the Djed column of Wsr)
Mzimu	- ancestral spirit(s)/mind
Nquzo	- pillar (foundation)
Taabu tisa	- nine trials (of the warrior)
Mwili	- body
Akili	- mind, meditation, philosophy
Usemi	- speech
Kutengene zeka	- flexibility
Ulinganifu	- coordination

Fikira	- Meditation
Wepesi	- agility
Nguru	- strength
Sawaisha	- balance
Kadiri ya mwendo	- speed
Mwendo	- rhythm
Ishi	- endurance
Mfano	- form
Taratibu	- drill (exercise)
Nguruya Smau	- antidote
Mahali tano	- five positions
Machukio	- hatred
Kujivunia	- false pride
Tamaa Mbaya	- lust, greed
Wiva	- jealousy
Kulema	- stupidity, ignorance
Kazi	- work
Mkono	- hands (weapons)
Shindana	- defense (or to draw in)
Shambulia	- offense
Funganisha	- yoga
Mgoma	- music (drumming)
Mchawi Ngoma	- dancing or dance of the warrior
Uzima	- vitality
Chakula	- food
Pigana	- fighting, punching, kicking, kneeing, shouldering, butting
Shikana	- grappling
Silaha	- weaponry
Kipepo	- butterfly (hand formation)
Pingisha	- wrist opposing
Kulabu	- hooking
Bekus	- parry
Prudish	- Ascending hands
Shuka	- descending hands
Nyatia	- stalking (asi)

DuaraMkono	- circle hand
KupenyaMkono	- piercing hand
Shndisha Nje	- to shut out
Buni	- design (devise)
Moyo Baraza	- soul session
Ndugu	- brother
Udugu	- kinship
Hekalu	- headquarters, temple
Sifika	- be praised
Sifa	- praise
Sifu	- to praise
Jinyosha	- relax (rest time0
Shabaha	- targets, aim
Marahaba	- reply to shikamou (to accept one's greetings)
Fikara	- Meditation, an internal exercise involving positive breathing and mental aawareness
Ungamana	- be united
Unyago	- invitation
Kujichanguna	- self determination
Mkuki	- a spear
Upanga	- sword
Gongakiponde	- stick
Mwanafunzi	- student
Mwalimu	- teacher
Malenga	- physical and spiritual master
Mfundishi	- grand master or great teacher
Hekima ya kioo	- mirror- like wisdom
Hekima ya Fahamu	- wisdom of inner awareness
Hekima ya mamojo	- wisdom of equality
Hekima ya ujasiri	- wisdom of fearless accomplishment
Hekima ya ulimnemjo	- wisdom of universal consciousness
Nguvu	- antidote, strength, power
Umoja	- unity

Kuumba	- creativity
Nia	- purpose
Imani	- faith
Ngapi?	- how many?
Vitabu vingapi?	- how many books?
Watu wangapi?	- how many people?
Mara?	- time of how often?
Mara mbili	- twice
Mara mia	- hundred times
Sita mara tatu	- six times three
kitabu cha tatu	- the third book
Siku ya tano	- the fifth day
Mweza wa saba	- the seventh month
Watu wa swisho	- the last person
Hekima ya fahamu	- wisdom of inner awarness
Hekima ya mamajo	- wisdom of equality
Hekima ya ujasiri	- wisdom of fearless accomplishment
Hekima ya ulimnemjo	- wisdom of universal consciousness
Umoja	- unity
Ujima	- collective responability
Kuumba	- creativity
Nia	- purpose
Imani	- faith
Hesabu	- count
Na	- and
Kwa sababu	- because
Weusi	- blackness
Weupe	- whiteness

KISWAHILI NUMBERS

Moja	1
Mbili	2
Tatu	3
Nne	4
Tano	5

Sita	6
Saba	7
Nane	8
Tisa	9
Kumi	10
Kumi na moja	11
Kumi na mbili	12
Kumi na tatu	13
Kumi na nne	14
Kumi na tano	15
Kumi na tisa	19
Ishirini	20
Ishirini na mbili	22
Thelathini	30
Thelathini na tatu	33
Arobaini	40
Arobaini na nne	44
Hamsini	50
Sitini	60
Sitini na sita	66
Sabaini	70
Sabaini na saba	77
Themanini	80
Themanini na nane	88
Tisini	90
Mia	100
Mia na moja	101
Mia na kumi	110
Mia mbili	200
Mia mbili na hamsini	250
Mia tano	500
Elfu	1,000
Elfu mbili	2,000
Elfu tisa, mia tisa tisini na tisa	9,999
Millioni	1,000,000
Millioni tano	5,000,000

Mdw Ntchr

Among the classical languages of the Afrakan people, Mdw Ntchr is the oldest with a written literature. The Mdw Ntchr literature consist of medicine, mathematics, science, physics, metaphysics, ourstory, poetry, prose, tales, folklore, religious theology, and cosmology texts.

A large percentage of the Mdw Ntchr have been translated by Europeans and European-American translations who have translated the Mdw Ntchr from an Eurocentric perspective, not into an Afrakan-centric perspective, and the Mdw Ntchr is an Afrakan language.

The people of northeast Afraka called their language Mdw Ntchr, commonly known as ancient Egyptian. The written language was also called the Mdw Ntchr. The word Mdw (Medu) means ancient words of wisdom in the Kemet language of the Hapy Valley and was represented by the walking stick. Ntchr (Netcher) a white flag meant nature or the existence of the all (the totality of life and of all existence). Mdw Ntchr is the oldest language in the world having a vast and varied literature. The word Mdw Ntchr means "Divine Words of the Ntchr" or "Divine Words of the Creator."

The Afrakans of northeast Afraka along the Hapy (Nile) Valley used the word 'Km' (Kem) to designate themselves ethnically and designate their country. The root word 'Km' (burnt wood or black coal) etymologically signifies "Black." They called their country Kmt "The Black Community," not the Black land. The word for land was "Ta." Another name of Kmt was "Ta Mrry. The Beloved Land). The people called themselves kmtyu (kemetyu) " The Black People," or the "Blacks." Another name in Kmt used to designate themselves as 'Remetch' meaning human in the sense of "original man" or the people of the land within the cataracts of the Hapy Valley. The Kmtyu of the land of Kmt called the river that flowed through their land, Hapy. Km, the word for

Blackness was even described as the Ntchru (the super forces of the universe). Km, the Great Black (Asr).

Km, (Kem)- The Black male name of the Ntchr (Asr).

Kmt, (Kemet)- The Black female Ntchrt (Ast).

Snu Kmu, (Senu Kemu)- The Black men.

The word Egypt comes from a Greek pronunciation of the Afrakans 'Great City', Het-Ka-Ptah meaning "The House of the Soul of the Creator"- The great city, later called Memphis. The Greeks said 'Aegiptios' (ai-geep-ti-os). Later, Englishmen pronounced this as Egypt due to the phonetic nature of their langauge.

There were several different dialects of Mdw Ntchr, they were referred to as old Egyptian- 8,000 B.C.E to the 10th Dynasty. Middle Egyptian- The Second Golden Age, 11th Dynasty to the 17th Dynasty. New Egyptian- The Third Golden Agr, 17th Dynasty to the 26th Dynasty. (Late Egyptians and Coptic lasted until the Romans adopted culture of Christianity was destroyed completely by the Arabs with Islam). These represented both temporal and spatial differences, each of them having various dialects within themselves. Coptic, for example: Sahidic, Bohairic, Fayyumic, Achmimic, Sub-Achmimic. Sahidic Coptic pronunciation is very close to old Egyptian. They represented a close dialect.

There were also 'living' spoken languages which were closely related to Mdw Ntchr such as, Kiswahili from the interior of eastern Afraka and the most well known is Wolof, one of the western Sahara languages. The late Dr. Cheikh Anta Diop had made the genetic relationship of Mdw Ntchr and the Afrakan languages. Wolof, Ashanti Twe and Kiswahili, languages are closely related languages to the Mdw Ntchr.

Coptic is the only stage of the language where vowels are written, so it is by way of Coptic, and other related Afrakan languages (Diop, 1972) that we know something about the original pronunciation of words in the Mdw Ntchr. Since vowels are not always written, in order to pronounce words herein, you can insert an 'e' (as in English letters) where needed, for example: Kmt, after inserting vowels we will have 'Kemet.' Coptic and Wolof can be used as guides to the speaking of Mdw Ntchr.

Besides spoken dialects there were various scripts. Hieroglyphic, a Greek word meaning "sacred carvings" is the best known describing the Mdw Ntchr .

The very beautiful sacred glyphs of the temples took years to master. These symbols were so clear and articulate one could see the type and species of animals, birds and plants, and the colors were spiritual and brilliant. However, before a scribe learned to carve or paint the sacred glyphs, he probably learned the Hieratic script which was used during the Old Period in ancient Kemet. This writing was developed in the interior of Afraka (the south), and brought to the northern part of Afraka called Kemet. Even men, women and school children outside of the great temples learned to read and write this style of Mdw Ntchr by Afrakan priests who were part of their communities. All letters and daily correspondence were written in the Hieratic script.

In ancient Kash or so called Ethiopian 25th Dynasty, scribes had developed a very cursive form called Demotic (Greek demotikos "popular"). This was the late period in Kemet Ourstory. This was a very

fast way of writing and only a few people in the world can read this style today. The readers of the ancient Kemetik language today are Kemetologist, Egyptologist, and Afrakan Spiritual Priest Warriors.

The Hieratic script was the most widely written of the Mdw Ntchr. The Hieratic was always written from right to left, also the Demotic was always written from right to left. The Hebrews and the Arabs learned to write from the ***Ancient Kemetyu***. All one has to do is study their languages and you will innerstand that they have the same Afrakan root. Their number system is also Afrakan from the Kemetik Kulture of northeast Afraka. The written system of Mdw Ntchr is comprised of three (3) elements. The three elements are alphabetical signs, syllabic signs and pictorial signs.

In the writing of words, phrases and sentences, all three elements are used together in combination. The Mdw Ntchr will be phonetically written with the English alphabet. For example:

A. Alphabetical signs are those symbols which represent one sound in the langauge. For example, a picture sign of the Vulture 𓄿 represents the sound of 'a' 𓄿 (as in father), a picture of a leg and foot 𓃀 represents the sound of 'b' 𓃀 (as in boy). There are 26 such signs.

B. Syllabic signs are those signs which represent one syllable, or two or three consonants. A game board represents the syllable 'mn,' 𓏠 (m+n) and a heart and windpipe represents the sound of 'nfr' (n+f+r) 𓄤𓆑𓂋

C. Pictorial signs are pictures which depict what they represent either exactly or abstractly. For example, a picture of: 𓉐 means house, the sun, Ra 𓇳 means sun or it can mean other things such as time of day, etc... if a single line is written under the picture, then it is what it is Ra - Sun, 𓇳𓏤 Pr-House. 𓉐𓏤

[hieroglyphs] is translated into English letters as 'Htp De Nswt' (The sound values here are determined via comparison of Coptic, Kiswahili and Wolof. Coptic is the only stage of the langauge where vowels were written.)

Spiritual Warriors will have to re-Afrakanize the European version of Hieroglyphics (Mdw Ntchr). Our own Mdw Ntchr scholars, Ourstorians and linguist will have to come together in Pan-Afrakan operational unity and establish specific rules that are consistent with Ma'at and the Afrakan-centered Worldview. My physical objective mind has studied the Afrakan legacy for a little more than 40 years, but my spiritual subjective Konsciousness is as old as time itself, and therefore, as Jhutyms-Ka-en-Heru, The Spiritual Scribe of Jhuty Heru Neb-Hu, the ancestors have left us the following list of things that must be innerstood about Mdw Ntchr in order to follow the Kemet Spiritual System of high Spiritual Konsciousness on a Deep Thought level:

1. Alphabet, mono-syllabic signs.

2. Syllabic signs, bi- and tri-literals.

3. Complements.

4. Determinatives.

5. Numerical principles, numbers and adjectives.

6. Grammar rules, verbs and sentence structure.

7. Nouns and every day working vocabulary.

8. The study of Nature (the Earth & the Cosmos), and how it relates to Human Beings.

9. The study of Afrakan Kultures and ethnic groups along the Hapy Valley (Nile Valley, from Egypt to Tanzania) and across the Sahara, along with other indigenous Afrakan languages.

10. The study of indigenous Afrakan spiritual and religious systems.

11. In-depth study of Kemet festivals, celebrations and Holy-days.

12. The study of Afrakan folklore, stories, and proverbs.

13. The study of astronomy, astrology, numerology and the Kemet Kalendar System.

14. In-depth study of the Ntchru, mentally, physically and spiritually from a Pan-Afrakan Spiritual Worldview.

Dr. Cheikh Anta Diop was a Spriritual Warrior on the level of Imhotep in Ancient Kemet, a multi-level genius. Dr. Diop is author of ***African Origins of Civilization: Myth or Reality, Civilization or Barbarism, The Origin of the Ancient Egyptians, The Peopling of Ancient Egypt and Deciphering of Meroitic Script*** *and* ***The General History of Africa Studies and Documents, I and II.***

Dr. Diop is our Black shining "Heru" champion of Kemetology. Dr. Diop proved beyond a shadow of a doubt that the Ancient Kemetyu are Black people like the indigenous Afrakans in the interior of Afraka and that Kemet history is an Afrakan Ourstory and that Kemet kulture, its language and Spiritual systems are unquestionably Black Afrakan.

Ta Mry - The Beloved Land.

EXPLANATION OF THE MDW NTCHR

a - The hawk vulture is to be pronounced like 'a' or 'ah' in father. The sound of this letter does not vary in most dialects.

e - The reed leaf has several pronunciations. It expresses the sound of 'e' (as in bee). Yet at the beginning of words, it is sometimes pronounced as 'yah' or 'a' (ah).

y - The two reed leaves also express the sound of 'e' (as in bee). It always has this sound when it occurs in or at the end of a word. In this position, it may be written in its abbreveation for // (two diagonal lines).

a - The arm and hand expresses a range of sounds between and include 'a-o'. It is often identical with 'a'. In writing of foreign names, it is used to express certain vowel sounds which did not exist in Mdw Ntchr, such as 'a', as in hat, and 'e' as in let.

w u - The quail chick expresses several sounds, 'u' (as in true), and 'w' (as in we) and sometimes 'o'. When 'w' occurs on the end or in the middle of a word, it may be pronounced as 'u'. yet, when it is the first letter of a word, it may be pronounced as 'w'. For example: "wsb" "answer" (pronounced wesheb)

b - The leg and foot has the approximate sound value of 'b' as in english.

p - The mat or stool has the approxiamate sound value of 'p' as in English.

f v - The Horn Viper has the approximate sound of 'f' as in English. In the writing of foreign names, 'f' sometimes expresses the sound of 'ef', usually represents a masculine form (men). Greeks used 'v' for this sound.

m - The Horned Owl has the approximate sound value of 'm' in English.

n - The wave of energy, like the ripple of water has the approximate sound value of 'n' in English.

r - The lips have the approximate sound value of 'r' in English. In Mdw Ntchr, 'r is represented by this sign of open mouth.

l - The Lion is sometimes used in the writing of foreign names to express the sound of 'l'.

h - The court yard or reed shelter has the approximate sound value of 'h' in English.

h - The twisted rope or twisted piece of flax also expresses the sound of 'h' in English. It is distinguished from (the court yard) in translation by the diacritical dot underneath. However, they sound alike. In Mdw Ntchr, a single sound may be represented by more than one sign; this is the case with 'h' and h.

kh - Has the approximate sound of 'c' in 'sh' the English word 'cost' and in some dialects has the sound of 'sh' as in 'she' in English. At various times in Kemet Ourstory, these sounds were interchangeable. In translation, it is distinguished by the diacritical mark underneath. This sound came later in the middle and late periods: maybe a placenta or a seed?

k/q - An animal's belly or a tool for scarping or embalming. It has the same approximate value as the sign. Yet in coptic, it is usually pronounced as 'kh' in English. It is distinguished from the placenta and other "K's" by the diacritical line underneath.

s - The folded cloth and door bolt has the approximate sound value of 's' as in English. In the earlier period, the door bold may have been pronounced like 'z' in English. The door bolt is sometimes used in the writing of foreign names to express the sound of "z".

sh - The pool of water has the approximate sound value of 'sh' in English, like 'sh' in 'sheep'.

q - The hill slope has the approximate sound value of 'K' or 'Q' in English. It could be a tool of some kind, draftsman's tool.

k - The basket has the approximate sound value of 'k' in English.

g - The stool has the approximate sound value of 'g' in the English word 'girl' or 'go'.

t - The loaf of bread has the approximate sound value of 't' in English.

tch - The tethering rope (used to tie up animals or cattle) has the approximate sound value of 'tch' in the English word 'choose' or 'church'.

d - The hand has the approximate sound value of a 'd' as in English.

j - The Cobra Snake has the approximate sound value of 'j' as in English or dj.

Abed (month)

Early Kmt	**Middle Kmt**	**Late Kmt**
Abd wa	Jhuty	Tochit
Abd snu	Menhet	Paophi
Abd shmtu	Het-Heru	Athry
Abd fdu	Ka-her-ka	Choiak
Abd deu	Sefbedet	Tybi
Abd sesu	Rekh-wr	Meshir
Abd sfku	Rekh-nds	Phaememoth
Abd khmnnu	Renutet	Pharmouti
Abd psdju	Khensu	Pachons
Abd mdju	Khenti-hr	Paymi
Abd mdju wa	Epet	Epipi
Abd medj snu	Meso-ra	Mesori

Heru (day)

Heru-wa (Saturday)** I

Heru-senu (Sunday) II

Heru-shomtu (Monday) III

Heru-fedu (Tuesday) IIII

Heru-dew (Wednesday) IIIII

Heru-sesu (Thursday) IIIIII

Heru-sefeku (Friday) IIIIIII

Heru-khemnnu* IIIIIIII

Heru-psju* IIIIIIIII

Heru-medju*

** Ancient Kemet had 10 ∩ days in each week.*

*** These are names of Wazungu gods and we should not use them in our Kemet circle or Worldview.*

Mdw Ntchr List

Wedgy wr	- Meditterranean Sea (Great Green)
Ast	- Wife of Wsr and mother of Heru, the Black Madonna or Great Black Mother
Teken	- A tall phallic symbol with a Pyramid on top to symbolize Black manhood and strength associated with Ausar and Heru and also the great mound of creation- the Atm
Heru	- The great Falcon, Son of Wsr
Jehuty	- The Ntchr of speech, thought and writing
Shemsu Heru	- The followers of Heru, higher Konsciousness
Neb	- A great master or lord, or to have mastery of something
Esfet	- Destruction, wrongdoings, anti-balance.
Sema Tawy	- Reunited two lands or united two lands
Moyo	- Internal vital heart force connected to the Ntchr also called Sekhem
Ta-Mry	- (The beloved land) another name for Ancient Kmt (Egpyt)
Sais	- Another name for Ancient Kmt
Ma'at	- Truth, justice and rightousness, universal balance
Ka	- The spirit of the vital force or the double
Ba	- The Heart soul of the human spirit
Khat	- The physical body
Khaibit	- The shadow
Khu	- The spiritual soul and intelligence
Sahu	- The spiritual body
Sekhem	- The power
Ren	- Name
Kmt Mystery System	- The educational system of ancient Kemet
Duat	- The world in-between the spiritual and physical or the world of transition.

Wsrfied - The human body prepare like Wsr of Ancient Kmt when the physical body dies and is prepared for resurrection.
Mdw Ntchr - The divine words of the Creator.
Het Ka Ptah Theology- The spiritual creation of the ancient Kemetik story.
Na Swt (Nswt) - The King of South or ruler from the land of the Swt Plant.
Na Swt (Nswt) Bety - The King of upper and lower Kemet.
Bety - One who is of the bee or King of lower Kmt.
Wab - The pure (a priest)
Hem-Ntchr - "Servants of the creator" - Kemet Priest.
Khery Hed - Father of Ntchr- Priest of Kemet.
Hem Ntchr Tepy - High Priest
Hapy valley - The ancient name of the Nile Valley.
Ta-Merrian Martail Arts- Ancient name of Kupigana Ngumi.
Wsarian Drama - The story of the rise of Wsr, his death and resurrection and the training of Heru the son, as he prepared to avenge the slaying of his father Ausar against his Uncle Setsh.
Heru - The son of Ausar and Ast- The rising sun, the avenger of wrong doings
Setsh - The brother of Ausar and Ast, the mate of Nebt-Het, the one who rules the south by might
Aha - The first king of the 1st Dynasty in ancient Kemet from the south.
Wsr - The mate of Ast, brother of Setsh and Nebt Het and father of Heru- The great Black father of truth who dies and comes back to life again.
Htp - To offer peace or satisfaction.
Ee-m-htp - I come in peace
Shem-e-m-htp - I go in peace
Htpu - Peace to you all or much peace

Mdw Ntchr (*numbering System*)

1. Wa | One
2. Snu || Two
3. Shmtu ||| Three
4. Fedu |||| Four
5. Deu ||| || Five
6. Sesu ||| ||| Six
7. Sfkhu |||| ||| Seven
8. Khmnnu |||| |||| Eight
9. Psdju ||||| |||| Nine
10. Mdju ∩ Ten

15. ∩ |||||

20. ∩∩

30. ∩∩∩

35. ∩∩∩ |||||

40. ∩∩∩∩

45. ∩∩∩∩ |||||

50. ∩∩ ∩∩ ∩

55. ∩∩ ∩∩ ∩ |||||

60. ∩∩∩ ∩∩∩

65. ∩∩∩ ∩∩∩ |||||

70. ∩∩∩ ∩∩∩ ∩

75. ∩∩∩ ∩∩∩ ∩ |||||

100. 𓍢 200. 𓍢𓍢 1,000,000. 𓁨

Sht Sht snu Kha

2,000,000. Kha snu 3,000,300 Kha shmtu, sht shmtu .

𓁨𓁨 𓁨𓁨𓁨𓍢𓍢𓍢

Symbol	exponential equivalent	English equivalent
𓏺	10^0	units (1)
𓎆	10^1	tens (10)
𓍢	10^2	hundreds (100)
𓆼	10^3	thousands (1,000)
𓂭	10^4	ten thousands (10,000)
𓆐	10^5	hundred thousands (100,000)
𓁨	10^6	millions 1,000,000)

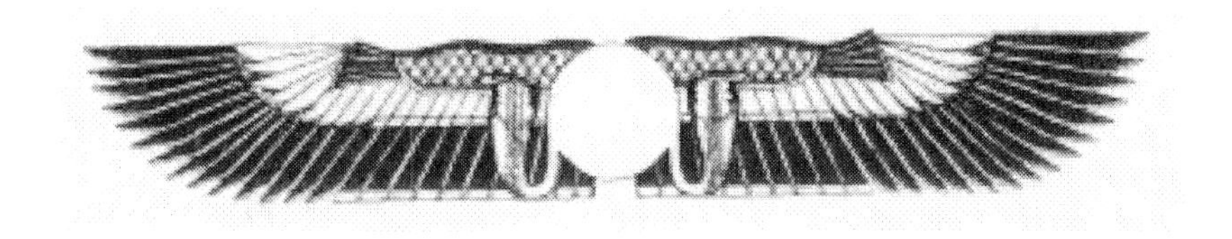

Example:

The following amounts of various kinds of geese were compiled and totaled up in the (shefedu) papyrus of Ramesses III:-

"

=6,820

=1,410

=1,534

= 150

=4,060

=25,020

=57,810

=21,700

= 1,240

= 6,510

---

totals (10,000x9)+(1,000x32)+(100x40)+(10x25)+4= 126,254" [17]

European languages will be taught in all the Afrakan-centered schools for foreign communication, but not for the government, schools, or mass communication for the Afrakan Worldview or the United Afrakan Nation. Afrakans must take control of their affairs, from an Afrakan-centered Kultural perspective. Language is the medium by which we process our thoughts. You can not liberate yourself with the thoughts of an opposing or contradictory Kultural center.

Among the classical languages of Afrakan people, The Mdw Ntchr is the oldest with a written literature. The Mdw Ntchr literature consist of medicine, mathematics, science, physics, metaphysics, Our-story, history, poetry, prose, folklore, religious theology, and cosmology texts. The word Mdw means ancient words of wisdom in the Kemet language of the Hapy Valley. Ntchr means nature or the existence of a A Divine Creator Force. Afrakans must embrace their ancestral roots from an Ourstorical and spiritual perspective. First we must recognize ourselves as an Afrakan people, then our languages and national communication must be restored, reclaimed, and resurrected so we will regain our Kultural genius, along with our scientific and technological memory. When our spiritual memory returns, healing on a scale that the world hasn't seen in 4,000 years, will return.

POINT 10; GOALS: One national language, Kiswahili for the United States of Afraka and the Pan-Afrakan community throughout the Diaspora. Kiswahili becomes a Pan-Afrakan language that links all Afrakans on the planet. Mdw Ntchr becomes Afraka's classical language. Our classical Afrakan legacy can still be studied on papyrus from Kemet, or on the walls of timeless tombs (time capsules) and temples in modern day Egypt and Sudan. Afrakan-centered Afrakans will have to reclaim, resurrect and modernize The Mdw Ntchr for daily use in our re-Afrakanizied lives.

Science and technology must be based on Ma'at and the law of correspondence. Modern Afakan technology must remain in harmony with the forces of nature.

Spiritual Warriors of the mind and science: Left, Dr. Yosef ben-Jochannan, and Dr. Richard King, right, Dr. Na'im Akbar

Below, Master Deep Thinkers: Dr. John Henrik Clarke with Mfundishi Jhutyms Ka n Heru El-Salim. Right, Dr. Martin L. King Jr. and Malcolm X, El Hajj Malik El Shabazz.

11. Afrakan-centered Kuumba System of Art, Inner-attainment and Relationships

The Afrakan Kuumba System is designed to reshape the way Afrakans view the world, and each other, as Afrakans. Afrakan people are divine and all art, music, dance, sports, and creative expressions should maintaining that divinity and oneness with the Ntchru, and ultimately The NTCHR.

Blackness is a state of perfection, a Konsciousness, the essence and beginning of life for human beings. Blackness as expressed through the Black Dot is Divine. In the Kemetyu ancient educational system of Kemet, Blackness was an ideal and an ultimate expression of the Ntchru. This perfection called Blackness was distorted and rearranged by Caucasian male domination, racism. Our Afrakan-centered Kuumba System refocuses our energies towards Ma'at and reconnects with our divinity, as well as recognizes the divinity that has always been within us: The Divine within us lying dormant waiting to be resurrected.

The concept of beauty is a fundamental element of one's Kulture, as expressed in art, music, literature, icons and architectural images. New expressions are created that enhance one's Kultural expression in a healthy society, but in our case, Afrakan Kulture was consciously undermined as our Afrakan civilizations were destroyed. Re-Afrakanization is the mission of Spiritual Warriors, to rebuild a new Afrakan-centered Kulture that recognizes our Blackness from melanin as beautiful and divine, and this must start at birth otherwise the battle will be extremely difficult, but we will win the minds and souls of our people.

Art if it is to be purposeful and liberating it must be introduced before rebirth, after rebirth, and as often as possible in our physical lives on this earthly plane. We have to raise Afrakan children from rebirth in an Afrakan centered environment where positive Kultural images and sounds reflect their Afrakan heritage. Our leisure expression is as important as our work expression as well as our spiritual expression. How we feel about ourselves will also determine how we look, dress, and what we aspire to and who our role models are. We must always look for Ma'at. Even in our inner-attainment and relationships, Ma'at must be supreme. The interests of Afrakans are best served through the pursuit of self-determination, as a people. That pursuit begins with activities that enhance your Kulture, helps perfect your Kulture, or brings clarity to your Afrakan Kultural heritage. Our relationships must be Afrakan Kultural inspired, because we want to be with people who also have our best interest at heart and who have a similar Afrakan-centered Konsciousness. When someone says, "Oh, color doesn't matter", you know they are not Afrakan-centered or in their right Afrakan mind. A Spiritual Warriors say's that color should not be your sold determining factor when making an intelligent decision. However, color does matter or there would not be any colors.

Each Afrakan has the potential to be an artist, which gives you a life-giving responsibility to Afraka, and to Afrakan people and to the universe. However, each Afrakan is also a human being and this gives them another set of responsibilities. We must receive life-giving forces, for what goes around comes around. Therefore, the Afrakan artists, and Afrakan citizen, feed off of each other's energy, which must be Afrakan-centered in order to support an Afrakan reality. Afrakan artists must make our reality or perception of the world clear. If the world were already clear, art would not exist. Art in its purest sense simply captures rhythms and relationships of a people's innerstanding or lack of understanding. Artists who innerstand our harmonious relationship with nature enlighten us or light us up. New Spiritual Warrior Artists will have to teach us through imagery, how to "BE" with clear images, mentally, physically and spiritually of "The Way".

Social activities offer Afrakan-centered people the opportunity to spend positive and purposeful time together in an Afrakan environment. Afrakan-centered games, music, sports, and other life-giving activities provide outlets for tension, stress, or anger, as well as provide an arena for social inter-activeness with other positive Afrakan-centered people or human beings.

Afrakan artists must emphasize the symbolic relationship between the spiritual connection, the Kultural connection and the natural order of nature in their artistic forms. Spiritual Warriors innerstand that Kulture must have a harmonious relationship with nature. If nature is disturbed it must be in a life-giving, non-environment polluting, life-sustaining way. All Afrakan-centered artists are creators, and life-givers, because each artist is giving birth to an art-form. Therefore, the artists have a Kultural obligation to their Afrakan roots and center. Spiritual Warriors, who are artists, must lead by example. By showing their Afrakan-centered reciprocal relationship, their art is wholistic, functional, and full of Kultural symbolism, creating Afrakan beauty that is consistent with traditional Afrakan artistic expressions, and yet innovative, new and functional at the same time.

Afrakan music must be inspirational, yet political, Kultural and spiritual. All Afrakan people have access to music, regardless of their economic class, or state of Konsciousness. Afrakan Spiritual Warriors must be in control of our music industry, and in control of Afrakan musical artists. Together we must launch an Afrakan Konsciousness campaign to flood the Konsciousness of Afrakan people with positive images, suggesting that Afrakan Kulture is a medicine. To embrace Afrakan love, unity, and Nationship, we must transform all Afrakan traditional relationships and make them relevant to our contemporary *united* Afrakan needs. Today the opposite is happening. Certain elements in today's Afrakan music in America have been used as a weapon to maintain an enslaved matrix white male domination relationship. Re-Afrakanization will correct this mistake.

Afrakan Spiritual Warriors must re-emphasize the use of the Afrakan drum, our first and most sacred instrument other than our voices back into our music, all aspects of our music: Jazz, R&B, Blues, Rap, Hip Hop or Spirituals. The drum is Afraka. Dance is the soul of Afraka. When we combine these two inseparable modalities, we are expressing both the simplest and most complex, yet the deepest aspects of Afrakan philosophy or Deep Thought. Music, dance and the voice becomes a connecting thread that ties Afrakan people's earthly experience with and to the cosmos. When we as Afrakan people are connected to this life force, via the drum, dance and voice, we know profoundly that the universe is whole. This wholeness is The NTCHR, and we become part of its rhythm. This rhythm allows your Sekhem - (your spiritual life force) and the Ntu -

(the universal life-force) to become One, and you then innerstand your divinity. This divinity is so powerful that the rest of the human family can see and feel this spiritual force we call Art, soul and creative expression in everthing we do. We are divine spiritual energies having an Afrakan human experience..

POINT 11; GOAL: All Afrakan Art must have Afrakan Konsciousness, form and feeling that expresses the soul of Afrakans and or Afraka. In the Pan-Afrakan world, the functionality of any artistic expression will be the most significant criteria for its artistic classification. To have all Afrakan Artists committed to Afrakan-centeredness, Ma'at, love, defense - mentally, physically and spiritually, universal harmony and Nation building is the goal.

Spiritual Warriors of literature and the spoken word. Left, is Sonia Sanchez, author of We A bbaDDD People, A Blues Book for Blue Black Magical Women, Love Poems, Under a Soprana Sky, poet, political activist and proponent of Black Nationalism. Right, Amiri Baraka, author of The System of Dante's Hell, A Black Mass, Reflections of Jazz and Blues, The Dead Lecturer, as well as the Autobiograph of Leroy Jones, poet, dramatist, essayist, play wright (award winning play, "Dutchman") and political activist.

Spiritual Warrior of literature from the continent of Afraka. Chinua Achebe from Nigeria is a poet, essayist, and author of <u>When Things Fall Apart, No Longer At Ease</u>, <u>A Man of the People</u>, <u>The Arrow of God, Ant Hills of the Savannah</u>, and <u>The Heinemann Book of Contemporary African Short Stories</u>.
Spiritual Warrior, Paul Robeson left us a legacy as tall as Imhotep, for he was a dynamic athlete, scholar, as well as actor, singer, autobiographer. Bottom right, Spiritual Warrior, Kwame Toure, political activist and Black Nationalist.

Spiritual Warriors of Drama and the Spoken Word: *Ossie Davis and Ruby Dee with Mfundishi Jhutyms Ka n Heru El-Salim of Black Gold Theater Company at Cross Roads Black Theater, New Jersey. Bottom, Brother Abiodun Oyewole of The Last Poets, master of the spoken word.*

12. The Maangamizi Memorial System of Reciprocity, Reverence, Reparing, Restoring, and Reparations For Afrakan Healing.

There are two Afrakan words used to describe the Afrakan Black Holocaust: Maafa (ma-ah-fa), and Maangamizi. The Maafa is defined as the 447-year period from 1441 to 1888, commonly referred to as the enslavement of Afrakan people by Caucasian Europeans and the continuing physical, and cultural conditions resulting from that period in history and Ourstory. We as Afrakan Spiritual Warriors and Konscious Afrakan people totally reject the definition of "slavery," or the "European Caucasian slave trade." First of all, the Afrakans that were enslaved were free people, kidnapped, stolen, tricked, or bamboozled into enslavement. Some of these enslaved Afrakans were prisoners of war, Priests and Priestesses, scientists, engineers, doctors, teachers, farmers, traders, housewives, market women, and above all innocent children victimized by Caucasian Europeans, Arabs and insane Afrakan collaborators. However, 98% of the Afrakans enslaved were free men, women and children, not slaves. The word "Maafa" comes from the Kiswahili language and is defined as, "catastrophe" or "disaster" which suggests an accidental act of destruction, like a car crash or an earthquake.

The Afrakan Holocaust is perhaps the most significant experience in modern Ourstory for people of Afrakan ancestry. The devastating trauma of millions of people kidnapped from their homes, beaten, raped, mutilated, separated from family, made to witness horrors, made to live horrors, taken to a foreign land, enslaved, worked literally until they dropped, spiritually assaulted, and psychologically manipulated, has been grossly underestimated and largely ignored. There is no way to deny the impact of pure savagery on the behalf of Caucasian Europeans and Arabs against Afrakans for centuries. Most of our mental and psychological confusion, and dysfunctional families and community disorder has its origins in the conditions of this Holocaust.

Because this Holocaust was deliberate, planned, and outright barbaric and savage, some Afrakan Deep Thinkers think we should use the word, ***Maangamizi***. This Kiswahili word makes it clear that the destruction, "catastrophe" or "disaster" was not an accident, but esfet, a deliberate act, which causes destruction, pain, and imbalance, the very opposite of Ma'at.

Today Spiritual Warriors agree that Maangamizi, the deliberate destruction of Afrakan people, their Kulture and their land, is still alive and part of the ongoing personality of Caucasian Europeans and Arabs Holocaust against Afrakan people. Only the illusion of physical enslavement has ended, in reality, Caucasian Europeans have just created a more sophisticated form of physical enslavement call the prison industrial complex system. Moreover, many Arab Muslims still practice slavery and the enslavement of Afrakans on the Afrakan continent and in the Arab world today in the 21st century western time and 63rd century new Afrakan time.

Afrakan people must also reject the term "European slave trade," When we use this term it hides the facts that we are dealing with a murderous, inhumane, barbaric transaction of genocide perpetrated against Afrakan people by Caucasian Europeans and Arabs. Moreover, when we call this horrific act trade, we make it sound like we are trading tomatoes or oranges and some of the crop went bad. We as Spiritual Warriors and as Konscious Afrakans must tell it like it was and is, this was definitely not a "slave trade," but a murderous, insane, barbaric transaction of genocide and human enslavement perpetrated against Afrakans by Caucasian Europeans and Arabs for profit.

We must also briefly talk about Afrakan collaborators. Yes, some greedy, ignorant, insane Afrakans took advantage of the profit factor in the Maangamizi and sold their brothers and sisters to Caucasian Europeans and Arabs. However, we will not be tricked into believing we enslaved ourselves and created our own genocide, and therefore should not receive reparations because of the Afrakan Holocaust. Every Holocaust that has ever been recorded has had collaborators. The Jewish Holocaust had Jewish collaborators at every level. There were Jewish officers in the German Army during Hitler's Jewish Holocaust. There were rich Jews that financed Hitler. There were Jewish informers who identified other European Jews, but no one is saying European Jews victimized themselves, enslaved themselves and therefore should not received reparations as a result of the Jewish Holocaust. Yes, that would be crazy, and not even entertained, and we as Afrakan Spiritual Warriors will not entertain it either. Reparations to Afrakan people for the Afrakan Holocaust perpetrated by Caucasian Europeans and Arabs will become a reality! This is a promise to our ancestors!

Afrakans throughout the Diaspora were never offered or given therapy for the hundreds of years of intense trauma, nor was "The Maafa" defined as traumatic. As a Spiritual Warrior and as an Afrakan Ourstorian, I am stating that not only was the Maangamizi traumatic, it was a horrific crime against humanity. However, a great many of the problems Afrakans face today in the Americas, mentally, physically and spiritually are the direct or indirect results of our forced, enslavement by the institution of Caucasian European male domination or white supremacy and its aftermath.

Spiritual Warriors must teach the Maangamizi from a liberating spiritual healing perspective, "the way out is back through". The inhuman atrocities of cataclysmic proportions committed against Afrakans by Caucasian Europeans and Asians must never be forgotten, so that it's crystal clear who they were and who they are! The Maangamizi was an incomprehensible process of murder, captivity, enslavement, rape, and torture. The trauma that is inevitable from this horrific experience has not yet been healed or even addressed. We carry the pain and scars of generations before us. This collective pain creates a collective crazy that haunts Afrakans mentally, physically and spiritually. In order to begin the process of healing from the horror of his-story and Our-story, we must revisit it. Spiritual Warriors must create an opportunity for the Kemetyu to squarely face our collective horrors, and come to grips with issues that Afrakans have Konsciously and sub-Konsciously run away from since our surrender or enslavement. It is a principal as clear and widely accepted as any that exists. "The Way Out Is Back Through." Nevertheless, we must be in charge of the return trip through our healing institutions and with our Healing Spiritual Warriors. The Kemet Spiritual system, and other indigenous Afrakan spiritual systems, like Akan, Yoruba, Voodoo etc., can provide a vehicle for this healing. However, Afrakan Spiritual Warriors must do the healing from our Afrakan-Centered, Spiritual Pan-Afrakan Worldview.

Part of our healing is the knowledge of knowing that we fought back, that we did not just surrender, and let our egos collapse in the presents of our enemies. There was Konscious resistance in an environment of hostile oppression then and we are still resisting today. To not to resist is insane, and a betrayal of our Afrakan ancestors. Despite what many of us have been taught, Afrakans resisted vigorously during The Maangamizi. From ambushing "European slave ships" and all the ships of enslavement in the Horrid Middle Passage were Caucasian European or American and European Jewish owned. We tried to stop the ships before they left the shores of Afraka or we tried to overthrow the ships while at sea. Afrakans resisted by uprisings with arms on the plantations and whereever we were, there was resistance. King Zumbi of Palmares, the free nation of Afrakans and indigenous inhabitants of Brazil resisted enslavement. The nation was called the Republic of Palmares and they successfully defended themselves against Dutch and Portuguese "enslavers" for more than 100 years in the 1600's. The knowledge of successful Quilombo societies in the midst of enemy territories, are all-important liberating acts of healing and repairing. Afrakans revolted and overtook the slave ship, Little George, in 1730, and made a 9-day return trip to Afraka. Boukman, an Afrakan traditional Voodoo priest, initiated the Haitian Revolution (1791 - 1804) for which Jean-Jacques Dessalines, Henri Christopher and Tousaint L'Overture defeated Napoleon and the French navy. Gabrel Prosser leads a revolt in Virginia 1800. Denmark Vessey leads revolt in South Carolina, 1822. Nat Turner leads revolt in Virginia, 1831. Acheampong Nanny and Cudjoe are amongst the leaders of the Maroons in Jamaica that defeated the British. In addition, Doming Bioho leads a revolt in Columbus, South America, and this list goes on, but most of all this is healing and repairing information that Afrakans need to hear from an Afrakan centered perspective!

Spiritual Warriors of the 63rd century new Afrakan time must build and maintain a national shrine in reverence to all the lost and forgotten Afrakan souls of the Maangamizi. This shrine will honor the Afrakans lost at sea during the savagery of the Middle Passage, Afrakans inhumanely destroyed in America, in the Caribbean Islands, in South America and on the Afrakan continent. We must develop an ancestor day dedicated to the Maangamizi, and it must be a National Holiday for all people of Afrakan

descent wherever we are in the world. This space must be a liberated space that we as Afrakan people control, not beg, borrow or rent from our oppressors. We must visit the closest Maangamizi memorial for an organized memorial service. Afrakans must stay home from work on that day. Afrakan employers should close businesses. Afrakan students should not attend school and Afrakan schools should be close. Maangamizi flags should be visible at homes, businesses, schools and hung wherever it is appropriate, so that everyone will remember the inhuman, barbaric and savage treatment inflicted upon Afrakan people by Caucasian Europeans, Arabs, and insane Afrakans. The Maangamizi must be taught in the school systems. This Maangamizi education should include the facts of the Arab and Caucasian European enslavement of Afrakan people and the contributions of insane Afrakan collaborationist as well as the European Colonist called Americans contribution to the Maangamizi.

Once we come to grips with reality, about who we are, and who our enemies and allies are, we than can actively struggle as one united Pan-Afrakan people for freedom and liberation at home, Afraka and throughout the Diaspora. This re-education from an Afrakan centered spiritual Worldview will eliminate the myths and lies that have been planted in our Konscious minds. We cannot regain all our stories that were lost and stolen but we can reclaim our Afrakan names, and a new positive, life-giving, Kultural Spiritual Worldview. This re-Afrakanization is not only for the healing of Afrakan people worldwide but it is also for the healing of our ancestors souls. This re-Afrakanization is about reclaiming our Afrakan minds and identity. It is about reclaiming and liberating our homeland Afraka, and most of all it is about sovereignty wherever we are!

A few quick facts about The Maangamizi: The Eurasians starting with the Assyrians and Persians, than the Greeks to the Romans rise to power was definitely part of the Afrakans fall from grace. Then the Arabs through the spread of Islam 640 C.E., continued the Maangamizi and then the Portuguese started a new era of the Maangamizi with the kidnapping of Afrakans from the continent in 1444. Over 200 million Afrakan people were uprooted and displaced and another 100 million sold into the European and Arab institution of enslavement from the Afrakan continent.

It is estimated that the casualty rate during the Middle Passage was as high as 40 - 50%. As many as half of the Afrakans kidnapped from their homeland died before arriving to the Americas and or the Caribbean. The Maangamizi involved Afrakans being sent to many places throughout the western and eastern hemisphere, not just the United States. Enslaved Afrakans who were victims of this insane savage, barbaric Caucasian European enslavement business were sent to places such as Brazil, Haiti, Cuba, Jamaica, Suriname, Barbados, the Bahamas, all the other parts of Central and South America. The inhumane savage Arab Muslim enslavers took Afrakans to many parts of Asia. We must remember and teach about the exploitation of Afraka, and North America, the Afrakan Holocaust and enslavement, forced free labor of Afrakan people, and all these crimes against humanity on other lands throughout the Diaspora.

As Spiritual Warriors, we also recognize the suffering of other indigenous people who were massacred, raped, wiped out, drugged insane, and hypnotized by Caucasian male domination. Now these drugged people are out of their minds to the point that they love the matrix of Caucasian male domination and feel good about their new language of Spanish, Portuguese, French or English, by the British, Dutch, Portuguese, Spanish, French, Germans, Belgians, Italians and other Caucasian European nations. Almost every European nation bears a measure of accountability for The Maangamizi, having participated in the kidnapping, raping, selling, and trading of enslaved Afrakans in this inhumane barbaric act of horrific proportions perpetrated against Afrakan people, on one level or another. Moreover, all the European nations have profited from the Maangamizi, through Caucasian male domination or white supremacy.

The Maangamizi prevention re-education must deal also with the present and the future. Moreover, this curriculum should take place for the whole school year, and not Black History month (February). Dr. Ani Marimba states, "We have been duped into believing that we are free and healthy, but we are still living in the Maafa. Only by going through the pain and the grief can we find our way to Sankofa, an acceptance of our being, our spirit." Only through this re-Afrakanization process, can we innerstand the true nature of the Wazungu and Asiatics, in relationship to Afrakan people, and melanin people, and the planet Earth.

Afrakan Warriors must bring justice to our Afrakan ancestors by having reciprocity met for all our ancestors. We must eliminate all the conditions that allowed the Maangamizi to exist. Reciprocity in the form of reparations must be paid from the American government for its participation in the Maangamizi as a whole. This is restitution/compensation for the crimes committed against generations of Afrakan people. However, each state that allowed the enslavement of Afrakans must also pay so that local state shrines and monuments may be set up for visitation along with the National Maangamizi Memorial. Reparations must also come from the Arab governments in Afraka and Asia, and all the European governments that participated in the Afrakan enslavement and Maangamizi, like the Berlin conference of 1885. Even proven Afrakan collaborationist from certain countries and towns must also pay reparations with land, money, citizenship, resources or several combinations of the above suggestions. Afrakan Spiritual Warriors must be so focused that there is no rest until there is Pan-Afrakan unity and reciprocity for the Maangamizi.

Reparations should been given to a national council of Afrakan elders and experts, in which the local people through the guidance of Spiritual Warriors elect to represent them, not the hand picked Negroes, and African-Americans elected or appointed by the U.S. Government. Land must be at the top of the list. Land here in America and the Afrakan continent. Free college education, no taxation, and free transportation home to Afraka if we choose. Political prisoners should be released from the modern American enslavement plantations. Trillions of dollars to support re-educational programs, business, and spiritual rehabilitation and physiological therapy given by Afrakan Spiritual Warriors. In addition, billions of dollars to help rebuild, repair, and re-Afrakanize our homeland Afraka from the continuing conditions of the Maangamizi.

"The events which transpired five thousand years ago; Five years ago or five minutes ago, have determined what will happen five minutes from now; five years from now or five thousand years from now. All history is a current event."

- Dr. John Henrik Clarke -

Ourstory has taught Afrakan people, the modern Kemetyu through the Maangamizi, that Afrakan people should never be at the mercy of Caucasian Europeans or Asiatics individually or collectively in anything, anywhere on the planet. We should never depend on them or let them be in control of our jobs, institutions, education, social activities, community or personal protection, music industries or **Kultural reinforcement. Do not let the Wazungu in your family, or your personal life.** They collectively do not have the spiritual capacity to have our best interests at heart and they do not make good reliable partners. As a Spiritual Warrior this is clear, their humane record is clear and this is how we must operate as Afrakan people from now through eternity.

Spiritual Warrior Mfundishi Jhutyms Ka n Heru El- Salim on New Jersey cable TV, with the Host Doris Roberson, speaking out against Racism, the Maangamizi and the need to heal through Ma'at, Afrakan love, Kulture, and an Afrakan Spiritual Pan-Afrakan Worldview.

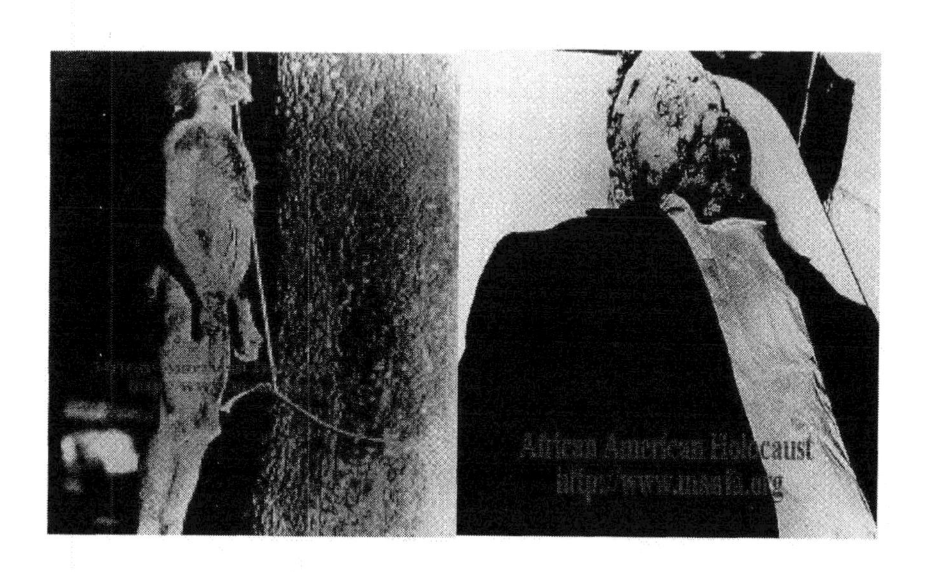

Top left an Afrikan raped, shot and hung. Top right, Emmitt Till, 14 years old, was murdered for allegedly whistling at a Caucasian woman. He was shot in the head, one eye was gouged out, and his head was smashed in on one side. Bottom left, this Afrikan was shot & lynched. Bottom right a dual lynching in Marion, Indiana.

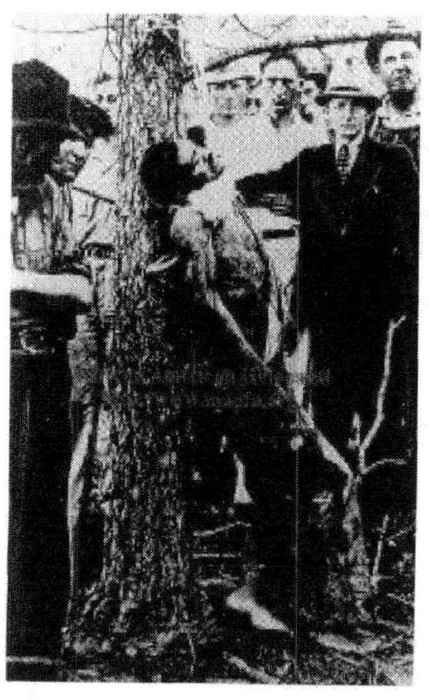

An Afrakan in American being burned by a Caucasian European American lynch mob Omaha, Nebraska -1919, The ***Maangamizi*** *continues...*

POINT 12; GOAL: To develop a council of Esteem Elders and experts to oversee the re-Afrakanization, self repair, self healing, self restoration and reparations, and these Spiritual Warriors are elected by the people. To build and maintain Maangamizi Memorial centers in Afraka and throughout the Diaspora. To revere and remember all Afrakan Ancestors and to pay yearly homage in terms of a Holy Day for their remembrance and honor. To awaken and re-educate the world to the enslavement of Afrakan people in both the western and eastern Hemisphere as a human atrocity, a Holocaust and to further the process of healing. To collect reparations from all those who have participated in the Maangamizi. To bring back the laws of reciprocity and harmony and balance into the universe. Land must be a major priority in reparations in America and in Afraka. To use reparation money to build the national and international shrines and monuments in the Diaspora for Afrakan people. Reparation money, some will seed the redevelopment of

the United States of Afraka, and some will fund Maangamizi re-educational programs and Institutions seeking to honor those Afrakans who perished, strengthen those Afrakans who survived, inform and educate all of humanity of the atrocities, and guide those Afrakans yet to come into self empowerment.

Heal a woman, heal a family. Heal a family, heal a community. Heal a community, heal a nation and only a strong healthy Black nation can heal the world. And only Spiritual Warriors can heal women and men. Let the healing begin Spiritual Warriors.

Spiritual Warriors are Healers: Spiritual Warrior Healer Sis. Prema, also a poet and community activist with Mfundishi Jhutyms at Wp Renpt - an Afrakan Kemet New Year celebration in New York.

1. Defense System
2. Educational System
3. Wholistic Health Healing System
4. Language Re-covery and Communication System
5. Ujamaa Economic System
6. Ma'at Afrakan Governance System
7. Food Production, Labor and Manufactory System
8. Kuumba Art and Inner-attainment System
9. Science and Technology System
10. Transportation System
11. Maangamizi Never Again Memorial System
12. Afrakan Spiritual and Religious System

"Let the Healing Begin"

CHAPTER IIIIIIIII (9)

Somo la Tisa

Kwanzaa: A Re-Afrakanization Ritual

The Pan-Afrakan community and the Spiritual Warriors innerstand and embrace Kwanzaa, an Afrakan-American holiday, created by Dr. Maulana Karenga in 1966. Kwanzaa is based upon Afrakan tradition and the Afrakan in America's experience. The Afrakan in America was stolen, ripped from the womb of Afraka, brutalized, de-humanized, dekultured, traumatized and reprogrammed for self-hatred and self-destruction, The Maangamizi. The Maangamizi is still happening today and like any entity propelled in motion, will continue unless met by an equal or opposing force. Kwanzaa is one of those forces that can help redirect our energies towards solving our own problems. Kwanzaa is a healing festival that helps Afrakans in America recapture their pride, dignity, and Afrakan Kulture as Black human beings. Kwanzaa is a Re-Afrakanization ritual.

Kwanzaa is a non-religious, non-political, non-heroic holiday dedicated to Afrakan Kulture and spirituality. Kwanzaa means in the East Afrakan language of Kiswahili: "The first fruits of the harvest". This is a very unique Afrakan holiday in America. It celebrates the richness and diversity of millenniums of Afrakan Kultures and values that still survive in the Kultures of Afrakan people in the Diaspora. Kwanzaa has become a forum for Afrakan derived Kultures to explore their Kultural roots, and to recognize their uniqueness.

Kwanzaa Roots

In August 1965, an uprising erupted in Watts, a predominately Black community of Afrakans born in America in Los Angeles, California. Afrakans in the community were angry about the crumbling houses, low-paying jobs, rising unemployment, and racism they faced day after day. On August 11, the anger, frustration, and hopelessness that many Afrakans in America feel came to a boiling point.

An uprising broke out when white police officers arrested Marquette Frye, an Afrakan born in America motorist. Some bystanders felt that Frye was treated too roughly by the white policemen. During the long, hot August night that followed, police and passing cars were bombarded with bricks, bottles, and slabs of concrete.

The uprising continued for the next four days. Four thousand people were arrested, hundreds were injured, thirty-four were killed. Cars were overturned. Windows were broken. Many buildings in the community were looted and set on fire, and the smoke from the flames could be seen for miles around. Police sirens wailed morning and night. More than two hundred million dollars' worth of property damage and loss resulted.

When the uprising was finally over, many places in the community were reduced to smoke and ashes. Hundreds of people were left homeless. Broken glass littered the sidewalks. Several businesses closed and moved to other locations. Watts looked like a war had been fought there. But in the aftermath of the uprising, something began to change in Watts. Afrakans born in American in Watts and across the city, joined together with a purpose, to rebuild Watts and make the community stronger and better.

Maulana Karenga was finishing his last year of graduate school during the Watts uprising. He too wanted to help rebuild Watts and bring Afrakan-Americans together. Karenga felt his people had lost touch with their Afrakan heritage. After receiving his Ph.D., he began teaching

Afrakans in America Ourstory at California State University, Long Beach. He also began studying ways that Afrakans in Americans could help themselves and each other. He wanted to unify his people and instill in them a sense of pride in their Afrakan Kulture. Dr. Karenga felt that there should be a special time during the year, set aside for this purpose. He began to research ancient Afrakan harvest ceremonies, and "first fruit" celebrations.

Dr. Karenga studied the Kulture of the Yorubas, the Ibos, the Ashantis, the Zulus, Ancient Kemet, and other Afrakan Nations. Although each Nation celebrated the harvest festival a little differently, there were many things the festivals had in common.

The harvest festival was a way of rewarding all the members of the nation or village for their teamwork during the year. Seeds could not be planted, fields could not be gathered unless the entire community worked together as a group. Everyone in the community, from the smallest child to the oldest adult had a job to do. By working together, the entire community had food to eat throughout the year.

The harvest festival usually lasted several days. The king or chief said a prayer for the health and wealth of each member of the community. He also gave honor to the community ancestors. Sometimes, a special cup was filled and passed around in the group in memory of those who had died long ago. After the ceremony was over, there was feasting, music, and dancing all night long. The Afrakan harvest festival was a time for community members to remember their ancestors, celebrate good fortune, and plan for the coming new year.

In 1966, Dr. Karenga created Kwanzaa, a Kultural holiday based upon the ancient customs of Afraka. He added an "a" to the Kiswahili word for first, kwanza, to create the name for the holiday. Kwanzaa is celebrated from December 26th through January 1st. Each day of Kwanzaa is dedicated to one of the seven principles of the Nguzo Saba. The Nguzo Saba are the seven principles of Kwanzaa established by Dr. Karenga to be memorized, discussed, and acted upon during the seven days of Kwanzaa. The Nguzo Saba is to serve as a guide for daily living not only for the seven (7) days of Kwanzaa, but for 365 days of the year, every year! Each day family members discuss the meaning of one of the principles, and lights a candle in the Kinara, which is one of the traditional symbols in Kwanzaa. This rich Afrakan based ritual will help Afrakans in America instill in them a sense of pride in their Afrakan Kulture.

Kwanzaa is not a religious holiday or one that honors a heroic person. It is not a holiday that is celebrated in Afraka. Kwanzaa is an original Afrakan-American holiday. Kwanzaa is a time when Afrakans in Americans join together to honor the traditions of their Afrakan ancestors. Planning for the year to come and working on ways to make themselves a better community are important parts of the holiday. Kwanzaa is a celebration of the past, the present, and the future, what we call the infinite now in the Kemet Spiritual System.

Dr. Karenga also incorporated many Afrakan customs, traditions, symbols, and words from the Kiswahili language when he created Kwanzaa. Kiswahili is a non-tribal Afrakan Bantu language that is spoken in East Afraka and many Kiswahili words and phrases like "Habari gani?" (What's the news?) And " Harambee!" (Lets pull together!), are used as part of the Kwanzaa celebration.

Dr. Karenga is an Afrakan Spiritual Warrior by deeds and action. He is an Afrakan who has dedicated his life towards the development of himself and Afrakan people. He exemplifies tradition and reason, combined with critical thinking, followed by dynamic action. This is how the re-Afrakanization must be carried out from community to community, state to state, and nation to nation. We call this operational unity. Kwanzaa is one small example of how ritual must be revised, and rejuvenated to reaffirm Afrakan-centeredness in our daily lives, mentally, physically and spiritually.

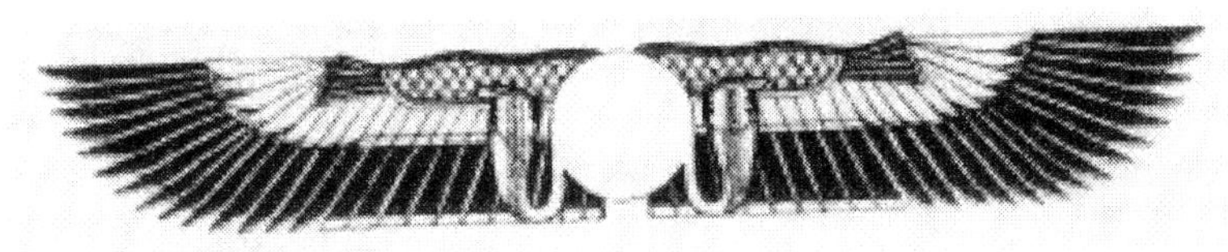

Kwanzaa paraphernalia

1. MAZAO (Crops i.e., fruits and vegetables)

The Mazao have significance because they symbolize the rewards of collective productive labor. Moreover, as Kwanzaa means first or First Fruits, it was patterned after the traditional celebrations that take place among Afrakan agrikultural societies at harvest time. At harvest time the fruits of collective labor abound and it is a time of great joy and togetherness, a time for Thanksgiving and remembrance. The Mazao therefore, represent the Ourstorical roots of the holiday itself.

2. MKEKA (Place Mat)

Dr. Karenga states, "The Mkeka is the symbol of tradition and extended Ourstory." He adds, "Since Kwanzaa seeks to inspire appreciation and practice of values which aid us in our lives and struggle, the stress is on tradition and Ourstory, for they form the foundation on which correct knowledge and true innerstanding is built. The ancestors innerstand this clearly, as illustrated by the following Afrakan proverb: " If you know the beginning well, the end will not trouble you."

3. KINARA (Candle Holder)

The Kinara is symbolic of the continental Afrakans, our parent people. In incorporating this symbol, Dr. Karenga used a Zulu concept. In early Kwanzaa celebrations, the Kinara was used to symbolize Nkulunkulu, the first born, the father of both our people and our principles. Since the early days of Kwanzaa, the Kinara has come to symbolize our ancestors, as a collective whole.

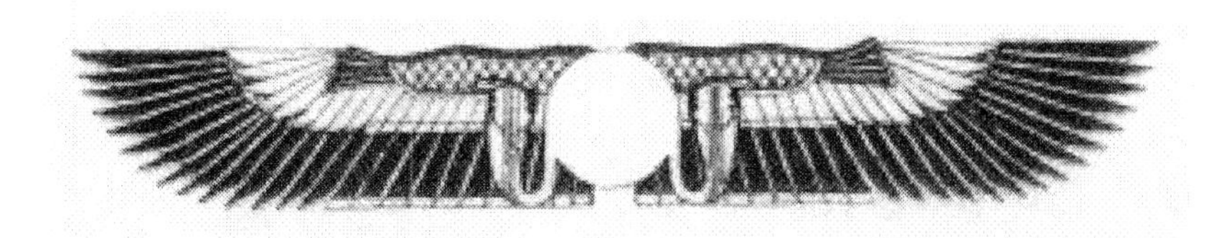

4. VIBUNZI (Ears of Corn)

The Vibunzi represent children thus, each family uses as many ears of corn as it has children. Karenga states," In traditional terminology, the ears of corn represent the produce of the stalk and the potential of the offspring to become stalks or producers and reproducers of themselves, thus ensuring immortality of the people or nation. "Emphasis is placed on children, for they truly represent the hope for the future. Therefore, if we instill the proper values in them and teach them the benefits of mutual respect, we insure a brighter tomorrow when they become elders.

5. ZAWADI (Gifts)

Zawadi should be given as reward for commitments made and kept and are usually exchanged among members of a nuclear family. They should be given to reinforce personal growth and achievement which benefit the collective. Gifts given during Kwanzaa are not given automatically, but are rather based on merit. They should be educational or otherwise beneficial in nature. Books make excellent gifts. Items for gifts that are handmade are encouraged. One should not fall victim to commercialism that presently characterizes Christmas, or the feast of mass consumption. Kuumba (Creativity) is greatly encouraged and Ujamaa (Cooperative Economics). So buy from Afrakan people, keeping the money in the community and supporting Afrakan business. The following is a suggested list of excellent Kwanzaa Zawadi:

- Books written by and about Afrakans from the Continent or the Diaspora.
- Wood carvings and sculptures created by Afrakan people.
- Authentic Afrakan masks, prints of Afrakans, created by Afrakans.
- Paintings by Afrakans, educational games, Afrakan clothing and accessories.

- Jewelry from Afraka or created by Afrakans, Afrakan fabrics.
- Tickets to Afrakan Kultural events, and Afrakan oils.
- Handmade Afrakan crafts and toys created and made by Afrakans.

6. KIKOMBE CHA UMOJA (The Communal Unity Cup)

Clearly, as the name suggests, the Unity Cup symbolizes the first, and most important principle of Kwanzaa, Unity. It is used to pour Tambiko (Libation) in the direction of the four winds (north, south, east, and west), in remembrance of the ancestors. The Unity Cup may then be passed among members of the family and guests who may either choose to sip or make a sipping gesture. This is done to honor the ancestors and to promote the spirit of Oneness.

7. MISHUMAA SABA (The Seven Candles)

The Mishumaa Saba represent the Nguzo Saba (The seven principles), which are at the heart of the value system that is the foundation of Kwanzaa. According to Dr. Karenga," The Nguzo Saba have their roots in research of Afrakan Kultures which revealed recurrent emphasis on values. Values that reinforced the bonds between people and increased their human possibilities for a meaningful and fulfilling life." As each Candle represents a distinct principle, beginning with Umoja (Unity, the black center candle), a Candle is lit each day from left, (red Candles representing the struggle) to right, (green Candles the fertile reward of struggle and proper preparation) after the Umoja Black Candle has been lit.

Spiritual Warriors and Afrakan Priest Scientists start every special occasion off with Tambiko (Libation) because it is tradition to pour Tambiko, in remembrance of the ancestors on all occasions. Kwanzaa, is such an occasion, as it provides us with an opportunity to reflect upon our Afrakan past and American present. Water is suggested for Tambiko as it holds the essence of life.

NGUZO SABA
(The Seven Principles)

1. UMOJA (Unity): To strive for and maintain unity in the family, community, nation and race.

2. KUJICHAGULIA (Self-determination): To define ourselves, name ourselves, create for ourselves, and speak for ourselves instead of being defined, named, created for and spoken for by others.

3. UJIMA (Collective Work and Responsibility): To build and maintain our community together and make our sisters' and brothers' problems our problems and to solve them together.

4. UJAMAA (Cooperative Economics): To build and maintain our own stores, shops and other businesses and to profit from them together.

5. NIA (Purpose): To make as our collective vocation the building and developing of our community in order to restore our people to their traditional greatness.

6. KUUMBA (Creativity): To do always as much as we can, in the ways we can, in order to leave our community more beautiful and beneficial than we inherited it.

7. IMANI (Faith): To believe with all our hearts in Afrakan people, our parents, our Afrakan centered teachers, our Afrakan centered leaders, and the righteousness and victory of our struggle.

These principles must be rooted in a powerful Afrakan-centered spatial prospective. These positive Afrakan values represent the best of Afrakan Kulture and act as a foundation for the re-Afrakanization of people of Afrakan descent. In addition, the Nguzo Saba will educate non-Afrakans about the power and beauty in Afrakan Kulture.

The First-Fruit Celebrations are recorded in Afrakan Ourstory as far back as Kemet and Kash and appear in ancient and modern times in classical Afrakan civilizations, such as Ashanti land, Yoruba land, the Zulus kingdom, and many smaller societies like Matabole, Thonga and Lovedu, etc.

Kwanzaa was not the name that was used by these societies for their First Fruit Celebration. As such, the First Fruit Celebrations in Ancient Kemet, was called "Pert-en Min" (The coming forth of Min). Among the Zulu, Umkhosi; among the Swazi, Incwala; among the Matabele, Inxwala; among the Thonga, Luma; among the Lovedu, Thegula; among the Ashanti, Afahye or Odwira; among the Yoruba, Eje, Oro Ologin or Odun Ijesu.

Five Values and Practices

There are at least five common sets of values and practices central to Afrakan First Fruit Celebrations, which formed the development of Kwanzaa:

1) Harvesting

Harvesting refers to people, as well the crops. It is a harvesting of the people, a bringing together of the most valuable fruits or products of the nation. Its human harvest, the people themselves.

2) Reverence

Reverence is an expression of Afrakan spirituality which here means intense emotional and rational appreciation for the highest ideals and values of the Black human. "Inherent in the Afrakan reverence for the creator is an ultimate respect for creation, so that a significant part of prayers and other rituals is a concern with being in harmony, with nature and the universe. In Ancient Kemet, the First Fruit Festival, the coming forth of Min (Pert-en-Min), was seen as a reaffirmation of the harmonious interlocking of the divine, natural and human social oneness. In Ancient Kemet, Kemet rituals were conducted to restore, renew, refresh, rejuvenate and reinforce the fertility of the Earth, and the life and strength of the people.

3) Commemoration, especially of the ancestors. This profound respect for the ancestors is because they are: a source and symbol of lineage; models of ethical life, service and social achievement to the community; and because they are spiritual intercessors between humans and the Creator.

4) Recommitment, this is the highest and most fundamental Kultural value in both thought and practice. Kulture as defined by Maulana Karenga, is the total life pattern involving the spiritual, historical, social economic, political, creative, psychological, etc. In Kwanzaa, the value system is the Nguzo Saba. In ancient Kemet, it was Ma'at - truth, justice, righteousness, and harmonious balance. The guiding principles were the Laws of Ma'at covered in Chapter 3. Others are Papa, Dinka, Ire among the Yoruba. These values are the Kultural and spiritual good, which benefit humans and satisfies the Creator, according to Maulana Karenga. Therefore, recommitment involves a reaffirmation and rededication in thought and practice to cooperation, peace, truth, justice, righteousness, sistership, brothership, harmony, reciprocity, creativity, collective work and responsibility, sharing the determination and Kultural integrity of the people, and all other values which serve as grounding and social glue for community.

5) Celebration, it is rejoicing of our great Kulture, Our story, our love, the praising and honoring of our labor, fruits, and ourselves. We are celebrating life and its goodness as we communion with the Creator and Creation, with the Ancestors and the Ntchru. In this way, the Afrakan families, communities, and Kulture are preserved, reaffirmed and renewed.

All Afrakan Spiritual Warriors, Pan Afrakanist, Kupigana Ngumi mwanafunzi na mpigani are encouraged to celebrate Kwanzaa. The Afrakan Spiritual Warrior and Priest Scientist must and will play key role in educating the community. Afrakan parents have the key role in educating the children in the values of the Nguzo Saba, the seven basic laws of Kwanzaa. From December 26th until January 1st, each day and night of Kwanzaa, when we meet other Afrakancentric people we greet each other as follows;

- "Habari gani?" (What is the news?).

- On the first day of Kwanzaa, Dec. 26th, you reply "Umoja!" (Unity) Asante, habari gani?

- On the second day, Dec. 27th, the reply is "Kujichagulia" (Self-determination) Asante, habari gani?

- On the third day, December 28th, reply, "Ujima" (Collective Work and Responsibility) Asante, habari gani?

- On the fourth day, December 29th, reply, "Ujamaa" (Cooperative Economics) Asante, habari gani?

- On the fifth day, December 30th reply, " Nia " (Purpose) Asante, habari gani?

- On the sixth day, December 31, reply, "Kuumba" (Creativity) Asante, habari gani?

- The seventh and last day, January 1st when someone asks Habari gani? You should reply "Imani" (Faith) Asante, habari gani?

Decorating the Home and the Community

An Ancestor table should be set up in a very visible location. The Kinara and all the Kwanzaa symbols should be in the center of the table. The table should be covered with traditional Afrakan cloth, with the Kwanzaa designs on it. The room, house, or hall should be decorated with the Kwanzaa colors which are Red, Black and Green. Seven added decorations are Afrakan prints, posters, mask, wood carvings, sculptures, flowers and plants.

The last day of Kwanzaa is the Karamu, the big feast or Afrakan family party. The Afrakan Spiritual Warrior recommend a vegetarian menu for the feast, Afrakan clothes, Zawadi (gifts) of books, art, and Afrakan Kultural items. Afrakan songs should be sang, dancing, drumming, a celebration of Afrakan beauty and work (Kazi). At the end of the evening, a *unity circle* should be made with everyone joining hands to affirm our togetherness and to vow to make the values of the Nguzo Saba throughout the coming year. At this point, everyone holds up their right fist and the oldest person in the group, or one of the elders chant "Harambe Kwa Umoja" (Let's Pull Together for Unity). Then everyone chants Harambe seven times, holding the last Harambe for as long as they can. In conclusion, everyone should hug each person, if it is a small group. If it is a large gathering, hug at least seven people.

Below is a model for the Karamu program which can possibly be of use in planning for your own program.

"A REINFORCEMENT OF OUR ROOTS"

A KWANZAA KARAMU

1. KUKARIBISHI (Welcoming)

a. Tamshi la Tambiko (Libation Statement)
b. Introductory remarks
c. Recognition of distinguished guests
d. Kultural expression

2. KUKUMBUKA (Remembering)

a. Reflections of an mzee (elder)
b. Reflections of a woman
c. Reflections of a man
d. Reflections of a youth
e. Kultural expression

3. KUCHUNGUZA TENA NA KUTOA AHADI TENA (Reassessment and recommitment)

a. Introduction of distinguished guest lecturer
b. Distinguished guest lecturer

4. KUSHANGILIA (Rejoicing) Karamu (Feast)

a. Tamshi la tambiko (Libation Statement)
b. Kikombe cha umoja (Unity cup)
c. Kutoa majina (Naming)
d. Ngoma (Drums)
e. Kultural expression

5. ASANTE NA TUTAONANA (Thank you and we shall see each other soon).

Tamshi la Tutaonana (The farewell statement).

In review, the Afrakan Spiritual Warrior Priest Scientist would like to answer the most commonly asked questions about Kwanzaa.

Questions and Answers about Kwanzaa

Question: What is the origin of Kwanzaa?

Answer: Kwanzaa was founded in 1966 by Dr. Maulana Karenga, a Black Studies professor who describes himself as a Kultural Nationalist. Kwanzaa originated as a Kultural idea and an expression of the nationalist," Us organization," which was headed by Dr. Karenga.

Question: Is Kwanzaa a Christmas substitute?

Answer: No, because Dr. Karenga recognized the undue hardship that the overcommercialization of Christmas has for Black people, and others who are at the lowest point of the social strata who are kept economically oppressed. Therefore, those who find Kwanzaa to be more meaningful to them, now have an option and can still be part of the holiday season.

Question: How important is gift giving during Kwanzaa?

Answer: Gifts may be exchanged during the Kwanzaa though it is suggested that they not be given if they present undue hardship. When gifts are given it is suggested that they be creative i.e. handmade or functional like a book. Whether handmade or purchased, gifts should come from Afrakan merchants and store owners not large white corporations or people outside the Afrakan Kulture or community.

Question: How is Kwanzaa celebrated?

Answer: Kwanzaa can be celebrate in a number of ways. At a bare minimum a table should be prepared with the following items: a place mat (Mkeka) usually made of straw, a candle holder for seven candles (Kinara); seven candles (Mishumaa Saba); a variety of fruits (mazao) ears of corn. (Vibunzi), representing the number of children in the home; gifts if any, Kikombe (Unity Cup) for pouring and sharing libation. Each day of Kwanzaa a candle should be lit beginning with the black candle, which is placed in the center of the holder. Candles are then lit alternately from left to right. Three green candles should be placed on the left and three red candles should be placed on the right. Each day an Nguzo Saba principle should be recited when the candle is lit.

The importance that each principle has for the person reciting it should be expounded upon. Other suggestions can be found in this chapter.

Question: Why is Kiswahili used?

Answer: Kiswahili was chosen because it is a non-tribal Afrakan language that encompasses a large portion of the Afrakan Continent. An added benefit is that Kiswahili pronunciation is extremely easy. Vowels are pronounced like those in Spanish and the consonants, with few exceptions like those of English. The vowels are as follows: A = ah as in father, E= a as in day, I= ee as in free, O= oo as in too. The accent is almost always on the next to last syllable.

Question: How does one dress for Kwanzaa?

Answer: The first thing that must be stressed is that Kwanzaa is an Afrakan Kultural Holiday. This is a time for Afrakans to pay tribute to their rich Afrakan heritage and Kulture. Afrakan clothes and fabrics should be worn all seven days of Kwanzaa especially at dinner when the candles are lit each night, and at the feast on January 1st, the last day of Kwanzaa. Afrakan clothes should also be worned at pre-Kwanzaa and post Kwanzaa programs. Ultimately we are exposing Afrakans to their own beautiful clothing. This is part of the re-Afrakanization process Afrakans throughout the Diaspora must go through. This Kultural ritual will show the beauty of the rich Afrakan Kultural heritage. The power and beauty of our dynamic Kulture, may inspire Afrakans in America to wear Afrakan clothing, even when Kwanzaa is over.

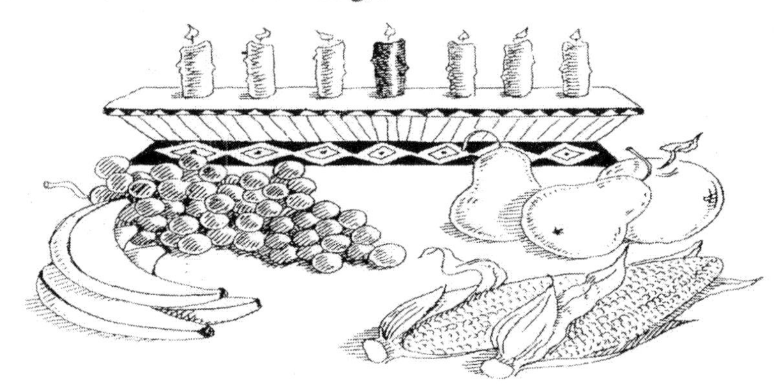

Kemklusion

Kwanzaa is an expression of Kujichakulia, the right to define ourselves, name ourselves and speak for ourselves. Kwanzaa has become part of our re-Afrakanization process of returning to our right minds, our Afrakan minds. As Spiritual Warriors, we will not, and must never, seek the advice nor permission of alien oppressors in practicing and perpetuating the Kultural heritage of our ancestors! Spiritual Warriors give respect to those pioneer practitioners and preservers of Kwanzaa tradition from its inception. Praise is due to creative and intellectual talents of Dr. Maulana Karanga for the germination of the Kwanzaa movement. As Afrakans and as Spiritual Warriors, Kwanzaa is our symbol of:

a. **Reclamation of Afrakan traditions.**

b. **Reverence to Afrakan ancestors.**

c. **Reinforcement and strength for family and Community stabilization.**

d. **Inter-generation respect and adherence for Afrakan Kultural values.**

e. **Self-determination, self-esteem, self-reliance and self-defense.**

f. **Preservation of our collective goal of Nationship, in theory and in practice, through Black empowerment.**

g. **Kwanzaa must be used as a re-Afrakanazation healing ritual, not just a social gathering or Black Christmas.**

"Sticks in a bundle are unbreakable." ***Bondei proverb***
"When the brothers fight to the death, a stranger inherits the father's estate." ***Ibo proverb***
"Emotions are good servants, but poor masters." ***Kemet proverb***

Dr. Maulana Karenga the founder of Kwanzaa.

Kwanzaa Setting by Mfundishi Jhutyms Ka n Heru El-Salim

FOR THE SPIRIT OF KWANZAA

For the Motherland, cradle of civilization.
For the ancestors and their Spiritual guidance.

For the elders, from whom
We can learn much.

For our youth, who represent
The promise for tomorrow.

For the unborn,
Who hold the keys to immortality.

For our Kemetyu,
The original Black people.
May you return to your right mind, because you are the
Seeds of humanity.

For our struggle and in remembrance
Of those who have struggled
On our behalf.

For the Nguzo Saba,
The divine principles which should
Guide us in all that we do.

For the Creator, who provides
All things great and small.

Amen Ra Na Swt Ntchr
Aten Ra Neb en Ankh
De en Nu Ankh Ujah Seneb
Amen Ma'at.

CHAPTER ∩ (10)
Somo la Kumi

Spiritual Warriors

All that exists is manifested through spirit. Spirit is the essence of all things. All reality is governed by a set of laws that protect and defend its existence through spirit. Thus, spirit is everywhere all the time, but not all things are always Konscious of its divine presence. Spirit and soul, the *Ka* and the *Ba*, are the vital principles in all humans. There are many types of spirits, but they all are manifestations of the One, The NTCHR.

Spirits that protect, defend and help perpetuate the existence of human beings are called Guardian or Warrior Spirits. When human beings have dedicated their lives to the development of their mind, body and soul to receive the divine spirit, and they allow the Guardian Spirit to guide their life with great efficiency, they become Spiritual Warriors. When the Spiritual Warrior is in harmony with The NTCHR, he or she are fulfilling their destiny through the act of living a spiritual existence within Ma'at and with no fear of death in the maintainance of Ma'at. However, whenever esfet exists, the Spiritual Warrior attacks it mentally, physically, and spiritually, just as the human immune system attacks all and any entities that would harm or threaten the human body-temple. When the Spiritual Warrior is successful in re-establishing peace and harmony, healing is taking place. Healing is the bringing of Ma'at or Htp into existence within the human body-temple. Becoming a Spiritual Warrior or the essence of the foundation of becoming a Spiritual Warrior is the essence of this gift I give to you, so that true healing can take place at home in Afraka and in Amenta, the land of death, Amerikkka and throughout the Diaspora, wherever Afrakan people are.

We are living in a time when esfet (division and disharmony through might and force) appears to be ruling the day. The Kemetyu, Afrakan people and the majority of the planet's population seem to be out of balance. The very soul of the planet has summoned the original Spiritual Warriors to lead the Kemetyu back into their right mind so that the healing can begin. As you read this book, you are already involved in the healing process. The healing has begun. The Earth cannot be healed until we, the Kemetyu, Afrakans are healed or involved in the healing processes on a high level of spirituality and commitment to Ma'at. The Kemetyu of today must align themselves with Ma'at from a Pan-Afrakan Worldview so that what they want and what they need, equal the healing necessary to bring all of us into our right Ntchr-like Afrakan minds. This will start the healing of the whole planet, as we evolve back into "The Way", Heru Konsciousness.

Wholistic healing of the whole body-temple, mentally, spiritually, along with the physical, must take place daily. Any aspect of the body-temple that holds any part of itself in denial loses Konscious spiritual presence or Sekhem, allowing disease to take control. The germs or energies that cause most diseases have always been present, but the human body, when in balance, a state of Htp, an aspect of Ma'at, has a Heru immune system that battles esfet or disease with a total commitment. Esfet therefore is not strong enough to enter, damage or disrupt the harmony of the body-temple as long as your spiritual Konsciousness is in harmony with the soul.

Ntchr Ntchru is given everything that it needs to become, to evolve and to fulfill itself. Human beings also have been blessed like the Ntchr Ntchru, but many human beings are unkonscious of The NTCHR, or we are in denial of its presence and power. As a result, we become helpless and oblivious of our spiritual healing powers. We must embrace the love of NTCHR, which is eternal love. Once we have accepted the Divine Spirit of The NTCHR, we will innerstand that we are divine manifestations of its love, allowing self acceptance and self love to come into our hearts.

This divine self-love must come first so that we can do what we came forth into being to do. Divine self-love is extended self-identity, including family, community, nature and the Afrakan personality. The Way of The Spiritual Warrior is to manifest a great mastery of divine love, a spirit that embraces and nurtures all things.

There exists in every human being a place that is free from disease, or esfet. In this place there is no pain, or anger, you cannot age, because you are ageless and timeless. There is no death, because death is an illusion. When you go to this place, limitations which all of us accept, cease to exist. They are not even entertained as possibilities. This is the heart of the Spiritual Warrior.

At the heart of the Spiritual Warrior is an unconditional and unlimited love for The NTCHR. This love is not an emotion, it is the essence of the Spiritual Warrior's very being, Ma'at. We must reject and let go of everything that does not allow us to fulfill our destiny of being, while being One with The NTCHR. You must do this at a time that is right for you and in the way that is right for you. If one is a Spiritual Warrior, this "letting go" needs to feel good and not like mere self-denial. Love of self becomes a prerequisite of all Spiritual Warriorship. When there is no enemy within, the enemy outside the body-temple cannot hurt you or poses no threat to your mission. The greater the Spiritual Warrior's spiritual focus and mastery over one's own breath, the stronger one gets, giving an infinite capacity to love and share. The greater the spirit, the more the warrior wants to fulfill its own destiny. This destiny is to bring harmony or Ma'at into existence. This harmony or state of Htp is the spiritual energy that manifests healing.

One of the many roles of the Spiritual Warrior is that of the **Healer**. The Afrakan Spiritual Warrior has an advantage over other humankind because the Afrakan Spiritual Warrior has been blessed with the Sankofa Spirit. This spirit carries millions of years of healing experience locked within its DNA, because of our unique Melanin enabling us to experience a greater spiritual connection with The NTCHR. The Sankofa Spirit brought forth from our collective Konsciousness, herbalists, diviners, and spiritual healers with infinite knowledge of the mineral, plant and animal spiritual systems. This same Divine Konsciousness developed the harmonious system of Ma'at in ancient Kemet. These resurrected spiritual healers represent millions if not infinite years of healing knowledge. They hold the secrets of Afrakan spiritual rituals that act as resource guides for the Spiritual Warrior to tap into, so that healing and restoration of balance, and our Afrakan minds, may come forth into being.

Spiritual Warriors must master the power of the Nommo in their healing. The Kemetik spiritual energy called Jhuty; the spiritual Ntchr of articulate thought, speech and divine writing, teaches us the power of the "Word". The word is the Nommo if it carries the Konscious Divine Spirit of The NTCHR. For the Spiritual Warrior the Nommo is a healing tool. The "Word" came into existence only after thought, Konscious and reasoning. Words are the children of High Konsciousness. Only words that were created after divine reasoning shall divide the light from the darkness. Knowing ignorance can strengthen ones life but ignoring knowledge is a weakness that guarantee early death and destruction (esfet). As sure as the sun will rise, Afrakan Spiritual Warriors are being developed. The Word has been spoken through the Nommo, so let the healing begin.

Healing is a Form of Liberation

Liberation is accomplished through action guided by Ma'at. Each person that is Konsciously involved in the healing process must reflect on the "One Spirit", and within this reflection, they must make a personal commitment towards healing. There is no mediator between humans and his or her salvation or liberation. There are many paths that lead to liberation. But liberation for Afrakans must be the state of truth, happiness and a feeling of completeness or Oneness. Real liberation in any field: physical, political, mental or spiritual is to be in Konscious harmony with The NTCHR. The world or universe, to the untrained mind that is out of balance and out of harmony with The NTCHR, appears to be a multiplicity of many different objects, people and reflections. However, the reality is that they are all a manifestation of the "One," The NTCHR.

Therefore, if you think you are a warrior fighting for liberation and the liberation is not truth, Oneness, universal harmony, cosmic Konsciousness, enlightenment, salvation, balance, and Htp, then you are not involved in liberation. To the Spiritual Warrior liberation is the healing of the whole people. If you are not involved in the healing, you are being used as a pawn of esfet, disharmony and destruction and you are part of the problem.

Spiritual Warriors are healers because they live with divine truth, the essence of love and happiness. This divine truth is Heru Konsciousness. Spiritual Warriors are fighters for liberation on all fronts: mentally, physically and spiritually, turning esfet (that which is out of balance, out of harmony with nature) into Ma'at (truth, justice, righteousness and harmonious balance). They recognize the ignorance of others and are strong enough to exercise compassion, as they teach the spirit of Heru Konsciousness to those who want to be taught. From this position of love, it will be possible to do the greatest good and create the conditions for healing, mentally, physically and spiritually. Liberation for Afrakans must be the establishment of Heru Konsciousness as a way of life or a state of "Being."

Spiritual Warriors must return us to Ma'at or recreate an atmosphere where Ma'at and spiritual development is a way of life, giving us an innerstanding of the harmonious natural laws of the universe. This spiritual Konsciousness of the vastness of the cosmos must harmonize within the hearts and minds of Afrakans and all people seeking wisdom through Spirituality and Ma'at.

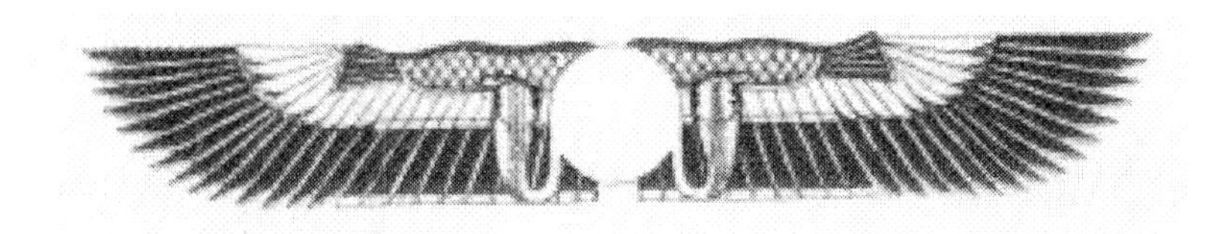

Community Spiritual Warriors: Mfundishi Jhutyms H.K. Salim, Kamau Kenyatta & Leslie Carter.

Kemet Kem-Unity Leaders: Abu Kha-f-Ra & Mfundishi Jhutyms Ka n Heru at a meeting of the Afrakan Masters and Grand Masters in N.Y.

Healing the Body - Temple

Spiritual Warriors are humans who love impersonally; they are humans who realize in their deepest heart that there is no reality outside of The NTCHR. Spiritual Warriors innerstand that every moment is in the infinite now, and he or she is only a manifestation of The NTCHR, as are the trees, birds, insects, rocks, air and stars. The Spiritual Warrior innerstands that "The Spirit "is using their body and all things are a part of them. They realize that they are not just in the universe, but it is the universe that is within them. Therefore Konsciousness becomes very clear to the Spiritual Warrior and they innerstand that they can never die, even when the physical body dies, decomposes and transforms, their spirit still exists. When one has no fear of dying, death possesses no threat to living. At this point, if your actions are based on Ma'at, which is love for NTCHR and love for your people who are also NTCHR, then the healing of a whole people can take place. This healing causes a positive state of transformation, bringing Ma'at into existence.

We the Melanin human beings, Kemetyu (Black people), Afrakans are spirit, housed in a physical body with a mind and a special soul. This spirit and soul is an energy that flows from The NTCHR. We are aspects of the One, because only The NTCHR exists. The spiritual energy of The NTCHR flows to the minds and transforms it into physical energy. The proper flow of energy promotes excellent health and the improper flow of energy leads to poor health, disease, illness and eventually transformation (death of the physical form). Ma'at Akhw Ba Ankh is an ancient method of directing the proper flow of this spiritual energy of The NTCHR into the mind, body, and soul. Utilizing this ancient method promotes high levels of mental, physical and spiritual performances necessary to maintain and perpetuate Ma'at.

When the body-temple is receiving the correct flow of spiritual energy a feeling of Htp, love, satisfaction and peace exists, along with contentment, harmony, equanimity, and Ntchru innerstanding. Feelings of anger, hate, fear and passionate desire cause blockages in the flow of spiritual energy through parts of the mind and body, thereby causing imbalance, disharmony, disease and illness. This prolonged physical transformation leads to physical dis-ease, disabilities or death. Anger held inside eats its host. In addition, depletion of energy occurs when the energy dissipates or flows out of the body due to mental attention on outward worldly objects (illusions), desires, worries, esfet, passions, and unhealthy sexual ejaculation. Many humans do not have sex for the right reasons. These activities cause an improper flow of the spirit energy and allow the body-temple to use up needed energy sooner or unnecessarily because Ma'at is not the objective. Lust is esfet and will move you further away from the divine energy. Love is Ma'at and will move you closer to the divine energy. Therefore, one of the functions of the Spiritual Warrior is to promote ways of preventing this foolish loss of Ntchr energy, or the Moyo. Today's Kemet Spiritual Warriors use Ma'at Akhw Ba Ankh, Ari Ankh Ka, meditation, yoga, Kupigana Ngumi and other Martial Arts to improve concentration so they can heal and Kultivate balance of this sexual energy.

Disease is, therefore an imbalance in the flow of energies of the body-temple which are controlled by the mind and which emanate from the spirit. Healing is accomplished by re-balancing the energies and vibrations of the mind and body-temple, and the spirit through the love of NTCHR.

Healing of the body-temple can be accomplished through specific changes in one's life-style and mental attitude and state of awareness (Konsciousness). When a human is aware of the lack of Ma'at in their body-temple, and lack of love for themselves, this is the first step towards healing. When they seek the help of Spiritual Warriors, this is the second step towards healing. Moreover, when a human follows the path of becoming a Spiritual Warrior himself or herself, loving The NTCHR through themselves, this is the third step towards healing. The path of Spiritual Warriorship also includes, learning to eat wholistically. Food is the essence of energy that perpetuates life, the first building blocks of our very being. Having knowledge of nutrition and following what we already know is a key ingredient in self-empowerment. Knowledge through wisdom is power allowing correct foods to be your first and best medicine. One must learn about herbs whose ingredients have balancing qualities with respect to the particular ailments. Healing also involves a thorough innerstanding of one's environment, using sound, color and smell in effecting harmonious

vibrations to cause a harmonious effect in the energies of the body-temple. All Spiritual Warriors must have a good exercise program to promote muscle tone, strength and excellent use of the physical body-temple.

Excellent health is the just result when a human's whole being, mentally, physically and spiritually, is in alignment and Konsciously connected to The NTCHR. This alignment includes maintaining harmonious relations with the spiritual forces, the physical self, the mental self, the community and the Afrakan Nation. There must not be any separation between the mental, physical and spiritual energies. Healing occurs when the proper physical, mental, social and spiritual order has been restored. This is the re-Afrakanization process, the alignment with NTCHR, the life-giving affirming spirits. Afrakan humans must help themselves first or be in the healing process before they can align themselves with other humans, the animal and plant world and the mineral world. All life must be respected, including the planet and its ecosystem.

Spiritual Warriors, you must learn to make all of nature your ally by using the Ntchru to help you give your gift. Let Jhuty and Ma'at guide your words and actions, but most of all - **Be Heru** so you can protect that which you develop and love. Heru Konsciousness will allow you to rise to the necessary level of greatness at any given moment. When you become the Golden Heru in Konsciousness, fire cannot burn you, gravity cannot limit your movements, and even mass, such as a mountain cannot prohibit your forward progress. Time and space cannot limit you, it becomes possible to move from other dimensions of space at will, and the past, present, and future are Konsciously happening in your mind simultaneously. The power of the infinite now are Konscious tools that Spiritual Warriors must carry with them for healing. With this NTCHR power of Moyo or Sekhem, disease can be transformed into ease which is the ultimate human healing state. Therefore, the path of the Healer is one with the Spiritual Path of the Spiritual Warrior who is in harmony with the cosmic universe. Spiritual Warriors innerstand that correct actions are the proper fruit for Afrakan spiritually guided humans. Correct actions are in harmony with Ma'at. The goal of life is to Konsciously bring yourself into harmony with the Ntchr Ntchru by revealing one's true identity. You are an aspect of The NTCHR only in human form.

Spiritual Warriors can provide spiritual counseling to promote innerstanding of reality, but only through the innerstanding of the Ntchr Ntchru, which are aspects of The NTCHR, can you perceive absolute reality. Being able to distinguish reality from the illusion will reduce the conflict in the mind. Meditation or Ma'at Akhw Ba Ankh, or Ari Ankh Ka can be used to quiet the mind to allow the direct flow of energy from the spirit of NTCHR to heal or energies you.

Spiritual Warriors innerstand that the Afrakan human mind and body-temple must be gradually retrained in a balanced manner. It must become attuned and accustomed to greater levels of energy by increasing the level of Heru Konsciousness, and reducing the level of resistance caused by holding on to their colonial or oppressor's system of Caucasian male domination or Arabism. In order for Afrakan people to heal themselves, they must develop an undying love for themselves as Afrakan human beings, their extended Afrakan self-idenity and for the One Divine Spirit, NTCHR. If human beings, especially the Kemetyu, Afrakans throughout the Diaspora and at home on the Afrakan continent are to heal, one needs to release all the negative judgments you can find in yourself and let personal love, divine love and knowledgeable innerstanding come in its place.

Afrakan people must use the Sankofa Spirit to recapture who we are, and from whence we came so that we can go forth as a whole people. We must recapture our spiritual thirst for the truth, "The Way", for NTCHR. In fact, Ourstory will teach us that spiritual awareness permeates all aspects of Afrakan life. Our spiritual Konsciousness is what affirms Ma'at, and Ma'at affirms excellent health, and divine order. The mission of the Spiritual Warrior is to acknowledge that we cannot perceive all that is real. However, the reality of The NTCHR perceives us and we the Kemetyu, the original humans who originated first on this planet, millions of years before humankind came into being innerstand that Black melaninted human beings operating in their right Afrakan mind can perceive the sum total of all that has existed, which is locked inside their DNA or ancestral memory.

The Spirit of NTCHR, which is perfection, is inside us and we are committed to returning to NTCHR as whole beings, Konsciously. Only whole people have the power to love unconditionally. Only whole people have the power to build for eternity. The process of re-Afrakanization is recreating a whole spiritual Afrakan human being.

Spiritual Warriors of Healing the body-temple
Mfundishi Jhutyms Ka n Heru & Queen Afua, she is the Nebt of body, mind and spirit purafication.

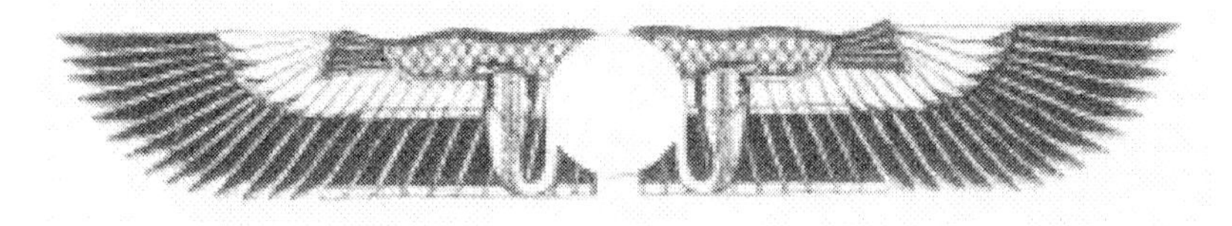

Spiritual Defense

As Spiritual Warriors, we are servants of our people and we are healers of our people. One of our biggest concerns must be the safety and protection of Afrakan people and the descendants of the Kemetyu from outside and inside the system of Caucasian male domination and Arabism. Afrakan Spiritual Warriors must be, and are prepared to live and die on the battlefield defending a Pan-Afrakan Worldview. Until now, recently, Afrakans have failed in our attempts to neutralize or destroy our oppressors' psychological attacks, beginning with the despiritualiztion of Afrakan life and our Afrakan Worldview of Ma'at.

Spiritual Warriors are engaged in a constant never-ending development of a defensive system that is built on spiritual principles. A spiritual defense system will minimize and /or eliminate those esfet forces designed to dehumanize and destroy Afrakan people. Afrakan Spiritual Warriors are therefore, simultaneously venerating and inspiring Afrakan people. They work from a Ma'at foundation with Jhuty and Heru as their guides to stop the destructive forces of esfet, Caucasian male domination,and Arabism as they elevate Afrakan people Kulturally and Spiritually. The Spiritual Warrior must at all times reflect the spirit of Afrakan people by being living examples of our Kultural greatness. We must protect the human integrity of Afrakan people and the Afrakan continent. If we do not learn to secure our space in the World community by maintaining our humanness and claiming our Afrakan continent, we will not be able to liberate ourselves from the doers of esfet (Caucasian male domination and Arabism). Our Kulturally enriched melaninated educational centers are a critical component in recovering and rediscovering our humanity, our true identities. They are also a central component of our spiritual defense system. If we, as Spiritual Warriors do not aid in the development and protection of our kulturally enriched, melaninated educational centers, we will not have intellectual enlightenment for self-sufficiency, now or in the near future.

Spiritual Warriors are not only healers, but they are the deep thinkers of the Pan-Afrakan World. As we unify around an Afrakan-centered Worldview with wholistic healthy goals, we will reclaim our role of leadership in the World community. Afrakans have always had great leaders during every time period of Ourstory, but white male domination has been successful in creating the illusion of disunity, confusion and weak leadership. The Wazungu have been successful by using the old "divide and conquer" methodology. White male domination has also mastered the power of definition, who ever defines the situation, controls the situation. Spiritual Warriors will have to eradicate this false illusion of weak Afrakan leaders by showing the discrepancies between His-story and Our-story, and only then will every one be able to see the truth of "The Story." We still have some of the greatest and most innovative leaders the world has ever seen. However, we as Afrakan writers and Ourstorians will have to tell our own story to our people and the world.

Spiritual Warriors become greater healers as they transform from being a lesser material being into a greater spiritual being. The essence of the Afrakan-centered Worldview is Spiritual. Healing is spiritual and before any substantial healing can take place among Afrakan people the Spirit of Sankofa must be manifested. We must go back to our ancestral memory banks and retrieve the legacy of our great existence. The Spirit of Sankofa will guide all of us to the future. The Spiritual Warrior innerstands clearly that the Kemetyu Spiritual Healing cannot be separated from our total mental, physical and spiritual experience, which includes education, health, nature, kulture, politics, economics, science, relationships and defense. The wholistic approach must be the only real approach we as Afrakan Warriors should even entertain.

It will also be the mission of Spiritual Warriors to teach about the Maangamizi and to point out our weaknesses as a people so that the Maangamizi will never happen again. As long as we have not learned from our mistakes, we will be destined to repeat them. We must clearly innerstand that the system of white male domination and Arabism are systems of esfet. We must not imitate these systems of esfet, but we must eliminate them from our minds, hearts and most of all, out of our Kulture. We are not at war with the Wazungu, Caucasian people, Arabs or Asians who follow a western life-style like the Japanese capitalists. We are at war with their value system and their culture. The western culture is materialistic, anti-nature, anti-spirit and promotes greed, injustice and esfet.

Western culture is the system of Caucasian male domination or Euro centrism. Euro centrism is a system of despiritualization of life. A minority of this planet's population, only 8% controls over 80% of its used natural resources. This Caucasian European and American culture is oriented towards perpetual conflict. In order for the Wazungu and Caucasian male domination to survive, it must continuously subdue and rape nature. Nature, in this sense, refers to everything that is not European. But the real truth is that Caucasian male domination has to lie to everybody, white, Black, rich and poor, Europeans, Asians and Afrakans, so that the illusions of those who have can keep control over those who have not.

The Afrakan Worldview, which is based upon the respiritualization of Afrakan life and Afrakan Kulture, views Euro centrism and Caucasian male domination as the enemy of nature and therefore the enemy of Afrakan people worldwide. This must be crystal clear to the Kemetyu, Afrakans. This is not racism in reverse this is self-preservation of Afrakan people and our way of life. The Caucasian European Worldview and the Arab Worldview are the enemies of the Afrakan Worldview, thus Euro centrism and Arabism are the enemies of Afrakan people and Afrakancentrism. We must not apologize for our position or shuffle our feet in the presence of our enemy. The key is to know thy self and Ourstory will reward all research. Their capitalistic, melanin deficient, anti-Afrakan Kulture and anti-Afrakan-spiritual way of life is directly opposed to nature. Therefore, anyone who believes and follows Euro centrism and Arabism are our enemies, regardless of their melanin color, nationality, economic status or religion.

The Spiritual Warriors of Afrakan descent must teach the Kemet system of Ma'at through our own educational institutions. In ancient Kemet, we used Sba, a Kemet term which refers to the teachings of Kemet wisdom, and the study of ancient Kemet. Spiritual Warrior Dr. Asa Hilliard and his brilliant research proved that it was Sba that produced the great Afrakan civilizations of antiquity.

The spiritual teachings of Ma'at also teaches us that today's Spiritual Warriors must use the Whmy Msu, a Kemet term that means the repetition of the birth, or a reawakening. Each Spiritual Warrior must go through a *Whmy Msu,* a personal healing, long before they can do or direct healing among Afrakan people today.

Afrakan Spiritual Warriors must be focused towards wholistic healing. No matter what illusionary route our oppressor takes us on, as Afrakan people we must follow our own Afrakan Worldview. We must prepare our bodies, minds and souls through spirit, to wage a total intellectual and spiritual war. The main battle for Afrakan liberation will be fought in the minds of Afrakan people. Spiritual Warriors must prepare the Kemetyu spiritually and psychologically to fight with our Kulture and our Ancestral Spirits. This way we have the power of millions of cumulative years of experience on our side, as we invoke the spirits of Afrakan Warriors since humanity began. We are boundless and limitless when we fight for righteousness and liberation. With the power of The NTCHR, the Spiritual Warrior stands for the wholistic healing of the Spirit of the Kemetyu, and all life.

Today's Spiritual Warriors innerstand that the Maangamizi has not stopped, and it has become more sophisticated in its destruction. It has shifted gears and uses more psychological warfare on the oppressed masses to aid in their own oppression. The nature of the addict is to think that more of the drug will make them feel better and in this case, more acceptable by the dominate Caucasian European society. However, the reality is really the opposite. What is clear to the Spiritual Warrior is that these conditions will continue to worsen unless an opposing or greater force redirects them. The Spirit of Ma'at, directed by Jhuty, will give spiritual identity, purpose, and direction to the Kemetyu, Afrakans collectively. When there is a lack of purpose, identity and direction the main ingredient is usually, the wrong culture and religous system. Kulture is the foundation in which all progressive ideas and collective thoughts are based, in order to move a collective group of people together and forward. If we take a close look at the conditions of Afrakan people globally in the 21st century, western time, we can tell if they lack purpose, Identity and direction. If they were in their correct Kulture, then they would also be in their correct state of mind and Konsciousness.

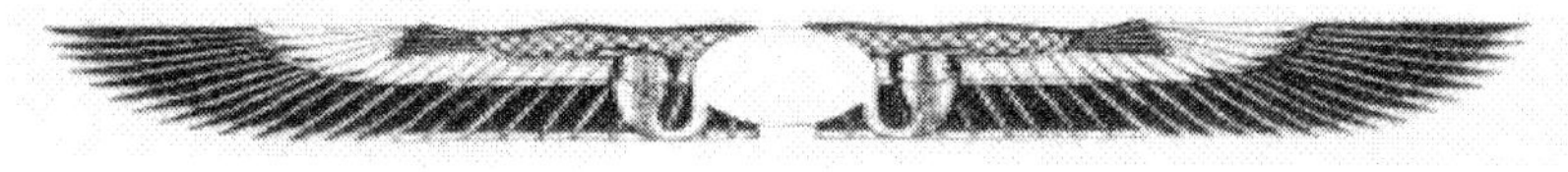

A Reality Check of Afrakan People in the 63rd Century, Sema Tawy, New Afrakan Time.

1. There is no strong Afrakan identity and pride in our Blackness, or Afrakaness worldwide. We must embrace a Pan-Afrakan Spirituality; we are powerful manifestations of The NTCHR. We must have a non-compromising love for the Pan-Afrakan Family, Black Afraka our continent and the development and protection of the United States of Afraka.

2. We have not taken a united stand and defended ourselves globally from a Pan-Afrakan-center. If we did this, then regardless of what country we are in or what language we speak, we would first identify with Afrakan Kulture, and our great Afrakan ancestors from the continent of Afraka. Our New Afrakan defense force must be as effective as an excellent immune system, protecting the human body-temple. The Wazungu, Europeans like the French and white Americans cannot teach Afrakans how to defend and protect themselves, this is something Afrakan Spiritual Warriors will have to do. Afrakan life has to be treated divine and sacred worldwide, and by Afrakan people first.

3. We do not have operational unity in our Spiritual System. Afrakan people do not have a common indigenous Spiritual Kulture as a base. We have abandoned Ma'at, which is "The Way". This is why we have adopted Christianity, Judaism, and Islam, and the main reason we participated and continue to participate in the Maangamizi. We have lost "The Way." However, "The Way" is still available. It has always existed; we have just been blind to its existence, disconnected only through our lack of Konsciousness. "Do not look where you fell, but where you slipped."

-Afrakan proverb-

4. Afrakan people have not collectively defended themselves against foreign cultures who have tried to dominate our land, our Kulture, and our economy. Once we were ignorant of the white man, and Arabs and the desires of the western culture, but now His-story and Our-story, rewards all research and we know their nature and their collective intent. western culture expressed through white male domination, Arabs through Islam wants to dominate the world through a system of exploitation, military

domination and disrespect for all life, not just Black life, but even the ecosystem of the very planet itself.

5. Afrakan people are not in control of their educational institutions from an Afrakan-centered Kultural Base, not in Afraka, North America or anywhere else that Afrakan people are collectively in the world. Afrakans must validate themselves through their own Worldview and perpetuate this perspective through their own political, economical and educational institutions worldwide.

6. Afrakans are not in control of their healing institutions or food base, which is our first medicine. Afrakans must be able to feed all Afrakans on the continent of Afraka and throughout the Pan-Afrakan world. Afrakans must return to herbology, and a natural wholistic healing system. We must also use our divine way of living to insure a divine life-style and excellent health.

7. We have no collective aim as the Kemetyu or Afrakan People. Afrakans on the continent or in the Diaspora have not defined short, medium or long-range goals collectively as an Afrakan people. Operational unity means that we vote together, and buy together. Thereby giving us a united political agenda, like a nation within a nation, no matter where we are in the world. "Sticks in a bundle are unbreakable." - Afrakan proverb -

8. We do not teach the Maangamizi and its global effects on Afrakan people Worldwide, so that the conditions that led up to the Maangamizi will not repeat itself. Afrakan people worldwide are still suffering from a massive state of traumatization caused by the Maangamizi. Caucasian male domination cannot cure this trauma, nor can Arabism and Islam, because they are the main causes of the pain and insanity. Remember we are still only recovering addicts of Caucasian male domination at our very best. We need an active recovery plan that involves mental, physical and spiritual Afrakan healing on its highest spiritual level. Without a re-Afrakanization program that is Afrakan-centered, we are powerless against this deadly drug called Caucasian male domination, which is destroying the planet and Arabism, which holds one third of our continent Afraka hostage.

9. We do not have an effective communication system in place to deliver information to Afrakan People on the continent of Afraka or the Pan-Afrakan Community Worldwide. Afrakans need a Pan-Afrakan Communication Network System, developed, maintained and operated by Afrakan people with an Afrakan-centered Worldview. Total Liberation is not possible until Afrakan people innerstand the need to control the communication within their own family, communities, institutions and nations.

10. We do not have a wholistic plan to reclaim the continent of Afraka, or to eliminate European imposed borders between countries. To reclaim stolen land by invading Arabs. To remove unwanted foreigners, or enemies of Afrakan people from the continent of Afraka. To change desert wasteland into fertile farmland. In addition, to develop Afraka for Afrakans by Afrakans to form the United States of Afraka.

11. We do not have an Afrakan plan for a continental economy that would support Afraka and Afrakans in the Diaspora. The Afrakan economy would have to be based primarily on the philosophy of Pan-Afrakanism as well as what Afraka has in terms of natural resources, technical skills, human resources, and Afrakan resources in America.

12. Afrakans have not developed their own transportation centers where they control transportation on land, air, or on water, which is totally independent of the western world. There is no reason why we have not created an Afrakan automobile. We know how to put them together, because we have been the major labor force for the American automobile industry. We are a billion people. Surely, we can support our own transportation system. Powerful economics is a Kultural and political statement at home and abroad.

13. Afrakans have not developed adequate housing for Afrakans from an Afrakan-center that is kulturally and environmentally harmonious with nature in the modern era. Afrakans must create from their own Worldview, even our architects must be Spiritual Warriors because courage allows you to be creative. We created architectural science, and we will have to make the natural harmonious changes for our new Afrakan life style.

One thing is for certain, if you do not plan to succeed, you are actually planning to fail. If these things are not on our planning board, than we are in for greater oppression and Caucasian European dependency in the 21st century. Spiritual Warriors innerstand and live by the philosophy to know yourself is to heal yourself. "***When there is no enemy within, the enemy outside cannot hurt you.***" - Afrakan proverb -

Spiritual Warriors are in the best possible position for healing Afrakan people because they have mastered the first level of healing and that is to heal ourselves. Afrakan Spiritual Warriors have to be at the base of Afrakan Liberation. We believe in ourselves and we believe in the genius of Afrakan people. However, the highest on the list is the fact that we accept and innerstand Afrakan Kulture and Spirituality and we are living the Afrakan Legacy by example, every day. The heart of the Spiritual Warrior is impeccable and unconquerable. It is the essence of love and total harmony with nature or the Ntchru. Moreover, this is the love that will heal Afrakan people. This is the love that will develop a re-Afrakanization program for the 63rd century new Afrakan time. It is our love for "The Way", divine love, which is eternal love of The NTCHR, which will heal Afrakan people and defeat the drug of Caucasian male domination and Arabism.

Mfundishi Jhutyms Ka en Heru and Spiritual Warrior Heru Pa-Ur Tehuty se Ptah - Spiritual Wood Carver, Meditation Facilitator, Food Preparation Instructor and Soul Sweat Facilitator.

Spiritual Warriors of Defense: Mfundishi Jhutyms Ka en Heru & Dr. Khalid Abdul Muhammad

Below, (Grand Master) Mfundishi Jhutyms Ka n Heru El-Salim & (Master) Malenga Heru Ur Nekhet of the Afrakan Martial Arts system Aha Kemet Wanyama Saba. We must develop, and defend our Kem-Unity or communities, Mentally, Physically and Spiritually.

Hearing and Listening

Spiritual Warriors are trained to hear sounds that most humans do not hear. They are trained to see things that most humans do not see. Moreover, of the humans that does hear and can see most do not comprehend or are not receptive to what they are hearing and seeing. When the Spiritual Warrior studies the forest or nature, they are involved in a unification ritual. This is a request on the part of the Warrior to become one with its environment. They become the trees, the leaves, the rocks even the very Earth. In return for this spiritual union, nature speaks back, revealing its secrets and special healing powers. The Spiritual Warrior must be a listener before being a healer, so they know the correct actions to take. Therefore, listening and hearing are prerequisites in wholistic healing.

When the Spiritual Warrior can read the sacred symbols of nature, the act of listening and hearing is on a higher level. Abstract and critical thinking is done from a spiritual level, because the spirit is guiding you. At this level, the Spiritual Warrior becomes a sacred Deep Thinker and real healing can take place mentally, physically and spiritually. Nature is NTCHR, The NTCHR is Nature, and when we listen to Nature, we are listening and reacting to an aspect of ourselves. By listening and observing the birds, the animals, the insects, and the plants, we may discover objects that have medicinal properties for humans. The Spiritual Warrior inner-stands that it was not just the bird, the animals, the insects, or plants, but Nature or NTCHR itself revealing the very essence of the universe to all those who are receptive and ready to receive its blessings.

Education vs Miseducation

Spiritual Warriors of Afrakan descent around the globe have come to a common Kemklusion about the conditions of Afrakan people globally in the 21st century, western time. This Kemklusion is that we, Afrakan people are out of our right minds, our Afrakan minds and we are Kultural-ly insane. We are in fact, addicts of a very sick, retarding, mental drug called Caucasian male domination and or Arabism. Caucasian Europeam male domination is a materialistic, capitalistic economic system based upon greed, material worship, lies, selfishness, fear and racism (esfet). Arabism is anti-Afrakan Kulture and anti-Afrakan Spirituality. It has enslaved us mentally and physically as well as stolen our land in North Afraka. 70% of all Arabs live in Afraka today. I believe the records will show that Afrakans were not paid or compensated for our land. There are 127 million Arabs in the world and there are over 200 million Afrakan Muslims, but Arabs control and represent the power elite of Islam. Arabs control the government, land, oil, and natural resources of North Afraka. Afrakans are enslaved physically and spiritually and or they are second-class citizens in their own homeland.

Afrakan Spiritual Warriors around the globe also recognize the fact that even the most Afrakan-centered of us, who live in the western world, at best are recovering addicts of Caucasian male domination or Arabism. Just like a recovering addict of alcohol, or hard drugs like cocaine or crack, the threat of a relapse is always possible and self-destruction is guaranteed. The Caucasian European American western educational system was designed to perpetuate, develop, and maintain Caucasian male domination worldwide. It is a psychological myth that melanin deficient beings, presently called Caucasian Europeans, the Wazungu or white people or Arabs are superior mentally, physically and spiritually to the original Melaninated Black people and all other melaninted people. The very nature of public education in America, Europe, the Caribbean, and anywhere western thought is being perpetuated, or Arabism under the banner of Islam, especially in the colonized world, is a despiritualizing institution based upon deception and lies.

Education for the new Afrakan must have a Spiritual Afrakan-centered focus that takes place at home, in our institutions, in our music, and art, which binds and heals our communities. We need a Pedagogy that trains the Afrakan community to transmit Kulture for healing and longevity. Afrakan-Centered pedagogy addresses the educational needs and concerns of Afrakan people from their particular Kultural spacial perspective and worldview. This Spiritual focus will liberate and heal Afrakan people wholistically, and at the same time create an unmovable love for themselves and for their Afrakan Kultural expression. Afrakan Spiritual Warriors of today must innerstand that the price for freedom is death, and death poses no threat in the struggle of freedom from an Afrakan-centered perspective.

This new spiritual and Kultural Pan-Afrakan-centered education must focus on the Spirit of The NTCHR first, then the Ntchru, our Kulture and Ourstorical experience as we are centered in our spiritual relationship with the universe. It must be crystal clear that we are spiritual beings which are manifestations of The NTCHR. Therefore, our first commitment is to NTCHR, and becoming **One** with nature again, to create a harmonious and perpetual state of existence with ourselves as Afrakan people. In return, the Afrakan-centered school must develop Spiritual Warriors that believes that every Afrakan has a mind that can be refined - like Jhuty or Seshat, a body that can be trained - like Heru or Sekhmet, and a soul that can be Kultured and centered - like Asr and Ast.

The first medicine for any recovering addict is to embrace their ancestral memory, Sankofa (to go back and fetch what you have lost or forgotten). For Kulture and Spirituality is the foundation or core of all real healing. Any recovery void of Kulture and Spirituality will be superficial and illusionary, at best. As recovering addicts of Caucasian male domination, our educational system must explain The NTCHR and our relationship with the One energy that is All. Secondly, we the Kemetyu - Afrakans, must recognize and see ourselves as Afrakan people throughout the world. Thirdly, we must innerstand our relationship with The NTCHR so we can relate to nature and the universe the same way we would relate to ourselves. Moreover, we must only relate to ourselves with *LOVE*. This energy must be developed, maintained, protected, and perpetuated wholistically, for spiritual healing of Afrakan people and the planet.

Afrakan people can only be healed through an Afrakan Kultural healing system that connects them to The NTCHR. Thus, Spirituality must be at the center of the healing for the Kemetyu, Afrakan people. Learning must be liberating, meaningful and spiritual, all at the same time. This is what is meant when Spiritual Warriors talk about an Afrakan-centered education.

Afrakans or melanin people anywhere on the planet, who are affected by the deadly drug of Caucasian male domination, must unlearn this life threatening capitalistic philosophy of the Wazungu. Their philosophy is anti-nature, anti-NTCHR and therefore, anti-Afrakan and anti any melanin people. It is the nature of Caucasian European culture to destroy, and/or oppress any foreign culture at its center before understanding it first.

Since Ourstory bears this to be true, Afrakan people and other humans, cannot liberate themselves with the culture and thinking process of the Wazungu or the Caucasian European American educational system.

It is important to innerstand the nature of all things possible, especially oneself. Based upon the spiritual innerstanding of Afrakans and the lack of spiritual understand of the Caucasian-Europeans and Americans and any where cacasian male domination exist, it becomes critical that we take control of our spiritual and educational processes so we can regain Konsciousness of our right mind. The Kemetyu, Afrakan people, and all melanin people must be able to develop and defend our spiritual and educational Institutions, because they feed the social-political, economic systems. If the nature of the society you live in is oppressive, was founded on oppression and maintains oppression, then the educational system supported by that society will reflect and perpetuate the same oppression.

Most Afrakans are disconnected only mentally, from The NTCHR and their own Kultural center here in America. Because of this mental disconnection, they are drowning in this Caucasian-European American educational system. They are having an anti-achievement dilemma. Caucasian male domination has stolen their spiritual center; militarily it has conquered their land, and has colonized their minds. Part of the dilemma is that these Afrakans want to be like the very people who are responsible for their destruction, because Caucasian male domination is in control of their desires. The western world, which is controlled by Caucasian male domination, teaches that all things belonging to the cucasian expression of the human race is superior to the Afrakan or any other groups of humans. Now these Afrakans feel that they must be validated by a cultural group that wants to destroy them and/ or enslave them mentally and physically. Consequently, the Wazungu and American values, particularly those having to do with excellence have little importance to them because of the destructive picture Caucasian male domination has painted.

The presentCucasian European and American educational system has white male domination at its center. These mis-educational institutions begin at nursery school and go straight through to graduate school, private or public. To participate in them for validation is like taking the deadly drug crack or cocaine to feel good or build positive self-esteem or independence; this is not going to happen. The very nature of these educational institutions is to destroy, oppress and enslave Afrakan people or any melanin people. "Powerful people never educate the victims of their power in how to take power away from them." Carter G. Woodson, the father of Black History Month in the 1930's, stated that because of Americas miseducational institutions the most educated Black persons would be our new enslavers. He also states that the nature of this miseducation is so backwards that we will demand to go to the back door even if there was no back door; our insanity would demand one. Many Afrakans in America have college degrees, but because they were trained instead of educated, they are not using their skills and tools for liberating Afrakan people. The majority of our college graduates work for or represent the very institutions that are responsible for our oppression. I personally know Afrakan professors who would never go out their houses unless they were wearing a European suit and tie. They are unconscious of the cultural statement they are making with these garments and cultural philosophical attitude. In addition, these are our most educated scholars. This is very scary, Spiritual Warriors.

The Nature of our Miseducation is so great that if you enter these institutions asleep, you will graduate with a degree asleep. The real tragedy is that most of these sleeping beauties do not want to wake up. There are always a few exceptions to the rule. If an Afrakan is awake, it is possible to use this system to your advantage. However, remember the main objective for writing this book is to empower Afrakan people to do for themselves, to heal themselves, to educate themselves and to validate themselves from an Afrakan-center instead of always being validated by the oppressor or the very institutions responsible for your enslavement.

If an Afrakan is awake and there is no other option at the time, they could however, make the mis-educational system work for them. With extreme caution, if one is centered in their own Spiritual and Kultural center, one could use the information at these Caucasian racists' institutions to their own advantage. Just as poison can be used as anesthesia, Caucaian male domination can be used in small amounts to aid in getting specific information, training and results. However, a careful plan of action with purpose, identity and direction must be intact or you will become part of the problem instead of the solution.

The kind of education and assistance that the Afrakan needs in the 21st century, western time, is more spiritual and Kultural, than academic. If Spiritual Warriors are in control of our Afrakan Kultural centered education and information banks, the performance of our students will expand to excellence. And our many achievements in every known field will be to benefit Afrakans first, mentally, physically and spiritually and then the rest of society, and the world.

Afrakan Spiritual Warriors of Afrakan-centered schools: Left, Mama Pat, former Principal and teacher at APAS. right, Dr. Shujha co-founders of APAS, CIBI Ndundu member, and CIBI President for ten years ending Nov. 2001. with Mfundishi Jhutyms Ka n Heru El-Salim, CIBI Ndundu member and former teacher at Afrikan Peoples Action School (APAS).

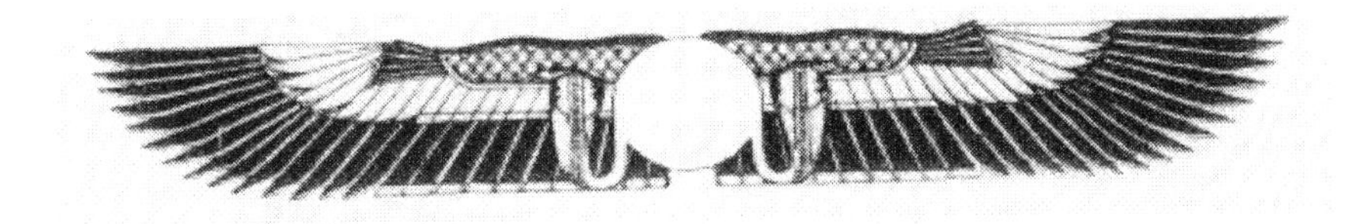

Spiritual Warriors Are Healers When We Think Truth, Speak Truth, And Do Truth.

The true Spiritual Warrior sees with exceptional clarity - Sia, then their tongue speaks with divine authority and power - Hu, then the body-temple obeys with extraordinary effectiveness, these Spiritual Warriors are Shemsu Heru. This is how Moyo or Sekhem (the divine vital heart energy) is used in healing; this is also "The Way of Ma'at", "The Way of The Spiritual Warrior," and "The Way of Heru."

In the 8th century about 700 B.C.E. or 3,540 S.T., the great Nswt Kashta ruled over the great Afrakan country Kash, which lies up south of Kemet and north of Punt in the great lakes region of Nyanza. This was a glorious period for the Kashite Nation for it was a time of prosperity. However, Kashta and his family were troubled and disappointed about the affairs of their neighbor country, Kemet.

Ancient Kemet had been a great nation for thousands of years and was a strong trade partner and ally of Kash and they shared the same bloodline. Because of Kemet's strength, no foreign nation from Europe or Asia could invade Kash's borders. However, gradual erosion of Kemet Kulture and its spiritual way of life started as early as the reign of the Nswt Pepy of the Old Period or First Golden Age, around 2,700 B.C.E. or 1,540 S.T., and then again during the Hyksos invasion and humiliation around 1,500 B.C.E., or 2,740 S.T. The Hyksos invaded Kemet from Asia as a wild warrior barbaric clan with superior war machinery like the horse and chariot. They were not interested in high culture or the spiritual way of life that existed in ancient Kemet; they only wanted the material wealth of Kemet. The Hyksos plundered, robbed, killed, raped and destroyed the beauty of Kemet and the glorious Afrakan way of life. These Asiatics made the Ntchr Setsh their Supreme god. Even in the Third Golden Age, the so-called 18th dynasty, the Nswt Akhenaten was greatly influenced by these factors and the dynamic spiritual balance between the Priestship and the royal family, which had been in harmony for more than 2,000 years had been destroyed and replaced with distrust and compition.

During the Third Golden Age, the so-called 19th and 20th dynasties, the name of the Ntchr Setsh still remained in the title of many rulers of Kemet and by the so-called 21st dynasty the distrust grew to the point where the Priestship under foreign support by Libyans ultimately undermined the Nswt and ruled a large portion of Kemet in the northern delta. This was the height of the third Intermediate Period of chaos in Kemet. It is at this point that the great Nswt Kashta of Kash and his royal family knew that something had to be done. Kemet had become so chaotic that little in the way of Kultural cultivation and maintenance took place. The Nswt Kashta his brother Pianky and his son Shabaka set out to Mt. Choke, (The Mountain of the moon) that led to Lake Tena the beginning of the Blue Hapy River in Kash to seek the wisdom of the great Spiritual Warrior, Grand Master Jhutyms.

When the Nswt Kashta, Piankhy and Shabaka arrived at the mountain, they found the great Spiritual Warrior Grand Master sitting peacefully on a small rock looking out at the Hapy Eterw. After the Nswt Kashta had explained their situation to the Spiritual Warrior Jhutyms, they waited patiently for the great Spiritual Warrior to speak. Contrary to the Nswt Kashta's expectation, however, the Grand Master Jhutyms whispered not a word. Rather, he smiled softly and gestured for the Nswt Kashta and his royal family to follow him. Silently they walked along the bank of the Hapy Eterw, whose end could not be seen. Hapy is the longest river in the world, traveling more than 4,160 miles long. Hapy was a Kultural highway where early civilization flourished in Afraka, while the rest of humanity was still asleep or was not even born yet or discovered. They all sat near the rushing waters watching its stability, fluidity and strength. The Spiritual Warrior Jhutyms only used four words to explain that they were using an ancient form of meditation called Ma'at Akhw Ba Ankh. After about three hours of Ma'at Akhw Ba Ankh, Jhutyms set out to build a fire. When at last, it was lit and the flames were aglow, the Spiritual Warrior Grand Master had the Nswt Kashta and his royal family sit by his side. There they sat for hours on end as the fire burned brilliantly into the night.

With the coming of dawn, when the flames no longer danced, Grand Master Jhutyms pointed to the Hapy Eterw. Then, for the first time since the Nswt Kashta and his royal family arrived, other than to say Ma'at

Akhw Ba Ankh, the Grand Master spoke, "Now do you innerstand why Kemet cannot sustain the greatness of its ancient predecessors?"

The Nswt Kashta looked perplexed, he looked at his brother Piankhy, but the great general of his armies, who was undefeated in battle in over 20 military campaigns, had no reply. Kashta looked towards his son the great Shabaka who was his most skilled scribe and Vizier of all Kash, but Shabaka bowed his head in shame because he too had no answer to give to his father the Great Nswt Kashta. Great Grand Master and Spiritual Warrior Jhutyms Kashta said," forgive us in our ignorance, for the wisdom you just imparted to us, we cannot comprehend." The Great Spiritual Warrior Jhutyms then spoke for the second time. "Reflect, Nswt Kashta, on the nature of the fire as it burned before us last night. It was strong and powerful. Its flames leapt upward as they danced and cried in vain glorious pride. Neither strong trees nor wild beast could have matched its mighty force, just like the power and greatness of ancient Kemet that we so dearly remember. With ease, our fire as ancient Kemet could have conquered all that lay in its path."

"In contrast, great Nswt Kashta, Piankhy and Shabaka, consider the Hapy Eterwr. It starts as but a small stream in the distant mountains. Sometimes it flows slowly, sometimes quickly, depending on the nature of its contributors, but always it sails downward, taking the low ground as its course. It willingly permeates every crack in the earth and willingly embraces every crevice in the land, so humble is its nature when we touch it, water can scarcely be felt, so gentle is its nature like Ma'at. My esteemed guests, yes, Kemet used to be like this, too. It's great Kulture has touched us all, there is almost no civilization that has not been effected by it's glorious wonders in math, architecture, science, it's festive holidays, astrology, and religious and spiritual gifts that Kemet gave to the civilized world. "Yet in the end, what is left of the once mighty fire? Only a handful of ashes remained. For the fire is so strong, Kashta, that it not only destroys all that lies in its path but eventually falls prey to its own strength also like ancient Kemet in its colonial days set the stage to be consumed by its own life-style. This, Kashta, is not Ma'at. It is not so with the calm and quiet river. For as it was, so it is, so it will always be: Forever flowing, growing deeper, broader, ever more powerful as it journeys down to the Wedgy Wr (the great Green), providing life sustaining waters and the Afrakan Kulture which brings sustenance to all."

After a moment of silence, the Great Spiritual Warrior Jhutyms turned to the Nswt Kashta and his royal family. "As it is with nature great Nswt Kashta, so it is with rulers. For as it is not fire but water that envelops all and is the well of life, so it is not mighty and authoritative rulers like the fire we saw last night, but rulers with humbleness and deep-reaching inner strength like the rivers of civilization, much like Hapy that captures the people's hearts and are springs of prosperity to their states and neighbors. Reflect, Nswt Kashta," continued the Great Spiritual Warrior Jhutyms "on what type of ruler and neighbor or ally, you and your royal family are. Perhaps, the answer that you seek will be there within the flowing stream of Ma'at."

Like the rays of Ra, the truth seized Kashta and the royal family. All of their hearts seemed to open at the same time. No longer proud but embarrassed as Spiritual Warriors themselves, they all looked up at the Great Spiritual Warrior Jhutyms with enlightened eyes. They all knew that the destruction of any group of Afrakans anywhere meant the eventual destruction of all Afrakans everywhere and they all knew what had to be done. As Ra was rising majestically over Hapy, the royal family gave their farewell greetings of peace and blessings and love.

The Nswt Kashta, his brother Piankhy and his son Shabaka led a campaign to liberate Kemet from foreign domination and national division, which had considerably violated the traditional Afrakan Kulture. From their power base in Kash, these mighty Afrakans reunited their two nations together through military victory and immediately started an ambitious project to restore the almost forgotten Kemet values of the Old and great Middle Period of ancient Kemet. When Shabaka became the Nswt, he commissioned the engraving of damaged and lost ancient texts to commemorate the restoration and re-Afrakanization of Kemet. The Kashites brought a fresh supply of wisdom from the interior of Afraka just like the new waters from the mountains to the Hapy Eterw to revive Kemet, which had been corrupted by an inundation of foreign and Asiatic

influence. The creativity and wisdom clearly shows that Kash and the spiritual flavor of the indigenous Kultures of central and eastern Afraka were the original parents of Kemet and not the reverse. Kemet was only the mouthpiece of the dynamic spiritual and collective knowledge that existed in inner Afraka that flowed down north from up south of Hapy. Hapy became a Kultural express super highway bringing the Kulture and almost all of its spiritual and religious paraphernalia from inner Afraka's three mountains of the moon to Kemet and from Kemet to the rest of the civilized world. These three centers are Mt. Choke that feeds Lake Tena in Ethiopia, the source of the Blue Nile, Mt. Mwenzuri in Uganda, the source of the White Nile, and Kilimanjaro the tallest mountain in Afraka that lies east of Lake Nyanza, the largest lake in Afraka and birth place of the human family.

Like the Great Spiritual Warriors of yesteryears, such as Kashta, Piankhy and Shabaka, the Spiritual Warriors of today must become one spirit, so that we can revitalize our focus, and develop a national direction! Moreover, like the waters of Hapy, we must flow through the hearts and minds of Afrakan people everywhere, revitalizing and resurrecting our great and glorious Kulture. For it is our Spiritual Afrakan Kulture, indigenous Afrakan languages, Ourstory (told through our Afrakan Worldview), and our Spiritual Afrakan rituals that are the healing medicine this Spiritual Warrior offers to you, my fellow Spiritual Warriors and friends, AMEN RA.

The Spiritual Warrior family of Kera Jhuty Heru Neb-Hu and se Ptah; left to right Sn Hassan Iman, Sn Heru Pa-Ur, Mfundishi, an elder and Sn Sniedy

Spiritual Warriors in the great Afrakan tradition of deep thinkers : Grand Master martial artist, Ahati Khalindi Iyi & Abdel Salaam dance choreographer and artist with Mfundishi Jhutyms Ka n Heru El-Salim. Below Spiritual Warrior wholistic massage therapist Najami holding the Ankh. Right, Bro. Hannabal, Ourstorian, writer and businessman.

Kemklusion

Spiritual Warriors know that in order to heal Afrakan people throughout the Diaspora, we must have a clear Afrakan memory, so that our Sankofa Spirit can guide us towards the universal truth. The innerstanding of Afrakan Kulture is the foundation of that truth, which must be grounded in an Afrakan reality. With this innerstanding of Afrakan Kulture, we can then use ***tradition*** and ***reason*** to plan collectively and positively for a collective great Pan-Afrakan future. "History is to the human race, what memory is to the human mind" - Diop.

Spiritual Warriors from around the planet must plan for this positive future with their respective ethnic groups. When we know our Spiritual center, and we have a clear innerstanding of our nature, and our enemies' nature, plus a clear innerstanding of our Kulture, and our enemies culture, we can then function at our optimal human potential within the Ntchru or forces of nature.

Afrakan Spiritual Warriors must become Heru, so that we can defend the right to be right, the right to be Afrakans in our right minds from an Afrakan-centered Kultural reality. Afrakans who are involved in the healing process are embracing a Pan-Afrakan Kultural educational system. It is Afrakan Kulture manifested through Spiritual Warriors that will assist us in the healing of ourselves, mentally, physically and spiritually. It is this type of healing that embraces Afrakan Spirituality and Afrakan-centered Kulture that will be able to liberate Afrakans in Afraka, America and throughout the Diaspora, and eventually the whole human family.

The power of the Spiritual Warriors lies in their innerstanding of The NTCHR and the Ntchru. Spiritual Warriors clearly innerstand that the power of healing comes from the spirit within, which is connected to Ma'at. In addition, through their unlimited internal vital energy emanating from The NTCHR, called the Sekhem, excellent health can be developed and maintained. This attitude comes from years of **disciplined** training in the mental, physical and spiritual wholistic arts from the ancient Kemet civilization that was developed in Afraka thousands of years ago. When we think of ancient Kemet (Egypt) we think of the Pyramids, the only standing wonder of the ancient world. We think of its colossal monuments, magnificent statues, and unparalleled architectural genius. However, the ancient Kemetyu's most magnificent gift was its Spiritual system, which gave birth to philosophy, religion, dynamic governance, mathematics and science. In ancient Kemet, the ultimate prototype of the Spiritual Warrior was created. The foundation for other Spiritual Warriors seeking enlightenment and spiritual Konsciousness was laid down in ancient Kemet. Much later in human Ourstory, through the influence of Kemet Spiritual Warriors, other cultures from Asia, like the Susa (Elam), the Indus Kash Valley Civilization, India and the Shang Civilization in China and through Buddhism and Taoism, would also develop Spiritual Warriors. This Black Spiritual genius from central and eastern Afraka would also reach the shores of North and Central America through the Olmec, Mayan, Aztec and Inca civilizations. In fact, the 16 Crucified Saviors before Jesus the Christ are all followers or were greatly influenced by the Kemet Legacy and Spiritual system from ancient Kemet and Kash of northeast Afraka.

At the Jalapa Museum of Anthropology in Mexico City, Mexico, a great tribute is given to Afrakan people as the founders of the Olmec Nation. These words are carved in stone at the entrance of the museum:

"Attention Mexicans: This is the root of your history, its cradle and its altar. Listen to the most silent voices of the most ancient culture in Mexico, the mother of the civilization of our continent. The Olmecs converted rain into harvest, the sun into a calendar, stone into sculpture, cotton into cloth, pilgrimage into commerce, mountains into thrones, jaguars into religion and men into gods."

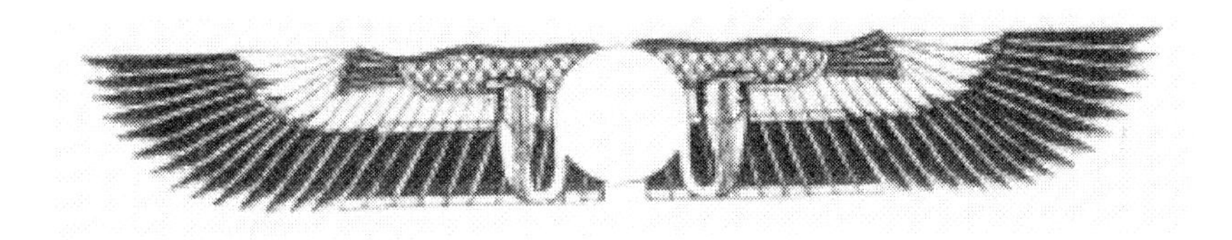

Olmec heads in Mexico of Afrakans from Kash, wearing Kashite soldiers helmets. More than 16 heads have been identified of Afrakan origins in Ancient Mexico.

The ultimate healing power of the Spiritual Warrior lies in their ethical code of human conduct and their respect for all life and the perpetuation of Ma'at. This Spiritual life is empowered through a state of Heru Konsciousness. The innerstanding of this Konsciousness is a gift from the ancient Spiritual Warriors of Kemet and Kash. It was the ancient Spiritual Warriors of the Kemet and Hapy Valley Civilizations that developed and gave to the world the concept of Ma'at (truth, justice, balance, harmony, reciprocity, order, propriety, righteousness, straightness, natural law, and integrity). Remember it was the Spiritual Warriors that built the temples and the pyramids to honor the dead and their ancestors. It was the Spiritual Warrior that gave bread to the hungry, water to the thirsty, clothes to the naked, carried those that had no boat to dry land, buried the aged, and saved the weak from those who were stronger.

In ancient Kemet, Spiritual Warriors left very articulate records of their deeds as examples for the masses to follow. *From the Book of Declarations of Virtues,* Middle Period, the Second Goldeb Age c3,000 B.C.E., 1,240 S.T. Harwa, chief official of the High Priestess of Amen-Ra says: "... I put an end to pain and erased wrongdoings. I buried the blessed, supported the aged and satisfied the needs of the have-nots. I was a shelter for the child and help to the widow; I did these things knowing their value and knowing their reward from the Neb of Ma'at, in a word, to endure in the mouth of the people without end, to be well-remembered for years and years to come." Djedkhonseankh, prophet of Amen-Ra, says: ..." I kept my mouth free from attacking those who attacked me. My patience turned my foes into friends and my enemies into allies. I controlled my mouth and was skilled in response, yet I did not submit to evil doing. No one spoke evil of my parents because of me. My parents were honored greatly because of my worthiness. Indeed, they found me helpful while they lived upon the earth. And I provided offerings for them now that they have departed." Among the Spiritual Warriors in ancient Kemet were revealed some of the finest qualities of humanity of any human society in recorded Ourstory or history. Moreover, like ancient Kemet, it will be the Afrakan Spiritual Warriors, keepers of our legacy, custodians of Afrakan Kulture and rituals, followers of Ma'at and Jhuty, through the spirit of Heru that will bring about the healing we need as an Afrakan people. It will be Heru Konsciousness brought forth by Afrakan Spiritual Warriors, that will re-Afrakanize, re-civilize Afrakan people and bring humanization to the whole human family. But we must rise up and seize the moment. We must rise up and take control and Kemtrol of our minds through the alignment of our spirit, soul and body-temples with Ma'at. Spiritual Warriors, we must rise up, Now!

Spiritual Warrior Priests; Baba Heru Ankh Ra Semahj and Mfundishi Jhutyms El-Salim with Mpigana Mbaheru left, and Mpigana Zuwena Kheper Salim right. Below, the Twin lions of yesterday and tomorrow, Shu and Tefnut. Each Spiritual Warrior must master the twin lions within themselves. The key is to master the self, to be in tune with the infinite now, and you will know yesterday and tomarrow.

SUN CHILDREN WILL RISE AGAIN

...will rise, will rise, will-will rise again
Giving birth to Konsciousness so that light could be born
Creating space, bringing Kheper into being
Sun beings that recognize their divinity, are the essence of enlightenment
I am the Blackness that allows light to be seen
I am the father of Ra
I am that which was, before there was existence
I am pure Konsciousness manifesting itself through spirit and soul
Yet, I am you and the Sun simultaniously
I am the light
My mind gave birth to planets, solar systems and Galaxies
I willed myself into this existence through the creation of Ma'at
Your perception of me is only what I allow you to see of me
I have always been here
Time is an irrelevant concept, used by humans who are mentally disconnected from the Oneness of existence, and in their ignorance they are trying to hold on to their illusionary perception of backwardness
There is only the Spirit!
The Spirit of The NTCHR and The NTCHR is all existence, manifesting itself through the known and unknown like Ptah, Ra, Amen, Heru, Jhuty, Seshat, Ma'at, Ast, Mut, Het-Heru
Inside my spirit is the eternal sperm of life, the seeds for yesterday and tomorrow
I am the creator of the Twin lions
I am the seed and the crop, call me Asr
Today is here only because you have been entrapped by time
There is only the infinite now, the eternal moment
You can't control time
Control is the illusionary entrapment of energy
Ma'at is the positive use of this energy, which creates freedom, void of time
Esfet is the negative use of this energy, moving energies out of balance, which creates a prison, and called western time
Aha!

Now are you beginning to see the picture, America is a prison.
Amerikkka is a giant penile colony of European cacasian domination, a drug that imprisons your mind from innerstanding the truth, the light, and enlightenment.
You look stunned and confused?
Wondering how did I get here, locked up in this prison?
What was the charge?
(Being the original people, having a divine shade of Black, a seeker of righteousness, unlimited creativity, speed, having tight kurly hair, locks, being blessed with divine melanin inside and out, and the worst crime of all, a giver of infinite love)
Was there a trial?
Was the millions killed in the Maangamizi- bail money?
Was the European Caucasian and Arab enslavement of Afrakans the sentence?
Was the Middle Passage death row?
And it should have been obvious that we got several life sentences, because 400 years later we are still doing time **in prison!**
Amerikkka
Focus - Sankofa, *refocus using your subjective unlimited mind*
Traveling through Northeast Afraka retracing thoughts past millions of years
Reprogramming our drugged, retarded, enslaved, Western mis-educated Afrakan minds
So that we can once again become one with the beauty of nature
Feel high from the spiritual hypnotic rays of the Sun
Golden in it's magnificence, yet connecting all life forms to one existence
I am Jhutyms Ka-en-Heru, the light, coming forth like Ra
I know you have been drugged white in deathly happiness and you are desperately trying not to hear me
Nevertheless, like Ra, the truth is always present, even if it is not visable, so am I and I am you!
Resurrect yourself, let go of time, become reborn, let this Western nightmare vanish with its suicidal, retarted, cacasian male

perverted desires
Claim your birth-right, use your story and Kulture like a human map to guide you back to Blackness, which is Heru Konsciousness
Reclaim your land - Afraka, your family - Afrakan people, your mate - The Black, brown, tan, golden sisters and brothers of the planet Earth
We must transform into great falcons, the original melaninated sons and daughters of the Sun
We are sun children
Swifter than swift, creators of divine math, establishers of Ma'at
We are the ones who took council from Jhuty, the divine mind of the Creator
The One Konsciousness
Through this Ntchr Konsciousness we can rise up out of the ashes of Caucasian male domination, like the Ben Ben bird of Ancient Kemet
We can rise up out of our physical and illusionary prisons
Leave your programmed limited objective mind behind and rise!
Our ancestor souls are with us, our guardian spirits are with us, the Divine Spirit is **with us**
I am with us, and we are with us
We are the children of the sun
Through Heru Konsciousness, we must give birth to ourselves so that we can ***BE!***
Give birth to light, and enlightenment, follow "The Way"
We are what the wazungu fear the most
Unlimited, Subjective, Black Spiritual Beings
Rise up, rise up, rise, rise, ***rise UP, NOW!***

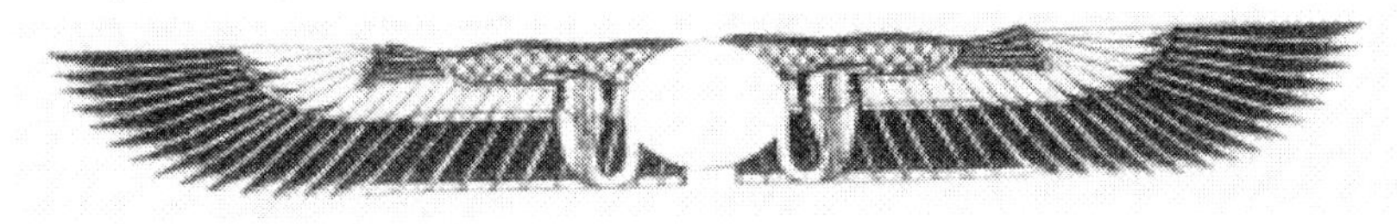

SELF MASTERY
of the Spiritual Warrior

A real master is one who controls their own happiness
Forges its own positive outlook on life
Develops its own light from the brilliance of Blackness
This is a Spiritual Warrior
The more you learn to love yourself
The more others learn to love you
The closer you come to self perfection
The more you are imitated and respected
We all live our dreams through each other
For only you are ultimately responsible for your own happiness
Not your mate, not your parents, not your friends, not even your children
They are all supposed to share and enjoy your happiness
The better you feel about yourself
The better others will feel about you
Send yourself flowers, work out, fine tune your health
Do it for you and we shall all rejoice in your victory
Be forgiving, patient, and kind to yourself
Most of us are very cruel and unforgiving to ourselves
What goes around comes around
But charity always starts at home
Use every moment possible learning about yourself
which is a reflection of the world
Because you must give your gift to the world
Just like a certain fish must swim home, a certain bird must fly south
You have a responsibility to Afraka and your sacred ancestors
Only those who are constantly in a state of perfecting, and giving their gifts, can truly be called Masters
And these Masters are Spiritual Warriors
Give your gift and fulfill your destiny
Because spiritual fulfillment is the greatest happiness...

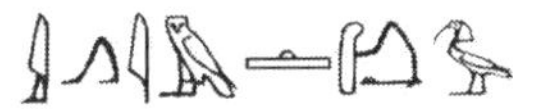

Spiritual Warriors Are Healers When We Think Truth, Speak Truth, And Do Truth.

Top left, Nswt Bety Tut-Ankh-Amen, who made lies an abomination and top right, Nswt Bety Kha-f-Ra, builder of the second largest Mer (Pyramid) in Kemet and repaired Heru em Akhety, this is doing Truth.
Amen Ma'at

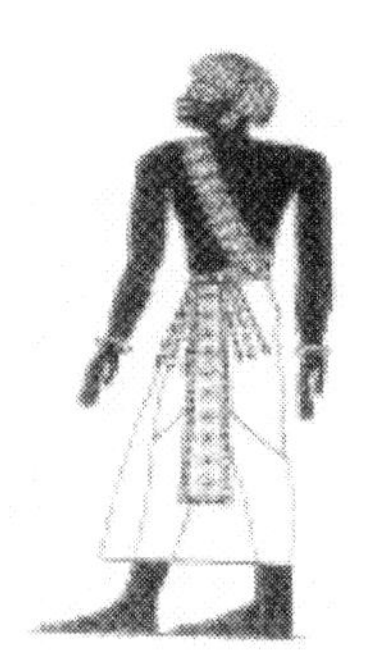

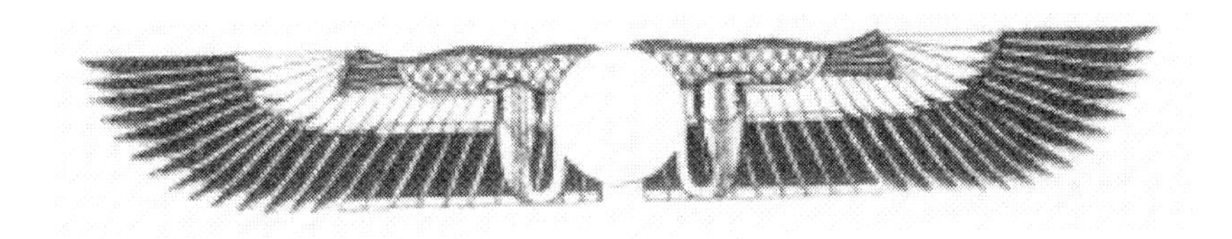

CHAPTER ∩1 (11)
Somo la Kumi na Moja

Ma'at Akhw Ba Ankh

The science of Ma'at Akhw Ba Ankh teaches us how to use and maintain Moyo, the power of the NTCHR that is within each of us. It connects us to Heru Konsciousness or Ma'at thinking so that we may innerstand who we are, why we are here, what our gifts or life missions are and how to recognize our Oneness with The NTCHR.

Ma'at Thinking brings balance to your life through the sum total of all your actions. Whenever and wherever Ma'at exists, it creates a state of htp. Self-mastery is the art of attaining Ma'at while creating Ma'at in your life giving endeavors. This is stability at its highest form. When there is stability humans can live their lives to the fullest human potential.

Remember Ma'at thinking is a state of Heru Konsciousness, which creates balance, and this balance is responsible for sustaining and perpetuating high levels of happiness and peace. Ma'at thinking is a perception and attitude that we can learn through Ma'at Akhw Ba Ankh. One may accomplish this attitude through the combination of Afrakan-centered thought, proper breathing, meditation, yoga, dynamic tension, balancing drills, and slow moving fighting dances for coordination and inner harmony, which are all part of the Kemetyu Ma'at Akhw Ba Ankh system.

This internal Art is also taught in Kupigana Ngumi (The Kemetyu mental, physical and spiritual fighting arts of northeast Afraka).

Ma'at Akhw Ba Ankh teaches you that you are Divine and that it is your state of Konsciousness that allows you to recognize your Oneness with the Supreme Wisdom, the One NTCHR. The process of recognizing your Divinity, your Oneness with The NTCHR is therefore, the same as *Ma'at Thinking* or Heru Konsciousness. This Konsciousness has no limits; there exists only unlimited possibilities. Time becomes relative, because yesterday, today and tomorrow are all existing now. The ancient Kemet spiritual system teaches us that when we are aligned with the Ntchru we are connected with all existence, having all knowledge, all power, yesterday and tomorrow are in the very present. This is called the infinite now.

Spiritual Warriors regard their physical bodies as an instrument for their journey towards perfection or Oneness. Ma'at Akhw Ba Ankh and Kupigana Ngumi are tools that are used to help fine tune your physical, mental and spiritual instruments to reach those goals. When the spirit and the soul are in alignment with the Konscious mind, a flow of energy that cannot be explained happens. This flow of energy is called by many names: trance, Holy Spirit, *Ma'at Thinking*, Heru Konsciousness, or a mystical experience. Meditation may be used as a deliberate way to seek a mystical experience and to train the mind in order to reproduce this experience at will, eventually possessing a form of "double Konsciousness" wherein the absolute and relative realities are equally perceived. Concentration and control of the mind allows meditation to occur. Ma'at Akhw Ba Ankh, (Ancient Kemet breathing poses and slow moving meditation) is practiced to enable the practitioner (Mpigana) to establish contact with the inner forces for the purpose of relaxation and alignment which lead to the development of physical power, mental astuteness, and spiritual illumination.

Ma'at Akhw Ba Ankh is based upon the ancient spiritual Kemetyu meditative systems along the Hapy Valley. Modern Spiritual Warrior Priests have translated the papyrus scrolls, the sacred hymns and writings confirmed that Ma'at is recognized as the natural vehicle for the balancing of the elements of the body, mind, and soul through correct breathing, correct posture, and correct Konsciousness. To the Ancient Kemetyu Priest Scientists, correct Konsciousness was a harmonious innerstanding of nature, or the Ntchru, because everything that existed in the Ntchru existed in the Kemetyu themselves. Part of this innerstanding was to innerstand the soul. In the book, *Stolen Legacy*, George G.M. James outlines the study of the soul by the Ancient Kemetyu Priests of Kemet as the following:

The 9 Tones of the Soul

1. Ka- the energy body (your double)
2. Ba- the heart soul
3. Ab- the physical heart
4. Khat- the physical body
5. Khaibit- the shadow
6. Akhw, (Khu)- the spiritual soul (intelligence)
7. Sahu- the spiritual body
8. Sekhem- the force or spiritual power
9. Ren- the attribute of manifestation (name)

In the modern resurrected Kemet shrines of today, there are Kemet Priests and Priestesses who can explain these nine tones of the soul. When a student is studying the Ma'at Akhw Ba Ankh System, all these steps are outlined in great detail. Ma'at is the harmonious balance or alignment. Akhw means the power of the blessed spirit. Ba means the power of the physical and spiritual heart soul. The Ankh is the knowledge and wisdom behind eternal life. Together Ma'at Akhw Ba Ankh means the harmonious balance and alignment between the spirit and the soul for Konscious living and everlasting life.

Kemet breathing postures and meditation should not be practiced without supervision in the beginning. A spiritual director is essential, for self-deception is possible. Those who have a high degree of proficiency in Ma'at Akhw Ba Ankh, the Kemet breathing and meditative postures, are called or known as Mfundi, Malenga, Mfundishi, Kupigana Ngumi Priest Scientists, Kemetyu Spiritual Healers, or Kemet Priest or Priestess.

The Breath and Breathing

The human breath is the cosmic force, which bridges the Nine (9) Tones of the Soul, the link between matter and spirit. The Ancient Kemet priest-scientists recognized the fact that the same force that held the Atoms together, also maintained similar energy patterns within the human organism.

It is by way of the breath that the mind is calmed and the body relaxed, two of the basic requirements for good health and good quality of the length of physical life. The main purposes of most of the breathing exercises are to regulate and harmonize various functions of the body-temple, mind and to direct the Moyo. The Moyo is the internal vital life energy force, of the heart of Heru Konsciousness. This harmony can be achieved by breathing a very specific way, according to the various exercises. When the Spiritual Warriors' breath wanders, the mind is wandering also, but when the breath is still, so is the mind of the Spiritual Warrior.

Calmness of the mind will not be achieved without the discipline of breathing. In fact, breathing is a vehicle to help the focusing of mind and transporting the internal vital forces throughout the body. Meditation refines the energy of the external air (Shu) and converts it into the internal vital force Sekhem, or Moyo. The two most commonly used breathing methods by most athletes, martial artists, dancers, singers, yoga practitioners and meditators are abdominal breathing and reversed abdominal breathing.

In abdominal breathing, the air is driven by the movement of the diaphragm. As the breath is drawn into the body, it is directed to the diaphragm forcing it down. When the diaphragm is forced down, the lungs expand and they vertically inhale. At the same time, the abdomen is compressed by the diaphragm and obviously extended as if the air filled all the way down until the abdomen shrinks inward. The tongue touches the roof of the mouth when inhaling and drops naturally down when exhaling.

In Reversed Abdominal Breathing, the abdomen shrinks inward when inhaling as the diaphragm is forced down. When exhaling, the abdomen is swollen.

There is however another invaluable breathing technique-The Kupigana Ngumi breath. In the Kupigana Ngumi breath, the mouth should be closed, and all your muscles relaxed, with your tongue rolled and touching the roof of your mouth.

1. Inhale deeply through your nose until you feel naturally the breath is moving downward with your diaphragm instead of outward with your chest, the belly protruding to its natural extent while the lungs fill with air. Breath slowly counting to six (6), but without noise or needless effort.

2. Exhale through your nose until you feel naturally empty of air. Keep the mouth closed during the entire exercise. Continue this deep breathing for 5 minutes. As your concentration develops, you should begin to feel the Moyo (the vital energy) traveling through the nose to the lungs and around the entire body, and then up and out again. The basic principles of the discipline of the breath are as follows:

1. Meditation- Calmness of breath; clarity of mind.

2. Dancing and physical Postures- Restoration of body physical/ psyche. Nine Tones of the soul; the opening of the heart.

3. Heru Konsciousness- Wisdom of the ancestors which explains the knowledge of the Ntchru.

Correct breathing is the link to everything in the universe. The universe has a pulse, just as we do. Through meditation we can tap into this rhythm, the eb- the heart of The NTCHR. When we breath correctly and with the knowledge of Kupigana Ngumi, or Ma'at Akhw Ba Ankh we will maintain and innerstand a relationship with The NTCHR, the One Great

Force. We are also able to develop and maintain a relationship between our ancestors, parents and the not yet born. Correct breathing will put you in touch with the self, the direct link to The NTCHR. And, breathing will help you to innerstand the link between you, the community, and your race because your people are your life force in human form.

Konscious Relationship Are The Keys To Harmonious Life

The NTCHR is Konsciousness
This Konsciousness sustains all existence, far beyond our comprehension
Shu is the spiritual breath of the Ntchr Ntchru
There is nothing outside the breath of Shu
Shu is a manifestation of The NTCHR
Shu, the breath is your link to every living force in the universe
The universe has a pulse, a rhythm, just like we do
This rhythm is part of our relationship with the Creator
Are you Konscious of this relationship
Or is this connection happening inspite of our ignorance

Konsciousness then is the key
Be Konscious of and maintain a relationship with the Ntchr Ntchru
This state is living spiritually, it gives you integrity, the greater the connection the higher the spirituality, since the essence of being is spirit
Be Konscious of your relationship between you and your ancestors
Your ancestral memory is your life force, they carry the keys to your story, your Kulture and your value system
Be Konscious of your relationship with your gift from the Creator, so that your mission in life will be in tune with Ma'at (truth, justice righteousness, reciprocity and harmonious balance)
Be Konscious of your relationship with words, Jhuty (articulate thought, writing, speech and righteous actions), for the ability to change or alter reality can occur through utterances
So good speech is praised because it is the light of wisdom and the light of wisdom is the lamp that lights the way to all knowledge and just deeds are more precious than gold

Be Konscious of your relationship with love, for love is the foundation for righteousness
Only the loving are Konscious of our Oneness with The NTCHR
This Oneness gives you infinite innerstanding
Innerstanding creates the power to love: love your mate, your family, your friends, your gift, your mission and Ma'at
This is the love that maintains harmony in the universe...

Meditation

Meditation was a fundamental practice among the Kemet Priestship. The Ntchru, which are the internal, external, and Duat forces, were the foundation and basis of the spiritual practice of ancient Kemet. The disciplines of chanting and dance have been handed down through the centuries through many indigenous Kemetyu Kultures. These disciplines, along with breath control, and specific Kemet postures left for us on the walls of Kemet Temples, form the nucleus of Kemet meditation, which we call Ma'at Akhw Ba Ankh, at the Shrine of Jhuty Heru Neb-Hu.

Excellent meditation is a pure state of Konsciousness that emerges from within the innerkonscious, also called the Heru Konsciousness or your ***First Eye***. Meditation in general is an internal process involving posture, breathing, and mental awareness. Wherever the mind reaches, the feelings are also there; wherever the feelings reach, the Moyo is also there; wherever the Moyo reaches, the power is also there. The focusing of the mind at various points of the body can facilitate the development of the vital force of the human body called Moyo, causing the strength to be manifested accordingly. Because the focusing of the mind requires mental concentration and inner tranquility, the general condition of meditation is therefore emphasized as the calming of the mind or stopping the world (a process of storing energy). Meditation seems to induce the experience of an altered and higher state of Konsciousness, and through the study and use of meditation, human beings can create and achieve on a level much closer to that of the divine. Ma'at Akhw Ba Ankh manifests stillness of mind within the dynamic movements of the body, combining activity with stillness which is consistent with the Kemet laws of complements.

Meditation is absolutely spiritual and must be used as part of the healing system of Afrakan people. The root of meditation, "medi", like medicine, means to heal, and Afrakan people worldwide need a healing. Meditation brings mental, emotional and spiritual balance, which is the key to enlightenment. Meditation is a process, which enables you to control the true self, eliminating all external interruptions.

In our daily lives, our thoughts are projected outwards, thinking of what must be done in order to accomplish our goals. However, meditation is a Konscious focus inward with controlled breathing. All our thinking is directed inward, with full awareness, into the universe of our inner mind (Innerverse). In this relaxed state, we are able to communicate or become Konscious of other worlds that exist beyond the boundary of the physical. The deeper we enter into this inner life, the more we are able to perceive the different qualities of the spiritual worlds. Like plants, we can grow spiritually towards the light of our inner divinity.

To the modern Kemet Spiritual Warrior who uses Ma'at Akhw Ba Ankh, meditation is regarded as a manner by which individuals encounter the nature of the Divine within themselves. This procedure is based upon "The Way", the ancient Kemetik teaching of Ma'at. This level of innerstanding liberates the mind through Heru Konsciousness. Heru Konsciousness is the level of the mind that few of us ever encounter. This is Konsciousness where the Divinity resides, along with the spiritual soul, Ba and the Divine Spirit, Ka. This alignment brings forth the light of your true self or *Enlightenment. This enlightenment allows you to experience your connection to nature or greater aspects of The NTCHR.*

Some people think they don't have time to meditate. Spiritual Warriors know the truth: if you don't meditate, you will not have time to do what you really need and want to do. If you don't have time to meditate, you don't have time to really live and experience your own divinity. We are divine and meditation permits us to experience the divinity that exists in all of us. When meditation is done correctly, it is like a continuous flow of perceptions or thoughts, like the flow of water in a river connecting you to the infinite power of The NTCHR, which is consistent with the Kemet laws of complements.

Meditation may be used as a deliberate way to seek Ma'at and train the mind towards Afrakancentricity. In a state of meditation, one undergoes definite shifts towards more efficient biological functioning such as lowered respiration, reduced oxygen consumption and decreased metabolic rate. The Ancient Afrakan Kemet Spiritual Warriors discovered some vital keys towards self-mastery through the awareness taught in meditation long before Europe or Asia emerged from savagery and barbarism. Awareness alone can control mental and physical realities, even the so-called effects of time, which is only an illusion. By thinking divinely, we reproduce divine thoughts from Heru Konsciousness. With consistent repetition, we will be able to reproduce Ma'at at will, eventually possessing a form of "double Konsciousness", wherein the absolute and relative realities are equally perceived giving the Spiritual Warrior the power to heal through Ma'at Thinking.

To practice Ma'at Akhw Ba Ankh or Afrakan meditation correctly: One must calm the mind through correct breathing, so the spirit can be felt. One must cleanse the body-temple from all dirt, so that the soul can be felt. One must cleanse the soul from malice, selfishness and desires, so that Jhuty, Heru Konsciousness can be heard. Once you innerstand your Oneness with the divinity of creation, you can appreciate your gifts from The NTCHR and the sacredness of Love. In addition, once you innerstand the sacredness of love, you will know that The NTCHR is Divine Love and you are a disciple and messenger.

Everyone can do meditation, the simplest way to get started is to sit quietly in the nest of nature, or your local park, or even a quiet spot at home. Clear your mind and listen and allow your natural environment to be your teacher. Do this every day or two or three times a week for 30 minutes. By doing this you are preparing the mind for the seeds of Wisdom. Only when the mind is clear can the power of wisdom and enlightenment enter uncontaminated.

Posture

The posture, as used in this work, is defined as the position or bearing of the body, assumed for special purposes. Kemet Priest Scientists utilized a variety of postures based upon the powers of nature and the characteristics of certain animals held sacred for the purpose of balancing, integrating, stimulating, and transforming psychological energies. Many of the postures can be seen to this very day having been carved into the temple walls along the Hapy Valley in ancient Kemet and Kash (modern day Egypt and Sudan). The Ntchru, the forces of nature — Shu- the air, atmosphere; Tefnut- water, moisture; Geb- earth, mass; Nut- sky, force field; Ra- the sun, light and energy; Amen- the hidden force — represented the powers within the human being, the Moyo. In addition to these forces, these Black Afrakans of the Hapy Valley combined the natures of animals such as Heru, the hawk or falcon, Jhuty, the Ibis crane, Nekebet, the Vulture, Bast, the Lioness, Uatchet the Cobra, Ean, the Baboon, Sobek, the Crocodile, and Enpu, the Jackal, — Tese animals and more were studied and thier most dynamic qualities were incorporated into the training of the Kemet Priest-ship.

Many of the priests and high officials of ancient Kemet wore the skins of many of these animals for the purpose of strength and a sense of identification with the power of that Ntchru. The skins, bones and feathers that were worn in ancient Kemet were only symbols of the infinite power they possessed that also exist inside each of us. When practicing the various breathing techniques, of Ma'at Akhw Ba Ankh, Kupigana Ngumi, Kemet yoga, Kemet meditation and other forms of breathing therapies, you should always maintain a proper posture.

In Ma'at Akhw Ba Ankh there are three basic positions that all of the postures fall under:

1) The erect position- standing positions; using various postures standing on one or two legs.

2) The sitting position- either on a chair or on the floor or ground.

3) Lateral position- Lying on the floor or ground or floating in water.

The posture or form of a Spiritual Warrior does not become perfect or impeccable until the effort of achieving it vanishes and you become the embodiment of that posture or form at your highest level.

The Moyo

The Moyo is the vital energy emanating from The NTCHR that allows your Konsciousness to create balance to achieve and maintain excellent health in your illusionary physical form.

The Moyo is similar to electricity. Although you cannot see it, you know it exists because you can feel it or see its effects. When your Moyo is centered with the spirit and Konsciousness, the physical and mental body can find balance and we say you are healthy. When you are in an emotional state, your Moyo, if untrained can become unbalanced, allowing your body-temple to suffer from stress or depression and those negative emotions create physical disharmony and disease.

Moyo is also the subtle energy that propels the universe, the vitality that propels creativity, and the spirit that holds all things together from the smallest atom to the largest star system. In ancient Kemet Moyo was called Sekhem.

Ma'at Akhw Ba Ankh is the spiritual balance of the living soul and spirit within the physical body-temple. The techniques in Ma'at Akhw Ba Ankh are used to increase positive Moyo and release or decrease esfet (life threatening energy). Innerstanding and using the postures in Ma'at Akhw Ba Ankh will help develop and maintain your Moyo, the source of your internal strength and give you the balance needed to heal our minds and bodies.

Moyo is not just energy; it is the use of the life force. Moyo is the vital internal energy that maintains our lives on a high mental, physical and spiritual level. Without the knowledge of Moyo, or the development of what Afrakan Spiritual Warriors call Moyo, you will become tired and ill, and the physical body-temple will not be able to defend itself from esfet, causing you to expire early (death).

Ma'at Akhw Ba Ankh allows you to develop your Moyo by helping you concentrate on soft, internal relaxation and steady training movements with postures moving from soft to hard and back again from hard to soft. Each practitioner is trying to achieve an equal balance of left and right functions, which will allow you to hear and be directed by The Spirit of The NTCHR, thus increasing the use of high levels of your Moyo.

The Moyo is the vital energy flowing through the body-temple from your Heru Konsciousness. Your Konscious mind can also direct some of this energy that carries out body functions that was thought to be only controlled by your inner mind. The more control one has over your Konscious mind, in terms of focus and the ability to stop any outside illusionary interferences from distracting you from your purpose in life, the greater the Moyo. When the Moyo is great and you are Konscious of this connection you can direct the body-temple towards a wholistic state of being, allowing you to become a healer, or giving you greater healing potential.

The human body-temple consists of a brain, which houses the Heru Konscious, and Konscious mind, which controls several systems. These systems control all the human characteristics and body functions. Each system has several organs within it and the Moyo exist in each organ of the body-temple, as well as in the Konsciousness of all human beings.

If the Moyo is weak, or you are in a state of unconsciousness, you will have little to no control over your state of health, or your Konsciousness. Unconscious human's use only 1/2 of their brain at a time. While the other half is dormant of the half that is operational, only about 5 to 10% is used.

The majority of the population is consciously dormant and mentally unkonscious. This is why the masses struggle to survive instead of Being. However, if your Moyo is great, then your Heru Konsciousness can control the various systems in the human body-temple, which are the respiratory system, the digestive system, muscular system, the nervous system, the circularity system, the endocrine system, the urinary system and the skeletal system. Each system channels the Moyo differently. These channels that flow through the body-temple, giving it energy and vitality, are called meridians. The flow of Moyo through these meridians is referred to as the Subtle Body. The mastery of the flow of your Moyo through these meridians can keep you youthful, vigorous, alert and in a state of balance. This balance is call wholistic health. Wholistic health should be one of the goals of all human beings. The greater your wholistic health, the greater your spiritual potential, because you now have the strength to meditate and tap into your Heru Konsciousness, The NTCHR.

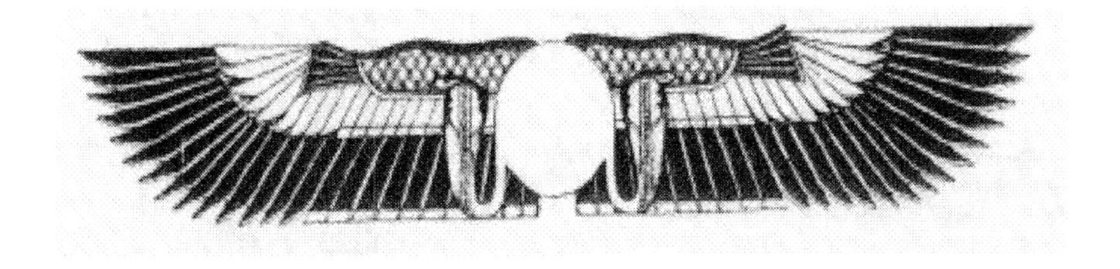

Kemet Yoga-like Postures

Many of the postures that you see look like Asian Yoga, only because Asian Yoga has its roots from Afraka. These same postures can be found on the walls of Ancient Kemet in Afraka, thousands of years before Yoga came into existence in India, China or other parts of Asia. However, the concepts are the same: to bring harmony to the mind, body and soul. Ma'at Akhw Ba Ankh, like the practice of yoga, serves to re-unite the individual self with the Absolute or pure Konsciousness. These postures exercise every part of the body, stretching and toning the muscles and joints, the spine and the entire skeletal system. By releasing physical and mental tension, the mind is able to liberate vast resources of energy that we call the Moyo or in Mdw Ntchr, Sekhem.

The Spiritual Warrior perceives the physical body as a vehicle, with the mind as the driver, and action, emotion and intelligences as the three forces, which pull the body or vehicle. In order for the body-temple to run smoothly and efficiently, all three elements have to function as one. Correct breathing controls the physical health, and the meditation techniques ensure peace of mind. Having awareness of your Kulture and Ourstory completes your connection with nature. Now as a Spiritual Warrior, you can give your gift much easier, because the road is much smoother on the highway called your mission.

Dr. Hapi & Mfundishi Jhutyms Ka en Heru. Dr. Hapi is a Spiritual Warrior in the Healing Arts, specializing in Kemet (Egyptian) Yoga and massage therapy.

Massage Therapy

Spiritual Warriors of ancient Kemet developed and used a form of massage therapy to treat and heal the whole body-temple more than 5,000 years ago in Afraka. These Spiritual Warriors used a series of techniques they called pressure therapies as preventive and therapeutic medicine. A healer could bring back balance were it no longer existed, or set up the conditions were balance could be maintained, by treating the individual as an wholistic entity representing the mind, body and spirit. Their function was to bring the whole person into harmony - Htp, a state of equilibrium. Pressure therapy could also treat specific organs, muscles and diseases, but the goal was to create Ma'at, to eliminate the cause, not just treat symptoms.

These Spiritual Warriors innerstood the sacred science of developing the Moyo, which was an entity in itself. Learning to Kemtrol and control the Moyo, the flow of this Ntchr like energy, which makes up our esoteric body-temple, constructively and productively can determine the quality of the life we lead spiritually, mentally, physically and emotionally. The Moyo flows through energy centers in the human body-temple called chakras. Your personal body-temples consist of major and minor chakras. These centers control and energize the internal organs and they also control and affect one's psychological condition. By energizing and controlling the energy that flowed through these centers, one could promote self-healing. Once these centers were energized, the healing process could begin.

Spiritual Warriors of today must carry these ancient healing secrets, because we are dealing with an Afrakan people who have been Spirituality and Kulturally assassinated by white male domination and Muslim Arabism. As a result, not only are they out of their Afrakan mind, they have inherited a host of sickness and diseases, ailments and conditions such as: asthma, heart disease, hypertension, diabetes, alcoholism, drug addiction, sexual disorders, psychological disorder, stress and this negative list could go on simply because we have adopted someone else's culture and Worldview.

We as Afrakan people have been given by The NTCHR, all that we need for survival, all that we need to be whole human and spiritual beings. However, in order to be whole, we need our Afrakan mind back and a wholistic spiritual Afrakan Kulture, with a Pan-Afrakan Worldview or we will just be treating the symptoms instead of the problems. And our major problem at this moment in Ourstory is white male domination and their Wazungu Caucasian European culture's strangle-hold on Afrakan people worlwide.

The human body-temple, the mind, emotions and the spirit all are responsible for our wholeness. If each of these components of self are healthy and whole, and synchronized with each other, life will be in a state of Ma'at or Htp. Nevertheless, if you are Afrakan and you are out of your Afrakan mind, you will be forever trapped in the Matrix of white male domination, which seeks to control even your very soul. Take a closer look; the system of white male domination already has humanity in danger of being trapped in this world of western destruction with adolescent morals. The capitalists of the western world are like termite people destroying everything in sight, even the very water, air, and land that it needs to survive itself and is a society void of spirit and spirituality with a superficial understanding of the mystery of the atom, but with no innerstanding of The NTCHR, and Ntchru. The western world with all their materialism is stumbling blindly through a spiritual darkness while toying with the precarious secrets of life and death. The Matrix of white male domination has achieved brilliance without wisdom, power without Konsciousness. The western world has developed nuclear giants and ethical infants. White male domination knows more about killing than about living. Brothers and sisters, we must abandon the matrix of white male domination and Muslim Arabism, and return to your Afrakan Kulture as Spiritual Warriors.

This is the oldest documentation depicting pressure therapy, dated around 3,000 B.C.E., Old Period, the 1st Golden Age ancient Kemet from the time capsule tomb of Ankmahor, a physican from Het ka Ptah.

Water

We must drink plenty of clean water for optimum wholistic health. Water is essential for life. 50 to 75% of body weight is water. Water should be drunk daily on an empty stomach, and in large quantities. Drink from one quart up to a half a gallon daily for proper cleansing and internal purification depending on your body-temple. Do not drink water with or directly after a meal. This dilutes the digestive process and diminishes the absorption of nutrients gained from the food you eat. In addition, there is no substitute for water, not herbal tea, coffee, soda, or juice. Anything in water besides H_20, the body treats as food. Only clean water acts as a cleansing and purifying agent essential for removing wastes. Water also regulates body temperature. It keeps all body functions going and helps prevent constipation.

Drink an 8 oz. glass of water about 1 hour before class on an empty stomach. You will lose a tremendous amount of water from the body while doing this practice. If you do not replace this fluid, you are at risk of dehydration. However, do not drink directly after practice, let the body cool down. In hot climates this may vary, drink during and after workouts to avoid dehydration. Then about thirty minutes after practice drink another 8 oz. glass of water. Develop the habit of drinking water the first thing in the morning on an empty stomach, and the last thing at night before going to bed. Be the Neb-Hu (master of your senses), the master of yourself.

Food

Always practice on an empty stomach. Eat two to three hours before practice and eat light. If you are hungry before class, have a piece of fruit, like an apple, or an orange or a piece of watermelon for energy. Practicing with food in the stomach might cause discomfort, dizziness, or nausea. Create another good habit by always going to the restroom before class. It is best that the bladder and bowels be empty, as well.

When we do eat, we must eat to live. Eat live foods full of energy. Since the essence of food forms the fuel for the mind, it is important to eat a natural diet. An excellent diet for a Spiritual Warrior is based on fresh, light, nutritional food such as fruit, grains, vegetables, legumes, nuts and seeds. This type of diet keeps the body-temple lean and limber and the mind clear and sharp. The Spiritual Warrior must eat moderately and abstemiously; otherwise, however clever, the Warrior cannot gain high levels of Heru Konsciousness and success.

A Wholistic Diet, with the Innerstanding that Food is the Fuel for your Universe

In order to stay in excellent mental, physical and spiritual condition and maintain optimum health, you need to follow a wholistic diet made up of largely fresh vegetables, fruits, beans, nuts, seeds and grains. This is a vegetarian diet. Consume no dairy products. Most people of Afrakan descent are lactose intolerant and should not consume dairy products like cow's milk, cheese, eggs and milk by-products like yogurt and ice cream. Calcium and vitamin D, which is good for the human body, should almost exclusively come from plant food, such as broccoli, cauliflower, celery, avocado, carrots, cabbage, and leafy green vegetables along with plenty of sun light.

A vegetarian diet, with plenty of exercise, will also help maintain a low blood cholesterol level. Your cholesterol level is related to all degenerative illnesses, because high cholesterol prevents oxygen from going to cells. Those with high cholesterol levels are prone to the diseases of affluence (wazunguism) - cancer, heart disease, and diabetes. Scientists maintain that the healthiest blood cholesterol is under 180 mg/dL, and an ideal blood cholesterol level is below 160 mg/dL.

We should also have diets that are rich in fiber. Research and studies shows that among many Afrakan tribes, because of their high-fiber diet, Afrakan people have little or no incidence of intestinal cancer. A high-fiber diet has been shown to be protective against heart disease, as well.

Fiber binds with cholesterol in the intestinal tract and thus, causes it to be eliminated from the body-temple in greater quantities.

What Foods Are High In The Nutrients We Need For Excellent Health

Afrakan Spiritual Scientists show that the cabbage family is a powerhouse for Afrakan people. These include broccoli, cabbage, kale, brussels sprouts, collard greens, and mustard greens. Such vegetables contain a group of compounds called indoles, which prevent tumors and cancer.

Additional green, yellow and orange foods rich in phytochemicals and other cancer fighters include citrus fruits, carrots, parsnips, squash, celery, and parsley. Soybeans and soybean products, such as tamari, miso, and soy sauce, contain a compound called genistein. Genistein prevents blood vessels from attaching to tumors, which prevents tumors from obtaining essential oxygen and nutrients to survive.

Afrakan Spiritual Scientists encourage the use of garlic because it promotes health in a wide variety of ways. Garlic stimulates the liver to more effectively identify poisons and turn them into harmless, water-soluble compounds. Garlic also encourages a variety of detoxifying enzymes to be produced by the body-temple, some of which directly attack cancer cells and tumors. Garlic is most effective when eaten raw, but it also promotes excellent health when eaten cooked. The onion also contains many of the sulfur chemicals found in garlic, but in smaller quantities.

Foods rich in vitamin B should be consumed daily. The B vitamins strengthen the immune cells, increase their number, and help to regulate hormones. Good sources are whole grains, such as brown rice, broccoli, leafy greens such as collard and kale, beans and peas, potatoes, walnuts, green peppers, soybeans and soybean products, wheatgrass, wheat germ, sprouts (all kinds), and fruits like dates, figs, prunes, cherries, and raisins.

Holistic Food Combining Chart

POOR COMBINATION

ACID FRUITS

All Citrus, Cranberries, Grapefruit, Lemons, Limes

Oranges, Pineapple Pomegranates, Strawberries, Tangerines, Tomatoes

Some Acid Fruits such as Lemons & Limes become alkaline in the body

Good

SUB-ACID FRUITS

Apple, Apricots, Berries, Cherries, Fresh Figs, Grapes, Guava, Kiwi, Mango, Nectarines, Papaya, Peaches, Pears, Plums

Good

SWEET FRUITS

Bananas, Coconut, Dates, Dried Fruits, Figs, Jack Fruit, Persimmons, Plantain, Prunes, Raisins

Soak Dried Fruits for 4-hours.

******FRUITS for BREAKFAST******

Electric Cleansers

After eating fruit, allow 15-30 minutes before eating other foods.

MELONS

Cantaloupe, Honeydew, Watermelon

Eat melons alone or leave them alone *

Avoid eating fruit for at least 3-hours after eating other foods.

MAKE FOOD COMBININATIONS ABOVE THIS LINE OR BELOW THIS LINE

POOR COMBINATION

PROTEINS

Lunch*

Magnetic Builders

Ackee, Avocado, Coconut, Dry Beans/Peas (Legumes), Green Algae, Identity-Preserved Organic Soya Beans, Soy Products, Spirulina, Olives, Nuts, Seeds, Sprouts, Wheatgrass

Pre-soak all Nuts & Seeds for 12 hours and Sprout Legumes.

EXCELLENT

LOW & NON-STARCHY VEGETABLES

Lunch & Dinner* Electro-Magnetic Stabilizers

Alfalfa Sprouts, Asparagus, Artichokes, Beet Greens, Beets, Bok Choy, Broccoli, Brussels Sprouts, Cabbage, Callaloo, Carrots, Cauliflower, Celery, Chard, Collards, Corn, Cucumber, Eggplant, Garlic, Green Beans, Kale, Leafy Greens, Lettuce (no Ice Berg), Mung Bean Sprouts, Mushrooms, Mustards, Okra, Onions, Peas (Fresh), Parsley, Radish, Sea Vegetables, Peppers, Scallions, Spinach, Turnips, Watercress, Zucchini

EXCELLENT

CARBOHYDRATES STARCHES

Dinner* *(Magnetic Builders)

Artichokes, Bread (whole grain or sprouted), Chestnuts, Corn, Dry Beans/Peas(Legumes), Grains/Cereals, Pasta, Potatoes, Pumpkin, Winter Squashes, Yams

Pre-soak Grains & Legumes for 12 hours & Sprout all Grains & Legumes.

POOR **GOOD** **POOR**

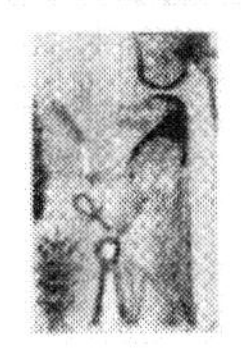

FATS

Avocado, Coconut, Olive

OILS

Avocado, Flax Seed, Nut Oils, Olive, Seed Oils, Sesame

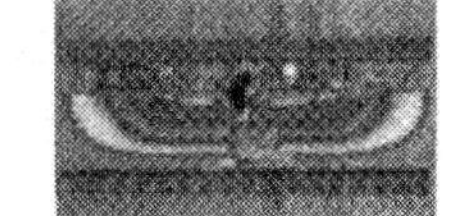

Special Combinations

***Avocados combine well with acid & sub-acid fruits, vegetables & tomatoes.**

***Tomatoes combine well with non-starchy vegetables, avocados, nuts & seeds.**

*** Soaked or sprouted nuts & seeds can be combined with fruits.**

NOTE: Learn more about DNA-melanin, in-season, non-hybrid and organic, whole foods for optimal health. Many foods listed in this chart would be considered *transitional* foods. Consultations or workshops are recommended for clarity.

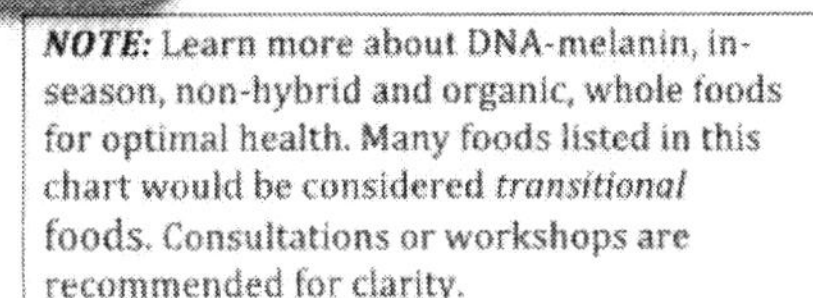

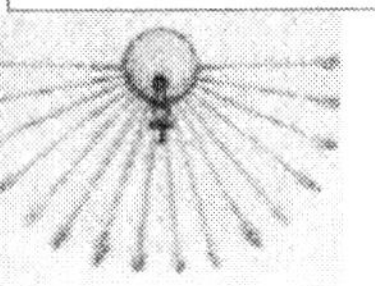

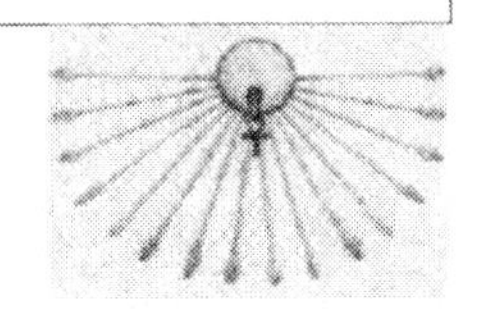

HOLISTIC FOOD TIME TABLE

Seneb Ma'at (Harmonious Health)

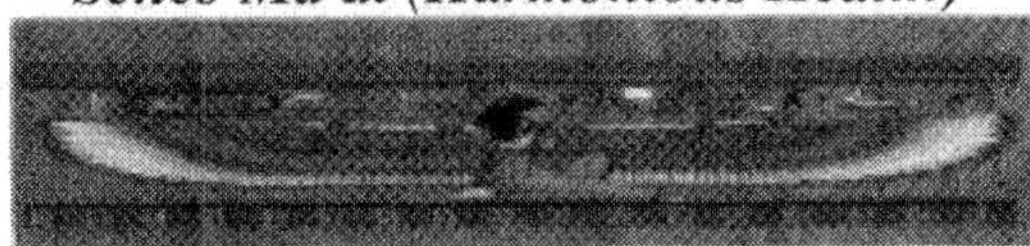

Elimination Time (4:00am-12:00pm)

4:00am - 6:00am

6:00am - *Pure Water (4 cups)

*(By end of day consume 1/2 your body weight in ounces) or Coconut Water

7:00am - Fruit Juice (Lime or Lemon Juice is an option)

(Green Drink is an Option)

8:00am-11:00am

8:00am - Breakfast (Fruit) (Supplements are an Option)

9:00am-11:00am (Herbal Tea is an option)

11:00am - Pure Water or Coconut Water

Intake Time (12:00pm-8:00pm)

12:00 pm - Nut Milk

(*Mixed with Vegan Protein Powder is an Option)

1:00pm--4:00pm

1:00 pm - Lunch (Protein & Vegetables) (Supplements are an Option)

4:00pm-Pure Water or Coconut Water

5:00pm - Vegetable Juice (*Green Drink is an option)

6:00pm-8:00pm

6:00pm-Dinner (Starch & Vegetables)

Reparation (Body repairs & rebuilds itself) (8:00pm-4:00am)

8:00pm-4:00am (Fast on Oxygen)

Disclaimer: The health and wellness information contained in this book and handouts are for educational purposes only. This information is not for a prescription or diagnosis of disease. See your medical profession for medical advice.

**The basis of the health and wellness information is a synthesis of works and research by Dr. Aris Latham, PhD, Dr. Laila O. Afrika, Dr. Sebi, Queen Afua/ Mut Nebt Het, Mfundishi Jhutyms Ka n Heru El-Salim and Hemet Ntchrt Seshatms Ma'atnefert El-Salim.*

Behold The Power of Cheese!!!

The United States population in 1970 was 203 million. In that same year, the dairy industry produced 2.2 billion pounds of cheese, which translates to 10.8 pounds of cheese per person. In 1990, America's population had grown to 248 million, but the average American ate 24 pounds of cheese per person. Now we are in the 21st century western time and America's cheese consumption is more then 30 pounds per person.

Got milk? Got Pus! Eighty percent of milk protein consists of casein, a tenacious glue. Casein is the glue that is used to hold labels on bottles. Have you ever tried to scrape off a label from a beer bottle, then consider the effects of casein in your body. Casein is the glue that holds together wood in furniture. The American Food and Drug Administration (FDA) allows 750 million pus cells in every liter of milk. In Europe, regulators allow 400 million pus cells per liter. Foreign cheese from France and Italy is better then American cheese because it has less pus! One slice of American or Swiss cheese contains over 468 million pus cells. Got cheese? Got Pus!

Mucus is produced as the result of drinking milk or eating cheese or their by products like ice cream, yogurt, and cheese toppings. Mucus congests internal body organs. The average person in America lives his or her life with a gallon of mucus clogging the kidney, spleen, pancreas, tracheal-bronchial tree, lungs, and thymes. Cow's milk is a killer, but cheese is ten times more deadly because it is more concentrative with pus and cow hormones that the human body was never supposed to consume. Cheese can also contain mycobacterium paratuberculesis, which causes diarrhea and irritable bowel syndrome. Eighty percent of the Afrikan population is affected by cow's milk and cheese in the most negative way. Got milk? Got Colds! Got Danish Cheese? Got diarrhea! Got pizza? Got bad bowels! **Behold the Power of Milk & Cheese!**

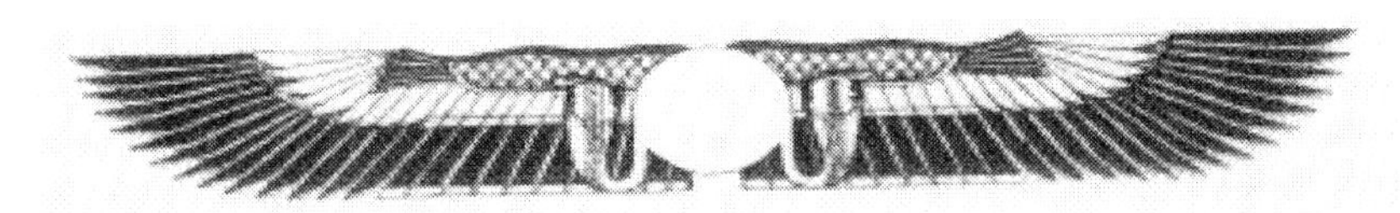

Food Alternatives

Low Vibration food	****High Vibration Foods*** ****Includes trnsitional foods***
Cow's Milk	Soy Milk, Nut Milk, Rice Milk Mother's Milk
Ice Cream	Soy Ice Cream, Fruit Sorbet, "Rice Dreams"
Cheese	Soy Cheese, Grated Tofu, Pureed Nuts & Seeds
Butter & Margarine	Soy Margarine, Cold-Pressed Olive Oil
Yogurt	Soy Yogurt or other non-dairy Yogurt
Eggs	Scrambled Tofu, Mashed Avocados
White Bread	Whole Wheat, Cracked Wheat Bread, Sprouted Bread
White Pasta	Whole Wheat Pasta, Sprouted Pasta, Quinoa Pasta
White Flour	Whole Wheat Flour, Barley Flour, Quinoa Flour
White Rice	Brown Rice, Wild Rice, Couscous, Quinoa Grits
Grits	Soy Grits, Barley Grits, Quinoa Grits
Pancakes	Buckwheat, Whole Wheat, Bran or Flaxseed
Commercial Cereals	Whole Oats, Granola
Commercial Oils	Cold Pressed Olive Oil, Sesame Oil, Coconut
Corn Starch	Arrow Root Powder
White Sugar	Raw Honey, Fructose, Organic Maple Syrup
Canned Vegetables	Fresh Vegetables (steamed or raw)
Salt	Sea Salt, Kelp, Vegetable Salt, Soy Sauce
Animal Flesh Protein	Sprouts, Tofu, Sunflower, Seeds, Green & Yellow Peas, Blackbeans, Pinto & Kidney Beans, Deep Green Leafy Vegetables, Algae
Canned or Bottled Fruit Juice	Fresh Squeezed/Pressed Fruit Juice
Soda, Kool-Aid, Fruit Drinks .	Fresh Juice, Organic & Unsweetened Fruit Juice
Commerical Peanut Butter	Fresh Unsweetened Peanut, Almond, Sesame Butter
Chocolate	Carob

Super Fruits

Kiwi : This is a good source of potassium, magnesium, Vitamin E & fiber. It's Vitamin C content is twice that of an orange.

Watermelon : Composed of 92% water, it is also packed with a giant dose of glutathione which helps boost our immune system. They are also a key source of lycopene - the cancer fighting oxidant. Other nutrients found in watermelon are Vitamin C & Potassium.

Strawberry : Strawberries have the highest total antioxidant power among major fruits & protect the body from cancer, causing blood vessels clogging free radicals.

NOTE: This list is mostly "transitional" foods. Inquire about workshops, DVDs and CDs, for higher levels of Food Energy and Holistic Living.

Twelve Ways of Protecting Yourself Against Disease and Promoting Excellent Health.

1. Eat whole grains and whole grain products daily. Whole grains include brown rice, barley, oats, millet, corn, quinoa, kamut, and wheat. Whole grain products include bread, pasta, and whole grain flour products. Whole grains are rich in complex carbohydrates for stable and long-lasting energy. They contain minerals, such as zinc and selenium, which boost immune response. They provide protein and also offer many essential vitamins, including vitamin E, an antioxidant and immune booster. Finally, whole grains provide an abundance of fiber, which promotes intestinal health. Ensure you have an active life-style that includes exercise when cooked grains are in your diet. If you consume cooked grains, then 20% or less are in your diet for a proper balance Alkalinity and Acid (80%/20%). For higher nutritional value and alkalinity, use sprouted grains and sprouted grain products. Seek to transition to whole plant foods and chlorophyll whole food supplements for the same benefits.

2. Eat at least three to seven vegetables per day. Vegetables are rich in vitamins, minerals, and fiber. Many contain beta-carotene, an immune enhancer and antioxidant. You should vary your vegetables, but the ones to emphasize are:

* Leafy greens, such as collard greens, mustard greens, kale, and cabbage
* Broccoli, brussels sprouts, and onions
* Squash: All the squashes are rich in beta-carotene and strengthen the immune system
* Roots, especially carrots, rich in beta-carotene

3. Get your protein from beans, sprouts and whole grains. All the essential amino acids are located in beans, grains, and vegetables.

4. Eat sea vegetables, such as wakame, arame, hijiki, nori, and spirulina. These are rich sources of trace minerals (including zinc, iron, magnesium, manganese, and selenium).

5. Eat organic and locally-grown foods that are pesticide chemical free.

6. Eat health-protecting foods, such as shiitake and reishi mushrooms, miso, tamari, shoyu, and garlic. All of these boost your immune system. Also maintain zinc in your daily diet. Optimal zinc levels increase the number of circulating immune cells. Zinc causes antibodies to mount a stronger attack against a disease carrying agent. Pumpkin seeds, whole grain, such as brown rice, whole wheat, bulgur, whole wheat bread, cashews, most beans and black-eyed peas are good sources of zinc.

7. Eat at least three to seven pieces of fruit per day. Eat sugars that are natural or less refined and part of a whole grain food, such as oatmeal cookies sweetened with apple juice or barley malt, cakes sweetened with apple juice or rice syrup and natural fruit juices. At the same time, minimize or avoid white sugar. White sugar is a drug and it also robs the body-temple of essential minerals and vitamins.

8. Don't smoke or use tobacco products, and stay away from drugs and unnatural products. Tobacco and many drugs are a major free radical producer, which destroy the cells.

9. Get regular exercise, such as Kupigana Ngumi, Ma'at Akhw Ba Ankh, three times a week. Fast walking four to five times a week for 45 minutes. Bicycling, and aerobic exercise three times a week, and sports are also recommended. All of these promote excellent circulation, which brings oxygen and nutrients to cells and serves as antioxidants.

10. Seek balance in life through Ma'at. Be spiritually centered. Stress is a major factor in the onset of disease and unhealthy living. There will always be challenges and problems; let's find a wholistic way to put them in perspective, and if you are of Afrakan descent, that should be Afrakan-centeredness, based upon Afrakan Kulture and an Afrakan spiritual system.

11. What foods you should avoid: meats, dairy products, processed foods, sugar, salt, junk foods, saturated fats, shellfish, and fried foods.

12. Intimacy with your relationship with the Creator, with a mate, keeps human beings healthier and allows us to live longer. Men who are married and live with their wives, or who have a close intimate relationship with a woman live on the average 10 to 15 years longer than men who live alone and who do not have a close intimate relationship with a woman. Single elderly Women seem to have closer relationships with family or bond with other elderly women and stay healthier and live longer than their male partners in all divisions of the human family. The greatest and healthiest relationship a human can have is with the Creator. This relationship is expressed best through your mental, physical and spiritual rituals, as a way of life.

The Gaze

Every posture in the practice of Ma'at Akhw Ba Ankh and Kupigana Ngumi has a gazing point. Sometimes the gaze is up, sometimes at the tip of the nose or straight out past the end of the nose, and sometimes to the side. Generally, the gaze is simply directly straight ahead. Gazing will improve the vision by exercising the eye muscles and the optic nerve, while increasing the blood flow. The important thing is to practice keeping the eyes focused on one point. This attention on the breath and the gazing begins the whole process of practice for developing concentration. Eventually, this will lead the mind to be steadfast and still. Every cell of the body should be focused and ready to begin practice.

Your Map, The Blue-Print For Success

Training the Spiritual Warrior can be compared to developing a magnificent Kultivated garden. Each of our individual gardens has different contents, and varies in size and shape, based upon our individual or collective needs. Some gardens are covered with multicolored flowers and herbs, surrounded by evergreen trees and running water. The perfection of our gardens represents the Kultivation of our many gifts and talents as we perfect our mission in life.

Wherever you now stand in your garden, even if it is just in the planning stages or you are in the mist of harvesting y our fruits, vegetables, or flowers, it is wise to have a map or plan of what your garden is suppose to look like. This map is your blue print to success. It tells you what to plant, when to plant it, and how to Kultivate it with the right love and attention to obtain the right results relative to your goals and objectives. From your map, you will also get an idea of the obstacles in your path, and gauge the effort that will be required to complete your goals.

Realistic vision allows you to choose the right plants, flowers, vegetables, herbs, fruits, trees and even grass or stones for your garden. Some of these combinations may not work together. Innerstanding this, you can retrace your steps if necessary, make a new map with the appropriate preparations, and redefine your immediate plans or goals.

Some people would question this and say, "Come on, Mfundishi, a map just for a garden?" However, they would not be Spiritual Warriors, because nothing should be left for chance. Your map is your blueprint, as Ourstory is a human map and it is your first vital element in the successful Kultivation of a magnificent garden of life. Innerstanding your vision is the proper beginning. You have to perceive it in order to achieve it. If you do not have a definite plan for success, then *no plan* is an excellent plan for failure.

The Four Principles of Ma'at Akhw Ba Ankh and Aha Kemet wa Kupigana Ngumi

Ma'at Akhw Ba Ankh and Kupigana Ngumi teach softness in the face of hardness - absorbing, neutralizing, and redirecting force. They also teach blending with another's energy rather than resisting. The basic knowledge of Kupigana Ngumi and Ma'at Akhw Ba Ankh contains four major principles: nonresistance, accommodation, balance and Konsciousness. These principles will enhance Moyo or Sekhem and greater spiritual development. These movements are easier said than done, but it must be mastered by all Spiritual Warriors. For every action there is an equal and opposite reaction.

1. Nonresistance

Nonresistance is a dynamic aspect of Ma'at. It is like a willow bending in the wind, going with the flow, yet it is ready to spring back, unharmed and prepared to continue its life's journey. This lesson takes passions and excellent breath control. Most of the tension is a subtle pain, and like any pain, it is a signal that something is wrong. When you are not in harmony with life, you will feel this tension. In life, we have to learn to let certain things happen naturally, based upon the natural flow of life's circumstances. Use life and learn to be one with its natural forces. This is the way of the Spiritual Warrior. When life gives you lemons, make lemonade. Innerstanding the spirit of nonresistance, you become partners and one with nature. Partnership or Oneness with nature is an excellent characteristic of a Spiritual Warrior.

Do not try, BE! The word "try" itself implies a weakness in the face of a challenge. The moment you try, you are already tense; therefore, trying is a primary cause of error and failure. When you sit down in your chair, you do not try you sit down, it is a natural flow. When you walk, you do not try, you just move easily. We must learn to flow easily even when a challenge arises. Consider this example of the effects of trying too hard. If you walk across a five-inch plank of wood twenty feet long, suspended a few inches from the ground, you would not have any problem. You would flow across with ease. Now transport that same five-inch plank to a height of twenty-five feet, and over a snake pit. Suddenly you begin trying harder. It is the same plank, but you have changed your mental state. A lack of Konsciousness can cause stress and tension. Moreover, with the correct Konsciousness of nonresistance, and innerstanding your oneness, you will flow with the forces of nature as its partner.

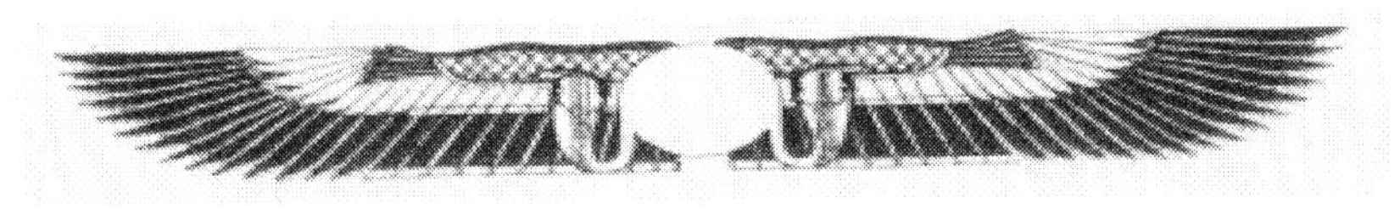

2. *Accommodation*

Accommodation is a dynamic aspect of Ma'at. Gentle running water can cut through solid rock with focus and persistence. By innerstanding the natural principles of Ma'at, you develop a realistic and harmonious approach towards challenges in your life. Training mentally, physically and spiritually is a process of development through gradual, realistic, increasing demands. Actions of the modern human family directed by white male domination are attempting to either push or slow down the winds (Shu) of life rather than flow with things as they are. If you create confrontations, you invite turbulence, and turbulence is felt in the human body-temple as physical, mental, and emotional tension.

Even grinding hard rocks with the correct tools slowly, and with Konsciousness, will cause them to naturally accommodate by changing their shape. However, if you try to grind too quickly, or with the wrong tools, the rock may break. Life works in a similar fashion. The demand for knowledge, wisdom and innerstanding must be gradual, consistent and with Konscious purpose. Working in your garden of life is the same. If you plant seeds in the wrong season, nothing will grow, even if they were excellent seeds or wonderful ideas. The law of accommodation is a law as profound and as certain as the law of gravity.

Let us give an example of the law of accommodation. Choose a physical action that is presently a little beyond your reach. It could be a one-arm push-up, a headstand or handstand. Once you have chosen your feat, attempt to perform it several times in the morning and again in the evening. Do this every day. With each attempt, you are asking your body-temple to change. Ask politely, but do not over do it, and most importantly be consistent and focused. Continue for a month, see what happens. Do not "try," just do it each day, and you'll find your body-temple complying with your polite request. It is the same with any change you would like to make in your habits or your personal life-style. It only takes a little time, and a lot of passion. And most importantly, be consistent. The body-temple, the mind and the soul will adapt and accommodate according to our Konsciousness. Spiritual Warriors know that your success depends upon the realistic demands you are willing to make on yourself, and your commitment to completing the goal, then success, psychic security and harmonious clarity of mind is yours.

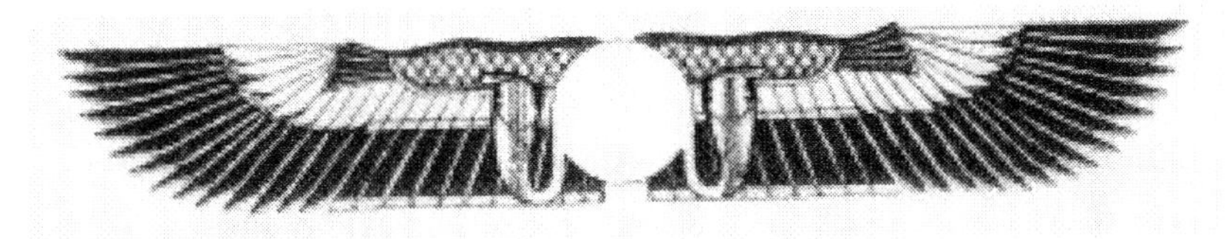

3. *Balance*

To have harmony, not too much, nor too little. To be centered is to have balance. Balance and Ma'at are synonymous. This is why we say Afrakan Spiritual Warriors must be Afrakan-centered in order to be in harmony with nature, their Kulture and the spirit of their ancestors. The word "centered" has to be a state of Konsciousness with the Spiritual Warrior, because it refers to a state of simultaneous physical, mental, emotional, and spiritual balance.

Balance itself is a state of Konsciousness. If you are relatively calm and happy right now, stand up and balance yourself on one leg. Now do it with your eyes close. Make a mental note of the relative ease of this act. The next time you are upset, angry, fearful, or distracted, use it. Give yourself this same balance test with eyes open, then closed. You will notice that one of two things will happen: If you are meditating on your upset nature, you will lose your balance easily. If you are meditating on your balance, you will lose your upset nature. Physical balance and emotional upset are like fire and water; they do not mix.

It is important to maintain balance in everything we do. In Ma'at Akhw Ba Ankh and Kupigana Ngumi all forms and drills are done with eyes open and close, right and left side. We also count forward and in reverse, so that balance and harmony becomes a way of life, and a life giving habit.

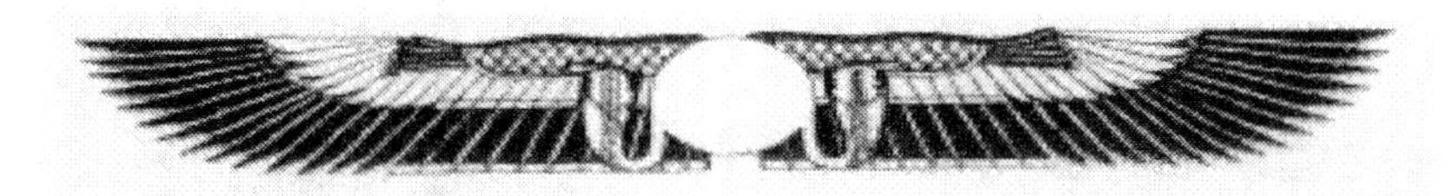

4. Awareness

Heru Konsciousness or Ma'at thinking is a state of awareness. This form of awareness transforms life's lessons into wisdom. It can translate confusing circumstances and events into useful knowledge. Awareness, then, is the beginning of all life's lessons. Through Ma'at thinking—which includes nonresistance, accommodation and balance—the Spiritual Warrior becomes aware of his or her Oneness with nature and The NTCHR. This allows the Spiritual Warrior to use his or her body-temple as a vehicle of expression to give his or her gifts, explore his or her talents, and give them freely to the world as part of our healing.

How to practice Ma'at Akhw Ba Ankh.

Who - Human beings who are seeking Ma'at in their life. Also Afrakans who are in the healing state of re-Afrakanization. Moreover, any human being who wants a healthy life-style consistent with Konscious preventive health maintenance. One should only spread the Kemet wisdom of Ma'at with those who are interested and ready, and who are evolved enough to receive the blessings of our wise and sacred ancestors.

When - Each practitioner should be consistent in the amount of time, as well as the specific time of the day. It is best to start each day off, in the morning with Ma'at Akhw Ba Ankh. This will keep you sharp and focused during the day. However, any time you can make to practice is a good time. When we practice at the end of the day our body-temple is more flexible, so postures are easier and practice seems relatively better. At the same time, our energy is generally lower and our concentration is not as clean and clear at this time of day. Still, the practice of Ma'at Akhw Ba Ankh later in the day is relaxing as it removes fatigue from the day's strain and tension and encourages a deep and peaceful sleep. The important thing is to be as consistent as you can so the body-temple can maintain a rhythm.

Where - Pick a location in your home, your yard or park where you will not be interrupted during practice. Choose a quiet and peaceful spot with a good aura, and practice there consistently. When you have found an excellent teacher, visit the school consistently on the same days and time each week, so that you will develop a rhythm, or spiritual flow.

How - The following are step by step instructions for beginning your practice of Ma'at Akhw Ba Ankh.

1. Drink 8 oz. of water 30 minutes before practicing.
2. Wash the body-temple before practicing.
3. Start practice with prayer or positive affirmation.
4. Ulimwengo or Asr Djed posture, (The battle of Heru).
5. Hekau mazoezi, chanting and breathing meditation.
6. Shu postures, deep breathing standing and sitting.
7. Mazoezi, stretching and strengthening exercises.
8. Ma'at Akhw Ba Ankh forms, slow moving postures for mastering life and to bring forth Ma'at.
9. Asr Karst posture. Lying down meditation.
10. Kemet Legacy, the teachings of ancient Kemet (Sankofa).
11. Reflection time on new and old information.
12. End practice with prayer or positive affirmation.
13. Drink 8 oz. of water 30 minutes after practicing.

14. Wash the body-temple after practicing.

15. Practice giving your gift, or reflect on your mission.

Meditative postures

These are positions that aid the body in harnessing energy, the Moyo, as well as strengthening the body-temple, mentally, physically and spiritually. Please do not force, or strain yourself in any of these postures. These postures should be practiced several times weekly in a scientific program with expert supervision. Consumption of clean drinking water, a proper diet and plenty of rest is important to bring about optimum wholistic health.

Ulimwengo: *Holding the Universe* - You are standing upright with your feet about shoulder width apart, back straight, knees bent like sitting in a high chair, looking directly in front of you and your arms are held heart level like you are holding a large invisible ball. You must focus only on one spot for several minutes. Breath deeply from the diaphragm, mouth closed, only breathing through the nose.

a) Length of time: beginners, 5 to 10 minutes daily or at least 3 times a week. Intermediate students, 12 to 20 minutes, and advance students 30 minutes.

b) Benefits: Develops strength in the legs and back. Increases internal strength in arms. This meditative posture will also help develop focus and concentration.

The Ulimwengu Posture used in Ma'at Akhw Ba Ankh and Kupigana Ngumi is based upon the Djed (Djed- one who endures), the stability of Asr and Ptah.

Mfundishi practicing the Ulimwengo Posture on three continents; top, Kemet (Egypt) - Afraka, bottom left, Brazil - South America, and bottom right, New Jersey, North America. Ma'at Akhw Ba Ankh and Aha Kemet Wanyama Saba wa Kupigana Ngumi are based upon the Djed (Djed- one who endures), the stability of the Ntchrw Asr and Ptah.

Kukaa Hekau Posture:

Sitting With Legs Folded - You sit on the floor or ground by placing your left leg behind the right until you are sitting with your legs crossed. Your back must be straight, hands resting over your knees with your longest finger and thumb touching by making a circle. You are looking straight ahead at one point, with focus and concentration.

Mfundishi meditating in the Kukaa Posture, positions 1 & 2.

Ma'at Akhw Ba Ankh, Kukaa Posture.

Mfundishi meditating in the Kukaa Posture, positions 3, 4 & 5

Ma'at Hekau Posture:

1. The Ma'at posture represents the first step in the path of self mastery ("I laid the foundation through Ma'at. I created forms of every kind. Ra's description of creation.")

2. The Ma'at posture symbolizes the harmony of heaven and earth through the human mind.

3. The Ma'at posture serves as the basis for all subsequent actions (Kupigana Ngumi techniques and principles).

4. The emphasis is placed upon mental tranquility and controlled respiration.

5. The nine elements composing body, mind, and spirit are in actuality the life force vibrating at various frequencies under the direction of the mind (Ptah). These frequencies correspond to a nine note musical scale.

Mfundishi El-Salim in the Ma'at posture

Mfundishi practicing the Ma'at meditative posture in Kemet. At the top photo Mfundishi is standing on The Mer Khut of Khufu (the Great Pyramid), middle, he is at Mahez, an ancient center for Afrakan Martial Arts, and at the bottom photo Mfundishi is at Edfu in front of Heru, the great Spiritual Warrior.

Mfundishi Jhutyms smoking a Native American peace pipe at a Native American sweat and meditation session upstate, New York.

MA'AT AKHW BA ANKH

First Level (approx. 8 weeks)

Ulimwengo 10 min.
Kukaa Hekau
Ma'at Hekau
Nut
Mazoezi: a) head roll b) shoulder roll c) waist roll d)knee roll
e) toe roll f) ankle roll g) mazoezi tumbo - 10 times
h) hip raises i) neck bridges...
Shu
Shu wa
Heru djed - count 30 on each side
Kiungu Cha Mkono mazoezi
Asr
Hesabu (count) 1 to 30 in Kiswahili and 1 to 30 in Mdw Ntchr

Define: Ma'at Akhw Ba Ankh:

Ma'at:

Jhuty:

Heru:

NTCHR:

Chapter 2 has these Ntchru in it if you need assistance or consult Kera Jhuty

Heru Nub-Hu Flash cards of the Ntchru of ancient Kemet.

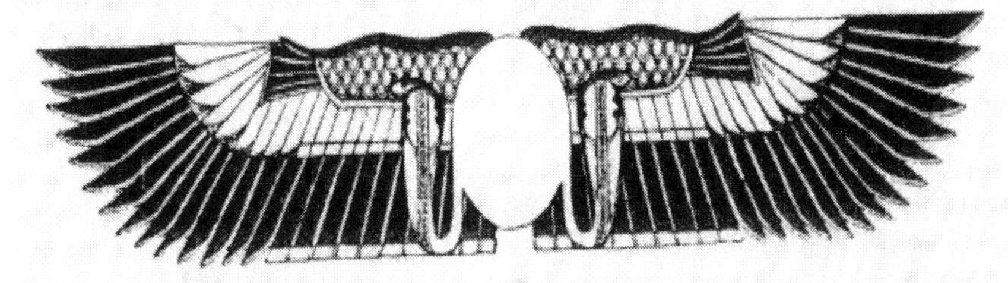

MA'AT AKHW BA ANKH

Second Level (approx. 8 weeks)

Ulimwengo 15 min.
Kukaa Hekau
Ma'at Hekau
Nut
Mazoezi: a) head roll b) shoulder roll c) waist roll d) knee roll
e) toe roll f) ankle roll g) mazoezi tumbo - 15 times
h) hip raises i) neck bridges j) arm bridge k) Geb
l) shoulder stand m) Geb twist...
Shu
Shu wa
Shu senu
Shu shomet
Heru djed - count 60 on each side
Jhuty Kaa - count 60 on each side
Kiungu Cha Mkono mazoezi
Kiungu Cha Mkono taratibu (1/2)
Asr
Hesabu (count) 1 to 60 in Kiswahili and 1 to 60 in Mdw Ntchr

Define: Asr

Ast

Nebt Het

Nut

Geb

Chapter 2 has these Ntchru in it if you need assistance or consult Kera Jhuty Heru Nub-Hu Flash cards of the Ntchru of ancient Kemet.

MA'AT AKHW BA ANKH

Third Level (approx. 8 weeks)

Ulimwengo 20 min.
Kukaa Hekau
Ma'at Hekau
Nut
Simba Rafu
Mazoezi: a) head roll b) shoulder roll c) waist roll d) knee roll
e) toe roll f) ankle roll g) mazoezi tumbo - 20 times
h) hip raises i) neck bridges j) arm bridge k) Geb
l) shoulder stand m) Geb twist...
Shu
Shu wa
Shu senu
Shu shomet
Shu fedw
Heru djed - count 60 on each side
Head stand
Jhuty Kaa - count 60 on each side
Kiungu Cha Mkono mazoezi
Kiungu Cha Mkono taratibu
Asr
Hesabu 1 to 100 in Kiswahili and 1 to 100 in Mdw Ntchr
Greetings in Mdw Ntchr and Kiswahili
Define: Shu
Tefnut
Amen
Ptah
Het Heru

Chapter 2 has these Ntchru in it if you need assistance or consult Kera Jhuty

Heru Nub-Hu Flash cards of the Ntchru of ancient Kemet.

MA'AT AKHW BA ANKH

Fourth Level (approx. 8 weeks)

Ulimwengo 25 min.
Kukaa Hekau
Ma'at Hekau
Nut
Simba Rafu
Twa Bow
Mazoezi: a) head roll b) shoulder roll c) waist roll d) knee roll
e) toe roll f) ankle roll g) mazoezi tumbo - 20 times
h) hip raises i) neck bridges j) arm bridge k) Geb
l) shoulder stand m) Geb twist...
Shu
Shu wa
Shu senu
Shu shomet
Shu fedw
Shu dew
Heru djed - count 60 on each side
Head stand - count 30 in each leg posion
Jhuty Kaa - count 60 on each side
Kiungu Cha Mkono mazoezi (2 levels)
Kiungu Cha Mkono taratibu (2 levels)
Ra
Asr
Hesabu 1-1,000 in Kiswahili and Mdw Ntchr
Greetings and classroom vocabulary in Mdw Ntchr and Kiswahili
Define: Ra
Sekmet
Bes
Set
Enpu

Chapter 2 has these Ntchru in it if you need assistance or consult Kera Jhuty

Heru Nub-Hu Flash cards of the Ntchru of ancient Kemet.

MA'AT AKHW BA ANKH

Fifth Level (approx. 8 weeks)

Ulimwengo 30 min.
Kukaa Hekau
Ma'at Hekau
Nut
Simba Rafu
Twa Bow
Mazoezi: a) head roll b) shoulder roll c) waist roll d) knee roll
e) toe roll f) ankle roll g) mazoezi tumbo - 25 times
h) hip raises i) neck bridges j) arm bridge k) Geb
l) shoulder stand m) Geb twist...
Shu
Shu wa
Shu senu
Shu shomet
Shu fedw
Shu dew
Shu sesu
Heru djed - count 100 on each side
Head stand - count 100 in each leg posion
Jhuty Kaa - count 100 on each side
Kiungu Cha Mkono mazoezi (3 levels)
Kiungu Cha Mkono taratibu (3 levels)
Ra
Eah
Asr
Hesabu 1- 1,000,000 in Kiswahili and Mdw Ntchr
Greetings and classroom vocabulary in Mdw Ntchr and Kiswahili

Define: Seshat, Sobek, Khepr, Heru Ur, Neb Hu.

Chapter 2 has these Ntchru in it if you need assistance or consult Kera Jhuty

Heru Nub-Hu Flash cards of the Ntchru of ancient Kemet.

Hekau

. The Kemet Warrior Priest Scientists taught that humans could learn to purify their minds through the discipline of Ma'at Akhw Ba Ankh, the Kemet meditation and breathing postures of Ma'at. One of the tools used in Ma'at Akhw Ba Ankh is Hekau. Hekau is the repetitious use of divine sound, vibrations, word or words to evoke Ma'at thinking. Moreover, when Ma'at thinking occurs it is possible to transcend the "physical" and mental reality of esfet (physical illusion), and attain the higher spiritual visions while still alive in your human form.

Hekau may be safely used by anyone to help steady the mind and to train it to focus on the wisdom or spiritual teachings which will transform or prepare the mind for mental transformation. Some forms of Hekau may be spiritual or religious songs or scriptures, but they must be innerstood by the speaker who uses words of wisdom based on Ma'at.

The Hekau must be repeated over and over for several minutes, the more mental power you have the greater your Moyo, and when your Moyo is great you can place yourself in a calm state. It is in this calm state that the power of the Moyo allows you to receive and transport yourself to a higher psychological and spiritual plane of Heru Konsciousness.

Heru Konsciousness is special vibration patterns, just like emotion, reason, fear, will, and desire are accompanied by vibrations, a portion of which are projected and then received by energy fields in close proximity. Hekau can produce certain vibrations that can stop the mind, and when the ordinary consciousness is stopped, the images of your illusionary reality also stops. Now through your Heru Konsciousness your mind is open to a much greater range of information and possibilities.

When Hekau is done everyday it is like you personally visit the Temple, shrine, church or Holy place of spiritual worship. You become closer to your goals because your focus becomes sharper and clearer until they are manifested into physical, mental or spiritual reality. This discipline of chanting also includes dance and has been handed down to us through the centuries, forming the nucleus of the Kemet mediative systems, we now call Ma'at Akhw Ba Ankh.

Hekau should be repeated aloud first, until the student has mastered the sounds or words and its innerstanding. Once there is a clear level of innerstanding, empowerment begins and it is a form of self empowerment between you and The NTCHR. Hekau is also extremely effective when done silently or mentally, which also means it can be done anywhere, at your own alter or shrine, your own home, at a Temple or class, or even while riding on a bus, train, plane or subway. Sometimes Hekau is done as a prelude to meditation or done while in certain meditative or breathing postures.

The following Hekau is used by the shrine, Jhuty Heru Neb Hu and were selected by the author:

1) ***Ankh*** - divine life.

2) ***Sah en Ma'at*** - spiritual protection and harmonious balance.

3) ***Sah en Ankh*** - spiritual protection and divine life.

4) ***Hotep Ankh Ujah Sneb*** - May you have peace and satisfaction and may you live long, be prosperous and have good health.

5) ***Jhuty Heru Neb Hu*** - May the Ntchru Jhuty, the spirit of articulate thought, speech and writing, along with the Ntchru Heru, Higher Konsciousness and physical protection, be manifested through the mastery of our senses.

The following Hekau can be done as call and response:

1. ***Ankh Pu Ntchr- Ba Er Pet Sat en Ta***
I am the supreme divinity- soul is of heaven, body belongs to the earth.

2. ***Amen Ra Na Swt Ntchr - Aten Ra Neb en Ankh***
The unseen and the seen mind of the universe is the Na Swt or Divine Ruler, among the Ntchru. The energy of the Ntchr of light is the master of life.

Hekau, the chanting of the MDU NTCHR, words of power, is our way of invoking the spirits of our ancestors and the power of the Ntchru who reside within us all.

Our ancestors, in their infinite wisdom, created and developed Mdw Ntchr during the ancient civilization of the Hapy Valley, from which Kemet emerged. They knew that certain sounds had specific effects on our environment and us. The sounds that are in the Mdw Ntchr are just one of our many tools to reclaim and use the power that is ours for our re-Afrakanization.

Some of this knowledge was delineated in the burial chambers (time capsules of knowledge) in Kemet. There were four guardians who protected the vital organs of the body. These organs were put in Messu Heru jars; each jar top depicted the image of a guardian. Each of these guardians had many pieces of information ascribed to them. Among the information was the knowledge of how to cure and control those vital organs. For example, by saying Hapy, the guardian of the lungs, the lungs will become empowered and conditioned. This is the type of knowledge that is waiting for you in the modern Kemet shrines, and today's Spiritual Warriors are waiting for you lost Afrakan Warriors to return home, mentally and spiritual first, so that Afraka can become whole and great again.

Hekau is a powerful tool left by our ancient Afrakan ancestors for us to use and assist us in our daily sojourn through life. Afrakan Spiritual Warriors must, or should, chant in the tongue of our sacred ancestors for they are waiting to assist us. When we use an Afrakan language, we allow the message to resonate through our very beings from a Kultural perspective. During Ma'at Akhw Ba Ankh, many phrases in Mdw Ntchr are chanted, all designed to empower ourselves, to empower our ancient homeland, and to assist our re-Afrakanization process and us. Hekau is an opportunity to share with each other our Afrakan Kulture and enjoy yourself in a healthy spiritual way.

Affirmation

To affirm means to "make firm". Our mental commentary influences and directs our feelings and perceptions about what is going on in our lives and it is these thoughts that ultimately attract and create everything that happens to us.

Spiritual Warriors use positive Afrakan affirmations like they use Hekau. It is an external dialogue that speaks to the internal mind called your Heru Konsciousness. Behind this dialogue is our inner, deeper, wiser intuitive mind. Affirmations can be done silently, spoken aloud, written down, chanted or even sang. Most people of Afrakan descent in the West, especially in Americas and the Caribbean have been cut off from their true Afrakan Kulture and their awareness of whom they are. They have lost their Konscious connection with their higher self, their Heru Konsciousness, so they have lost their own sense of power and responsibility for their lives. Positive Afrakan affirmations can restore this connection giving you infinite energy or unlimited Moyo.

In order to Re-Afrakanize our people, positive Afrakan Affirmations must be as important as healthy foods and clean drinking water. They should be done 5 to 10 minutes daily, powerful affirmations can replace negative, non-productive thoughts that have been in your mind since childhood.

Below are a few common, but powerful affirmations:

1. **Every day is magnificent and wonderful and every day I'm getting better and better, and Afrakan people are getting better.**
2. **I am a radiant Afrakan being, filled with light and love.**
3. **I am the master of my life.**
4. **I am Afrakan and I have everything I need already within me.**
5. **The more I have, the more I have to give to Afrakan people.**
6. **I am the spirit and I'm naturally enlightened.**
7. **Perfect wisdom is in my heart.**
8. **The more I love myself, the more love I have to give Afrakan people.**
9. **It's O.K. for me to have everything I want.**
10. **I am vibrantly healthy and radiantly Black and beautiful.**
11. **My higher self is guiding me in everything I do.**

Positive Affirmation should always be phrased in the present tense. Say what you want, affirm it in a very positive way, and always keep it short and to the point. Affirmations are often most powerful and inspiring when they include references to spiritual sources, like the NTCHR, Ntchru, the divine love, the light and universal intelligence. Positive Afrakan Affirmations can be done in an Afrakan tongue or in any language that you know. The first step in healing for Afrakan people is the desire, the commitment and the will to be healed. Place a positive, inspiring, and uplifting book by your bedside. Read it every morning and every night. These positive Afrakan Affirmations can be shared with loved ones and friends in a study group, at school, house of spiritual worship or with family. We must first **Be,** then we must **Do**, before we **manifest** what we Want.

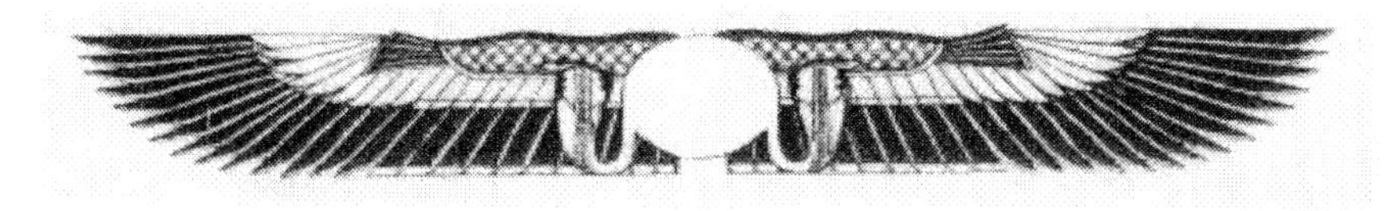

Every Spiritual Warrior must communicate Konsciously with The NTCHR daily. This communication could be Hekau, with Positive Afrakan Affirmation, or prayer.

Afrakans should do this in an Afrakan language, if possible. This communication with The NTCHR is for alignment, allowing the Divine Spirit to come in harmony with your soul, your Konscious mind and your body. This alignment puts you in rhythm and harmony with all that is good for you, as you refocus on Ma'at. When the Spiritual Warrior has reached the advanced stages of his or her training, he or she will innerstand the power of the spirit, which is pure. It is beyond old age and death, because it is One with The NTCHR. This is the Asr Spirit waiting in all of us. This is the essence of Ma'at Akhw Ba Ankh.

Affirmations For Spiritual Warriorship

Morning: ***I declare myself a divine being, a manifestation of The NTCHR. And as a Spiritual Warrior, I am on duty to co-create with the Ntchru and implement Ma'at wherever esfet exist. Use my spirit for good, and guide me Great NTCHR, so I may guide others who are lost and blind.***

Day time: ***I release all my fears, anger and negative thoughts and attitudes to love and guidance of The NTCHR, and wait for guidance as I choose harmonious balance to direct my positive action towards Ma'at. Joy and love are my confirmation of right choices and Ma'at, and pain and discomfort are my teachers of bad choices and esfet.***

Bed time: ***I forgive myself, my love ones, my family, and others, for any actions today that moved me away from my greatest potential and highest good. I release myself to the Divine Konsciousness and will of The NTCHR as I sleep and dream and recharge for a righteous tomorrow.***

Kemklusion:
Ma'at Akhw Ba Ankh
(Kemet breathing and Meditative postures)

The spirit of the Creator dwells within us
The innerstanding of this spirit can be developed through
Ma'at Akhw Ba Ankh
The unity of the mind, body, and spirit through:
Kemrect breathing
Kemrect relaxation
Kemrect diet
Kemrect exercises
Kemrect thinking
Kemrect innerstanding of Self
Kemrect konscious spiritual kemmunikation with the Supreme Wisdom, The NTCHR
When two or more of the above are united, some degree of happiness is developed.

You are what you eat and if you eat junk, you become junk!!!

1). Your body is like a fine machine, like an autooibile: use the best quality fuel and get the best results in return. (i.e.; eat and drink good, wholesome foods and you will be healthy). 2). Tune up your machine frequently (i.e.; keep the colon and internal organs cleansed and free of toxins, chemicals, drugs and harmful germs. 3). You will receive the full value of your purchase (i.e.;it's your Ntchr-given right to enjoy a long healthy, dis-ease-free life and prosperous life).

Every 60 to 90 days your body renews its cells. The foods you eat and drink are the only source of fuel and building material your body has. Be careful what you eat, because it will become you!!!

In order to create and maintain mental, physical, and spiritual happiness, Ma'at must be Konsciously in your life and Ma'at Akhw Ba Ankh is one such vehicle that allows you access to your infinite power, by developing the perfection of character, which must be a daily ritual...

The Spiritual Dance
Ma'at Akhw Ba Ankh

Come... Take my hand...
We shall glide effortlessly over fallen leaves and tender grasses
Blending with the wind as we vibrate with the pulse of the universe
Moving in-between palm trees without disturbing the tranquility of our surrounding beauty...

With grace, subtle movements are transformed into meditation
Which becomes prayer to the Body-temple stylized through a graceful dance
An ancient Kemetik ritual form, that aligns the spirit and the soul
Ma'at Akhw Ba Ankh
Illuminating awareness of your divinity
When the Cosmic energy merges with the human energy
A state of Spiritual Balance is recognized
This healing energy called by modern Afrakan Priest scientists as Moyo
When the Moyo is released, the vibration of this energy awakens your Heru Konsciousness
This Konsciousness directs healing
When this level of awareness permeates the spiritual dance
It expands the heart
All levels of existence are integrated into the moment
At this point the spiritual dance directs the healing of all those who become one with the movements of the moment...
Amen-Ra.

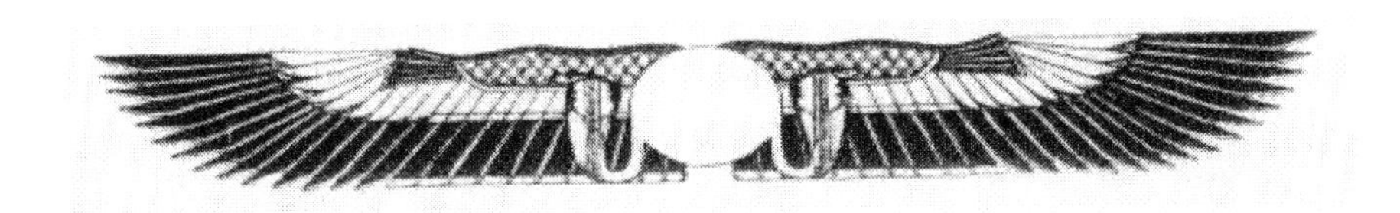

CHAPTER ∩ I I (12)
Somo la Kumi na Mbili

Kupigana Ngumi

Kupigana Ngumi From the Kemetik Shrine of Jhuty Heru Neb Hu

Kupigana Ngumi is the essence of martial science from the Global Afrakan experience. It is expressed through the body, mind and spirit disciplines preserved within Afrakan Art, Dance, Music, Religion, Spirituality and Kulture.

The Words:

*Kupigana- Method of combat *Ngumi- Fist, arm or hand.
*Kupigana Ngumi- Method of combat utilizing the fist, arm, hand or any part of the anatomy or weapon of extension.
*Mpigani- Practitioner of Kupigana Ngumi.

The word Kupigana Ngumi is an adopted term for the collective fighting arts of the entire Afrakan Continent. Kupigana Ngumi literally means "way of fighting with the fist." Every nation of people in Afraka has its own language and word for warrior and warfare. Kupigana Ngumi is from the Kiswahili language. It is a non-tribal trade language used in many countries in east Afraka. The term was first used by **Shaha Mfundishi Maasi**, a warrior and martial artist of the Royal Guard of King Nana Kablam I, and **Nganga Mfundishi Tolo-Naa**, a warrior and traditional healer. When they collaborated in the early 1970's they used the term Kupigana Ngumi to form the Pan-Afrakan Kupigana Ngumi Federation.

Kupigana Ngumi utilizes the traditional and contemporary martial arts techniques, drum rhythms, and dance movements of Afraka. Its diverse repertoire includes graceful acrobatic techniques, flying kicks, strong punches, sweeps, traps, throws, psychological techniques and Mnyama Mapigana (Animal Fighting Techniques).

Kupigana Ngumi is the synthesis of the Afrakan Warrior experience. It imparts a view, which recognizes the inherent capacity of the martial arts to impart life-cultivating benefits, as well as defensive and offensive capabilities. Kupigana Ngumi reveals the power to serve the needs of Afrakan people and to strengthen their capacities towards human refinement.

The essence of Kupigana Ngumi is to train the mind, body, and spirit to become a Spiritual Warrior. Kupigana Ngumi practitioners should be as skilled in speech as they are in fighting. The tongue of a person is his or her sword. Many times effective speech is stronger than all fighting. However, when speech fails, and all other forms of communication break down, you should be like a mighty storm and a skillful lion on its prey. As Ourstory witnesses, to develop anything of value or anything of beauty and not be able to defend it, is like not having it at all. The doers of esfet, like the Europeans and Asiatics, will steal what is yours and claim it as their own if you do not defend your space, your kulture, your story, your people.

Thirteen Sub-divisions of the Kupigana Ngumi Training System:

Warrior Arts - Pigana (boxing)
Mnyama Ngoma (animal dance or form)
Shikana (grappling)
Silaha (weaponry)
Fikiri (meditation)
Afrakan intelligence agency and strategy center

Kultural Arts- Mchezo Ngoma (Afrakan Kultural music & dance)
Ma'at Akhw Ba Ankh (Harmony of the breath aligned with the spirit and soul)
Ourstorian Hekima (Ourstorical wisdom)
Chakula (food)
Ngoma (music)
Uzima (health)

One of the main objectives of Kupigana Ngumi is to realize that the physical being and the spiritual Self are one with the absolute-they co-exist. One is part of the other. The other a whole of whose nature the one partakes. Total realization of the unconditioned, unlimited Self is complete liberation for the Spiritual Warrior. This information and transformation is possible for all human beings. Kupigana Ngumi training is not only the mastery of the physical body-temple, but also the development of the mind and the soul. Kupigana Ngumi and Kemet breathing postures are a way of life that helps you to innerstand the knowledge that is within you, which is a part of the greater union of Self and The NTCHR. Its essence is to discover the eternal presence of The NTCHR by living each moment in complete awareness of The NTCHR. Today Spiritual Warriors call the Kemet breathing and meditative postures **Ma'at Akhw Ba Ankh,** which is the central core of Kupigana Ngumi centers in the New York, New Jersey, Philadelphia, Maryland and Washington D.C. (Kemet Shrines of Kera Jhuty Heru Neb Hu).

In the Kemet shrine of Jhuty Heru Neb Hu, the Kupigana Ngumi Warriors are trained in the spirit of the ancient Kemet traditions along with modern techniques and reasoning, based on Afrakan-centered thoughts and principles and we call this system Aha Kemet Wanyama Saba. The synthesis of knowledge between the old and new is for the complete liberation of all our initiates. Afrakan people are still suffering from the Maafa or Maangamizi- the deadly effects of white male domination on all levels of mind, body and soul exploitation.

In our modern system of the ancient Afrakan martial art form (today called, Aha Kemet Wanyama Saba wa Kupigana Ngumi), we, the Kemet branch, under the Kemet shrine of Jhuty Heru Neb Hu, have embraced some basic spiritual principles, so that Ma'at may always be at the foundation of whatever we do. Each Spiritual Warrior must walk in the path of Heru. The following is part of that path:

1. The way of spiritual Konsciousness
2. The way of works
3. The way of knowledge
4. The way of devotion
5. The way of love

The following outline illustrates:

The Three Levels of Mastery in The Kupigana Ngumi Kemet Spiritual System

I. Those who seek the light, the Mpigani and the Kaka and Dada.

A. Meditation (upon the principles of nature-Ntchru)
B. Posture
C. Breathing
D. Motion
E. Focus

II. Those who have the light, the Mfundi and Malanga.

A. One becomes the Mfundi, Malanga, Mfundishi, the embodiment of Ma'at.
B. The harmonizing of the nine (9) Tones of the Soul.
C. The realization of (soul force), the Moyo or Sekhem.

III. The sons and daughters of Light, the Mfundishi.

A. National Unity- The soul of all human beings are of one essence.

B. A Spiritual Warrior is the link between heaven and earth.
C. Spiritual Warriors and the society are divine parts of the divine universe.
D. The points of power lies in the present moment.
E. For the Spiritual Warrior, today is a good day to Die...

In ancient Kemet, the Priests and Priestesses of the temples were divided into three main classes, the lower called Wab, literally "The Pure". The second level Priest or Priestess was called by the title Hem- Ntchr, literally the "Servants of the Creator." These were the scholars, Warriors and master teachers. Other titles of the second group were Lector Priest, Ka Servant, Priest of Heru, and the Priest of Enpu. In addition to these two groups of priest were the elders, who were called Khery-Hed "Father or mother of the Ntchru." At the head of the whole temple staff was the Hem Ntchr Tepy, the "High Priestess or Priest." She or he was usually one of the Sons and Daughters of the Light. In today's society this degree of mastery is also called the Mfundishi in the Kupigana Ngumi system. The Kemetyu believed in the essential unity of all things in the universe and Innerverse, as well as the belief in One Supreme Creator. This belief was practiced before ancient Kemet and during every time period in the Kemet Ourstorical Periods. As expressed on numerous temple walls: "There is only one Creator who is nameless, incomprehensible and self-Created."

The Kemet Priest Scientists were great messengers who taught that each person was a microcosm of the Creator, and by knowing the Self, they would know the Spirit. Through the spirit and the power of the Moyo or Sekhem, they would gain experience, internal and eternal strength and peace. Tradition spread to the southern part of Eurasia and became known as "Shamanism." This became the earliest known form of martial dance (or form) practiced by the initiates of the ancient Kemet Mystery System of Ta-Mrry, Sais, and Kemet (names of Egypt used by the indigenous Kemetyu). Additionally, these practices were prevalent in the Sudan, Nubia, Kash, Ethiopia, Morowe, Kenya, Uganda, and Tanzania, and the entire inner continent in general.

Ngoma (dance), being a series of motions, aided the initiate in focusing and directing vital energies for the following purposes:

1. *Awakening the subtle senses*

2. *Body alertness*

3. *Freedom from body-minded tension*

4. *The ability to withstand stress*

5. *Centering and focusing one's thoughts*

6. *Kultural connection*

These were ancient methods used by our Kemetyu ancestors of the Hapy Valley and they are still used today by many Afrakan Spiritual Healers, as well as the martial artist of the Kupigana Ngumi training centers. The warrior dance and drumming was designed for the development of the Moyo.

War-dance performed by Kemetyu and Kashite soldiers before a battle, Old Period Ancient Kemet.

"The modest person is strong, and one who is true in word and just in deed is praised. Houses are opened to the humble, and a wide seat is given to one who is gentle in speech and conduct. However, sharp knives stand ready for the unrighteous intruder. For there is no entrance except for the righteous." This is from the Husia translated from ancient Kemet text by Maulana Karenga. Kupigana Ngumi is one of the methods available to each human being who wishes to be true of voice, and strong of heart, yet gentle in speech and conduct. This art is also for those who wish to have the knowledge of self-defense, and the ability to defend their family, mentally, physically and spiritually.

Why is Kupigana Ngumi necessary? Because it is a tool that is instrumental in undoing the mis-education of European Caucasian supremacy and for constructing a healthy Afrakan body, spirit and mind. If you cannot defend yourself, mentally, physically or spiritually, then everything you do, build, or create is in serious jeopardy of being stolen. It is the principle of KUJICHAGULIA or Self-determination in action: "To define ourselves, name ourselves, create for ourselves, and speak for ourselves, without being spoken for by others." Dr. M. Karenga, the Nguzo Saba. We utilized the Kujichagulia principle of Self- determination, because Afrakan people must no longer allow themselves to be "enslaved" by the Worldview of others. We must assume responsibility for our own racial integrity. This integrity is the basis for Kupigana Ngumi and the development of Spiritual Warriors.

Ancient Kemet Ahau, Afrakan Warriors of ancient Kemet, Old Period, 1500 B.C.E. or 2740 S.T.

Afraka, The Original Birthplace and Home of Martial Science

The origins of the Spiritual Warrior along with its sciences, art, and spiritual philosophy are steeped deep in ancient Afrakan antiquity. These great warrior skills, philosophy and sciences stem from ancient nations from the interior of Afraka: the Zhing and Ta Khuy Empire which surrounded the great lakes region of Lake Nwanza, present day Tanzania, Kenya, Uganda, Burundi, Rwanda, the Congo, Malawi and Mozambique. Marcus Garvey got the idea of the red, black and green Flag from the Zhing Empire. There was also the great Empire of Kash, which stretched from Sudan up to the Sahara, to Ethiopia, across the Red Sea into Arabia, and India. Ta-Sety (land of the bow) located in northern or Lower Kash at present-day Qustul, in the Sudan, where great Afrakan warriors were known for their military skills with the use of the bow and arrow far into antiquity.

More than 5,000 years before the Nswt Narmer and Aha united Upper and Lower Kemet into one nation called Kemet, the Black Community, this area was considered a colony of ancient Kash. The royal family headed by the Nswt (ruler from the south where the swt plant grows) and Nswt Hmt Wrt (the great royal wife) was already in place along with a system of worship of the Ntchru and sacred laws of governance, temple building and a military Army and Navy to protect the Empire. The fighting sciences were only a small fragment of the total knowledge that each student of the Kash universities and temples had to master. This was the greatness that the Kemetyu of Kemet was to later inherit.

The Kashites built the famous statue Heru em Akhet, Neb Hu, mis-labeled the Great Sphinx, when Kemet was just a colony of Kash. The sciences of math, astronomy, astrology, masonry, engineering and writing were already ancient in Afraka during the building of this great monument of mental, physical and spiritual mastery. These Afrakan sciences were all developed pre-flood, before the last ice age melted or pre-Wazungu (the Caucasian Euroasiatics). In the book "**Wonderful Ethiopians of the Ancient Cushite Empire**" by Drusilla Dunjee Houston, informs us that

the Kashite warriors who later became the cornerstone of Mediterranean and Oriental mythologies such as Dionysus, Hercules, Saturn, Asr, Zeus and Apollo were in fact Kashite kings of the pre-Eurasia historical ages.

The Afrakan warriors of central-east and northeast Afraka of ancient Kash, and much later Kemet, became the prototype of all ancient and modern Spiritual Warriors. The Spiritual Warrior was not just a great fighter and military person but a well rounded, mentally, physically and spiritually complete individual.

The Warrior Priests that were later recorded in the legends of the famous Shaolin monks, Buddhist monks, Ninjas, Samurai Warriors of Asia and all their spiritual temples that taught the fighting arts as a science, even the knights of the round table in Europe, can also trace their attributes of the warrior priest to examples from Kemet and Kash.

The oldest records written or illustrated of warriors in training as a military science is in Kemet. These records were recorded around 2,800 B.C.E. or 1,440 S.T. during the Middle Period of ancient Kemet in the province or spt of Mahez, the providence of the antelope.

At Mahez (present day Beni Hassan in Egypt) are large murals or wall painting in several time capsules or tombs. These are the earliest known findings of empty hand combat instruction in the world. It is to date, the most important of Afraka's great martial arts legacies. On the walls in these time capsules are thousands of separate drawings of Black Afrakan fighters executing hand to hand combat, Nuba wrestling, grappling techniques, weapon training, navy strategies, and military techniques for protecting and destroying a castle complex. Yes, castles. In the book Nuba Wrestling, The Original Art, by Nijel Binns, he clearly illustrates ancient castles from Ta-Sety even before the unification of Kemet by The Nswt Narmer and Aha. Brother Nijel illustrates beautifully castles and fortresses in Kemet and Kash from the Second Golden Age in Kemet, around 2,800 B.C.E. or 1,440 S.T. from the time capsules of three high officials: Baqet lll, Khety, and Amenemhat.

TEMPLES, FORTRESSES, AND CASTLES EXISTED IN AFRAKA, ANCIENT KASH AND KEMET BEFORE EURASIA

Illustrated by Nijel Binns

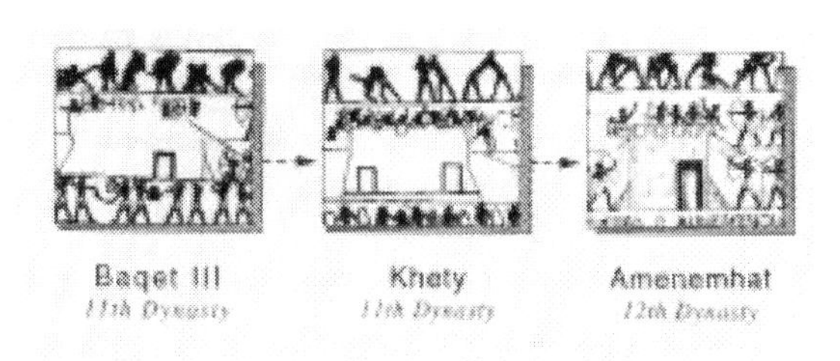

Detailed section of Amenemhat's Time-capsule

A. Kash wrestlers as they were drawn over 2,800 B.C.E. or 1,440 S.T., they are all Afrakan.

B. Modern pen & ink version by the European Perry Newberry, attempts to make it appear that these are Black and white wrestlers, however there were only Black Afrakan wrestlers in all the time capsules.

C. Kash archers in clearly identifiable castle.

D. Two warriors covered by a testudo, and using a long range lance to attack the opponent 2,500 years before the Romans.

Seal found in Siali showing the sign for "Ta-Sety" " Land of the bow." This is an Afrakan Nswt, Shemsu Heru, hundreds of years before Aha and the so-called first Dynasty of ancient Kemet.

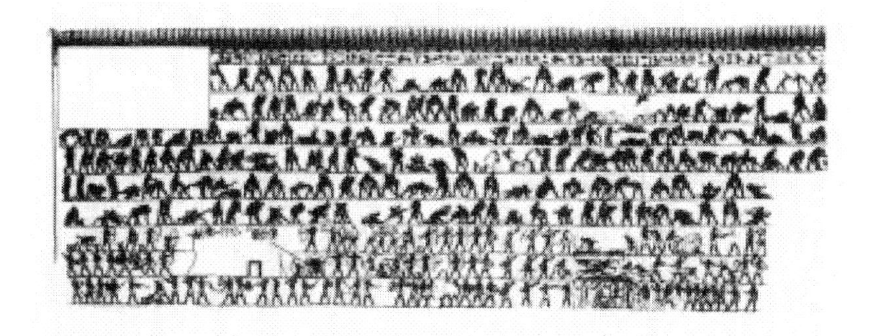

Baqet's time capsule contains 227 wrestling figures, below, Khety's time capsule contains 221 infantry men, archers, and the siege of an Afrakan castle.

Since the date of the paintings inside the time capsules of wrestling illustrations at Mahez are from about 2,800 B.C,E. or 1,440 S.T., this predates the Greek Olympics (776 B.C.E.) by over two thousand years, it is certain that western wrestling began its tradition with the Greeks, most of whom received their training in Kemet and Kash.

These are Kash warriors from the Middle Period of ancient Kash, the most famous Bow men in the world.

The Black Afrakan armies of the Hapy Valley were considered the most formidable of ancient times. Taharqa was one of the great Nswtu of Kemet in the Fourth Golden Peroid, the so-called 25th Dynasty of Kashite rulership who held great warrior competitions. Afrakan warriors ran 30 miles through the Nubian desert at night and this took five hours to complete. Taharqa followed his warriors on horseback and was so pleased with their performance that he rewarded every one who completed the journey. Taharqa saw no winners and losers only victorious warriors in his contest. These are the ancestors of the east Afrakan runners that dominate the marathon and all the long distance races worldwide today.

The warrior tradition and military knowledge from Ta-Sety, Kemet and Kash that spread into Arabia, which once was also a colony of Kash allowed the Moors who are the descendants of the Kemetyu, to occupy Spain and parts of Southern Europe for more than 700 years.

Above, is a photo of two finely detailed wooden models of soldiers from the tomb of Mesehti at Asyut. Buried around 2,000 B.C.E. or 2240 S.T,, they represent 40 strong detachments of Kemetyu spearmen from Kemet and Kemetyu archers from Kash. It is clear that the people of the Hapy valley, northeast Afraka made no racial difference between Kemet and Kash, only a political national difference, they were both Black Afrakan people.

Mfundishi Jhutyms El-Salim with Spiritual Warrior Bro. Runoko Rashidi. Bro Rashidi is an Afrakan research Ourstorian, specializing on the study of Afrakans in the Diaspora, like Asia and also the Hapy Valley, northeast Afraka.

Aha Kmtu (Kemet Warriors) Navy ground soldiers and wreslting techniques from Mahez, ancient Kemet, Middle Period, ancient Kemet 2800 B.C. E. or 1380 S.T. .

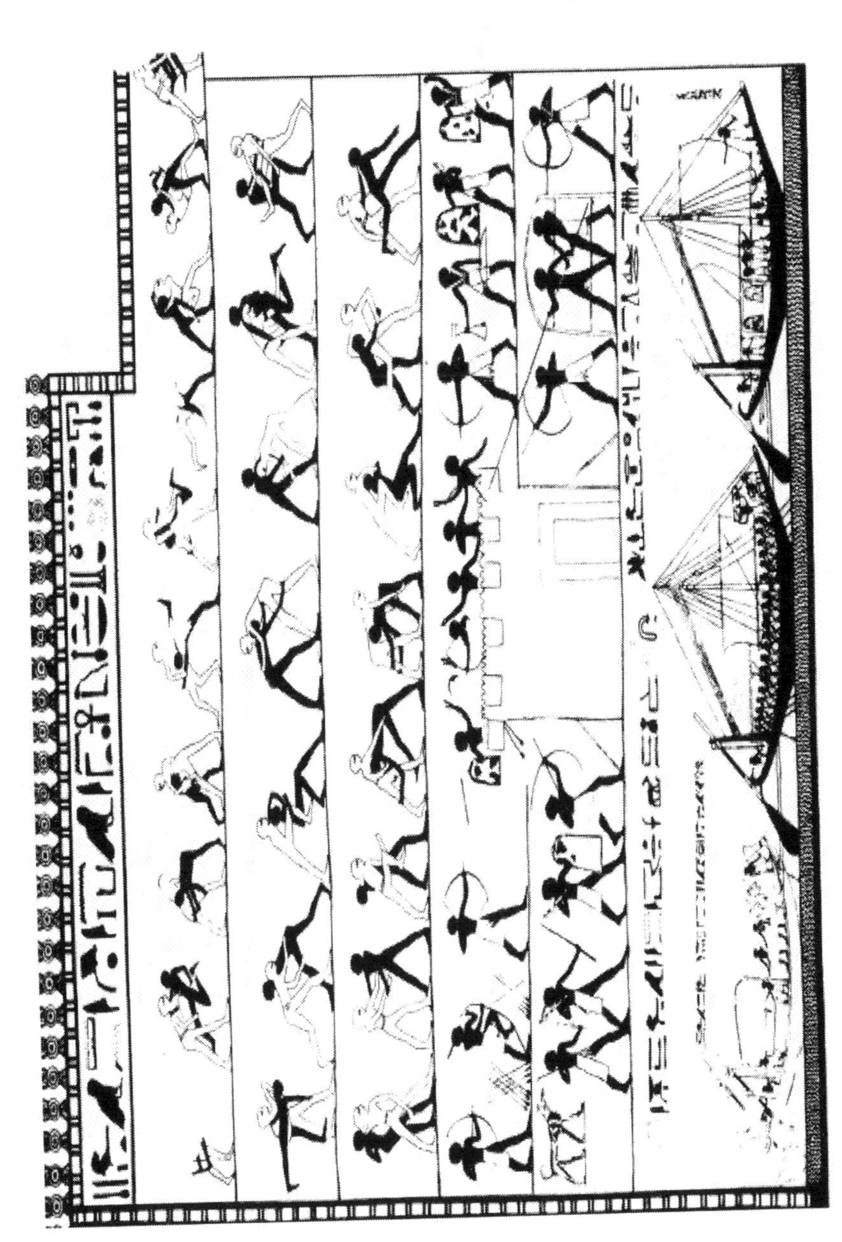

Middle Period, ancient Kemet 2800 B.C. E. or 1380 S.T.

Middle Period, ancient Kemet 2800 B.C. E. or 1380 S.T.

Aha Kmtu (Black Warriors) performing stick fighting, wrestling, boxing and grappling techniques at ceremonial games during Middle Period, ancient Kemet 2800 B.C. E. or 1380 S.T.

Aha Kmtu at Mahez, ancient Kemet demonstrating an Afrakan Navy as well as hand to hand combat, weaponry and the defense of an Afrakan castle, Middle Period, ancient Kemet 2800 B.C. E. or 1380 S.T. .

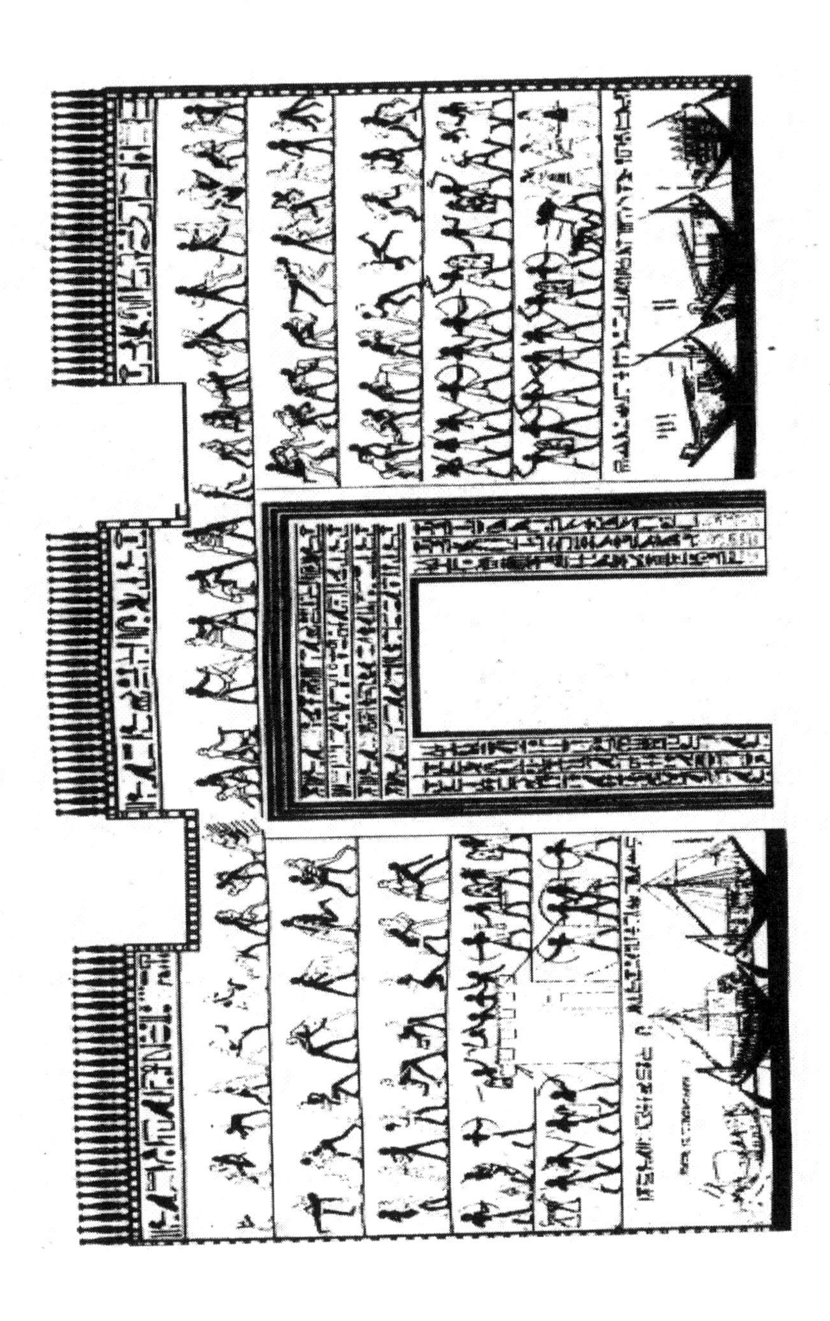

Kupigana Ngumi warriors from ancient Kemet, Middle Period at Mahez, Kemet. (Wrestling, grappling, and weaponry)

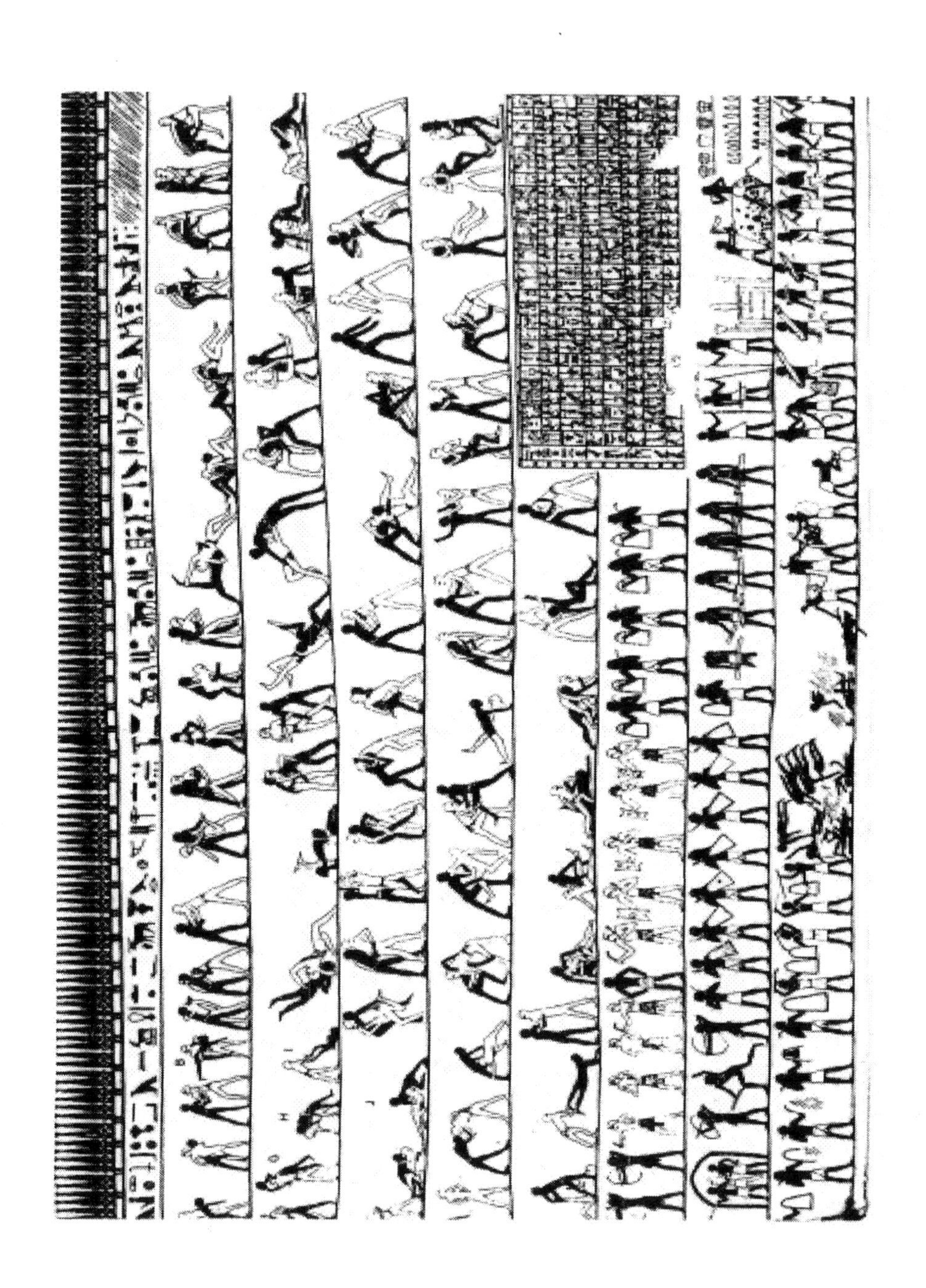

Kupigana Ngumi warriors from ancient Kemet, Middle Period at Mahez, Kemet. (Wrestling, grappling, and weaponry) , ancient Kemet 2800 B.C. E. or 1380 S.T.

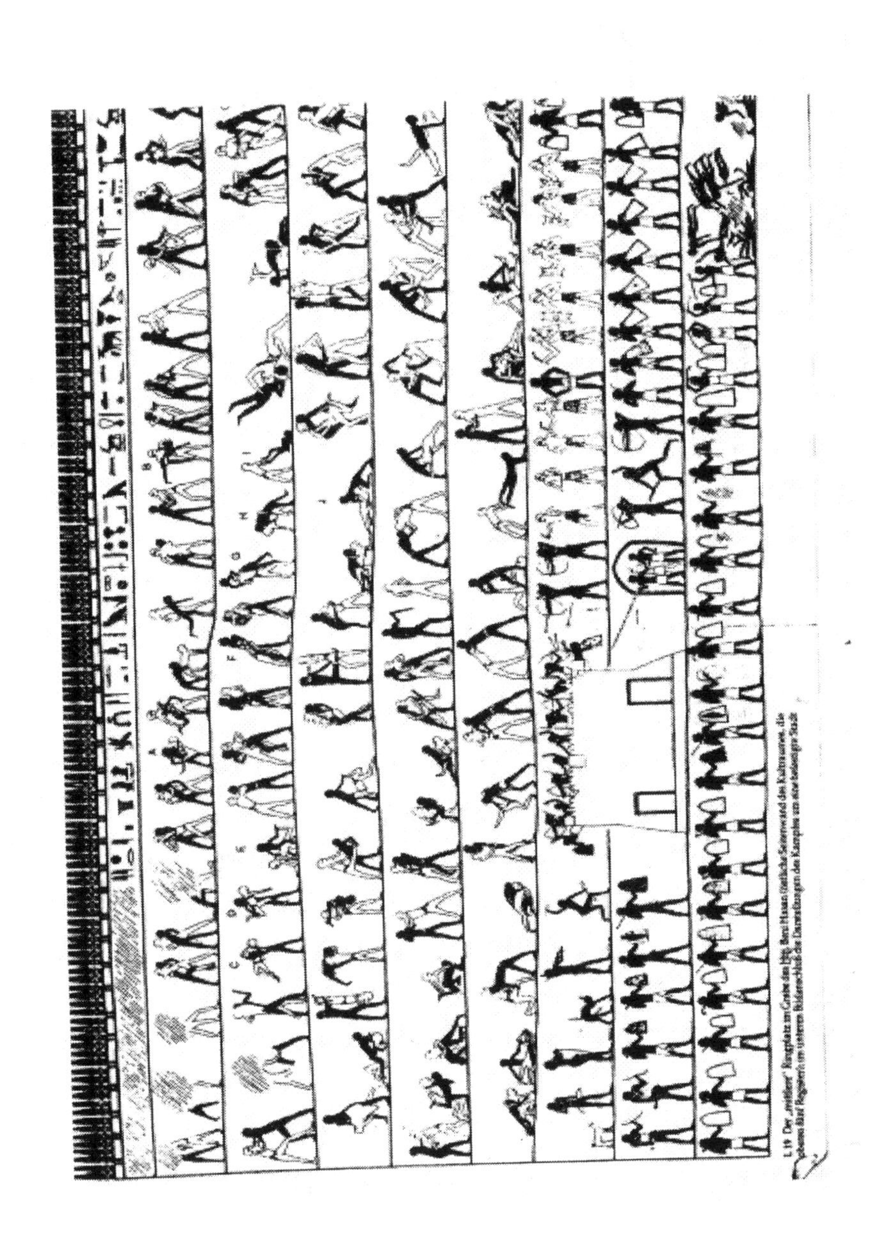

Baqet III's Time Capsule, East Wall. Middle Period, Mahez, Ancient Kemet. Contains 227 Afrakan wrestling figures, infantry men and archers, as well as a siege of an Afrakan castle.

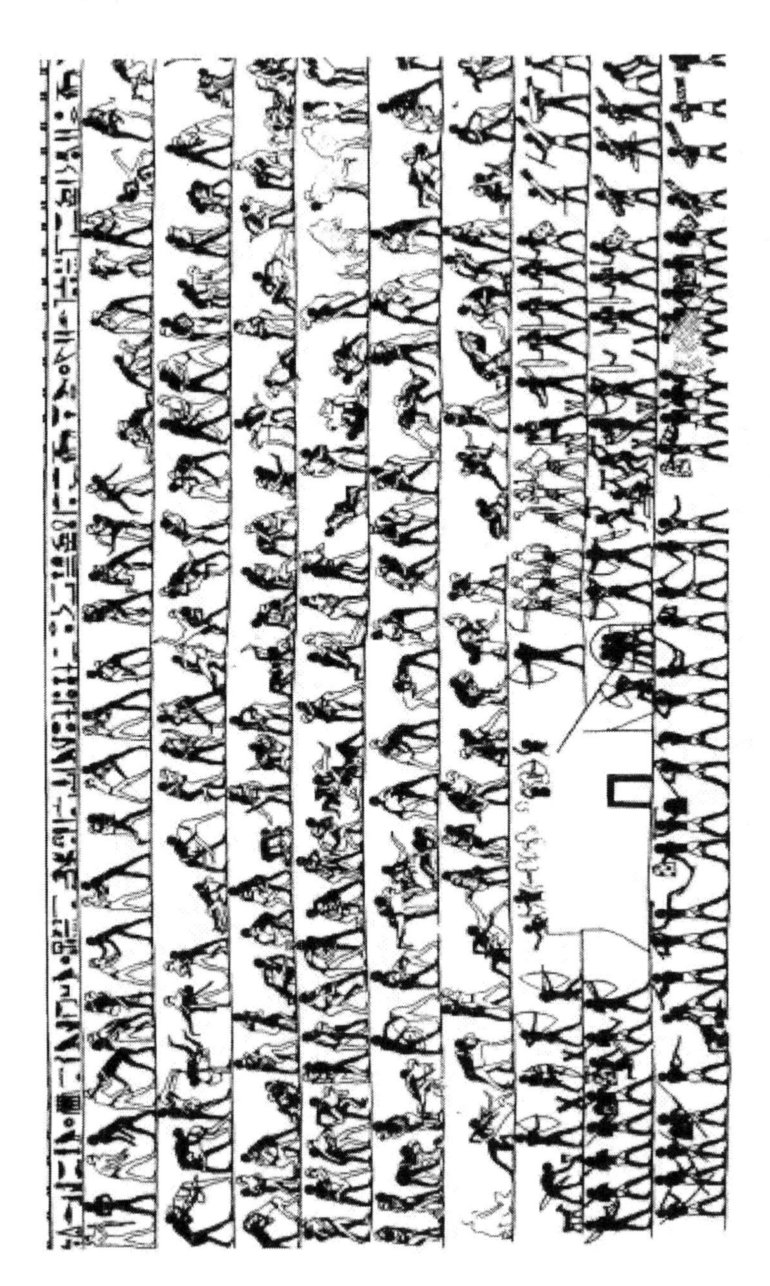

Baqet III's Time Capsule, continuation of the East Wall. Middle Period, Mahez, Ancient Kemet. Contains 227 Afrakan wrestling figures, infantry men and archers, as well a siege of an Afrakan castle.

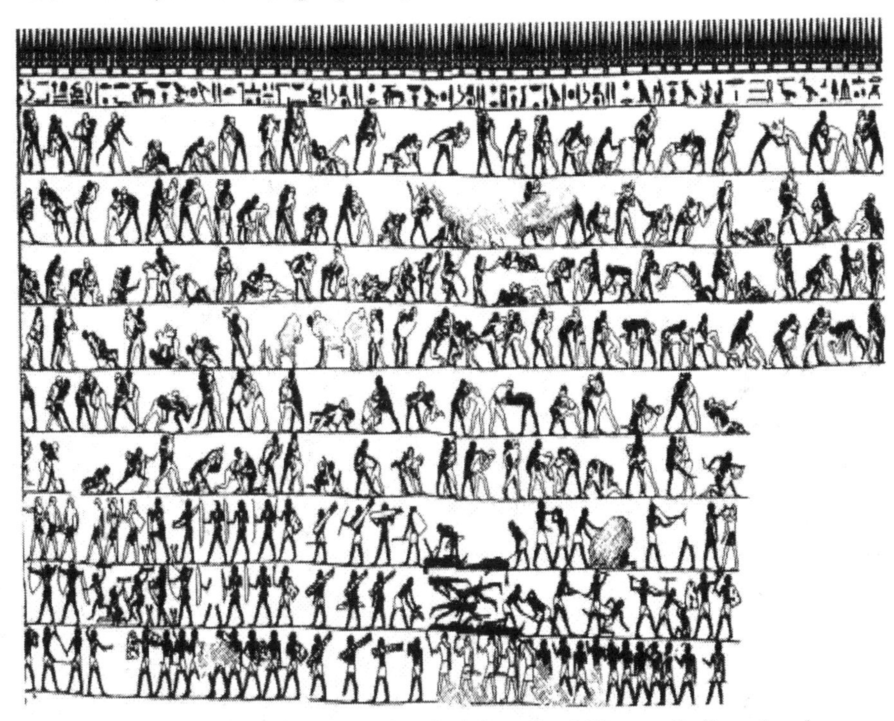

Below is Mfundishi Salim at Mahez (Modern Beni Hassan in Egypt), where the above freezes and all the wrestling and warrior freezes were found.

The wall-paintings at Mahez (Beni Hassan), Kemet and the wrestling freezes from the Tomb of Hotep Ptah in Sakkar, the First Golden Period, the so-called 5th dynasty shows that almost every hold and throw known to modern wrestlers was known to the Kemetyu 4,500 years before our common era.

Open hand, close hands, grappling, throwing, wrestling and weaponry was emphasized in training soldiers during their military service in Ancient Kemet and Kash.

Above, stick fighters atop a cabin, tomb of Khons ll, 31 the Third Golden Period, eighteenth dyn. Wrestlers and stick fighters before the statue of Jhutymes, Tomb of Amenmes, TT 19, so-called nineteenth dynasty

Above, wrestlers and stick fighters in competition beneath the audience window of User maarRa MeryAmum (Ramesses lll), Medinet Habu, also New Period.

Ancient Afraka gave birth to many Warrior Societies: the Bambara and Mandika of west Afraka, the Maasi of east Afraka, the Zulu of southern Afraka and the Nuba wrestlers of Kash, and the Medjay Warriors of north Afraka to name only a few. Ourstory teaches us that the warriors of Segu, from central west Afraka lived by a code of valor and honor equal to that of the Samurai of Japan. However, we are only presented with the image of "Tarzan" single-handedly defeating armies of confused, fearful savages. Clearly, this is indicative of the point of view many of us have of ourselves to this very day. Living on a steady diet of such negative propaganda has caused many Afrakans in the Americas to look to others for protection, inspiration and excellence. We are told that Black youth are facing a crisis in identity. Is it just possible that the seeds of confusion were sown via the constant exposure to negative information concerning the Afrakan persona? It is also obvious that any attempt at Self-determination on the part of Afrakan people in America, is looked upon as being subversive and unpatriotic, remember the **Black Panther Party For Self-Defense**? We are even told not to use our own judgment in determining the sincerity of Black Leadership, but rather to adopt the views of so-called "fact finders." However, with the power of an Afrakan-centered Worldview at our fingertips we begin to see world history in a new light. In this light, the fantasies, excuses, fabrications and straight up lies heretofore to accepted as historical fact, are seen as rationalizations for the exploitation of the Afrakan continent and Afrakan people throughout the Diaspora and nothing more.

We now know that Chaka, the Great Zulu King, developed one of the most unique military strategies of all times, and the Zulu nation fell upon both the Dutch, Boers and English invaders with a unique genius in military history. It took the might of Europe and the British Navy to finally eliminate his military presence in South Afraka with false treaties and trickery. They, the Caucasian European, were only victorious because of superior destructive war technology, like the Gatling gun, invented in America in 1818. What is usually unknown is that Chaka Zulu's concepts are still studied at the U.S. Military Academy at West Point and in Eurasia today, along with the military tactics of Hannibal Barka of Carthage and Queen Nzinga of MbandeNdongo and Matamba.

We speak of the Burmese-British Wars of 6064 S.T. - 6123 S.T. (1824 C.E. -1883 C.E.), and the Japanese resistance to the attempted Mongolian invasion in 5514 S.T. (1274 C.E.), as being historic testimony of bravery and tenacity in the war for Self- determination. However, no mention is made of the Maroons, descendents of West Afrakan Warriors living in Jamaica who fought and defeated the British, eventually making them sign a treaty in 5895 S.T. (1655 C.E.). The Spanish or the British never defeated the maroons. They fought with inferior weapons, but with superior spirit. This is the Spirit invoked in Kupigana Ngumi. Furthermore, no mention is made of the Afrakans in Haiti who under the leadership of Bookman, Toussaint and Dessalines, defeated the French Army under Napoleon. Again, no mention is made of the Si Mo Society of West Afraka, who for centuries remained the soul of the Baga fighting legions. The Priests of this society accompanied the Baga armies into battle and were themselves fierce warriors. To this day, this society restricts its initiates to the confines of a chosen few families and remains a secret society. The novice warrior endured the initiation known as "the strengthening of the will" which included hunger, thirst and exposure to the elements and much more. And of course, there are the magnificent warriors of the Akan nation, under the Ashanti people, who courageously fought the Dutch and the British until the 20th century. The Ashanti were never defeated on the battlefield. Only through the deceit of European negotiations they finally fell. The great Soninke Warriors, warriors of ancient west Afraka, present day Ghana, knew how to make iron in 4540 S.T. (300 C.E.), and were the best swordsmen in all of north and west Afraka. They were also never conquered from outside forces, from 4540 S.T. (300 C.E.) to 5240 S.T. (1000 C.E.). There was also the Matamba Warriors who fought and defeated the Portuguese slave traders for nearly 30 years, forcing the badly beaten Portuguese to negotiate a treaty in 5896 S.T. (1656 C.E.). These are just a fraction of the facts previously hidden and usually never exposed in this miseducational system of Europeam Caucasian domination. Kupigana Ngumi is the adopted term for the collective fighting arts of the entire Afrakan continent. Kupigana Ngumi takes on the essence of those ancient Afrakan principles of spiritual and physical harmony, which gave birth to all martial arts and forms of yoga and meditation.

Conditions That Lead to The Maangamizi

All the conditions that lead to the Maangamizi (the deliberate destruction of Afraka, its people and their Kulture) still exist today. Through intense and thorough physical, mental and spiritual investigation we must consider these seven factors:

1. The dismantling of the Afrakan family structure.
2. The disruption of the practice of spiritual traditions.
3. The enforced non-use of ethnic Afrakan Languages.
4. The lost, Ourstorical map of our past greatness and connection to our Afrakan Ancestors.
5. The dismantling of our defense systems, so we could not protect ourselves under European invasions, mentally or physically.
6. Control over Afrakan peoples' educational system and standards of beauty and excellence.
7. The control of production and distribution of our food supplies, housing and transportation.

These seven elements constitute the basis of a peoples' Kulture. Due to the systematic destruction of these vital elements during the enslavement of Afrakan people, much of what is to this day treasured by all independent ethnic groups was lost or stolen from the Afrakans in the Diaspora, and to some extent on the continent itself.

Using the all seeing eye of Heru or Heru Konsciousness, it becomes clear what we must do, as Afrakan Spiritual Warriors, to reverse this crippling effect. This devastation has put Afrakan people in a state of backwardness on the entire Afrakan continent, and its families throughout the Diaspora. We must take each of these seven steps and reverse, mend and heal them. Then we must create a strong defense system within our Afrakan Kulture, which will make sure that this will never happen again.

These seven factors have been covered in Chapter 8 in depth, dealing with the New Afrakan Kulture and re-Afrakanization, but the problem is so severe that we will highlight these particular factors again.

1. The Dismantling of the Afrakan Family Structure

The Afrakan concept of family includes children, parents, grandparents, uncles, aunts, brothers, sisters, as well as departed relatives and the unborn. In addition, each group has its own social and political organization. To be removed from the family was equal to death, and there must be serious consequences for betrayal of the family or a family member. Spiritual Warriors must teach us how to heal our families and to eliminate all traders and uncle toms and "aunt jamamas."

2. The Disruption of the Practice of Spiritual Traditions

With regard to spiritual practices, we must be made aware that religion accompanies the Afrakan from before birth to long after death. To be without spiritual practice amounts to excommunication from the entire society. The spiritual practice of Afrakans must embrace The NTCHR as the ALL. In addition, we must innerstand that we are Divine, we were not born in sin, and our Afrakan Kulture helps us maintain our divinity. This also means that Afraka is the Holy Land for Afrakan people, and we must treat our continent and Afrakan people and all of nature with the ultimate respect and reverence. Afrakan people must re-evaluate our relationship with Christianity, Judaism and Islam and reclaim our own Afrakan Spiritual systems using logic and reason.

3. The Enforced Non-use of Ethnic Afrakan Languages

Language is the best medium of communication for innerstanding a Kulture and preserving of Kulture. Afrakan Ourstory was lost with the forced stripping of our Afrakan languages. Many of our Afrakan oral folklore traditions could not be transmitted from generation to generation. This dekulturalization process removed Afrakans from the flow of kultural practice and placed them in Kultural shock, to say the least. We must re-learn our Afrakan tongues and Afrakan scripts, like the Mdw Ntchr, Wolof, Asante Twi, Mandinka, Yoruba, Ibo, and Kiswahili and use them in our families, schools, spiritual services, rituals, and in our own businesses and institutions. If you do not use what you have, you will lose it, or some one else will steal it and claim it for themselves. (In all the Museums in Europe and America or the western world, Egypt has been taken out of Afraka and placed somewhere in the middle east, wherever that is. We must challenge all these lies.)

4. The Lost, Ourstorical Map of Our Past Greatness and Connection to Our Afrakan Ancestors

Our Afrakan story is our legacy and lifeline. It is the Kultural map of where we are, where we have been and where we are going collectively as a people. Once your Ourstorical roots are removed, you destroy yourself. We must build new institutions that glorify and tell the true story of our great ancestors in all the fields that define us in the world community in economics, politics, defense, technology, science, communication, transportation, and agrikulture. We must build universities that are Afrakan-centered, and whose only purpose is to wholistically develop and re-Afrakanize Afrakan men and women for self-reliance.

5. The Dismantling of Our Defense System, so We Could Not Protect Ourselves Under European Invasion

A people who cannot defend themselves are a doomed people. **To develop something and not be able to defend it, is like not having it at all.** The Europeans and European-Americans have destroyed or greatly distorted Afrakan Kulture. Only Afrakans can rebuild it and defend it. Kupigana Ngumi is a key in the defense of self, family and nation. Ma'at Akhw Ba Ankh must be embraced by the whole family, so we can regain our focus on Ma'at, and have the discipline to do what we must do for survival and flourishing as an Afrakan people in the 21st century. Afrakan people must have a defense force in every Black community to protect

Afrakans and defend our best interest wherever we are in the world, especially here in Amerikkka.

6. <u>The Control of Production and Distribution of Our Food Supplies.</u>

A people who cannot feed themselves by nature will be slaves and dependent on those who control their food source. Afrakans throughout the Diaspora must seize control of the production of our own wholistic food source. We must grow and produce the types of foods that are the best for Afrakan people. We must also seize control of our own transportation and the buildings of our own housing and communities. We must support this with our minds, bodies, souls, and economic strength and remain in total control of distribution and production.

7. <u>Control over Afrakan Peoples' Educational System and Standards.</u>

Europeans have taken control of our education or our miseducation, as one of their first steps in colonization, along with giving Afrakans their European version of religion. We must develop independent educational institutions that are Afrakan-centered. If we cannot kemtrol the minds of our children, we will not have a future. We, as Afrakans, must redefine education from an Afrakan-centered perspective, and not imitate Europeans, by just adding a Black history section to a system that has meant death and destruction to Afrakan people.

Afrakan Spiritual Warriors are the inheritors of the ancient science of human development by way of body-mind-spirit discipline. As such, we must re-kindle the spirit of the sacred lineage handed down to us over these many centuries. "We must concern ourselves with the overriding importance of Kulture and lineage," Mfundishi Maasi.

The Way of the Warrior

Martial Arts or the protective sciences were developed in Afraka many thousands of years ago. The way of the warrior was developed along with the domestication of animals and the development of agrikulture. It was first created out of the necessity to defend livestock from predatory animals, and later to defend against invaders attempting to seize their grazing land, livestock, or crops. Since Afrakan people were the first to create civilized societies of herding and farming, it is only natural that they developed the first *Martial Arts* systems to defend these civilizations.

All Afrakan Kultures were rooted in nature. Therefore, the warrior sciences developed in Afraka were based upon being in harmony with nature. Afrakan warriors replicated the movements of the best fighters in the animal world, as well as the movement of celestial bodies in their orbits. Not only could Afrakan warriors replicate the movements of animals, they actually took on the spirit and sometimes transformed into the animals. Afrakan warriors did not separate the physical aspect of combat from the mental and spiritual realms. Through the use of sacred music, dance, invocations, herbs, talisman, communion with the ancestors, and the forces of nature, they were able to create warriors unmatched by any other martial artists or at least equal to the very best on the planet in skill, strength, or bravery.

Afrakan warriors were highly skilled in both empty hand and armed combat. The time capsules called tombs of ancient warriors found in Mahez (present day Beni Hassan), ancient Kemet reveal the sophisticated grappling system that our Afrakan ancestors developed and is still using in many parts of West Afraka today. Our ancestors also mastered a wide array of weapons including the spear, staff, mace, sword, bow and arrows, blowguns, various knives and swords, poisons, claws, and much more. Afrakan warriors combined sorcery, weaponry, and unarmed fighting to produce the most sophisticated martial arts to ever exist. These Afrakan systems existed while Eurasia was still in a barbaric and savage state.

Traditionally, you had to be initiated into the warrior societies of a village to learn the sacred martial sciences. Today, here in America, there are Afrakan masters who make available to you ***The Way of the Warrior.***

The Way of the Warrior is the Way of Heru. Afrakan legend tells us that Heru was the righteous warrior who did battle against the principle of esfet (Set). Heru was the avenger of the wrongs done to his mother and father and the Ma'atian way. He was the Uniter of his father's kingdom, and the protector of the sacred, harmonious balance of nature, Ma'at. The Way of the Warrior then is about defending all of our Afrakan mothers and fathers, the elders (Wazee), and any others unable to defend themselves. It is about protecting the sovereignty of the home, village, or nation. One of the greatest roles of the warrior within a society is also to protect nature from the destructive ways of the ungrateful parasites on the planet. The warrior's sole task is to bring order where there is disorder. The warriors' struggle for order starts within, and then projects itself onto the outside world. The warrior must epitomize that which he fights to maintain. The warrior must constantly battle within to maintain harmony and righteousness. The warrior must, in the face of fear and danger, do whatever is necessary to bring back harmonious balance and order (Ma'at). The warrior must detach himself or herself from fear, pain and emotions in order to carry out what is necessary in battle. In this task, the warrior can leave no room for negligence, and no room for surrender.

The greatest warriors refuse to lose. Knowing that death lurks around every corner, the Spiritual Warrior takes on every challenge as if it is his or her last and greatest battle. The Spiritual Warrior holds back nothing for tomorrow. Spiritual Warriors must have so much confidence in their personal power, and faith in the righteousness of their struggle, that they win every battle before it is fought. Using the simple formula of evaluation, preparation, and execution that has come to them through the spirits of great warriors who now reside in the realm of the ancestors, warriors become unconquerable. This attitude takes you beyond the normal limits, making you more powerful each time you overcome your enemies: internally, externally, mentally, physically or spiritually.

Afrakan Spiritual Warriors must learn from our glorious Ourstorical experience that if the Wazungu (melanin deficient Europeans and their descendents in the Diaspora) want to sign a treaty with you, then you are winning, so keep fighting to the end or until they surrender. Then we can dictate and define our own reality from an Afrakan Center. Every treaty the Wazungu in Europe or America has signed with melanin people they have lied and broken their promise. **A treaty to them is a way of buying time to regroup so that they can get the upper hand to destroy you**. According to the ancient Greeks, Romans and even Napoleon and George Washington, "History is the lie agreed upon." As Afrakan Spiritual Warriors, we must re-evaluate our own formula of evaluation, preparation before dynamic action. Moreover, if we do this with a critical eye, we would see each time that we confronted the Eurasians, we underestimated their lack of humanity, their lack of respect for the Ntchru or NTCHR. We never really knew who they were, and therefore we never really innerstood the level of esfet we were dealing with.

Spiritual Warriors, we have learned much from our glorious past, and now it is time for dynamic action! We must use the spirit of our Sankofa Spirits for liberation and salvation. We are at War! However, this war is not to conquer other lands, or to conquer other people, but a war to liberate our minds from white male domination! It is a war to protect the Afrakan nation against chaos and esfet, to protect the Afrakan community and its nation building Institutions from esfet, to protect Afrakan families and individuals from esfet. So the Spiritual Warrior accomplishes the will of Ma'at by building and protecting the nation, by creating and maintaining the community, by building, creating and maintaining its Nation-building Institutions, by re-creating and strengthening the chaotic disorder of the Afrakan family and by developing a positive atmosphere that is inspirational for all Afrakans to grow, dream and follow their visions and missions.

Opposite page shows Kupigana Ngumi Instructors, standing (left to right): Mfundishi K. Vita (Atlanta), Mfundishi Jhutyms El-Salim (New York & New Jersey), Nana Kweku Sakyi (Bono Priest, Miami), Mfundishi Olafemi (Chicago), Malenga Ohave (Damona, Israel). Sitting (left to right): Mfundishi Tayari Casel (Maryland), Nganga Mfundishi Tolo-Naa (Milwaukee), Mfundshi Russ Meeks (Chicago), Ahati Kilindi Iyi (Detroit).

Mfundishi Jhutyms Ka n Heru El-Salim and Malenga Khalid Maasi who was setting in for his father, the Shaha Mfundishi Maasi at a meeting of the Afrakan Masters in New York City the eve of the Million Man March at Washington D.C., 1995.

Kupigana Ngumi Ranking System

(from Kera Jhuty Heru Neb-Hu Aha Kemet System)

Unlike the Asian martial arts, there are no multicolored belts worn in Kupigana Ngumi. You can tell a skilled warrior by the way he or she carries himself or herself. The accomplished warrior moves and talks with an evident sense of power. This power is not arrogant, nor domineering: it is the power of one who bears harmonious balance within. Within Kupigana Ngumi, there is recognition of accomplishment. Titles are bestowed upon those who have survived their tests of mental, physical, and spiritual challenges. There are six titles with multiple levels under each title that exists in Kupigana Ngumi. They are Wanafunzi, Mpigana, Dada/Kaka, Mfundi, Malenga and Mfundishi.

Dr. Maulana Karenga introduced the ranks and titles, which are utilized by many of the Kupigana Ngumi practitioners in the Pan-Afrakan Federation, in the mid 1960's. Shaha Mfundishi Maasi was the first Afrakan in America to be bestowed the title of **Mfundishi**. This title was granted as a reward for loyal service and commitment to the cause of Afrakan Liberation and excellence in martial arts.

The second person to receive the title was Mganga Tolo-Naa who has made a number of sacrifices on behalf of Pan-Afrakanism and Martial Art excellence. He has suffered long and hard, and was rewarded by the Shaha Mfundishi in order to show recognition and admiration for the skill and intelligence of this loyal son of Afraka.

The third and fourth persons to receive or be promoted to the rank of Mfundishi were Tayari Casel, root student of the Mganga, and affiliated student of the Shaha. And Jhutyms Ka en Heru Hassan K. Salim, root student of the Shaha Mfundishi Maasi, and affiliated student of The Mganga. The skills learned by the above men, and brothers in the Struggle of Afrakan people to liberate themselves from white male domination are not only in martial arts but also represents the exceptional insight required of one who will one day assume International responsibility for the cause of Pan-Afrakanism. It must be clearly innerstood, that the title symbolizes an introduction to the higher process and not the end results. This determination is based upon the Afrakan principle which states that "a name must be grown into and the attributes manifested over time and trial".

Mwanafunzi is a student of life. All entering initiates have this title, as well as the greatest warriors. For the true warrior forever remains a student of life. Mwanafunzi have an internal battle to fight in order to prepare themselves physically for the challenge of becoming a warrior. They train to develop correct breathing, correct focus, and correct posture. They have nine challenges to overcome in order to be promoted. (See first level student, Mwanafunzi page.)

Mpigana is one who practices **Kupigana Ngumi**. In the Shrines of Jhuty Heru Neb Hu, in the East Coast Shule, there are two levels of Mpigana (Mpigana moja & Mpigana mbili). There are nine new challenges on each level of Mpigana dealing with the foundation of warriorship. The Mpigana begins to develop techniques of interpersonal combat. They also begin to temper their bodies, minds, and spirits to be able to handle combat. (See second and third level student, Mpigana page)

Dada, Elder sister, **Kaka** Elder brother, are intermediate level students. By this time, they have a good mastery of the physical aspects of combat, are skilled in some weaponry, and are now striving to master the mental and spiritual aspects of a warrior. They must now gain a mastery of the Afrakan Ourstory, language, Kulture, and spiritual philosophy of their Afrakan ancestor's rituals. (See fourth level student, Kaka or Dada page).

Mfundi means master craftsman. An Mfundi is an advanced initiate. There are in most schools or shule at least three levels of the Mfundi. There is a saying in Kupigana Ngumi, "If you drop an Mfundi in the middle of the desert, when you come back a year later there will be a thriving civilization." An Mfundi has a good grasp of the mental, physical, and spiritual aspects of being a warrior. It is on this level that one can truly call themselves a warrior. It is on this level that the warrior is constantly being called into service. The Mfundi is the active warrior who has taken on the way of Heru. (See fifth level student, Mfundi page.) The Mfundi must be an active teacher for at least 10 years for recommendation for Malenga. The rank of Mfundi will be probationary for three (3) years from the date of promotion.

Malenga is a mental, physical and *Spiritual Master.* A Malenga is one moving beyond the physical battle, into the spiritual realm. They spend less time dealing with earthly wars. They are on the road to becoming a Priest Scientist. A Malenga is a master teacher. There are three levels of Malenga in the Shrine of Jhuty Heru Neb Hu Kemetik Shule. These Warriors are the Captains, Lieutenants and Generals; they must be strong in order for the system to be strong. Members of this group may be recommended for the intelligence agency and strategy center along with the Mfundishi. A Malenga must have at least 10 years of experience as a master teacher and a community activist, before a recommendation can be made for Mfundishi. The rank of Malenga will be probationary for three (3) years from the date of promotion.

Mfundishi is the Grand Master Priest Scientist. One who no longer needs to fight on the physical level. They can easily overcome challenges with little or no physical effort. They are the wisdom keepers. They are the vessels that contain the knowledge of great past warriors. They are the ones closest to the realm of the Ancestors, and therefore have the greatest access to it. These Warriors are your Generals, Majors and Chiefs. The rank of Mfundishi will be probationary for three (3) years from the date of promotion. With regard to the title of Mfundishi, holders of the title must have attained the age of at least fifty (50) years of age by the end of the probationary period for the purpose of entering the council of elders. (This is a traditional requirement and will not be subject to deviation.)

There are several active Wafundishi or Afrakan Grand masters in America: **Shaha Mfundishi** Maasi, **Nganga Mfundishi** Tolo-Naa, **Mfundishi** Jhutyms Ka en Heru Hassan Kamau Salim, **Mfundishi**

Olafemi A. Watangulizi, **Ahati** Kilindi Iyi, **Akan Priest** Baba Kwame Ishangi, **Mfundishi** Tayari Casel, **Mfundishi** Bakari Kulinda, **Mfundishi** Khalil Maasi, **Mfundishi** Akili Alleyne, **Mfundishi** Denise Brown, **Nana** Porter, and **Mfundishi** Kijana Vita, Plus several honorary title has been granted to a few long term masters in the Afrakan struggle, one is brother Russ Meeks and several other great Afrakan community leaders for their long standing service to the Afrakan community. However, it must be clearly innerstood that this is strictly honorary and carries neither authority or official responsibility.

Reviews will be held yearly at a National Kupigana Ngumi Retreat and certified by The Grand Council of Wafundishi or the Mfundishi in charge. The following infractions will be deemed sufficient to deny certification:

1. Insufficient knowledge of Afrakan Ourstory.

2. Insufficient knowledge of Afrakan Traditions.

3. Insufficient knowledge of key Afrakan Spiritual Principles.

4. Insufficient knowledge of Ourstory of Kupigana Ngumi and the Afrakan Martial Arts.

5. Insufficient knowledge of Afrakan Martial Literacy and language.

6. Insufficient knowledge and application of "Ngumi" skills as determined by the Grand Council or the head Mfundishi in charge.

7. Insubordination (here is a clue: martial equals military and in the military when skills or decorum are not up to par, one is stripped of rank).

The Kupigana Ngumi MFUNDISHI (Grand Master) is a person of love, action and principles. (*An okra does not show its seeds through its skin.* A man's face does not have to reveal all he knows). The Kemetyu believed that only through the development of the Moyo or Sekhem could a person be one, or in great harmony with the absolute NTCHR. The

Mfundishi is a Spiritual Warrior of discipline, love and focus, which allows their Moyo to be a healing force for Afrakan people. Each of the Grand Masters listed in this book are masters of different Afrakan Systems. The views in this book are the views of Mfundishi Jhutyms Ka en Heru Hassan Kamau Salim, Hem Sem-Tpy (High Spiritual Warrior Priest of Kera Jhuty Heru Neb-Hu), a Kemetik Afrakan Spiritual Society and Grand Masters of "Aha Kemet Wanyama Saba System"-The Black Spiritual Warrior Seven Animal System.

"Aha Kemet Wanyama Saba System"
KUPIGANA NGUMI

Kupigana Ngumi teaches Control and Kemtrol
Control is the mastery of your mind in relationship to nature
Kemtrol is the mastery of your spirit, the ultimate tool of wisdom
With wisdom, one can command their thoughts
When the thoughts are clear so will your speech be clear
When your speech is clear it's like a sharp spear
Powerful motion becomes fluent, and unpredictable
Control and Kemtrol over oneself becomes natural
Only through the mastery of self
Can one be the master of others
Through this mastery,
Self restraint and composure are developed
Htp
When one develops Htp, one becomes reserved
The Kempassionate and reserve warrior is a superior martial artist...

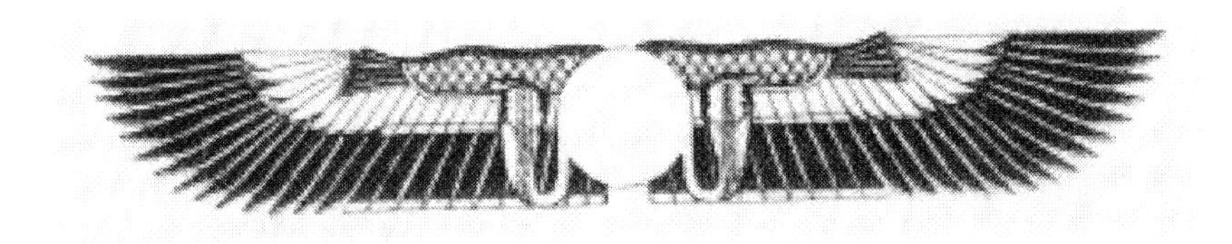

From left to right; Mfundishi Maasi, Mfundishi Talo-Naa, Mfundishi Casel, & Mfundishi El-Salim, The first four Wafundishi at a meeting of the Grand Masters in Washington, DC

Above are wanafunzi Nalani & Shadiyah in the New York shule. Bottom right, Mfundishi Talo-Naa, Mfundishi Jhutyms El-Salim & Malenga Kenny at a Afrakan martials arts retreat in Georgia.

The Nswt M-haty-Amen an Afrakan ruler, represented as a Hem Sem Tpy-priest wearing locks, royal necklace and a leopard skin cloak. From Medinet el-Fayum in Kemet during the Second Great Golden Period, around 1,800 B.C.E .or 2,940 S.T. And right Nswt Taharqa from Kash, who ruled Kemet around 690 B.C.E. or 3,550 S.T. the Fourth Golden Period. These Afrakans were the prototypes of Spiritual Warriors who ruled by example with excellence. These Afrakan rulers were Shemsu Heru.

The following information is taught in some of the Kupigana Ngumi centers around the country within the ranks of Mwanafunzi to Mfundi. For greater clarification consult a Mfundishi, Malenga or Mfundi.

A) **Weapons** (instruments of defense/offense):

1. Major - most well developed instruments ,i.e., fist, fingers, foot, knee, elbow, etc.
2. Secondary- second most well developed instruments (supportive weapon) like the head- butt, or shoulder.
3. Potential- (spontaneous counter offense) for instance, opponent ducks to avoid your punch and in so doing, created an opening for a new blow, like a knee.

B) **Targets** (anatomical weakness):

1. Major- based upon major deficiency of opponent, weakest target of the anatomy, etc. (joints and pressure points).
2. Secondary- second most critical defence.
3. Potential- spontaneous opening created by opponent's attempt to cover primary and secondary lines of attack.

C) **Logistics** (lines and angels of delivery):

1. Short Range- shoulder, elbows, knees, feet, head-butting.
2. Medium Range- striking with hand and feet.
3. Long Range- kicking and leaping techniques.

Note: Each of the above logistical classifications are composed of mainly circular routes of delivery. Three important things must always accompany any Kupigana Ngumi movements: correct breathing, correct focus and correct posture.

D) **13 Major Weapons:**

1. Fist
2. Palm
3. Forearm
4. Elbow
5. Shoulder
6. Hip
7. Knee
8. Fingers
9. Heel
10. Instep
11. Side of foot
12. Sole of foot
13. Head

E) **Major Targets:**

1. Head
2. Neck and Throat
3. Solar-plex and Stomach
4. Spine and Kidney
5. Groin
6. Knees
7. Shins and Calves
8. Ankle, Instep, Toes
9. Elbows
10. Wrist
11. Fingers
12. And all pressure points and joints

F) **6 Major Logistical Examples and 8 Logistical Drills:**

1. Direct- attacking forward (circular when touched) All strikes are quick and circular and all blocks are smooth and circular always conserving energy until the last moment of impact.

2. Withdrawal Attack- striking forward as withdrawing.

3. Lateral Attack- punching, kicking laterally as stepping forward, backward, cross, or side, etc.

4. Circling Attack- delivering blows as spinning, stepping, sliding in a circular manner.

5. Dropping Attack- stepping in any manner with angular or circular blows which descend upon target(s), leaping and jumping also utilized.

6. Rising Attack- delievers circular or angular blows which rise to the target as stepping, sliding etc.

Flexibility Drills- excercises for relaxing the body, releasing trapped energy and increasing the range of motion.

Balance Drills- exercises fordeveloping the ability to maintain control during movement by way of correct body alignment.

Agility Drills- exercises which enable the individual to move with speed and power from any angle.

Coordination Drills - exercises which enable the individual to integrate all the powers and capacities of the mind and body into effective action.

Speed Drills - exercises for learning to focus attention and maintain suitable postures for explosive movement.

Posture Drills - exercises to carry the body in such a way as to minimize wasted motion and wasted energy.

Endurance Drills - hard and continuous exercises for producing respiratory and muscular strength.

Rhythm Drills - exercises designed to develop a sense of timing and momentum.

Take note that in China, the eye of Heru is known as Tai-yih (Tai chi). Additionally, according to Koichi Tohei (a Japanese master): " It is at that point at which a person gives themselves completely to the universe, that universal power pours into the body." Ma'at symbolizes that act of giving oneself to the universe physically, mentally, and spiritually. Specific techniques of utilization regarding Ma'at will be presented in Kupigana Ngumi Federation Training Centers across the country. I will explain just a few postures and techniques in the next few pages.

1. The Ma'at posture represents the first step in the path of self mastery ("I laid the foundation through Ma'at. I created forms of every kind"). Ra's description of Creation.

2. The Ma'at posture symbolizes the harmony of heaven and earth through the human spiritual mind.

3. The Ma'at posture serves as the basis for all subsequent actions (Ma'at Akhw Ba Ankh and Kupigana Ngumi

techniques and principles). The emphasis is placed upon mental tranquility and controlled respiration.

4. The nine elements composing body, mind, and spirit are, in actuality, the life force vibrating at various frequencies under the direction of the mind (Ptah), and corresponding to a nine note musical scale.

And finally, the mastery of Ma'at is the mastery of Moyo or Sekhem, the Ntchru force in all human beings that connects us with the universe.

"The head of a human being is a secret storage place.
The point of power can be found in the present moment.
Thoughts shape your life and experiences.
The way to control your life is to control your choice of words and thoughts.
No one masters your mind but you."

We have learned that for every effect in our lives, there is a thought pattern that precedes and maintains it. Our consistent thinking patterns create our experiences. Therefore, by changing our thinking patterns, we can change our experiences.

In the ancient Kemet Spiritual Systems, there were three grades of students, and we still use the same foundation laid down by our ancient Afrakan ancestors of the Hapy Valley in the Shrine of Jhuty Heru Neb-Hu.

1. The mortals- probationary students who were being instructed, but who had not yet experienced the inner vision. (Mwanafunzi, Mpigana, Dada and Kaka).

2. The intelligences- those who had attained the inner vision and discriminating mind, and have a degree of mastery. (Mfundi, Malenga, Mfundishi),

3. The creators or sons and daughters of light - those who had attained spiritual Konsciousness. (These were the sages, the Mfundishi, the great prophets, and great teachers recorded throughout Ourstory and history.)

The ancient Kemetyu built their temples as replicas of the human body. The Kemet Priest Scientists knew that the same powers present in the universal macrocosm were present in the human's microcosm. Thus, they painted the ceilings of their temples blue to represent the starry Heavens. The walls carried the sacred teachings of the elders, sages and creative priests and priestesses and Sons and Daughters of Light. The doorways faced east to share the light of Ra. Moreover, all statues stepped forward on their left leg, the side of the heart and receiving from The NTCHR. This is noted so that all Spiritual Warriors, regardless of color or ethnic background, know that we must study and digest this wisdom if we are to return Ma'at back to Civilization.

Spiritual Warriors Know Thyself

Spiritual Warriors Know Thyself. This is the fundamental principle of the psychology of Kemet. Every human being is composed of a body-temple, an immortal soul, called the Ba, and the Holy Spirit, called the Ka. The ancient priest and Spiritual Warriors taught that *Self-knowledge* is the basis of all knowledge. The Ancient Spiritual System requires as the first step, the mastery of the passions, which makes room for the occupation of unlimited powers. In the second step, the Mwanafunzi is required to search within him or herself for the new powers, which had taken possession of them. The third step requires a person to become one with the Moyo, the universal power, which connects you with all things. When one attains the power to use the Moyo, through the influence of Ma'at, he or she becomes one with the power of creation, The NTCHR.

In the ancient Kemet Spiritual System, and in the advance levels of Ma'at Akhw Ba Ankh and Kupigana Ngumi, the wanafunzi are required to manifest the following soul attributes:

Soul Attributes:

1. Control of thoughts.
2. Control of actions.
3. Steadfastness of purposes.
4. Identity with spiritual life or higher ideas based on Ma'at (truth, justice, and righteousness).
5. Evidence of having a mission in life.
6. Evidence of wanting to belong to the Priestship in the Kemet Spiritual System.
7. Freedom from resentment when under the experience of persecution and wrong.
8. Confidence in the power of the Kemet Priest Scientist, Masters, Mfundi, Malenga and Mfundishi as teachers.
9. Confidence in one's own ability to learn.
10. Readiness or preparedness for Initiation - "When the student is ready, then the master will appear."

Spiritual Warriors In Pursuit of Nation-building

1. Control of thoughts

Learn to mediate so that you can control the way you think and how you think, as well as what you think. Analyze every situation before you react. You must be a warrior for Ma'at, that is to bring about order if there is none.

2. Control of actions

Each Spiritual Warrior is in the process of mastering their thoughts, so they can create right thinking. In order for the Spiritual Warrior to influence others, they must consistently produce right action.

3. Steadfastness of purpose

Staying Power! If you believe in all your heart in your mission then you must have fortitude. Being steadfast is holding to your Afrakan Kemetik principles.

4. Identity with spiritual life or higher ideas based on Ma'at (truth, justice, and righteousness)

We are divine spirit in a human form, this is our first and foremost identity. Our human identity is with Afrakan people worldwide and throughout time.

5. Evidence of having a mission in life

The Maangamizi speaks of our need to liberate ourselves. Ma'at is our mission in life. The development of our gifts are the vehicles which will help us accomplish our mission. We must only be concerned with Ma'at and the liberation of Afrakan people, and we must plant the seeds of liberation in every preceding generation.

6. Evidence of wanting to belong to the Priestship in the Kemet Spiritual System

Once you have seen the mission and innerstand its importance, then you must move in that direction. And the only direction that can liberate us is towards becoming "A Spiritual Warrior". Spiritual Warriors are Konsciousness. Spiritual awareness is Heru Konsciousness.

7. Freedom from resentment when under the experience of persecution and wrong

With Heru Konsciousness comes enlightenment. One who is enlightened sees change as a must because the alternative is death for Afrakan people, mentally, physically and spiritually. Now comes the conflict. Your parents, family and friends don't see, can't see what you see. You can't follow their path and they don't see yours. They will act negatively towards you as you follow your mission as a Spiritual Warrior. Only courage will help you stay on the path of Ma'at and that courage comes from within. That courage will keep you from being resentful against those who don't see; and that same courage will stop their resentment from getting in you and slowing you down.

8. Confidence in the power of the Kemet Priest Scientist, Masters, Mfundi, Melanga and Mfundishi as teachers

If you have come to the level where you want to develop or change, then the best thing to do is to become the student of someone more advanced in the path of liberation into Ma'at. Do your research and make sure you are following a master teacher who is someone who has demonstrated their attachment to Ma'at through their actions not just their words, and that they are a Spiritual Warrior for Afrakan people.

9. Confidence in one's own ability to learn

The greatest teacher cannot teach unless the student is willing to change. The only thing that prevents change is the unwillingness to change.

10. Readiness or preparedness for Initiation - "When the student is ready, then the master will appear."

Once you've received Ma'at, are you prepared and willing to change. We are continuously receiving knowledge on many level, but most of the society has not changed for the better. The receipt of knowledge is worthless unless change follows. We must be prepared to change and grow into Spiritual Warriors.

Mfundishi Jhutyms El-Salim, Shaha Mfundishi Maasi, Ahati Kilindi Iyi, and Mfundishi Tayari Casel at a Kupigana Ngumi Warrior Workshop in Harlem, New York at the Shrine of Jhuty Heru Neb-Hu.

THE DJED COLUMN (The Ulimwengo Posture)

The Spiritual Warriors of Kupigana Ngumi of the Shrine of Jhuty Heru Neb-Hu embrace the teachings of the Kemet legacy. The ancestors direct us to utilize the power of the universe for physical, mental and spiritual needs.

The Djed column of "Asr"and "Ptah," or the Ulimwengo posture of Kupigana Ngumi by Mfundishi Jhutyms Ka n Heru El-Salim

Phase Wa I Gathering:

The Djed column of 'Asr', or the Ulimwengo posture, symbolizes stability (endurance, patience and re-birth), and the balancing of the four primal elements.

1. Air- Dry

2. Fire- Hot

3. Water- Wet

4. Earth- Cold

All of these elements provide the continuity of life (Re-birth) and the reunion of body, mind and spirit.

The Ulimwengo Posture of Kupigana Ngumi is based upon the Djed (Djed-one who endures).

At the center of the Innerverse is Moyo.
At the center of the universe is Moyo.
At the center of your mental, physical and spiritual essences of life is the Moyo.

Hence, the Djed or Column of Asr and Ptah is the Principle of Stability, bearing the four elements, which make for formal existence. Below are three forms of the Djed Column.

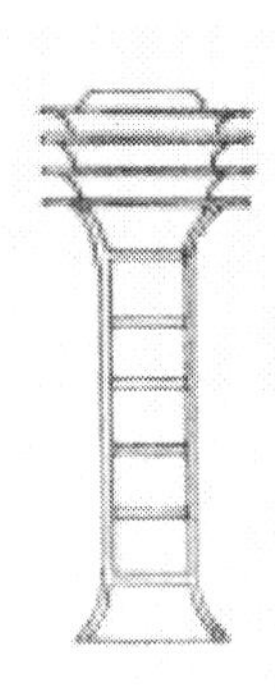
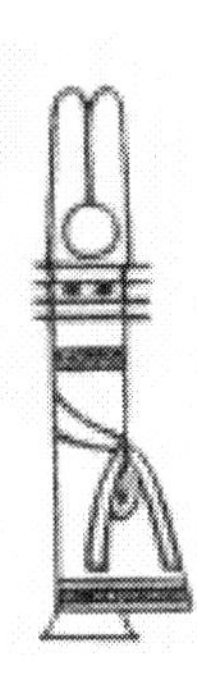

Djed becomes Ka through the distinction of spirit, soul and body, which makes this interaction possible. This will come about through direct or the indirect methods.

The column of Asr is truly the symbol of stability of continuity within life. The principle Djed next becomes the Ka, the element of nourishing support, giving form to spirit and to the soul.

The diligent practice of the Ulimwengo Posture (meditation- Ma'at Akhw Ba Ankh) bestows the state of Hotep, Peace, Spiritual union. In the lower stages, the power of Ulimwengo is made manifest in the statement of:

1. Balance, stability
2. Footwork, mobility
3. Striking power
4. Ability to withstand stress
5. Co-ordination of hands, feet, torso
6. Intuitiveness
7. Instinctive distancing
8. Relaxed agile movement
9. Stimulation of self testing energy
10. Internal Power

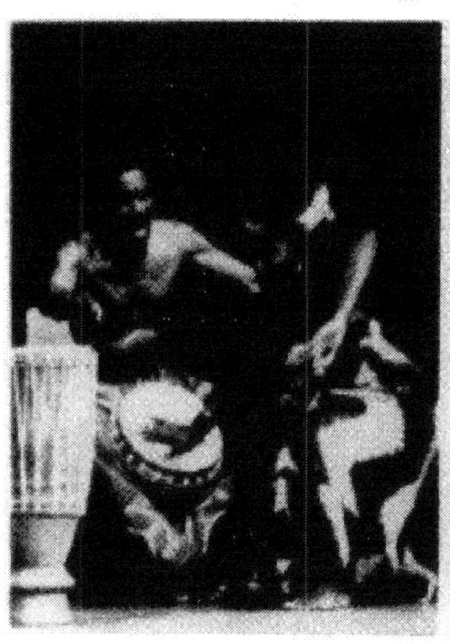

Spiritual Warrior Baba Kwame Ishangi, drumer, dancing, and martial artist.

When the body is totally limber and relaxed, the Moyo (energy) begins to flow smoothly throughout the entire system, energizing:

1. The physical body- the gross pattern
2. The breath - the bridge between body and mind
3. The subtle body- the vital centers

All are woven in a complex manner to sustain and enhance ***Ankh*** ☥ life.

Below are Kupigana Ngumi instructors; (left to right) Malenga Heru Ur, Mfundishi Jhutyms Ka n Heru, and Kaka Heru Khuty. They are also teachers of the Kemet Spiritual System.

Phase Senw II Distribution:

The next phase of training involves the Fungasnisha Drills (basic, energy distribution drills).

1. Atum - the complete one
2. Enpu - the opener of ways
3. Asr - the regenerator
4. Heru - one who is strong and powerful
5. Humet- potentiality
6. Heka - effective action
7. Hehity- one who seeks
8. Askai - one who is exalted
9. Nut/Geb- Heaven/Earth

Phase Shmtw III Application:

This phase of training involves the application of Moyo (learning to utilize Moyo in martial applications)

1. Nyatia- stalking (Footwork, balance, coordination)
2. Duaria- the perfection of mobility and stability

Phase Fedw llll Tempering A:

The phase of Heru sharpening mkono: basic hand movements from all 7 animals of The **Aha Kemet Wanyama Saba System** of the Kera of Jehuty Heru Neb-Hu form of Kupigana Ngumi.

1. Jhuty - Crane - Karanga,
2. Maa Hes - Lion - Simba
3. Erat - Cobra (snake) - Nyoka
4. Heru - Falcon - Mwewe
5. Mew Km - Black Panther - Paka weusi
6. Ean Ma'at - Baboon - Nyani
7. Sobek - Crocodile - Mamba

Phase Dw lllll Tempering B:

The phase of Heru sharpening miguu: basic leg and foot sharpening movements from all 7 animals of "the Aha Kemet Mnyama Saba System" of Kupigana Ngumi.

1. Forward

2. Side

3. Circling

4. Hooking

5. Backward

6. Sweeping

7. Leaping

Phase Sesu lllllI Sparring: Cheza Ngoma

The Sparring Phase

1. Pigana l - mastering the hand and foot techniques of fighting

2. Mnyama- animal fighting

3. Shikahs- grappling

4. Pigana ll - mastering the body posture, the shadow

5. Silaha- weaponry

Phase Sefkh lllllII Spiritual Dancing Forms:

The dancing phase/Dancing the Mchezo

A. Shen

1. Defending the circle

2. Trapping within the circle

3. Cuffing through the circle

B. Mnyama

1. Understanding the animal

2. Mastering the animal movements and nature

3. Seven fighting animal system

4. Becoming the animal

Mdw Ntchr --- Kiswahili --- English

a) Jhuty	*Karanga*	*the crane*
b) Maa Hes	*Simba*	*the lion*
c) Erat	*Nyoka*	*the cobra*
d) Heru	*Mwewe*	*the falcon*
e) Mew km	*Paka weusi*	*the black panther*
f) Ean Ma'at	*Nyani*	*the baboon*
g) Sobek	*Mamba*	*the crocodile*

The Kupigana Ngumi System Aha Kemet Wanyama Saba (the ancient Kemet, Black Warrior fighting seven animals), was developed by Mfundishi Jhutyms Ka en Heru Hassan Kamau Salim. Its origin is from the Hapy or Nile Valley of east and northeast Afraka. All of the animals in this System are from eastern Afraka. Mfundishi Jhutyms Ka n Heru El-Salim has trained and studied in America with Mfundishi Maasi, and on the Afrakan continent with several Grand Masters. Within the System of Kupigana Ngumi Pan-Afrakan Martial Arts Federation, there are many styles and spiritual philosophies. The author of this book, Mfundishi Jhutyms Ka n Heru El-Salim, is a Kemet Spiritual Warrior Healing Priest, but not all of the Kupigana Ngumi Masters and Grand Masters follow the same Spiritual system. All of the Kupigana Ngumi Masters and Grand Masters are Afrakan and follow one of the indigenous Afrakan Spiritual Systems.

Another style of Kupigana Ngumi is called the "Kiungo Cha Mkono," a Kiswahili term which translated means: Shackle Hands, Pharaonic Hands, Paired Hands, Connected Hands or Helping Hands. This term and idea was developed by Ngana Mfundishi Tolo-Naa in the early seventies. It is based on the Afrakan concept of Kujichagulia ("defining for self"), and applied to the principles of the science of Martial Arts. The principles of shackled hands proved very efficient, in that it eliminates the dual aspect, which existed in other martial arts: that of blocking and striking, and combined it in one action (the Afrakan concept of Shield and Spear). Shackle Hand is also symbolic of Afrakan peoples' Ourstory of enslavement; and the practice of this art form can serve as a vehicle to break the chains of our mental bondage. Over a period of years, Ngana Mfundishi Tolo-Naa developed eighteen hand functions, which are the foundation of the Shackle Hand System. The system is taught on three levels:

A. Hands joined closed as though cuffed.
B. Hands joined shoulder width apart as though shackled.
C. Pharaonic Hands - Crossed to symbolize the holding of the crook and flail, from our ancient Kemet past.

The Art of Hearing and Listening

The Kupigana Ngumi practitioner embraces silence rather than useless chatter, or unnecessary physical confrontation. The Spiritual Warrior who is skilled in Kupigana Ngumi must work with the guidance of Jhuty and the power of Heru, but the balance of Ma'at must always be present so that aggression will always be directed towards the enemy at the correct time, and never inward towards the self and family.

Spiritual Warriors should be in a position to give every day. They must be humble, because greed is the root to most violence. White male domination is rooted in unchecked greed, called free enterprise or capitalism. The greed that is rooted in capitalism can set violence in motion at an individual or collective level, if one is not rooted in Ma'at. Ourstory clearly shows that since the dawn of time Ma'at has never been in the European value system. This is why it is clear that the European system of white male domination or white people collectively, is the enemy of Afrakans - Black people collectively. And especially, the enemy of all those people of color who embrace Ma'at (truth, justice, righteousness and harmonious balance). Therefore, the true Spiritual Warriors who have high levels of mastery of Kupigana Ngumi are healers because they are hearers and listeners of nature and the people. Only those who love to hear nature, and who have mastered the skills of listening can act on what is said in a giving way. This is why Spiritual Warriors love to give. We are givers and leavers, not takers; this is "The Way."

Hotep Ptah

In ancient Kemet, a Spiritual Warrior named Hotep Ptah, left some very profound writing behind, so that Spiritual Warriors that followed him would have a guide towards righteousness. The following is from a book entitled, *Hotep Ptah:*

Hotep Ptah

1. ***Hearing means accurate perception***
2. ***Accurate perception becomes a habit***
3. ***Hearing well is speaking well***
4. ***Hearing well is useful to the hearer***
5. ***Hearing is best of all***
6. ***Hearing is beloved of The NTCHR***
7. ***Hearing is a matter of Konsciousness***
8. ***Hearing will help one innerstand good action***
9. ***Lips are straight when speaking Ma'at***

Each Kupigana Ngumi Spiritual Warrior must study and master the ancient teachings of our Afrakan ancestors. The words of Hotep Ptah teaches us to control our heart, our mouth, our thoughts, our desires and our speech. Be deliberate so as to say things that count.

Spiritual Warriors of Defense returning Home to Kemet to study and master the ancient teachings of our Afrakan ancestors : Mfundishi Tayari Casel and Mfundishi Jhutyms Ka n Heru El-Salim at the Great Temple in Waset.

KUPIGANA NGUMI

AHA KEMET

Wanyama Mpigana Saba Shule

First level Mwanafunzi

Ulimwengo 10min.
Kukaa Hekau
Ma'at Hekau
Nut
Mazoezi: maruka 1 - 5, 10 X
Urafu 1 - 5, 10 X
Mazoezi tumbo - 10 X
a) hip raises, b) neck bridges, c) arm bridge, d) shoulderstand,
e) Geb, f) Geb twist, h) 9 pushups - 5x, i) frog leaps - 25
Shu
Shu wa
Heru djed - 30
Kusimama taratibu
Piga take mazoezi - moja
Piga Mkono mazoezi
Kulinda taratibu - moja
Jhuty Kaa -30
Kiungu Cha Mkono mazoezi
Piga take taratibu - moja
Jhuty taratibu
Kupigana Ngumi mazoezi na taratibu - moja
Asr
Hesabu 1 - 30 in Kiswahili and Mdw Ntchr
Define: Kupigana Ngumi -
Kemetik Aha -
Wanyama Mpigana Saba -
Mdw Ntchr -
Kiswahili -

Mehez, Kemet -

KUPIGANA NGUMI

AHA KEMET

Wanyama Mpigana Saba Shule

Second level Mpigana mbili

Ulimwengo 15 min.
Kukaa Hekau
Ma'at Hekau
Nut
Shu, Shu wa
Shu senu
Heru djed - 60
Mazoezi: maruka 1 - 5, 20 X
Urafu 1 - 5, 20 X
Mazoezi tumbo - 20 X
a) hip raises, b) neck bridges, c) arm bridge, d)shoulderstand,
e) Geb, f) Geb twist, g) head stand, h) 9 pushups 10x,
i) frogleaps - 25
Kusimama taratibu
Piga take mazoezi - moja, mbili
Piga Mkono mazoezi
Kulinda taratibu - moja, mbili
Jhuty Kaa -60
Kiungu Cha Mkono mazoezi - 2 levels
Piga take taratibu - moja, mbili
Jhuty taratibu - 2 levels
Mnyama tano taratibu
Kupigana Ngumi mazoezi -moja
Kupigana Ngumi taratibu - moja
Simba taratibu
Kiungu Cha Mkono taratibu
Long pole - mazoezi - moja
Asr
Hesabu 1 - 100 in Kiswahili and Mdw Ntchr

Define: Asr, Ast, Nebt Het, Set, Heru Ur, Nut, & Geb

KUPIGANA NGUMI

AHA KEMET

Wanyama Mpigana Saba Shule

Third level Mpigana tatu

Ulimwengo 20 min.
Kukaa Hekau
Ma'at Hekau
Nut
Shu, Shu wa,
Shu senu, Shu shomet
Heru djed - 60
Mazoezi: maruka 1 - 5, 20 X
Urafu 1 - 5, 20 X
Mazoezi tumbo - 20 X
a) hip raises, b) neck bridges, c) arm bridge, d) shoulderstand,
e) Geb, f) Geb twist, h) head stand, i) 9 pushups -10x,
j) frog leaps - 50
Kusimama taratibu
Piga take mazoezi - moja, mbili, tatu
Piga Mkono mazoezi
Kulinda taratibu - moja, mbili, tatu
Jhuty Kaa -60
Kiungu Cha Mkono mazoezi - 3 levels
Piga take taratibu - moja, mbili, tatu
Jhuty taratibu - 3 levels
Mnyama tano taratibu - 2 levels
Kupigana Ngumi taratibu - moja, mbili
Simba taratibu - 2 levels
Kiungu Cha Mkono taratibu - 2 levels
Paka weusi taratibu
Long pole - mazoezi - moja
Miti mifupi (short sticks) - mazoezi - moja
Hesabu 1 - 1,000 in Kiswahili and Mdw Ntchr

KUPIGANA NGUMI

AHA KEMET

Wanyama Mpigana Saba Shule

Fourth level Kaka / Dada

Kimbia - 1 mile (10 min. or Under)
Ulimwengo 25 min.
Kukaa Hekau
Ma'at Hekau
Nut
Shu
Shu wa
Shu senu
Shu shomet
Shu fedw
Heru djed - 100
Twa Bow & Arrow
Mazoezi: maruka 1 - 5, 25 X, Urafu 1 - 5, 25 X, tumbo - 25 X
a) hip raises, b) neck bridges, c) arm bridge, d) Geb, e) shoulder stand, f) Geb twist, h) head stand, i) 9 pushups - 10x, j) frog leaps - 50
Kusimama taratibu
Piga take mazoezi - moja, mbili, tatu, nne
Piga Mkono mazoezi - moja, mbili
Kulinda taratibu - moja, mbili, tatu, nne
Jhuty Kaa -100
Kiungu Cha Mkono mazoezi - 3 levels
Piga take taratibu - moja, mbili, tatu, nne
Jhuty taratibu - 3 levels
Mnyama tano taratibu - 3 levels
Kupigana Ngumi taratibu - moja, mbili, tatu
Simba taratibu - 3 levels
Kiungu Cha Mkono taratibu - 3 levels
Paka weusi taratibu - 2 levels
Nyani taratibu - 2 levels

Fourth level Kaka / Dada
continued...

Nyoka taratibu
Heru taratibu
Long pole - mazoezi - moja, mbili
Miti mifupi (short sticks) - mazoezi - moja, mbili
Hesabu 1 - 10,000 in Kiswahili and Mdw Ntchr
Define: The most popular Kemet Cosmology of Creation.

Mfundishi Jhutyms Ka n Heru at Wp Renpt in New York with Mfundi Sankhu Kheper, Head Kemet Priest of Temple of Anu in New Jersey playing the drum in the background.

KUPIGANA NGUMI

AHA KEMET

Wanyama Mpigana Saba Shule
Fifth level Mfundi

Kimbia - 1 mile (8 min. or Under)
Ulimwengo 30 min.
Kukaa Hekau
Ma'at Hekau
Nut
Simbarafu
Shu, Shu wa
Shu senu, Shu shomet
Shu fedw, Shu dew
Heru djed - 100
Twa Bow & Arrow

Mazoezi: maruka 1 - 5, 50 X, Urafu 1 - 5, 50 X, tumbo - 25 X
a) hip raises, b) neck bridges, c) arm bridge, d) shoulder stand
e) Geb, f) Geb twist h) head stand, i) 9 pushups 10x,
j) Frog leaps - 100

Kusimama taratibu
Piga take mazoezi - moja, mbili, tatu, nne
Piga Mkono mazoezi - moja, mbili
Kulinda taratibu - moja, mbili, tatu, nne
Jhuty Kaa - 100
Kiungu Cha Mkono mazoezi - 3 levels
Piga take taratibu - moja, mbili, tatu, nne
Jhuty taratibu - 3 levels
Mnyama tano taratibu - 3 levels
Kupigana Ngumi taratibu - moja, mbili, tatu, nne
Simba taratibu - 3 levels
Kiungu Cha Mkono taratibu - 3 levels

MFUNDI continued

Nyoka taratibu 3 levels
Heru taratibu 3 levels
Sobek taratibu 3 levels
Long pole - mazoezi - moja, mbili, tatu
Miti mifupi (short sticks) - mazoezi- moja, mbili, tatu
Kisu kifupi (short dagger)
Long sword - moja
Ta Merrian dances and grappling techniques
Pressure points
Weapon fighting
Hesabu 1 - 1,000,000 in Kiswahili and Mdw Ntchr
Mdw Ntchr classes and Kiswahili classes

Below, Mfundishi Salim with a medium pole. The long pole, medium and short sticks must be mastered by the fifth level - Mfundi.

KUPIGANA NGUMI

AHA KEMET

Wanyama Mpigana Saba Shule

Mfundi mbili and tatu (senior)

1. Pressure Point Manipulation

   A. Identifying a multitude of points on the body that allow you to dominate any size opponent with little effort.
   B. Innerstanding the auto kinetic response to being struck in these points in order to effectively plan combinations.
   C. Using the body's natural weapons to strike pressure points effectively.

2. Joint Manipulation

   A. Use of compression and hyperextension of the joints to subdue opponents.
   B. Escapes from holds using simple moves that require no strength.
   C. Ground fighting without wrestling.

3. Research and document Ourstory of Afrakan warfare and spiritual training in Afraka and in the Diaspora.

4. Research and document aspects of the psychology of fighting (i.e. fear, aggression, adrenaline, offensive vs. defensive mindset, etc.)

5. Research and demonstrate aspects of personal combat as they relate to the present circumstances and environment.

6. Demonstrate personal assimilation of Kupigana principles in modern and improvised weapons techniques.

7. Demonstrate personal assimilation of Kupigana Ngumi and principles by creating and explaining application of breathing and meditation forms.
8. Demonstrate personal assimilation of Kupigana Ngumi and principles by creating and explaining application of stance, weapons and fighting forms, using animals as well as the elements.
9. Ulimwengo for 30 min.
10. Fighting multiple opponents and continuous fighting for 15 minutes with a new opponent every two minutes.
11. Explain Kemetik principles of science as it applies to survival in the city and in the country as a Warrior.
12. Kimbia - 3 miles (30 min. or under)

Afrakan Grand Masters of Asian and Afrakan martial arts systems. Center: Grandmaster Kham, left; Grandmaster Dr. K.T. Padu, Grandmaster John Dimkims, Sensei Louis Hatchett, Malenga Maasi, Prof. Prince Shemyahudah, Master Elder Aladjo,Mfundishi Jhutyms Hassan K. Salim. Right center: Grandmaster Rico Guy, Master Daniel Stewart, Master Marvin Gatling, Sensei Vernon Johnson, Baba Pa-ur Tehuti Se-Ptah, Sensei Talib Shabazz, Heri Abu Khafra. This photo was taken by Edmund Herman of Umoja Photography on the eve of the Million Man March, 1995.

The Poetic Teachings of Kupigana Ngumi

Kupigana Ngumi teaches wisdom
Wisdom is motion, thoughts, and speech in action
The power of dynamic motion can only be mastered after unlimited and relentless repetition
The mastery of motion can stop the world clearing the thoughts so that the infinite knowledge of the ancestors may guide your speech
Good speech is the light of wisdom
The light of wisdom is the lamp that lights the way to all knowledge
For, when the mouth stumbles in darkness
It is much worse than the foot...

Kupigana Ngumi Teaches Patience

Patience is unlimited will
Will is an unconquerable force
that rests at the feet of all success

If one waits long enough
If your will is strong enough
Even an egg will walk

Endurance is the soul of patience
One moment of patience may ward off great disaster
One moment of impatience may ruin a whole life...

CHAPTER ∩ I I I (13)

Somo la Kumi na Tatu

The Divine Drama

Let it be known that Spiritual Warriors are Healers. We are resurrecting the Kemetyu Legacy of Asr and we are truly on the path of becoming Heru. Each student of the Kemet Legacy as well as Afrakan Spiritual Warriors and Martial Artists of Kemet Aha Wanyama Saba wa Kupigana Ngumi serve to embrace the Spirit of Heru. The Asrian Drama reenacts the proverbial battle between harmony and disharmony (Heru vs. Setsh or Ma'at vs.Esfet, the oppressed vs. oppressor). We utilize these teachings not only as a preface to the warrior mentally, for overcoming esfet and white male domination, but also to recapture "The Way" a state of Being Heru, "The Whm Msu" or living in Ma'at.

The Hapy Valley Basin of northeast Afraka presented the oldest scientific systems of combat in the world. They were the first fighting methods of an esoteric nature and were bestowed from the Ntchru themselves. One such system was "Aha," today called Aha Kemet Wanyama Saba wa Kupigana Ngumi (The Kemet fighting 7 animal system). This Ancient Kemetyu fighting method was based on the battle between the Ntchru Heru and Setsh, representing the principles of complements. This battle was known as the "Asrian Drama", or The Divine Drama and it symbolized the forces of nature, realigning itself with Ma'at.

Ahati Kilindi Iyi, a present day Spiritual Warrior of the Kupigana Ngumi family, in a position paper entitled, "The Essence of Ta-Merrian Martial Arts" emphasizes the religious / philosophical basis of Afrakan-based disciplinary fighting arts. The art and struggle of the Spiritual Warrior is essentially expressed on three levels:

1. **The celestial battle of the sun as it descends into the Netherworld.**
2. **The Human being's day-to-day battle on earth in our fight for survival and enlightenment.**
3. **The human being's spiritual battle in the space between death and the next stage of existence.**

These are the elemental aspects of struggle for the Spiritual Warrior and the essence of them continues unchanged. Ahati Kilindi Iyi goes on to say that, "Combat exemplifies the movements of the planets in their orbit and also certain animals held sacred." Each Spiritual Warrior was empowered with a particular animal force. The practitioner was then taught the sacred dance, music and songs in order to invoke the sacred powers within the very psyche of the warrior.

The Asrian Drama, which embodies the above three struggles, was reenacted by Priest Scientist and Kemet Spiritual martial artist of Kemet Aha Wanyama Saba wa Kupigana Ngumi, once a year at a special ritual festival called the "Divine Drama." This dramatic dance symbolized the rebirth, life, death, and resurrection of Asr, through Heru, the royal avenger. We learn that Heru grew strong of body and mind through assiduous training and developed his powers by learning the language of the Ntchru, the forces of nature. When the time came to claim his rightful position, Heru consented to enter into combat with his uncle Setsh. Setsh is the slayer of Heru's father Asr and he is the ruler or personification of the force esfet, or division through might and force. Setsh of the south and Heru of the north, both wore the 'White and Red crown'. This symbolism reflects that each warrior possessed positive and negative forces that must be directed each and every day.

Today, followers of the Kemet legacy practice the Divine Drama because it reminds us of the battles we must go through in our daily lives to be resurrected and re-Afrakanized. The Asrian Drama is a symbolic portrayal of the sun's rebirth, life, death and resurrection, with each deity representing one of these elements. In our daily lives, we must evoke the aspects of the positive spiritual forces to aid in combat against white male domination, or esfet. Music, dance, meditation, special Afrakan rituals like the pouring of libation, lighting of candles, incense, chanting, and the reading of the sacred words of the ancestors are also used to prepare and protect warriors. These are regarded as sacred and inseparable from the warrior's training. Today as European Caucasian supremacy attempts to rear its head in every aspect of our lives and the conditions of the Maangamizi continue, these practices can protect and aid Afrakans as we resurrect our ancient spirits and the Spiritual Warriors within us, while we rebuild the new Afrakan mind and nation as we return to "The Way".

In the Asrian Drama, it is written that Asr was the first of five human characteristics born of the Ntchru Geb and Nut. The other four being Heru Ur, Setsh, Ast and Nebt Het. Each represented part of the human personality that developed the whole being, so we each possess these energies. Symbolically, the five personalities formed two unions, or two sets of complementary energies. The fifth energy, Heru-Ur represented a neutral force for balance and protection, the warrior, and the prototype for Heru the son.

Asr and Ast headed the northern domain. The divine spirit of Asr (Asar), began domesticating animals and growing food, (the birth of agrikulture). This was the start of "civilization." Humans no longer having to look for food, became less nomadic and had more leisure time to reflect and draw innerstanding from nature. Ma'at became the law of the land and Asr instructed the people of Kemet in the science of spirituality. Asr was loved and revered for his great contributions to the birth of civilization as we now know it. Asr was the first force to "discover" the secrets that enabled one to achieve the human divine potential. He was thus, able to harmonize all the divergent and competing interests of society and lead the people to a life of peace, prosperity and love.

A Greek writer Plutarch, who lived in the first century C.E., whose narratives *On Isis and Osiris*, was compiled from various oral and written sources, was responsible for making the Kemet myth of the death and resurrection of Asr well known to the Greeks and Romans. Everyone knew that the Christ story was an Afrakan story, which later developed into the New Testament. "When Asr was born, a voice proclaiming the birth of the lord of creation was heard throughout Kemet. Geb, the Neb of the Earth, crowned or proclaimed Asr, the Nswt. Asr devoted himself to civilizing his subjects: he taught them husbandry, instructed them in worship of the Ntchru, and established a code of laws. When Kemet was at last peaceful and flourishing, Asr set out to bring his teachings to the other nations of the world." This sounds like we have heard all this before, but this version is older than the Old, and New Testament of the Jewish, and Christian Holy Bible, by thousands of years.

Setsh, his younger brother, became jealous of all the adulation and love and special homage paid to Asr. While Asr was traveling to spread his wisdom to other lands, Setsh plotted to do away with him. During Asr's absence, his wife Ast, who shared rulership of Kemet with her husband Asr, ruled Kemet and it continued to flourish. Throughout Afrakan traditions, women shared rulership with men. In ancient Kash and Axum, they had as many women rulers as men. Spiritual Warriors are not defined by sex, but by attitude, control, commitment, and mastery of Spiritual Warrior skills, and their innerstanding of "The Way".

Ast is associated with the art of healing. She is the great wife who loves her subjects and cares for the weak and helpless. She is the Divine Mother to whom we call and turn to in time of grief. Like her complementary force, she also played an important role in the development of civilization. She taught the art of growing corn, cultivation of grains, fruit trees, making cloth and designing garments. She also instituted marriage and instructed her people in the art of healing diseases. She learned her magical powers from the Ntchr Jhuty, the master teacher of "The Way" (Jhuty is your Heru-Konscious mind). The throne of Ast symbolized a birthing chair and was a symbol of rulership. Her throne was the seat that gave birth to authority and rulership in ancient Kemet.

A statue of the Ntchrt Ast protecting her mate and or complement energy, the Ntchr Asr.

Heru was the symbol of Higher Konsciousness and Warriorship that exist inside each human being. Heru is the spirit that fights for righteousness and eternal truth(Ma'at). Above Heru wears the etef crown of ancient Kemet.

Setsh and Nebt Het headed the southern domain. Setsh was the Ntchr of the sky by night and the downward motion of the sun. He rules by might and force. Certain situations call for the energy of Setsh. Therefore, you can never eliminate Setsh. You must have control over that energy within your life. Nebt Het is the sister and best friend of Ast. She is the nurturer and represents the bond of sistership and friendship.

Setsh masterminded a plan to kill his brother at a welcome home party; he planned in Asr's name. Setsh had a beautiful coffin made, a *Karast* of gold, saying to the guest that whoever could fit the *Karast* would receive it. During ancient times, a *Karast* was a prized possession because it insured that the body would be preserved and it served as a vehicle for rebirth, protection and resurrection.

Seventy-two people and one of the female rulers from Kash, or present day Ethiopia, named Aso joined Setsh's plot and they were all promised wealth. All the guests tried to fit inside the *Karast*, but only Asr could fit because it had been made to his exact measurements. Asr laid in the *Karast* and within all the excitement Setsh and his conspirators sealed it with molten lead. The *Karast* was then thrown into the Hapy River where it sailed to the Wedgy Wr (Mediterranean Sea). After drifting for many days, the *Karast* floated onto the shores of Byblos. There, an Acacia tree sprang up around the *Karast* and enclosed it. The tree was so magnificent that the king of Byblos had it cut down to be used as a pillar in his temple. When Ast found out what had happened to her husband, she set out in search of his body. Through the power of faith and relentless struggle, tools of all Spiritual Warriors, she was able to find and return Asr's body back to Kemet. Asr placed his body in a state of hibernation until he was resurrected with love from his mate and family. Ast and Nebt Het hid Asr for protection. Setsh, hunting wild boars by the light of the full moon discovered Asr's Karast, realizing that it was his murdered brother. A wild and fearless rage enveloped him and he ripped Asr's body into 14 pieces (symbolic of the waning of the moon in a lunar cycle) and scattered them throughout the land. This can also symbolize the Maangamizi of Afrakan people, the deliberate destruction and the ripping apart of Afrakan families, Kultures and the ancestral memory of the Afrakan genius, by Europeans and Arabs. Moreover, the scattering of our broken pieces remain throughout the Diaspora.

Nebt Het, who was married to Set, left her husband, furious about what he had done to their brother. Later with her sister Ast and her son Enpu, the guide searched and found all the parts of Asr's body except his phallus, which was believed to have been eaten by Hapy River catfish. (This explains why scavenger fish were not eaten in Kemet.) She then erected a new phallus from black clay enriched with the spirit of the Ntchr with the help of the Ntchr Khnum. This became the New Moon and the 14 days of resurrection into wholeness. Later monuments in honor of her husband's lost but regained regenerative power were carved from solid stone. (Those special monuments were called the Tekhn and they were placed always in front of the entrance of Kemet Temples). Ast also buried an image of each member of Asr when it was found and erected a tomb which became a place of worship to Asr their beloved Nswt. Not all was lost, however Ast, using her magic or spiritual will, transformed herself into a Hawk. Fluttering above the body of Asr, Ast received his spiritual essence and became impregnated. This is still depicted on the wall today in the ancient city of Ta en Tarert, later called Denderah by the Greeks, (Egypt) at the Temple of Sety Mry-n-Ptah and User-Ma'at-Ra Stp-n-Ra Much later in history Asians and Europeans will copy this divine birth story.

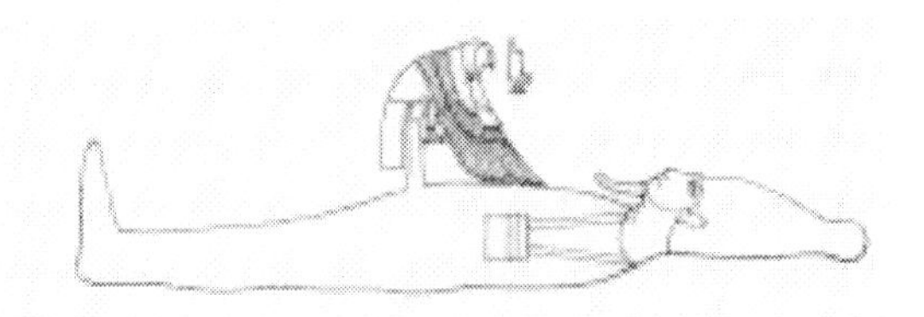

Fluttering above the body of Asr, Ast received his spiritual essence and became impregnated with Heru.

Enpu, with his Aunt Ast and Mother Nebt Het, mummified the body of Asr with all the original parts and wrapped them in linen bandages, with the divine help of the Ntchru Jhuty and Ra. This was the beginning of mummification and the Enpu Priest, which flourished in ancient Kemet until the Christian era or the coming of Asiatics and Europeans. Today, a mortician is a poor copy of the ancient art of mummification and body preparation for transformation.

In the papyrus swamps of the Delta, Ast gave birth to a son, whom she called Heru. Her son was named after his uncle, "Heru The Elder (Heru-Ur)" or "Heru The Great" and even today in most Kultures of Afraka the uncle and nephew share the greatest bond of any family members. The uncle is responsible for the development of his nephew just like Heru-Ur and Heru. As a result of this great bond, Heru grew strong of mind and body. Ast, his mother trained his power so that he could avenge his father's death, resurrecting Ma'at as the dominant energy in the land. Through his mother's magic, he communed with the Ntchr of knowledge, Jhuty. All the secrets of the Innerverse and Universe were revealed to him. The Kemet Legacy of Heru teaches that these same forces are in each of us waiting to emerge. (**We must take the brothers from the streets and place them**

in protective Afrakan-centered schools and Kultural centers, and give them the Kemet legacy of Heru, guided by the wisdom of Jhuty and Ma'at.) This will be a major key towards returning to Asr our highest level of spirituality through the Warrior Heru. Initiation was the only way to gain the knowledge of Jhuty and Ma'at, "The Way".

The time finally came for Heru to go before the Divine council of Ntchru to claim his rightful position. However, Setsh was among them and stated that Heru was illegitimate and had no right to the Double Crown of Kemet. Heru and Setsh consented to enter into combat to decide who would rule Kemet and wear the Double Crown of Asr. The battle was long and fierce during which time the two fighters transformed into different animal principles on which the movements of Aha, the ancient Kemet fighting systems were based. Today, Aha is called **Aha Kemet Wanyama Saba Kupigana Ngumi.** During the battle, Setsh threw dirt in Heru's eyes and later he was able to Blind Heru. Today, esfet, white male domination, has blinded Afrakan people with wazungu desires, because it seems like we cannot see the poison of white culture and the destruction of white male domination not only in our lives, but also in the world. Moreover, just like Heru lost his left eye, but it was restored by the female healing powers of Het Heru and the wisdom of Jhuty. We as Afrakan people will have to call on our healing sacred sisters and the ancient wisdom of Jhuty to give us back our sight, so that we too can heal and do battle like Heru. The battle was finally won when Heru hurled his mighty spear. This battle was shown on the walls of the temple at Edfu dedicated to Heru in present-day Egypt. Heru prevailed over Setsh, avenged his father's death, and regained Ta-Merry or Kemet, known today as Egypt. Heru did not destroy Setsh. He was victorious over him in battle. He subdued Setsh so that he could restore Ma'at. Esfet must exist, but if there is to be balance, it must be controlled by the greater force: Ma'at, which is truth, justice, righteousness and harmonious balance. Heru's victory came from humbling himself to the intuitive guidance of wisdom. Intelligence has always defeated might and strength when it has prepared itself for battle. Initiation, purification, meditation and liberation are the first steps towards being a Spiritual Warrior. This was the way in Ancient Kemet and it is still the way to liberation today.

After Heru finally defeated Setsh he turned his uncle over to Ast for her to administer the Judgment, but she refused to kill him, on the grounds that Setsh was her brother and she could not destroy family and set him free. Outraged, Heru cut her head off, but the Ntchr Jhuty replaced it with a cow's head. Ast was transformed into the divine cow, Het Heru. Jhuty, Ast, Nebt Het, Enpu and Heru performed the opening of the Mouth ritual on Asr's sah (mummified) body and Asr was brought back to life through the eye of Heru by Jhuty. Through the council of Ntchru, Asr was declared the Judge and Nswt (ruler) of the Dead or the Duat, the underworld, while Heru was to be the Nswt of the living. Setsh objected, but a council of 42 Ntchru with Atm as the leader and Jhuty as the Judge, found Heru to be Maa Kheru, True of voice or word. Thus, the Divine Drama was settled based on right over might. Afterwards all the Nswtu of Ancient Kemet was Shemsu Heru, followers of Heru, and took on a Heru name from 4240 B.C.E. or 1 S.T., the time from the Nswt Narmer until the coming of the Europeans from Greece and Rome and the Asiatics.

This Asrian drama in all its lessons and symbolism is the foundation for warrior training. The principles of the Afrakan warrior arts and the sacred arts of traditional Afrakan Kultures were and are intertwined. "The human of occult powers was the incarnation of intelligence, agility of mind, thought, cunningness, shrewdness, and foresight." (Budge: *Asar, and the Egyptian Resurrection)* Prior to war it was the custom of the Afrakan Spiritual Warrior Priest or Shaman to place his forefinger upon each weapon in order to empower it. This is an example of the powerful spiritual rituals used to empower Spiritual Warriors. Dancing also served as a medium used by the Warrior Priest. So ritual dance is as important as combative training in the developing of Spiritual Warriors. Gestures and steps, coordinated with subtle body movements served as a vehicle to call forth the Warrior Spirit. Because of this tradition, the Mchawi Ngoma (dance of the Warrior Priest) is one of the high points in the training of the Kemet Aha Wanyama Saba Kupigana Ngumi Spiritual Warriors.

Prayer and positive affirmation is also a functional and important part of Warrior training. The Mchawi Ngoma is as powerful as prayer, not simply an attempt at artful embellishment or imitation of nature but rather the tapping of the very forces of nature. Beginning with the Ulimwengo posture (symbolic of the Djed column of Asr), the Mpigana reenacts the agony, death, and rebirth of Asr through his son Heru. The next stage of preparation for the dance involves the Ma'at and Ka postures, representing the balancing and refining of inner energies and the receiving of divine power. These postures are explained in Chapter 10 and they are part of Ma'at Akhw Ba Ankh and the Kemetik Aha martial arts system. The Mpigana then encounters the postures of the Divine elements, which distribute and guide divine power along with the innerstanding of the sacred seven animals of the Aha Kemet Wanyama Saba wa Kupigana Ngumi system. These postures of divine elements and sacred animals are only aspects of each warrior in his or her innerstanding of themselves as nature.

"Nyatia" is the art of stalking and is symbolized by "Ochosi" the hunter of the Yoruba tradition. Nyatia and Ochosi are linkages from the Ancient Kemet tradition, to the Yoruba of west Afraka. Ochosi is the master hunter and lord of the swift arrow (i.e., the skills of closing the gap and piercing the enemy). "Nyatia" also involves "msing," (stepping) and "duria" (circular gesturing).

"Bastalisha" means to reduce the enemy's effort to nothing. This skill brings the ability to avoid the actions of the opponent and to deliver "Mkono" (striking gestures with the hands, arms and legs) to the face, head, body, arms, legs and joints and pressure points of the opponents. Like Heru, this enables one to subdue the opponent rather than destroy him.

In other dances, silaha (weapons) are utilized, some of which are:

1. Spear- Mkuki
2. Sword- Upanga
3. Stick- Gongo or Kipande (short, medium and long)
4. Dagger- Kupumau\Kuhema (short, medium and long)

In order to master the above skills and the 'Dance stage' of the Aha Kemet Wanyama Saba Kupigana Ngumi, the practitioner must realize the power of the "Nine Attributes," which were previously mentioned under the Nine Principles of Ma'at. For the purpose of clarity and to demonstrate the connection between the Ma'at posture and physical preparedness we mention them again:

1) Balance- Sawazisha;
2) Coordination- Ulanginiful;
3) Rhythm- Mwendo;
4) Strength- Nguvu;
5) Endurance- Ishi (Ustahimilivu);
6) Flexibility- Kutengene Zeka (Kunama);
7) Agility- Wepesi;
8) Speed/Quick- Upesi;
9) Posture- Mfano.

The nine trials tell Ourstory of the Ancient Afrakan. The songs of the warrior brothership and sistership, tell of the royal ancestors who are reflected in the arts and skills of the Afrakan Diaspora. Some of the arts that the warriors had to master for both discipline and skill were weaving, pottery, ground painting, hair art, dying and tinting, food preparation and the construction of dwellings. These were used in their everyday lives in order to maintain a prosperous community. Afrakan Spiritual Warriors must update, refine and master functional skills to be able to develop and maintain our own Afrakan communities today.

We the Kemetyu, Afrakan Spiritual Warriors of today must avenge our ancestors' deaths. We are, because, they were. There is a lot of unfinished business between us and the doers of esfet, the wazungu and Asiatics. What goes around comes around. The present day Afrakan from Afraka, America and the Diaspora, who are the descendants of the members of the great continent of Afraka are the sons and daughters of Asr and Ast. We are also the sons and daughters of the Maangamizi victims. We are the reincarnation of Heru and like Heru; we have to prepare for a battle of liberation of our people for their Afrakan minds and our continent. On the next page is a physical war shirt by an Afrakan warrior from the Akan Nation in west Afraka. We, the Kemetyu of the 63rd century S.T. must develop mental, physical and spiritual warrior protection as we prepare for battle against the matrix of European Caucasian domination.

A war shirt (Batakari), the Akan people, Ghana west Afraka.

Below Mfundishi sharing spiritual powers with two ancestrial Afrakan Nswtwy: Nswt Jhutyms Aa-Khpr-n-Ra and Nswt Metchuhotep Neb-khrw-Ra of ancient Kemet.

Shemsu Heru

{Sankofa Story of the Second Golden Age or Middle Period of Ancient Kemet as told by Mfundishi Jhutyms Ka-n-Heru Hassan Kamau Salim}

Like our great and victorious Spiritual Warriors of our glorious Afrakan past, we must reclaim, and resurrect the Heru Konsciousness lying dormant in our Black minds. We must master past lessons so we can move into the future, wise, courageous, victorious, and once again in Kemtrol (total Black or Afrakan control of our destiny).

In the 2nd Golden Age or the Classical Period (so-called 11th Dynasty) of Ancient Kemet, the Glorious Middle Period of the reunification of Ancient Kemet, the Nswt Intef-sa-Ra 2069 - 2060 B.C.E. or 2171 - 2180 S.T., sent his son, Mentchhotep, to the great temple at Waset to study under the great Warrior Master Priest of Amen because Prince Mentchhotep was to succeed his father as ruler of Southern Kemet. The great Warrior Priest at the temple of Amen was to teach the boy the basics of being a good ruler, and a silent, mighty Warrior for Ma'at.

When Mentchhotep the Prince arrived at the great temple of Amen, the Hem-Sem-Tpy (High Priest) sent him with one of Kemet's greatest Warriors, Jhutyms Ka-en-Heru, to the tropical rain forest in Kash. Ancient Kash was a great Afrakan nation that was located up south of Ancient Kemet. After three years, the prince Mentchhotep was to return to the temple to describe what he had learned and in detail explain the sounds of the great Afrakan Rain Forest.

When the prince Mentchhotep and the Spiritual Warrior returned, the Hem-Sem-Tpy asked the boy to describe all that he felt and heard in the great rain forest of Kash. "Hem-Sem-Tpy", replied the prince, "I could hear the great falcon call, the leaves rustle, the Ibis crane flying over my head, the wind whisper and holler, the peaceful sounds of the waters, the night roar of the lion, the rumble of zebra herds and wilder beast and the chatter of baboons as they gave praise to the morning sun, Ra". When the young prince had finished, the Hem-Sem-tpy asked. "What did you learn from Jhutyms Ka-en-Heru, your spiritual guide?" The young prince Mentchhotep replied, "He did not speak much, only in riddles. Pain seemto be his favorite lesson, how to inflict pain from many positions. These various positions he called them postures and stances. We stood in Ulimwengo, Ka, Ma'at, Heru Djed everyday for hours. We sat in Kukaa, laid in the Asrian posture for days, silent. We watched and imitated various animals: the crane, baboon, lion, the black panther, the falcon, the cobra, and the Hapy (Nile) crocodile." When the young prince finished this time, the Hem-Sem-Tpy told him to go back to Kash alone to the great rain forest and listen to what more he could hear and to practice everything that Jhutyms Ka-en-Heru had taught him. "You have missed the very essence of our lessons." The prince was puzzled by the Hem-Sem-Tpy's request. Had he not discerned every sound already? Hadn't he endured enough pain for a lifetime? Is this what his father wanted him to learn?

Mentchhotep traveled alone back to the ancient land of his ancestors, Kash. This time he even traveled deeper into the heart of the rainforest to the very source of the Hapy Eteru (Nile river) and all the Mountains of the Moon. For days and nights on end, Mentchhotep practiced every posture, every stance, meticulously studying every animal, every plant, and paid strict attention to his diet, eating only once a day and fasting monthly. Nevertheless, he heard no sounds other than those he had already heard. Then one morning, as the young prince sat silently under a tree, in one of his meditative postures from Ma'at Akhw Ba Ankh, he started to discern faint sounds unlike those he had ever heard before. The more acutely he listened, the clearer the sounds became. The feeling of enlightenment enveloped the prince. "These must be the sounds that Jhutyms Ka-en-Heru and the Hem-Sem-Tpy wished me to discern," he reflected.

When Mentchhotep returned to the great temple of Amen, the Hem-Sem-Tpy and his spiritual guide Jhutyms Ka-en-Heru could feel a great energy surrounding the prince. He was surely not the young boy who had left not long ago. When asked what more had he heard responded Mentchhotep reverently, "Hem-Sem-Tpy, when I listened most closely, I could hear the unheard - the sound of flowers opening, the sound of Ra warming the Earth, and the sounds of the grass embracing and drinking the morning dew."

The Spiritual Warrior Jhutyms Ka-en-Heru and the Hem-Sem-Tpy nodded approvingly. "To hear the unheard," remarked the Hem-Sem-Tpy, is a necessary discipline to be a good Nswt. For only when a ruler has learned to listen closely to the people's hearts, hearing their feelings and uncommunicative pains unexpressed, and complaints not spoken of, can a leader hope to inspire confidence in the people. This level of Konsciousness allows the leader to innerstand when something is wrong, and meets the true needs of the citizens. The demise of countries comes when leaders listen only to superficial words and do not penetrate deeply into the souls of the people to hear their true opinions, feelings and desires."

Mentchhotep had experienced Heru Konsciousness. His training was like that of Heru in the Asrian Drama and he was now ready to do battle with the forces of esfet. Armed with this new power of Heru Konsciousness, Mentchhotep was able to liberate and unify his people from the hands of chaos. The reign of Mentchhotep reached its pinnacle some years after he came to the throne with the reunification of Kemet. The political progression of his career is eloquently attested by the series of Heru names he adopted: first, "He who gives heart to the Two Lands," then "Master of the White Crown (Upper Kemet)," and finally, "Uniter of the Two Lands."

The Nswt's birth name, Mentchhotep - meaning "Mentch is content," Mentch being the Waset Ntchr of war - also seems appropriate, since the first part of his reign saw a great deal of bitter fighting. Mentchhotep enjoyed an unusually long reign of 50 years, the latter part of which, following reunification, saw a return to peace and prosperity in Kemet. Great trade was developed and maintained with Kash the land south of the sixth cataract. Building works at numerous sites - El Kab, Gebelein, Tod, Deir el Ballas, Denderah and Abydos - all testify to the stability brought forth by Mentchhotep. One of Mentchhotep's greatest projects, however, was the temple tomb he erected on the west bank at Waset, in the impressive great bay of cliffs at Deir el Bahari. The design of this temple was innovative, a great stepped podium with square cut pillars around it, and the next terrace with a hypostyle hall at the rear at the base of the cliffs. In the 3rd Golden Age (so-called 17-18th Dynasty), Hemet en Ntchrt and Nswt Hatshepsut Amen would copy his design leaving their footprints boldly behind forever. Shemsu Heru.

Kemklusion

In closing, it must be clear that we, the Kemetyu, resurrected Afrakans must do BATTLE, mentally, physically and spiritually for the liberation of our souls, our minds and our physical bodies. Power only concedes to more power and European Caucasian domination and Eurasians, which represent Esfet, must be killed, subdued and mentally held in check within the minds of Afrakan people. Only then can we collectively return to "The Way." We defeat white male domination by conquering ourselves. We are at war with the western mind and philosophical value system, not white people. We must stop imitating the western system, which is opposed to nature, and begin to embrace that which is ours: Ma'at.

In order for the modern Kemetyu, resurrected Afrakans to be victorious in battle, we must become Heru in spirit and master ourselves. As Spiritual Warriors, we must study Ourstory with a falcon's eye, innerstanding our strong and weak points. A critical and analytical study of the Maangamizi is a prerequisite for the liberation and redemption of Afrakans Worldwide. We must manifest the utmost courage and faith and never give in to anger, fear, or aggression. If we give in to esfet, then destruction is our destiny along with our oppressors.

We, as Afrakan Warriors, must see that just like Asr's body was ripped into pieces and scattered by Setsh, which also represents esfet, white male dominations has ripped us apart, and scattered us around the world. What is left of our great civilization is now hidden in Western museums, technology, science, and the world's religious systems. As Spiritual Warriors, we must follow Heru, who favors the guidance of Jhuty and Ma'at. The falcon Heru is symbolic of the harmony of the Warrior. Just as the night submits to the light of day and winter submits to the warmth of summer, Afrakans will rise again. This epic battle of Heru and Setsh stands as a classic example of how humans should confront the negative presence on earth, called white male domination ...then harmony, based on Ma'at, will be established as the order of the new day.

This new day for Afrakan people must be a new kind of freedom. Afrakans, who had been conquered by Europeans and/or enslaved by their system of European Caucasian domination, thought of freedom as a place, rather than as a continuation of a struggle. Even today, insane and mis-educated Afrakans think freedom is a goal, rather than a launching pad from which to reach our goals. Afrakan people will not find freedom or happiness until we have a collective Afrakan purpose. Without Kultural identity and Kultural direction, which a people get from their Kultural Ourstorical ancestral map, freedom is irrelevant. No one can give you your freedom. Freedom is something you earn through struggle, like Heru, and Mentchhotep, freedom is something ultimately that you take! If we are truly to become healers, our very first patient must be our loved ones, family, friends, and ourselves. The family is the smallest unit of a nation. If we cannot heal our families, the communities and the nation will forever remain sick, oppressed and without freedom, which is the opposite of "The Way."

The quest of every Spiritual Warrior is to become whole, like the divine spirit of Asr, through self-healing, this lays down a spiritual foundation for healing the family. Only whole families can heal a community, only whole communities can heal a nation, and only whole nations can heal the planet Earth. Spiritual Warriors must bring Ma'at back into our lives, and make her our spiritual mate or complement. Afrakan men, we must seek spiritual mates like Ma'at, Het-Heru, Ast, and Nebt-Het, if we are to raise strong and powerful families again as we become Heru with the Ntchr Jhuty as our eternal guide. Afrakan women, you must become Ma'at, Het-Heru, Ast, and Nebt-Het, as we all re-Afrakanize ourselves in the 63rd century new Afrakan time. Only with wisdom can we do battle with European Caucasian domination, which is the modern version of Setsh. Only then, can we stand before Asr resurrected and whole. Falcons, it is time for us to fly. Up you mighty Warriors! Shemsu Heru (followers of righteousness). You can accomplish whatever you will! BECOME HERU! AMEN MA'AT.

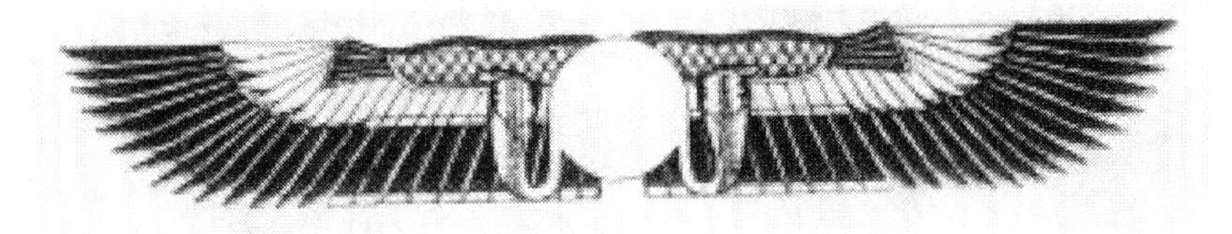

Mfundishi Jhutyms touching and sharing the spiritual power of the Shabaka Stone now in the British Museum. Below the Ntchr Asr -Left & Ast and baby Heru right. We are, because they were, so lets BE! **Shemsu Heru!**

Becoming Heru

Each Afrakan Spiritual Warrior must become Heru
Heru fights for liberation and freedom through excellence
When the Human Body Temple is functioning with excellence
Mentally, physically, and spiritually
It turns against and eradicates dis-eased tissues
It destroys any element that would try to choke or disrupt its internal harmony.
When we become Heru, we act with excellence
Mentally, we become Heru Konsciousness and Ma'at thinking
Physically, we develop Strong, toned, conditioned sacred body-temples
Spiritually, we are surrounded by love and we become konscious of our connection to the Ntchru
As Heru we are in constant battle with the poisonous elements that are destroying Afrakan Kulture and Spirituality
We must oppose European Caucasian domination and the European Worldview that exsist within us
It is like a poison to Afrakans, and all Melanin domanated people and nature itself.
Afraka for Afrakan people and Afrakan-centeredness for all Afrakans at home and throughout the Diaspora
One people, one mind, one aim, one goal
Excellence!
Ma'at through an Afrakan Worldview
Mentally, physically and spiritually
Because the time has come for the Kemetyu, resurrected Afrakans
To reclaim our rightful position as guardians of Afraka and its people
Like Heru, we must defend what we develop
Until our last breath
Shemsu Nu-n-Heru
Amen Ma'at...

Chapter ∩ I I I I (14)
Somo la Kumi na Nne

" The Moyo"

How to Kultivate and use your Personal Power

The Moyo is the center force of your personal power. It is the internal vital life force energy of the heart and Heru Konsciousness. Spiritual Warriors must teach the masses how to Kultivate and master their Moyo. Once the Moyo is Kultivated and consistently maintained at high levels, it can also be utilized for healing. It is the strength of the Moyo that is at the center of the spirit of the Afrakan Spiritual Warrior. This spirit will help defend our legacy - mentally, physically and spiritually, and like Ra, we will live for eternity. "The Aha Kemet Mnyama Saba System" of Kupigana Ngumi and Ma'at Akhw Ba Ankh meditations and breathing postures are methods of developing your personal power so that you can **"Become Heru,"** through the mastery of oneself. *Geb, the Neb of the Earth along with Nut, the livable atmosphere, are symbolic of Mother and Father Nature,* and they represent a symbolic book with endless chapters on the secrets of the universe. With the assistance of the Kemetik Legacy, Mdw Ntchr, an Afrakan-centered Worldview, "the Aha Kemet Mnyama Saba System" of Kupigana Ngumi. and Ma'at Akhw Ba Ankh, we will learn to read these symbols of nature. At the same time, we will learn to listen to our own eternal spiritual energy, which is only a microcosm of the outer temple of nature. Only with the power of the Moyo will we have enough personal power to overcome white male domination, and replace it with a new Worldview, with an Afrakan-centered Worldview.

Our bodies often tell us the path of **NTCHR,** which is part of our innerkonscious minds and links us to the Oneness of All. The only problem is that many of us have forgotten how to listen to ourselves, and even more of us have become ignorant to the appropriate steps to take when action is needed. The beauty of the human mind is that we have the power of action or the lack of action. The creative wisdom of The **NTCHR** has endowed us with at least seven senses. These seven senses are touch, taste, smell, sight, hearing, knowing - intuition, and will. When these senses are in harmony with the self, which is linked to the All, we become the Ntchr through our actions. The levels of self-destruction will depend on the level of disharmony. We have a choice to be slaves of our senses or we can be masters of them. In ancient Kemet, this great mastery of harmony was called Neb. We can be the Neb of Self and seek the path of the Afrakan Spiritual Warriors, or perish in Esfet (destruction, wrong doings, white male domination, a destructive imbalance).

The Stages of Life

One of the major keys to successful living is to learn that human beings are creatures of habit. To be successful, we must learn and practice life-giving habits, and acquire the skills needed to complete one's personal mission or goals. There is no magic or great secret in mastering life. Basically, minimize your life-threatening habits and replace them with life-giving habits. And never stop learning, never stop perfecting your skills, always be on a mission, never stop dreaming and reaching for Ra- the stars. Remember, Spiritual Warriors are always seeking balance, developing themselves mentally, physically and spiritually with Ma'at in their hearts, Jhuty in their minds and Heru as their guide.

Look at your life as if it was a garden, and you are the gardener. Your garden can be well attended, well watered, richly fertilized, full of beautiful flowers and plants, neatly groomed, a true joy to be in and full of positive attributes and experiences. However, without a true Kultural center and Pan-Afrakan Worldview (plan of action), your garden will be overrun by weeds, poorly kept, not watered and containing no flowers, no true Kulture at the center, only negative thoughts and emotions, and it will be extremely difficult to heal ourselves through a European Worldview. The choice is yours. If you want positive results, you must plan well in advance and follow through with positive action, for action is the fruit of all real knowledge.

The process of developing the necessary tools and knowledge that will allow a human being to navigate into maturity for any people is Kulture, so Afrakan people must use Afrakan Kulture within a workable Pan-Afrakan Worldview. With a positive life-giving spiritual Afrakan Worldview, they can travel through their missions as captains of their own human and spiritual vessels, which is the healing formula for Afrakan liberational institutions. In addition, this same healing formula will enable them to give their gifts to the world as they complete their life's purpose.

All Spiritual Warriors know and must teach that every action (including inaction), has a definite result. If you do nothing in your garden, something still happens. Weeds seem to appear out of nowhere and they will not go away but continue to grow on their own. It takes hard work and a definite plan to replace them. Life is the same way: The NTCHR has given you talent and precious gifts, but if you do not Kultivate them, perfect them through hard work, your life will be overrun with weeds. Who, what, and where are the weeds of life? They are the negative thoughts, emotions and negative experiences or our reactions and interpretations of negative experiences. The seven aspects of esfet are fear, pride, wrath, gluttony, luxury, avarice, and envy. These negative thoughts, emotions and experiences will not go away by themselves. If you do not change your life-threatening habits and take action to remove the weeds with life-giving habits, like the seven Virtues - faith, hope, charity, strength, prudence, temperance, and justice - your talents and gifts will be consumed by the weeds of esfet, and wasted away. We all know or knew someone who was very talented, but never lived up to their potential and ended up a loser. Weeds consumed their garden and their existence.

Spiritual Warriors must teach one of the most important lessons of life, the realization of the stages or seasons in life. If you are to Kultivate your garden, you must harmonize the right seasons with the right action. There is a season to plow and prepare the ground before any planting can take place. After developing a strong, fertile foundation, you have a planting season, growing season, and harvest season. Life has stages just like the seasons; only life's stages are based on your thoughts, attitudes, emotions, maturity and associations at particular periods in life. If we are to be successful we must master certain life skills in each stage of our lives, or there will be even greater challenges in the next stage of life.

FIVE STAGES OF HUMAN LIFE

1) The NTCHR, the unborn spiritual forces and the sacred ancestral memory are all One inside the womb of creation at birth. You are re-born divine.
2) Birth to 21 years of age - We learn, practice, and master most of our life-giving and life-threatening habits in this second stage. You do not choose this education or mis-education; it is given to you from parents, friends, media, society, etc. Each human baby develops four spiritual centers that are inherent in every human and automatically according to DNA blueprint. These spiritual centers are temporal and obey the agreed upon laws of physics. Each spiritual center opens and receives light or is activated at basic stages of development. Spiritual center one at rebirth - Infant - Nourishment survival spirit Kem-necked to Mother. Spiritual center two - toddler - locomotion, 3-D (space). Spiritual center three - child - language, 4-D (time). Spiritual center four - adolescent - puberty, sexual and emotional spirit (heart).
3) 22 to 49 years of age - This is the adultship stage. Use of all that was learned in the previous stages is used to flourish and create. But if you have not done well previously, all of your vices are materialized and begin to show clearer in day to day situations and circumstances and you get sucked into the

illusion of white male domination. In this stage most addictions are learned to help deal with the illusion of what is perceived to be reality or simply escape from an unprepared reality. In this stage, your education or your mis-education is external. It is an education you allow yourself to have, through your actions or lack of action. Here the potential for the activation of Spiritual centers five through eight becomes available. These Spiritual centers are increasingly transcendental nature, where centers one through four are analytical in nature, centers five through eight are intuitive and psychedelic in nature.

4) 35 to 77 years of age- Personal Power- Mastery of the laws of success and practicing them. Successful experiences enable the Spiritual Warrior to have the greatest success. In this stage, only perfect practice with direction leads towards perfection. Perfection is a state of Konsciousness. You are in control or someone else is in control. The real leaders of life emerge during this fourth stage of life. Spiritual centers five and six are the keys they are the euphoric spirit - developed by Athletics, Drama, Literature, Music, and Meditation. Spiritual center six being in tune with biorhythms, vibrations or the Art of Magick.

5) 50 years of age and up- Elders to Ancestors- Once you have purpose, identity and direction you can accomplished your life goals. This accomplishment is the act of giving your gifts to the world with pleasure. Your life is successful because you completed your goals, followed your plans, developed your gifts and now you are surrounded with family, friends and all the magnificence and harmony that a productive garden can produce. This harmony is called Ma'at or Htp. This is one of the ultimate goals of all Spiritual Warriors and healers. This seventh Spiritual center is the Collective Konsciousness, Ancestorial memory. But if you failed to remove all the weeds from your garden during your first four stages, and if you have not prepared the foundation for success with a carefully

well thought out plan, you will never be able to give your gift to the world. And without Kultural direction even great talents will be manipulated and used or exploited.

Rites of Passage for Men and Women

Men:	Women:
a. Mother Training - birth to 7 yrs.	**a. Mother training-birth to 7yrs**
b. Ntchru Training - 3 to 14 yrs.	**b. Ntchru training- 3 to 14 yrs**
c. Manship (warrior) Training - 14 to 42 yrs.	**c. Womenship training- 11 to 22 yrs**
d. Reproductive Cycle - 21 to 63 yrs.	**d. Reproductive Cycle- 14 to 42 yrs**
e. Leadership Training - 33 yrs & up	**e. Leadership Training - 33 yrs & up**
f. Elders - 50 yrs & up	**f. Elders - 50 yrs & up**

The Way of the Warrior is not mandatory among the women, but is encouraged at the basic level within Womenship training

Initiation or rights of passage are the processes of developing the necessary tools and knowledge that will allow a human being to navigate into maturity or citizenship within that society. The initiated citizen then at this state of empowerment can travel through their missions as captain of their own human and spiritual vessel enabling them to give their gifts to their people, the world as they complete their life's purpose within a Kultural system.

These stages of life are initiations and they are also called rites of passages, because they mark significant stages in a human being's development from rebirth, to a responsible adult, to eldership. Spiritual Warriors must make sure these rites are grounded in the principles of Ma'at - truth, justice, balance and righteousness, with their ancestral Ourstory and Afrakan-centered Kulture, then a Spiritual center can be activated - Universal Spirit, Cosmic Konsciousness, which are aspects of The NTCHR Spirit. Traditionally, all Afrakan people had rites or initiations that showed the development and positive growth, from one stage to the next. However, the Maangamizi has destroyed this Kultural connection. The ancient Kulture has been destroyed or distorted within most Afrakans in Afraka and in the Diaspora. Spiritual Warriors will have to reintroduce these programs from an Afrakan-centered perspective to re-Afrakanize the complete Afrakan family, at home in Afraka and throughout the Diaspora. Who ever controls the minds of our children, families and the voice of our communities, truly controls our future. We, as Afrakan people, must regain control of our minds, our youth, our families, our elders our Institutions and the security and voice of our communities. The elders and the Institutions in our communities need the rites of passage program as much as the youth, they all must help teach each other and give purpose to the whole community or nation. Only at this level of healing can we Kultivate our gardens, families, communities, and ourselves so that we can become a strong Afrakan people, developing strong Afrakan families, Kem-unities (communities), and nations wherever we are geographically.

The First Stage

The first stage of life is the spiritual stage. In the beginning, there was only The NTCHR, and The NTCHR was All. The universal intelligence that directs all things is manifested through spirit and spirit is in everything, everywhere all the time. The Divine Spirits are reflections of the One Creator, The NTCHR. Some of these spiritual forces have special interests. Our sacred Afrakan Ancestral Spirits have mastered certain life forces while on the physical plane and are available like the Jegnoch to guide us towards our gifts or special talents.

When we are re-born, at physical birth, The NTCHR gives each of us an ancestral memory bank that is like a timeless capsule holding all the keys to who we are, where we came from and what we must do. Your DNA holds all this information, along with our special talents and gifts and then another copy is placed in our Melanin and locked in our Pineal gland. Some Afrakan Priestesses and Priests can communicate with the unborn child while it is still in the sacred womb of the woman, and learn something about who the child is and what their mission is, so that they can prepare for their reentrance back into the physical world of human beings. All this knowledge is lodged in the unkonscious mind of the child and can be transferred to the child's Konscious mind in later stages of its development. Because the womb of a woman is so sacred it is important that she prepare herself mentally, physically, spiritually and kulturally for the first stage of human life which is inside her sacred womb. This is just another reason why every woman should be treated with respect and dignity, for she is the sacred keeper of human life. It is equally important that women learn to respect themselves because of their responsibility to humanity. Seeds of respect, responsibility, self-discipline, love, warmth, caring and sharing start in the womb. Mama and Baba should stroke the abdomen as they talk, pray and sing to the unborn child.

In Ancient Kemet, there were birthing houses built next to the Sacred Temples, so that the right atmosphere could be created as each new life re-entered the physical world of human beings. The birthing house was prepared for ultimate comfort and ease, both aesthetically and spiritually pleasing and in tune with the ancient knowledge. Kultural images and artifacts donned the walls and halls. Several midwives carried the birthing knowledge embodying love and tradition, creating a positive Kultural and spiritual atmosphere for both mother and child. Today, Ma'at Akhw Ba Ankh, the way of the Ancient Kemet meditative and breathing system, is an excellent form of exercise and mental, physical and spiritual development that can prepare women before and after childbirth on how to be a dynamic house for themselves and their family. Once the child is reborn through natural childbirth, with love and Kultural healing custodians to guide the new/ancient life force, then a melaninated atmosphere at home will set the tone for the second stage of life. Spiritual Warriors if we are to truly create Ma'at and maintain Ma'at we will have to re-create our own healing and health centers with birthing departments within them that reflect Ma'at. We must stop having our children and delivering our children in the killing, Institutions called Hospitals of white male domination.

The Second Stage

The second stage of life starts from re-birth and lasts until about 21 years of age. Almost all of your formal education or mis-education that is given to you by other people will come during this time period.

During the second stage, you are learning the rules of the game of life within your society. It is also during this stage that you develop your attitude towards other people, society, your people and the world in general. But most important, your self-image is developed during this second stage of life.

When a strong foundation, based upon Ma'at has been laid, with the discipline of Heru Konsciousness and Afrakan-centered Kultural awareness, all things are possible. If young Spiritual Warriors are properly nurtured and prepared to pursue their mission in life by perfecting and giving their gifts, then the family, community and nation will be blessed. At this point, the young Spiritual Warriors will be ready for stage three in life. But, if the young adult did not receive a life-giving education, was not nurtured properly at home, there were no social institutions in place to help develop their lives, and if their self-image was developed on the streets, by TV, movies and the mis-educational system of white male domination during this critical stage in life's development, he or she will enter stage three mentally enslaved. Nevertheless, prepared or not, if you live long enough you will enter the third stage of life. At around 7 years of life, reason develops; at 14 years of age, puberty, and at 21 years, the age of maturation. However, because of mass insanity, improper diets and Kultural retardation, reasoning does not happen at 7 years of age, but much later if at all. Puberty starts much too early and maturity evades some youth forever. Your success will depend on how well you have adjusted to being a student of life. To the Spiritual Warrior, Ma'at must be at the heart of your struggle. If in this second stage of life you are given lemons, make lemonade, regroup and adjust your plan for success.

The Third Stage

The third stage of life starts around 22 years of age and lasts until a person is around 49 years old. If one has been properly prepared, this is the stage of inside education, or spiritual education. The education you receive during the third stage is by choice or lack of choice, but the decision is totally in your hands. Young Spiritual Warriors follow their mission by choosing a field of study or work that will help sharpen their NTCHR given gifts. Stay away from dead end nowhere jobs and backward people who are going nowhere fast, or people who do not have a positive mission. They will drain your Moyo instead of charging it, these people are weeds. Focus is the key at this point because your journey has not really started until you have left your parents or guardians' house and moved out on your own. Once you are responsible for all your own bills, rent, food, clothing, transportation, etc., you are experiencing the rituals of survival and the everyday challenges of life in this society. If you have not mastered discipline, control of passions, along with perceptive financial skills in the second stage of life, you will pay dearly during the early part of the third stage of life.

There are very few Spiritual Warriors before this stage of life, because this is where control of thoughts, emotions, and appetites are tested. If you fall, or fail in the second stage of life your parents or family is there to pick you up, dust you off, kiss you and tell you that it will be all right. However, in the world of illusions and white male domination, it is not quite like that. Some people get overwhelmed in this stage for a variety of reasons. Some start out too young and unprepared, before they have mastered life-surviving skills. There are babies having babies, and unprepared young men impregnating women. Then there are some people who were so sheltered that they do not even have a clue about the real challenges of survival. Then there are those who slept or partied through the second stage of life and now they are in for a rude awakening. These unprepared people are crushed, eaten and destroyed by this system of capitalism and white male domination, which feeds off the ignorant and unprepared souls. If you think this is bad, double all of this pain and grief if you are Black or Afrakan because you have been conquered and enslaved by white male domination. Now another person can use you, you can be subdued by a sensation, a feeling, a drug, or some negative addiction, as a means to escape or cope with the illusion of "real" life situations in an insane society.

All of nature's inhabitants must quickly learn to master the skills of survival or they become fuel for some other creature's journey, or they simply perish. The major challenges of the third stage are centered on self-discipline, focus, and personal mastery of your mental, physical and emotional appetites. Spiritual Warriors must be anchored spiritually from a wholistic life-giving Worldview. Even with these skills if one does not have ethnic and Kultural integrity and knowledge, one will be used as a pawn in the game of life under the control of white male domination.

The Fourth Stage

The fourth stage of life is the stage of personal power. This stage starts around the age of 35 and takes you into your senior years. Some special people may enter this stage around the age of 33 years. This is the stage where it all comes together or falls apart. The experiences of the first three stages have given you the skills to make things happen. It is at the fourth stage that Spiritual Warriors attain their greatest success. It is also when the average person has some success, or experiences their greatest failures.

Spiritual Warriors are empowered mainly during this stage because the years of discipline, focus, correct breathing, and physical training have helped them to master the laws of success and to achieve their goals and to help heal themselves and their families. These Spiritual Warriors were the major players of life in the third stage. Now they are the controllers of the players, the owners, coaches, directors, healers, financial wizards, coordinators and your Kultural custodians. Ma'at has become part of their lives, they have a clear vision of life, a dynamic innerstanding of ethnic pride, Kultural integrity, and they are at peace with themselves and in harmony with the cosmos.

Spiritual Warriors at this stage are healers, because they are giving their gifts to the world. They innerstand that human beings are creatures of habit and you either have life-giving habits or life-threatening habits. The healing comes with the giving of their life-sustaining gifts. These Spiritual Warriors are doing what they love and loving what they do. It is the Moyo that promotes internal healing and it is the Moyo that extends outward to heal others.

The masses, who do not innerstand The NTCHR and who are not followers of Ma'at, will have very limited Moyo. They will have to repeat lessons, which should have been mastered in previous stages. And those human beings whose life-threatening habits out weighed their life-giving habits will experience poverty, bad health, poor attitudes, sickness, disease and early death, or a long unfulfilled life of spiritual death, which is slavery.

In the final analysis, your consistent actions will determine your success or failure in life; you can become a Spiritual Warrior or a fool, or something in between. It is not what you say, but what you do and how consistently you do it that determines the out-come.

The Fifth Stage

At stage five are the Elders, the ones who are the closest to the Ancestors or who have achieved a higher Konsciousness or the mentally, physically, spiritually and Kulturally uncompromised masses. This stage is usually from around the age of 50 years of age, until you recycle your physical energy back into the universe as spirit. If you were never a Spiritual Warrior and you reached this stage, then you are a pawn in the game of life. If you were a Spiritual Warrior who has become an Elder, your next stage is an Elder of immortality. You have given your gifts and followed your dreams and healed a multitude of sick humans. The society needs to have you sit at the round table of Esteem Elders as one of our Spiritual Visionaries who will help us create tomorrow's reality and secure yesterday's dreams.

These visionaries of immortality see far pass their personal desires or ego. They use the Sankofa Spirit for building the future, and they center themselves within the Afrakan-centered society by reflecting positive realities for the immortality of Afrakan people. These positive realities will revive Pan-Afrakanism and the concept of a nation within a nation here in America for Afrakan people or wherever we are in the Diasopra.

In the fifth stage, Spiritual Warriors have realized their visions for immortality. Their gifts and talents are healing their people and it is their state of total faith in The NTCHR and in themselves as a manifestation of The NTCHR that make them the great visionaries of our times. These are the grand masters, the Wafundishi, the sages, the prophets and sacred poets of the people. They are impeccable Spiritual Warriors who are healers just through their very presence. Their Moyo or their physical, mental, spiritual and psychic powers are stimulated to an unlimited, uncharted level of excellence. Consequently, these elders are still Spiritual Warriors who are magnetic, attracting people and resources on all levels and helping to remold and re-Afrakanize the Kemetyu of today. With this spirit, Spiritual Warriors are invincible and cannot be stopped or defeated. We will be victorious against esfet and the European American system of Caucasian male domination as long as the spirit of the Spiritual Warrior lives and is manifested in each generation.

If Afrakan people are to recapture and reclaim their spiritual, intellectual and technical genius, and control their own destiny in the 63rd century new Afrakan time, it will be because we have allowed our Spiritual Warriors, through corporative operational unity, to take control of our collective lives as Afrakan people. We, Afrakan people, are catching hell from the system of white male domination collectively; the racist's laws of the land affect us collectively. Discrimination affects us collectively, and it will take a collective effort to heal us, as Afrakan people. Once we as a people decide to teach Afrakans that only Afrakans can save Afrakans and that our wealthy and the wealth that the collective masses have, can help stop this destructive pattern of the maangamizi and help finance our own liberation. Afrakan Spiritual Warriors must teach Afrakans through Afrakan Kulture and a wholistic Spiritual Worldview how to love ourselves, because only Afrakan people have our own best interest at heart, we will then be able to stop the system of white male domination from giving us hell on earth. Pan-Afrakan operational unity is the key, once we innerstand that we are Afrakans, and therefore have an obligation to Afrakan people, the Afrakan continent and to Ma'at, then we can liberate ourselves and remain sovereign.

There are a growing number of Afrakan millionaires, and an even larger number of very affluent Afrakans in America, but collectively Afrakans are still poor. Collectively we have the worst education, live in the worst housing, and have the lowest paying jobs. We are poor because of the collective desires of white male domination - racism. In addition, Afrakan people have been programmed, just like European Americans have been programmed, that white is right, and therefore better. So our rich, Afrakans in Americas or Afraka spend their money at the same places, on the same things that their European counterparts do. We give the wealth back to our oppressors without the masses of Afrakan benifiting from this enormous wealth. Somehow, someway, someone, or some group of Spiritual Warriors will have to teach Afrakans that only Afrakans can save Afrakans.

These five stages will mean nothing if we do not use this information for liberation. Collectively, we must support these Elders who have become Spiritual Warriors, the ones who are the closest to the Ancestors and the ones who have achieved Higher Konsciousness. These are the Spiritual Warriors who will master the Eight Spiritual centers that will lead us to infinity. Eight is the infinity sign side-ways. These visionaries of immortality are in the best position to collectively lead us as Afrakan people to total Liberation, a state of Htp for eternity.

The Seven Types of People in The World

There are at least seven types of Afrakans in the Western world of the European-American Caucasian dominated system of the matrix. The matrix system wants to control the minds, the bodies, the souls and desires of all of the people of the world, along with all of the planet's wealth (natural resources). In addition, it has become partners with esfet in this conquest, the enemies of Ra (the spiritual world in which Afrakans are indigenous of).

The matrix of European Caucasian domination is void of a mature spiritual connection. The Spirit is not only in every living being but it encompasses the planet, the cosmos and beyond, which is unlimited and all-powerful and reaches far beyond the boundary of our comprehension. Thus, the Spiritual Warrior can penetrate the matrix at will, because all things are of spirit, and this spirit cannot be bought, tricked, or manipulated. Even physical death poses no threat to the Spiritual Warrior. The matrix is powerless against the spirit. European Caucasian domination tries to control the physical world through definition and illusion. It defines the paradigm of your world through false values and desires to enslave you, if physical enslavement does not work. The power of the Western world uses an illusion, and the image of powerlessness of Afraka, the richest place on the planet, and weak mindless greedy Afrakans, is also an illusion that the matrix is coercing you to see. The Spiritual Warrior can see through the lies of the illusion of the matrix, and ***esfet is not tempting to an evolved spirit***. This is why the Spiritual Warrior spends a lifetime developing his or herself, and mastering ones own appetite and personality. In order to develop the "Moyo", one needs to make your own life the subject of intense inquiry, in this way you will discover your personal goals, directions, gifts, and destiny. The process of freeing your mind, innerstanding the spirit, kultivating the soul, and controlling the senses is the essence of the Spiritual Warrior, the reward will be clear insight.

There are at least seven types of human beings operating in America, and within the influence of white male domination. Let us examine these seven personalities:

1. The "Doers" - The "Doers" are a small elite group with vision, creativity, and foresight. They are the controllers of the power in the game and they are the makers of the rules. The doers are the visionaries that see even what the best of the players cannot see. They reach stages beyond their own personal goals. They have the ability to Kultivate the forces and vibrations which are the keys to life. The doers are the makers of Ourstory. They are magnetic, attracting the people and the sources needed to realize their vision. They become impeccable warriors in the game of life. They are difficult to defeat, and no matter what obstacles that stand in their way, they are victorious, because they refuse to accept defeat, and death poses no threat. These Doers are at the top of the pyramid of life. They are the Grand Masters, Masters, the Gurus, the Wafundishi,and the C.E.O's. Most of the Doers are in the 4th or 5th stages of life. They are the power masters and the elders. In the beautiful garden of life, they are the owners, the ones who planned the garden and willed the garden into existence, and ultimately payed for the Kultivation and maintenance of the garden.

Remember there are Physical Masters and Spiritual Masters. The Physical Masters are still entrapped by materialism and the American Illusion. Only the Spiritual Master can liberate his or her soul from the deathly grips of the matrix.

2. The "Players" - The "Players" use their power to make things happen. They generally do what they love and love what they do. They are also the very best at what they do and therefore, they reap the rewards of their efforts. The "Players" are the ones who take the risks and pay the price but, also reap the reward. These Players are in the second level of the pyramids, and the third stage of life where experience by doing the game is the teacher of the day. They are the professional athletes, directors of corporations, major entrepreneurs, and manufacturers. In martial arts they are the Malenga and Mfundi, the modern day Black Belt. In the beautiful garden of life, they are the master gardeners, the physical creators of the beauty. They are not necessarily the owners but they are the keepers of the garden. They make all our dreams happen. The masses of people in the matrix of white male domination, live their dreams through the players. The players are usually programmed around individual, capitalistic goals that keep them in the heart of the European America Caucasian domination system of the matrix. The star players are highlighted and given extra recognition so that they can keep the masses of the people chasing after an illusion. This is why the life of spirituality, "The Way of Heru" becomes the guide of the Spiritual Warrior, not the acquisition of material objects, fame or fortune.

3. The "Watchers" - Watchers are the spectators who watch the game from the outside on the bleachers. They are close to the action, they can smell it, feel the sweat, and they usually are the "wannabes" with a thousand excuses why they are not playing the game themselves. They watch others play the game of life. Watching someone else get paid. Watching the players get the recognition and the personal security they wish they had. Some of them dream of being a Player, or they may even be ex-Players who did

not plan for the future. Watchers are generally people who had dreams but let them be compromised. Watchers often say "I should have done this, or I could have been that, but I have a good life." So, Watchers run other people's businesses instead of their own. They manage or direct for someone else. A few get paid well, but most never get paid their worth. They make just enough money from their job to get a seat in the game of life. (J.O.B., just over broke) The Watchers are in the second, third and fourth levels in the stages of life. Most Watchers are the middle management, educators, small business people. In the Martial Arts, they are the Mpigana and the under belts who have not mastered their trade. In the beautiful garden of life, they are the ones that pay admission to see the work of the Spiritual Warriors. They pay the salary of the owner and Kultivator, only they don't have a garden of their own. They admire the beauty of the garden and usually die saying, "I wish I had a garden as beautiful as this." They recognize the beauty in others, but they do not recognize it in themselves. They very rarely seize the moment. They are the foundation of the matrix system, the unconscious working middle and upper middle class who are hypnotized by materialism. What this group is lacking is Konsciousness, an awareness of their Afrakan Ancestral memory, and a plan of recovery, re-Afrakanization and liberation.

4. <u>The "Listeners"</u> - Listeners are people who read about the game and listen to the game from the parking lot. They may even be the couch potatoes who watch the game on TV but they always get second hand information. They are never there. They are always on the outside of the event. These are the people who live their lives working for others at the bottom of the scale of life. They are the masses of the population who never live out their dreams. The Listeners know the game is going on, they just have not developed themselves enough to participate in the game. Most of the Listeners could not afford the tickets to the game, or don't even know who to buy tickets from

because they are overwhelmed with just survival and working from day to day. They live their entire life responding to others and developing other people's programs. They are always wondering what went on; they often see the world in terms of would have, could have, and should have. Most of the Listeners are in the second, third, and fourth stages of life. They are the everyday workers in every society. They are over worked, under paid and unappreciated, but the most needed commodity called human labor. They are the bottom section of the pyramid of life. In Martial Arts, they are the wanafunzi, the white and yellow belts. They have seen all the martial arts movies and need the skills, but have mastered very few. In the beautiful garden of life, these people have never really paid too much attention to it because they have been too busy working. They have only looked at the garden in books, magazines, TV, and movies. They don't think the beautiful garden is a realistic attainable goal. Many Afrakans in this group cannot help themselves because they are not Konscious that the matrix is controlling their desires and aspirations. The masses of Afrakans in America think that they are not capable of defeating white male domination, or even worse, they are not really sure who their real enemies are. So even in the name of progress, these confused masses enslave themselves even more. And just like the garden they don't have, they don't think that Afrakan liberation and independence is a realistic attainable goal so they get lost in the illusion of American insanity.

5. The "Clueless" - The Clueless don't even know a game is going on, and have no plans to find out what is going on. They live from moment to moment, and nothing really matters to them but the bare essentials. They definitely can be found at the base of the pyramid. The Clueless have loosely defined goals or unrealistic goals compared to their skill level. Along with not having clearly defined goals, they usually have shallow roots or don't innerstand their

family or Kultural roots. They are ruled by their addictions and their appetites. The Clueless are from the second, third, and fourth stages of life. They are the jobless, the homeless, sometimes the minimum wager and the underachiever. In martial arts they are the ones who don't know what martial arts is about, or why anyone would want to know it. Some of the clueless promise themselves that one day they will take a class. In the beautiful garden of life, they don't even know it exists and if they see one, they think that they don't have time to Kultivate it, or that it is an unattainable goal and therefore, a waste of time. These are people who have lost their vision, and have stopped dreaming in color. These are the casualties of the matrix system of white male domination, and they ***no longer reach for Ra, or any of the stars.***

6. The "Spiritually Konscious" - The Spiritually Konscious has always existed. Before the matrix system of European Caucasian domination took control of our societies, the Spiritually Konscious was the average Afrakan or melanin dominated human. This is before any contact with foreign influence of Asiatics and caucasians. Today these people are partially under the control of the matrix. They are Konscious that the matrix exists, and that it is not their friend, but are not unified enough to resist it totally. The Spiritually Konscious usually have a religious or spiritual system that is not Christianity or Islam. Many speak another language, that is not European, and at home practice another Kulture that is not part of the matrix system of white male domination. In the Black community, they are Afrakan-centered, or at least Afrakan Konscious. They read Afrakan-centered books or at least Afrakan authors. They are usually a little more health Konscious than the average citizen in the matrix, but not necessarily. They celebrate or support Kwanzaa; they have a few Afrakan outfits that they wear at special occasions. The main tragedy here is that they think they can't exist without economically depending on the matrix system of white male domination. Their success and failure is still defined by the white

male domination. They can be Black professors at white universities, or members of the Ph.D. club. Sometimes they are well trained managers, directors and even players of the matrix. These Spiritually Konscious Afrakans are in the middle class. But the majority of the Spiritually Konscious are still at the bottom of the pyramid of life because they either do not totally innerstand the game of white male domination or they just refuse to play the game. The reality of the Spiritually Konscious, is that they are also pawns in the game of white male domination. What is missing is organization. If these Spiritually Konscious humans could operate as a nation inside a nation, they could economically step outside the matrix and white male domination and control their own destiny. They must learn about the "laws of collectivity," operational unity and the Spirit of One, The NTCHR" or practise what you teach!

7. The "Spiritual Warrior" - The Spiritual Warrior lives in the society for one reason and one reason only: to bring about its destruction and to liberate those who want to be liberated from the matrix of white male domination. The Spiritual Warriors have spent their entire lives developing the tools of self empowerment so that they can deliver their gifts to the world. These tools are sometimes keys that allow them to open major doors within the matrix so that they can move freely within the system of white male domination. They are usually self employed, or they are working and networking with other Spiritual Warriors. Their full time occupation is usually teaching, healing, organizing and providing positive guidance and inspiration for liberation outside of the system of white male domination. The Spiritual Warrior teaches by example. They are humans of principles, and these principles are based upon Ma'at and are the power tools of healing and developing personal power. Only with personal power can you free yourself from the illusion of the matrix system of white male domination, a drug that is destroying, Afrakan people, all people of color and the planet.

Mfundishi Jhutyms at Black Gold providing Spiritual Warrior training in the way of Heru on the left. On the right, Mzee Hannibal Afrik, Marimba Ani, Mfundishi and Djifa Richards at target practice, serious survival training. Bottom left and right are 20th century Jegnoch's of all Afrakan-centered Spiritual Warriors; El Hajj Malik El Shabazz and Brother Khalid Mohammed.

THE SEVEN PRINCIPLES OF PERSONAL POWER

1. Only the Spirit of the Soul Endures.

2. Only with love in one's heart can one succeed.

3. Only through persistence can you be successful.

4. Only through the innerstanding of the Ntchru can you be one with time.

5. Only when one becomes the Neb Hu of themselves can one know the Creator, The **NTCHR.**

6. Only through the innerstanding of the Black Dot, can one innerstand the uniqueness of the Black genius.

7. Only through the knowledge of one's own Kulture and story can one act correctly for liberation.

Above are a list of some of the Spiritual Warrior's tools, also known as the seven principles of personal power.

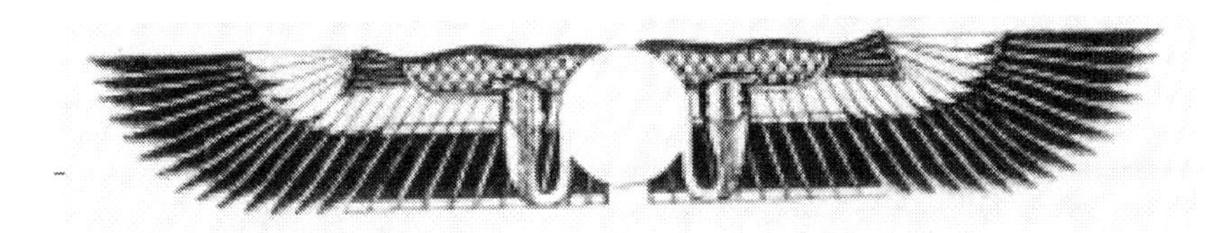

First Principle

Only the Spirit of the Soul Endures. A victorious soul is the ultimate success. Principles are steps on a ladder that helps you reach your goals. The human soul is part of the infinite energy of the Creator. It lives temporarily in your mind as it baths in a sea of melanin, a magnificent molecule of energy that directs our creative genius. Blackness, called melanin in the human body-temple, is the material, which is the foundation of the innerkonscious mind. This same innerkonscious mind links you to every melanin-dominated mind that ever existed. So locked deep within your innerkonscious mind is the knowledge and wisdom of everything that has ever happened, that was recorded by a human mind. However, wisdom and knowledge are irrelevant if one does not act on what one knows. Spiritual Warriors must teach that when you see and innerstand Ma'at, you must teach and discuss this truth with those who are blind. There are many scholars drowning in drugs and lining the gutters of our society. All the failures and misfortunate people of the world are not dumb and ignorant. They have never learned the power of self, nor do they innerstand the spirit of the soul. Strong principles build a powerful ladder that can endure far beyond the physical body. This type of ladder is called an institution. Principles that create institutions are the foundation for harmony in the soul and in the society.

The key to innerstanding the soul is to communicate with it. Tell yourself, I shall be the Neb of good habits. I shall develop those habits, which will help me master my senses. When my senses are in harmony, they will keep my body, mind and soul in harmony. This harmony is self-empowerment. When I think of Afraka or Afrakan people, I will think of good habits, the re-Afrakanization of our minds and good habits are the key to success. When I embrace Kupigana Ngumi or Ma'at Akhw Ba Ankh, I am standing with and in the company of my sacred Afrakan Ancestors and they are guiding me towards self-respect, self-determination, and self-defense. Ma'at Akhw Ba Ankh, the Afrakan meditative spiritual system uses the pyramid as a symbol for developing good habits so that we may rise on the pyramid of life.

Human beings are creatures of habit. We can be enslaved by bad habits and remain at the base of the pyramid of life forever or we can be the Neb of ourselves, the choice is ours. Failure is a person's inability to reach their own personal goals in life, whatever they may be. The main reasons for failure is that one's bad habits outweigh one's good habits on the scale of Ma'at (Truth, Justice, Righteousness and Harmonious Balance). Each day that you practice Kupigana Ngumi and Ma'at Akhw Ba Ankh you must say to yourself," I shall develop good habits that will be the mastery over my senses, which is the self." Everyday you should check off your list of good habits that will help you be the Neb of self. A lost day cannot be retrieved, nor can it be substituted. Live each day as if it is your greatest day! Be excellent, Will excellence into your life. This is the spirit that lives to eternity, remember only the spirit of the soul endures.

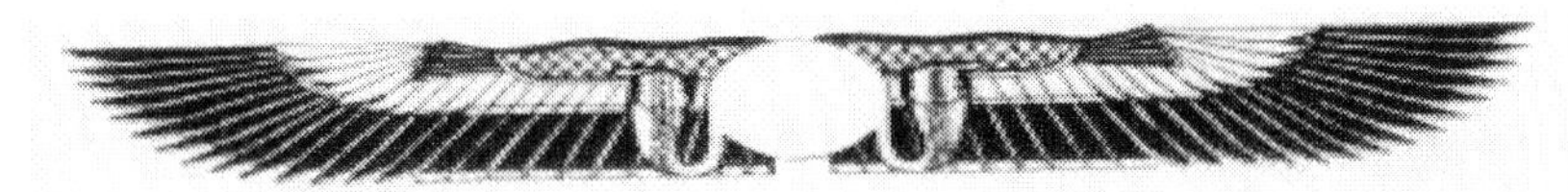

Second Principle

Only With Love In One's Heart Can One Succeed. I will greet each and everyday with love in my heart for self, family, friends and the spirit of my people, the cosmos and The NTCHR and I will succeed. Spiritual Warriors must teach that gentleness is one of the first steps of love, like the gentle loving care given to a new baby, or a new idea. With the power of love of Self, I will succeed because if I do not love self, it will be difficult to love anyone or anything else. Without love of Ourstory and the Kulture of your people, the Self will self-destruct (while indirectly you are destroying your people)! Love is a person's greatest instrument but not blind love, for love is like a doubled-edged sword. More love of others than for yourself is dangerous to you and your people. Love is a powerful energy force and like any great power, it must be directed. Spiritual Warriors must teach that we should love happiness, for it enlarges your heart, yet, we must endure sadness for it opens your soul. Yes, even have a love for the lessons learned in your failures, for they are only challenges that we must learn to master.

A fool is someone who does not love Self, or loves their enemy more than Self. This kind of person should be avoided and watched, because they become enemies of our people and must not be trusted. These fools are your uncle toms, overseers, police informers, modern day drug pushers and they, like the Ntchr Set, have always been around. We can no longer ignore them, or make believe they don't exist. This energy must be destroyed in our community or held in close check. These fools sold us out during slavery; they kept us enslaved during the European conquest of Afrakan people and they are still all around us pulling us apart and spearheading disunity today. Remember the fool does not love self, and actions speaks louder than words, so don't be tricked by their rhetoric. We must take control of our own lives, and our own communities. Only Spiritual Warriors can deal with these fools, and they must be dealt with in the 21st century. We must make the profession of the fool become extinct like the dinosaur or the most short-lived profession in our community.

Once you have accepted the challenge to move up the pyramid of life, you must be able to develop a wholistic approach towards your thinking. You will zealously inspect all things which enter your body, your mind, your soul, and your heart, for the glory of heaven is within. You will cherish your body with cleanliness, physical conditioning and moderation in all things. Even too much of a good thing is bad. Remember that love is your greatest asset, love of Self, family, friends, and your people. If you have no other qualities, you can succeed with love alone in your heart. And you need no reason to be happy other than you're alive. So smile, laugh, be happy just because you can. Exercise your will to love each moment of life, that is power alone. Without love of Self, family, friends, Ourstory and the Kulture of your people, you will fail. You may possess all the abstract knowledge and skills of the world, and even have money, but your soul will still be empty and void and you will remain at the bottom of the pyramid forever. Please do not confuse blind love with respect. It is suicidal to love your enemy. If you have love in your heart, you will respect them, but you may have to neutralize or destroy them and only through respect will you know all you must know to defeat them. At the beginning and end of each work day, or Kupigana Ngumi class when you perform the salutation, you must think, "I will greet each and everyday with love in my heart for Self, family, friends and the spirit of my people, for we are The NTCHR, and I will succeed."

The Five Keys To Love

Knowledge of self creates the power of inner peace
Inner peace creates the power to Listen
Listening creates the power to Communicate
Communication creates the power to innerstand
Innerstanding creates the power to Love
Love of Self is the key to all life
All life is The NTCHR
The NTCHR is Love...

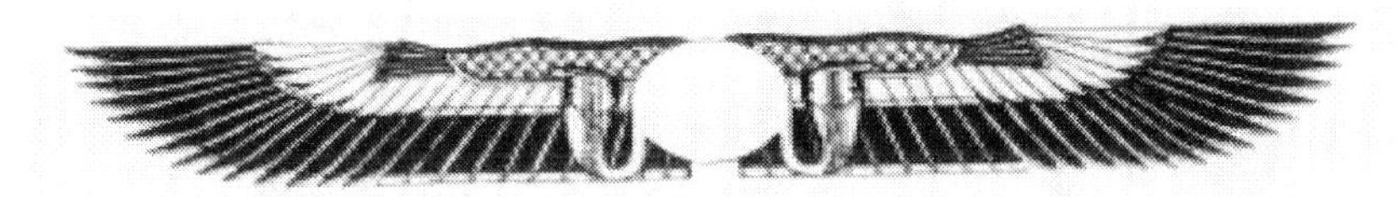

Third Principle

Only Through Persistence Can You Be Successful. "*I will persist endlessly until I succeed or transform in the struggle.*" Spiritual Warriors must innerstand the law of persistence. Kupigana Ngumi teaches you that you must do, and do, and do, and do again until it is correct. Never try, try is a weak word, do until you cannot do it any more, than still do it! There is no substitute for constant repetition. Only through endless and countless practice, can one perfect one's movements, skills, emotions, and mind. Each obstacle is simply a detour to your goal and you must accept and meet each challenge. Learn well everything that challenges you, for you will gain strength through your experiences. Life is like the ocean, if you are to cross it, you must learn to handle its waves and thunder, as well as its calm beauty. You must end each and every day with a personal victory; never allow your day to end in failure. You must plant the seeds for tomorrow's success. Just like you need apple seeds to plant apples trees, you must think successful to be a success. When you end each day in success, you gain an insurmountable advantage over those who cease their labor at a prescribed time. We as Afrakan people must re-program ourselves for success. In sports, we were told once, that we could not play as good as whites. We proved them partially right; we don't play as good as whites, we are better! We must now take this attitude into every aspect of our lives, but from an Afrakan center.

You must greet each new sun with confidence that this will be the best day of your life and that you will be the best you can be. Not the best anyone else can be, but your best! Your re-Afrakanization pledge will be "*as long as there is breath in my soul, I shall persist.*" This will teach you the power of consistency. When you innerstand the great power locked behind the door of consistency, you will have learned patience. In East Afraka, there is a proverb that goes, "with patience and consistency, even an egg will walk." I will persist endlessly until I succeed.

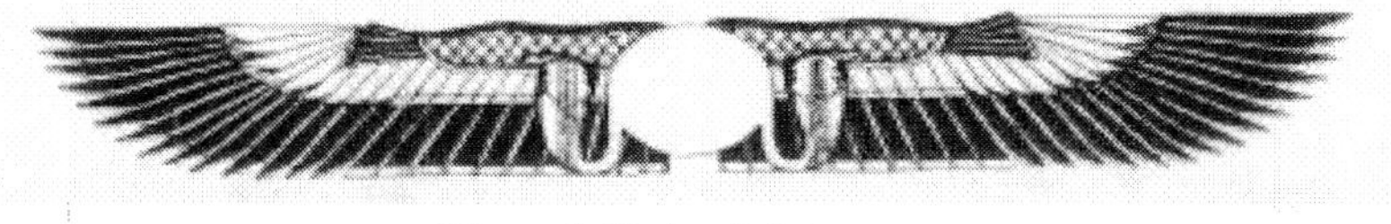

Fourth Principle

Only Through the Innerstanding of the Ntchru Can, You be One with Time. "*I will live each and every day as if it is my last and I will succeed.*" The Spiritual Warrior must innerstand and teaches that what is important is now! Yesterday and tomorrow is all part of the infinite now! Moreover, when we find Ma'at or harmony within the mind, body, and soul, we can see tomorrow as plain as you can read these words. All of this is only possible, because locked within the hidden door of Heru in your innerkonscious mind; there is only the infinite now. This infinite now is all time and no time, seen and unseen, perceivable and unperceivable, the energy of the All. Since here and now is what is important, you must not waste anytime mourning yesterday's misfortunes, deficits and aches of the heart. Instead, use this experience wisely so you do not repeat yourself. History should be innerstood so we know what our enemies did and why our enemies did it. Ourstory should be recorded so we know what to do and what not to do. The sun will never rise where it sets nor will it set where it rises. Even the greatest Kupigana Ngumi Master or Mfundishi cannot retrieve pain that was caused yesterday; he or she can only heal it in the moment. If you waste today, you may destroy the last page of your life. Therefore, you should live every hour of this day by Ma'at, you should cherish each day for it can never return. Plan your life. Don't be afraid to use pencil and paper; it was invented by Afrakans thousand of years ago to record actions that moved the spirits of people. Write your goals and objectives down. Write at least nine actions to reach every personal goal.

Each and every day check your list and make comments as needed. Bydoing this, you will avoid the killers of time.

All Spiritual Warriors must destroy Procrastination with action, doubt must be drowned by faith, and fear must be dismembered and replaced with confidence. Be careful not to spend energy condemning those who procrastinate and those who doubt the power of The NTCHR. Let your action be your teacher. Where there are idle mouths and wrong teachings, listen not. Where there are idle hands and wrong doings, linger not. Where there are backwards and idle bodies, visit not. It is important that you know that misery loves company, and people who do not take action, and who are miserable, are that way because they received a lot of practice. Surround yourself with people who want Spiritual Healing and with Afrakan people who are involved in the healing process.

Each morning look at your children, your family as if it may be the last time you will ever see them. Be affectionate with your children while they are young; tomorrow they will be gone, and so will you. Today embrace your woman, women embrace your man with sweet kisses, for tomorrow they will be gone, and so will you. Today call your dear friends and your parents, tell them how important they are in your life, because tomorrow they will be gone and so will you.

Each day you should be building steps for your ladder of success. Maybe today your ladder will be strong enough to be an institution. In addition, we must build institutions for our people. Afrakan people must build positive Afrakan-centered Institutions that will ensure an Afrakan tomorrow. Institutions empower dreams. A people without dreams and visions are a dead people. And a people without institutions to empower their dreams and visions are a people without a positive future.

Afrakan Spiritual Warriors teach us that people of Afrakan descent, modern day Kemetyu, melanin-dominated human beings and all people who have Ma'at in their heart, must make every hour count and that each minute should only be traded for something of value. You must labor harder than ever before and push your muscles until they no longer move; push your mind until it no longer thinks, then you must endure.

Now in the 21st Century, we are living under the deadly, retarded system of white male domination. We the Kemetyu Afrakan people, must eliminate the European and American Worldview and value system from our hearts, and our Kulture. If we fail all melanin dominated human beings, our planet and all life as we know it, is doomed. We must plan for positive results, because white male domination has a plan for our demise as a people. We must be aware of our Konscious minds, so that we can use our Heru Konsciousness at will. We must clearly innerstand that only the spirit of the soul survives so we must Kulturally Kultivate our souls for victory in the 21st century.

Spiritual Warriors must innerstand and teach that the spirit of the people is greater than any technology that can be invented by esfet (Western mind-set). We must be the Neb of Our Self. To surpass the deeds of others is unimportant, but to surpass your own is your ultimate goal. Maintain your Kultural dignity and your character will be strengthened by your actions. Live each and every day as if it is your last day, and you will succeed.

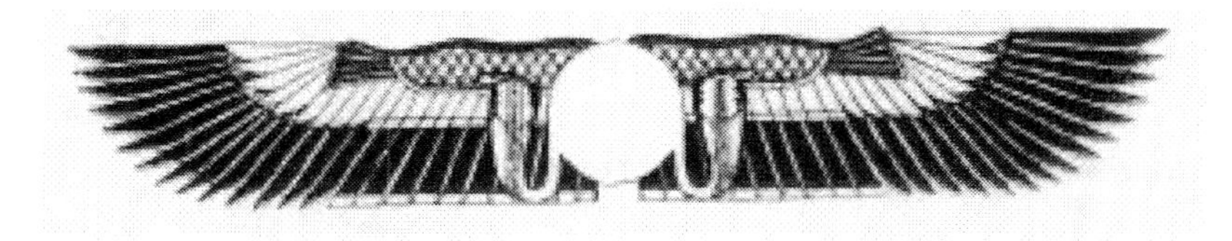

Fifth Principle

Only When One Becomes The Neb Hu, Master Of Your Senses Can You Know The Creator. "*Today I will be the Neb of my emotions and I will succeed.*" I will act positively, causing my thoughts and aura, my personal energy field around me to be positive. The common person allows their environment and their thoughts to control their actions. What is happening here is that someone else or something else is controlling your destiny. If it rains, your emotions are down simply because you cannot see the rays of the sun, or you had a car accident in the morning and because you're upset, the whole day is ruined. With this attitude you will remain at the base of the pyramid of life. Spiritual Warriors, are they who permit their thoughts to control their actions and the strong are they who utilize their actions to control their thoughts. If positive energy is being transmitted from your being, you will affect everyone and everything around you. You have to be in charge and direct your emotions. In every person, there is a wheel constantly turning from sadness to joy and all other emotions that fall in between. From exaltation to depression, from happiness to melancholy. And all these emotions are good but we cannot dwell on any of them for a long periods of time. If something happens that is sad, feel the emotion, then let it go and now institute the positive energy. If there is pain within from a tragedy, feel it then let it go and now institute the positive so that your life can go on. Yesterday's joy will become today's sadness; yet, today's sadness will grow into tomorrow's joy.

Spiritual Warriors innerstand that knowledge of Self grows into wisdom. Wisdom is the action with purpose and that is powerful! Knowledge is only potential power. We must act on what we know without compromise. Good intentions are not good enough, make positive corrections and proceed again until one succeeds. My mother, may her spirit rest in Htp, use to say , "the road to hell was paved on good intentions". One must remember that today's dead flowers carry the seeds for tomorrow's bloom. Plan your actions well, and the magnitude of your success will even surprise you.

If you innerstand the wheel of emotions that affect every human being, make sure that you do not judge a person on one meeting alone. When you meet a person, look deep into their eyes, make hand contact gripping them firmly. If your contact is deep, you can feel their strength or weaknesses in their eyes or their body. And at all times keep a positive aura about yourself. Master your own moods through positive action. When one masters their own moods, they will control their own destiny. "Today, I will be the Neb of my emotions and I will succeed."

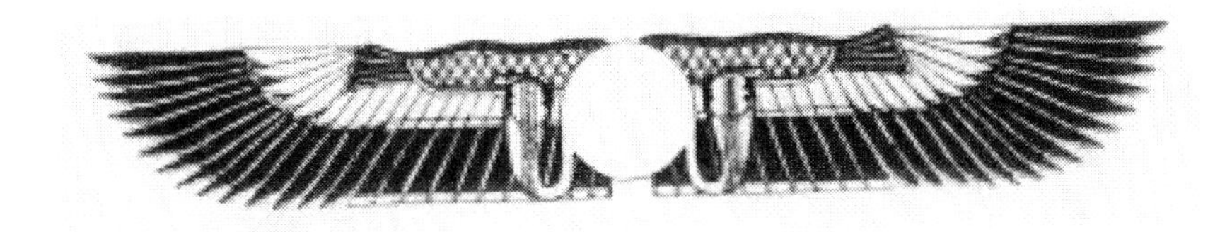

Sixth Principle

Only Through the Innerstanding of the Black Dot, Can You Innerstand the Dynamics of the Black Genius. I am a unique creation of nature. I am rare and there is value in all rarity; therefore, I am valuable. I am the sum total of millions of years of evolutions; therefore, locked deep in my innerkonscious mind at the core of my Black Dot is the infinite knowledge of my collective ancestors. With the power of discipline expressed through Kupigana Ngumi, Ma'at Akhw Ba Ankh, or the Kemet Legacy, I can be better equipped in both mind and body than my predecessors and many of the wise persons who preceded me. I must tap into my inner mind and use this energy, my Moyo which comes from the Black Dot at the center of my innerverse. With this energy, I can develop my skills through my innerstanding of the Black Dot, so I can give my gift to the universe.

Since the beginning of time, never has there been another human being with my mind, my heart, my eyes, my ears, my hands, my hair, my mouth, my soul, and there will be none after me. None can produce my child. With Kupigana Ngumi, no one can duplicate my kick, and my strike, no one can duplicate my fighting style and no one can do Kupigana Ngumi exactly as I. Hence forth, I will take advantage of this difference for it is an asset to be promoted to the fullest. And this is why, the Priest Scientist and Spiritual Warriors stress, know thy Self! Surely the key to personal power is in innerstanding the self with the discipline and power to move or act on what you know.

I must concentrate my energy on the challenge of the moment and my actions will help me seize the moment. Nature knows no defeat. It emerges victorious and so will I and with each victory the next struggle becomes less difficult. I will win. I will become a great human being by mastering myself. I will be a Spiritual Warrior and I will be the Neb of myself and master the innerstanding behind the Black Dot and the dynamics of my own Black genius and I will succeed.

Seventh Principle

Only Through the Knowledge of One's Kulture and The Wisdom of Ourstory and History Can One Act Correctly. I will act with the collective memory of my ancestors. My correct action will be my Afrakan-centered Worldview. To act, think, move, live, buy and love Afrakan will be my food and drink, which will nourish my Afrakan success. I will be armed with the knowledge of Afrakan Kulture and the spirit of the Ancient Afrakan Ancestors. They will guide my action into the positive energy. All actions must be based on Ma'at and the spirit of an Afrakan Worldview, because without a positive Afrakan Worldview you will be helping your enemy without your knowledge, just like junk food is not the proper nourishment for the body and mind. Only action that is guided by the Afrakan ancestors that is rooted in the Kemet legacy gives us our true Afrakan Ourstory and Kulture that will yield the proper fruit of knowledge of Afrakan success. Afrakan-centeredness is the proper fruit for people of Afrakan ancestry.

I will look for growth in every situation, especially those considered to be bad. Spiritual Warriors must make good things better and bad things good. Time discriminates against no one. We all have 365 & 1/4 days in a year, 168 hours in a week, and 24 hours in a day. It does not matter if you're Black, Brown, Red, Yellow, or White. Time is like change; it is constant and one does not manage time, but more of a case of managing ourselves on the use of time. This is why Spiritual Warriors must stress knowing thyself through Ourstory, and our Kulture. The ancestors will guide your purpose, identity, and direction, because only through the knowledge of Afrakan Kulture and Ourstory, will Afrakans return to their right minds and succeed as human beings, and heal ourselves and the planet. Only Through the Knowledge of One's Kulture and The Wisdom of Ourstory and History Can One Act Correctly.

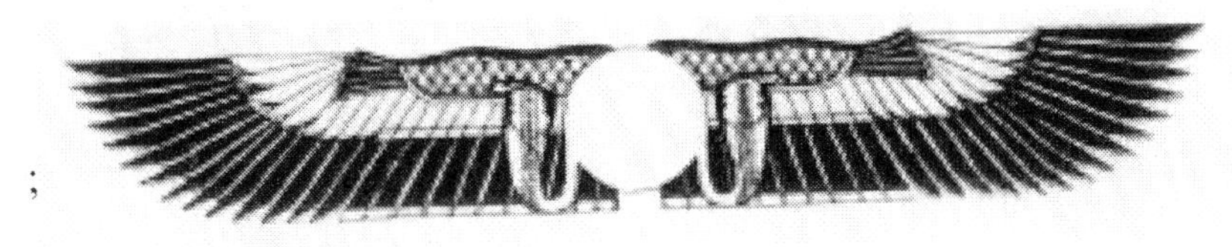

Now that we have explored these seven principles, let's look at how to incorporate them into your life through there practical applications. In the next few pages, I will present a layout to maximize on life-giving habits, which lay the foundation for becoming a Spiritual Warrior.

Affirmations:

The power of affirmation can change your thinking, your attitude, and finally your behavior. Affirmations help to change what happens in your life by strengthening and changing your thoughts, attitudes and habits to support the goal you wish to achieve. Use affirmations to produce the positive results you desire. Write your affirmations for each area in your life for your personal goals and on the 12 point re-Afrakanization Kultural system. Put your affirmations on 3 X 5 cards and keep them with you, frequently reading and reminding yourself of your important goals. Keep your affirmations in your wallet or purse, in your daily planner, have them on your think pad or flashing on your personal or work computer screen. Tape your affirmations on your mirrors, to your closet door, even in your car. At night, have your affirmations near your bed so you can read them with other important reading materials before you go to sleep. In the morning, when you wake up read your affirmations again. Any worthwhile accomplishment requires an investment of time and effort. Make reading your affirmations a daily ritual until it becomes a habit, and it will empower your life.

You may use affirmations of others to inspire and motivate yourself. But I find that usually the most effective affirmations are those you write or create yourself. Powerful Spiritual Warriors combine both, their positive affirmations along with the most powerful affirmations available to them.

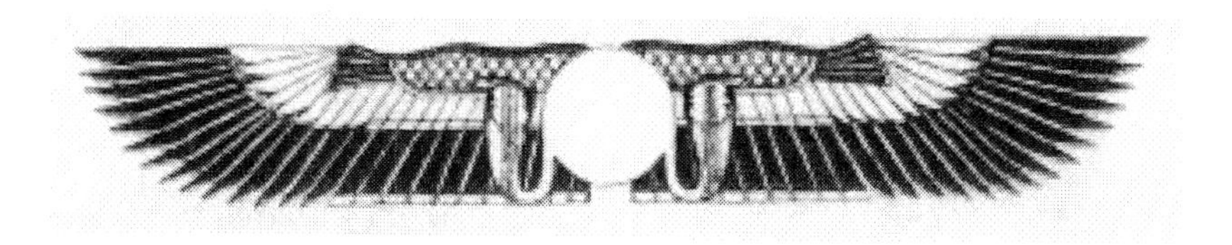

Goals for Success:

List personal goals:

A. Family

B. Education

C. Travel

D. Defense

E. Work

F. Spiritual

G. Community

H. Social

I. Economics

J. Physical

K. National Pan Afrakan

L. Kultural

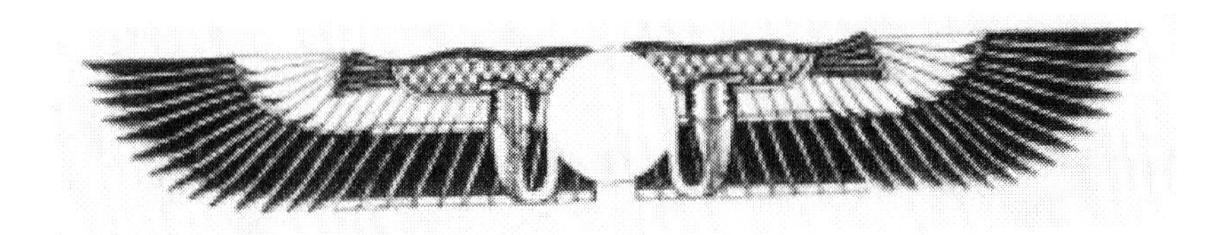

Goals for Success:

PERSONAL

A. Family goals:

a) The kind of mate I want. b) Activities with children. c) Time with family. d) Time spent with extended family. e) The kind of living space I want.

Rank:

1.
2.
3.
4.
5.
6.
7.
8.
9.

Action steps to achieve my goals:

1.
2.
3.
4.
5.

Affirmations:

____

____

____

Obstacles and road blocks:

____

Visualization, how I want it to be.

____

____

How I will benefit from achieving these goals.

____

How Afrakan people will benefit, when I achieve these goals.

____

Goals for Success:

PERSONAL

B. Educational goals:

a) The time, effort, and money I am willing to invest in my mental Afrakan-centered educational development. b) How will this Re-Afrakanization affect other areas of my life. c) How will this new education effect my family.

Rank:

1.
2.
3.
4.
5.
6.
7.
8.
9.

Action steps to achieve my goals:

1.
2.
3.
4.
5.

Affirmations:

____

____

____

Obstacles and road blocks:

____

Visualization, how I want it to be.

____

____

How I will benefit from achieving these goals.

____

How Afrakan people will benefit, when I achieve these goals.

____

Goals for Success:

PERSONAL

C. Travel goals:

a) Use travel as a form of education. b) Travel to Afraka. c) Encourage other Afrakans and family to visit Afraka and use Afrakan travel agents.

Rank:

1.
2.
3.
4.
5.
6.
7.
8.
9.

Action steps to achieve my goals:

1.
2.
3.
4.
5.

Affirmations:

____

____

____

Obstacles and road blocks:

____

Visualization, how I want it to be.

____

____

How I will benefit from achieving these goals.

____

How Afrakan people will benefit, when I achieve these goals.

____

Goals for Success:

PERSONAL

D. Defense goals:

a) Self defense. b) Defense of the family. c) Community defense and security.

Rank:

1.
2.
3.
4.
5.
6.
7.
8.
9.

Action steps to achieve my goals:

1.
2.
3.
4.
5.

Affirmations:

____

____

____

Obstacles and road blocks:

____

Visualization, how I want it to be.

____

____

How I will benefit from achieving these goals.

____

How Afrakan people will benefit, when I achieve these goals.

____

Goals for Success:

PERSONAL

E. Work goals: (Employment and career)

a) What I want from a career, finance, advancement and work satisfaction. b) The time and effort I am willing to give to career advancement. c) How will my career help my family, community and Afrakan people.

Rank:

1.
2.
3.
4.
5.
6.
7.
8.
9.

Action steps to achieve my goals:

1.
2.
3.
4.
5.

Affirmations:

Obstacles and road blocks:

Visualization, how I want it to be.

How I will benefit from achieving these goals.

How Afrakan people will benefit, when I achieve these goals.

Goals for Success:

PERSONAL

F. Spiritual goals:

a) The importance of spiritual matters in your life. b)The time I give to spiritual development. c) Developing a spiritual family and community. d) Meditation daily & Kultural Rituals.

Rank:

1.
2.
3.
4.
5.
6.
7.
8.
9.

Action steps to achieve my goals:

1.
2.
3.
4.
5.

Affirmations:

____

____

____

Obstacles and road blocks:

____

Visualization, how I want it to be.

____

____

How I will benefit from achieving these goals.

____

How Afrakan people will benefit, when I achieve these goals.

____

Goals for Success:

PERSONAL

G. Community goals, also organizational goals.

a) Afrakan nation building. b) Nation within a nation.

Rank

1.
2.
3.
4.
5.
6.
7.
8.
9.

Action steps to achieve my goals:

1.
2.
3.
4.
5.

Affirmations:

____

____

____

Obstacles and road blocks:

____

Visualization, how I want it to be.

____

____

How I will benefit from achieving these goals.

____

How Afrakan people will benefit, when I achieve these goals.

____

Goals for Success:

PERSONAL

H. Social goals:

a) How I value Afrakan people. b) How I work with other people. c) How I use my leisure time - social activities.

Rank:

1.
2.
3.
4.
5.
6.
7.
8.
9.

Action steps to achieve my goals:

1.
2.
3.
4.
5.

Affirmations:

____

____

____

Obstacles and road blocks:

____

Visualization, how I want it to be.

____

____

How I will benefit from achieving these goals.

____

How Afrakan people will benefit, when I achieve these goals.

____

Goals for Success:

PERSONAL

I. Economic goals:

a) Planning money use. b) Use of credit. c) Financial responsibility. d) Afrakan nation building contributions. e) Investing in and saving gold and silver, along with gems and valuable stones. f) Soverignity. g) UCC 1 form.

Rank:

1.
2.
3.
4.
5.
6.
7.
8.
9.

Action steps to achieve my goals:

1.
2.
3.
4.
5.

Affirmations:

Obstacles and road blocks:

Visualization, how I want it to be.

How I will benefit from achieving these goals.

How Afrakan people will benefit, when I achieve these goals.

Goals for Success:

PERSONAL

J. Physical goals: (Health)

a) The importance of physical conditioning and health in my life. b) The time and effort I give to physical and health matters. c) How my physical condition and health affect other areas of my life.

Rank:

1.
2.
3.
4.
5.
6.
7.
8.
9.

Action steps to achieve my goals:

1.
2.
3.
4.
5.

Affirmations:

____

____

____

Obstacles and road blocks:

____

Visualization, how I want it to be.

____

____

How I will benefit from achieving these goals.

____

How Afrakan people will benefit, when I achieve these goals.

____

Goals for Success:

PERSONAL

K. National Pan-Afrakan goals:

a) Afrakan nation building. b) Afrakancentered Institutions. c) Solverignity

Rank:

1.
2.
3.
4.
5.
6.
7.
8.
9.

Action steps to achieve my goals:

1.
2.
3.
4.
5.

Affirmations:

Obstacles and road blocks:

Visualization, how I want it to be.

How I will benefit from achieving these goals.

How Afrakan people will benefit, when I achieve these goals.

Goals for Success:

PERSONAL

L. Kultural goals:

a) How I value Afrakan people. b) Spiritual activities. c) Kultural pursuits. d) Daily Kultural Rituals.

Rank:

1.
2.
3.
4.
5.
6.
7.
8.
9.

Action steps to achieve my goals:

1.
2.
3.
4.
5.

Affirmations:

____

____

____

Obstacles and road blocks:

____

Visualization, how I want it to be.

____

____

How I will benefit from achieving these goals.

____

How Afrakan people will benefit, when I achieve these goals.

____

Purpose:

Make priorities and objectives specific and realistic:
List in order of importance:

Rank	Date started	Progress 1	2	3	4	Date achieved
1.						
2.						
3.						
4.						
5.						
6.						
7.						
8.						
9.						
10.						
11.						
12.						
13.						
14.						
15.						
16.						
17.						
18.						
19.						
20.						
21.						
22.						
23.						
24.						
25.						

Check off your progress list quarterly.
Every three months review your progress.
Keep a record of your progress in a journal and reflect on monthly and yearly progress.

Goals in the 12pt. Afrakan Kultural System

	Starting date	*Target date*	*Achieved date*
1.Spiritual System-			
2.Afrakan-centeredness-			
3.Defense: Internal & External- (Kupigana Ngumi)			
4.Rituals-			
5. Afrakan-centered Education-			
6.Pan-Afrakan Political Goverance-			
7.Ujamaa Economy-			
8.Ma'at Akhw Ba Ankh-			

Goals in the 12pt. Afrakan Kultural System

continue *1.Starting date 2.Target date 3.Achieved date*

9. Afrakan Council of Elders- (Halls of Ma'at) 1 2 3

Short______

med.______

long______

10. Afrakan Language- (Kiswahili / Mdw Ntchr, etc.)

Short______

med.______

long______

11. Afrakan Kuumba- Art, Music, Dance & Inneratainment:

Short______

med.______

long______

12. Maafa/Maangamizi Memorial & Education-

Short______

med.______

long______

Habits:

Good habits are your keys to good personal management.

Area : Good habits	Bad habits	*Progress*	*Starting*	*Target*	*Achieved*
1.					
2.					
3.					
4.					
5.					
6.					
7.					
8.					
9.					

Ask others to tell of your bad habits.
Ask others to tell of your good habits.
Make priorities of which bad habits you must change first.
Check off your progress list quarterly.
Complete this yearly.
Keep in a journal to reflect yearly progress.

Parasites or Obstacles to Self-Renewal:

Time wasters, like TV. How much TV do you watch?
Per/ week_______________ hours _____________per/ month
If you watch more than 8 hours per week or 40 hours per month, than you need to cut back.

A. Television (Look at TV guide and check off programs relevant for progress), record with VCR relevant programs. If they have Euro-centric commercial, edit them out and review before sharing with family or friends.

How often do you talk on the telephone? Is the conversation life-giving or life-threatening. Are your calls relevant to your goals?
Per/ week _______________ hours _______________ per/ month
If your calls are more than 2 hours per/ week or your personal bill is $100 per/ month, than you need to cut back.

B. Telephone calls, eliminate busy talk or gossip. List calls relevant to your success, in all aspects of your life, than get off the phone! Use cell phone for emergencies or business on the go, that are top priorities.

Transportation, do you use the most efficient way to travel to work, or to take care of business or pleasure? How much time are you spending on the commute to work?
Per/ week _______________ hours _______________ per/ month
If you spend more than 15 hours per/ week or 60 hrs per month, than you need to reevaluate your transportation!

C. Waiting for buses and trains (always carry reading or working materials if you must travel this way). Sometimes mass transit is more productive then your own personal car. But this usually can be ascertained from the specific circumstances and stress factors involved.

The goal is to eliminate one parasite each quarter of the year.

Look at each parasite as a personal challenge.
Analyze your mail, and try to handle each piece of paper no more than twice (sort all your mail into daily mail folder).

D. Handling mail: Do you waste time on your mail, or does your mail pile up on you?

1. An action folder- immediate attention, do now or today!
2. Hold - "working file" for on going, new, long and short range projects.
3. A file for special projects.
4. Information folder- read on the train or bus or at night or at breakfast.
5. Deferred folder- periodicals, read at spare moments or when you need to break up your day or work load.
6. Junk mail - put in the garbage!

Procrastination:
Stop rationalizing and you'll be more likely to act. You must overcome inaction, indecision and the fear of the unknown.

A. Is being on time an issue for you? Yes_____ No _____
Be on time! Always try to be 15 minutes early. Move your personal watch ahead 15 minutes or your clocks in your house.
B. Is the decision of what to do first an issue? Y__ N __
Learn to do it now!
C. Make a "To Do" list everyday and do it! Anything left from yesterday's list becomes the first things on today's "To Do" list.
D. Visualazation, you must see it to achieve it. Spend 2 or 3 minutes a day on visualizing the end product through meditation.

(Spend only 15 minutes at the beginning or end of the day planning for positive results). It is the effective use of time that will make you powerful, not how much time you spend on a project.

Personal:

Basically be good to yourself! What can you do to be good to yourself?

A. Enough rest. Awake (correct breathing). Sleep (at least 6 to 9 hours daily).
B. Balanced diet (eat one or two meals a day and color coordinate your meal. Vegetarianism if possible).
C. Regular exercise program (like Kupigana Ngumi-martial arts, Ma'at Akhw Ba Ankh or meditation, yoga, running, biking, etc. at least 3 times a week)
D. Take time out for your family and special friends, call and visit at least once a week.
E. Read and join a study group (a community that inner-stands the truth is a strong community and only a strong community can affect positive changes).
F. Work for yourself and the collective human nation.
If you use this wholistic approach towards developing the self, you will have increased energy and a decrease in tension and stress.

Poor Self - Image

The masses of Afrakans in the world are suffering from poor self-esteem.

1) Putting the blame on someone else.
2) Running away from your challenges and problems.
3) Criticizing other people constantly, instead of working on your self.
4) Waiting for someone else to solve your problems and challenges.
5) Pretending that everything is okay.
6) Utilizing a Euro-centric standard of beauty and success.
7) Trying not to look Afrakan, physically or spiritually.
8) Fear, expecting to fail.
9) Distractions, listening to the opinions of others who are not where you want to be.

Things that Affect your Self - Image

1. Thoughts - Afrakan-centered Konsciousness, emotions and feelings developed by a Afrakan value system, and education based upon Ma'at.

2. Environment - Develop and surround yourself in a Melanin enriched atmosphere at home and at work.

3. Associations - Surround yourself with friends, family and people who think positive and progressive like you do, or want to.

4. Security - Know how to defend yourself, your family, and your people. Your nation, family, or organization is only as strong as your weakest link.

5. Spirituality - If you are Afrakan, than your spiritual system should reinforce your Afrakanity through your Kulture and your respect for nature as you become Konscious of your Oneness with The NTCHR.

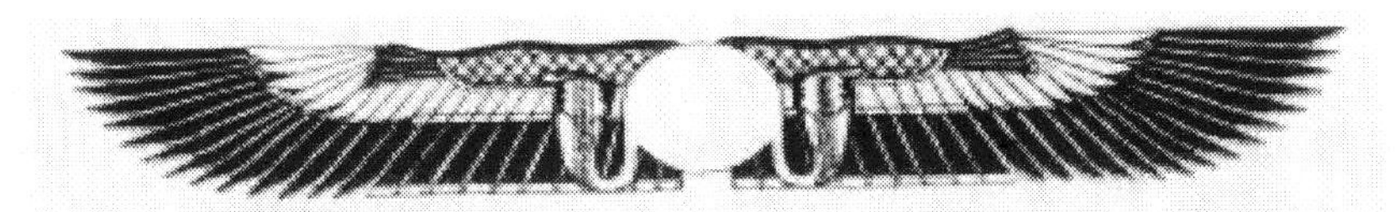

13 Ways To Improve Your Self Image

1. Be honest with yourself don't destroy your possibilities for growth and improvement.

2. Develop your imagination, by focusing on Ma'at. Where your imagination leads, your reality will follow. If you can visualize it, you can become it, or achieve it.

3. Be able to relax. Learn to breath correctly so that the infinite flow of energy from the Creator can be used in your life for positive transformation and healing.

4. Have that winning attitude. Everyone loves a winner. If you can think it, you can do it.

5. Kultivate excellent habits. We make our habits, then our habits make us.

6. Aim to be happy. Expect happiness and be happy. Happiness is a state of Konsciousness. Make happiness a habit.

7. Be real. If you are not true to yourself then harmony or Ma'at cannot exist in your reality. Only the truth can set you free.

8. Have compassion with innerstanding based upon, not just your personal experience, but also your ancestors. You are your people.

9. Grow from your mistakes. Nothing beats failure like success. Mistakes are life lessons in wisdom. Try not to make the same mistakes over again.

10. Acknowledge your weakness. If it is not acknowledged it can not be overcome.

11. Be spiritually centered. Even when success is reached you must continue to grow in knowledge, innerstanding and Konsciousness if you are to maintain success. From whom much is gained through innerstanding, much is to be given (reciprocity).

12. Believe in the Spirit because the Spirit is The NTCHR, and the Spirit is in all things.

13. Be spiritually centered, live your life by the power of the Divine Spirit and have a sense of harmony with all things. Only this centering can bring Ma'at back into the world so that real healing can take place.

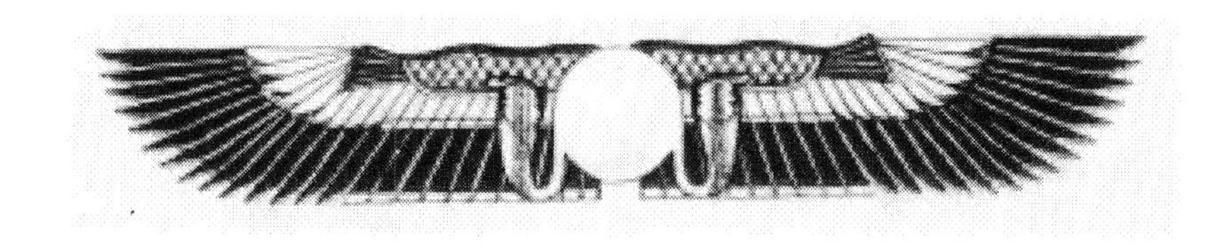

Guidelines for Self-Improvement & Healing for New Afrakan People & Spiritual Warriors

1. Pay close attention to everything that goes on about you, and how it relates, not only to you, but to Afrakan people and Afraka.

2. Love and Respect Yourself First, and others will respect you. You are an Afrakan and there is no one greater than yourself.

3. Maintain an open mind and avoid forming opinions about those subjects about which you have no, or a little knowledge.

4. Patience and Consistency are necessary in order to develop sharpness in mind, body, and spirit.

5. You are what you make of yourself. Think highly of yourself, and Afrakan people.

6. Keep a clean, drug free head and body. If you have a clear head you will always know what is happening to you.

7. Check Yourself at the end of each week, month and year, to see how much you have learned and improved.

8. Remember that the first goal on the road to self-improvement is the ability to overcome laziness, illusion, procrastination, doubt, stagnation, fear and time wasted on distractions.

9. Friends must be treasured. Never mistreat a friend for they are hard to find. Treat your friends the way you want to be treated. Call once a week or write often if you are not close by.

10. Good friendship is one of your greatest assets, treat your friends special, and you will be treated special.

11. When in doubt go to the proper source for clarification. Idle gossip only adds to confusion.

12. Be in control of your environment, surround yourself with beauty or things that make you feel good. That which is good for you is beauty. If you are Afrakan, then Afrakan Kulture should be visible in your home, or personal space. Make your space Melanin enriched.

13. You are what you eat Put only those things in your body-temple as "nourishment" that maximize your overall efficiency. Work towards Vegetarianism and live, raw foods.

14. Your power is linked to the Creator (NTCHR) and the spirit of your people, so meditate several times a day for centering.

15. Always make an attempt with the certainty that you will succeed. If you have tried to do something and failed, you are vastly better off than if you had tried to do nothing and succeeded.

16. Spiritual Warriors must teach that the state of a nation, institution, organization or a family is simply a function of the capacities of its people.

17. Fast at lease two or three days a month. Purification for liberation.

18. Have your colon cleaned at least once a year or quarterly.

19. Have a personal physical check up, complete with blood work once a year.

20. The power of prayer, hekau and positive affirmation are unlimited, so start and end each day with them, and before eating any meals or snacks.

21. Read at least one new book every two weeks. Join a study group to expand your world, and your knowledge of the Afrakan Family.

22. Learn an Afrakan language, Mdw Ntchr, Kiswahili, Twi, Yoruba, Wolof, etc. You must learn to think in a language outside of your oppressor's thinking.

23. Visit Afraka at least once in your life time; take your children, because it is our Holy Land.

24. Konsciously practice positive Afrakan values, and Spiritual systems, like the Nguzo Saba and the Laws of Ma'at.

25. Surround yourself with Positive Afrakan images, icons, Art, even dress Afrakan, because your clothes are part of your self-esteem and part of reconstructing our New Afrakan minds.

26. Organize! Belong to a organization that is involved in Afrakan Nation building.

27. Develop a love for Afraka, your ancestral home land, as well as your self.

28. Develop knowledge of your heritage, for to know nothing is bad, but to learn nothing is worst. Travel to Afrakan-centered conferences and share in Afrakan Heritage festivals.

29. Develop and defend a positive Afrakan-centered role of men and the role of women, in your personal relationship.

30. Develop discipline and control against lust, desire, and material wealth.

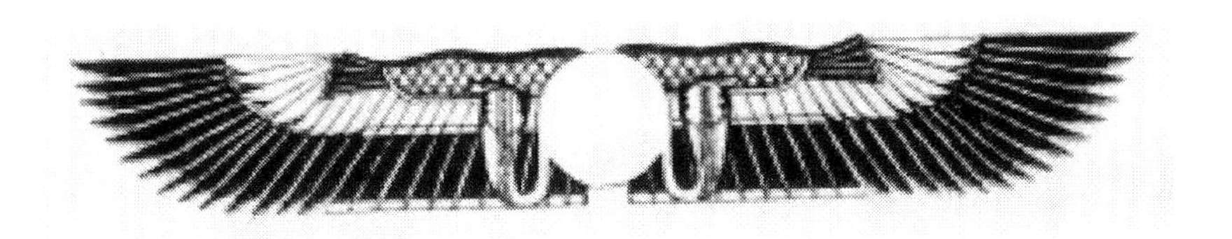

Goals I have achieved

In my personal life this year______________ Date completed

1. ______________________________

2. ______________________________

3. ______________________________

4. ______________________________

5. ______________________________

6. ______________________________

7. ______________________________

8. ______________________________

9. ______________________________

10. ______________________________

11. ______________________________

12. ______________________________

This section serves as a powerful affirmation and demonstration of your ability to achieve worthwhile personal goals. This section gives you clear visualization of your achieved successes.

Review this section frequently. Celebrate your progress! This is your self motivational section. And it can also inspire and motivate others, like your family and friends.

Goals I Have Achieved

In the 12pt. Afrakan Kultural System this year.

_______________ Date completed

1. ____ | ______
2. ____ | ______
3. ____ | ______
4. ____ | ______
5. ____ | ______
6. ____ | ______
7. ____ | ______
8. ____ | ______
9. ____ | ______
10. _______________________________________ | ______
11. _______________________________________ | ______
12. _______________________________________ | ______

This section serves as a powerful affirmation and demonstration of your ability to achieve worthwhile goals in the 12pt Afrakan Kultural System. This section gives you clear visualization of your Pan-Afrakan collective, unified, nation building achieved successes.

Success encourages success so review this section frequently. Celebrate your progress, and success! This is your self motivational section. And it can also inspire and motivate others, like your family and friends.

Worksheet for Spiritual Warriors

1. Identify your gifts and special NTCHR given talents.

   a. ____________________

   b. ____________________

   c. ____________________

   d. ____________________

   e. ____________________

2. Based upon your special gifts you can identify your life's purpose.

   ____

   ____

   ____

   ____

   ____

3. Based upon your purpose, identify and establish at least three (3) clear goals.

   a. Short range goals:

      1.____________________

      2.____________________

      3.____________________

   b. Middle range goals:

      1.____________________

      2.____________________

      3.____________________

   c. Long range goals:

      1.____________________

      2.____________________

      3.____________________

   d. Other goals:

      1.____________________

      2.____________________

      3.____________________

4. Research all the information pertaining to your goals. List all the doable steps necessary to achieve each goal and where the information came from. Also list the date the information was collected.

a.____

b. ____

c. ____

d. ____

e. ____

f. ____

g. ____

5. Prioritize these doable steps into a logical sequence. Develop a check list with dates you began and projected time of completion, with monthly or quartly progress checks to make sure you are on target.

	Progress			*Starting*	*Target*	*Achieved*
a.						
b.						
c.						
d.						
e.						
f.						
g.						

6. List daily affirmations, prayers and rituals in a Melanin dominated Kultural Language. Memorize them, make them habits that become part of your daily life.

____

____

____

____

____

7. As a Spiritual Warrior, you must maintain and constantly reenergize a positive spiritual energy force field (The Moyo). Make it a habit of doing Ma'at Akhw Ba ankh every day and the complete practice, with exercises, postures and forms three times weekly. Kupigana Ngumi should also be practiced mentally every day, but with a formal class once or twice a week. Remember it is what you do outside of the class that will allow you to develop the Moyo, so you can heal yourself and others.

8. Give your gift everyday, if you have developed it. Show that you love yourself everyday by your personal rituals. Tell someone that you love them everyday! Help somebody, give something to someone everyday. Make it part of your mission! The more you give the more you will receive; therefore, you are healing and you are constantly being healed.

9. Re-evaluate and re-assess your plan towards your life goals, purpose and mission. If you are not all you want to be, reconfirm your goals and purpose and repeat steps 2 through 8. If you can feel the blessings of your mission in abundance and Ma'at has become your world, and you are giving your gifts and living as Heru and Asr, you are at the highest level of the Spiritual Warrior.

10. Spiritual Warriors are healers while actively involved in the state of Warriorship (righteous struggle). It is the spiritual act of becoming that allows you to **Become Heru.** All Spiritual Warriors must evolve through stages, and one of the stages must be Heru (Higher Konsciousness). You are your people. Your whole experience at this moment is a healing to every Melanin dominant human being who are receptive to healing.

This power called the Moyo will also heal Melanin deficient human life-forms who are receptive to Ma'at and who have a similar mission to create and maintain Ma'at with The NTCHR. One of the goals of all Afrakan Spiritual Warriors is to be a healer, through becoming Heru and Asr, the power and the glory on earth as it is in heaven.
Amen Ma'at.

POWER IS PEACE

Power is the control of the will
Will is the sum total of your vital Force
The use of the Moyo or Sekhem
And to rule your own force
Is the ultimate control
Your control must be reflected
In your inner and outer forces
Balance is harmony
Love is divine
Oneness is Peace
And power is a prerequisites of eternal Peace...
HTP.
AMEN MA'AT

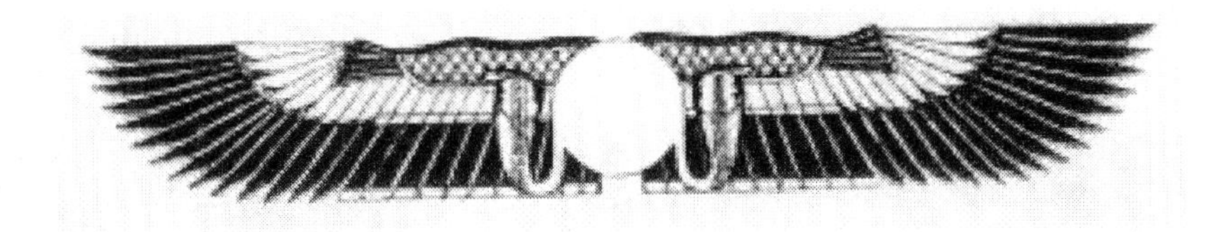

Appendix I - Poems, Hymns, Proverbs, Quotes

Appendix I - Poems, Hymns, Proverbs, Quotes

Appendix I - Poems, Hymns, Proverbs, Quotes

Appendix I - Poems, Hymns, Proverbs, Quotes

Appendix II - Illustrations and Pictures

Appendix II - Illustrations and Pictures

Appendix II - Illustrations and Pictures

Appendix II - Illustrations and Pictures

Appendix II - Illustrations and Pictures

Appendix III - Points of Interest

Appendix III - Points of Interest

Appendix III - Points of Interest

Appendix III - Points of Interest

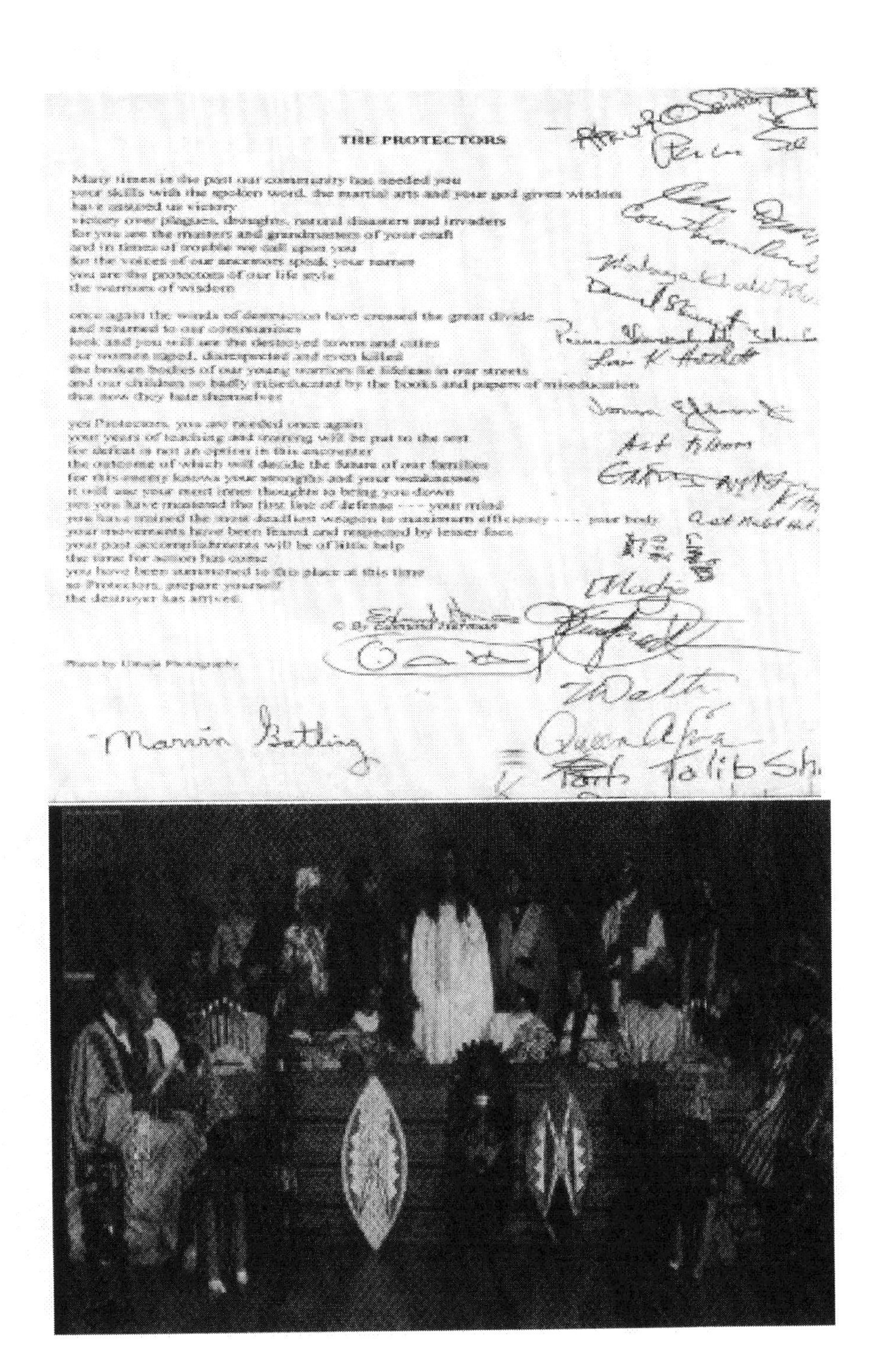

THE PROTECTORS

Many times in the past our community has needed you
your skills with the spoken word, the martial arts and your god given wisdom
have assured us victory
victory over plagues, droughts, natural disasters and invaders
for you are the masters and grandmasters of your craft
and in times of trouble we call upon you
for the voices of our ancestors speak your names
you are the protectors of our life style
the warriors of wisdom

once again the winds of destruction have crossed the great divide
and returned to our communities
look and you will see the destroyed towns and cities
our women raped, disrespected and even killed
the broken bodies of our young warriors lie lifeless in our streets
and our children so badly miseducated by the books and papers of miseducation
that now they hate themselves

yes Protectors, you are needed once again
your years of teaching and training will be put to the test
for defeat is not an option in this encounter
the outcome of which will decide the future of our families
for this enemy knows your strengths and your weaknesses
it will use your most inner thoughts to bring you down
yet you have mastered the first line of defense --- your mind
you have trained the most deadliest weapon to maximum efficiency --- your body
your movements have been feared and respected by lesser foes
your past accomplishments will be of little help
the time for action has come
you have been summoned to this place at this time
so Protectors, prepare yourself
the destroyer has arrived.

© By Edward Harman

Photo by [illegible] Photography

Mfundishi and Sister Mansura Khnam the first editor of Spiritual Warriors Are Healers, at Black Gold Afrakan Kultural Center, New Brunswick, New Jersey.

Below, Zuwena Salim graduating from Norfolk State U., with her father and mother, Mfundishi and Cynthia Salim. Right, Mfundishi with his niece Sesheny.

Glossary

Ab/ ib - Also spelled: Ieb or eb, represents the heart. The Kemetyu believed the heart was the center of all konsciousness, even the center of life itself. When some one died it was said that their "heart has departed." It was the only organ that was not removed from the body during mummification. In the Coming Forth By Day, an ab was the heart that was weighed against the feather of Ma'at to see if an individual was worthy of joining Asr in the after life.

Abd - A Mdw Ntchr word meaning month

Abu - A Mdw Ntchr word meaning elephant.

Afraka - The Living flesh or land and soul of the light of the Creator. The new, but ancient name given to our home land, the birth place of all humanity. An Afrakan name meaning **"land of the sun"** from northeast Afraka. This definition is an act of Kujichagulia, self-determination, we as Afrakan Spiritual Warriors will define ourselves and name ourselves and will refuse to be definded by the Wazungu.

Akh - A portion of the spiritual anatomy known as the higher self.

Akhet - The third of the three seasons of the Kemet Kalendar, the season of harvesting. It was both a four month period of the civil Kalendar and a season of the natural year. Also, the Akhet represents the horizon from which the sun emerged and disappeared. The horizon, thus, embodied the idea of both sunrise and sunset. In the New Period, the double horizon was represented by the double lion. And the proper name of the Great Sphinx is called Heru Em Akhety (Heru in the Double Horizon).

Amen - Amen was self produced at the beginning of time, self existent, an almighty and eternal force, who created all the Ntchru and gave form to all things. The Ntchr of air and wind. The unknowable unconditional self. The unseen and "unseenable" creative force that is spirit, and all thoughts

Amen Ra - The unseen and seen life force of creation. The Afra kan spiritual life force of the cosmos. Center city of wor ship was Wast. Triad - Amen, Mut and Khonsu.

Amenta - The west, the land of the dead. It represents the Under world or Land of the Dead. Originally it meant the horizon of the sunset. Later, it became the symbol of the west bank of Hapy (Nile), where the sun set and also where the Kemetyu traditionally buried the dead.

Amu - A Mdw Ntchr word meaning the Indo-European, Caucasian or wazungu.

Ancient Afrakan - A term used by modern Spiritual Warriors for the original Homo sapiens population of Afraka, who were physically small and Black, and their immediate descen dents who populated the world between circa 100,000 B.C.E. and 25,000 B.C.E., from whom have come the Caucasian, Mongoloid, Semitic, and Amerind branches of the human family.

Ankh - A Mdw Ntchr word meaning life, union of male and female principles, which perpetuate life. Symbolizes the union of the male staff and the female eternal circular womb and the children as the crossbar. The symbol of eternal perpetual life, eternal life, the union of comple ments.

Anpu - The Ntchr who guides the Ba (soul) to the scales of Ma'at and weighs the heart for judgement. The opener of the way. Also. pronounced Enpu.

Apep - A Mdw Ntchr word meaning the great enemy of Ra or the great snake of darkness found in the Duwat.

Ast - The great Black mother. The Ntchrt of mothership and maternal devotion; mother of Heru, wife of Asr. Her Greek name is Isis.

Asr - The great Black. The Ntchr of ever lasting life, death and resurrection, the father of Heru and complement of Ast.

Aryan - Caucasoid speakers of the Indo-Iranian branch of the Indo-European language family. Nomadic Aryan tribes invaded Persia and northern India from the north around 1500 B.C.E., imposing their language and culture.

Atheism - The belief of Salvation by doing what makes you happy. A belief system that there is no God, NTCHR - only existence, which just happened on its own without any help.

Atef - The Atef Crown was worn by Asr. It is made up of the Rams horns, the white crown of Upper Kemet and the red feathers are representative of Busiris, Asr's Sacred City in the Delta.

Atum - The Ntchr that is represented as the complete One.

Ba - A Mdw Ntchr word meaning the soul life force. It is the non-material spirit that gives each entity its unique self. The Ba is what is called someone's personality. It would leave the body at the time of death. During the day, the Ba would make itself useful, at night it would return to its time capsule (tomb). At this time, it would look for the person to which it belonged. This would be the sah (mummy), however, often the Kemetyu would supply the Ba with the statue in the likeness of the deceased in case the mummy was lost or damaged.

Bantu - A major Afrakan ethnic group and language family that spreads from west Afraka across equatorial Afraka to East and Southern Afraka. Kiswahili and Mdw Ntchr are in this same Afrakan family.

Bes - A Ntchr of protection for the home and children. He is also known for music and dance. He is associated with Ra and is often in the image of a short Afrakan Twa.

B.C.E. - Before the Common Era.

Bhdt (Behdet) - Winged Solar Disk - This is a form that the Ntchr Heru of Edfu takes in his battle with Setsh. The Ntchr Jhuty used his will to turn Heru into a sun-disk with splendid out stretched wings.

Book of the Coming Forth By Day or Light - See Prt em Heru.

Bennu - A sacred bird associated with the Ra, which rose from the primeval hill at creation. From the Mdw Ntchr word weben, "to shine".

Candle - The candle holds deep mystical symbolism. Four elements of creation: fire, earth (wax in solid form), water (wax in liquid), and air. All are consumed in the burning process and all of them come together to produce light. This light represents Konsciousness (enlightenment) illumination.

Cataract - A formation of rocks or waterfall in the Nile River (Hapy) making the Nile impassable by boat; there are six cataracts in the Nile River between Khartoum, Sudan (Ancient Kash) and Aswan, present day Egypt (Ancient Kemet).

Caucasoid - Members of the human race possessing a physical type resulting from adaptation to the Eurasian climate and environment, characterized by such features as minimal to no skin pigmentation, straight to curly hair with color variations, heavy body hair, orthognathism, high-bridged, narrow noses, etc. Caucasoids (Caucasians) include Nor dic, Alpine, Basque,Germanic and Slavic populations.

Coffin Texts - See Karast Sbayt.

Coptic - The language and culture of Roman and "Christianized" Egypt and Ethiopia; related to the Coptic church, the Coptic script is the Kemetik language written in a modified Greek alphabet, used in religious services.

Cosmogony - The theory of creation, as of the world or of the universe.

Cuneiform - A Mesopotamia script characterized by nail-shaped wedge imprints in clay tablets.

Dalit - The name in which the Black Untouchable caste of India have given themselves.

Dietary Degenerates - Individuals whose regulated course of eating and drinking (mentally, physically and spiritually) is degraded or deteriorated and does not support life-giving habits.

Deshret - A Mdw Ntchr word meaning red crown of the north.

Diaspora - Any place outside of the Afrakan continent for Afrakan people.

Djed - A Mdw Ntchr word meaning stability and represents strength. It is believed that the Djed is a rendering of human backbone. It was originally associated with the creation Ntcher, Ptah, himself being called the "Noble Djed". As Asr's Sacred City took hold, it became known as the backbone of Asr. A djed column is often painted on the bottom of coffins, where the backbone of the deceased would lay, this identified the person with the Nswt of the underworld, Asr. It also acts as a sign of stability for the deceased's journey of the afterlife.

Djew / dju- Which means mountain, the symbol suggests two peaks with the Hapy (Nile) valley in the middle. The Kemetyu believed that there was a cosmic mountain range that held up the heavens. This mountain range had two peaks, the western peak was called Manu, while the eastern peak was called Bakhu. It was on these peaks that heaven rested. Each peak of this mountain chain was also a symbol of the tomb and afterlife, probably because most Kemet tombs were located in the mountainous land bordering the Hapy valley.

Djhuty - See Jhuty.

Dravidian - One of the native Black Kultures that inhabit South ern India and their language group is part of the Elamo-Dravidian branch of the Afro-Asiatic family, including Tamil, Malayalam, Kanarese, Kurukh, Telugu, etc. They had inhabited most of India before the Aryan invasion of 1500 B.C. E. or 2740 S.T.

Dsrt - A Mdw Ntchr word meaning red land or the desert.

Dwat - A Mdw Ntchr word meaning the underworld or the world of transformation.

Eah - A Mdw Ntchr word meaning moon.

Ement, imnt, Ament - Mdw Ntchr word meaning west or land of the dead.

Ementy - Mdw Ntchr word meaning right.

Esfet - Disorder, wrong doings, the opposite of Ma'at,.

Geb - The Ntchr of the earth, or Neb of the earth. Geb is the source of terrestrial authority. He was born of Shu and Tefnut, his mate and sister energy is Nut. Together they bring five children energies into being; Asr, Heru Ur, Setsh, Ast and Nebt Het. These five children also represent the five days above the year.

Grh - Mdw Ntchr word meaning night, dark or obscurity.

Hall of the Double Ma'ati - "Hall of the Two Truths," the judgment hall where one's heart is weighed against Ma'at's feather of truth by Enpu, as Jehuty records the result. Those who pass are declared "pure" and led by Heru to His Father Asr. Those who do not are fed to Ammit, a Ntchr whose purpose is to utterly destroy wickedness.

Hat / Haty - A Mdw Ntchr word meaning that which is in front of or mayor, leader or prince.

Hedjet - A Mdw Ntchr word meaning the white crown of the south, Upper Kemet.

Hem Ntchr - "Servant of Ntchr," the commonest title of an ordained priest. Feminine form Hemt Ntchrt or ordained priestess of Ntchr. Sometimes the word Ntchr is replaced with the name of the Ntchru served: Hem Khepera or Hemt Ptah.

Het Ka Ptah - "House of the spirit of Ptah," the Kemetyu name for the city and national capital of Men-Nefer in nothern Kemet.

Heru - The Ntchr of Higher Konsciousness that fights to defend Ma'at. The son of Asr and Ast. The avenger of his father against Set. He is the Ntchr that appears as a falcon, or a falcon headed man or a sun disk with falcon wings. Heru is the embodiment of divine rulership in Kemet or Priest of higher Konsciousness. Heru means that which is above, heaven or that which is righteous.

Heru em Akhety - One of the oldest Afrakan monuments in ancient Kemet. It has the body of a lion and the head of an Afrakan. (Misnamed by the Greeks as "The Sphinx"), also **Heru Khuti**

Heru Konsciousness - A state of heightened awareness, where one is in tune with nature and the spiritual world simultaneously.

Hotep (Htp) - A Mdw Ntchr word meaning to offer satisfaction, supreme peace or calmness through nutrients like bread and water on a table *(the Mdw Ntchr symbols for Hotep).*

Hdj - A Mdw Ntchr word meaning mace of the ruler or chief.
Hmt - A Mdw Ntchr word meaning wife or woman.
Heh - A Mdw Ntchr word meaning millions or eternity.
Hu - A Mdw Ntchr word meaning authoritative utterance.
Hyksos - Semetic invaders who occupied the Delta Region of Lower Kemet during a period of decline between 1786 B.C.E or 2454 S.T. and 1567 B.C.E. or 2673 S.T. This was ancient Kemetyu's second Intermediate Period. They were later expelled by Black Afrakan rulers from the South (Kash and Upper Kemet).
Ib - A Mdw Ntchr word meaning heart.
Indo-European - A major language branch that encompasses the majority of languages spoken in Europe and areas of European settlements. The languages include Anatolian, Indo-Iranian, Greek, Italic, Germanic, Armenian, Celtic, Baltic and Slavic. In Kemet, these people were called the **Amu.**
Iwn - A Mdw Ntchr word meaning column.
Iwnu - A Mdw Ntchr word meaning the name of a famous city Annu in Kmt.
Indus Valley Civilization - The first high civilization of India, located in present-day Pakistan, established ca. 3000 B.C.E. or 1240 S.T.
Jhuty - The Ntchr of Good Speech, Intelligence, Wisdom, and articulate Action. The scribe of the Ntchru. Other versions Djhuty or Tehuti.

Ka - A Mdw Ntchr word meaning the divine spirit force of life. Ka is usually translated as "spirit". The ka came into existence when an individual was born. It was believed that the ram-headed Ntcher Khnum crafted the ka on his potter's wheel at a persons birth. It was thought that when someone died they "met their ka". A person's ka would live on after their body had died. Some tombs included model houses as the ka needed a place to live. Offerings of food and drink would be left at the tomb entrance so the ka could eat or drink.

Kantake - A ancient Kash title that means Queen-mother. A line of Kash queen-mothers of Meroitic Kash between 300 B.C.E. or 3940 S.T. to 300 C.E. or 4540 S.T.

Karast - The sarcophagus (casket) that the sah (mummy) is placed.

Karast Texts - A collection of funereal texts written directly onto the coffins and sarcophagi of noblemen and women from the Middle Period. These were a carry over from the Old Period's Mer-Khut (Pyramid) Texts, which provided for safe passage of the ruler through the afterworld.

Keku - A Mdw Ntchr word meaning the darkness as associated with the condition which existed before time began.

Kemet (Kmt) - "Black Kem-unity (Community)," the name the Black indigenous people of the Hapy Valley gave to their country.

Kemetyu - The name of the indigenous Black people of the Hapy Valley. Translated from the Mdw Ntchr as the Black people.

Kemklusion - A conviction reached in consequence of investigation, reasoning, and logic based on Afrakan Kemet Deep Thinking.

Kha - A Mdw Ntchr word meaning rise, shine or appear. Another word spoken kha, a lotus bud or leaf can mean 1,000.

Khemennu - The city of the Eight Ntchru, the Ogdoad. A group of cosmic principles connected to the formation of matter. They are the inner secret of the formation of matter or what we perceive as matter.

Khepresh - The blue crown was a ceremonial war crown often worn in battle by the Nswt only. The style represented an Afrakan hairstyle from up south from Kemet. It was worn beginning in the New Period after the Hyksos expulsion from Kemet.

Khepri (Khepr) - "Becoming", or coming into being. The Ntchr of creation and the rising sun.

Kher-Heb - "Lector-Priest or Priestess," the title given to the servants who recites the spiritual words of power in the temple. In antiquity, sometimes equated with the "learned" member of the Priestship, who could read Mdw Ntchr and therefore" knew the words of power."

Khet - Represents a lamp on a stand from which flame emerges. Fire was embodied in the sun and in its symbol the uachet which spit fire. Fire also plays a part in the Kemet concept of the underworld. There is one terrifying aspect of the underworld which is similar to the christian's concept of hell. Most Kemetyu would like to avoid this place with its fiery lakes andrivers that are inhabited by fire demons.

Khu - Part of the spiritual anatomy known as the enlightened self.

Khufu - A Nswt of the Old Period and builder of the Mer Khut en Khufu (the Great Pyramid).

Maafa - The destruction of Afrakan people and their Kulture by the hands of Europeans and Arabs. Also known as Maangamizi or the "Black Holocaust".

Maa Hes - Mdw Ntchr word meaning lion, and Mai hsa is ferocious lion.

Maangamizi - The deliberate destruction of Afrakan people and their Kulture by the hands of Europeans and Arabs. Also known as the Maafa or the "Black Holocaust".

Ma'at - The Ntchr of order and harmonious balance in the cosmos. The spiritual and ethical principle of truth, justice, righ teousness, and right action. The Ntchr Ma'at is usually portrayed as a woman wearing a headdress with an ostrich feather attached. Some Ntchru are often seen standing on the Ma'at symbol, as if standing on a foundation of Ma'at.

Ma'atian - The Afrakan deep thought or philosophy of truth, justice, righteousness, and harmonious balance as a way of life.

Maroons - From the Spanish word cimarron runaway. Freedom-fighting Afrakans or Afrakan descendants who escaped from enslavement in the Americas. The independent communities they formed ranged from elusive bands to established towns and small nations.

Matrilineal - The line of family or clan descent determined through the mother. In traditional Afraka, the woman, even in marriage, retains her individuality and her legal rights and continues to bear the name of her family.

Mdw - Mdw Ntchr word for "words".

Mdw Nefer - Mdw Ntchr word meaning good speech.

Mdw Ntchr - (Mdu Ntchr, Metu Neter) Translated as Divine Words, Language, or Speech of the Ancient Kemet. The Divine Language or words of the Ntchru through the Kemetyu.

Melanin - An important organic chemical that produces Black pigmentation in skin, hair, eyes, internal organs, etc. The Melanin molecule is found in all living beings on earth in varying quantities, and is considered by some scientists to be the molecule of life.

Menat - The Menat was a heavy necklace with a crescent shaped front and a counter piece at the rear. It was a symbol associated with the Ntchrt Het Heru and her son, Ihy. Het Heru was some times called the "Great Menat". We often see Het Heru using the Menat as a conduit through which she passes her power. It was representative of the ideas of joy, life, potency, fertility, birth, and rebirth.

Menhed - A scribe's pallet. Writing was a very important skill to the ancient Kemetyu practiced by a group called scribes. The writing equipment used by scribes consisted of a palette, which held black and red pigments, a water jar, and a pen. To be ascribe was a favorable position, even some of the Nswtu and nobles are shown proudly displaying the scribe's palette.

Men Nefer - Mdw Ntchr words translated "Established Beauty". A sacred city in Kemet. It was the site of the first capital of ancient Kemet.

Mer Khut - (Mr Khut, Mr Khuti (two Mr Khut), Mr Khutu (more than two Mr Khut). Kemet sacred structure with a four sided base rising to one point, used as a time capsule (tomb), temple, observatory, Initiation Hall, etc. Also known as the "Great Mounds" in Kemet. Misnamed by the Greeks as the "pyramid(s)".

Mer Khut Sbayt - A collection of funereal texts provided for the dead ruler in their Mer Khut (pyramid) time capsules (tombs) in the Old Period. They are the oldest surviving religious texts of Kemet. Misnamed the "Pyramid Texts."

Mht (Mehet) - A Mdw Ntchr word meaning papyrus.

Moors - Afrakan population inhabiting northwest Afraka that, after converting to Islam, conquered the Iberian peninsula in 711 C.E. establishing Moorish Spain. The Moors descended from the ancient nomadic Afrakans of the eastern Sudan region, described during the Greco-Roman period as "Libyans" and Maures". They range from Libya to northeast Afraka. They also sailed to the Americas long before the European Caucasians.

Mountains of the Moon - Several mountains, including Kilimanjaro, in the great lakes region, modern day Tanzania of east Afraka, Mount Mwenzori, also in the great lakes region in present day Uganda, and Mount Choke in modern day Ethiopia are all sources of the Nile River; the ancient Kemetyu proclaimed these regions to be the home of their ancestors.

Moyo - A Kiswahili word meaning heart, referring to your vital spiritual life force, which is directed by the heart or Heru Konsciousness.

Nb - Neb - To have great mastery of or the master of.

Nbty - A Mdw Ntchr word meaning the two ladies, Wadjet & Nekhebt.

Nebw - Nbw (Nub) - This is the Kemet word for gold, which was considered a divine metal. Its polished surface was related to the brilliance of the sun. Gold was important to the afterlife as it represents aspects of immortality. By the New Period, the royal burial chamber was called the "House of Gold."

Neb Er Tchr - The will of the universe.

Nefer (Nfr) - Mdw Ntchr word meaning good or beautiful. Its Mdw Ntchr symbol is the heart and the trachea. It symbolizes that which is the most beautiful thing, the highest good and the greatest achievement.

Nehesy (Nhsy) - A Mdw Ntchr word meaning the land south of Kemet. Today, it would be in northern Sudan.

Nekhbet - A Mdw Ntchr word meaning vulture. A Ntchrt portrayed as a vulture, the protectress of Upper Kemet.

Nemes - A striped (royal blue and gold) head cloth worn by the Nswt.

Nswt - The Heru ruler from the south ruling all of Kemet, north and south as one unified land. The one who is of the Swt plant. Nswt is like the word King but spiritual.

Nt - The red crown of Lower Kemet.

NTCHR - The All, the Divine Creator, the One Konsciousness in which we are all connected to by essence and spirit. Divine nature and all spirits are aspects or manifestation of NTCHR.

Ntchr or Ntchrt - A masculine or feminine divine principle, respectively.

Ntchru - Divine principles and laws that are manifestations of the NTCHR, that govern the cosmos and every living energy force.

Nubia - This name comes from the Mdw Ntchr word Nub, which means gold. The southern land where gold was found was later called, the land of gold.

Nwu (Nnw, Nun) - Mdw Ntchr word meaning the personification of the primeval waters, the eternal never ending, never beginning, primeval darkness from which the NTCHR Created Itself.

Orisha - "Powers," the name for Ntchru and divinities in the indigenous Afrakan religion of Yoruba, Akan, Voodoo and also several Afrakan-Caribbean derivatives, like Sanataria .

Papyrus - A plant that grows naturally and abundantly in the Hapy (Nile) Valley. In ancient Kemet and Kash it was used for making paper, ropes, baskets, boats, etc.

Paradigm - an interconnected set of ideas, beliefs, values, and actions that comprise a complex model of thinking and behaving with silent, hidden boundaries.

Patrilineal - The family line or clan descent determined through the father. In patrilineal societies, in marriage the woman usually loses her family name and legal identity.

Peret - The second of the three seasons of the Kemet kalendar, the season of growing or planting. It was both a four month period of the civil kalendar and a season of the natural year.

Pet (Pt)- A Mdw Ntchr word meaning heaven or sky. This symbol depicts the sky as a ceiling which drops at the ends, the same way the real sky seems to reach for the horizon. This sign was often used in architectural motifs; the top of walls, and door frames. It symbolizes the heavens.

Primordial Hill - The ancient Kemetyu believed that during creation this hill rose out of the sea of nothingness to create dry land or matter. The idea of this hill rising had a profound effect on the Kemetyu, being used as everything from temple layouts to the possible inspiration behind the Mer Khutu (Pyramids).

Prt em Heru - Mdw Ntchr for "Coming Forth by Spiritual Light (Enlightenment)". Becoming one with Heru. A collection of funeral texts popular from the end of the Middle Period forward, basically a papyrus form of the previous era's *Karast (Coffin) Texts.* Available to any member of society who could afford to have a copy made for them. These chapters basically reflected the ancient Kemetyu beliefs about the afterworld and the soul's progress through it.

Pshent - The Double Crown, the red crown and the white crown put together to represent a unified Kemet. Narmer or Mena was the first Nswt recorded wearing this crown around 4240 B.C.E. or 1 S.T.

Punt (Puanit) - An East Afrakan nation or country, located some where south of Ancient Kemet and Kash, near present day Somalia, that had extensive commercial interactions with the Hapy Valley civilizations.

Pyramid - See Mer Khut.

Pyramid texts - See Mer Khut Sbayt.

Quilombo - Afrakan-Brazilian name for a maroon stronghold or community.

Ra - The sun was the primary element of life in ancient Kemet. Some of the most popular Ntchru had a solar connection.

Remetchu - A Mdw Ntchr for original humans. Interchangeable with the word "Kemetyu".

Rennent - "She who nourishes", the Ntchrt of good fortune and destiny.

R.E.M. - Rapid Eye Movement. A state of deep sleep.

Rift Valley - The greatest depression (fault in the earth) in the world from East Afraka, Kemet to Mozambique. Traceable by the lakes and seas filling its elongated pockets. This area is where the oldest remains of humans (Homo Sapiens) were found. It is the most fertile land and sections, such as Tanzania and Mozambique have the largest population of animals per square miles in the world. It has the greatest source of thermal energy (a pure, non-polluting energy source) known to humans.

Rn (Ren) - A Mdw Ntchr word meaning name, to the Kemetyu the act of naming was a sacred act because it called a principle into existence.

Sa (Saa) - A Mdw Ntchr word meaning protection. It is believed to represent a papyrus life-preserver used by ancient Kemetyu boaters. From early times the sa plays an important part in jewelry design. It is often used in conjunction with certain power symbols, particularly the ankh, was and djed signs. We often find Taurt, the hippopotamus Ntchrt of childbirth, resting her paw on a standing sa sign.

Saa - Divine wisdom and protection.

Saba - A Mdw Ntchr word meaning star.

Sah - Mdw Ntchr word meaning mummy. Sahu is plural for many sah, three or more. Another version in Mdw Ntchr is "wi".

Sba - A Mdw Ntchr word meaning to teach.

Sbayt - A Mdw Ntchr word meaning a teaching text, book or teacher.

Sankofa - An Akan word meaning return to the past in order to retrieve what was lost so that one can move forward.

Sanskrit - The ancient language of the Hindus of India.

Scarab - The dung beetle associated with Khepr (Khepr-Ra) in Ancient Kemet that represents transformation. The Kemetyu observed the nature of the dung beetle as it rolled a ball of dung across the ground which was similar to the sun being rolled across the sky (as above so below).

Sekhem - A scepter or symbol of authority, also a word that means internal power.

Sekhemty - The double crown of ancient Kemet, the double power of Upper and Lower Kemet, the red and white crowns of the united Kemet.

Sema (Smai, Semy) - Mdw Ntchr word that means union. Its glyphs (symbol) is the lungs and trachea attached to the windpipe that represents the unification of Upper and Lower Kemet. Spiritually, it symbolizes the union of the Higher Self and the lower self leading to "The One".

Shabaka Stone - An inscription dating from the reign of the Nswt Shabaka c 710 B.C.E.or 3530 S.T., to record an earlier, worm-eaten papyrus concerning a sacred drama of the coronation of the Ntchr Heru, but most importantly, the mythology of the Ntchr Ptah and the creation of the world, cited by modern scholars as evidence of a deeply spiritual and abstract religious philosophy in Kemet.

Senet - A Kemet board-game consisting of moving a number of pieces around a board with squares, popular among the noble class of ancient Kemet.

Serekh - A Mdw Ntchr word describing the Nswt name represented inside a palace facade with Heru standing on top.

Seshat - The female Ntchrt of mathematics, measurement, literature, a complement and mate of Jhuty; often shown as a woman wearing a seven pointed star on her head with horns of the great cow or mother energy. She carries a reed pen and palette recording the deeds of the Nswtu.

Seshen - A Mdw Ntchr word meaning Lotus Flower. This is a symbol of the sun, of creation and rebirth. Because at night the flower closes and sinks underwater, at dawn it rises and opens again. According to one Kemet creation myth it was a giant lotus which first rose out of the watery chaos at the beginning of time. From this giant lotus, the sun itself rose on the first day.

Sesh-Per-Ankh - "Scribe of the House of Life." the title of the Priest or Priestess whose temple duty is to record temple occurrences, oracles received from the Ntchru, etc. The sesh-per-ankh in antiquity was also in charge of the temple libraries and a holder of great knowledge.

Set/Setsh - The manifestation of blind force. The Ntchr of esfet, darkness, the opposite of his brother Asr. He ruled by might and force.

Shemsu Heru - Ancient Kemetyu: Followers of Heru. An Afrakan population from the south who entered the Kash and Kemet Hapy Valley region, introducing writing, coppersmithing, goldsmithing, and ironsmithing.

Shmty - A Mdw Ntchr word describing the double crown.

Shemu - The first of the three seasons of the Kemet kalendar, the season of inundation. It was both a four month period of the civil kalendar and a season of the natural year.

Shen - A Mdw Ntchr symbol of a loop of rope that has no beginning and no ending, it symbolized eternity. The sun disk is often depicted in the center of it. The shen also seems to be a symbol of protection. It is often seen being clutched by the Ntchru Heru the falcon, and Mut the vulture.

Shenu - A Mdw Ntchr word "shen" which means "encircle." The shape represents a loop of rope in which a name is written for protection. Misnamed "cartouche".

Shepsu - Venerated ancestors.

Sistra (Sistrum) - A musical instruments similar to the rattle, sacred to Het Heru. This sacred percussion instrument was made of a wooden or metal frame fitted with loose strips of metal and disks which jingled when moved. This music was thought to attract the attention of the Ntchru. There are two types of sistrum. An iba, was shaped in a simple loop, like a closed horseshoe with loose bars of metal above a Het Heru head and a long handle. The seseshet had the shape of a naos temple above a Het Heru head, with ornamental loops on the sides. The rattle was inside the box of the naos. They were usually carried by women of high rank.

Sma - Union or united.

Sn-netchru - The Mdw Ntchr word for "Incense". Incense invoke divine awareness through the sense of smell.

Sovereign - A free Konscious and very powerful person. A human being that innerstands their Ntchr given rights of freedom along with the natural law of Ma'at.

Spat - A Mdw Ntchr word meaning district, like a nome.

Spdt (Sepdet) - A Mdw Ntchr word describing a very special star. The rising of Spdt was celebrated as the rebirth of Ast. It was also the star called Sirius A, the Dog-star, or Sothis, whose helical rising marked the start of the inundation.

Sphinx - See Heru em Akhety.

St - A Mdw Ntchr word meaning throne,divine seat, woman or place.

S.T. - Sema Tawy, The re-unification of "The United Two lands of Upper and Lower Kemet". The 1st Golden Age of Kmt.

Swt - The Mdw Ntchr word for a plant found in southern Kemet and Kash that grows in the Hapy. Sometimes it can also mean south.

Ta Khui - The land of enlightened spirits, east central Afraka.

Ta Ntchr - The land of Divine Spirit, east central Afraka.

Ta-Seti - The land of the bow, northern area of Ancient Kash. The birthplace of the Royal Nswt civilization several generations before the rise of Ancient Kemet. In Kash, Ta-seti they established an early political unity and led these Black Afrakans to a great Kultural distinction that the world has marveled at for millennia.

Tawy - The two unified lands called Kemet

Tepra - Oracle.

Tepra En Ma'at - The 42 utterances or oracles of righteousness.

Tekhen - A very tall four-sided pillar with a Mer Khut on the top. This represent rebirth, a phallic symble of fertilty pointing to Ra, placed infront of divine Temples from the 5th Dynasty.

Tiet - A Medw Ntchr word associated with Ast and is often called "the knot of Ast." It seems to be called "the knot of Ast" because it resembles a knot used to secure the garments that the Ntchru wore. In the Late Period, the sign was also associated with the Ntchru Nebt Het, Het Heru, and Nut. In all these cases it seems to represent the idea of resurrection and eternal life.

Time Capsule - Enclosed sacred compartments comprised of information and materials preserving "life-giving" knowledge of Ancient Afrakan (Kemet) civilization. Misrepresented as only tombs and symbols of death.

Twa - Any of the physical small Africoids generally in the forest regions of central Afraka. During the ancient period, they inhabited most of Afraka.

Udjat (Uachet)- The sound eye of Heru. The Udjat was a symbol of healing and protection.

Ushabtis - A statue place in the tomb of the deceased to do work in the after life. A Mdw Ntchr word literally meaning "to answer." In some tombs of the late New Period, whole gangs of ushabti workers were included with different tools for doing different work. A complete collection would consist of 401 Ushabiti: One for each day of the year, 365 days plus 36 foreman.

Vandals - A Germanic tribe that invaded Western Europe around 350 C.E., ravaging Gaul, Spain, and crossing the Mediterranean Sea, invaded North Afraka. In 455 C.E., the Vandals sacked Rome.

Wadj - A Mdw Ntchr word meaning green papyrus or the color green.

Wadjet - The cobra-Ntchr of the Delta; tutelary deity of Lower Kemet, appearing on the royal diadem, protecting the Nswt.

Was - A Mdw Ntchr word meaning power and dominion. The Was scepter is carried by Ntchru as a sign of their power. It is also seen being carried by the Nswtu and later by people who held high ranking positions in the ancient Kemet society.

Wast - Mdw Ntchr word meaning Seat of Power: Political center of Kemet, home of the remains of the finest temples in the ancient world; Ipet Reset (Luxor Temples), Ipet Sut (Karnak Temples).

Wat - Mdw Ntchr word meaning road.

Watoto - The Kiswahili word for children.

Wazungu - Kiswahili word for Caucasian people or the collective Melanin deficient Caucasian Europeans of western Asia..

Wdj - Mdw Ntchr word meaning spirit door for the after-life to communicate with the living. Also called a stele.

Whm Msw (Weheme Mesu) - Mdw Ntchr word meaning rebirth, renewal and restoration.

Wennefer - An epither of Asr, "Perfect Being".

Wepwawet - A jackal Ntchr, who "Opens the Way", especially the ways to the Duat for Asr. This is an aspect of the Ntchr Enpu.

Winged Solar Disk - This is a form that the Ntchr Heru of Edfu takes in his battle with Setsh. The Ntchr Jehuty used his will to turn Heru into a sun-disk with splendid outstretched wings, called the Behdet.

Yabet - Mdw Ntchr word meaning east.

Yabety - Mdw Ntchr word meaning left.

Spiritual Warriors at a CIBI (Council of Independent Black Instiutions) Conference in New Jersey. Left to Right: Mwalimu Shujaa, Mfundishi Jhutyms Salim, Uhuru Hotep and Arataymis Ma'at. Below Sat en Khufu, the high priestess, who was the daughter of the Nswt Khufu, of The Great Mer.

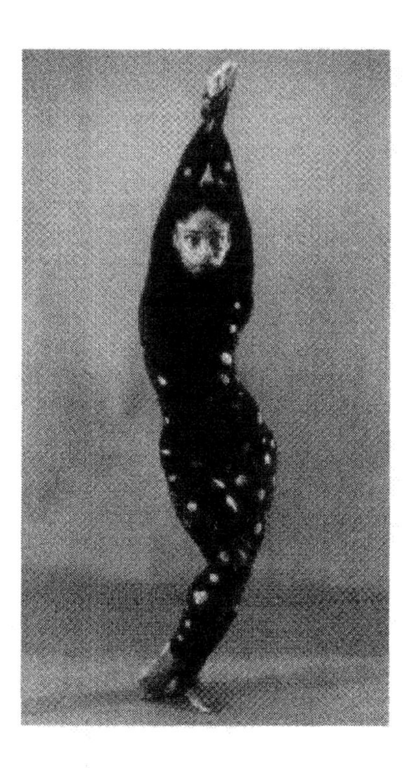

Spiritual Warrior Diane Salaam, choreographer, and Dancer of Forces Of Nature Dance Company, Harlem, New York. Below center, Spiritual Warrior Stanley Jordan, world famous guitarist with Mfundishi& Hemet Ntchrt Seshatms.

BIBLIOGRAPHY

<u>Note</u>: *Afrakan names are written in correct order to maintain their proper meaning and spiritual energy. *European names are written last name first unfortunately this represents ownership or possession from a Euro-centric perspective.

Adams, Hunter. *Afrikan Observers of the Universe: The Sirius Question*, Journal of Afrikan Civilizations.

A. Ajamu (1997). *From Tef Tef to Medw Nefer: The Importance of Using African Languages, Terminologies, and Concepts in the Rescue, Restoration, Reconstruction and Reconnection of African Ancestral Memory.* In J. Carruthers & L. Harris (Ed.). African World History Project: The Preliminary Challenge. Loas Angeles.

A. Borishade (1996). *Re-aligning African Heads: Yoruba Curatitves for Maafa-Related Ailments.* Jacksonville, FL: Sankofa Productions.

Alexander, Curtis, E. *Reference Works of Yosef Ben-Jochannan: A Study of Our History in Afrika.* P.O. Box 15004, Chesapeake, VA: Great Bridge Station.

Alexander, Curtis, E. *Cheikh Anta Diop: An Afrikan Scientist.* P.O. Box 15004, Chesapeake, VA: Great Bridge Station.

Anderson, S. (1995). *The Black Holocaust for Beginners.* New York: Writers & Readers Pub.

Anvatsky, B.. *Isis Unveiled,* Vols. 1 and 2.

Aptheker, H. (1965) (1965). *One Continual Cry: David Walker's Appeal to the Colored Citizens of the World, 1829-1830.* New York: A&P Publishers.

Aschmide, Peter & Avery (1978). *Journal of Afrikan Civilizations & Science*, Vol. 201.

Ayei Kwei Armah (1979). *Two Thousand Seasons.* Chicago: Third World Press.

Banfield, Beryl. *Africa in the Curriculum.* New York: W. Blyden Press.

Barneja, R. (1977). *Competitive Binding Between Cocaine and Various Drugs to Synthetic Levodopa Melanin,* Journal of Pharmaceutical Science, 66 (11): 1544-1547.

Barnes, Carol (1987). *Melanin-The Chemical Key To Black Greatness: The harmful Effects of Toxic Drugs on MELANIN Centers in the Black Human* Vol. III. Houston, Texas: Black Greatness Series.

Barr, F.E.(1983). *MELANIN: The Organizing Molecule, Medical Hypothesis*, VOL. 11: 1-40, MAY.

Bennett, Lerone Jr. (1999). *Forced into Glory: Abraham Lincoln's White Dream.* Chicago: Johnson Publishing Company.

Brown, T. (1998). *Empower the People: A 7-Step Plan to Overththrow that is Stealing your Money and Freedom.* New York: Wm. Morrow.

Bunkley, C. (1996). *The African American Network: Get Connected to More than 5, 000 Prominent People and Organizations in the African American Community.* New York: Plume/Penguin.

Bloom, A. D. (1987). *The Closing of the American Mind.* New York: Simon and Schuster.

Cabral, Amilcar (1973). *Return to the Source: Selected Speeches by Amilcar Cabra*l. New York: Monthly Review Press.

Campbell, Horace (1987). *Rasta and Resistance.* Trenton, New Jersey: Africa World Press.

Carruthers, Jacob H. (1999). *Intellectual Warfare*. Chicago: Third World Press.

Carruthers, Jacob H. (1997). *African World History Porject: The Preliminary Challenge*. Los Angeles: The Association for the Study of Classical African Civilizations.

Carruthers, Jacob H. (1984). *Essays in Ancient Eyptian Studies.* Los Angeles, California: Timbuktu Publishing Company.

Cheikh Anta Diop. *The African Origin of Civilization*. New York: Lawrence Hill & Company.

Clegg, C. (1997). An Original Man: The lfe and Times Elijah Muhammad. New York: St. Martin's Press.

Collins, P. (2000). *Black Feminist Thought: Knowledge, Consciousness, and the Politics of Empowerment*. New York: Routledge.

Conniff, M. & Davis, T. (1994). *Africans in the Americas: A History of the Black Diaspora*. New York : St. Martin's Press.

Cruse, H.(1967). *Crisis of the Negro Intellectual: From Its Origins to the Present.* New York: Wm. Morrow.

Cuddy, D. (2000). *Now is the Dawning of the New Age World Order.* Oklahama City, OK: Hearthstone Publishing.

Chandler, Wayne B (1999). *Ancient Future: The Teachings and Prophetic Wisdom of the Seven Hermetic Laws of Ancient Egypt*. Atlanta, Georgia: Black Classic Press.

Chinweizu (1987). *Decolonizing the African Mind. London*: Sundoor, BCM Box 4658, London WCIN 3XX, England.

Chinweizu (1987). *The West and the Rest of Us*. London: Sundoor, BCM Box 4658, London WCIN 3XX, England

Churchward, Albert (1921). *The Origin & Evolution of the Human Race*. London: George Allen & Urwin Ltd.

Clarke, John Henrik (1991). *Notes for An African World Revolution: Africans at the Crossroads*. Trenton, NJ: African World Press.

Cleary, T. (2000). *Ways of Warriors, Codes of Kings : Lesson in Leadership from Chinese Classics*. Boston: Shambhala.

Colins, Janet. *Lectures on Egypt*. 5502 Girard Avenue, Philadelphia, PA: Harambee Institute.

Crum, W.E (1989). *A Coptic Dictionary*. Oxford: Claredon Press.

Cruse, H.arold (1967). *The Crisis of the Negro Intellectual*. New York: William Morrow.

Davidson, Alison & Veggi, Athon (1995). *The Book of Doors Divination Deck: An Alchemical Oracle from Ancient Egypt*. Rochester, Vermont: Destiny Books.

De Lubicz, I. S. *Her Bak*, Vol. 1. New York: Inner Traditions International.

De Lubicz, I. S. *Her Bak*, Vol. 2. New York: Inner Traditions International

De Lubicz, I. S. *Opening the Way.* New York: Inner Traditions International.

De Lubicz, I. S. *Sacred Science.* New York: Inner Traditions Interna

De Rosny, Eric (1985). *Healers in the Night.* New York: Orbis Books.

Diager & Smith (1921). *Asian Fighting Arts.* Kodansha International, Ltd.

Douglass, F. (1845). Narrative of the Life of Frederick Douglass: An American Slave. [reprint 1968 Signet Books New York]

E. Addae (Ed.) (1996). *To Heal a People: Afrikan Scholar Defining a New Reality.* Columbia, MD: Kujichagulia.

E. Ayisi (1972). *An Introduction to the Study of African Culture.* London: Heinemann.

Edelstein, L.M (1977). *Can Blackness Prolong Life ?* Ebony, pp.124-127, June.

Edwards, L. (1998). *The Power of Ideas: The Heritage Foundation at 25 Year*s. Ottawa, IL: Jameson Books.

Edwards. *Black Gods/Osiris in the New World.*

Farrakhan, L. (1993). *A Torch for America.* Chicago: FCN Publishing

Faulkner, R. O (1978). *Middle Egyptian.* Griffith Institute.

Frankfort, Henri. *The Egyptian Religion.*

Funk & Wagnalls (1987). *New International Dictionary.* J.G. Ferguson Publishing Company.

Gadalla,Moustafa. *Exiled Egyptians: The Heart of Africa.* Greensboro, North Carolina: Tehuti Research Foundation, 1999.

Gardiner, A. H. (1978) . *Egyptian Grammer.* Griffith Institute.

Ghallowgiw, P. *The House of Life, Medical School of Egypt.* Israel Bulletin of Medicine.

Gillings. *Math in the Time of the Pharoah.*

Gorden, M., ed. (1959). *Structure of Melanin. In Pigment Cell Biology*, New York, Academic Press Inc,. pp. 563-581.

Greenfield, Moses (1982). *The Five Books of Moses.* Atereth Publishing.

Gtiaule. *Conversations with Oqotomell.* Oxford Univrsity Press.

Haich, E.. *Initiation.*

Hamilton, C. V. (1968). *Race and Education: A Search for Legitmacy.* Harvard Educational Review. 38(4), 669-684.

Hare, N. & Hare, J (1988). *Bringing the Black Boy to Manhood.* San Francisco, California: Black Think Tank.

Harris,Clarence J (1973) . "African Pantheism, Vol. 4," International Journal Environmental Studies.

Harris, Marc J. (1972) *African Communal Life and Government.* Brooklyn: Forum Magazine, African -American Teacher's Association.

Heller, K., Holtzman, W., & Messick, S., Eds. (1982). P*lacing Children in Special Education: A Strategy for Equity.* Washington, DC: national Academy Pree.

Herodotus (1958). *The Histories of Herodotus.* New York.
James, G.eorge, G. M. *Stolen Legacy.* San Francisco, California: Julian Richardson.

J. Olumide (1948). *The Religion of the Yorubas. Lagos.*

Jomo Kenyata. *Facing Mt. Kenya.*

Jones, Edward, L. (1972). *Black Zues.* Seattle, Washington: University of Washington.

K. Al-Mansour (1993). *Betrayal by any other Name: An Honest Appraisal of Black & Hispanic American Leadership Over The Past 100 Years.* New York: First African Arabian Press.

Kaka Ankshashak Heru-Khuty (1993). *Per n Rek m Netcheru (Book of Knowing the Netcheru).* From an unpublished work.
King James (Version) (1652). *The Holy Bible.* Philleppe De Champagne.

Kilindi Iyi (1988). *The Essence of Ta-Merrian Martial Arts.* Detroit.

Kilindi Iyi (1988). *Aha Martial Arts of the Nile Valley.* Detroit.

King, Richard. *The Black Dot*, Vols. 1, 2, & 3.

Kwame Agyei Akoto & Akua Ison Akoto (1999). *The Sankofa Movement: ReAfrikanization and the Reality of War.* Hyattsville, MD. Oyoko Info Com Inc.

Kwame Agyei Akoto (1992). *Nation Building: Theory and Practice of Afrikan-centered.* Washington: PAWI.

Lane-Poole, Stanley (1990) *Moors in Spain.* Baltimore, Maryland: Black Classic Press.

Leakey, Richard E.. *Origins.* New York: E.D. Dutton.

Leakey, L. S. B.. *The Progress and Evolution of Man in Africa.* Oxford University Press.

Lewis, Mary C. (1988). *Herstory (Black Female Rites of Passage).* Chicago: African American Images.

Hillard, Asa G., III (1999). "*Race, " Identity, Hegemony, and Education: What Do We need to Know Now?* Presented to Chicago Urban League, University of Illinois Chicago (1999). In Rethinking Schools: Winter, 1999/2000 (pp. 4-6).

Hillard, Asa G., III (1998). *SBA: The Reawakening of the African Mind.* Gainesville, Florida: Makare Publishing.

Hirsch, E. D., Jr. (1987). *Cultural Literacy: What Every American Needs to Know.* Boston: Houghton Mifflin.

Huntington, S. P. (1996). *The Clash of Civilizations and the Making of World Order.* New York: Houghton Mifflin.

Hope. *The Way of the Cartouche.*

Ions, Veronica (1990). *Egyptian Mythology.* New York: Peter Bedrick Books.

Jackson, John G. (1982). *Journal of African Civilizations*, Egypt & Christianity, Vol. 4.

Kotkin, J. (1993). *Tribes: How Race, Religion, and Identity Determine Success in the New Global Economy.* New York: Academic Press.

Kozol, J. (1991). *Savage Inequalities: Children in America's Schools.* New York: Crown.

Lichtheim, Miriam (1984). *Ancient Egyptian Literature,* Vols 1, 2, & 3. Los Angeles: University of California.

MacIver & Randall, Wolley. *Journal of African Civilizations.*

Marimba Ani (1994) Yuruga: *An African-centered Critique of European Cultural Thought and Behavior.* Trenton, NJ: Africa World Press.

Majani Mareful (1981). *Technical Skills for Black Self Reliance.* Box 236, Pennsylvania: Jamia.

Majani Mareful (1979). *The Story of Black People & The USA.* Box 236, Pennsylvania: Jamia.

Majani Mareful (1979). *Community Building & Learning Technical Skills.* Box 236, Pennsylvania: Jamia.

Mason, H.S. (1948). *The Meaning of Melanin, Special Publication,* N.Y., ACAD. Sci., VOL 4:399.

Massey, Gerald. *Ancient Egypt.*

Maulana Karenga (1987). *The Husia.* Los Angeles, California: Kawaida Publishing Company.

Maulana Karenga & Jacob H. Carruthers (1984). *Kemet and the African World View*. Los Angeles, California: University of Sankore Press.

Maulana Karenga(1977). *Kawaida Theory*. Inglewood, California: Kawaida Publishing Company.

Maulana Karenga (1977). *Kwanzaa.* Los Angeles, California: Kawaida Publishing Company.

Mfundishi J. H. Hassan K. Salim & Shaha Mfundishi Maasi (1994). *Kupigani Ngumi: Root Symbols of The Ntchru and Ancient Kmt,* Vol 1. Plainfield, New Jersey.

Moses Greenfield, Moses (1982). *The Five Books of Moses.* Atereth Publishing.

Matteson, Barbara J. *Mystic Minerals.*

McIntosh, S & R (1982). *Finding West Africa's Oldest City.* National Geographic.

Molefei Kete Asante, Abbary, A. (Eds.), (1996). *African Intellectual Heritage: A Book of Sources.* Philadelphia: Temple University Press.

Molefei Kete Asante (1987). *The Afrocentric Idea*. Philadelphia: Temple University Press.

Molefi Kete Asante (1987). *Afrocentricity.* Phildelphia: Temple University Press.

Mwalima J. Shujaa (1995). *Too Much Schooling, Too Little Education: A Paradox of Black Life in White Societies.* Trenton, NJ: Africa World Press.

Nacimento, A. D. and Nacimento, E. L. (1992). *Africans in Brazil: A Pan-African Perspective.* P. O. Box 1892, Trenton, NJ: Africa World Press.

O. K. Owsu (1994). *Origins of World Civilizations: A Wholistic Worldview of Cultures and Civilizations.* Baltimore, Maryland: Cultural Eye Productions.

Osei. *The Afrikan Concept of Life and Death.*

Parkinson, R. B. (1991). *Voices from Ancient Egypt: An Anthology of Middle Kingdom Writings.* Oklahoma: University of Oklahoma Press.

Putnam. *Osiris and The Egyptian Resurrection.* Vols. 1 & 2.

Quirke, Stephen (1995). *Ancient Egyptian Religion.* New York: Dover Publications.

Ra Un Nefer Amon (1987). *Metu Neter.* Bronx, NY: Khamit Corporation, March.

Ravitch, D. (1996). the Last Word on Afrocentrism? In Hot Topics: June (On-line), Available: http://www.edexcellence.net/hottopic/afrocent.htm.

Rwkty Amon Jones. *Introduction to Mdu Ntr.*

Sanders, W. I. Rivers, J. C. (1998). *Cumulative and Residual Effects of Teachers on Future Students Academic Achievement.*

Sen-Ur Heru Ankh-Ra Semahj se PTAH and Queen Afua. *Contributions from Abu't Neferty MuKham Ma'at's Smai Tawi Sacred Woman Priestess Training*, Brooklyn, New York: Smai Tawi Heal Thyself / Know Thyself Afrakan Wellness Center.

Schlesinger, A. M. (1998). *The Disuniting of America: Reflections on a Multicultural Society.* New York: W. W. Norton.

Schmoker, M. (1996). *Results: The Key to Continuous School Improvement.* Alexandria, Virginia: Association for Supervision and Curriculum Development.

Sertima, Ivan Van. *African Presence in Ancient Asia.*

Skyrtic, T. M. (1991). *The Special Education Paradox: Equity as the Way to Excellence.* Harvard Educational Review, 61(2), 148-206.

Shorter, A. W. (1972). *The Egyptian Gods.* Seattle, Washington: Nencastle Publishing.

Singer, Ronald (1982). *The Middle Stone Age at Klasies River Mount in South Africa.* Chicago: Chicago Press.

Snell, R.S. (1963). *A Study of the Melanocytes and Melanin in a Healing Deep Wound.* JANAT., VOL. 97:243.

Stanford, Eva. *The Mediterranean World in Ancient Times: The Intellectual Adventure of Man.*

Stoller & Olkes. *In Soreeny and Shadow.*

Swan, G.E.(1963). *The Chemical Structure of Melanin*, Ann. N.Y., Acad. Sci., VOL. 100: 105.

Teish, Luisah. *Jambalaya.* San Francisco, California: Harper & Row Publishing.

Thathachari, Y.T.(1969). *Physical Studies on Melanin II X-RAY Diffraction*, Biophys., J., VOL. 9:77-89.

Thompson. *Flash of the Spirit.*

Tomkins, Peter. *Secrets of the Great Pyramid*. Harper & Row.

Volvey, C. *Ruins of Empires*.

Weatherwax, John. *The African Contribution, Vols. 1 & 11*. Ancient Africa. Los Angeles, California: Aquarian Spiritual Center.

Williams, Chancellor (1974). *Destruction of Black Civilization*. Third World Press.

Winters, Clyde-Ahmad. *Iron-Smelting in East Africa.* Journal of African Civilizations.

Wilson, Amos (1998). *Blueprint for Black Power: A Moral, Political and Economic Imperative for the Twenty-First Century.* New York: Afrikan World Infosystems.

White, P.L. (1958)., *Melanin: a Natural Occurring Cation Exchange Material*. Nature (London), 182:1427.

Woodford, James., *De-Melanizing Solution as Attachments to Marijuana Urinalysis Testing Devices-* Submitted for Publication.

Woodson, Carter G., (1977). *The Miseducation of the Negro*. New York: AMS Press Inc. (First published 1933.)

Yosef Ben-Jochannan. *Black Man of the Nile and His Family*. 209 W. 125th Street, Suite 21G, New York City: AlkebuLan Books.

Yosef Ben-Jochannan. (1972). *Cultural Genocide in the Black and African Studies Curriculum.* New York: Alkebu-Lan.

Zaslavsky, Claudia. *Africa Counts*. New York: Lawrence & Hill Company.

About the Author

MFUNDISHI JHUTYMS KA-EN-HERU HASSAN KAMAU SALIM was born in Newark, New Jersey. He has lived in Tanzania, East Afraka and now lives in Montclair, New Jersey. He was educated at Norfolk State University, Livingston College, Rutgers University Graduate School, The Kemetik Institute and the University of Dares Salam, Tanzania. Brother Salim holds degrees in Afrakan Studies, History, Education, Kultural Anthopology and Kemetology. He is one of the few teachers of *Mdw Ntchr* (hieroglyphics or Ancient Egyptian Writing) in America who teaches it from an Afrakan-centered holistic spiritual perspective.

Brother Salim is a Professor of Afrakan and Afrakan-American History and Ourstory, a Kemetologist, poet, playwright, actor, and Grand Master Martial Artist. He has taught Elementary School, High School, Junior College, Undergraduate and Graduate School. He has served as Assistant to the Dean, Student Activity Coordinator, and also as Associate Dean of Special Affairs at Livingston College, Rutgers University. Brother Salim has received hundreds of awards, trophies, and certificates as a poet, playwright and actor. He holds an Eight Degree Black Belt (red sash) in Chinese Shaolin Hung-gar Kung Fu and is also a Grand Master (Mfundishi) in Kupigana Ngumi (Afrakan Martial Arts) and founder of the Aha Kemet Wanyama Saba System. He is a High Priest in the Kemet Spiritual System of Jhuty Heru Neb-Hu, and he has studied extensively in Afraka.

Brother Salim has appeared on numerous occasions on New Jersey cable television, Black Entertainment Tonight (BET), 9-Broadcast Plaza, New Jersey; In The Black, and several talk shows and radio shows in America and abroad including Trinidad, Jamaica and several Afrakan countries.

As an international traveler, Brother Salim has traveled to 23 countries on the Afrakan Continent, he has traveled throughout the Caribbean, Southern Europe, and South and Central America. He has lectured or performed at more than 160 Universities.

Brother Salim has written several books of poetry: Seven Shades of Black , In America Not of America, and I Love The Night. Many of his poems have appeared in large and small theaters and poetic publications. 1985 New York cable -Best amercure Playwrite for 7 Shades of Black. More than 250 of his poems have been published in the United States. He has written three children's books: Kemet, Kuku Kamau, and The Chicken and The Falcon; a best seller: Kupigana Ngumi: Root Symbols of Ancient Civilizations, and his latest book: Spiritual Warriors Are Healers. He has also been selected as Who's Who in America 1991, 1992, 1993, 1994, 1995, 1996, 1997, 1998, 1999.

Mfundishi Jhutymes Ka en Heru Hassan Kamau Salim is founder of Black Gold Theater Company, the Ma'at Institute for Children and Adult Education, The Kemet Shrine of Jhuty Heru Neb Hu, and Black Gold Afrakan Kultural Arts Center, with locations in New Jersey and New York. Mfundishi Salim is also the creator and founder of the Aha Kemet Wanyama Saba wa Kupigana Ngumi System of Afrakan martial arts and Ma'at Akhw Ba Ankh -Ancient Kemet Meditation and Spiritual Breathing System.

Mfundishi Jhutymes is a member of the Ndundu Council which oversees The Council of Independent Black Institutions (CIBI) - governing and accreditation component. This organization is celebrating 35 years plus of leading Deep Thinking in the Afrikan-centered schools in Afrika, Europe and North America. He is also a member and lecturer for A.S.C.A.C. The Association for the Study of Classical Afrikan Civilizations. Mfundishi is also the founder of The Pan-Afrakan Kash Kemet Mdw Ntchr Outreach Society.

Black Gold Sacred Living
Kera Jhuty Heru Neb Hu
P.O. BOX 1396 Montclair,
New Jersey 07042
866-227-3170
e-mail - Mfundishijhutyms@bww.com

Zuwena and Hassan Iman Salim, left-top 1993, right 1992 and bottom 2003

Mfundishi with his two watoto (children)top 1990 & 1996. The bottom as adults with Malenga Heru Ur in 2003 Kemet Inititation.

SPIRITUAL WARRIORS ARE HEALERS

Spiritual Warriors Are Healers
Bringers of light
Agile spiritual sunrays
Transforming darkness into light
Ancient ancestral messengers
Carrying codes not visible with matrix sight.

Spiritual Warriors Are Healers
Deep thinkers, the creators of Ma'at
Great spiritual and physical masters who can also fight
Kultural Kem-stodians, who carry the secrets of the night
The original enlighteners of the wisdom of life
We maintain the harmonious rhythms that promotes life
Afrakan rhythms, funky drum rhythms
Spiritual can't touch that, hear that, but feel that rhythms
Quintessential rhythms, which are the very aspects of the essence of existence.

But, between the nature of things
And the state or perception of things
The untrained mind has become hypnotized by the deception of things
Unconsciously imitating European seduction of corruption
Breathing tainted air polluted by western insane productions
Murdered by the by-products of wazungu progress
Disguised by western technology a prologue to Afrakan disaster
Clones of misguided souls nourished by self ignorance
Reflecting mirrors of mass annihilation and the end to any Afrakan nation.

Therefore, the Ntchr sent forth Spiritual Warriors
With metaphors hiding sacred codes of information
For spiritual transformation and Afrakan liberation
Transforming life-threatening habits into life-giving gifts

SPIRITUAL WARRIORS ARE HEALERS

Translating Mdw Ntchr, our ancestral inheritance
And Afrakan Kultural memory coded in glyphs
Kulture gives meaning to the totality of comprehensible reality
This reality is not just now, or then, or for me, but to eternity.

Spiritual Warriors Are Healers because we innerstand
That the greatest weapon against the ignorance in humans
Is our ability to choose one thought over another and make a stand.
Spiritual initiation into the rituals of Afrakan liberation
Is a powerful formula that can help Afrakans build a sovereign nation.
Afrakans must be trained in Afrakan-centered spiritual education
So that we can make a total spiritual transformation
When the Spiritual Warrior combines the unity of matter and spirit
Healing is achieved through this divine alignment
Heru Konsciousness changes your vision, your possibilities
We become our ancestors
Transforming sickness into wellness
Backwardness into dynamic progress
Wazunguness into Afrakan spiritualness
Even the boundaries of ordinary space and time become limitless
For only knowledgeable and spiritual people
Wise in the rituals and Kulture of their ancestors
Can heal them-selves, rule them-selves, and maintain sovereignty among them-selves.

Spiritual Warriors Are Healers
Bringers of light
Agile spiritual sunrays
Transforming ignorance into light
New ancient ancestral messengers
Transforming and whispering Mdw Ntchr chants into the night
Decoded codes not seen by matrix sight
Causing our enemies and the wazungu to take flight
However, the daylight will not hide them
Moreover, Spiritual Warriors, ***we rule the night!***

OTHER WORKS AVAILABLE BY THE AUTHOR

Spiritual Warriors Are Healers Workbook and Study Guide

Kupigana Ngumi: The Striking Mind, Body & Fist.

Seven Shades of Black, the Play and the Poems

In America, Not of America

I Love the Night

The Trial of El-Hajj Malik El Shabazz, Malclom X

A Framework for Rites of Passage Programs and Afrakan-centered Education

DVD's

1. Ma'at Akhw Ba Ankh 1-1
2. The Importance of Afrakan Languages
3. Introduction to Mdw Ntchr 1-1
4. Mfundishi as Guest on Cable TV Show: "Ancestors House" Hosted by Camille Yarbrough. Show Theme: "The Study of Ancient Kemet"
5. Mfundishi as Guest Host of Cable TV Show: "Ancestors House" Show Theme: "The Study of Mdw Netcher and Pan Afrakan Mdw Netcher Conference"
6. Mfundishi Salim on "The Importance of Mdw Netcher"-Guest on Afrakan Warrior Scholarswith Shiek Omar
7. Mdw Ntchr Beginners Class Set 1-11 (11-DVDs)
8. Mdw Ntchr Beginner Intermediate Class Set 1-12 (12 DVDs)
9. Mdw Ntchr Intermediate Set
10. Pan-Afrakan Kash Kemt Mdw Ntchr Conference DVD Set 1-5
11. Mfundishi Jhutyms at the First Pan-Afrakan Mdw Ntchr Conference
12. Self-Healing with Colors and Crystals

For more information on these works contact the Author at:

Black Gold Sacred Living / Kera Jhuty Heru Neb Hu
PO Box 1396, Montclair, NJ 07042
www.BlackGoldSacredLiving.com
MfundishiJhutyms@bww.com
1-866-227-3170

Kupigana Ngumi Aha Kemet
(Afrakan Martial Science)
&
Maat Akhw Ba Ankh
(Ancient Kemet Meditation & Breathing Forms)

Pan Afrakan Kash Kmt Mdw Netcher Outreach Society (PAKKMNOS)

Notes

Notes

Notes

Notes

Food For Thought

Suggested quotes from this book for Back inspired by the spirit of Jhuty and Heru:

(1) Wa
"Freedom is irrelevant if it is not connected to the Divine Spirit within the foundation of your own Kultural center. No one can give you your freedom. Freedom is something you earn through struggle, like Heru, and Mentuhotep, freedom is something ultimately that you take! If we are truly to become healers, our very first patient must be ourselves, our loved ones, and family..."

(2) Snu
I tell Spiritual Warriors to say and internalize ... "Today is a good day to die! If you have nothing to die for, then you have nothing to live for. Fear prevents you from living a full and satisfying life. Eliminate the fear and nothing can stop you from fulfilling your visions."

(3) Shmtw
"Spiritual Warriors are healers because they are living, walking examples of their Kulture. They are spiritual beings directed by spirit. Their souls are at Htp (peace) and they are giving their gifts and living by divine order, which is Ma'at."

(4) Fdw
"Like the Great Spiritual Warriors of yesteryears - Kashta, Piankhy and Shabaka, the Spiritual Warriors of today must become one spirit, so that we can revitalize our focus, and develop an Afrikan national direction."

(5) Dew
"Working for the liberation and Nationship for Afrikan People is crucial, but, it means nothing unless it includes first developing one's self, as a Spiritual Warrior, than, working on building and maintaining unity in one's own family."

M mr nfr (With Perfect Love), Mfundishi Jhutyms Ka-n-Heru Hassan Kamau Salim, Ankh Udja Snb Nb